D1391606

it
could
never
happen
here

Also by Eithne Shortall

Love in Row 27
Grace After Henry
Three Little Truths

it
could
never
happen
here

eithne shortall

CORVUS

Published in hardback in Great Britain in 2022 by Corvus, an imprint
of Atlantic Books Ltd.

Copyright © Eithne Shortall, 2022

The moral right of Eithne Shortall to be identified as the author of this work has been
asserted by her in accordance with the Copyright, Designs and Patents Act of 1988.

All rights reserved. No part of this publication may be reproduced, stored in a retrieval
system, or transmitted in any form or by any means, electronic, mechanical, photocopying,
recording, or otherwise, without the prior permission of both the copyright owner and the
above publisher of this book.

This novel is entirely a work of fiction. The names, characters and incidents portrayed in it
are the work of the author's imagination. Any resemblance to actual persons, living or dead,
events or localities, is entirely coincidental.

10 9 8 7 6 5 4 3 2 1

A CIP catalogue record for this book is available from the British Library.

Hardback ISBN: 978 1 83895 184 9
Trade paperback ISBN: 978 1 83895 185 6
E-book ISBN: 978 1 83895 186 3

Printed in Great Britain

Corvus
An imprint of Atlantic Books Ltd
Ormond House
26–27 Boswell Street
London
WC1N 3JZ

www.corvus-books.co.uk

MIX
Paper from
responsible sources
FSC® C018072
FSC
www.fsc.org

For my dad, Billy Shortall, who made me coffee while I wrote and always served in a Seamus Heaney 'Inspiration' mug...

In case you thought I didn't notice.

1
·····

ABERSTOWN GARDA STATION

The parents and staff filed into the police station. Pristine coats hung from their confident shoulders, and huddles quickly began to form. A few threw glances in Garda Joey Delaney's direction and he did his best to look authoritative from his position behind the reception desk. He lifted his blink-and-you'd-miss-it backside from the swivel chair, placed both hands on his belt and yanked it up, ready for action.

'Delaney, get in here!'

The young guard swung around to see his superior, Sergeant James Whelan, already disappearing back into his office.

He gave the belt one further hoist and quick-stepped it in after him.

'The first batch seem to all be here now, sir.'

Whelan lowered himself into the chair with a groan. The sergeant was forty-six – exactly twice Joey's age – but he moved like a man of far greater years. Garda Corrigan pointed this out to him once and Whelan snapped that being tethered to useless eejits such as him was slowing him down.

'Did you mark their names off the list?'

1

Joey had expected the parents to approach the desk and formally check in, but most of them had ignored him entirely. 'I'll go around now and do a roll-call.'

'You do that. I'll just finish up in here, and then we'll get started.' The sergeant lifted the remains of what looked like a chicken sandwich from his desk and took a bite.

'Do you think they'll know anything, sir?'

'If there's anything to know, that lot will be in the loop.' The sergeant nodded towards the door, to the staff and parents of Glass Lake Primary beyond. 'They pride themselves on it.'

Glass Lake was a sought-after school located one town over in Cooney. Curtains were due to go up on its annual musical tonight and even Joey had a ticket. He wouldn't normally be too keen on watching a bunch of twelve-year-olds perform *The Wizard of Oz*, but the other officers insisted the school's shows were always unmissable. 'West End quality at West Cork prices,' was how Corrigan had put it. Not that it mattered now. There would be no musical tonight, or any other night this week. Obviously.

Joey nodded, hands on belt, as he marched out of the sergeant's office and over to the desk where he had left the clipboard of witness names. He was determined not to be another useless eejit slowing the sergeant down.

He cast an eye over the list and then over the busy waiting area. Yesterday evening, this lot had been up at Glass Lake, getting the auditorium ready. Now, they were in Aberstown Garda Station preparing to give their two cents on the body that had been pulled from the River Gorm while they were busy painting the Yellow Brick Road and putting finishing touches to Munchkin costumes.

They were still waiting on the initial post-mortem results and

Joey knew the most likely cause of death was accidental. Eleven months he had been a qualified guard stationed at Aberstown and, until yesterday, there hadn't been a reason to switch on the siren of the station's sole patrol car.

This wasn't a part of the world where robberies happened, never mind murders.

Still, thought Joey, as he hitched up his trousers and strode over to the whispering masses, there was no harm in keeping an open mind.

Extracts from witness statements, as recorded by Garda Joey Delaney

Mairead Griffin, school secretary

It was pandemonium yesterday evening. It's been pandemonium ever since the parents learned this year's musical was going to be on television. They've been turning up in their dual roles of legal guardians and Hollywood agents, and God help us all if their child isn't standing right where the cameras are going to be. If a single one of them noticed anyone was missing – if they noticed anything other than how high their child's name was listed in the programme – then let me know and I'll keel over right here and die of shock.

Susan Mitchem, parent

I fully support postponing the musical – a mark of respect, absolutely – but I had a casting agent coming to see my son and I've had no clarity on when to reschedule the train tickets for. I'm in serious danger of losing my money. The whole thing is tragic, one hundred per cent, but as the old maxim goes: the show must go on.

Mrs Walsh, teacher

It's just so sad, isn't it? Imagine how cold it must be in the water, especially at this time of year. A tragic, tragic accident – and this town has had enough of those. My thoughts are with the family. You hear about these things on the news, but you don't really think about it, not properly, not until it happens to one of your own.

2

•••••

The front door opened, and Christine Maguire leapt from the sitting room into the hallway, knitting needles and almost-completed teddy bear left languishing on the sofa.

She held her index finger to her lips and gestured up the stairs. 'Well?' she whispered. 'Did you find him?'

Her husband removed the thick thermal gloves the kids had bought him for his birthday. 'I've got four pieces of news,' he said. 'Three pieces of good news and one piece of bad news.'

'Jesus, Conor. Did you find the cat or not?'

Christine was the only member of the family who hadn't wanted a cat. Hers was the one vote, out of the five of them, for a dog. (Brian wrote 'porcupine' on his piece of paper, but given the options were 'dog' or 'cat', her son's ballot had been registered as spoiled.) The animal had sensed Christine's outlier position from day one and returned the disdain ten-fold. And yet here she was, unable to go to bed until she knew the damn creature was safe.

'I found him,' said her husband, undoing his jacket. 'Porcupine is alive and well.' (Such was Brian's aggrievement at being excluded from the democratic process that they'd allowed the seven-year-old to choose the pet's name.)

'Thank God.' Christine leaned back against the wall and glanced up the stairs. 'Maybe now Maeve will go to sleep.'

'They're the first two pieces of good news.'

She watched him jostle with the coat rack. 'What's the third?'

'He's being very well cared for in Mrs Rodgers' house.'

'Mrs Rodgers, of course! Why didn't we think of that?'

Rita Rodgers was an older lady who lived at the end of their street and spent a lot of time tending to her rose bushes – a real jewel in Cooney's Tidy Towns crown. The local pets were known to stop by and keep her company while their owners were out. She'd lived a fascinating life – literally ran away with the circus – and she exuded a worldly calm. Christine often said they were lucky to have Mrs Rodgers on their street; she was a reminder to stop and smell the (prize-winning) roses.

'Good old Mrs Rodgers, ay?' she said. 'We should drop her down a box of chocolates, to say thank you. I can pick something up tomorrow. I'll go tell Maeve that all is well.'

Their middle child had added Porcupine's disappearance to her ever-expanding list of things to lose sleep over. Other items included the teddy bear she was supposed to have finished knitting for school tomorrow (hence Christine currently committing late-night forgery) and a sudden, strong fear that she would not be involved in the Glass Lake musical.

Maeve didn't want to act in the production, which was a pity; she was the only one of Christine's children with the looks for stardom. (She wasn't a bad mother for thinking that. Maeve was her prettiest child, but Caroline was the most intelligent, and Brian the most likeable. Everyone went home with a prize.) Maeve wanted to work on costumes, but some other girl was already signed up to do that.

Christine didn't see the problem. It was a school show staged by a bunch of pre-teens. Surely the attitude should be: the more the merrier.

'Hang on,' she said, as Conor continued to mess around with the coat rack. It did not take that long to hang up a jacket, even if you approached things with as much precision as her husband. 'What's the bad news?'

'Hmm? Oh.' Conor frowned at the woollen collar as he attached it to a hook. 'She doesn't want to give him back.'

'*What?*'

'Mrs Rodgers, yes. I was surprised too. But she was quite firm about it. I always thought she was dithery, but I guess that was ageism. She's actually impressively sharp. She knows we're gone from the house for at least seven hours every day and that Porcupine is left on his own. She did this bit where she opened the front door wide and told Porcupine that he was free to go. *Go on now if you're going,* she said. And Porcupine looked up at her and meowed. Now I know he meows all the time, especially when he's hungry or when it's early and—'

'Yes, Conor, I'm familiar with the cat's meow.'

'Right. But this was different. This meow sounded like a word.'

'Excuse me?'

'A human word, I mean.'

Christine squinted at her husband, who was supposed to be the brains of the family. He raised his hands in a wait-for-it gesture.

She waited.

'And it sounded ... like, "No".'

Christine smacked her lips.

Conor nodded.

'*What?*'

'I know,' he said, still nodding. 'Crazy. Porcupine did not budge. I took off my hat, so he'd recognise me, but nothing. He just stood at her feet, loyal as you like. I have to say, it was very impressive.'

'What did you do?'

'What could I do? She was very nice about it. She explained that we were very busy – which is true, you said the same thing when we first talked about getting a cat – and probably didn't have a lot of time. But she has plenty of time and lots of space. She's an animal person, and she'd really cherish the company. I could almost hear her rattling around in the place, the poor woman. You know her husband died?'

'Yes, forty years ago, Conor! And they were separated. She left the man for a tightrope walker!'

'If we were separated and you died, I'd still be sad.'

'What? Conor, no! She stole our cat!'

Now it was her husband's turn to put his finger to his lips and gesture towards the stairs. 'Porcupine looked happy. I know it's only been a couple of days, but he looked fatter.'

'That cat couldn't get any fatter.'

'I don't know why you're so annoyed, Christine. You never liked him anyway.'

'She *stole* our cat! She cannot just steal our cat!' Christine caught her voice before it escalated to a full-on roar. That woman, their nice, old, butter-wouldn't-melt neighbour, had abducted their pet. How many times had Mrs Rodgers called out 'Busy today?' as Christine hurried past her house? When Christine called back 'Up to my eyes, Mrs Rodgers', she'd assumed she was making polite chitchat, not fashioning the noose for her own hanging. 'I should have known,' she raged. 'I should have known she wasn't the person she said she was. The Tidy Towns committee asked everyone on the street to leave some grass and dandelions in their gardens, but she just eviscerated it all. Animal person, my foot! She doesn't give a damn about the bees!'

'To be fair now, Christine, we're not too worried about the bees ourselves. I just haven't got around to fixing the lawnmower.'

'And how, exactly, could Porcupine look happy? That animal has one expression and it is smug.'

'Well,' Conor conceded, 'he looked sort of smugly happy.'

'Doesn't she already have a cat? A white and ginger thing?'

'I have a memory of seeing her with a brown one,' said Conor, 'but maybe not. That was a while ago.'

To think how many times Christine had stopped to compliment Mrs Rodgers on her 'organic' roses, knowing full well the charlatan was using chemical fertilisers. The Maguires lived on the same street, they had the same soil, and they could barely grow grass. But Christine never said a word. And when Mrs Rodgers won the intercounty garden prize, she'd written an article about it – she'd even pushed to get a picture of the old bat and her performance-enhanced bushes on to the front page.

'So, what? We leave him there? And then what? What are we going to tell the kids? What are *you* going to tell Maeve?'

'We'll just explain that Porcupine is an individual,' said Conor. 'He was a kitten but now he's a cat and he's decided to move out, like the three of them will one day ...'

Christine threw her head back and hooted.

She prided herself on being able to see her children for who they were. In Maeve's case, that was an anxious, conscientious little oddball. Dr Flynn had diagnosed her constant worries as 'intrusive thoughts' and said some children found comfort in prayer. But Conor was resolutely atheist – except when it came to ensuring their children got into Glass Lake Primary: then he was all for standing beside a baptismal fountain and shouting 'Get behind me, Satan' – so he bought her a set of worry dolls instead. Christine could have sworn their sewn-on smiles were already starting to droop.

Then, right on cue, their eleven-year-old daughter appeared at the top of the stairs.

'Why aren't you asleep, Maevey?' Conor called up.

'I was saying prayers for Porcupine. Did they work? Has he come home?'

'I've found Porcupine,' said Conor, ignoring the first portion of the question. 'And he's alive and well.'

Maeve gasped and started to run down the stairs.

'No, hang on, hang on. He's not here. He's at Mrs Rodgers' house.'

'Why is he at Mrs Rodgers' house?' Maeve directed this question towards her mother but, with a swing of the head, Christine lobbed it on to Conor.

'He's, well ...' Conor looked to his wife, then down at their daughter, his lips curled into a smile that didn't reach his eyes. That was his first mistake. Kids could spot a 'bad news' smile a mile away. 'When we got Porcupine, he was a kitten. But now, now he's all grown up. He's graduated from kitten college. He's passed his feline driving test. He's an adult, he's a cat ...'

Maeve's face shifted involuntarily.

'... and when people, and animals, grow up, they move out of home. When I was a child, I lived with your granny and grandad, but then I grew up and now I live here with you ...'

10

There it was again, a spasm just under the left eye. Christine winced in sympathy. A twitch. Wonderful. Just what the girl needed.

'... and when you grow up, you'll move out of this house too.'

'But I don't want to move out.'

'It won't happen for a long time.'

'I don't want to move out,' repeated Maeve, her voice creeping higher. 'I want to stay here. Mom? Do I have to move out? What if a baddie broke in or the house went on fire and I didn't know because I was asleep and there was nobody there to wake me or what if—'

'This is way, way in the future, Maevey,' explained Conor as the child's breathing grew louder. 'By then you'll be big, and you'll want to go. Caroline will move out first—'

'*Caroline's moving out?*'

Conor flinched. 'No, she's—'

'*Why is Caroline moving out?!*'

'I just meant because Caroline's older, she's fourteen and you're only—'

'Shush now, Maeve, breathe normally. It's all right. Caroline's not going anywhere,' said Christine, deciding her daughter's mental well-being should probably trump a learning opportunity for her husband. 'None of you are. We're all staying here, until we're old and grey and roaming around the house with walking sticks. All right? Okay?'

'And Porcupine is staying too? Until he's old and grey?'

'I'm not sure ... Conor?'

'Dad?'

'He's ...' Conor suddenly looked very tired. 'Yes. Porcupine is staying too. He's just having a sleepover at Mrs Rodgers' house.'

'A sleepover.' Maeve rolled the word around, deciding whether to believe it.

'Exactly. Like when you stayed at Amelia's house for her birthday and slept in sleeping bags and ordered pizza. I'd say Porcupine will have pepperoni, what do you reckon?'

Maeve smiled. 'He does like meat.'

'He loves meat,' said Conor, taking the reprieve and running with it. 'I'd say he'll ask them to bring a couple of portions of garlic sauce too, for dipping. Does that sound like Porcupine?'

'Cats can't dip, Dad.'

'No,' he agreed.

'He's having a sleepover?'

'Yes.'

'And he'll be home tomorrow?'

'Absolutely.'

'That's great news,' Christine chimed in, parodying her husband's enthusiasm. 'I look forward to seeing him then. Now, Maeve, back to bed.'

She followed her daughter up the stairs and into her room, which had the same animal wallpaper and curtains as when she'd first moved into it. Maeve had always been young for her age. She had an innocence that even Brian, four years her junior, was starting to shed.

The bedroom's centrepiece was a large noticeboard covered in drawings. Currently, it was dedicated to costume ideas for the Glass Lake musical and multiple, very similar pencil sketches of Porcupine. She'd done a good job of capturing his sly, soulless eyes. The noticeboard was always so singular in focus, and the artwork so concentrated, that it gave her daughter the air of an obsessive stalker. Maeve had got her single-mindedness (and her peculiarity) from her father. When Christine first met Conor – at a party in a squat in what felt like another lifetime – she couldn't believe anyone

12

grew up wanting to be a dentist. Yet by all accounts her husband's childhood bedroom had been much like this, only his noticeboard had been a shrine to teeth.

'Thank you for helping me with the teddy bear,' said Maeve as she climbed into bed. She took a tissue from the nightstand, wiped her nose, and pushed it under her pyjamas' sleeve.

'No problem.'

'And thank you for going to meet the Lakers tomorrow.'

Christine smiled tightly. 'No problem.'

The Lakers were the mothers, mainly alumni, who ran Glass Lake Primary from the shadows. The most ridiculous thing about the Lakers was that this was also how they referred to themselves.

'You can't be late, okay? The Lakers are never late, so I don't think that would go down well. If you're going to be late, you probably just shouldn't go at all.'

'I won't be late, Maeve.'

'And I was thinking maybe you could wear some legging things and a puffed waistcoat, maybe with fur on the collar ...'

'Like the ones Amelia's mom wears?'

'Yeah, kind of like that.'

Amelia's mom was Beverley Franklin, a prominent Laker and director of this year's school musical. She used to work at a pharmaceutical company but now she sold jellies that were 70 per cent vegetables on Facebook and spent too much time on the sixth-class parents' WhatsApp group.

'I'm not sure I have one of those jackets,' said Christine diplomatically. 'But it'll be fine, I promise you. I'm going to charm the pants off those other mothers, and I'm going to get you a position working on costumes.'

Maeve didn't look wholly convinced. 'You do know Amelia's mom, don't you?'

'Yes, I told you,' said Christine, tucking the duvet in around her daughter. 'I was in her class at Glass Lake – just like how Amelia is in yours.' *I just don't pin my entire identity on it*, she added silently. 'Me and Beverley go back years. Okay?'

Maeve gave a small nod.

'That's my girl.'

The Lakers organised annual golf outings and reunions (For a *primary* school!) and lucrative fundraisers. They had no say in the academics, thankfully – going on some of the stuff sent into the parents' WhatsApp groups, there were a few anti-vaxxers in their midst – but they had a regrettable amount of input into extracurricular activities. They met at the Strand café on Cooney Pier every Thursday morning, and if you wanted your child to make the swim team or get a solo in the choir or to work on costumes for the annual sixth-class musical, you better believe you were pulling up a chair and ordering a flat white.

Conor couldn't understand this because Conor was a blow-in – meaning he'd only been living in Cooney for sixteen years as opposed to being born, bred and, crucially, educated here.

'It seems insane that you have to take a whole morning off work to meet some women in a coffee shop just so Maeve can maybe be involved in the school play,' he said as they climbed into bed that night. 'Surely the teachers decide who gets to work on it.'

'It is insane. But that's Glass Lake. The parents are far too involved; they were even when I went there. But if it eases Maeve's mind, I can put up with them for an hour or two.'

'And where will Derek think you are?'

14

Derek was her boss at the *Southern Gazette*. He'd been editor of a national tabloid in Dublin until a heart attack, and his wife, forced him into a slower pace of life.

'I've told him I'm meeting a source.'

Derek regularly talked about tip-offs and whistle-blowers and sources. Christine, who specialised in hundredth birthdays and local council disputes, found it best to just play along.

'Anyway,' she said, 'you've got your own morning to worry about.'

'My Thursday's looking pretty relaxed,' said Conor, sleep making its way into his voice as he nuzzled into her. 'Nothing but routine check-ups until a root canal at noon.'

'I'm talking about the morning-morning, dear husband, and what exactly you're going to say when Porcupine doesn't turn up for breakfast.'

. . . .

Maeve Maguire didn't like getting out of bed in the middle of the night. The house was scarier and colder and sadder when the lights were off and everyone else was asleep. And she didn't like leaving her worry dolls unguarded. She lined them up under her pillow every night, and without her head to hold them in place, she worried they'd get up and run away.

In the daylight, Maeve knew they were only dolls and that dolls couldn't walk, let alone run. But at night, things were different. This was when the four tiny women in their bright dresses and dark pigtails would make a break for it. They would escape and tell everyone her secrets. She pictured them skipping along the streets of Cooney, avoiding the glow of the streetlamps and jumping over any deep cracks in the footpath (they were only teeny after all;

15

shorter than Maeve's middle finger) before they slipped into people's letterboxes, under their front doors and through any windows left ajar. She imagined them hopping up the stairs of these homes, sliding under doors and scaling the beds of Cooney's residents as they squeezed around pillows and climbed beside ears so they could whisper all the bad things that Maeve Maguire of Sixth Class, Glass Lake Primary, had done.

Maeve's biggest worry was that the dolls would achieve all this in the time it took her to get downstairs, do what needed to be done, and return to bed again. If Santa Claus could get around the world in a night, one little coastal town wasn't going to be much of an ask, especially when they could split it between four. If Maeve never knew they'd been gone, then she'd still go into school the next morning, where everyone would know her bad thoughts and bad deeds, and it would be too late to pretend to be sick.

She lifted her pillow and was comforted to see the dolls just as she'd left them. She looked away, then turned back extra quickly. They didn't move. She returned the pillow and slowly swung her legs out of bed. She crept out of her room and closed the door behind her. She grabbed a towel from the landing and pushed it against the gap under the door. She pulled the used tissue from under her pyjamas sleeve and squeezed it into the keyhole. Just in case.

Then, quick as she was able, and without making a sound, she snuck downstairs and did what she had promised to do.

3
· · · · ·

Beverley Franklin never wasted time. She did squats while brushing her teeth and jumping jacks when waiting for the kettle to boil. If suppliers placed her on hold, she put her phone on loudspeaker and cleaned a shelf of the fridge. She left floss beside her laptop and worked a thread of it around her mouth as she waited for the machine to load. And in the mornings, between shouting 'Rise and shine' and 'Let's go, let's go' at her two daughters, she did whatever household tasks could fit into the short window.

The first task this morning was to take delivery of the teddy bear. However, the taxi she'd ordered to collect the stuffed animal from Cooney Nursing Home had ignored either her precise timing instructions or the local speed limit and the driver was knocking on her door, package in hand, before she'd had a chance to deliver the first wake-up call.

'Twenty-six eighty,' said the driver, as she took the bag and removed the bear she'd commissioned several days ago. She'd read about the knitter in the *Southern Gazette*: an illustrious textiles career in Paris then London, where she made garments for the royal family. The article read like an obituary, but it had actually been to mark the woman's hundredth birthday. The centenarian played hard to get at first – retirement this, arthritis that, partial blindness the other – but Beverley kept phoning the nursing home and upping the fee until she relented. And, credit where it was due, the woman had delivered. The bear was navy blue with button eyes, a large white belly and a right arm an inch longer than its left. It was perfect, but not too perfect – just as Beverley had requested. She carried the thing through the foyer up the main flight of stairs to Amelia's bedroom and knocked on the door, ready to rouse her.

'Rise and shine, *ma chérie*,' she said, pushing the door open to reveal the pleasant surprise of her youngest daughter already up and dressed and sitting at her vanity table.

Amelia turned from the mirror. 'He's so cute!' she exclaimed, arms stretched out towards the bear. 'Thanks, Mum. I didn't even know you could knit.'

'If you have a problem, I have the solution. Now. Are you ready to wish your grandmother a happy birthday?' A lifetime of grafting had taught Beverley that when making morning to-do lists you should start with the task you most want to put off. 'I'll stand by the window. The light is better.'

She crossed the room to the bay window and pulled her phone from the pocket of her next-season Moncler diamond quilted gilet. (Shona Martin's mother was a buyer for Brown Thomas, and she'd gifted it to Beverley when she was announced as director of this year's Glass Lake musical.) She scrolled to video.

'Do you want to wish her a happy birthday, and I'll record it?'

'That's all right, *chérie*. She'd much rather see your lovely face.'

Amelia, thankfully, understood nothing of difficult mother-daughter relationships.

The girl gave her ponytail a firm tug and stood poker straight by her pale pink wardrobe. Beverley nodded and Amelia flew into action.

'Happy birthday, Granny, I love you so much!' she gushed. 'I can't wait to see you again. Thank you for being the best grandmother in the world! You're amazing!' Most people's eyes would be engulfed by a smile that wide, but Amelia's exaggerated features could take it. '*Happy birthday*,' she sang, then she blew three gorgeous kisses to the camera and it was all Beverley could do not to reach out to catch them.

'*Parfait!*' she enthused, pressing stop on the video. 'Absolutely perfect. That could have come straight from the account of an A-list influencer.'

Amelia smiled modestly. She had more than 2,000 followers on Instagram – double that of any other child in her class. 'Thanks, Mum.'

Amelia had inherited more from her mother than high cheekbones and excellent hair. She was driven and hard-working. She wanted to be an influencer and she had what it took to make it. That wasn't Beverley being a deluded parent, either. She wasn't like Lorna Farrell, who was convinced the school choirmaster had said Marnie was a 'pre-Madonna' and now believed her daughter was destined for world domination. Beverley actually *had* experience of the entertainment industry.

'I promised my followers I'd post my everyday make-up routine,' said Amelia, switching on the ring light they'd bought for her recent birthday. 'It's more authentic if I do it in the morning.'

'Authenticity is very important,' agreed Beverley, who had read a lot about social media strategies before launching Sneaky Sweets, the health food start-up she ran online. 'Don't forget to take off the make-up when you're finished. Glass Lake rules. Ten minutes, then downstairs for breakfast. You don't want me coming back in and ruining your shot.'

Although actually, wouldn't it be kind of cute to feature some candid bloopers? Beverley had toyed with suggesting she take a cameo role in Amelia's socials. Followers responded well to glimpses into family life. Amelia could post occasional clips from her acting days and then Beverley could talk about what a fun time it had been but how family was more important.

If only all this technology had been around when she was younger, her career could have been so different. Magazines and newspapers had been obsessed with Beverley – and what were they, if not the social media of their time? (Ella was forever telling her she was obsessed with things – herself, Amelia, cleanliness, Glass Lake – but this had been *real* obsession. There was a two-month period where she'd appeared in the *Sunday Independent* every single week.) More people had heard of Beverley Tandon (as she was then) than Pauline Quinn, the young temptress she'd played on *Cork Life*. Beverley remembered her agent telling her this like it was a bad thing: 'You're not Julia Roberts, Bev. You're a soap actress.' Now, though, self-promotion was an asset. She ran Sneaky Sweets almost entirely through Facebook and it was doing well. There were a lot of desperate parents frantically searching the internet for ways to feed their fussy eaters. But however good Beverley might be at selling jellies made from vegetables, she'd have been so much better at selling herself.

'*Mum!*' chided Amelia.

'Nine minutes,' she said, stepping back out on to the landing.

Phone still in hand, she opened the last recorded video. She wrote 'Happy birthday' and deleted it. Then she wrote 'Happy birthday, Mam.' 'Happy birthday, Frances.' 'On your special day!' 'HB, Mama.' 'Peace and light x.' The last one was definitely the most

Her Mother. She deleted it too and just clicked send. The video was self-explanatory.

Mentally ticking the task from her list, she strode along the landing. This was usually when she delivered Ella's wake-up call. However, last night she had politely asked her eighteen-year-old daughter if she had any plans for the weekend – she wasn't even that interested; she was just waiting for the Duolingo update to load – and Ella had responded by asking why she was so obsessed with her. (If anyone was obsessed it was Ella; and she was obsessed with the word 'obsessed'. Beverley should have said that last night. She always thought of retorts hours too late.)

She paused at the bottom of the stairs that led to the next floor. Ella's first lecture was at 10 a.m. – Beverley had her university timetable linked to the Alexa family calendar, along with Malachy's work schedule, Amelia's after-school activities, and her own myriad appointments – and if she didn't get up soon, she'd be late. But Beverley kept walking. If that was how she was going to speak to her mother, she could sing for a wake-up call.

Next up was the toilet bowl in the main first-floor bathroom. There were, as Malachy had so eloquently described it a few hours earlier, 'stringy particles' stuck to the edges. She ran the hot tap and pulled the bleach and a pair of rubber gloves from the box of cleaning supplies Greta kept in the bathroom cupboard.

Ella accused her of 'Catholic guilt' for cleaning before Greta came, and 'white privilege' for having a cleaner in the first place. Whatever about being white (everyone she knew was white!), the Catholic guilt accusation was untrue. Greta worked for all the Glass Lake mothers, and Beverley cleaned before she came for the same reason the Franklins did their banking in Cork City rather than Cooney and Beverley went all the way to Dublin to see her dermatologist. Because people talked. And she'd rather not give them anything interesting to discuss.

Pulling on the Marigolds, she grabbed the toilet brush firmly in both hands and applied brute force to the rim of the bowl until the debris came loose.

'It looks like bits of food,' her husband had said, as he stood at the foot of their bed at 5.30 that morning, stretching his glutes in preparation for his daily pre-dawn run. Malachy did not share Beverley's inherent drive – he'd been born wealthy instead – but when it came to his appearance, he found the motivation. 'I wouldn't be surprised if Ella has an eating disorder.'

'I doubt it,' Beverley had replied, as he placed his palms flat against the wall that separated their room from the second guest bedroom. 'It's probably just hard water build-up. I'll take a look.' Then, because he still wasn't appeased, she added: 'You look well toned.'

Flattery always settled her husband.

She carried the toilet brush over to the sink now and rinsed it under the flowing tap. It was important people thought she'd never dream of cleaning her own toilet, but the actual act of it was nothing. Hard graft and an eye on the future. That was how she'd secured such an enviable life.

Tick, tick.

The final item on Thursday's to-do list was admin. There were seventy-two unread WhatsApp messages. Being a Glass Lake mother was a full-time job and Beverley already had a full-time job, no matter what Ella thought. (It was hard to be a girl-boss role model for a daughter who dismissed your crusade to revolutionise the food industry as 'refreshing your Facebook page'.) Beverley was sometimes tempted to let elements of school life slide, but there were parents and children counting on her, not to mention the reputation of Glass Lake itself. She skipped the Sixth-Class Parents group, the Wonderful Wizard of Oz group, the School Trip to Dublin group and opened the Lakers thread.

Lorna Farrell said, 'Is it terrible that Thursday is my favourite day because I get to have a Strand café flapjack?' Fiona Murphy said, 'That's how I feel about Friday – aka Wineday.' Lorna Farrell sent two cry-laughing emojis. Claire Keating said, 'Wineyay!' and sent a gif of a monkey drinking a bottle of Merlot.

Beverley went to put the phone away – they were meeting in forty minutes, for Christ's sake, no wonder she was the only one who ever seemed to get anything done – when a new message came through from Lorna.

'Today's meeting is going to be extra special – get ready for BIG news, ladies!! Isn't that right @BeverleyFranklin?' This was followed by a wink emoji, and then a cry-laughing emoji. Lorna ended all her messages like this, even when it made no sense.

The top of the screen alternated between telling her Claire was typing and Fiona was typing. 'What's the news??' said one. 'Spill spill!' said the other.

Beverley's grip tightened.

She was director of this year's Glass Lake Primary musical. *She* was the one who'd lobbied the national broadcaster. Everything Beverley had done, from selecting the highly visual *Wonderful Wizard of Oz* to thinking big on set designs and casting the leads early, had been to catch the TV station's attention. She'd sent in headshots of Amelia and Woody Whitehead. (If anything proved

Beverley's commitment, it was her willingness to cast a Whitehead. They were a scourge on Cooney, but even she couldn't deny the youngest son had a face, and name, for stardom.) And it had worked. Lorna Lick-Arse Farrell was not going to steal her thunder.

Beverley composed herself and fired off a response–

'BIG news, ladies. HUGE. I've a hectic morning on here, but I'll do my best to get to the Strand early. *Á bientôt.*'

– then she locked her screen and slid the phone back into her pocket. She shoved the bleach and gloves behind the cistern – Greta would tidy them away – and hurried out on to the landing.

On Thursdays, Beverley had Amelia at school for 8.40, dropped Malachy's shirts to the dry-cleaner's when they opened at 8.50, and was over at the Strand café on the other side of Cooney for 8.55. She would hang back in the car until she saw a few other mothers go in. Just because she no longer worked in the city didn't mean she had time to be sitting around waiting on people. This morning, though, she'd be in there first. Amelia could be a few minutes early and the shirts could wait.

She walked purposefully along the landing – let's see who was obsessed with what when Ella was late for college! – and headed for her younger daughter's bedroom.

Had she thought about it, she would have knocked. They'd talked about privacy last summer and agreed Amelia was entitled to some.

But she was in a hurry.

Her mind was full of Lorna Lick-Arse Farrell and how the Yellow Brick Road still looked bronze and the way Malachy had watched himself in the mirror that morning.

She was distracted.

She wasn't thinking.

She turned the handle to her daughter's room without any warning.

'*Chérie,*' she was saying before she was fully through the door, 'we've to leave early so maybe you can do—'

Amelia looked away from her phone. She was standing near the window, holding the too-large device aloft in her too-small hand as she angled it towards her body. Her entirely naked body.

'Mum!'

Her daughter – her beautiful, ambitious, *twelve-year-old* daughter – was wearing a full-face of make-up and not a stitch more.

Her skinny arms pushed against her sides, causing her barely-there boobs to move ever-so-slightly closer together and the skin at her sternum to dent. Beverley had never seen her do anything remotely like that with her mouth, her cheeks, her eyes. She barely recognised the expression as belonging to Amelia. The prominent hip bones and faint wisps of pubic hair came as delayed shocks, and the sticky, cherry-coloured gloss bleeding up on to the skin above her puffed out lips made Beverley's stomach lurch. But it was the pleading look on her daughter's face that would haunt her. It said 'like me' and 'love me' and 'reassure me' but also, and this was too much for Beverley because she was sure her daughter didn't even know what it meant and didn't want to imagine where she'd seen it, it said 'fuck me'.

This pushed Beverley over the edge.

Shock, upset and fury reverberated around her body, rattling against her ribcage and up her trachea, before launching themselves into the pale pink room in a high-pitched guttural scream.

No amount of chalky blusher could stop the colour disappearing from Amelia's face; a blackbird fled from the window ledge behind her; and a teenage boy awoke in a room upstairs where he'd been sleeping, all night, entirely unbeknownst to Beverley.

4

· · · · ·

Arlo Whitehead's dream always went the same way. He and Leo
and Mike were playing on stage at a massive stadium that was
Madison Square Garden but also Cooney Parish Hall. Arlo had never
been to New York (he'd never been further than Lanzarote) but he'd
watched Tom Petty live at Madison Square enough times to know
the venue. Sometimes Neil Young was watching from the wings, and
sometimes it was the guy who'd driven their school bus. Whoever
it was, he was always totally impressed. It was all going well – until
the last song. Even though Arlo could never hear anything in his
dreams (he wished he could; the crowd were totally into whatever
they were playing), he knew they were falling out of time. When he
looked over at Leo, ready to shout at him to sort it out, he noticed
his best friend no longer had arms. Leo was just looking down at
the guitar hanging around his neck, screaming. Leo screamed and
screamed at the instrument until his face started to melt away.

Arlo had googled 'How to stop having the same dream'. The
most common suggestion was to write down the details so he could
interpret their meaning. But this was the only dream he ever had,
and it didn't take Freud to work it out.

So, when he was roused by an almighty roar, he wasn't overly
alarmed. He assumed it was Leo screaming about his missing limbs

and was relieved to have woken before his friend's face started to run down his body.

But then he remembered where he was, and that there was never noise in his dreams. ·

He pushed himself up in the still unfamiliar four-poster bed and looked over at Ella. She was also awake, and though she wasn't screaming, there was a look of mild alarm on her perfect face. (Ella's perfection was beside the point, but it was difficult not to register, no matter the circumstances.)

'That's my mum,' she said, and suddenly he was completely alert.

'Your mom?' He scrambled further up, grabbing his T-shirt and navy jumper from the floor before climbing out of the bed. 'What time is it?' His foot caught slightly on the under sheet, which had come untucked. 'Shit, Ella! I knew I shouldn't have come over last night!'

Ella's parents did not know about Arlo. Well, they *knew* about him, in the way that everyone in Cooney knew about him: as Charlie Whitehead's son, a subject of suspicion, and the only teenager to have walked away from the Reilly's Pass crash intact. But they didn't know about him in the way that mattered: as Ella's boyfriend, as the love of their daughter's life.

'Where are my trousers? Why didn't the alarm go off?' he said, lying on his front on the floor so he could see under the bed. The Franklins' carpet had to be felt to be believed; it was softer than his own bed at home. 'Maybe someone saw me sneaking in last night? There are so many streetlights around here. I don't think there's more than three in our whole estate. I knew it was too risky.'

'Arlo, breathe,' said Ella, climbing out of the bed. She had a red mark on her left cheek from how she'd slept and was wearing the

E&A necklace he'd bought for her birthday and his favourite Dylan T-shirt. They had cover stories ready for where both items had come from, but Ella's parents never asked. Her hair was dark blond and cropped. She'd cut it short to piss off her mother, which Arlo didn't condone, but it was sexy. Although it was sexy when she'd had it long, too. Her eyes were pale blue and hypnotic, like an ocean. He'd written that into a song, but he hadn't shown it to Ella yet. Lyrics without music were cheesy. And with Leo gone and Mike gone-gone, he'd be waiting a while for someone to put it to music.

His trousers were not under the bed.

'Maybe your sister told her. Would Amelia do that?'

He was back on his feet and Ella was coming towards him. Already he felt happier. The mark on her cheek was a perfect circle. Half of him marvelled at how that was possible, and the other half thought, 'Ah, but of course'. Everything about Ella Belle Franklin was perfect.

He'd never been in love before and it was amazing. Sometimes he'd be working away, thinking about nothing but expanding pipes or shelf brackets, and then he'd be overcome by a giddy, nervous feeling, as if it was Christmas Eve or the day of some amazing gig, but it was actually just because Ella existed and she wanted to spend that existence with him. Wasn't that incredible? Love was better than all the songs said, even Leonard Cohen's. He wouldn't go as far as to say it was better than sex, but it was definitely equally good.

'Amelia wouldn't do that,' she said, standing in front of him. 'My mum doesn't know.' Ella was the only person he knew who said 'Mum'. He'd thought only English people said that. But then the Franklins were very wealthy, which was almost the same as being English. 'Not that I'd care if she did find out.'

29

'I know, but I care. I need more time.'

A couple more months of working hard and word would get around (as you could rely on it to do in Cooney) that he was a pretty decent lad and not, in fact, 'just like his father'. Then Arlo could look his future parents-in-law in the eye and tell them how wonderful their daughter was. The plan involved turning up early to every job, putting in long hours, doing good work and never saying anything rude no matter what was said to him. The plan did not involve getting caught in Ella's bedroom with no trousers on.

'Relax. There's no way she knows. Bev is too wrapped up in her own life to notice.' Ella also called her mother 'Bev'. She did it to annoy her, even when she wasn't there.

'She was yelling about something.'

'She probably spotted a blackhead in the bathroom mirror. Or maybe Amelia wasn't wearing the exact Glass Lake regulation knee socks. Who knows why Bev does anything? But there's no way she's coming near this room. I told you, we're fighting.'

Arlo tried not to come to Ella's house too often – getting caught sneaking up the Franklins' stairs was also not part of the reputation rehabilitation plan – but whenever he did, Ella picked a fight with her mother. This was apparently a watertight guarantee that Beverley would not come near her bedroom. 'Not until I apologise,' Ella explained. 'She wouldn't give me the satisfaction.' Arlo had grown up in a house where arguments were loud, instant affairs; Mom got annoyed at Dad, Dad charmed Mom, and then it was over. Ella's logic was alien. And he felt bad for Beverley.

Do not feel bad for Beverley Franklin. She's a head melt. Trust me. Who cares if she likes you or not?

It's all right for you, Leo. Everyone in this town loves you. They cross the road when they see me. They think I'm cursed or a bad omen or something.

Really, Arly? You really think it's all right for me?

Arlo pushed his best friend from his head – they could talk on the drive to work – just as Ella stepped forward and kissed him on the lips. She slipped her tongue into his mouth and he grinned. Then he remembered the current situation.

'What time is it? My phone is in my – there they are!' His trousers were hanging off the couch at the end of the bed, which Ella had informed him was actually a *chaise longue*. 'Give anything a French name and Bev will pay three times more for it.' He pulled on his jeans and found his phone in the back pocket.

8.28 a.m.

Not late, so. Not yet.

Good.

If there was one job he couldn't afford to mess up, it was this morning's.

．．．．．．．．．．．．．．．．．．．．．．

'What are you doing?! Why would you do that?! *What is wrong with you?!*'

'I wasn't … I'm sorry!' Amelia shouted back, whipping a blanket from the end of her bed. 'Don't freak out, Mum, please! I'm sorry!'

The reverberation in Beverley's head continued. She looked at her daughter, face caked in make-up, then down at the phone lying on the bed. 'Jesus Christ!' she cried. 'Jesus, Amelia! *Jesus Christ!*'

'I'm sorry!'

Beverley took a moment and shut her eyes, only as soon as she did, she was assaulted by the image of her daughter pouting into the camera. Where had she seen such an expression? They flew open again.

'Who was it for?'

Amelia's doe eyes were smothered in blue shimmery eyeshadow. Beverley had not known she owned anything so cheap.

She repeated herself. 'Who was the photo for, Amelia?'

'I don't ... It wasn't for anyone.'

Beverley needed to think. She closed her eyes, but there it was again. Was the goddam image tattooed on to her eyelids for all eternity now?

'Don't lie to me.'

'Mum.'

'Do not lie to me!'

'I wasn't sending the photo to anyone,' she pleaded. 'I wasn't. I swear.'

Beverley took a deep breath but did not remove her gaze from her daughter.

'It was just for me. I just ... I wanted to see what it would look like.'

The girl cringed, but she didn't look away. She was shivering, in spite of the blanket.

After what she'd found on Malachy's phone in April, Beverley was bound to be sensitive. But not everyone was as perverted as her husband. Young girls experimented. She was only twelve, for God's sake. Who would she be sending it to?

'Amelia.'

'I swear on your life, Mum.'

God help her, but the child appeared to be telling the truth.

'You swear you weren't sending it to anyone?'

'I swear,' said Amelia emphatically. 'I wouldn't. That's gross.'

Beverley agreed. It *was* gross.

Amelia's face was bright red, and Beverley struggled to tell where the excessive blusher ended and the embarrassment began.

'All right,' she said. 'Well, thank God for that.' She let out a loud sigh. Amelia looked equally relieved. 'You know you shouldn't be taking photos like that regardless? You don't know who could hack into your phone, or if it got stolen, where they might end up. It's a very stupid thing to do.'

'I know. I'm sorry.'

Beverley threw back her head. 'All right.' She leaned forward so her hands rested on her thighs, then she straightened up again. 'Okay. Get dressed, quick. And take off that make-up. We have to get going. I need to leave early.'

Amelia hurried back to her vanity table, where she'd thrown her camisole and school shirt.

'No time for breakfast. I'll grab some fruit,' said Beverley, heading for the door. 'And I'll meet you out at the car.'

'Sorry for giving you a fright, Mum.'

Beverley turned back to her daughter, who was attempting a smile. Of course she wasn't sending erotic photographs of herself out into the world at twelve years of age. Had she that little faith in her own parenting skills? These were the kinds of tender moments she never had with Ella any more. She should cherish them.

'And I'm sorry I thought the worst,' she replied, instructing her own face to soften. 'Forgive me?'

Amelia grinned. 'Always.'

'Good.'

Her hand was on the doorknob and she had one foot out in the landing when she heard it. A vibration.

Quick as a flash, she turned.

'Mum—'

But Beverley was back in the room and over at the bed before Amelia had thought to move.

She looked down at the screen.

Her daughter had one new message.

Beverley did not recognise the App logo, but she knew the sender's name. There was no need to unlock the phone. The reply was succinct.

| Got it!!! Thanks!!!

For the second time that morning, Beverley emitted noises she had not known she was capable of making.

....

'Are you nervous?' asked Ella, sitting beside him on the edge of the bed as he pulled on his boots.

'About what?'

'Arlo.' She grinned.

'Oh, about Glass Lake!' he replied, bringing his hand to his forehead and generally making a joke of it even though he'd had an uneasy feeling in his stomach ever since he agreed to take on the job at the school. 'It'll be fine.'

'Of course it will.'

'I just have to be on time and do the best work I can.'

She kissed him on the cheek. 'I love you.'

She never seemed to mind that he didn't say it back. Probably because she knew he did love her – of course he did! – it was just that every time he tried to say it his tongue swelled in his mouth and his head got so hot that he thought it might actually go on fire.

'It's just part time, for a couple of weeks,' he said. 'I doubt I'll even see Principal Patterson.' His stomach flip-flopped. He *hoped* he wouldn't see her.

More yelling from the floor below. The only words he could decipher came from Beverley.

'Well, she's lucky to have you working there. You're so good with your hands.'

Arlo blushed, even though Ella hadn't meant it *that* way. Although, he hoped she did mean it that way too. He definitely put in the effort.

'This town, though. Some people can be real jerks.'

'I know.'

'They can be totally unfair and terrible …' She was trying to make him feel better, but the flip-flopping in his stomach had turned to sloshing. '… and just tiny-minded gossip lickers.'

'Gossip lickers?'

'Or whatever,' she said. 'You know what I mean.'

People had only recently stopped sticking 'For Sale' signs in the Whiteheads' front garden. And two weeks ago, while he was walking down Main Street, a man spat at him. He hadn't told Ella that. He didn't tell her any more than he had to, in case it sowed seeds of doubt. 'Yeah. I know.'

'That's why we're getting out,' she declared, throwing herself back on the bed and pulling him with her. 'One more year. Less than a year. Woody will be finished primary school in June, and then we go. Right?'

'Right,' Arlo agreed, pretending to do the maths even though he knew exactly how far away it was. 'Eight months.' *One week and four days.* 'Then it's goodbye Cooney, hello Cork city.'

'We'll rent an apartment, overlooking the river.'

'Or maybe a little house, with two bedrooms,' he said, lying back beside her. 'One for us, and one for Woody when he comes to stay, or Amelia.'

'Amelia can only visit if she promises not to tell Bev our whereabouts.'

'We'll get a little dog ...'

'Called Wisdom,' said Ella.

'Or Cooney.'

'Why would we call our dog Cooney? We want to *forget* Cooney.'

'Okay fine, Wisdom,' said Arlo. 'And we'll grow our own vegetables and we'll have friends over for dinner, and when you come home from university, we'll sit in our garden—'

'Or on our balcony.'

'Right, and we'll be so happy that we'll listen to songs about heartbreak and we won't have a clue what they're going on about.'

Ella laughed. 'And then you'll go to college ...'

'Maybe.'

'Arlo!'

'Maybe I will, or maybe I'll be such a successful handyman by then that I'll have my own business with lots of employees and I won't need college.'

'You're still planning to re-sit your leaving cert next year, right?'

'You're ruining the daydream here, Ella.'

'Have you applied for the re-sits?'

'Daydream disappearing. Daydream disappearing,' he said in an automated voice, moving his arms in a robotic fashion.

'Have you?'

'I will.' He wouldn't.

He pushed himself up, stood on the bed and peered out the skylight. Beverley's Range Rover was still in the driveway.

'Shoes!' Ella swiped at his feet.

'Sorry,' he said, clambering down. 'Isn't your mom usually gone by now?' The only thing that made sneaking into the Franklins' after midnight slightly less of a gamble was that Ella's parents had schedules you could set your watch by. Her dad was always gone before they woke, and her mom left to drop Amelia to school at 8.24. Arlo checked his phone again. 'I need to leave.'

Ella jumped up from the bed and pulled a cardigan from the floor. 'I'll go down and distract her,' she said. 'And when the coast is clear, I'll give the signal and you make a run for it.'

She was grinning now. Ella loved the espionage.

Arlo could do without it.

'Sounds risky,' he said.

She shrugged. The beige knit slid down her left shoulder. How was her skin so perfect? Like silky milk. *Silk milk.* That might actually work as a lyric. 'Let's just wait it out then,' she said, throwing herself back down on the bed, 'and you can be late.'

The mere suggestion brought him out in a sweat.

Arlo groaned. Ella gave a gleeful grin.

'We just need a signal ...' She looked around the room. Her eyes landed on a poster by the door. 'Hang ten!'

'Hang ten?'

'Hang ten,' echoed Ella, gravely this time. 'When you hear me shouting "Hang ten", you make a break for it.'

'How are you going to casually yell "Hang ten" at your mother?' Arlo thought about this and burst out laughing.

'What?' demanded Ella.

'Beverley ... On a surfboard. In her furry jacket thing ... And her face ...' Arlo tried to rearrange his face into the mildly pained expression Ella's mother always wore, but he was laughing too much.

Ella furrowed her brows. Fits of giggles were her thing, not his.

'Ah, yeah,' he gasped, wiping his eyes.

'Okay, chuckles. Keep the bedroom door open, and when you hear me say "Hang ten", go!'

5

· · · · ·

Beverley saw Ella approaching and shifted her expression to indifferent. A crisis with one daughter did not automatically bring the other back into her good books. The eighteen-year-old was wearing her lovely 'Ella & Amelia' necklace and that mangy old T-shirt she always slept in after they had a fight: yet another punishment for Beverley, who regularly ordered expensive matching pyjamas from Anthropologie for the three Franklin women.

'Shouldn't you have left by now?' said Ella, less defiant than usual. Beverley took the tone, and eye contact, in the apologetic manner it was intended. Ella glanced behind her mother: 'You're going to be late for school.'

'Being late is the least of your sister's problems,' said Beverley. 'Do you know what I just caught her doing? Do you?' Beverley hoped that somehow she would know because she honestly wasn't sure how she could put it into words.

'Was she applying make-up with her feet?' said Ella, stepping into the bedroom and closing the door. 'There's literally no space between your lip gloss and your nose, Amelia.'

Why was Ella closing the door? Beverley needed air. She did not need a closed door.

'Amelia, tell her. Tell your sister what you were doing.'

Amelia went to take the phone from the bed.

39

'Do not touch that, I swear to God!' Beverley picked up the device and flung it across the room. She didn't want to look at it, never mind touch it, ever again. 'And get some make-up remover. Now!'

'Jesus, Amelia, what *did* you do?'

The girl shrugged. 'I took a photo.'

'Of what?' said Ella.

'Of myself.'

'A selfie. Yeah, I think I've heard of them.' Ella kicked her left foot back, so the sole was resting against the still-closed door.

'Open that please, Ella.'

The teenager didn't budge. 'Great to hear you're trying new things, little sister.'

'She took a photo of herself *in the nip*. A sex picture, a whatever you call them ...' The confined space was making Beverley a little breathless. Was this the worst thing that had ever happened to her? No. Of course it wasn't. *Get a grip, woman!* But it was the worst thing since the last time she'd stumbled across a naked photograph. 'Can you open that door? I'm feeling a little light-headed.'

'A dick pic?' suggested Ella.

'Gross!' shrieked Amelia.

'Who was the dick pic for?'

'It's not a dick pic! It's a nude.' Amelia stuck her tongue out at her sister.

A nude. Jesus wept. She made it sound like she'd been posing for an early Renaissance masterpiece.

'A boy at school,' replied Beverley, struggling to accept she was having this conversation. 'A sick little toerag who is going to regret the day he laid eyes on my daughter ... I'm going to see Principal

Patterson this morning and I'll have him expelled before the day is out. Open the door, Ella!'

'So, you're taking dick pics now …'

'It's not a dick pic because I don't have a dick.'

'If you say so.'

'Mum, tell Ella to stop saying I'm taking dick pics! I don't have a dick!'

'Can you both *please* stop saying dick? Amelia, you're barely twelve. You shouldn't even know what a dick is.'

'I knew what a dick was when I was like eight, Mum.'

Beverley shut her eyes. 'Gah!'

'What?'

'Nothing, just my new internal screensaver.' She needed to get out of this room.

'It's not even a big deal.'

'Not another word, Amelia! Get your bag, get downstairs, and get in the car. We're going to the school. And bring the make-up remover. Sweet mother of God, Ella, if you do not open that door now, I am going to really lose it.'

'I'm doing it, I just …' Ella opened the door a fraction and started shouting. Then she shut it again.

'What are you doing? What is Hang Ten? I said "open", Ella. Jesus! You're too old to be competing for attention. Amelia – take the bear, come on. Do not touch that phone!'

'But we're allowed—'

'I said leave it. Ella, open the bloody door! Now!' Beverley grabbed her youngest daughter by the arm, walked around her eldest and yanked the bedroom door open.

A faint bang echoed from the hallway below. Beverley might have questioned it if it wasn't for the accompanying, and oh so welcome, cool breeze that it sent gusting up the stairs.

....

'Sweet Jesus!'

Christine opened the bathroom door to find her daughter standing in the threshold.

'Is Porcupine back?'

Maeve had already gone through her mother's wardrobe, seeking suitable clothes for her meeting with the Lakers. She'd found skinny jeans that Christine had forgotten she owned, and which were now cutting off her circulation.

'That's nothing to do with me,' she replied, sticking her fingers into the jeans waistband as she tried to eke out some space. 'You'll have to ask your father.'

Maeve followed her down the stairs. 'He said to ask you.'

'And I'm telling you to ask him.'

'I can't.'

'Why not?' she asked, catching a glimpse of herself in the hallway mirror. She looked like she'd eaten Beverley Franklin.

'Because he already left for work.'

'He *left*?' Christine stuck her head into the sitting room and the study before marching down to the kitchen. No sign of the coward. His surgery did not open until 9.30. Conor never left before her.

'Yes, when you were in the shower. He said it was a dental emergency. So? Is he back?'

'Who?' asked Brian, slurping his cereal.

'Are those Frosties, Brian? You know you're only allowed Frosties at the weekend.'

'No, cornflakes,' said her son, lifting the bowl and necking the evidence.

Her daughter was down on all fours, peering under the table and making *psssh-psssh* sounds.

'Maeve, breakfast, come on.'

'But I don't see him.'

'Who?' asked Brian again.

'Porcupine,' came the voice from under the table. 'He was at a sleepover in Mrs Rodgers' house last night.'

Brian looked sceptical. 'Says who?'

'Mom.'

'I did not. Your father said he was at a sleepover. I never said a thing.'

'Mom, Dad, same difference.' Maeve was opening the back door now. 'Here, Porcupine! Heeeerrrrre, Porcupine!'

'Okay, that's it, time to go.'

'But I didn't have my breakfast.'

'No time. Here' – Christine opened the cupboard and threw two cereal bars at Maeve – 'let's go.'

'I want cereal bars!'

'Do not push me, Brian. I can smell the sugar off your breath from here.'

'But—'

Christine rounded on her daughter. 'Do you want me to be late for the Lakers?'

Maeve shoved the bars into the side of her backpack. 'Come on, Brian, let's go.'

Her youngest child slipped down from the table and they both followed Maeve out of the house to the car.

'He's not at a sleepover, is he?' said Brian, dragging his schoolbag down the path.

'I don't know anything about it. Ask your father.'

She unlocked the car from the front garden and threw a glance down the street, but there was no sign of life from number one Seaview Terrace.

Brian climbed into the back seat beside his sister. 'I'm sorry, Maeve, but Porcupine is dead.'

Christine whipped her head around. 'What?! No, he's not! Brian!'

'He's at a sleepover,' said Maeve, her face doing that involuntary twitch thing again, as she glanced to the front seat for reassurance. She looked tired and Christine wondered if it was worrying about the cat or the musical that had kept her daughter up.

She slowed down as they passed Mrs Rodgers' house, nestled behind a garden of perfectly pruned rose bushes. The cheerful flowers had masked the truth for so long. But no more. She would be getting that cat back, and an apology with it. In another life, one before children and beyond Cooney, Christine had attended demonstrations and sit-ins. Her activism was rusty – the last thing Cooney had protested was a Starbucks opening – but you didn't need to be a member of Amnesty International to know stealing a family pet was wrong.

'When Pablo's gerbil died, his parents told him it had moved to China.'

'Porcupine is not dead, Brian.'

'He's at a sleepover. Both Dad *and* Mom say it,' said Maeve. 'Right, Mom?'

Christine turned left onto Reilly's Pass, towards Franklin Avenue, though she had a good mind to swing by the dental surgery instead. 'Right,' she said through gritted teeth.

Gerry Regan, the town pharmacist, was stopped at the lights. He was dressed in full Lycra, lit like a scrawny Christmas tree and yelling up at the driver of an oil tanker. Articulated trucks were not allowed on this stretch. Local opposition had intensified since the crash last February, even though that had involved a single car.

Christine honked her horn and raised a fist towards Gerry in solidarity. (There was life in the old activist yet.) But now the carriage door was opening, and the driver was climbing down.

Brian twisted to catch a glimpse of the action as they sped on.

'A sleepover,' repeated Maeve, confirming the story to herself.

'Yes, Maeve, and one day we'll all be at that sleepover,' said Brian, placing a soft hand on his sister's knee. 'A big sleepover in the sky.'

....

Arlo had parked the van the next street over. He did this in case Ella's parents spotted it and started asking questions. After his dad went to jail, his mom wanted to sell the thing, and all the tools with it. But Arlo had been helping out since he was thirteen; he was well able to take over the handyman trade, or at least keep it going until his dad got out.

At the end of the road, he turned back and could just about make out Beverley Franklin bursting through her front door with Amelia trailing in her wake. He'd heard them talking as he skipped past the bedroom but hadn't hung around to get the details. Whatever it was about, he felt bad for Amelia. Arlo liked Ella's little sister. She knew about him and Ella but hadn't said a word. In exchange, she'd told him she fancied his little brother Woody and he'd promised not to say anything either.

Woody was the reason Arlo was still in Cooney. He'd have moved to Cork city the day Ella started university there, but his dad had made him promise one thing: to look after his mother and twelve-year-old brother. He couldn't say he was doing a great job of it, but Woody's entry into the moody teenage phase a year early was hardly his fault. Woody would be done at Glass Lake in June and heading to secondary school two towns over, where he might have a chance to be more than the son of a convicted killer.

Cooney didn't care that Woody was only a kid or that he'd had no say in what his dad had done or drunk or driven. People used to remark on how good-looking and fun Charlie Whitehead was and how he'd cut them a deal or done some extra job for free. Now they came up to his sons on the street and said their dad was a drunk and a chancer who had an eye for the women.

Arlo crossed the road towards his van. The path was carpeted in leaves and a woman was striding towards him, led by a cute dog in a fluorescent pink jacket. The woman swung her hips as she walked, and the dog waggled its butt, so that they kept perfect time.

Everyone hated Charlie Whitehead for what he'd done to Mike and Leo and their families, but also for what he'd done to the town. Cooney was supposed to be the home of Tidy Town wins and blue flag beaches, not a drunk driver who'd killed one teenager and left another in a wheelchair.

He smiled at the dog as it drew nearer, then up at the woman. She wore a sweatband around her head. It was an identical shade of pink to her dog's jacket.

'Shame on you.'

The woman was still in transit and Arlo didn't register what she'd said until she had passed.

He inhaled sharply and turned back, but she bustled on, hips picking up speed. Did she think he was going to run after her? Tackle her to the ground and demand she take it back?

It happened all the time, but it still knocked the wind out of him. He took three deep breaths, then opened the door of his van and climbed in.

He still had work to do, that was all. He just had to try harder.

He put his key in the ignition and tuned in the old stereo. He turned up the volume. Then he turned it up more.

Aren't you going to talk to me?

Can't. I need to keep my head in the game.

Pity you didn't do that the night my life was destroyed.

I'm sorry, Leo.

Or Mike's life. Do you spend enough time thinking about Mike's life? Do you spend enough time missing him?

I'm sorry. I'm really sorry, all right?

Not really, Arly, no. But I suppose it'll have to do.

6
· · · · ·

Christine was at the top of the queue, jabbing around in her bag, when she was struck by an image of her Keep Cup relaxing on the top drawer of the dishwasher. She'd meant to pack it while Maeve was having breakfast.

Feck.

Her eyes flickered to the stack of disposable cups already decorated in cheery Christmas imagery.

The barista smiled, waiting.

'I don't suppose your cups are compostable, are they?'

'I'm actually not sure,' he replied with an enthusiasm usually reserved for helpful answers.

Their deep red background and delicate snow scenes were so inviting, not to mention how much better the proportions were for retaining heat than the Strand café's vast ceramic mugs. But Maeve had recently informed her that a disposable cup took five hundred years to biodegrade. Christine had been outwardly horrified and quietly guilty. (Ice caps melting! Polar bears dying! All so she could keep her coffee warmer a little longer.) That was when she'd bought the Keep Cup.

She sighed, grabbing a two-pack of waffle biscuits from in front of the register. 'I'll take a mug,' she told the barista stoically.

She paid and moved to the end of the counter to wait on her flat white. Beth Morton, who taught at a boys' secondary school two towns over, was already waiting. Christine lifted a hand to greet the petite woman. Beth had three sons in Glass Lake, one of whom was in Maeve's class.

'What do you think of Lorna Farrell's hairband?' asked Beth as Christine stood in beside her. 'Too much, or just enough?'

She followed her gaze to the corner alcove where a gossip of women was huddled around three tables scattered with cups and phones and car keys. Christine had been in school with half of them. The difference was she'd left; she'd lived in other places, had other experiences, and while she had ultimately ended up back in Cooney, she did not consider it to be the centre of the universe. It wasn't even the centre of West Cork.

'I've never been able to wear them,' said Christine, watching Lorna's head dip towards her notebook, the emerald stones of her hair accessory catching the harsh café light. 'They always end up going more headband than hairband on me.'

'Same,' said Beth, taking her coffee (served in a lovely, cheery Christmas cup). 'Last time I wore one, my husband said I reminded him of Axl Rose.' She took a sip and licked her lips. 'What are you in for?'

'School musical. You?'

'Same. Feck it, anyway. I knew I should have come last week. Maeve's not after lighting, is she?'

'No. Costumes.'

'Well, that's something, I suppose.'

'Flat white for here!'

Christine took her mug, which was more like a bowl – did the surface area really need to be *so* wide? – and added two sugars.

49

'I'm just glad Ethan doesn't want to be in the thing. Zero stage presence, that lad. He's the only one of my boys I ever left at the supermarket. There has to be less competition for the backstage roles, right?'

'You'd imagine. And it's a school play; there's got to be something for everyone.'

'In a perfect world, sure. But we're not in a perfect world. We're in Glass Lake,' said Beth, taking Christine's discarded sugar sachets and throwing them in the bin. 'At least you're one of them. Oh, don't give me that look, Christine. You know what I mean. You went to the school. I'm not even from Cork.'

'Well, I don't think I'm in the Lakers' good books either. Lorna has been thick with me since an argument in the playground last year. She refused to let Brian on the other swing because Annabelle's imaginary friend was using it.'

'I'm supposed to be in double geography right now. I told them the boiler burst.' Beth blew air through her lips as she shook out her shoulders. 'Christ on a bike. I feel like *I'm* the one auditioning. Why do we do this to ourselves?'

'I have no idea,' replied Christine, who should have been at her desk, working on an article about cuts to West Cork's bus service. She didn't know what she was going to do when she got back to the office after meeting her 'source' and had no juicy information to relay.

'There are other schools.'

'Absolutely,' agreed Christine, though they both knew that if you lived in West Cork and didn't at least try to get your kid into Glass Lake you were basically negligent.

There was a child in Brian's class who travelled out from Cork city every day. He only got into Glass Lake because his mother took a job as a special needs assistant. Halfway through his first year, she quit, and they couldn't very well kick him out. Heaps of parents gave grandparents' and third-cousins-once-removed's addresses as their own to secure places. Christine didn't feel wonderful about sending her children to such a privileged school, but they lived in Cooney, and she was a past pupil. This, combined with the baptisms, which *she* had no problem with, had made her lot a shoo-in. She wasn't about to send them further away just to prove her egalitarian credentials.

Beth took a deep breath. 'Right, come on. Before your coffee goes cold. You know if you get it in a takeaway cup, it stays warmer longer?'

When they reached the group, Claire Keating was holding court. Claire was well known in Cooney for having three sets of twins. If the Keatings so much as went to the supermarket together, a photo would appear in the *Southern Gazette*'s social pages.

Lorna Farrell was to Claire's left, taking notes in a Glass Lake copybook. She was dressed in a Lakers '92 hoodie (which she'd clearly had made as the school didn't sell merchandise) and bejewelled hairband. In front of her sat a flapjack cut into tiny chunks. Fiona Murphy was slouched on another chair, texting on a phone held up so the Little Miss Fiona case covered half her face. She had multiple bracelets dangling from her wrists and her fingers were covered in delicate gold rings.

Christine and Beth took the two available chairs.

'I would have backed you up in the WhatsApp group, but you know how difficult it is to say anything there any more,' Claire was saying to a vaguely familiar woman with an auburn bob. 'God forbid you question one thing about your child's education, without everyone accusing you of undermining the teacher. Which obviously you weren't doing.'

Christine placed her coffee on the nearest table. It was the only ceramic mug. She should have just got a festive cup. She wasn't going to save the ice caps single-handedly.

'Obviously not,' said Auburn Bob. 'I *want* Ben to learn about climate change. I just don't think they should be using the parents' literal cars as examples of the worst offenders. He point-blank refused to get in his booster seat last Friday. He wanted to get the bus.'

'Rosie's started going through our bin and taking out everything we forgot to recycle,' said another mother.

'I told Ben the bus also ran on petrol and he called me a climate change denier.'

'I've got three kids, two pets, and a mother-in-law who asked to move into our house but is actually residing up my arse,' said the other woman. 'I'm *sorry* if I don't always have time to rinse out every yoghurt pot.'

'It's not good for their mental health,' added Auburn Bob. 'Climate anxiety. Right? Isn't that a thing?'

'I've never liked how they teach climate change at that school,' said Claire, drawing air quotes around the words 'climate change'. Claire had some questionable views, which she liked to share on WhatsApp and Facebook, but Christine kept shtum. Her plan was to say nothing until the musical came up. It was best to go softly-softly with the Lakers. They took this whole thing very seriously. 'Lorna?'

'Yep, got it.' Lorna tapped the notebook with her pen. 'Have a word with Principal Patterson. See if we can't get the third-class climate change module toned down.'

'Great. Thank you. And welcome to our latecomers. Christine ...'

Christine dutifully returned the finger waggle.

'... and excuse me, I don't know your name ...'

'Beth. Beth Morton. My son Ethan is in sixth-class. He was hoping to work on the musical this year.'

'Whoa!' Claire whipped her head back as though Beth had just gone to throw her Americano at her. 'Jump right in there, why don't you? That's fine.' She exchanged a look with a few of the others that suggested it was not at all fine. 'I'm afraid, Beth, we can't discuss the musical until Beverley gets here. She's our director.'

'I could actually give everyone an update on the musical,' said Lorna, whose full schoolyard name had been Lorna Lick-Arse Farrell. Christine had a feeling she'd started that moniker. 'I'm across that with Beverley.'

'That would be great,' enthused Beth.

'No,' said Claire, holding a hand up to Beth and, by extension, Christine. 'We're waiting for Beverley. Now. What else is there?'

'The Halloween party,' said Lorna, recovering quickly. 'And actually, sorry, can I just check? Did anyone have an issue with the sixth-class knitting assignment? Anyone think it was a lot to ask of the kids, or too much pressure, or ...?'

'I thought it was great,' said Fiona Murphy, using the straw from her iced water to pull at her lips. 'Made me think the new teacher might be worthwhile, and not just as something to look at.'

A few of the others nodded and Lorna made a show of crossing something out. 'No issues. Roger that.'

'Right. Halloween. Talk to me,' said Claire. 'Where are we on decorations?'

The Lakers debated whether the proposed skeletons were *too* scary and if safety scissors would suffice for cutting through pumpkins. Lorna was experimenting with 'organic' papier-mâché cauldrons and would let them know how she got on. Then they discussed hiring a photographer for the Glass Lake first holy communions next May, and Claire passed around ring binders containing sample shots. Christine was tempted to ask what was wrong with Seamus McGrath, the school caretaker and general factotum who took the official class photos every year free of charge. Although she suspected the free bit was the problem. She caught sight of the 'pricing structures' in one of the ring binders and realised these women were willing to pay more for photos than she was for a car.

These were the times when she couldn't quite believe she'd ended up in the exact place where she'd begun. Sometimes, when she was quick-fire buttering bread and flinging it into moaning mouths, she wanted to turn to her children and say: 'You've no idea! Mammy once lived in a squat and wrote for the *NME* and slept with a member of Suede!' It had only been three articles, and he was actually the band's sound engineer, but the squat bit was entirely true. A squat! She doubted if any of these women had even been camping.

Someone got a text from Beverley saying she was running late. Beth made a tutting noise and when Claire's eyes darted in their direction, Christine made sure to turn her attention to Beth too. No need to be taken down with her.

She took another mouthful of coffee and grimaced. It was stone cold.

'I'm going up for a refill. Anyone want anything?' she asked, pretending not to see the daggers thrown by the mother who'd been in the middle of bad-mouthing another part of the curriculum. 'No? Okay.'

She joined the queue behind Butcher Murphy, who ran the butchers below the *Southern Gazette*'s office and was an unlikely candidate for a takeaway coffee. Butcher had a head like a ham and even though Christine had known him since childhood, she couldn't remember if it had always been like that or if it was a career version of how owners start to resemble their pets. His real name was Simon, but nobody called him that.

'Well, if it isn't the vegetarian,' said Butcher, who called her this because three years ago she'd asked if he ever stocked fish. 'Ordering a double shot of salmon, is it?'

'Just a regular, old-fashioned Americano. Presume you're getting a soya chai tea?'

'*Heee*-yah,' he scoffed. 'Three euro for some dirty water? They saw youse coming anyway.'

'Next!'

Christine waited but Butcher didn't step up to order.

'Next!' called the barista again.

'She'll have an old-fashioned Americano,' said Butcher, swapping places with Christine.

'In a takeaway cup,' she added. She'd forgo the avocados next time she did a shop. 'Aren't you ordering anything?'

'I'm just here to keep an eye on things,' he said, peering over her shoulder towards the Lakers.

'Ah.' She understood the situation now. Butcher and Fiona Murphy had separated a couple of years ago and, even if you went on the mildest of local rumours, he had not taken the split well. Fiona had swiftly started dating again and relished letting everyone, including her ex-husband, know. She'd cornered Christine at the Easter fundraiser to ask if the *Southern Gazette* would be interested in a column about modern dating. Christine had pretended her raffle number was being called and excused herself in the direction of the stage.

'What do youse be talking about at these yokes?'

'I'm not the best person to ask. I'm not a regular.'

'Clothes, is it? And men?'

'I think it's mainly about the kids ...'

'*Heee*-yah. Sex, I suppose,' he added, suddenly forlorn. Sixty to nought in no time at all.

'I better get back, Butcher. Look after yourself.'

He gave her the Cooney nod – sharp, fast, diagonal – and shuffled behind the next queuing customer. She returned to the Lakers just in time to hear that Beverley would now not be making the meeting at all.

'She just texted. Some sort of emergency,' declared Lorna, holding her phone aloft.

Bloody wonderful. Would she have to come again next week? How would she swing that? There were only so many 'sources' Cooney could realistically have to offer. And wouldn't it be too late? The musical was in a fortnight.

But then Lorna removed a second copybook from her handbag and started brandishing it about. 'I can fill everyone in on the musical,' she said loudly, the café light bouncing from her hairband to the crisp white pages and back up to her taut forehead. 'I've been across the show, in a sort of producer capacity.'

Claire waved a hand in her direction as if to say, 'Continue'.

'That's great because my daughter Maeve—'

But Lorna ploughed on. 'We've actually had some really exciting news. Like, really exciting.' She looked around the group, slowly nodding her head. 'This year's musical ... is going to be on TV!' Lorna gave herself a gleeful round of applause. 'We submitted the script to RTÉ and it has been accepted. They're going to film *several* segments for *The Big Children's Talent Show.*'

Other mothers were clapping now. Even Christine was impressed. *The Big Children's Talent Show* might be the only thing her kids watched on telly that was actually made for telly.

Everyone was talking at once and several women were making the case for why their child should be in the show. She heard Auburn Bob reminding Lorna how she'd canvassed for her husband Bill's councillor bid, while Beth was frantically offering the woman the use of their holiday home if she ever fancied a trip to Tuscany.

'People, people! The leads have all been cast. We only have smaller roles left to fill.'

'Lorna!' shouted Christine, hoping the woman had never figured out where the Lick-Arse nickname came from. She pulled her chair in towards Lorna, who was basking in the scramble for her attention. 'Can you give Maeve a job on costumes, please? She really wants to be involved.'

'I see she registered her interest with Mr Cafferty, all right,' said Lorna, glancing down at her notebook. 'Has she any experience?'

'She's eleven. So, no.'

'Well, Shona Martin's already down to do costumes and her mother's a buyer for Brown Thomas so ...' The woman shrugged apologetically.

'Oh, come on, Lorna. Two people can work on costumes. Isn't it the taking part that counts? It's a children's play.'

'A children's play that's going to be on national television,' she corrected. 'I'm sorry, Christine, but I don't think we can fit her in. We do have an opening if she wants to sell raffle tickets at the interval ...'

Auburn Bob was pulling her chair into the circle now, blocking off Christine and nearly stomping on her foot. 'How much are they going to film, Lorna? Will they be talking to parents, or just the children?'

'Lorna?' Claire interjected from across the circle. 'Max and Geoff are down to play Munchkins, yes? I know they're selecting a few extras from fifth class. I'm not sure if Beverley confirmed that.'

'I have their names here, Claire. No problem at all.'

Another woman arrived into the middle of the circle in what was turning into a rather aggressive game of bumpers.

Christine stood, so she could be seen in the growing bottleneck, but she was knocked off balance by Auburn Bob. Then her mobile started to ring. Christine stepped out of the scrum, her left leg almost getting caught between two seated women hopping into the centre.

'Derek, hi,' she said before her boss could get a word in. 'I know I'm running a bit late, but my source has some good information. I'm hopeful I can get a decent story out of it.' She could find her way out of this white lie later. The more pressing issue was that Lorna was scribbling down names, and Maeve's was not among them.

'Drop it,' came the thick Dublin croak. Derek had swapped his sixty-a-day habit for thirty-a-day as part of his post-heart-attack life overhaul, but his vocal cords were fried long ago.

'Sorry?' Christine swapped the phone to her far ear and edged back towards the Lakers. She had to get back in there.

'Drop whatever it is you're doing,' barked her editor. 'I've got a scoop, Christine. I'm talking front-page material, and I want you on it right away.'

....

Garda Joey Delaney

How would you describe the atmosphere at the school yesterday evening?

Claire Keating, parent

I fail to see what that has got to do with a beloved member of our community being found dead in a river.

Delaney

For now, everything is relevant.

Keating

Bustling. Everyone was busy. Some were busy-bodying, but one way or another, we all had something to do. I, personally, was proofreading the programme notes.

Delaney

A few people have mentioned that tensions were high.

Keating

This was going to be on national television. So yes, tensions were high. I wouldn't read

anything into that, though. It's Glass Lake.
Tensions are always high.

Delaney

I heard some parents were annoyed.

Keating

There was a lot to be annoyed about. I'm sure
you read the newspaper reports – they didn't
help either. But really, it was down to how
the school handled things. You live here long
enough, and you quickly learn: do not piss off
the parents. The Cooney Welcoming Party is only
ever one slow day away from becoming the Cooney
Vigilante Party. And the photos, well, they
pissed a lot of people off.

Beverley's husband hadn't had an affair. He'd said that when she found the photos, and she'd been repeating it to herself ever since. He'd handed her his phone so she could see the Audi he was planning to purchase, only her thumb slipped and she scrolled back too far. There were dozens of them: crude, unprofessional shots with terrible lighting and awkward angles. Beverley couldn't understand how he found them arousing.

'I never slept with her. It was only pics.'

Pics.

She'd never heard him utter that word before in his life.

Beverley had taken it in her stride, mainly. She wasn't naïve; she knew men would be men. When she had the space to think about it rationally, she was able to feel sorry for him – which was a lot easier than feeling sorry for herself. The idea of Malachy standing naked somewhere – their bedroom? The bathroom? His *office*? – as he pointed the phone at his naked body was deeply pathetic. And saying 'pics' was almost as childish as taking them. He was nearly forty-one, for God's sake.

Beverley came to a stop at the traffic lights beside the empty shop unit where a Starbucks had been for all of five minutes. The Keep Cooney Independent committee had formed a picket line and the multinational had slunk back to the city where it belonged. Lorna Farrell's husband Bill was a recently elected councillor (something she didn't let anyone forget) and he said an interiors studio specialising in louvre shutters was going in there now. Which was much more in keeping.

In the rear-view mirror, she watched her daughter rub at the last of the blue eyeshadow. A small mound of used cotton pads sat on her knee.

The light turned green, and Amelia looked up as Beverley returned her attention to the road. They hadn't spoken since they'd left the house.

They drove on past the newsagents and Regan's Chemist. Mrs Rodgers, who Beverley knew from the Tidy Towns committee, was heading into the pharmacy. She checked the mirror as the older woman disappeared inside, but it was hard to get an idea of what might be wrong with her. She hoped it was nothing serious. Mrs Rodgers had the most fabulous red roses; last year's judges' report had, quite rightly, singled them out.

She turned the car on to Franklin Avenue. Beverley was eight when she found out the meandering road that led from Main Street up to Glass Lake was named after Malachy's family. She'd immediately set about gathering intelligence on the boy in the year above. She learned that the long navy car that collected him every afternoon was driven by an employee and that his mother sat in the back seat, pushing the door open for him, but never getting out. She heard that at his tenth birthday party, the same driver was sent into Cork city to collect McDonald's and bring it back to Cooney, and that a woman who was not his mother had opened the door to the guests. As far as Malachy was concerned, Beverley knew nothing of him until they met at a local disco when they were sixteen. Even though she could have handed in a dossier by then.

Malachy had accompanied her to last year's Southern Pharmaceuticals Christmas party. This was before she'd quit that multinational cesspit and made a career pivot into health food entrepreneurship. (She had not been fired. She had *quit*. And she could not be happier about it.) Malachy had been in a foul mood until Benny from advertising asked if he'd ever considered modelling.

Her husband had laughed self-deprecatingly and blamed the Yuletide Slammers Benny was knocking back. 'I'm forty this month,' he'd said, patting his non-existent belly. 'I think I'll leave the acting to my wife.'

'Do you act, Beverley?' Tamara from development had asked, dragging her gaze away from Malachy's chest.

'I used to. A long time ago.'

In Cooney, Beverley's acting career was fundamental to her identity. She was the most famous person her friends knew, and she wasn't even famous. But she'd never mentioned it at work. Those people made fun of soaps.

'She was in *Cork Life*,' Malachy supplied. 'And she was phenomenal.' He was always so generous when his ego had been sated.

Beverley had looked at him and seen what the others saw. Sparkling blue eyes, a weather-beaten ruggedness, and thick sandy hair carefully cut so it always flopped to the left. Nobody could tell he'd had a small area transplanted from the back of his head. He looked like he might work on a yacht, but also like he could own a yacht – so that no matter what kind of man you were attracted to, you were always attracted to Malachy.

Tamara from development had mouthed *Wow* at Beverley and a slightly drunk woman from research shouted: 'The slutty babysitter! I knew I recognised you!'

'Not slutty. Sexy,' Malachy corrected, looking at Beverley in a way that said nothing – not even Tamara's ample cleavage and too tight dress – could compete.

That night, they'd stayed in a hotel in the city and made love on the bed, by the window, in the bathroom. Beverley's thighs throbbed and her heart soared. She'd instigated positions she wasn't aware could be done, let alone by her, and almost a year later, even while on a mission to defend her daughter's welfare, the memory still made her blush.

About ninety metres from Glass Lake, traffic ground to a halt. The Lakers had run a campaign to encourage parents to drop their kids off farther away from the school gates. It made little difference. Twice, she'd caught Fiona Murphy *parking* in the middle of the road, while she got Ciara out of the vehicle. What did they expect if they didn't lead by example?

The other Lakers didn't have the same loyalty to the school that Beverley had. Enrolling her at Glass Lake was the one great thing her parents had done for her – and even then, it was only because her mother had got a job in Cooney and the school was on the way. So much of her parents' lives had been about getting by and not drawing attention, that there was no space for big dreams. Her acting ambitions were never taken seriously. But Glass Lake had opened her eyes to a better world. Learning about the Franklins had given her a defined goal, yes, but one way or another she'd been working towards this life since she was five.

Of course, her own mother's life now was unrecognisable from the one she'd led when Beverley was small. As soon as Beverley's youngest sibling had finished school, her mother had left her father and their West Cork home for a retreat in India. Having endured years of her husband deriding her appearance, specifically her weight, Beverley had assumed it was a boot camp – sort of Eat, Pray, Love without the Eat – but no. It had been a hippy sex retreat. Now her mother, who lived in Dublin and was sixty-six *today*, could talk of little else, and Beverley was embarrassed by her in a whole new way.

She had made the mistake of confiding in her mother about Malachy's 'pics'. That evening she'd received a one-line email – Take the time to heal your relationship with yourself. Mam x – and a link to female-friendly porn. (Her mother. Sixty-six! Was *nobody* capable of acting their age?)

It was 9 a.m. Amelia was now officially late for school, which meant everyone ahead of them was late too. At least Beverley had a valid excuse. She blasted the horn.

'Mum!'

The car in front pulled into the right and she swerved around it, manoeuvring off Franklin Avenue and on to the short driveway that led up to Glass Lake.

When she read articles about the ubiquity of porn, she found herself wondering who all these viewers were. If it really was as prevalent as they said, then she must know a few of them. They couldn't *all* be in Dublin. She tried to imagine if her friends might be among the masses.

Claire Keating lived a heavily timetabled life. Three sets of twins was surprising, generally, but not given Claire's efficiency. Why do something six times when you could get the job done in half that? It was unlikely she saw sex as a leisure activity, and she certainly wouldn't make time for anything as discretionary as watching *other people* have sex. Lorna Farrell was far too won't-someone-think-of-the-children to be condoning smut. She couldn't even bring herself to use the correct terminology for genitalia. She had recently sent a message to the WhatsApp group seeking a recommendation for a 'good front bum doctor'. The only Laker who seemed a likely candidate was Fiona Murphy. Even if Fiona wasn't watching porn, she'd be delighted to know someone thought she was.

Beverley had never seen any. The idea made her sad. All those people who'd started out dreaming of Academy Awards and luscious costumes and ended up with harsh lighting and polyester nurses' outfits. Journalists wrote about it as if it was a foregone conclusion that the next generation – Amelia's generation – would be reared on the stuff. But that kind of thinking was what was wrong with parents. You had to fight for what you wanted. Nothing good in life was just handed to you. Even the most blissful moments of Beverley's life, when the midwife placed her daughters on to her chest, had been preceded by hours (days in Ella's case) of horrific pain. Being wealthy meant, as she'd known it would, that there was less resistance – but you still had to fight.

She pulled into a staff parking space, right by the entrance. She popped a Rennie out of its blister pack, threw the carton back on the passenger seat, and undid her seatbelt.

'Out. Now,' she said.

When it came to her daughters, Beverley was prepared to kick and scream.

....

Principal Nuala Patterson's only child refused to speak to her. Her only husband had left her, and her only working ovary had finally ceased production, resulting in night sweats and insomnia. Yet nothing, but nothing, made Nuala as weary as arriving into work to find a note on her desk saying Beverley Franklin had phoned ahead and was on her way in.

Given the Franklins' affluence, Nuala would argue that when Beverley lost her job at Southern Pharmaceuticals earlier in the year (the school grapevine said she'd been fired), it was actually her, as principal of Glass Lake, who had suffered the most. Before, it was phone calls; now Beverley came to see her every time she had an issue with Amelia's test results or one of Seamus McGrath's set designs.

Nuala dropped her bags on to her desk. She pulled out her heels, sat in her swivel chair and undid her runners. 'Did Beverley mention what time she'd be in?' she shouted through her open door.

'Didn't say,' replied Mairead. The school secretary appeared at the office threshold, eating a particularly milky bowl of cereal. 'But it sounded like she was phoning from the car.'

Nuala hooked her shoe strap at the last hole. (Dr Flynn was amazed by how she'd managed to experience almost every possible side effect of the menopause, from thinning hair right down to swollen ankles. Nuala was not surprised. It was the cherry on top of the worst year of her life.) 'How did she sound?'

Mairead raised an eyebrow. 'How does Beverley Franklin ever sound?'

When Nuala first came to Glass Lake – as a teacher, straight out of university, at the age of twenty-two – Beverley had been in second class. Nuala hadn't taught her, but she remembered the happy, pretty, not particularly well-off child. Now Beverley was one of the wealthiest women in Cooney and while still objectively attractive (the grapevine reported she went to Dublin to get her work done), her face settled in a faintly pained expression, as if she'd constantly just bitten her tongue.

'What else have we got on today?'

'The social worker is calling at around eleven; we still need to sort out those forms to hire two more SNAs; and Claire Keating has an appointment to see you this afternoon. It's about the sixth-class history curriculum; specifically, Edward Jenner.'

'The smallpox guy?'

Mairead raised an eyebrow. 'Claire has an issue with how the textbook describes his invention of the vaccine. She says it lacks balance.'

'There is no balance. It's facts.'

'Not according to Claire. According to Claire, it's big pharma propaganda.'

They were only seven weeks into the school year and already the parents, who had always been the hardest part of her job, were surpassing themselves. But then, everybody and everything was more irritating than it used to be. Nuala couldn't seem to pass a car without the driver texting on their phone, and every café she went into was packed with diners watching videos and listening to music without a set of earphones between them. Maybe it was the menopause or maybe it was her family skedaddling off to the other side of the country, but every now and again she feared she would have to stop leaving the house, lest she go on a murderous rampage.

And then, just as quickly as the rage came on her, the apathy took over.

Nuala sighed.

The first school bell had yet to ring and she could easily have taken to the bed.

'Ten minutes with Beverley then you knock on that door, okay? Any excuse will do. Someone's got a pigtail caught in a pencil sharpener, the Minister for Education's on the phone. Whatever. Just get her out of here.'

....

Beverley was out of the Range Rover and pointing the fob at it when she noticed the white van parked two spaces down from her. The older Whitehead boy – Argo? Anglo? Some made-up name like that – was unlocking the back of it.

'I don't believe it.'

'Mum,' pleaded Amelia, quickening her step to keep up. 'Please! Don't embarrass me.'

The older Whitehead boy was the one who'd been in the car when his drunken father got behind the wheel and killed Mike Roche Junior, not to mention leaving another minor disabled. He'd been in Ella's year, they all had, which meant he'd graduated in the summer. Why he was still in Cooney was beyond her. And what was he doing in Glass Lake, of all places? Clearly none of the Whiteheads had an ounce of shame.

'These parking spaces are for staff only,' she snapped. 'You've absolutely no right to park here.'

'But, Mum, you're not—'

Beverley yanked her daughter in closer, cutting her off. The boy continued to stand there, mouth open like a dead fish.

'Well? Have you anything to say for yourself?'

'I'm ...'

Beverley put her free hand on her hip. Charlie Whitehead's sons might have got his looks but neither had inherited his gift of the gab.

'I'm working here,' he said eventually.

Beverley guffawed. 'At Glass Lake? I doubt that very much.'

'Honestly, Mrs Franklin, I am.'

'You're telling me Nuala Patterson hired you? That's a barefaced lie and you know it.'

'Seamus McGrath hired me. I'm helping him out for a few days.'

'Seamus?' she echoed. The lad nodded dumbly. Yet another bone to pick with the school caretaker. Was a Yellow Brick Road really too much to ask for? Not bronze, not gold – yellow. She was asking the caretaker for a basic colour, not a utopian impossibility.

She peered into the van and saw a ladder and some buckets. The Whiteheads' vehicle had been spotted on the road over from theirs a couple of times recently and when Beverley found out which of her neighbours was throwing work his way, she'd be making a swift cut to the Franklins' Christmas card list.

'You ...' she said, steadying herself. He began to wither under her stare. '... and your *whole* family ...'

'Mum,' whined Amelia, tugging at her hand, '*please.*'

A scourge, that's what the Whiteheads were. Beverley had graciously cast Woody in the school musical, and how had he repaid her? By exploiting her daughter, that was how. She could have swung for his brother. But Beverley did not do out of control. She did poised and enviable. This morning had been a blip. She did not enjoy feeling so feral.

Without another word, she yanked her daughter towards the heavy double doors that led to Glass Lake's foyer.

8

• • • • •

Mrs Rodgers pretended she didn't see the three people standing in line and walked straight up to the counter of Regan's Chemist. She slumped her shoulders as she did so, to remind the other customers that she was old. She didn't have as much time left for queuing as they did.

Gerry Regan looked from her to the small line and hesitated. She flashed her dodderiest smile, the one that exposed the upper right-hand side of her mouth, where she was missing a tooth. The other customers – who were all young and distracted by the phones in their hands – weren't going to make a fuss, so neither was he.

'Good afternoon, Mr Regan.' The bruise on his face was at the early stages but there was no pretending she couldn't see it. She allowed her smile to crumple into deep concern. She would permit two minutes for this exchange. 'Oh no, Mr Regan. What has happened to your eye?'

'Altercation with a lorry driver this morning, I'm afraid,' he said, bringing his hand up to what promised to be a significant shiner. 'I made some polite enquiries into the weight of his vehicle and whether it was permitted to be on Reilly's Pass, which of course it was not, and he swung for me.'

'That's shocking. You poor creature. Did you get his licence plate number?'

'I did. I was reciting it to myself, to ensure I remembered, when he hit me. I was on the bike, you see, no room for pen and paper in my cycling gear.'

'Well, of course,' said Mrs Rodgers, who had seen the pharmacist's cycling gear. There wasn't room for imagination, never mind a notebook.

'If he thinks I have concussion, he can think again. I've already phoned it in. And I've started a petition.' Mr Regan pushed the clipboard towards her. To live in Cooney was to be forever signing petitions.

Mrs Rodgers didn't like leaving Albert alone while he was still settling in. (She'd renamed the cat Albert, without any fuss. He was a clever so-and-so. He knew as well as anyone that Porcupine was a ridiculous name. The Maguires wouldn't have called their children Porcupine, and yet they wouldn't show a pet the same courtesy.) 'What is the world coming to, eh?' she said, scribbling her signature as illegibly as possible. 'Now, if you could lend me some assistance: I am looking to purchase hair dye.'

Mr Regan glanced at her white mane, which had never been dyed a day in its life. 'I see. Well, the hair colour is just here ...' He accompanied her to a small display with preposterously young women on the boxes. (Why would they need to dye their hair?) 'I'm afraid it's not my expertise.' He dipped his head slightly, acknowledging the loss of his own hair at a cruelly young age. 'But we have a few different shades and brands. What colour were you thinking?' He picked up a couple of boxes and read out the labels. 'Ashen blonde, maybe? Sandy brown?'

'Black.'

He paused. 'Black.'

Mrs Rodgers nodded. She removed a box from the shelf and scanned the back of it. 'Midnight Blackout. This will do. I'll take this one.'

'Are you sure?'

'I am.'

'All right ...' Mr Regan took the box and scanned it through. She caught him glancing at her crown again, no doubt trying to picture her with the hair of a moody, misunderstood teenager. She didn't have the time, or inclination, to explain. She'd told Albert she would be back for *The Chase*. When he used to visit her on weekday afternoons, that had been their show. He'd purred when she read out the TV listings this morning, so she wasn't about to let him down.

She handed over the money and waited for Mr Regan to bag the dye. He was very good at putting things in bags, slipping them in with sleight of hand and utmost discretion. She supposed that was an inevitable result of years spent selling piles suppositories and condom lubrication.

'**M**rs Franklin,' said Principal Patterson, rising from her desk, 'nice to see you. Again.'

Beverley pretended not to see the school secretary mouthing 'Good luck' as she quietly pulled the door behind her. She knew Nuala Patterson didn't like her, that she conveniently forgot about the thousands of euro Beverley fundraised every year and thought of her only as a nuisance and silly for being so invested in the goings-on of the school. No doubt she was counting down the days until Amelia graduated in June. *Both Franklin daughters finally gone!* But if she thought Beverley would let Glass Lake go to the dogs once she no longer had skin in the game, she needed to get out her dictionary and look up exactly what community was all about.

'I'm not here on pleasant business,' she said, pulling out the chair on the opposite side of the principal's desk.

'No,' agreed Nuala, retaking her own seat. 'What can I do for you?'

'I need you to expel Woody Whitehead.'

There was a faint sound of the principal sucking in air.

'This morning I went into Amelia's bedroom to call her for school ...' Beverley broke off. She produced a water bottle from her bag and took a swig. It turned out she didn't need to close her eyes to get a picture-perfect memory of her naked daughter. 'I went in to call Amelia for school, and I found her taking a photograph of herself. Naked. She was taking a naked photograph of herself.'

Nuala's eyes widened ever so slightly. 'Right.'

'Not just a naked photo but a – a sexual photo. It was explicit. And she was sending it to Woody Whitehead.'

'I see.'

No, Principal Patterson, you did not see. Trust me.

'That can't have been easy.'

'No. It wasn't,' replied Beverley matter-of-factly. She did not want sympathy, she wanted action. 'That boy, that Whitehead boy, was soliciting sexual photographs from my underage child. And I want him expelled, Nuala. I want him gone today.'

'Did Woody send a photo of himself naked, too?'

'That's my understanding of it. Yes.'

The principal leaned back into her chair, causing her neck to disappear and the weight gain to become more apparent. Beverley tried not to notice – she was sure it was down to grief – but it wasn't easy.

'So, what are you going to do about it?'

'I understand this is very distressing for you. But I can't just expel Woody Whitehead.'

'Why not?'

'Well, for one thing, if I was to expel Woody, I'd have to expel Amelia too.'

'Of course you wouldn't. Amelia is a twelve-year-old girl. She didn't do anything wrong.'

'And Woody is a twelve-year-old boy. They're both underage. What we usually do in these circumstances is get both sets of parents in, talk to them, talk to the children, and make sure everyone understands how serious the situation is and that it shouldn't happen again.'

'What you usually do? Are you saying this usually happens?'

'Sometimes.' The principal corrected herself, 'Occasionally. Rarely.'

But she'd said 'usually'. Beverley had heard it, and she had not liked it.

'Sometimes, children can think they're in relationships, boyfriend and girlfriend, and they're playing at being grown-ups. They get the idea somewhere that this is what grown-ups do.'

'It is not what grown-ups do,' said Beverley, barely allowing the woman to finish her sentence. 'And they're not playing house, Nuala. This is not *normal* behaviour. My daughter is barely twelve, and now there's a naked photo of her out there in the world. I don't think it's too much to expect that the boy be punished. And I didn't expect you of all people to be sticking up for a Whitehead.'

'I'm not sticking up for anyone, Beverley.'

'I saw the older Whitehead brother in the parking lot. He says he's working here. Did you know that?'

'I didn't hire him,' replied the principal, her tone cool. 'I will talk to Woody, and to his parents, to his mother, I mean. I'll talk to Amelia, and to Mr Cafferty. The class teacher usually has an idea of what's going on.'

There was that word again. *Usually.*

'Mr Cafferty hasn't been here a wet week,' she shot back, though, actually, the new sixth-class teacher was fine. A little overzealous maybe – between after-school activities and running her socials, where did he expect Amelia to find the time to knit

76

a whole bear? – but he was open to parental partnership. Some of the other staff acted like a weekly progress report was a massive burden. 'I'm not really interested in you talking to anyone except Woody's mother. I doubt she'd put up much of a fight. You think they'd be glad to move on to a different school, a different town.'

'What does your husband think?'

Beverley hadn't said a word to Malachy. The girls were her job. And in light of his own behaviour, she wasn't sure he deserved to know. Sending nudes was *not* something grown-ups did, not good grown-ups, and not when they were married to someone else. 'He agrees with me, of course,' she snapped. 'Neither of us think this is acceptable behaviour. I don't see how you can think it's acceptable behaviour.'

'I never said—' Principal Patterson cut herself off and sighed, as if Beverley were the errant child. 'If you want, I can get in touch with the Department of Education, talk to the district psychologist. They might have some advice, or they could talk to Amelia, if you're really concerned.'

Beverley leaned forward and banged the principal's desk (which the Lakers' 2017 Christmas extravaganza had paid for). She could feel her grasp on the situation weakening, her aim floundering. She took another swig of water. Her throat had been sore for months.

Poised and enviable, she told herself. *Poised and enviable.*

'My daughter doesn't need to see a psychologist, and certainly not a *state* one. I'm not concerned about her and you don't need to be either. What I'm concerned about is Woody Whitehead and how you don't seem to want to do anything about lewd behaviour in your school. I'm concerned that, instead of doing your job, you're trying to pass the buck.'

This wasn't just about her daughter; it was about Glass Lake. And Beverley was eternally loyal to this place.

Principal Patterson compressed her mouth in a way that did nothing for her lips. Beverley eyeballed her back.

'Technically, Mrs Franklin, none of this happened at the school.'

'That you know of,' she countered. 'And the school certainly didn't teach them *not* to do it, did you? The Lakers raised eighteen hundred euro last year to support the web-safety modules and I'm really starting to wonder where that money went.'

'We have done several web-safety modules with the students, and Amelia will do more this year. We also sent home an information booklet for parents on safe web use. It contained advice on restricting children's access to the internet as well as information on how best to monitor phone use. Glass Lake's advice is that parents refrain from giving children phones until they've finished primary school.'

'Oh, come off it, Nuala! School policy allows them to have phones in their bags in sixth class. Amelia is in sixth class. You can't wash your hands of this one. And a booklet isn't going to save you either. If you do not do something about this, I will be forced to take matters into my own hands, and I can promise you that will not be preferable.' She ignored the principal's raised eyebrows. 'Parents,' she stormed on, 'need to be made aware of what is happening at this school.'

'I don't think it is happening at the school.'

'And men – male students, I mean – need to be taught not to do it; not to make underage girls send them nude photographs and to generally have some decorum and class and self-respect!'

A sharp single knock on the office door. 'Sorry, Principal Patterson, there's a phone call for you.'

Beverley turned and glared at the secretary's head sticking around the doorframe.

'I've asked if they can wait, but I'm afraid it's urgent.'

....

Derek billed every story as 'front-page material'. A new heron in the park, trees felled without permission, a bicycle stolen from outside Connolly's supermarket; everything was a potential splash – until it was written up and he could no longer deny that it definitely was not. Christine admired his optimism. If only some big Dublin gangster would buy a holiday home in West Cork. It would make Derek's year.

'I'm on my way into the office this very second, Derek,' said Christine, who was still sidling up to the Lakers. Beth Morton was writing something into Lorna Farrell's notebook. She would need to get closer, but it looked like an Italian address.

'Forget the office,' came the thick Dublin croak. 'This is big, and I need my best reporter on it right away.'

There were only three reporters at the *Southern Gazette*, and Amanda was on holiday this week while Anthony operated a work-to-rule where he refused to cover anything but sport.

'I'm honoured.'

'This is juicy, Christine. It lives up to that great journalism mantra.'

'If it bleeds it leads?' Derek regularly shouted maxims at them. This one was a favourite. But it being Cooney, the nearest they'd come was when a Halal butchers opened on the outskirts of town.

'No,' said Derek. 'The other great mantra ... "Sex sells." And what sells even better is a sex scandal.'

'In Cooney?' replied Christine doubtfully.

'Right here in our own sleepy little town,' he confirmed. 'We had a phone call from an irate mother. She says some of the kids up at Glass Lake have been sending nude photos to each other, including her daughter. And since you've got a kid ... You do have a kid, right?'

'I have three kids, Derek. You've met them. Two of them are at Glass Lake.'

'Perfect! I knew you'd be the woman for the job. The mother wants to stay anonymous. She was gunning to name the boy involved, but obviously he's a minor so we'll keep that out of it. Still, pretty exciting stuff, eh?'

'Mmm,' said Christine, who thought it was a little icky and not particularly newsworthy. When Caroline was in sixth class, a girl had sent all the other kids a disgusting meme. Not for the first time, she'd been smug about holding out on giving her children phones until they got to secondary school. 'It isn't *that* unusual.'

'Yes, but we've got a parent giving out. And you know what that means? It means we've got a ...'

'A row,' supplied Christine reluctantly.

Beth and Lorna were now laughing. How had that turned around so quickly? Had Beth just bribed her son's way into the musical? Outrageous. Christine needed to get back there and see what she could barter for Maeve.

'A sexy row,' agreed Derek. 'And feel free to spice it up. Mention a few celebrities who've been caught sending around nudes and we can work a few of their photos in. Any of those Cork lads ever been caught out – Cillian Murphy, or Jonathan Rhys What's-it? That'll outrage the old dears. The letters will be flowing in.'

The previous editor of the *Southern Gazette* had heart palpitations any time someone complained about so much as a typo on the TV listings. But Derek relished the ire of his readers. 'Outrage means they're reading!' he'd shout with glee, slapping the missives down on Christine's desk. Christine oversaw the letters page as well as the local birthdays list.

The Lakers were packing up their stuff now. Lorna had slipped both notebooks into her Class of '92 tote bag and Beth was waving as she headed for the door.

'Can this actually wait until later, Derek? I was working on that story about cuts to the West Cork bus service and—'

'Forget buses. There's nothing sexy about buses. A bus accident, maybe. But cancelled buses? Definitely not sexy. No. I want you on this. Did I mention it's got front-page potential?'

Part of billing everything as a cover story was to incentivise them to work harder. But Christine had no interest in being on the front page, especially not for an underage sex scandal. She liked her comfortable life, down in the back pages of the newspaper, where she outraged nobody.

Now Lorna was heading for the door. Christine gave a silent moan. She could not return home to Maeve with no job on the musical and no sign of that Judas cat. There was no way the worry dolls would cut it; she'd have Christine and Conor up all night, encumbering them with her anxieties.

'I'll send you on the number,' Derek continued. 'The mother's name is Beverley. She lives in one of those McMansions on the southside of town. I said I'd get someone over to her today.'

'Beverley *Franklin*?'

'Ah now, don't tell me you're friends? This bloody town.

Everyone's someone's cousin! I'll have to see if Anthony will make a concession this once and—'

'No, no,' interrupted Christine, as the last of the Lakers packed up their things. 'I know her, but we're not friends. I can do it. Definitely. No conflict of interest.'

'Are you sure?'

'I am one hundred per cent positive.'

If Christine couldn't get Lorna to pencil Maeve in for costumes, she would have to take the matter up a level.

'That's the enthusiasm I like to see.'

She threw her bag over her arm and headed for the café door. 'So, you want me out there today?'

'This afternoon, yes. I'll send on her details. And remember, Christine: Outrage ...'

She caught the door just as Fiona Murphy swung it behind her. Butcher Murphy appeared from behind a nearby pillar.

'... makes a front page,' she chanted.

'Attagirl! Now go get 'em,' barked Derek.

....

Mairead placed the requested glass of water on Nuala's table and the principal chased down the Xanax rattling impatiently behind her teeth. When the secretary left, she popped a second tablet into her mouth. It was her recompense for not shouting at Beverley Franklin.

For years, Glass Lake had banned mobile phones. But parents had complained: what if they got delayed doing pick-ups? What if there was an issue with an after-school activity? So, the school amended its policy to allow, if necessary, sixth-class students to carry phones; they had to be kept in their bags and switched off for the duration of the school day. It was intended as an 'in exceptional circumstances' allowance, but instead students viewed it as the point at which they were *entitled* to a phone. So, every September, the sixth-classers returned with shiny new mobiles hopping about at the bottom of their backpacks and, within weeks, there was an incident. The staff referred to it as the Sixth-Class Curse.

Last year, two boys had watched porn and told their friends what they'd seen. It spread through the school like a virus, every student telling four more, the details multiplying and mutating as they went. Two years before that, a girl was sent an explicit meme by an older sibling and forwarded it to every student in her class. As sure as night follows day, parents had arrived at Nuala's office.

Never mind that none of it – the online bullying, the sexting, the viewing of inappropriate material – ever happened in the classroom. It occurred in the back seat of the car as the kids were driven home, or up in their bedrooms, or even when gathered together in the family room, the adults watching TV and the kids messing around on iPads, blocking classmates on TikTok as a joke or typing 'porn' into YouTube to see what would happen.

The parents had given their children the phones. But somehow, it was always the school's fault.

'Can you ask Mr Cafferty to come and see me at the end of the school day?' Nuala called after Mairead. The photos incident aside, she was due a check-in with the newest faculty member. Frank Cafferty, the sixth-class teacher, had come to them from an ultra-Catholic, rural, three-teacher school; she feared the Glass Lake parents would eat him for a post-workout snack. 'And can you get me the most recent sex and relationships curriculum from the Department, please?'

Nuala tried not to give in to the Beverley Franklins of her school. Nice and all as it was for the kids to have tennis rackets without holes and for the corridors to be repainted annually, the basic needs of the school, and Nuala's wages, were paid for by the state and she was not answerable to the Lakers. However, occasionally, and often accidentally, one of them had a point.

It had been a while since they'd updated the sex ed programme and, as far as Nuala could recall, there was currently no mention of online elements at all. It could be worth doing some contemporary modules.

Mairead appeared in the doorway. 'I've asked the Department for that.'

'Thanks,' replied Nuala, returning to the mound of paperwork on her desk.

The secretary didn't budge.

'What is it, Mairead?'

'Did you know Arlo Whitehead is working over in the auditorium?'

'Seamus hired him.' And she wasn't likely to forget with the whole world reminding her.

'Is that okay with you?'

The set designs for the musical had the caretaker swamped, and the gutters needed replacing. It was just for a week or two, he'd said. As if that made it any easier.

Nuala attempted a gracious smile, though she suspected it came out more like a grimace. 'I guess it has to be.'

The secretary nodded.

Nuala went back to her files. After a few seconds, she put them down again.

'You are now officially hovering, Mairead.'

'I presume you don't want me to send him in to you, for the usual greeting?'

Sitting on her desk, under the special needs assistant application forms and the folders for the social worker, were first-stage divorce papers. Nuala had printed off several copies in the weeks since she'd received them. There was an identical set spread across the back seat of her car and another sitting in an orderly pile on the kitchen table. But she couldn't bring herself to sign any of them.

The worst year of Nuala's life had many parts to it, but at the centre of everything sat Arlo Whitehead.

'No,' said Nuala, who hadn't spoken to the teenager since the day her only child lost the use of his legs in the Whiteheads' car. 'I don't think that's going to be necessary.'

10

Joey was standing at the entrance to the station, watching the last of his morning interviewees climb into a Range Rover, when the sergeant came up behind him.

'All done?'

'Yes, sir,' he replied, standing to attention. 'All done until the afternoon batch. Just have to type them up.'

'Anything of note?'

Joey pulled out the small notebook where he'd been marking down conversation topics all morning. Most of his notes consisted of half sentences – cut off at the point where he realised the tangent the witness had gone off on had nothing to do with the investigation. 'Not really ...' He flicked back through the pages. 'Someone saw the deceased in a heated debate with Principal Nuala Patterson a few hours before the body was found in the river.'

'Who said that?'

'A parent ... Lorna Farrell.'

'I don't see Nuala Patterson being caught up in this. She's about the only one of them who I'd give the benefit of the doubt. More likely that parent has a grievance against Nuala. I wouldn't be principal of that school for all the tea in China.'

'Is it worth following up on anyway?'

'No harm. Nuala's in this afternoon, so you can ask her about it. You've met Principal Patterson, haven't you? At that school information night you did?'

'Yes, sir.' Joey had met her once before that, too, the day her son was paralysed in a car accident.

It was early one February morning and the ambulance had just left the scene with Leo Patterson on a gurney in the back when Joey and the sergeant arrived at Reilly's Pass. They had to wait for a second ambulance to come for the boy who had died. His father was a star of the Cooney GAA scene, apparently. Joey didn't know much about Gaelic football, except that it was a big deal around here, but he'd committed the teenager's name to memory. Mike Roche Junior. His first body.

One of the remaining passengers had identified himself to Joey as the driver. He was distraught. His was another name he'd committed to memory. Charlie Whitehead. His first arrest.

It was five hours later, when the sergeant had gone to the hospital and Joey was left to guard the site until forensics arrived, that a car pulled up at the side of the road and Nuala Patterson got out. He tried to keep her away, but she was adamant. She explained that she was the injured boy's mother. He thought of his mam back home in Leitrim, and how if he was in a car crash, she'd probably turn up wearing a coat over her pyjamas too.

'The preliminary post-mortem should be back soon,' said the sergeant, lowering himself into the chair behind the reception desk.

'Do you think there's a chance of foul play?' asked Joey, trying to keep the hope out of his voice.

'There's always a chance,' said his superior. 'It's not likely around here, but I'm not ruling it out. The suicide risk on this one is low: gainfully employed, happily married – or as happy as any of us are. There's no sense of a desperate person teetering on the edge. Throw in the fact that we haven't got a plausible theory for why our DOA was out by the river when everyone else was up at Glass Lake. It doesn't make sense. And that makes me suspicious.'

Joey quivered. Half of him was giddy at the prospect of something exciting finally happening, and the other half felt guilty about it.

Lorna Farrell, parent

If tensions were high at the school, it wasn't down to the musical – it was because of the photos. I presume you know about that? The children were N-A-K-E-D in them. I was angry when I heard about it, of course I was. Show me a parent who wasn't and I'll show you a textbook example of negligence.

Beth Morton, parent

Glass Lake has always had feuds. One parent doesn't sign another parent's petition and suddenly people are getting kicked out of WhatsApp groups and children's birthday party invitations are being rescinded. But the stuff with the photos was different. Everyone was concerned. Personally, I don't think anyone should have handed in their resignation over it, but that's only an opinion.

11

......

Arlo didn't remove his head from under the sink, but he could feel the woman's eyes on his bent back. He tried to concentrate on the U-bend. He'd fixed this last week and somehow it was leaking again.

'Can I get you anything to drink while you're down there?'

'No thank you, Mrs Murphy,' he said, voice muffled as he reached behind him for a spanner. 'I'm fine.'

'What did I say about calling me that?' Her hand hit his shoulder and he gave a start. The Murphys' kitchen was so big, it echoed. It was disconcerting to never know how close she was. 'You're making me feel ninety,' she said. 'Anyway, it's *Ms* Murphy now.'

She laughed but Arlo could tell she didn't really find it funny, so he said: 'Fiona, I mean. Sorry. I'm fine for a drink, thank you, Fiona.'

'Are you sure?' She stepped away. 'A coke? Or a beer, maybe? I've some craft ale in the fridge, from this cool little microbrewery in Mayo.'

'No, thank you, Fiona, I'm fine. Thank you.' The heat rose in his cheeks. Could he not think of any new words? He wanted to reach behind and tug down the back of his T-shirt. But he didn't, in case she was watching.

The piping came away in his hand and Arlo peered up towards

the drain. How did he expect to win over the people of Cooney if the jobs they paid good money for weren't done properly? Word of mouth was everything in this business. His father had taught him that. He'd also taught him that, no matter how many adhesives you had in the van, charm was the best way to seal a deal.

But Arlo wasn't charming. His limbs were too long, and he blushed too easily. People said he looked like his dad, but no matter how much he studied his reflection, he never saw it. Sometimes he concentrated so hard on the mirror that his nose started to drift away from his face and he had to shut his eyes for as long as it took for the sensation to stop.

The footsteps halted. Arlo hoped she'd left the kitchen. Fiona Murphy was divorced, and she said it was a godsend to have someone to do 'manly things' around the house. She hired him a lot and always tipped. She was one of the few people in Cooney who was nice to him and he was grateful, but he made mistakes when he was also trying to guess if he was being watched or not.

She fancies you, boy.

Don't be stupid, Leo. She's like forty.

Remember that time she pressed her leg against your back?

She was reaching for a pillowcase.

Must have been a hard-to-reach pillowcase.

She's probably just afraid I'll steal something.

During the summer, a family out by Cooney Pier had hired Arlo to fix their boiler. They'd been so torn between not trusting a Whitehead and needing to go to work that they'd locked the doors to every room before they left, giving him access only to the hallway. It was the hottest week of the year and he couldn't open a window or get to the kitchen for water. He'd sweated so much he left a stain on the patch of carpet outside the boiler room and they'd docked him the cost of cleaning. The final payment hadn't even been enough to cover parts.

'I heard you were up at the school this morning.'

Arlo jumped slightly, banging his head off the exposed pipe. He scrunched up his face and cursed silently into the darkness until the worst of the pain passed.

'You know what some of those Glass Lake mothers are like,' Fiona continued. 'Keeping an eye on everyone's comings and goings, sending the details into WhatsApp like it's the Interpol messaging service.'

She laughed but the knowledge that people were actually discussing him, and it wasn't just in his head, made Arlo feel so exposed he could no longer resist the urge to emerge from under the sink and make sure his T-shirt hadn't ridden up his back.

'Mrs – Fiona – I would actually take some water, if that's okay?'

His shirt was still where it should be, but it was clammy, as was his face. He felt sweat around his eyes and he blinked.

Fiona, who was leaning against the far wall, walked over to the fridge and removed a bottle. 'Is it totally awkward?' she asked, crossing the room towards him. 'With Nuala Patterson?' She lowered her voice even though they were the only people in the kitchen. 'Does the woman just *hate* you?'

She unscrewed the water bottle and left it on the ground beside him, brushing her hand across his back as she straightened up.

Definitely looking for the ride.

Fuck off, Leo. She's talking about your mom.

Arlo spoke to his best friend in his head because Leo would no longer talk to him in real life. He'd sent him messages on Instagram and SnapChat, he'd even sent him a long email, but Leo ignored them all. Then a few months ago, he blocked him. So, the last thing he'd ever said to Arlo was still, 'You're a fucking wimp.' Two seconds later the car skidded off the road, and Leo and Mike were thrown up against a 200-year-old oak tree.

They'd been on their way home from a gig in Cork city. Donovan was playing, so they had to go. But Leo, Mike and Arlo were only seventeen, and the Triskel was strict on ID; they needed an adult. Arlo convinced his dad to take them. Arlo was supposed to drive them there and back, only he got drunk. People blamed his dad for that, but Mike was the one who snuck in the whiskey. His dad had only bought them one pint each, but it was true he'd bought himself several more.

What they should have done was left the car. They should have paid for a taxi. Arlo imagined this scenario all the time. In reality, nobody would have gone for it. It was an hour and a half's drive so a taxi would have cost at least two hundred euro, plus the hassle of coming back for the car the next day, and his mom needed it to get to work in the morning. Now, though, two hundred quid seemed like a pretty good price for his dad to avoid seven years in jail, Leo to keep his legs, and Mike to still be alive. Mike was the funniest fucker Arlo had ever known, and now he was gone for ever. And without Leo around, there was nobody he could really talk to about that.

'Nuala Patterson should be grateful,' said Fiona, watching him carefully from her seat at the kitchen table. 'At least her child is alive. I heard she didn't want to hire you. Is that true?' Her stare burnt into his skin and he knew he was going red again. 'That's discrimination. You could sue, you know? Does she ever speak to you? I bet she says *awful* things.'

There were people in Cooney who refused to hire him because of what had happened. But there were a few, like Fiona Murphy, who saw it as a bonus: your sink fixed by the one who escaped unscathed. Ella said they were like hyenas, tossing around his intact carcass, desperate for any remaining morsel of gossip. But it didn't help Arlo get through the day to think of them like that.

'We don't — she doesn't talk to me,' he said finally.

'Is that right?' gasped Fiona, as if he'd revealed something far more interesting. 'How *terrible*. You hardly made your father get behind the wheel drunk, now did you? And your little brother got a lead role in the musical – I'd say Nuala Patterson just hates that.'

Without thinking, Arlo lifted a wrench and placed the cool metal against his burning cheek. He switched it to the other side. Fiona caught his gaze and raised an eyebrow in a way that made him drop the tool. It clattered on the pale blue tiles and he quickly shoved his torso back in under the sink.

'I should get on with this,' he said into the airless dark.

'Absolutely, Arlo sweetheart.' He could hear the smile in her voice. Under his T-shirt and heavy jeans, his skin prickled. 'I'll be as quiet as a church mouse,' she said. 'I'm just checking in on my socials. Pretend I'm not even here.'

....

Frances Tandon was having a lovely sixty-sixth birthday. She'd started the day with scrambled eggs from her hens, who had been on strike for the past week but were now back laying with gusto, and some deep meditation where she came as close to reaching bliss as she had all week. She'd received several cards in the post and the students who rented the house next door had dropped in a box of 'special birthday brownies'. They'd underlined special a few times, lest they accidentally drug an unsuspecting, and newly minted, pensioner. Frances was saving them for this evening.

Then she'd hosted a particularly successful workshop for beginners. She knew it had been successful because ten of the twelve participants had signed up for Tantric Sex level two before they left, and everyone had removed at least one item of clothing for the concluding gentle touch session. While she had been slightly concerned about the man who started taking notes – 'How do you spell "solar plexus"?' – that same student got so into the shaking off his inhibitions portion of the afternoon that he'd knocked over the altar and sent the Shiva statue and incense burners crashing to the floor. So, all in all, excellent feedback.

Having seen off the students, extinguished the candles and gathered up the bedsheets from the floor, Frances was now making the ten-second commute from the renovated shed that served as her tantra studio to the main house, where she had happily lived alone for more than twelve years. She threw the sheets into the washing machine and placed a saucepan of soup on the hob's back-left ring. Her favourite ring.

She poured herself a generous glass of kombucha and tore a corner off one of the brownies; just a nibble while she waited for the soup to heat. Then she checked her phone for the first time that day. There were missed calls and birthday greetings from her children and grandchildren. Even Beverley, she was glad to see, had sent a message.

Frances opened the WhatsApp from her daughter. There was no text, only a video. She pressed play.

Happy birthday, Granny, I love you so much! I can't wait to see you again. Thank you for being the best grandmother in the world. You're amazing. Happy birthday!

Frances watched as Amelia blew three kisses to the camera. That was it. No sign of Beverley. Presumably she was holding the camera.

Frances pulled another chunk from the brownie – they were deliciously moreish and the hashish not at all noticeable – and watched it through again. It was, ostensibly, a lovely message. What grandmother didn't want to hear she was the best in the world? What person didn't like to be told they were amazing? Yet despite Amelia's exaggerated, effusive way of speaking, it was oddly hollow. It was like the camera had turned her granddaughter into a shiny, unauthentic version of herself. Frances would have preferred an awkward but simple 'Happy birthday Granny' and then for Beverley to turn the camera on herself and say the same. Better yet, a phone call, so she could have an old-fashioned interaction with her daughter and granddaughter. Ella was the only Franklin who ever actually phoned.

It wasn't that Frances was lonely. Far from it. She talked to her other children on the phone and saw a wide circle of friends in Dublin regularly. She had a busy and fulfilling second career, having given up badly paid pen-pushing at the same time she gave up her husband. She held tantric sex and massage workshops in her studio and travelled the country hosting retreats and classes. She took a lover, a retired chiropodist named Geoffrey, about once a week. They had sex and played Scrabble and generally succeeded in ensuring the lovemaking lasted longer than the board game.

So no, it wasn't that she was lonely for her daughter, it was just that she yearned to help her. Beverley reminded Frances of her former self. Her daughter would balk at that; she was slim and wealthy, things Frances had never been, and Beverley didn't allow her husband to call her names in front of her children. But it wasn't about external traits (a possibility Beverley would struggle to comprehend); it was about being so tangled up in yourself that you didn't realise you were your own prison guard, let alone that it was possible to be free. Her daughter had always been chasing the wrong things for the wrong reasons, and she accepted her role in that. She should have left her husband a lot sooner.

Frances had given birth to five children, but it was only when they were grown and she had travelled to India and discovered tantra – specifically, in the middle of a vigorous shaking session just outside Mumbai – that Frances felt she had finally given birth to herself. She was a woman renewed, freed from cultural baggage and people pleasing and western expectations. She had achieved bliss. And she desperately, oh so desperately, wanted even a sliver of that for her daughter.

Of course, Beverley had no truck with tantra. She acted as if Frances had chosen this path in order to continue a lifetime of embarrassing her. (Now her mother wasn't just fat – she was fat *and* she removed her clothes for a living!) But tantra wasn't only about delayed orgasms and pleasing a sexual partner – although Beverley's sex life didn't bear thinking about; Frances doubted if her son-in-law found anyone as attractive as himself – it was a spiritual practice that helped people to heal. It healed the relationships we have with ourselves. After an adulthood marred by verbal abuse, Frances had learned to love her body. Her daughter was so thin, so afraid of ending up like her mother, and yet she didn't love herself half as much.

Frances felt a faint tremor and took a deep breath, opening her channels and allowing the energy in.

Only it wasn't her body vibrating. It was her phone.

Her granddaughter was calling.

'Ella, my love, how wondrously cosmic to hear from you.' Frances leaned back in her chair and watched the evening light reflect off her glass wind chime and explode across the ceiling. 'You'll have to speak slowly. It seems your dear old grandmother has accidentally scoffed an entire hash brownie.'

....

Ella Belle Franklin had intended to go to Dublin for university. Her dad offered to pay for accommodation wherever she wound up, but Ella had planned to live with her grandmother. Her parents were surprised and delighted when, at the last minute, she swapped University College Dublin for University College Cork. They were even more delighted when she decided to live at home for her first year. Her father was rarely there, and her mother was perpetually disappointed in her: her hair, her clothes, the close bond she enjoyed with her grandmother. But her parents were controlling people, who liked to be in charge, and this way they knew where she was. Most of the time.

Ella had stayed in Cork, and Cooney, because of Arlo. Her parents would never have guessed that, and this fact delighted Ella. They could only see their daughter in their own image and so couldn't even consider that she might fall for someone they would deem wholly unsuitable. Not that she was with Arlo because it would annoy her parents. That was only a bonus. She had loved Arlo since fifth-year religion, when they all had to write about someone important to them. Most of the boys had picked footballers or YouTubers, but Arlo wrote about his little brother. Sister Tracey read out his essay and Arlo went so red that Leo Patterson threw cold water on him. This only made the boys laugh more, but Ella had felt this ache in her chest, like she needed to know everything Arlo thought as soon as humanly possible. She made more of an effort with her friendship with Leo then, because she knew they were close.

Arlo had stayed in Cooney for Woody, and she had stayed for him. Now, though, she couldn't wait to get out of the place.

On Thursdays her lectures were done by lunchtime, but she was reluctant to come straight home. Arlo worked long days so there was nothing to rush back for. Sometimes she went for lunch or coffee with classmates, but mostly she drove to the car park of the Lidl superstore just outside the town and sat and listened to music and watched as Cooney residents snuck into the chain outlet while pretending not to see each other. There was a very active Keep Cooney Independent campaign, and locals were supposed to shop at Connolly's supermarket. But Connolly's was extortionate, and their vegetables were shite.

Today she parked in front of a gigantic billboard advertising special offers on monkey nuts, skeletons and large, plastic cauldrons.

She had declined her parents' offer of a new car in favour of her grandmother's old Peugeot, even though the heater didn't work – Ella was currently wearing gloves and a scarf – and it often leaked oil. She loved this car because it reminded her of good times. Frances Tandon was the only woman who could make driving over a pothole, at speed, fun. Ella, however, never drove at speed.

The last time she heard from Leo Patterson was April. She and Arlo had been trying to contact him since the crash but neither had got a response. Then, out of the blue, he sent her this long email. He called her a slut and a tease and told her about the fight he and Arlo had been having when the car left the road. They'd been fighting about her and this was what had distracted Charlie Whitehead. She was the reason they'd crashed. She, he wrote, was the reason Mike was dead.

Sometimes, when she was driving, she thought about this so much that she could no longer be sure she was in control of the car. So, she'd pull over and do something else. Today, sitting in the Lidl car park, she'd called her grandmother.

Then she sat back, listened to loud hip hop and watched as Lorna Farrell, one of her mother's many frenemies, rolled a trolley laden with jumbo packs of toilet paper, shopping bags, several skeletons and a cauldron out of the supermarket in a pair of oversized sunglasses and a large floppy sunhat.

Ella gave an involuntary shiver. She checked the thermometer on the dashboard.

It was seven degrees outside.

12

......

A **few weeks** ago, Maeve went to a sleepover at Amelia Franklin's house. She was so excited to be asked, it didn't matter that every girl in the class had got an invitation. Christine hadn't slept properly that night. She kept waiting for the call telling her Maeve was homesick and sobbing in the Franklins' bathroom or walk-in wardrobe and to come get her. But her phone never rang. Maeve had a great time and arrived home the following morning with a goodie bag for herself and some interior design suggestions for her parents. Their nice but not particularly remarkable semi-D could do with more. More marble, more rooms, more gym equipment, and definitely more chandeliers.

'Even one would do. We could put it in the foyer,' the eleven-year-old had said, not a hint of irony as she gestured to the tiny damp porch with the peeling paint where the Maguires kept umbrellas, mucky shoes and Porcupine's kitty litter.

So, while Christine hadn't been inside Beverley's home since they were children, and she'd lived somewhere a lot less glamorous than this, she had an idea of what to expect.

The winding staircase, expansive foyer and entirely marble kitchen were all as to be expected from a neo-classical, *nouveau riche* home. Not that the Franklins were new to money – they'd made their fortune in printing two generations back and were as close to a dynasty as West Cork came – but Beverley was. The ostentatious light fixtures and shoe room – where Christine reluctantly left her ankle boots – were also predictable. Indeed, nothing in the vast pile took Christine by surprise until Beverley put her sitting at one of three marble breakfast bars and continued to yammer on about how her daughter had been wronged. As she glanced back across the floor, convinced her threadbare ankle socks had left sweat marks on the gleaming slabs, she spotted the fish.

An artificial pond, measuring about 3ft by 3ft and topped with a glass ceiling, had been built into the kitchen floor. Two colourful fish were swishing around the water feature, which had been made flush with the marble slabs. It was so decadent and so surprising – nothing about Beverley said 'quirky' – that all journalistic enquiries and representations on behalf of her daughter flew from her mind. All she wanted to ask was, *Why?*

'Apologies,' said Beverley, interrupting her own lengthy diatribe, the gist of which was: sexting is bad; Woody Whitehead is worse. 'My mind is in a million places. Would you like a coffee?'

'Sure, but I can make it.' Christine slid down from her stool. 'Where do you keep—'

'Alexa,' said Beverley, so sternly and decisively that Christine was sure the woman had forgotten her name despite being classmates for *eight* years, 'make coffee.'

A flicking switch echoed through the uncluttered room and on the countertop (also marble) over beside the silver oven, a stainless-steel coffeemaker started to gurgle.

Beverley pressed a cupboard door that, up to this point, Christine had assumed was a wall. The thing popped open and she removed two mugs.

'It's not even really about Amelia. Well, it is, of course, but I'm not *worried* about her, not in any greater sense. She's confident, you know, very talented, her own person. Have you seen her Instagram page? She's going to go far. I'm more worried about what this says about Glass Lake and that Principal Patterson doesn't seem to care. What might the Whitehead boy get some other young girl to do, someone more impressionable, with less attentive parents? Not everyone is as well-adjusted as Amelia. And we all know what the father was like. A drunk. You know about the crash, right? Out on Reilly's Pass?'

Christine nodded. Everyone knew about the crash. She had reported on it. She'd also written about Mike Roche's horrendously sad funeral and Charlie Whitehead's sentencing. Derek was livid when he pleaded guilty immediately – 'Do you know what a local manslaughter trial does for newspaper sales?!' – but Christine was glad they'd been spared a court case. It had been a grim few months in Cooney as it was. The *Southern Gazette* received a lot of letters and emails from people calling for the Whiteheads to be run out of town. Christine had chosen not to publish them. Connie Whitehead was getting a hard enough time of it in the real world without having to see the hatred in print. She'd be lying if she said she hadn't been slightly concerned when Maeve was put sitting beside Woody Whitehead at the beginning of the school year. But Maeve liked Woody, and Charlie's children were as much victims as anyone else. Plus, she'd googled it, and according to some study in Arizona, a criminal mind was not hereditary.

'So,' Beverley continued, 'you wouldn't exactly keel over from shock if his sons turned out not to be the greatest citizens either, would you? An expulsion would be the quickest, fairest and most discreet solution, but Principal Patterson just isn't on the ball like she used to be. I think she needs it pointed out to her that Woody is not the kind of student we want at Glass Lake.' She yapped on and on, her perfectly manicured feet stepping on the fishbowl's glass cover as she crossed the kitchen, turned on the cold-water faucet and filled a jug. 'I watched Woody at pick-up today – nobody there to collect him, *quelle surprise* – and you can tell, just by looking at him… It's his expression, or the way he walks or something. It's weird. *He's* weird. You know when you can just tell?'

Christine half felt like sticking up for the boy. Maeve made Woody sound like a sweet if slightly peculiar kid. The peculiarity was probably why they got on so well. And who was to say Amelia hadn't started the whole thing?

Still. Sexting.

Even the word was unpleasant. It was like something a snake might say before it lobbed its head forward and gave you a fatal bite. *Ssss-exting*. Kids would be kids; but she wasn't so sure she wanted them 'being kids' while sitting beside her overly naïve daughter.

Beverley put a jug – complete with mint leaves and slices of cucumber – and a glass tumbler in front of Christine. 'Nuala Patterson wouldn't even entertain the notion of expelling him. She basically said if he went, Amelia was going too. She threatened me, essentially. You'd think the Whiteheads would be her least favourite Cooney residents, given what happened to her son, but I guess I still win out. And that's it. It's a *fait accompli*,' she said, sounding out each syllable. 'Who made her judge and jury of Glass Lake?'

The Department of Education, thought Christine, as the goldfish continued to whip their tails around the dimly lit rectangle. Was

103

it soundproofed? Could fish even hear? And how did they get the food into them?

'He is not the kind of student we want at Glass Lake,' Beverley said for what must have been the fourth time now. 'We don't want a junior pornographer representing us on national television, for God's sake. I don't know if you've heard, Christine, but I've got this year's musical onto *The Big Children's Talent Show.*'

'I did hear that, actually, at the Strand this morning,' said Christine, pulling her attention away from the fishbowl and back to the rather tedious conversation. This was her chance. 'Well done. Seriously. It's such an impressive achievement. It's great to have Glass Lake represented on the national broadcaster.' Christine lifted the tumbler to her mouth and resisted the urge to blink. She needed to convey she was genuine – and not just a genuine suck-up.

'You were at the Strand this morning?'

She nodded as she swallowed. 'Mm-hmm.'

Beverley leaned forward. 'How did Lorna break the news about the TV appearance? Did she make it clear I was the one who organised the whole thing? Because I was. Her only idea was to send the director general of RTÉ one of her weekly thank-you cards. Have you ever got one of those? Awful things. Now that her husband's a councillor, she stamps the back of the envelopes with the Cork County Council crest. If you ever see one coming in the letterbox, bin it straight away. It doesn't matter how good your cleaner is, she'll never get the glitter out of your carpet.'

'I'll bear that in mind.'

'I was the one who—'

'I was actually at the Strand to talk to you,' Christine interrupted, unwilling to let the conversation move on. 'About the musical, as it happens. Maeve wants to work on costumes. She's very enthusiastic and she has loads of ideas already. I gave her name to Lorna Farrell but I'm not sure she heard me …'

'Lorna Farrell is a lapdog,' said Beverley dismissively. 'That's fine. Maeve Maguire for costumes. I'll remember. Woody, though, Woody is a lead.'

Christine let her shoulders drop. 'Great,' she enthused.

'Excuse me?'

'No, I mean, about Maeve, great. Just about Maeve.'

Beverley put her hand to chest. 'He's playing the lion. My God, I hadn't even thought about that. How does Nuala Patterson expect me to work with him now? No way. Absolutely no way.' She lifted the coffee pot and poured. Even the Franklins' technology could only do so much. 'For the sake of everyone in Cooney, he needs to be named.'

If one of the fish died, was there a way of getting the carcass out? Or did it just lie there decomposing under the LED lights until construction professionals came and pulled the whole thing apart? The Franklins had this place built, so presumably the fishbowl was their idea. It was just so hard to imagine that when they were drawing up the designs for the kitchen – plug socket here, gas line there – they'd thought to draw a little rectangle and write 'Fake Indoor Pond'.

'Named publicly,' clarified Beverley. 'As in, in the *Southern Gazette*.'

'We can't name him,' said Christine, as firmly as she could. 'I can write the piece without names, as I think my editor explained. But Woody's a minor. We've got to be careful around that. We wouldn't name Amelia either.'

'Well, of course you wouldn't name Amelia. She didn't do anything wrong.'

Christine took a slow sip of her coffee. 'Delicious. Thank you.'

'So, fine, no names. I don't think it'll take much for people to guess, anyway. Who else *would* it be?'

Beverley was deluded if she thought people would only be interested in the male party. Cooney was a small town. Christine ignored Derek's voice screaming in her head – 'Outrage Makes a Front Page! Outrage Makes a Front Page!' – and said, 'Are you sure you want to do this, Beverley? Children do silly things. Before she reaches adulthood, I'm sure Amelia will have done a lot worse.'

In her head, this sounded empathetic, comforting even, but from the expression on Beverley's face, it was clear that was not how it came out.

'Has your daughter done a lot worse than this?'

'No,' said Christine, before quickly adding, 'Not that I know of. But I mean, possibly.' She wanted to say that Maeve didn't have a phone but thought it might sound like she was gloating, which she was a bit. 'It's a full-time job, worrying about kids,' she said instead. 'My eldest is a vegan who doesn't like vegetables, so I have nightmares about her being diagnosed with scurvy and me having to explain myself to a team of doctors. And my youngest says everything that comes into his head. He goes up to complete strangers and asks why their face is so red or tells big burly truckers that his mom says tattoos are for criminals. I have disowned him in public more times than I care to admit. And Maeve' – Christine chortled. She talked fast as she tried to coax Beverley around – 'Maeve has to confess every bad thing that enters her head. She regularly tells me she worries she wouldn't be sad if I died, and I just have to smile and say it's fine. And then we've got this cat who abandoned us for a neighbour and ...' She shook her head. 'Anyway, trust me, it's a lot. My family, I mean. Not yours.'

Beverley's bottom lip protruded, and her eyebrows lifted. (And they did go up, even though her forehead didn't budge. Whoever did her Botox was very good.) 'Thank you for the concern, but I know what I'm doing.'

When they were at school, Christine had been paired with Beverley for a project on the *Titanic*. They were meant to go to Christine's house to work on it, but her mom got food poisoning, so they had to go to Beverley's over in Aberstown instead. It had been nothing like this place. As Christine recalled, they'd been given big plates of chips for dinner, which Beverley insisted they eat in her room while the rest of her family ate together downstairs. Beverley had shared a bedroom with two older sisters who painted their nails and taped songs off the radio. Christine, who never had chips for dinner and was an only child, thought it was amazing, but when her dad came to collect her, Beverley made her promise not to tell anyone in school about her house. They'd got on well working on the project, but they never hung out again after that. As an adult, she got that Beverley had been embarrassed, but she'd never understood of what.

Christine produced a Dictaphone and notebook from her bag. She didn't really need both, but they were good visual aids to remind people they were talking to a newspaper. 'Why would you want to remind them?!' she could practically hear Derek shouting. But Christine, like her daughter, needed a clear conscience to sleep at night.

She pressed record and flipped back the notebook cover.

'What was the school's response when you told them about the photo?'

13

......

Mrs Rodgers had to bribe Albert with a promise of two more episodes of *The Chase* to get him to sit still while she ensured he was thoroughly rinsed. She gave him a quick towel-dry and carried him into her bedroom where he stretched out on the eiderdown.

She took a hand mirror from her dressing table and held it up to him. 'What do you think? New home, new you?'

But Albert just yawned laboriously.

Mrs Rodgers ran her hand along the dressing table and idly picked up the hairdryer. She did a slow, exaggerated yawn of her own, so as not to rouse his suspicion (Albert was a very intelligent animal; he could have been on *The Chase*, and that show was so rapidly running out of gimmicks that a pets special was only a matter of time), then she pointed the contraption at the cat, pulled the trigger, and blasted him out of it. Albert gave a high-pitched whine and leapt up and out of the room. Mrs Rodgers sighed. It would have to do.

She turned the thing off, just as the doorbell went. Pulling back the net curtain from her bedroom window, she peered down on to the thinning crown of Conor Maguire from number seven.

Mrs Rodgers was surprised to see him back again. They had settled this last night.

She made her way slowly down the stairs, scooping up Albert as she went. Remembering at the last minute to hunch herself forward – frailty was her greatest weapon – she slowly allowed the front door to creak open.

'Hello?' she said, forcing her voice to croak. 'Who goes there?'

'Conor Maguire, Mrs Rodgers. Sorry to disturb you.' He was standing on her path, prancing on the spot like a boxer warming up for a fight, except he was wearing slacks and a shirt. 'I'm here about the cat. I talked to my wife and we'd really like him back, if that's all right. You see, the kids are missing—' He stopped jigging. His eyes had dropped to her chest. It was a while since a man's gaze had rested there. 'Is that Porcupine?'

She looked down, as if noticing the animal curled up in her arms for the first time. 'Hmm? Oh, no. This is Albert.'

Albert purred at the sound of his name.

Good cat, thought Mrs Rodgers.

Conor blinked.

'I haven't seen your cat in days, I'm afraid. But I will let you know if he comes calling again.'

'Mrs Rodgers, I was here last night. You had Porcupine then. That *is* Porcupine.'

'Al-bert,' she said, slowly, kindly.

'What happened to his …?' Conor's brow furrowed as he inspected the cat. When he looked at her, his face was flooded with a sort of horrified respect.

She smiled vacantly.

'Mrs Rodgers … did you *dye* his fur?'

'Whose?'

'Porcupine's! Our cat. The cat you're holding!'

'As I said, I haven't seen Porcupine. Maybe you should put up some Missing posters? I hear they can be very helpful.'

Conor opened his mouth, but no words came out. It took two more attempts before he spoke, though it was hardly worth the wait. 'That's my cat,' he said meekly. 'Please give me back my cat.'

'This is *Albert*,' she said again, patiently, though she needed to get back inside. It was chilly and Albert was still damp. Plus, it had been at least forty minutes since his last meal. 'Albert is *my* cat. I suppose he does look a little like Porcupine, but you couldn't get them confused, not really. Albert's fur is so distinctive, with this big patch of black on his back. See?' She nodded down to the animal, then looked back up at Conor. He had reverted to opening and closing his mouth.

She hoped he wouldn't cry. Animals were very sensitive to human emotions.

'If Porcupine has any similarly distinctive features, it might be an idea to mention them on the poster. You're a dentist. Maybe you noticed something unusual about his teeth?'

Albert purred, more insistently this time.

He was right, of course. It was getting late, and she had promised him two more episodes before bed.

'Well, thank you for the visit, Conor dear, and best of luck with the cat. Tell the children I was asking for them, and Christine. I do hope they're not working her too hard at the paper. Busy, busy!'

....

They were wrapping up the interview when Beverley heard Ella's old Peugeot sputtering its way up their porcelain-paved driveway. They had offered to buy her a new car, as a reward for doing so well in her exams, but she had taken her grandmother's banger instead. This had succeeded in pissing off both parents: Malachy because he did not like having a piece of junk in his driveway, and Beverley because it was a constant reminder of the close relationship Ella had with her mother, and not with her. She gave her girls everything she never had, and Ella just kept finding new ways to throw it back in her face.

Beverley picked up Christine's cup, and her own. She was halfway to the sink when she realised the journalist still had coffee left. But she couldn't bring them back; she'd look ridiculous. She was never at ease when an outsider was in her home, even though she'd spent years getting it just right for showing off. It was a hangover from childhood.

Her jitters were not helped by the fact that Christine was the only person from school who'd ever been in her house as a child. And of course, she'd had to be there for dinner.

Beverley's dad was constantly making comments about her mother's weight: lamenting that she was 'too good a cook' in front of strangers and calling her an embarrassment in front of the kids. But mealtimes were the worst part of Beverley's childhood. When her mother was eating, he said nothing. He would lay his own cutlery to one side, making it clear her consumption had his undivided attention. He refused to eat a morsel until she was done. He just sat there watching her. Beverley had watched too, not out of meanness, but because he made it seem so enthralling. Her mother never lifted her eyes from her plate. The day Christine came for dinner she'd insisted they eat in her bedroom, but she was sure she'd noticed anyway. How could she not?

Ella strolled into the kitchen, tapping away on her phone.

Beverley carefully moulded her lips into a smile: not too wide as to be needy, but not too tight as to be antagonistic. She never knew where she stood with her eldest daughter these days, and she did not want to have an argument in front of someone whose only familial complaint was that her daughter confided in her *too* much.

That had been a humble brag worthy of Lorna Farrell.

'Hello, darling,' said Beverley. 'How was college?'

Ella looked up from the screen and, though it took her a second, she returned the smile. If nothing else, the Franklins knew how to keep up appearances.

'Good,' she said. 'Grand.' She looked at Christine. 'Hi.'

'Hi,' the woman replied, raising a hand. Ella's gaze lingered on the Dictaphone.

'Ella, this is Christine Maguire. She's a journalist with the *Southern Gazette*.' Her daughter's face remained blank. 'That's the local paper. You know newspapers, darling? The physical things with words printed on them.' She'd meant it to sound jovial, a little ribbing, but playful was not a tone she excelled at. 'And Christine, this is my elder daughter, Ella. She's studying psychology at UCC.'

'I know what newspapers are, Bev. You've shown me your scrapbook enough times, all those articles from your time as an actor that never actually mention your acting.'

Beverley held on to her smile. 'It's not a scrapbook, darling,' she said, with just a hint of a warning. 'It's a few cuttings I happened to hang on to.'

'And laminate,' Ella muttered. 'Are you writing something about Bev?' she asked, louder. 'Has she told you about the time she nearly got Minnie Driver's part in *Circle of Friends*, but the director said she was too young and too thin?'

It was actually the casting director – her agent had been far too lazy to get her in front of the actual director – and those hadn't been his exact words, but years of auditions had taught Beverley to read between the lines.

'Christine is writing about Glass Lake and its complete rejection of any responsibility for how its students communicate with each other.'

'Is this about Amelia's nude?'

Beverley's nose wrinkled.

Still, at least 'nude' was better than 'pic', or indeed 'dick pic'.

'Yes. Although I'm an anonymous source – so you never saw Christine here, all right? And we will not be naming Amelia' – she turned to the journalist for confirmation – 'and you're not to tell anyone else about what happened.'

'Just the newspapers.'

'It's anonymous.'

'Nothing's anonymous in Cooney,' said Ella, pulling open the fridge.

The strained relationship with her eldest daughter pained Beverley more than she cared to admit. Ella had once referred to her mother as her best friend. That changed when she hit adolescence, which was fine, Beverley knew the importance of letting your children be who they wanted to be. She'd thought they'd have more time together after she left Southern Pharmaceuticals, but the sporadic bickering and animosity had only got worse. At first, she worried her daughter had been traumatised by that horrific car crash. Ella was in the same year as the boys and it must have been quite the shock to attend the funeral of a classmate. She had been friendly with Leo Patterson, and Beverley half-thought they'd been dating. She hadn't minded. It was slim pickings in Cooney and the son of a school principal and an accountant was at least a respectable first boyfriend. Anyway, Ella had laughed at the suggestion. They weren't even that friendly any more, she'd said. But if it wasn't the crash, then what was it? What had turned her into an argumentative teenager at the very point she should have been exiting that phase?

'So not a word to anyone else,' repeated Beverley. 'Got that, Ella?'

'Mmm.' Her daughter's head disappeared into the fridge. 'Except Granny.'

'No, including Granny.'

'Yeah, well, too late. I already told her.'

'*What?*'

Beverley brought her hand down hard on the marble worktop and waited for her daughter to show herself.

'You know, I think I have everything, so I can just—'

'Don't go on my behalf,' said Ella, emerging with a yoghurt, and speaking to Christine as if she was the only person in the room. 'I'm going upstairs now.'

'Ella Belle Franklin. What do you mean you told Granny?'

'I rang to wish her happy birthday, which I hear is more than you did.' Ella opened the yoghurt and slurped a bit from the carton. She did this to annoy her. Beverley resisted the urge to throw a spoon at the ingrate. Ella shrugged. 'Granny asked.'

'My mother asked if Amelia had sent any naked photos lately?'

'No,' said Ella, heading for the door. 'She asked how Amelia was, so I told her.'

'You couldn't just have said "Fine", no? You had to ...' From the corner of her eye, she could see Christine starting to gather her belongings. She still had to ask about copy approval and to see if they could get some vague reference to the boy's 'troubled family background' or how the family was 'known to gardaí' into the piece. 'We'll talk about this later, Ella.'

'Whatever you say, Bev,' sang her daughter, as she swung out of the door, and disappeared back into the foyer.

14

......

'**A**rlo? Is that you?'

He followed his mother's voice into the living room where the Nine O'Clock News was on mute. The house was always quiet now. Connie Whitehead was sitting on the couch, remote by her side and mobile in her hand.

'Hi, Mom.'

'How was today?'

'Long,' he said, throwing himself down beside her. 'And grand,' he added. 'Today was grand.'

It actually had been. He'd had an easy introduction to Glass Lake. Seamus had given him the tour and Principal Patterson hadn't been mentioned let alone sighted. Fiona Murphy's was a bit awkward but she'd added a sizeable tip. He'd had two jobs outside the town after that; neither family seemed to have feelings on him one way or the other.

'How was your day?' he asked. 'How was work?'

'Work was fine.'

His mother was a teller in a bank on Main Street. Arlo had wanted her to ask for a backroom position after the car crash, but she refused. She said people were welcome to bad-mouth her husband; she'd probably agree with them. But it wasn't just Charlie

Whitehead they bad-mouthed. After the trial, a man had come in, thrown a carton of eggs at her counter and demanded to know when she was going to get the fuck out of Cooney. Arlo only knew about it because the man, an uncle of Mike's, had come up to him in Connolly's and gloated about what he'd done. His mother hadn't said a word, which made him wonder what else she didn't tell him.

'Really?'

'Yes, really,' she said, throwing an arm around his shoulders. 'I had a call from Glass Lake, though ...'

Had he done something wrong? Had someone complained? Surely, they wouldn't ring his mother. He was eighteen. If Seamus had a problem—

'... about Woody.'

'Oh, right.' But the relief was short-lived. 'What about Woody? Is he okay?'

'He's been sending naked photos of himself to a girl in his class. And this girl has been sending them back to him. Amelia Franklin, you know, of *the* Franklins.' His mother shook her head. 'I've to go in and talk to Nuala tomorrow, which, you know, is not ideal, but it's fine.' She looked at him. 'Arlo, it's fine.' This was how it worked now; both trying to make the other feel better, both failing miserably.

'Amelia Franklin?' He hadn't spoken to Ella since he left that morning. He'd barely looked at his phone. But the clogs were turning now, things slipping into place. 'How did the school find out?'

Connie sighed. 'Well, that bit's even worse. The girl's mother walked in on her taking a picture. A picture of herself, like.' She winced. 'God help me, but the first thing I thought was, Rather her than me. Can you imagine if I'd walked in on Woody doing the same? Mother of Jesus. Anyway, Beverley – you know Beverley

Franklin? – was beside herself, which is fair enough. And she went up to the school.'

His mother didn't know about him and Ella, but for different reasons to the Franklins. Her husband had just been sent to jail and he didn't want to rub her nose in his happiness. Or at least that was how he'd reasoned it to Ella. He also liked having another world to escape to, one that was just for him, one where he didn't have to feel bad whenever he started to feel good.

'Did this all happen today?' asked Arlo, recalling the argument between Amelia and Beverley that morning.

'This morning. And I've talked to Woody, before you start. I've taken his phone off him. George says he's probably just acting out, missing his father's influence. He's offered to take him fishing or hiking or on some other male-bonding activity.'

'George from the bank?'

'My friend George, yes.'

'He doesn't even know Woody.'

'It was just a suggestion.'

'I can take Woody fishing.'

His mother gave him a look. 'Since when do you fish?'

'Since now, if it's what Woody needs.'

'George and I are just friends, Arlo.'

'I know,' he said defensively.

'George is happily married. Very happily.'

'So are you.'

A beat. 'Right.'

'I'm going up to talk to Woody,' he declared, sounding more confident than he felt. He was no longer sure how to speak to Woody. As a brother? As a father? As a friend? 'Is he in his room?'

'He is.' Connie watched her eldest son make his way towards the door. He was never comfortable being observed.

He could smell his own stale sweat. If he stank last night, he really stank now. He desperately needed a shower.

'There's a letter for you on the kitchen table. From your dad.'

'Did you open it?'

'No, I did not open your post.' Her gaze drifted back to the muted screen, where a beaming weather forecaster was now standing beside a massive map of Ireland. 'I just assume he's the only person writing to you from Cork Prison.'

Arlo moved out into the hallway. He didn't like the turn the conversation had taken.

'You don't have to visit, whatever he says,' she called after him. 'You don't owe him anything. None of us do.'

....

'So, you want to report a missing cat?'

'No, not missing,' said Christine, pacing the kitchen with her mobile stuck to her ear. 'Abducted. He's not missing because I know exactly where he is. He's at number one Seaview Terrace, probably stretched out on the couch, licking himself.'

Conor looked up from his seat at the dining table, where he'd been nursing a tumbler of whiskey since she'd arrived home from the Franklins' and poured it for him. He had relayed his latest attempt to retrieve their cat like a soldier detailing atrocities witnessed at the front.

'Seaview ... Are you at Seaview Heights? Did you already phone this in?'

'No. We're the next road over. This is my first time calling.'

'I have a record of a missing cat from Seaview Heights, in June.'

'The cat has only just been swiped. And I'm at Seaview Terrace, not Heights, number seven. Look, can I just speak to the sergeant?' She knew Sergeant Whelan through work. He was always good for an off-the-record quote.

'The sergeant really is in a meeting, Mrs Maguire. If I interrupt him for a missing cat, I'll lose my job.'

'But the cat's not missing!'

Conor caught her sleeve. 'Tell them about the fur.' He mimed his fingertips being stuck together, then slowly he pulled them apart. 'It was all ...'

'Listen, Garda Delaney, wasn't it?'

'Yes, Ma'am.'

'Our cat has been abducted by a woman called Rita Rodgers. She's our neighbour. If you send a guard out to have a chat with her, I'm sure she'll give it back. That's all it would take.'

'Have you tried asking this woman to give you back the cat?'

'My husband tried mediation but she's refusing to return the animal, so I felt I had no choice but to get the guards involved. She coaxed him into her house with food and treats, and then she assigned him a new identity.'

'It was matted together,' whispered Conor. 'You should have seen ... All these great big clumps ...'

She pushed his glass closer.

'So, can you send someone out? Get a guard to have a word? Tell her to hand over the animal?'

'Oh, hang on, is it Seaview Crescent? I have a missing cat here: brown, last seen in August. Is that yours?'

'It's Seaview Terrace. Terrace!'

Conor flinched. The line went quiet.

'Hello?'

'One second, Mrs Maguire.' There was a harsh rustle against her ear as the officer put his hand over the receiver. She could hear him explaining the situation to a co-worker: 'Missing cat ... abducted ... no, seriously ... I can't ... I don't think I should ...' She thought she heard someone laugh.

When he came back on the line, the phone was on loudspeaker.

'Look, I know this isn't exactly blazing-sirens stuff, but I'm phoning on behalf of my kids. They're distraught without Porcupine.' This wasn't entirely true. Only Maeve had enquired about his whereabouts when Christine got home, and even then, she had been distracted by news of her costumes position on the musical.

'Porcupine?' repeated the officer. 'I thought it was a cat.'

'It is a cat. That's his name.'

Some sort of snort came from further away, then someone else hissed, '*Shhh!*'

Christine clenched her free hand into a fist. 'Our son chose it. And now our deranged neighbour is calling him Albert. The name isn't really the point. The point is that our neighbour has stolen our cat and is pretending it's a different animal.'

'Why would she dye his fur?' said Conor to nobody. 'Why would a human being do that?'

'Okay, well, we'll get an officer on this as soon as one becomes available. Thank you for the call, Mrs Maguire.'

'What if it's a case of animal cruelty?' she said, before he could hang up. 'Then would you take it seriously?'

'I can assure you we take all complaints seriously, and in line with procedure, I have created a file and—'

'Yes, yes, yes, I know. But this is animal cruelty. This woman is abusing our cat.'

The line went completely silent as she was placed on mute. She could just imagine all of Aberstown Station enjoying a hearty chuckle.

'Animal cruelty?' said Garda Delaney when the line returned.

'Yes. She dyed his fur.'

'Excuse me?'

'He used to be a sandy colour but now he has a big patch of dark brown on his back—'

'Black,' whispered Conor. 'It was pitch black, like her soul.'

'I mean, black, a huge patch of black on his back, and all the hair was matted together from the dye.'

Conor took a large gulp of whiskey.

'She never sought his consent,' said Christine. 'Or ours. She just did it.'

The line went dead again.

'Hello?'

More silence.

'Hello? Are you still there?'

The background noise returned. '*Yes,*' said the officer, his voice now high and breathless.

Then the line went silent again.

'Oh, for feck sake.' She lowered her own phone. 'He's putting me on mute,' she hissed at Conor. 'So he can have a good laugh.'

A couple more seconds and the line returned. Christine rolled her eyes.

'I'm sorry,' said the young officer. 'We're hav— we're having some technical difficulties here.'

'I'm sure,' said Christine coolly. She wanted to read him the riot act, but she knew she was on loudspeaker and she needed to maintain some shred of respectability with the guards she occasionally dealt with for work.

The officer cleared his throat. 'I'll be sure to ... to add that detail to the file, Mrs Maguire. Thank you.'

More whispering in the background. 'Say it!' 'No.' 'Go on!'

Garda Delaney's voice returned. 'And, ah, I'll forward it on to the ISPCA, to, ah, to the hair and beauty department.'

The last bit tumbled out so fast and so squeaky that she barely caught it.

Then the line went dead.

'Well?' asked Conor, the whiskey entirely drained.

'Well, he had to get off the line before he gave himself a hernia from the hilarity.' Christine sighed. 'We need a Plan B.'

....

When Arlo opened the bedroom door and stuck his head around, Woody pulled his hand away from his mouth.

'Hey,' he said.

'Oh, hi. Hey.' Woody threw down the controller and turned away from the old TV set. 'I thought it was Mom. How – how are you?'

Arlo laughed, relieved. His brother could still be his old pre-teenage mutation self, awkward and earnest. 'Grand, thanks. How are you? You weren't just sucking your thumb there, were you?'

'No.' Woody went a shade of red that was familiar to Arlo, and he instantly regretted saying anything.

'Sorry,' he said, still standing in the doorway. 'How are you?'

'Fine.'

'Mom told me about the photos.'

'Oh.'

'Yeah,' said Arlo. The screen behind his brother was paused on a computer game image of two men in army combats firing at someone else. The gamer tag in the corner said 'Ruth'. If that was another girl from school, he didn't want to know.

'Are you mad at me?'

'Of course I'm not mad at you. But like, you know you shouldn't have done it, don't you?'

'Yeah, I know. I'm sorry.'

'Why did you do it?'

Woody shrugged.

'Do you want to talk about it?'

'No.'

'Okay,' said Arlo, relieved. His own cheeks were starting to burn at the idea of discussing his little brother's naked body – or worse, Ella's little sister's naked body. 'It'll be all right. Mom will calm down, and it'll blow over. If she can get past the car crash ...'

But Woody didn't smile, and Arlo stopped forcing his.

He didn't know why he'd said that. It wasn't funny.

'Amelia's mom is really mad.'

'Yeah ...' Of all the students Woody could have been messaging, Beverley Franklin's youngest daughter really was a bad choice. 'Maybe stay away from Amelia for a while.'

'I am staying away from her. She told me that, about her mom being mad. I didn't ask.'

'Good. That's good.'

Woody looked at him. Arlo nodded emphatically.

Neither of them had any more to say.

'Do you want to play with me? I'm in the middle of a mission but I can leave if you want?'

'I better have a shower. I stink.'

'Okay.' His brother turned back to his game and the screen started to move again.

He wanted to tell his little brother he loved him, but it seemed too dramatic for a Thursday night; it might sound like he was dying of cancer or off to kill himself or something. So instead he said 'Goodnight' and headed for his own room, ignoring the guilty sense of relief.

When their dad told them he loved them, he made it sound like the obvious next line in whatever mundane conversation they were having. How did he do that? Arlo couldn't even bring himself to say it to Ella, though he did love her, and he knew exactly what he wanted to say.

I love you, Ella Belle Franklin. You saved my life.

I'm going to stop telling you things if you're going to mock me.

Sorry, Arly, but that's not how it works. I live in your head now. I know everything you think.

He lowered himself down on to the pale blue sheets of his single bed and examined the envelope. His name and address were scrawled across the front, while Cork Prison was stamped on the reverse.

Leo hadn't come to Charlie Whitehead's sentencing. After the crash, he went to a physical rehab facility in Dublin and hadn't set foot in Cooney since. Mr and Mrs Patterson had been in the court gallery. They'd sat near the back, beside Mike Roche's parents. Arlo felt uncomfortable that he and his mother were in the front row, as if they were saying they were more important or something. When the sentence was handed down, Mr Roche had shouted, 'Is that justice? Is that justice?' Nobody had answered and sometimes Arlo still heard the question hanging in the air. Mr Patterson moved to Dublin shortly afterwards, and when Leo was able to leave the rehab unit, he moved in with his dad. Several of the women he did jobs for told him the Pattersons were getting a divorce, as if, somehow, Arlo might enjoy that piece of information.

Mike's parents had moved too. That really upset people. Mr Roche was the best coach Cooney GAA had ever had, and now he was gone. But the Whiteheads, who'd never added anything to the local football team, were still here. His family's only contribution to the town, if you listened to the current gossip, was death, misery and dodgy plug socket fixtures. He could appreciate why they were so annoyed.

Arlo's chest ached like it sometimes did when he thought about his dad. He tried to imagine him sitting down – in a cell? At a desk? – to write to him. Was he sad? Lonely? Nervous? Scared? Did he have friends in prison? Did people like him? Did they still laugh at his jokes and ask for his opinions? These were the things Arlo wanted to know but they were too childish to ask. He had spoken to his father twice by phone since May. Both times, he had felt like he was choking. He couldn't get the words out. Nothing seemed important enough to say. The more he thought about these calls the worse he felt and the more he avoided speaking to him again. But he wanted to talk to him – and talk about him. Nobody else did, though, not his friends, not his neighbours, not even his wife.

Or me. I don't want to talk about him either.

And I don't want to talk to you about him, Leo, so don't worry.

Are you going to open that letter, or are you too scared?

Why would I be scared of a letter?

It's you, Arly. You jump when people look at you.

Sometimes it seemed impossible that Cooney would ever like him. He was breaking his back for people who would never let him be unremarkable again because they needed someone to discuss and the Whiteheads were still the best offering.

He thought of Ella and felt both better and worse.

If she spent a day in his head, she'd understand why he couldn't study.

Are you actually feeling sorry for yourself? You're the only one who walked away with your former life fully intact.

It's not exactly intact. People literally spit at me on the street.

Boo fucking hoo. And you got the girl. Fuck knows you didn't deserve that.

His bedroom was suddenly all out of proportion. It felt like he was reclining in a matchbox. Everything was tiny while he remained the same size. Slowly, he stretched out his right arm, convinced it would touch the opposite wall, but of course it was several feet away. He closed his eyes and counted to twenty. He breathed in and out.

He would keep trying, keep working hard, and everything would come right.

It just had to.

15

......

ABERSTOWN GARDA STATION

Joey knocked on the sergeant's door and waited for the bark instructing him to enter. The man was sitting at his desk, eating another sandwich. This one appeared to be tuna.

'Sorry to disturb you, sir ...'

'Are the second batch of parents here already?'

'Not yet. I just wanted to drop in the transcribed statements from this morning – before we have to start round two.'

'Very quick, Delaney. Good job.'

'Thank you, sir. My mother taught me to type. I could do fifty-five words per minute by the time I was ten; sixty-five by the time I was twelve.'

'Did I ask for your life story, Delaney?'

'No, sir,' he said, dropping the pages on to his boss's desk and pulling up his belt. 'No, you did not.'

'Anything noteworthy in here?'

'A lot of talk about the kids sending naked photographs.'

'Yah, that came up with me too.' The sergeant caught a large dollop of mayonnaise with his tongue before it splashed out of the sandwich and on to the freshly typed-up pages. 'Anything else, though? Anything that might actually explain why we were fishing a body out of the Gorm yesterday evening?'

'It's hard to say.'

'I'll take that as a no.' The sergeant sighed, wiping at his mouth then throwing the half-eaten tuna sandwich down on to the crisp paper. Joey tried not to wince. 'They're an opinionated bunch, aren't they – the Glass Lake parents?'

'They are, sir,' he agreed. 'Very, ah, strong willed. I got that impression from the information night.'

'Yes, that came up a few times too,' said his boss, moving both hands to his lower back as he stretched it out. 'Is it true two of the fathers almost came to blows, right in the middle of the assembly?'

'It is,' said Joey, as the sergeant reached for his food. 'I gave the main speaker a police escort home. A few of them looked ready to charge the stage.'

....

Sally Martin, parent

On at least three occasions, I saw Mr Cafferty slipping files to parents. I don't know what was in them and I can't say if it's related or not, but it's worth looking into. I'm not exaggerating when I say 'slipping'. He was not just handing them over. There was something in there that he did not want anyone to see. I'm not telling you how to do your job but that, to me, is worth investigating.

Fiona Murphy, parent

I say this from a place of respect, friendship
and concern, but Beverley Franklin has been
acting unhinged for a couple of weeks now.
I'm her friend; Lakers for life. But if I was
looking for someone who might be capable of
pushing someone to their death, that's where I'd
start. And I wasn't the only one who noticed.
Ask anyone who was at the parents' information
night, for a start. That was when she began to
unravel.

16

· · · · · ·

TEN DAYS EARLIER

'Sexting' row at Glass Lake Primary

By Christine Maguire

A concerned mother has lodged an official complaint with Glass Lake Primary after her daughter was involved in a 'sexting' exchange with a male student.

The mother, who cannot be named to protect the children's identity, has called for the male student to be expelled and described the school's response to the situation as 'wholly inadequate'.

The male student, who is in sixth class, sent a nude photograph of himself to the female student, also in sixth class, and asked that the gesture be reciprocated. The girl did so shortly afterwards.

'Glass Lake has a responsibility to keep its students safe,' the mother said. 'It needs to ensure the children receive adequate education about the internet, and it also needs to remove any students who are a threat to the well-being of everyone else at the school.'

Nuala Patterson, principal of Glass Lake Primary, said the school did not comment on individual students, but that an information night is being organised for parents, with fifth- and sixth-class students due to receive two additional sex education workshops this week.

· ·

It was impossible to say what a typical autumn evening was like on the tree-lined stretch that wound its way from Franklin Avenue up to the main Glass Lake building because, typically, nobody was here to experience it. Arlo imagined it was very still; the only light

131

coming from whatever stars were not blanketed in clouds sent inland by the Atlantic, and the only sound the wind working its way in and out of the branches of the 200-year-old oaks.

He and Ella should walk up the avenue some night, see what the quietness was like. He'd bring his warmest coat, in case she got cold, and if they heard something rustling amongst the trees, he would walk on that side, an arm thrown protectively around her waist. And maybe, if they found a clearing, and the mood took them, they—

The short, sharp blast of a horn brought Arlo back to the present.

A man's head appeared out the driver's side of a year-old Merc. 'Oi, space cadet! Any chance we can hurry this up?'

Tonight was not a typical autumn evening on Glass Lake's avenue. Tonight was a parents' information night.

A cacophony of purring engines, tyres on fallen leaves, and honking horns ran the length of the private avenue that led up to the school. Dozens of impatient parents were waiting to be told where to park. The headlights and backlights were dipped, but still they created a glow in the sky above like the aurora borealis.

He tugged at the reflective jacket that kept slipping down his arm and gestured for the Merc to approach. The fluorescent stick Seamus had left for him was already starting to malfunction.

Arlo had never seen the aurora borealis. He wasn't even sure what country it was in or, come to think of it, what exactly it was. But still. Beauty was beauty. And it would make a good lyric. It had the bonus of rhyming with Alice.

Eh ... who's Alice?

Who was Eleanor Rigby? It doesn't matter. We'll write a song about her and then she'll be someone.

132

I'm pretty sure there are already a few songs about people called Alice.

And they'll all be sick that they didn't think of rhyming it with aurora borealis.

Go on so, Lennon and McCartney, what are you thinking?

Aurora borealis, a door for Alice.

Abbey Road, here we come.

Shut up. I'm brainstorming.

The Merc came to a stop beside him. The driver gave him a look.

'Here for the information night?' asked Arlo, cutting the father off at the pass. 'Are you fifth- or sixth-class parents?'

'Fifth,' said the woman in the passenger seat, and Arlo watched her face do the thing parents' faces had been doing all evening.

'Fifth, okay, so just park by the sports hall. There should be plenty of spaces. If you could keep in line with the other vehicles, that would be great. Thank you.'

He pointed his semaphore rod in the direction of the sports hall with such conviction that it flew from his hand.

He caught the beginning of the woman's comment to her husband – 'That's the boy who' – as their window rolled up and they drove on.

....

'Oh, for heaven's sake,' Beverley muttered when the young man in the fluorescent jacket pulled his head away from the window of Tony Moran's Mercedes and threw his traffic baton on to the path, causing it to extinguish.

'What is it?' Malachy glanced in the rear-view mirror and slowly moved the car forward. The gravel caught on the wheel underneath.

The entirety of the Lakers' summer fundraiser just two years ago had gone towards repaving the yard. This was what happened when they let Principal Patterson hire the contractor herself.

'That's the Whitehead boy, the older one,' she said, pointing through the front windscreen. 'The one from the car crash.'

'From Ella's year?' Malachy squinted into the darkness where Arlo had recouped the broken baton and was brandishing it furiously, as if trying to cast a difficult spell. 'Not exactly setting the world alight, is he?'

Malachy put the car into first and inched forward. Then he was rolling down the window and opening his face into a broad smile. In the generous, confident voice he always used with the people of Cooney – his dynasty voice, as Beverley thought of it – he said, 'All right, son? Cold evening to be standing about outdoors.'

If Beverley had been hoping for a show of paternal protectiveness when she told Malachy about Woody soliciting photos from their daughter, she hadn't got it. 'They're young,' he'd said. 'Young people don't think.' Beverley was tempted to ask what his excuse was so, since he was forty. But she didn't, of course. They never spoke about the photos she'd found on his phone. It was dealt with, over, nothing more to say.

'I hope they're paying you a princely sum for this,' Malachy continued, as Arlo stared dumbly into the car, his broken baton hanging by his side.

'Yes, sir,' the boy mumbled, glancing from Malachy to Beverley. 'It is cold.'

Beverley leaned out slightly so she could be seen. She raised her eyebrows. 'Are you going to grant us permission to drive on?'

'Yes. Yes, sorry. The sixth-class parents are in the far yard, up by the swimming pool. You can head on up.'

'Very kind of you.' There was something especially irritating about a Whitehead telling them where to park in the yard they had built, or at least paid to have resurfaced.

She didn't need to look to know Malachy was making his apologetic face. It was the one he used with waiters. It said: 'If you think not accepting tagliatelle as a substitute for linguine is bad, you should try living with her.'

The engine started again. 'Thank you, son, and try not to get frostbite. You're doing a great job.'

Beverley focused her eyes on the space just above the dashboard. It was about the only way she could stop them from rolling.

The window closed and Malachy released the handbrake. 'Those looks are wasted on that kid,' he said, as the car rolled forward. 'Not really at the races, is he?'

Beverley had had a bad feeling about this information night ever since she'd received the To-All-Parents email on Friday afternoon. When she said she wanted something done, she meant she wanted Woody Whitehead gone. She did not want free cheese and a lengthy lecture.

Malachy's priority was that nobody know their daughter was the girl being discussed. Of course he wasn't going to drive over to the Whiteheads and start pounding on their door; he had no interest in making a scene. It was for the best that the *Southern Gazette* article had ended up as a small piece on page nine, overshadowed by an obscenely large photo of the town pharmacist straddling a bike in Lycra and holding a hefty petition above his head with such pride you'd swear he'd won the Tour de France. Ella had agreed to keep quiet about a journalist being at their house, though Beverley knew the payback for that favour was still to come. And Malachy didn't read the local papers. Not unless he was in them.

'Go right here. We're not parking by the pool.'

'The boy said—'

'I don't care what he said. I'm not parking in a yard. Go up to the staff spaces. We paid for that car park; we can at least get some use out of it.'

As soon as the Audi was stationary, there was a tap on Malachy's window. He opened the door to reveal Fiona Murphy, dressed in a bright pink bomber jacket.

'Hi, Mal; nice scarf. Hi, Bev.' She bent over slightly and wiggled her fingers into the car.

Fiona had been particularly irritating the past few weeks. She kept grinning at Beverley and giving her the exact same knowing look that was currently plastered across her face. She was acting like she had something on Beverley. It had started long before the incident with Amelia and the photo, so at least it wasn't that.

'We better get inside, Malachy.'

'We still have a few minutes,' said Fiona, taking a half-step back so Malachy had just about enough space to exit the vehicle.

Beverley smiled at the lower-ranking Laker. 'You can squeeze in anywhere, Fiona — a real benefit of being on your own. It's much harder when you're in a couple.' She linked her husband's arm, aware of how enviable it and every other part of him was. 'We need to find two seats together.'

....

'Oh God,' said Christine, slouching down in the passenger seat. 'Can we park somewhere else?'

'Why?' asked Conor, eyes on the side mirror as he reversed slightly to better approach the parking space. 'Is this not where the young fella meant? It was hard to tell. A black stick in the darkness; not very helpful, is it?'

The Franklins were out of their Audi and talking to Fiona Murphy. Butcher Murphy was probably lurking somewhere nearby. She had been in for steaks that afternoon, and still he'd referred to her as The Vegetarian.

'I don't want to talk to Beverley Franklin. She'll be raging about the article. She probably thought it would be on the front page – complete with a cowboy-style Wanted poster for Woody Whitehead.' She watched Beverley link her husband, catching her hair with her other hand and tucking it into her sleek mac. 'I suppose it's hard being that wealthy; you must struggle to find things to worry about.'

'Everyone has their worries,' said Conor, eyes still trained on the mirror as he shifted the steering wheel ever so slightly to the right, then back to the left.

'Not Beverley Franklin. You don't know her. You should see their house. Literally fish in the floor.'

'I do know Beverley.'

'You're her dentist, Conor. You know her teeth.'

'You can tell a lot about a person from their teeth.'

'Well, I sat in the same classroom as her for eight years, and I'm telling you she expects to be the centre of attention, always. She will not like having been relegated to the bottom of page nine by Gerry Regan's crusade to stop trucks driving through Cooney.'

Christine was delighted the article had been relegated. She'd got a frosty response when she phoned Nuala Patterson for a comment. The principal had been more welcoming about her covering tonight's event. A story she'd been working on had fallen through (the local estate agent finally admitted it might not have been *that* Cillian Murphy he'd sold the house to) and Derek had gone for the sex education evening as a replacement. 'We can do spin-off lists,' he'd enthused. Derek loved lists. 'Five Signs Your Kids Are at Risk Online. Ten Things the Youngsters Aren't Telling You. Sexting: Six Ways to Tell if You're Doing it Right.'

'How's the alignment your side?'

Christine peered out into the pitch black where she couldn't tell the colour of the car beside them, never mind see the lines on the ground. From the glow at the school entrance, though, she could see that the Franklins had stopped to talk to someone else. 'I dunno, Conor, maybe another inch to the left.'

'On it,' he mumbled, rounding his shoulders.

She relaxed back into the seat, rubbing the condensation from the windscreen with the cuff of her coat sleeve. Malachy Franklin was probably the best-looking father at Glass Lake, though he was too suave for her. She preferred them gauche and earnest – or at least she had done the last time she stopped to consider how she liked her men, which was probably fifteen years ago.

Conor pushed his thin-rimmed glasses up and moved his face closer to the glass. 'Aim for perfection and you might just achieve it,' he muttered. He'd rather drive around all night than park a car that was even a degree off straight. It was the dentist in him.

The engine died, and he tapped the steering wheel with a satisfied sigh. 'Beautiful,' he said, before unbuckling his belt. 'Right, let's go.'

The Franklins were still chattering away. Christine could hear the echo of Malachy's big, hollow laugh.

'Do you want to phone Caroline and make sure everything's okay at home?'

Conor gave her a look. She was not the type of parent who spent the evening away from her kids worrying about her kids. Out of sight, out of mind was more her motto.

'I left my phone at home, charging,' he said, opening his door.

'I can do it?'

'No. Let's go.' The door swung shut after him.

Conor rapped on the window. Christine groaned.

'Fine,' she grumbled, pushing open her own door and clambering out.

The Franklins were standing in the entranceway talking to the Farrells, who also had a daughter in sixth class. Lorna Farrell was wearing a jacket identical to Beverley's and her husband Bill was sporting a large 'Farrell No. 1' badge on his lapel, even though he'd been elected to the council several months ago.

'Conor, how's it going? How's the teeth business?' bellowed Bill, as the whole group turned in their direction.

Beverley caught her eye, then immediately looked away.

'Fine, Bill, just fine. Thanks.'

'I must get in for a check-up soon. Hahaha.'

Bill was a patient with both dentists in Cooney, just like he bought meat from all three butchers and declared every pub his local. A true politician.

'We were just saying how much we're looking forward to being told our children should be playing with abacuses and spinning tops until they're eighteen,' boomed Bill. 'It's a brave new world, and we'd rather not be parenting in it, but here we are.'

Malachy smiled conspiratorially at Christine, who was mortified to find herself blushing. Was standing at the entrance to Glass Lake all it took to turn her into a schoolgirl again?

'How are you, Beverley?' she said, as Bill asked Conor something about rates subsidies and the group became divided along gender lines.

'Fine,' said Beverley curtly, as if this was a bizarre question to be asked. Had she really expected them to run an 'Off With his Head' type article? He was a twelve-year-old boy.

Lorna squeezed her lips into a wide, tight smile. 'I see you managed to get Maeve down for costumes, Christine. Weren't happy to accept my answer on it?'

'Well, I was talking to Beverley anyway, so I just asked if there might be space ...'

Lorna turned to Beverley. 'I thought you said the request came from the school.'

'I'm sorry, Lorna. Are you director of this year's musical, or is that me?'

'You.'

'Right, so stop asking stupid questions. Malachy' – Beverley reached for her husband's arm – 'we should get inside.'

The Franklins left and Lorna glowered at Christine as if she were the one who'd reprimanded her.

'Ready?' asked Conor, side-stepping over to her.

'Very,' she said, and gratefully accompanied him inside.

17
......

The parents trooped in and selected their seats: not too far back as to appear uninterested, not too near the stage in case they were asked a question to which they didn't know the answer. The perimeter of the auditorium was lined with long tables topped with tablecloths and refreshments. These were manned by teachers and volunteers – that curious breed who attend parents' nights, even when it doesn't affect their own children. Most of them were Lakers.

Christine took out her notebook.

Some 100 parents attended the information night held at Glass Lake Primary on Monday.

Which wasn't surprising. Glass Lake parents had better attendance records than their children.

Maeve's new teacher, Mr Cafferty, unstacked cups and saucers from plastic pallets and arranged them in four neat rows on a table in the far-right corner.

Teachers were on hand to help. Refreshments were served …

At the adjacent table, a younger Laker was removing the lid from the large tea urn and peering inside while Mrs Walsh, who'd been teaching Junior Infants and making tea for parents' nights since

Christine was at Glass Lake, watched on nervously. The Laker stuck in a cup, scooped out some liquid, swirled it around and sipped, like she was completing her sommelier qualifications. Across the room, Mr Peoples, the choirmaster, was laying out sandwiches and cakes, while another Laker clipped at his heels. Every time he finished a platter, she swooped in and rearranged it.

... with military precision.

She could have written this in her sleep.

'I'll get some tea,' she said, pulling Conor to one side as Fiona Murphy barrelled past, making a sound somewhere between a hush and a hiss as Butcher Murphy hot-stepped after her. 'You find the seats.'

'Here?' said Conor, gesturing to two empty chairs beside them, in the second last row.

'Are you insane? No. Somewhere in the middle.'

Mr Cafferty was taking tea and coffee orders while Mrs Walsh filled them, under the watchful eye of the designated Laker. Lorna Farrell and the Auburn Bob from the Strand last Thursday were in front of Christine in the line, interrogating the new teacher.

'You could come along the Thursday of the Halloween mid-term. You wouldn't have school then,' Lorna was saying, taking a cup without looking at it. 'There's no mid-term from parenting. And it is parents, usually, but we'd make an exception for a brand-new teacher. We meet every Thursday morning, all year.'

'Except Christmas,' added Auburn Bob.

Lorna nodded. 'The Strand is closed at Christmas.'

'I would love to come –' began Mr Cafferty.

'Excellent.'

'It's a date!'

'– but I'm away for mid-term.'

'Really?'

'Are you actually?'

'Yes,' he said, taken aback by the follow-up question. 'I promise.'

'That's a shame,' said Auburn Bob. 'It's just you teach our kids and we know so little about you.'

'We know you're married.' Lorna nodded towards his wedding ring. 'What does your wife do? Is she from around here?'

'What's your background?' added Auburn Bob.

'Do you have children?'

'Oh, well. Okay.' The man swallowed nervously but managed to retain his smile. 'I, I worked in tech before retraining as a teacher. This is my second school; I was in the midlands before. Jess is a wedding planner ...'

'Jess,' repeated Auburn Bob. Christine could almost see her opening a new mental folder and filing it inside.

'We don't have children.'

'Yet.'

Mr Cafferty laughed. 'Right,' he said agreeably.

The women's eyes lit up at this.

'So, you do want them?'

'Soon?'

'Sounds like soon to me. It's never worth waiting. You must be what, late thirties? How old is your wife? The same age, I imagine. You don't want to hang around too long.'

'That's right. Just ask Una Rawle.'

Lorna made a 'Mmm' sound, as if Una Rawle was recently deceased of shrivelled ovaries, rather than a living and perfectly happy (as far as she could tell of the local physio) mother-of-one.

'Okay, ladies,' said Christine loudly. 'There are several parched parents here, desperate for a cup of tea.'

Lorna looked around at her with that same psychotic smile. 'I'm surprised you're queuing, Christine. Why don't you just bypass the whole system and go back there and make your own tea? Isn't that how you like to do things?'

Christine no longer regretted the Lick-Arse moniker. One more comment and she was going to tell her, with relish, that she was the one who'd started it.

'Two teas please, Mr Cafferty,' she said instead. 'One with lots of milk, one with a dash.'

'If your mid-term plans fall through you know where we'll be,' said Lorna, giving the sixth-class teacher a meaningful look. 'And you'll throw me into the mix for those weekly progress reports, right? Beverley spoke very highly of the one you did on Amelia. Whatever you're doing for her would be perfect.'

The teacher nodded, and the woman moved on.

'Don't give them anything.'

'Sorry?'

'Don't tell them a thing about yourself,' she elaborated, as Mr Cafferty glanced at his phone then stuffed it back into his pocket. He took a tea from Mrs Walsh and passed it forward.

'Oh, it's fine, I don't mind,' he said.

'There'll be a pool going on your first offspring's date of birth by the end of this evening. And the most popular Google search in Cooney tonight will be Jess Cafferty wedding planner.'

His face twitched. 'We kept our own names.'

'Well, lucky for you,' said Christine, leaning forward to take the second cup that the teacher seemed to forget he was holding. 'And for her.'

The reverberating echo of a throat being cleared brought Christine's attention to the stage. Nuala Patterson was standing in front of a lectern embossed with the school crest. Balancing the two cups, Christine worked her way back across the hall.

There were three chairs set up on the stage. The principal had vacated one, while another was occupied by a young guard, presumably from Aberstown Station. (Cooney did not have its own police station. While this could easily have become a petition issue, residents embraced it as proof of Cooney's low crime rate.) The third chair was filled by Dr Cian O'Sullivan, a child psychologist from north Cork. The *Southern Gazette* had run several articles on him. He was also a second cousin of Nuala Patterson.

She slipped into the chair beside Conor and handed him his tea-y milk.

Principal Patterson welcomed them all and set out the evening's running order. She looked tired, but then maybe Christine was projecting. She'd heard rumours Leo Patterson and his dad weren't coming back. She couldn't imagine the strain something like that must place on a family.

The principal listed Dr O'Sullivan's many accolades – though only his local address got a round of applause – and said he would be talking about the parents' role in keeping their children safe online. He had agreed to do two workshops as part of the Relationship and Sexualities Programme with the sixth-class students, this coming Thursday and Friday, and would explain what they entailed. A few rows in front, Lorna Farrell blessed herself at the word 'sexualities'.

The guard would talk to them about the legalities of uploading and sharing images online. And finally – you could hear the defeat in the principal's voice already – there would be time for questions. Glass Lake parents never waited until the end to ask questions.

She did not recognise the guard and so suspected it was the same one who'd found Porcupine's abduction so hilarious. They'd told the children the truth now. Or the half-truth, in Maeve's case; Porcupine was on his holidays at Mrs Rodgers. Conor wanted to leave the cat – he still wasn't the better of being gaslit by a woman twice his age. But Christine wasn't giving up. She had a plan – working title: Operation Liberation – and currently had all three kids marking down Mrs Rodgers' movements in a notebook she'd left on the windowsill in the front room.

Principal Patterson retook her seat and Dr O'Sullivan approached the podium. He rested a few pages on the lectern and pushed his thin spectacles down his nose so his brown eyes were smiling over them. 'Everyone sitting comfortably enough to talk about sex?'

A nervous energy sparked through the auditorium as parents shifted in their seats. Lorna folded her arms as if to say, 'That sex talk's not getting in here.'

Christine wrote down the doctor's opening gambit, even though it would never make it into print. Derek talked a good talk, but they all knew the typical *Southern Gazette* reader was over seventy, politically conservative and mainly bought the paper for photos of their grandkids and death notices of their friends. The only time they were sitting comfortably enough to read the word 'sex', never mind talk about it, was in a highly serious context, preferably criminal.

The doctor talked about how technology and discussing sexual health had the potential to make us feel foolish. This got a low rumble of recognition, including from Conor, while others, such as Lorna Farrell, remained stony-faced.

'But your children are technology natives,' he said. 'So, let's gather up those awkward emotions and place them, at least for now, under our chairs.'

Across the room, a man mimed putting something under his seat. His wife yanked him back up.

Slides flashed up on the whiteboard and Dr O'Sullivan talked through them: sexting; inappropriate social media pages; explicit chatrooms; mislabelled videos; grooming; exposure to pornography, both accidental and intentional. Lorna's hand was flying up to her forehead with such regularity now that she should have just left it there. Her husband Bill cleared his throat loudly.

The doctor focused on sexting. He explained that some young people saw it as part of relationships or friendships. Others were mimicking what they'd seen in porn.

A dry cough spread through the hall.

A graph explained that five per cent of children had sent a sexually explicit image by the time they've finished primary school. 'If your child has engaged in sexting, process the information carefully,' he said, as a slide titled 'How Parents Should Respond' flashed up. 'Remember: they will be aware of your reactions.'

The Farrells were no longer the only people squirming. The collective murmur was now colliding with a faint titter and the sound rippled through the hall. Christine took down some of the bullet points as the doctor worked his way through them. These were more palatable and should work for one of Derek's beloved lists.

'I'm sorry,' came a voice from the back of the hall. A woman in a wine-coloured fur coat rose from her seat. She neither looked nor sounded particularly sorry. 'Can you stop, please? We're talking about children here, not teenagers. They're eleven and twelve. This isn't relevant. And, frankly, I don't think it's appropriate.'

A hubbub of agreement went up around the woman and she folded her arms defiantly.

Dr O'Sullivan leaned into the microphone. 'While sexting is concerning amongst primary school children, it's not uncommon. Remember five per cent have sent an explicit photo by the time they leave. That's one in twenty of your children.'

The woman's response was lost in a general swell of discontent. Bill Farrell was on his feet now.

'That's a country average,' he shouted up at the stage, chest puffed out. 'We're talking about Glass Lake.'

A sea of heads bobbed in agreement. Dr O'Sullivan frowned. He didn't understand the distinction. Which showed that while he was from near Cooney, he wasn't from Cooney.

'Isn't this the school's responsibility?' said a man near the front. 'Teachers are meant to teach. They just need to tell the students what is acceptable behaviour and what is not. That's it. We don't need to start talking to them about grooming, for Christ's sake!'

This got a small smattering of applause.

'I'm not suggesting I talk to the children about grooming. These slides are for the adults—'

But Fiona Murphy was on her feet now. 'It's not up to teachers to control what our children do online,' she said to the father near the front. 'Parents need to check their kids' phones. It's up to us to make sure they're not doing anything they're not supposed to. Right, Doc?'

'I'm not sure checking their phones is the best idea,' said someone else. 'It's better to talk to them. It builds trust.'

'I'm sorry,' said the not-sorry woman at the back, 'but we're here because of one incident. One boy and one girl sending each other pictures. At least, that's what the *Southern Gazette* said.'

Christine slouched in her seat.

Dr O'Sullivan looked to Principal Patterson, who nodded. The woman looked exhausted. And Christine was sure she wasn't projecting this time.

'That's right,' he said.

'Right,' echoed the woman. 'So why can't the school just talk to those parents, of the two perpetrators, and stop tarring everyone else's kids with the same nasty brush? It's ridiculous that we all have to come here for a telling-off. This has nothing to do with my daughter. She knows not to send naked pictures of herself. We raised her better than that.'

....

How dare Imelda Dargle call Beverley Franklin a bad parent? It didn't matter that Imelda – who was still wearing her coat even though the auditorium was warm, and it was hideous – didn't know she was talking about Amelia. She was implying the parents of *both* children involved had done a bad job. And after Beverley had cast Imelda's daughter as the Good Witch of the North. She made a mental note to cut some of her lines.

The so-called doctor was talking again now. More blame, no doubt, all directed at Beverley. Was he a real doctor, or just one of those people who'd spent too long at university? He had the air of the latter.

She could almost laugh at the irony of this man telling them not to judge or blame their children, while he was standing up there, judging and blaming her. His 'How Parents Should Respond' guide could have been re-titled 'How Beverley Got It Wrong'.

What should she have done, in the heat of the moment, when she walked into her baby's room to be confronted by ... *that*? Told Amelia to carry on? Offered to hold the phone for her? Suggested she try the bathroom, for better light?

Across the room, Christine Maguire was scribbling into a notebook. She must be reporting on this, too. What had the woman been thinking, talking to her on the way in? She might as well have got up on stage and pointed to Beverley: 'Ladies and gentlemen, my anonymous source!'

She did agree with Imelda on one point, though. It was ridiculous that they were having a public conversation. This could have been solved with a swift expulsion. Nobody was going to lobby to get Woody Whitehead back into the school. She'd spotted Connie Whitehead on her way in, seated in the back row – a sure sign that she didn't give a fiddler's about what was happening on stage.

The so-called doctor was now explaining how aside from sexting (who knew the man could talk about anything else?) he'd be giving the children the 'tools' they needed to stay safe online. Were the Lakers paying for this guff? Nuala Patterson was remarkably good at wasting other people's money.

'Shouldn't we name the children involved, so as to stop suspicion falling on the innocent kids?' said a voice from the front. 'Or at least name the male student. It's always the boys who start it.'

Beverley gave this a loud round of applause. Finally, someone was speaking sense.

'Spoken like the mother of a girl,' retorted someone else, to another smattering of applause.

'Hi, mother of a boy here,' came a familiar voice from the back of the hall. 'I'd be happy to hand over my son's mobile, should the school decide it does want to monitor phone use.'

'Well, we're not handing over our son's property to anyone!' retorted a father in Beverley's row.

'I'm just saying my son has nothing to hide.'

'I don't know who you are, lady, but that's not how it works here.'

'Sorry,' said the woman, whose voice Beverley recognised but couldn't place. 'I should have introduced myself. I'm new here. My name is Tamara Watson.'

Beverley froze.

It couldn't be. Surely.

She turned in her chair, eyes travelling up the aisle until they hit on the woman sitting at the edge of the second-last row, legs sticking out to the side, crossed and swinging.

Tamara Watson. In the flesh.

She looked exactly as she had when Beverley last saw her six months ago. She hadn't seen Tamara since she left Southern Pharmaceuticals, which was also the last time she'd felt this humiliated. And that time, it had all been Tamara's fault.

....

Nuala Patterson tried to muster up the vigour required to keep the Glass Lake parents in line. The young Garda Delaney had an odour of deep-fried chips. Leo had smelled like that sometimes, when he refused to change out of his football gear. She hadn't realised how much she'd missed it. She took her time crossing the stage to the podium, breathing it in deeply. But guilt-free thoughts of her son were impossible now, and before she had exhaled poor Mike

Roche was also in her mind. A lot of people in Cooney had spent more time mourning Mike Senior moving away than they had Mike Junior dying. Even Nuala felt she didn't give the late teenager the reflection he deserved.

'You try taking my son's property off him and I will have you charged with theft so fast you won't have time to open the photo gallery,' one of the school's older parents was saying to the new woman. 'You can't tar all boys with the same brush. Our son knows right from wrong.'

'I'm really not suggesting we check anyone's phones,' said the doctor, though nobody was listening to him any more.

'Our boy has never done anything like sexting,' the father continued, his bald head growing red and shiny.

'That you know of,' said Fiona Murphy, who was seated between Butcher and the new woman, Tamara. 'Kids are very good at hiding stuff.'

'We check his phone regularly,' shouted the father, jabbing his finger in Fiona's direction. 'Check his messages, check his Facebook. That's how I know my son's not up to anything.'

'Kids don't actually use Facebook, John. Maybe that's why you're not finding anything.'

'Also, children can have two accounts on any given social media platform,' came the voice of Claire Keating. 'One for their friends to see, and one for their parents.'

'I'm guessing you've never heard of Finstagram, John?' said Fiona. 'Fake Instagram. No? It's the cover account; the one they want adults to see. John Junior probably has about six of them.'

'I know exactly what my son has and exactly what he's up to. He's not even that interested in computers.'

Fiona made a half-arsed attempt at coughing. 'Okay, Boomer.'

The father's chair scraped against the floor as his wife's (much younger) hand flew up from the chair beside him and held him in place.

Butcher Murphy was also on his feet now, ready to defend his former spouse.

'He finds the internet distracting,' retorted the father.

'Get away out of that!' scoffed Fiona. 'I gave John Junior a lift home from summer camp this year, and the boy barely registered the car had windows.' Fiona mimed some sort of ape pushing buttons with his thumbs.

'How dare you!'

'He thought I Spy was a new Apple tablet!'

'You take that back,' the man shouted, fighting to break free of his wife's grip as Butcher pushed his way out into the aisle.

'Just try it, Slaphead!'

Nuala stepped in beside Dr O'Sullivan, who readily backed away from the podium. In the middle of the stage, Garda Delaney was looking worried. One didn't expect a parents' night to require riot gear.

Nuala pulled the mic towards her.

'Okay,' she said, as Butcher Murphy pretended to play bongo drums, 'let's take a break.'

18

......

Beverley moved both ham sandwiches to her left hand and reached out to the passing platter with her right to take a slice of fruit cake. The teenager carrying the tray was Arlo Whitehead. Did he now do everything around here? Would he be teaching Amelia's class next?

'The language the doctor used,' Lorna Farrell was saying, as she held a teacup in one hand and a saucer in the other. 'You wouldn't get it in a brothel. And I didn't care for his tone one bit. He's talking like the students are a bunch of criminals.'

'Taking or sending an explicit photo of a minor is a criminal offence,' said Beth Morton, who was also standing in their circle. 'We deal with this kind of thing regularly at secondary school.'

'But they're taking the photos of themselves,' said Lorna.

'If they're taking photos at all,' clarified Bill.

Sandwiches consumed, Beverley stuffed the fruit cake into her mouth. But the unsettled feeling in her stomach refused to be buried. She surveyed the room, turning her head as far as it would go without making it obvious she was looking for someone.

'It's still technically illegal, even if the images are of themselves,' said Beth.

'Well, I doubt that's true,' scoffed Bill, taking a bite of his own fruit cake.

Beverley had lost sight of Tamara Watson when everyone got up from their seats. She wouldn't fully believe the woman was here until she was standing in front of her. What would Tamara be doing in Cooney? And at a Glass Lake parents' night? Did she know someone else in this town? She had been sitting beside Fiona. Was that why Fiona was acting so smug lately? Did they know each other? Had Tamara told her what happened at Southern Pharmaceuticals?

The Whitehead boy passed them again, and she grabbed another sandwich, taking the opportunity to glance swiftly over her left shoulder.

Lorna caught her eye and smiled conspiratorially: 'Someday you'll have to tell me where you put it all.'

....

Arlo tried to wipe his forehead with the cuff of his shirt, whilst still balancing the two trays. Seamus had asked him to help with parking. Before and after the event. During it, he was supposed to be free. If he'd known he'd have to get up close with the parents, he'd have declined the job. He'd been sitting outside, alternating between trying to get the baton to work and rereading his dad's letter, when some woman had shouted at him to come inside and make himself useful. The torch from his phone must have given him away, not that he needed it. He didn't even need the letter any more. It was short, eight lines in all, and he knew it by heart. Charlie Whitehead wanted him to visit.

It was warm in the hall and he was bad at carrying things. He was trying to pass unnoticed by everyone whilst also making sure he was never gone from any group long enough for someone to complain. He'd made two failed attempts to get over to his mom, the well-thumbed letter in his pocket egging him on: *Look after your mother and your brother.*

'I see Susan Mitchem was at the wine again last night,' said a stocky father, taking an iced bun from Arlo's tray without looking at him.

'Saw that,' said the other man, also taking a bun. 'She must have sent that last meme five times. Doesn't she know the old maxim? If you can't identify the alcoholic in your parents' WhatsApp group, it must be you.'

Arlo waited for the men to each take another bun, before turning back towards the Franklins. He didn't want them of all people to think he was skiving. Beverley had taken several snacks from him already, which he chose to take as a good sign. He'd travelled about two metres when he was yanked to one side.

'Arlo!' exclaimed the woman, knocking one of his platters as she pulled him towards her. He managed to catch the tray but not before a row of sandwiches were sent flying to the floor. 'Oops, sorry about that.'

'Mrs Murphy,' he said, placing his trays on the ground and quickly gathering up the bread before anyone could stand on it.

'What did I tell you about calling me that?'

'Fiona, sorry.' Arlo glanced up at the woman.

'Let me help you,' she said, getting down on her hunkers. The women she'd been talking to stood in a huddle behind her, grinning.

'It's fine,' he said, stuffing the soiled sandwiches into a bunch of serviettes and then stuffing those into his pockets.

'This is *Arlo*,' said Fiona, elongating his name in a way that made him want to spontaneously combust. She placed a hand on his arm. 'He's my handyman.'

Arlo desperately needed to wipe his forehead, but he couldn't risk knocking any more food. 'Ah, hi,' he said, trying to move his neck away from the fabric of his shirt. 'Nice to meet you all.'

'If you ever need anything seen to around the house, Tamara, he's your guy.'

'I can see that,' said one of the women, glancing at his bulging pockets.

'I know you, don't I?' said another woman.

'I don't think so ...'

'I do. You're the guy whose dad killed Mike Roche's son.'

'He – he didn't ...' Arlo looked to Fiona, but she was still smiling at her friends as if they hadn't mentioned anything more inappropriate than the weather.

'Charlie Whitehead,' said another of the women, nodding. 'He did the wiring in our house. It kind of makes sense that he was a drunk; half the switches were upside down.'

'Is that the light in your hallway?'

'Mmm,' said the woman, watching Arlo.

'Sorry about that,' he said, pathetically, the sweat tickling his temples now.

'Stop, Sally, you're embarrassing the boy,' chastised the second woman, the one who'd breezily asked if he was the son of a murderer.

'He looks like him,' said the upside-down switches woman. Then, more accusatorily: 'You look like him.'

Arlo blinked. Fiona's hand was on his arm now and he was so warm he thought his head might burst into flames.

'Now, now, ladies,' she said, moving her hand up and down.

'There's absolutely nothing wrong with looking like Charlie Whitehead.'

Beyond the women, Nuala Patterson was working her way towards them. She approached the tray, reached for a sandwich, saw who was holding it and pulled back her hand like it had been bitten.

'Oh,' she said. Arlo caught her eye for the first time in months. Then she turned on her heels and disappeared into the crowd.

All the women, and Arlo, watched her go.

The upside-down switches woman gasped. 'Unbelievable.'

'Told you,' said Fiona.

'Oh my God, you were right.' The woman turned to Arlo, eyes shining with sheer delight: 'It's like you don't even exist.'

....

Malachy was regaling the group with a story about the time Ella and Amelia baked a lemon cake for his mother's birthday, only for their grandmother to slice the thing open and find congealed, raw egg.

'They didn't realise you were supposed to whisk them. *You never gave us that instruction, Daddy!*'

Everyone laughed. One mother even nudged him playfully. Women loved to touch Beverley's husband.

He did make it sound charming, even if it had actually been a sponge cake and neither Malachy nor his mother were laughing at the time.

'Beverley. Coo-coo. Beverley.' Fiona Murphy was approaching them, and she sounded positively gleeful. 'I've got someone here I believe you know.'

Bill Farrell moved to one side as Fiona and her little posse joined the group.

'I've been meaning to reacquaint you guys for ages,' Fiona was saying, though Beverley only had eyes for the dark-haired woman standing behind her. 'I helped Tamara here find a house to rent in Cooney, and we just got chatting. She mentioned that you used to work together. Isn't it a small world? She has so many interesting stories about you, Beverley.' Fiona wriggled her eyebrows, or at least that was what she was trying to do; but she got her Botox done locally, and cheaply, so nothing above her eye sockets budged. 'It's been so interesting to hear about you as a co-worker, when of course we only know you as a friend. I believe you were a real go-getter. Tamara says you really *attacked* whatever task you were given.'

Beverley tensed. Her hunch was correct. This was why Fiona Murphy had been so insufferable of late. She'd met Tamara Watson and Tamara had told her how Beverley came to lose her job.

'Hello, Tamara,' said Malachy, stepping forward to kiss the woman on the cheek. 'Long time, no see.'

'Hi, Mal,' she said, receiving the kiss graciously before giving Beverley a smile. 'Hi, Bev. You're looking well.'

When Beverley didn't respond, her husband spoke again. 'Everyone, this is Tamara Watson. She and Beverley were colleagues at Southern Pharmaceuticals.'

Tamara lifted a hand in greeting.

'And you live in Cooney?' asked Lorna.

'Yes, just moved here. Myself and my husband separated. He got the house, but I got the kid. Fiona here was my estate agent. She found us a lovely little rental out by the pier.'

'I said she must come to a coffee morning at the Strand, Beverley,' added Fiona, still beaming. 'Her son is starting in sixth class this week.'

'Absolutely,' gushed Lorna.

'Yes, we're both very excited. I remember you telling me how good the primary school was out here, Bev. I couldn't believe it when there was a space.'

'You must have got Marcus Birch's place. His dad got a job in London. The whole family just moved over.'

'So, you used to work together? That's fun,' trilled Lorna. 'You can tell us all Beverley's secrets.'

'Oh, she really can,' said Fiona.

Tamara smiled demurely.

'If you'll excuse me,' said Beverley, dumping a half-eaten salad sandwich on a passing tray. 'I must use the bathroom before Principal Patterson has us all back in our seats.'

....

Arlo was hiding in the corridor beyond the main auditorium. He'd come out to dump the soiled sandwiches, which he still hadn't done. Every time the double doors swung open, he jumped, convinced another parent was about to give him a task. Occasionally, he glanced in through the windows. He was keeping an eye on things, and by things he meant Nuala Patterson. He wondered if Seamus understood just how awkward he had made matters when he decided to throw a few weeks' work Arlo's way?

He stepped away from the window and took his phone from his shirt pocket. He was sending Ella updates, detailing the breakthroughs he was making with her parents, particularly her dad.

She responded:

> Trust me, Mal acts like he likes everyone.

He hit reply:

> I'm telling you I have cracked him. He called me mate. And
> he winked at me. He tipped me a fiver!

It was slightly annoying how Ella automatically thought the worst of her parents. They were old and conservative, but they were there for her. Last summer, her dad offered to buy her a new car. And yet she had only contempt for them. She didn't appreciate how lucky she was.

He pulled the napkins from his pockets and began to empty them into the bin. The double doors swung open and Beverley appeared. She did not look happy to see him.

He stalled for a moment, then he flung the last bits of bread into the trash, gave her a sort of awkward bow – he didn't know why; it just came out – and walked on down the corridor, not having a clue where he was going.

When he rounded the corner, he kept walking until he could no longer hear the hustle and bustle from the hall. He pushed his back against the wall and took a few breaths.

His phone beeped again.

> He tipped while people were watching, right? I'd say Bev
> just loved that.

....

Beverley could hear Malachy coming after her, but she didn't quicken her step and she didn't turn back. She couldn't bear to see the others

161

gently interrogating Tamara, who would be only too delighted to tell them all about the time Beverley Franklin attacked her.

She exited the auditorium to see Arlo Whitehead chucking a pile of sandwiches into the large bin.

He bobbed his head awkwardly and hurried away.

Beverley marched over to the bin and, without really thinking, pulled the sandwiches from the top of the mound. She shook her sleeves down over her hands to hide the food and headed into the girls' bathroom, past the line of grown women hunched over child-height sinks, and into the only free cubicle. She locked the door and began to stuff the bread into her mouth.

Bread was always best.

The last time Beverley saw Tamara she'd been standing beside the microwave in the first-floor kitchenette of Southern Pharmaceuticals laughing at something a colleague had said. Beverley saw red and lunged for her. The fall wouldn't have been so dramatic if Tamara had been wearing appropriate lab shoes – or if she'd had her cleavage strapped down. The woman was a teetering inverted triangle waiting to topple.

Principal Patterson's voice echoed through the speakers out in the main hall.

If everyone can take their seats, we'll wrap this up as quickly as possible.

One by one, the other cubicles opened, doors banging back against the stalls. Faucets squeaked on and off and hand driers blasted. A final pair of heels clip-clopped out of the bathroom and the main door swung shut again.

The only remaining sound was the buzz of the two long fluorescent bulbs.

Beverley counted to ten, just to be sure.

Then she leaned over the miniature toilet bowl and vomited.

....

Frank Cafferty was doing his best to stack the dirty cups without making a racket. The acoustics in the auditorium were phenomenally good. His last school didn't have acoustics, or an auditorium for that matter.

He'd insisted Mrs Walsh, the Junior Infants' teacher, sit down; he'd clean out the tea tanker and stack the crockery. The Glass Lake mother who'd been supervising the pair of them all night had got distracted by some misaligned mini quiches across the hall and disappeared. Frank was grabbing the opportunity to tidy up unobserved.

Principal Patterson was back on stage, addressing the audience.

He told himself to concentrate on what she was saying, on the dirty cups, on the four additional weekly student reports he'd somehow already agreed to this evening – on anything but the buzzing in his pocket. Five missed calls now, and all from a withheld number.

'Are you sure you don't need a hand?' Mrs Walsh asked from the plastic chair where she sat massaging her knees.

'Not at all,' he replied, flashing his widest smile. 'You have a rest. I'll fly through the rest of this.' Sometimes he forced himself to smile the whole drive to work, and when he arrived at the school, he really did feel happier.

As the buzzing stopped, Frank looked around the hall for a hand disappearing into a breast pocket or a phone being dropped into a handbag, but there was none. All his parents were here. Which meant it wasn't one of them tormenting him. He took some comfort from this. It wasn't exactly the same as what had happened at his old school, so.

He stacked the cups carefully, mindful of the superior echo. Then he transferred each stack into the plastic crate.

'Look at you go, Mr Cafferty. You could have taught my husband a thing or two. Lord have mercy on his useless soul.'

'I'm used to tidying, Mrs Walsh. Don't mind it at all. I do all the housework at home.'

'I'd well believe it,' marvelled the older woman, shaking her head in awe. 'I hope your wife knows how lucky she is. Sure, you're as good as two women.'

19
. . . . . .

Why hadn't their man been at Glass Lake? He was supposed to be at the school, helping with musical preparations, but instead he was out walking by the River Gorm. Why? This was a puzzle at the centre of the case and one Joey was desperate to crack. Imagine if he came up with an answer. The sergeant couldn't possibly mistake him for a useless eejit then.

Joey took out his notebook and considered the possibilities. There was no way their man had gotten lost – he knew how to get to the school, they all did. The officers had been instructed to leave the car for forensics to examine, but it was parked neatly nearby. No signs of a crash or that it had broken down.

'Was there any unusual action on his mobile phone yesterday, sir?'

'One call to the wife at lunchtime, just as there was every day this week and every other week. Nothing else. Nothing unexpected.'

Joey brought his pen to his lower lip and tapped. 'Curiouser and curiouser ...'

Whelan frowned.

The younger officer dropped his hand and cleared the embarrassment from his throat.

'Don't you have a second round of witness interviews to get started on?'

'Yes, sir. I'm just going in now, sir.'

'Well, don't let me keep you.'

'Right you are,' said Joey, as gruffly as he could manage. 'I'll let you know if there's anything of interest.'

....

Fiona Murphy, parent

The whole thing with Mr Cafferty and the quote-unquote mystery files was just progress reports. He was giving a few of the more interested parents updates on how their kids were doing. Nothing sinister about it. Of more relevance is the fact that Beverley was fired for anger management issues. She has form on lashing out, so who knows what else she might be capable of? She attacked Tamara Watson - just ask her. They used to work together.

Bill Farrell, parent

Of course I knew the man. I'm a public representative; it's my job to know all the men, and women. It was a terrible, tragic accident. He slipped and fell. It's awful, and I will be raising the need to rebuild the fence along the Gorm as a matter of urgency at the next council meeting. But you lot asking questions - looking to find out if the man had any enemies - you're needlessly dragging our community's reputation through the mud. Cooney has a Tidy Towns competition to concentrate on.

Tamara Watson, parent

I don't want to land poor Beverley in it, and like this all happened months ago, long before I came to Cooney or anyone drowned. But yes, it's all entirely true. Beverley attacked me in the office kitchen. She shoved me right into the recycling bin. I sprained my ankle. And before you ask, Officer, I haven't a clue why she did it. Not an iota. I was more surprised than anyone.

20

......

In her teens and early twenties, Beverley had made herself vomit. Being a thin person who didn't eat was dull and obvious but being a thin person who put away vast quantities of calories was exciting and commendable. Where possible, she did media interviews over dinner, knowing the journalist would write about how she'd consumed a whole pizza (Hollow legs! Where *does* she put it? Not your typical actress!) but wouldn't waste ink on her going to the ladies' room afterwards to touch up her lipstick. What started as an alternative to dieting soon became a source of comfort. When she was upset or uncertain or anxious, she'd eat too much, and almost immediately start to panic. But she knew that if she kept going, she would get to the point where she could easily expunge it all: the calories, the panic, the niggling possibility that she was nothing special. She'd stopped when she got pregnant with Ella. Nineteen years ago. And she hadn't done it again, not once, until she found those photos on Malachy's phone in April.

At first, she hadn't recognised the woman – her face wasn't exactly the focus – but eventually there was a wider shot that took in the familiar flared nostrils and thick dark hair falling either side of her neck.

'Tamara Watson? From development? From *my* job?' she'd yelled, standing in their pristine marble kitchen, waving the phone at her husband.

Malachy had been more taken aback than panicked. He'd pushed the door shut and told her to calm down. 'The girls are upstairs.'

'You don't know Tamara! She lives in the city. You've never even met ...' And then she remembered. 'The Christmas party? Are you serious? Has this been going on since then?!'

'It hasn't been going on at all. It's just pics. So please calm down.'

And Beverley had calmed down, as she always did. Malachy slept in the guest room that night, but the following evening, he was back in their bed. 'That's enough now, Beverley,' he'd said, undoing his cufflinks, and she'd rolled onto her side without another word. She wasn't going to leave him, so what was the point?

'Beverley?' said Claire Keating now, sitting in her usual chair in the alcove of the Strand, a disposable cup in her left hand. 'What do you think?'

What Beverley thought was that Malachy had phoned her three times in the ninety minutes she'd been here and still hadn't got the message. This happened whenever he worked from home, but today she would not be answering questions about the whereabouts of coffee filters (same cupboard as always) or why Alexa was ignoring him (because Beverley had been so pissed off after Monday night's school meeting that she'd deleted his voice profile). She pressed decline, again.

'Beverley?'

Claire's voice was sharper now, and Beverley let the phone fall back into her bag.

'Yes, Claire,' she said, just as curtly. 'I was checking my notes.'

The Lakers did not have an official chair. Given she'd been a parent the longest – Ella was three years older than anyone else's child – Beverley was the obvious honorary leader. But since Claire had her last set of twins, she'd been acting as if quantity, rather than quality, gave her seniority. 'What I *think*,' she continued, 'is that we need to go big on marketing.'

Lorna Farrell was cutting a flapjack into tiny pieces, and Fiona Murphy was idly tapping on her phone. She'd given Beverley an overzealous welcome when she arrived and made some pointed, apropos-of-nothing comment about Lorna *attacking* her dessert. Beverly couldn't tell how much Fiona knew, or what, if anything, she'd told anyone else. None of the others were acting like they had anything on her. Which was something, at least.

'We need every seat in that auditorium filled and people queuing up outside for returns. Nothing's as desirable as something you can't have – and all those bodies will look great on TV. So, we need to get the word out. Let's pitch the musical as a feel-good story to local media: radio, newspapers, websites. Have we any leverage there?'

'We got Buddy Reilly's son on to the spelling bee team last year,' said Lorna.

'That's right.' The local radio mogul's youngest had cost Glass Lake a place in the semi-finals and made them a temporary laughing stock on the Cork spelling circuit when he forgot the 'e' at the end of 'heroine'. 'Let's hit Buddy up for a couple of free radio ads, and a bit of editorial coverage.'

'And my sister works at *Cork Now* magazine,' offered someone else.

'Fine,' said Beverley, shaking her head as Lorna proffered the decimated cake around the group. She'd had nothing but coffee since dinner the night before. Things were back under control. 'Who wants to make some calls to the papers? You.' She pointed to the woman who'd come to the Strand to secure her son a place on Glass Lake's soccer team and had clearly zoned out of all other conversations. 'You can ring around the local press.'

'I'm actually not great on the phone,' said the mother of the aspiring soccer star. 'I have a bit of an anxiety disorder ...'

'It's the twenty-first century. We all have anxiety disorders,' snapped Beverley.

She never stuck her finger down her throat. All she had to do was a sort of internal lurch, like she was burping from her stomach, and everything came gushing back up. Apart from a couple of dentists, who could see the erosion on her teeth, the only person to ever remark on it was her mother. But then Frances did not understand the desire to be thin. Her mother had been absent the day that memo was sent to all women.

Still, she'd never done it anywhere as public as the Glass Lake bathroom. The lack of self-control had frightened her. It no longer made her thinner. It didn't even make her feel good any more. So, yes, that was it. She was done with it.

'What position did you say your son was interested in?' she asked, turning to face the mother.

'Goalie.'

'Yes, I think goals is actually oversubscribed at the moment ...'

'For what age group?'

'For *all* age groups,' said Beverley, who had little time for fair-weather parents who came to Lakers meetings when they wanted something for their individual child, but had no interest in the greater, holistic well-being of the school.

171

Fair-Weather Soccer Mom looked around the group. Lorna and Claire nodded. 'Always a lot of competition for goalie,' said Lorna. Nothing bonded the Lakers like a mother with no community spirit.

'Actually, you know, it's fine, I can make some calls.' The woman reached into her tote bag for a biro. She grabbed a napkin. 'So, *Cork Now* ...'

'*The Examiner,* the *Southern Gazette* ...' Beverley watched as she took down the details. 'No harm in trying the nationals either.'

Tamara had propositioned Malachy at that Christmas party, but he'd turned her down. (He'd paused after telling her that. *Well done, Malachy!* she hadn't said. *Well done on not falling into her bosom right there in the middle of the Southern Pharmaceuticals function room!*) They did, however, swap phone numbers. 'Not with any ulterior motive,' he stressed, though what sort of above-board reason there could possibly have been he didn't say. Tamara started texting him (he said) and a month later, with no coaxing (again according to him), she sent a pic.

A *pic.*

She spat the word from her brain.

'You okay, Beverley?' asked Lorna.

'Fine,' she replied, turning the grimace into a smile.

'You could get Christine Maguire to write something,' Claire told Fair-Weather Soccer Mom. 'She works at the *Southern Gazette*, and she's got kids at Glass Lake. Did you all see her article this morning? About Monday's information night?'

Lorna put down the eighth of a flapjack she was slowly nibbling. 'I could not believe they got a quote from Orla Smith, of all parents, giving out about kids accessing technology. I mean, come on.'

'What's wrong with Orla?' someone else asked.

'Surely you heard what her son did on the first day of Junior Infants? No?' Lorna's eyes widened as she jumped her chair forward. 'He picked up a book and ...' She lifted her left hand and dramatically dragged the air to the right. '... he swiped!'

'*No!*'

'Yes. He swiped *a book*! As if he'd never seen one before. Oh my God, Orla was *mortified*. She's been trying to make up for it ever since. Every afternoon, she's there shouting at Reuben to go back in and get a more difficult book to bring home. *Get a red one, Reuben. You know your level's RED.* And she's eyeballing all the parents as she shouts it. Annabelle's in his class and by the sounds of it the poor boy can't even spell "red" but she's making him bring home *War and Peace*, or whatever. I mean, Annabelle *is* reading at red level, but I wouldn't scream about it. It's nobody else's business if she found *Animal Farm* obvious or not.'

'Parenting's not a competition,' agreed Fair-Weather Soccer Mom.

'Exactly,' said Lorna. 'When Marnie was nine, and she was rereading *Romeo and Juliet*, Bill wanted to post a picture on Facebook but—'

'You said no because you didn't want to be boasting,' interrupted Claire. 'Yeah, you've mentioned it.'

What had hurt Beverley was that Malachy hadn't been remorseful. He'd acted like Tamara had just sent him the number for a good mechanic, and she was making too much of it. 'You don't even like Tamara,' he declared, and while it was true – Tamara was loud and cheap and brash – she had never told him that, which meant Tamara had. 'I don't like my friends either,' she'd snapped. 'But that doesn't mean you can send them a picture of your penis!'

'Any joy with getting a copy of the syllabus for what this quote-unquote doctor is going to be teaching our children, Lorna?' asked Claire.

'I managed to corner Principal Patterson after school yesterday, but she was less than courteous. She told me I could download the syllabus from the Department's website. But that's hardly going to tell us anything, is it? We were there Monday night. The man is clearly a renegade.'

'I had a snoop on Twitter,' said Fiona.

'And?'

'He has his pronouns in his bio.'

'Now? See?' said Lorna, looking around the group with an air of inevitable doom.

'I check Ciara's phone,' said Fiona. 'Girl or boy, you have to know what they're up to. You need to get to kids early, before they learn about sex from porn.'

Lorna spluttered, losing several precious flapjack crumbs. 'Fiona!'

'It's the reality, Lorna. Kids watch porn.'

'Stop saying that word.' Lorna looked around, lest anyone else might be listening to their conversation. 'Jesus! We don't even let Marnie watch *Friends*!'

'If someone started talking to my boys about pornography, I don't know how they'd cope,' said Fair-Weather Soccer Mom.

'Oh, come off it,' guffawed Fiona. 'Your eldest is twelve. Of course he's heard of porn.'

'If we're going to keep talking about this, can we at least call it something else?' squeaked Lorna. She took another morsel of flapjack and composed herself. 'Beverley and I are in the school this afternoon for musical rehearsals. I can snoop about a bit, see what I can find out about what Dr O'Sullivan is teaching.'

Beverley had agreed to have Lorna as an assistant director because it was Glass Lake tradition to have one and because she hadn't realised the woman would turn up to every run-through dressed like a has-been ballerina and deliver the 'fame costs' speech to any child who stood still for more than two seconds.

'But we still don't have an answer to the big question,' added Lorna.

'What question?'

'Who are the two kids that were sending the photos?'

'Well, I know we have a few sixth-class parents here, so let's not put anyone on the spot,' said Claire, drawing out the last word, so her conversation shutdown sounded more like a question.

'Not my kid,' said one mother with such immediacy that, had she not known the truth, it would have made Beverley suspicious.

'Or mine,' said Fiona. 'Though if Ciara was involved, I wouldn't be ashamed.'

'I'd say you're raging Ciara's *not* involved,' said Claire, and a couple of the women laughed.

Fiona shrugged, lifting her coffee cup. 'I can neither confirm nor deny.'

They weren't taking it seriously. It was because it was still a faceless – bodyless – act. If they knew who was responsible, they wouldn't find it so amusing. Beverley knew she couldn't identify Woody without casting suspicion on Amelia, but she comforted herself with the fact that he was the most obvious candidate. They would get there eventually.

'That new kid turning up just when this all happened is pretty suspicious,' said Lorna eagerly.

'What new kid?'

'The boy who took Marcus Birch's place. You were talking to his mother at the information night, Fiona. What was her name?'

'Tamara Watson,' said Fiona, answering Lorna's question but smiling at Beverley. 'I helped them find the house they're renting.'

'And?' pushed Lorna.

'And what? Does she seem like the mother of a sexual deviant? How would I know?' Fiona shrugged. 'Beverley might, though. And actually, Beverley, on the subject of Tamara ... Ciara would really love to have a bigger role in the musical. Something with lines? Would that be possible?'

'What's the musical got to do with the new woman?' asked Lorna.

Beverley did her best to keep her tone light. 'As you know, Fiona, all the roles have been well cast by this stage. The show goes up in one week.'

'It's a bit of a tricky one, I know, but I was thinking you could throw some ideas around?' Fiona smiled sweetly. 'Tamara said you were good at that, in work, I mean, throwing things around.'

'That's right,' enthused Lorna, taking another piece of flapjack. 'You used to work with the mother, Beverley. Any insights? Do you think it was her son?'

'I don't think it was the new boy.' Beverley tried to minimalise the authoritative tone that came so naturally to her. She continued to eyeball Fiona. The woman was as thick as two planks and yet somehow she was blackmailing her.

Lorna was crestfallen. 'Do they not seem the type to be up to something inappropriate?'

'Oh, they do,' replied Beverley. 'They absolutely do seem the type. But it wasn't him.'

As much as she would love to have the Lakers blacklisting Tamara Watson before she'd even received the Cooney welcome basket, suspicion could not be allowed to shift from Woody Whitehead. It annoyed her that he was still walking around, free of blame, and that his mother had sat in the auditorium on Monday night without anyone challenging her.

'How do you know it wasn't the new boy?' asked Claire.

Lorna lowered the flapjack square. Claire raised an eyebrow. The whole group was looking at her now. Faking self-doubt was harder than it seemed.

'Well, I don't *know* ...' Beverley picked up her own coffee. 'I just think there might be other candidates.' How could they *not* suspect the Whitehead boy? His father was literally a murderer!

'My money's still on the new fella,' said Lorna.

Fiona nodded.

So did Claire. 'I mean, it makes sense—'

'It was the Whitehead boy!'

Suddenly everyone was gasping and saying 'What?' and 'No!' and 'How do you know?' She had hoped they'd get there by themselves, but if they needed a little push, so be it.

'I can't say how I know, but I do.'

'The girl's not Amelia, is it?' asked Fiona, still grinning like she knew more than she did. It was highly unlikely Tamara had told Fiona *why* Beverley had sent her crashing into the recycling bin in the Southern Pharmaceuticals kitchenette. It was much easier to identify yourself as a victim than a homewrecker.

'No,' lied Beverley. 'How dare you, Fiona Murphy?'

The woman held up her hands. 'Just wondering ...'

'Christine Maguire has a daughter in sixth-class,' mused Claire. 'She's written two articles on the whole thing now. Where better to get the inside story than from inside your own house?'

Lorna gasped. 'Maeve Maguire? Do you think?'

Claire shrugged. 'It's one possibility.'

'I think you might be right,' said Fiona excitedly. 'Ciara is always giving out that Maeve gets to sit beside Woody. I think Ciara has a bit of a crush on him. Don't look so appalled, Bev, the Whiteheads might be criminals, but they're very handsome criminals. Anyway, yeah, apparently, they're friends, maybe *good* friends.'

'Beverley?' said Claire, and the group's collective head turned in her direction again.

She should contradict them, but what sacrificial lamb could she offer up in place of Christine's girl? She was rolling through the various parents that had crossed her recently – if only Tamara had a daughter! – when her phone started to buzz at her feet. 'Sorry. I have to check this.' She reached down and pulled the thing from her bag. Malachy's name flashed on the screen. She pressed decline. Although now she had no reason to avoid answering. And they were all still looking at her.

'Well? If the boy's Woody Whitehead, is the girl Maeve Maguire?'

Lorna was biting her lower lip. It may have been a coincidence, but her index and middle fingers were crossed. Claire's coffee hovered in front of her face. Fiona tilted her head slightly.

'It wouldn't be my place to say,' said Beverley eventually, her tone more knowing that she'd intended.

The Lakers exchanged smiles and loaded glances, while the Fair-Weathers – there were three in attendance today – looked as clueless as usual. Why have children if you weren't going to keep up with what was going on in their world?

At least Christine wasn't a member of the group. If people were going to talk about you, it was best to be in the dark about it. Beverley didn't have that luxury. Everyone in Cooney knew her, and she knew everything that went on.

'Can we discuss sets now, please?' she said, feeling mildly uncomfortable despite knowing she hadn't said or done anything wrong. (Could she help it if she was an assertive person? It was just how she spoke. It didn't *mean* anything.) 'Lorna, have you spoken to Seamus McGrath again? The man keeps presenting bronze bricks and insisting they're yellow and, honestly, I am running out of patience.'

There was a lot of musical business to get through. Despite her many reminders that he was made of heavy metal, the tinman kept flying across the stage in his rush to get his scenes over with, while Woody was still tiptoeing around the stage when he was supposed to be a lion. Their glaring faults highlighted just how good Amelia was in the real lead role, but they were dragging down the overall quality. Mr Cafferty was helping with movement; she'd be on to him this afternoon.

Fiona brought up a speaking role for Ciara again and, through gritted teeth, Beverley said she would see what she could do. As it happened, the girl playing the Wicked Witch of the West had just come down with a bad case of tonsillitis, but Beverley wasn't going to deliver this good news just yet. She didn't want Fiona thinking she could hold the Tamara incident over her head for ever. One fair-weather mother, who had been trying to 'augment' her son's role since Beverley cast him as Munchkin Number Seven, started

179

talking about character development, but Beverley cut her off. This was what happened when people found out television crews were coming. *Me, me, me.* They were so transparent.

'Beverley!'

The holler came from behind, and the familiarity stopped her mid-sentence. A hush fell over the group as they shifted in their seats to see where the commanding voice was coming from.

'Isn't that ...?' Lorna trailed off and Beverley turned to see what the rest of the Lakers saw: a heavily overweight woman with grey hair slicked behind her ears making her way towards them. The woman moved as though she was wading through mud rather than skirting a few tables. She was dressed incongruously in a girly pink kaftan, rimmed with silver foil and beads. A large purple gemstone hung from a necklace, banging against her ample chest.

'Beverley, *a stór*! Hello, hello, hello! And oh my days, is that Claire Potter?'

'Keating, now,' replied Claire. 'Hello, Mrs Tandon.'

'Miss, now.' The older woman winked. 'But I've kept the Tandon because it goes so well with tantric.' She put her hands on her hips and surveyed the group. 'Aren't you a fine-looking group of girls? A bit on the thin side, but great hair all round.'

A few of the women tittered with delight.

'What are you doing here?' said Beverley through gritted teeth.

'I'm here to see you, of course. I'm doing a workshop in Cork city for a few evenings. You weren't answering Malachy's calls, so I said I'd come on over. And wasn't it great that I did? Now I get to meet your friends! I see the puffer waistcoat is still in fashion, anyway.' She beamed at the seated women in amazement. 'If I didn't know one of you was my daughter, I'd swear you were all sisters. Like the

Corrs, but blonder, and without the conspiracy theorist brother.'

'Who is that?' whispered Fair-Weather Soccer Mom, and Fiona, who could hardly contain her delight, said, in a far louder voice: 'That's Beverley's mom.'

21

......

'What are you thinking about?' asked Ella, as they lay side by side on her bed, the rain pounding the skylight above.

'Nothing.'

Arlo was thinking about the crash.

It was almost noon. They hadn't moved in hours, not since Ella's grandmother turned up at the house without notice and Ella went downstairs to investigate. The drops exploded against the window above his head and he was right back in the car, watching them collide with the windscreen.

'You always hold my hand like that.'

Arlo turned his head and looked down at the narrow space between them where his fingers were curved around her palm and vice versa. 'Like what? That's how you hold hands.'

'Mm.'

'Ella, that's a standard hand-hold right there.'

'Sure, if you're a businessman.'

'Excuse me?'

'Glad the merger worked out, old boy,' she barked. 'A pleasure doing business with you.'

'All right then, show me how you'd do it.'

The mattress shook as Ella separated their hands, then reconnected them. 'There.'

Arlo glanced down. Their palms were perfectly aligned, fingers interlocked.

'That's how lovers hold hands.'

Arlo had had his driver's licence four months by the night of the Donovan gig. He'd been looking forward to chauffeuring them in and out of the city – and he had driven in without a hitch. Mike kept joking about how smooth his transitions were, but Mike hadn't a clue what he was talking about. He couldn't even start a car. Leo didn't comment, but only because he was jealous. He'd started lessons ages before Arlo and only recently passed his test.

He turned his face towards Ella, reassuring himself with her presence. 'It does feel more secure,' he conceded.

'The other way is a bit platonic. A bit ...'

'Business meeting.'

'Yes, or a father and daughter crossing the road.'

'Well, that's not what we're going for.'

'No,' she agreed.

The rain continued to fall, and Arlo heard the skid and screech and surprisingly low thud of Mike's body being crushed.

'What are you thinking about now?'

'Still nothing.'

'You must be thinking about something.'

If only Mike hadn't snuck in the whiskey. If only Arlo hadn't drunk it. If only they'd all stayed sober. If only his dad had stayed sober. If only the rain hadn't been heavy. If only the roads had been dry. If only the bend hadn't been sharp.

'I'm not.'

He was supposed to be at a job this morning, assembling furniture for a new woman called Tamara, but on the way to Ella's last night, she'd texted him to 'reschedule'. He wondered who she'd spoken to, and what they'd said.

A bit of being bad-mouthed is getting off lightly, Arly. Wouldn't you say?

Arlo concentrated on the rain.

Arrrr-leee … Hello?

Bam-bam-bam went the drops.

Hello? Are you just going to ignore me?

'Are you thinking about the visit to your dad?'

'No.'

'But you're booked in for tomorrow, right?'

'Doesn't mean I have to go.'

'I thought the prison already confirmed.'

'I got an email this morning confirming the time for tomorrow afternoon, but I don't *have* to go. I can just not turn up. Dad said he'd understand if I didn't feel like it and what's he going to do anyway? It's not like he can come after me.'

He hated how defensive he sounded. He would love nothing more than to talk about his dad, to tell someone about the real Charlie Whitehead. He wanted to tell Ella how his dad had taught him to affix a plug socket – the right way up! – and how readily he said he loved him and Woody and that it came so easily because it was true. Ella would listen because she loved him, but he knew she didn't want to hear. She didn't understand how he could say good things about the man who killed Mike and maimed Leo. And Arlo was caught between what he wanted and what everyone else wanted.

'I'll decide tonight,' he added, relaxing his tone.

'Your mum's right, you know,' she said carefully. 'You don't owe him, like, at all. He owes you and Leo and everyone else.'

I knew the girl still thought about me. Tell her I said hi, Arly. Tell her when she gets bored of you, she should give me a call. She knows I'm funnier and smarter and much better craic.

Arlo's stomach began to churn. 'It's not that simple.' He pushed himself up from the bed. 'I'd better go. I'm at the school for the rest of the day and I've to pick up paint on the way. Your mom has been on Seamus's case about the sets again. This is our fourth tin of yellow.'

Ella rolled her eyes. 'The woman's insane.' She held out her arms and he pulled her up to standing. 'You know Bev hasn't said a word to Amelia about the photos in the week since she walked in on her taking them? She's talked to the press and she continues to hound Principal Patterson, but she hasn't said a word to Amelia. She went straight back to being Bev's golden girl. And Amelia's so blasé about it I honestly wouldn't be surprised if she instigated the whole thing. How's Woody? Did he get into trouble?'

'I haven't spoken to him much since it happened.'

'Yeah, give him space. He'll come to you if he needs to.'

'Yeah,' agreed Arlo, ignoring the niggle in his chest.

'I'll go distract Mal,' she said. 'I'll ask him about that time he completed a triathlon in less than four hours. That should keep him talking.'

'Is your granny definitely gone?' Arlo had heard a lot about Ella's grandmother, and apparently, she'd heard a lot about him. This had worried Arlo, but Ella insisted that just because her granny knew about him, it didn't mean Beverley did. 'Their mother-daughter relationship is even worse than mine and Bev's,' Ella had explained. 'Bev acts like Granny's the embarrassment, when really it's her.'

185

'She's gone to track down Bev, who will hate that,' she said now, delighted. 'So, the path should be clear.'

....

'You didn't have to leave on my account,' said Frances, pink kaftan billowing as she followed Beverley out of the Strand and across the road to where the Range Rover was parked, right by the pier.

The wind made the rain worse, drawing it in on them from all directions. Beverley caught the driver's door before a gust took it. She absolutely did have to leave on her mother's account. Five minutes after she'd shown up at the café, Frances was pulling up a chair and reading the Lakers' sexual fortunes.

'This line here? This means you're going to have a long sex life. Actually, you're probably already in the middle of it.'

Fair-Weather Soccer Mom had roared with delight at this. 'Don't be telling them all my secrets, Miss Tandon.'

Beverley had tried to bring matters back to the musical, but Claire waved her protestations away. She wanted to know if she was going to have more children.

'Beyond my expertise, I'm afraid,' Frances had said, inspecting Claire's palm. 'But I can tell you're putting the effort in.'

'We are,' giggled the woman formerly known as Claire Keating, but who had clearly been invaded by some sort of body snatcher. 'We actually are.'

They'd all lost their minds.

They were howling and shrieking as if they'd downed a bottle of Bacardi as opposed to a couple of Americanos and low-fat flat whites. Her mother was sitting in the middle of it, oblivious to how she was making a complete fool of herself – and, by association,

Beverley. When Lorna divulged that she called Bill 'Councillor' in bed, Beverley had made their excuses and left.

Her mother had this effect on people. They automatically opened up to her, and it was all the more incomprehensible because Beverley's reaction was always the complete opposite.

Frances went around the other side of the car and clambered into the passenger seat, Beverley snatching away the half-empty Rennie packet and bottle of water before they were flattened. She opened the glove box and fired them in.

'Why do the seats need to be so far off the ground? It's not as if we're going cross country. Would you consider getting yourself a nice Mini, *a stór*?'

Beverley grimaced at her mother's pet name for her but said nothing.

'Do you remember the Mini we had when you were small? The five of you piled into the back, screaming at us to speed up anytime there was a bump in the road.' Her mother laughed to herself. 'You'd all beg us to go faster so youse would go flying up and bounce your heads against the ceiling.'

'That wasn't me,' said Beverley, bringing her hand to her chin. It barely seemed possible but, yes, there was another spot.

'Of course, that was before the EU introduced its nanny state rules.'

'Seatbelts are basic safety. We should have been wearing them. There were seatbelts in the car.'

'Yes, but only for three of you. And what were we going to do? Pick our favourite kids?' Frances chuckled lightly. 'Anyway, it was more fun without the seatbelts. I can still hear you roaring: *Faster, Mam, faster!*'

Beverley couldn't speak for her siblings – although childhood brain trauma would explain a lot – but she knew for a fact she had never goaded her parents into giving her a concussion. Her mother loved reflecting on their childhood as if it had been this idyllic time, and if Beverley interjected with the truth, she was the uptight party-pooper.

'Your friends seem nice. That Claire is a howl. And Lorna. I only ever met them once or twice when you were a child, but I remember you speaking about them. It's wonderful you're still friends.'

Beverley motored on along the seaside stretch, her jaw clamped shut. Her main memory of the Mini was the day they'd arrived home to find her dad had sold it. She now knew he'd sold it because they needed a vehicle with space for all the children, but that hadn't stopped him making the same cutting joke over and over: 'Your mother's too maxi to be driving a Mini.'

Beside her, Frances quietly exhaled. 'It's breathtaking around here,' she said, gazing out the window. 'I'm so truly happy for you, that you get to live somewhere so tranquil. I love my life in Dublin, but I miss the Atlantic, and all the open space. Of course, Aberstown was never as nice as this, but it had its charms. In the countryside, the rain makes everything greener. In Dublin, it just accentuates the grey. It's much harder to keep your doshas balanced in a city.'

Beverley felt a short surge of acid reflux, but she was not about to reach over her mother for the glovebox. Nor was she going to give her the satisfaction of asking what doshas were. She did her best to swallow down the reflux.

Her mother rolled down the window and took some dramatically deep breaths. The rain splashed in, hitting Beverley at the side of her eye.

'Does Ella know you're coming?'

'I saw Ella when I called to the house this morning. I like the short hair. She's such an impressive young woman. So many opinions on so many things. I haven't a clue where half the countries she talks about are. What's that election she's obsessed with at the moment? Bangladesh? Or Barbados? I can never get them straight. Is Barbados even a country? It's great to see that passion. You've done a wonderful job with her. I hope you know that.'

She hadn't a clue what her mother was talking about. Ella never instigated conversation with her any more. 'Ella should have been at university,' she said, knocking on the indicator earlier than necessary.

Her mother hit her gently on the arm. 'I don't remember you sticking to your lecture schedule too diligently.'

The difference, she desperately wanted to respond, *is that Ella's mother cares.*

'She told me about this business with Amelia and the photos. I can imagine that had you very worried, *a stór*. I'd love to help if I can.'

'So *that's* why you're here. Of course. That makes much more sense.'

'I really am doing a workshop in the city. Tantric sex, three nights, starting tomorrow. You can look it up online. I just thought, while I was in the area, I'd see if I could be of any service.'

Beverley nodded to herself, tightening her grasp on the steering wheel. 'You don't think I can handle this. You thought this would be an opportunity to remind me that I'm a big old prude.'

'I'm receiving your negative vibrations, *a stór*, but I'm finding it difficult to track the origin.'

189

'Why didn't you stay in a hotel, so? I'm sure the workshop organisers would have put you up.'

'They would,' Frances agreed. 'But I'd rather see you. And I thought I could speak to Amelia too, if you wanted.'

'To give her some pointers, is it?'

The wipers swished over and back, fighting a losing battle with the rain. The wind rattled in the branches as they began the incline up to the Franklins' street.

Her mother pulled the seatbelt away from her chest and sat straighter. 'I'm sorry you have such a low opinion of me, Beverley. And I mean that genuinely. Amelia is only twelve. I take this seriously. And if you're concerned, then I'm concerned.'

Frances opened the beaded handbag on her lap and removed a bottle of what looked like silage. She took three large, loud gulps. Beverley's reflux surged.

She dropped to second gear as they approached the house. Ella's car was still in the driveway. Was she planning on going to classes at all today?

'Maybe we could spend some time together this afternoon?'

'Can't,' said Beverley, killing the engine. 'I've rehearsals for the Glass Lake musical shortly. I'm directing this year.'

'Of course! *The Wizard of Oz*. No better woman for it. You always loved putting on plays.'

'I was a professional actress, Mother.'

'Oh, I know, I know. Amn't I always telling people? But it's the love of it that counts, not whether you once made money from it. I'll come along to that. Rehearsals! So glamorous.'

'No way,' said Beverley as they exited the car, her mother doing an unnecessary jump down on to the recently resurfaced driveway.

'Oh, go on, Beverley. I'd love to see Amelia in action.'

'No.'

'All right. I'll just stay here so.'

'Yes, you will.'

'Give me a chance to talk to Malachy. I never did get to give him a good dressing-down about his own nudes. Speaking of which, did you ever watch those erotic films I sent you? Some exquisite shots in there. I suppose I could root out a bit more of that for you while I'm home this afternoon too—'

'All right, all right! Fine! You can come. But you cannot say a word and you must remember I'm in charge and it's not a game, it's a school musical that is going to be on national television.'

Beverley was almost at the front door when she turned back to point the fob at the car. Her mother disappeared from sight.

'Mother?'

A sudden loud warble came from the far side of the car and Beverley rushed over. Frances was on the ground, her pink kaftan gathered up at her waist as her black-legginged legs splayed outwards.

'Mam!' She tried to help her up. 'What happened?'

'I lost my ... my footing ...'

'Mam? Are you okay?'

'Just give me a moment,' said Frances, her voice faint.

Her mother's gaze settled somewhere behind her. Beverley snapped her fingers. 'Mam? Can you focus? Can you see me?'

And just as suddenly Frances was back. 'Sorry, a stór. I'm fine,' she said, gently pushing her daughter away and getting to her feet as nimbly as a cat. 'The damn rain. I must have slipped. These tiles are a bit slippy, aren't they?'

Beverley exhaled loudly, sending her eyes skywards. 'This is porcelain paving, not tiles, and it's not slippy, it's expensive. You're carrying too much weight, Mam. That's the problem. It's not good for your balance.'

Frances dusted off her leggings and readjusted her bosom so the large gemstone sat right in the middle. 'Oh, my darling girl,' she said cheerfully, 'don't you know my vastness is one of the most spectacular things about me?'

....

Arlo didn't dare turn back until he was at the very end of the street. Even then, it was only a surreptitious glance. The rain blurred his view. He hoped it would blur Beverley Franklin's too.

So that was Ella's grandmother.

One of Arlo's grannies only wore black (her husband died when she was forty, and she wasn't going to let anyone forget it) and the other still worked the farm and dressed as such. Ella's granny didn't look like either of them. And she certainly didn't look like Beverley. Ella's granny looked like she'd been to Woodstock.

As Beverley disappeared inside the house, the older woman stopped and looked around. Could she see him? Should he wave his appreciation for her brave act of diversion? He hoped she hadn't hurt herself.

He'd thought he was done for when he opened the front door to find the woman looking right at him, and Beverley on the cusp of turning back in his direction. He was about to say something – 'Sorry' was the word that had been forming on his lips – when suddenly the grey-haired hippy was throwing herself on to the tarmac. (She was sort of how Janis Joplin might look, if she'd had a chance to grow old.) Arlo didn't hang around for directions. He legged it.

His dad had a pirated DVD of Arlo Guthrie playing Woodstock. He'd rooted it out of the attic for him and Leo one Saturday night. They'd watched it over and over until they could mimic every gesture Guthrie made on stage. Arlo's brother was named after Woody Guthrie, and he was named after his son, Arlo, who was also a folk musician and who Charlie Whitehead regularly argued was as good as, if not better than, his father.

Leo had thought Charlie was so cool, all Arlo's friends did. Their parents had never even heard of Arlo Guthrie. Leo had once told him, in the deepest confidence, that he was named after Leo Sayer. Arlo had never heard of the singer, so he looked him up. Then he rolled around his bedroom floor laughing for at least an hour.

Jogging up to his van now, Arlo laughed again. 'When I neeeed you, I just close my eyes and I'm with you ...' he sang softly, as he opened the driver's door.

The fuck you bring that up for? Haven't I suffered enough?

Leo Sayer! He's even naffer than Cliff Richard. You should have just lied, boy. Leo Varadkar would have been cooler than that!

So you're talking to me again, then? I thought you were throwing me under the bus for your girlfriend. Or should that be my girlfriend?

She was never your girlfriend, Leo.

She almost was, and she would have been if it wasn't for what happened. And that's why you don't like to talk to me when she's about. You're a wimp.

Don't call me that.

Wimp, wimp, wimp. It all worked out really well for you, didn't it, Arly?

That's not true.

You were never exactly competition. You had to butcher me just so you could stand a chance. You're scrawny and gangly and anytime anyone speaks to you, you look like a fucking tomato – a tomato with a wonky nose. I'd have won hands down.

Arlo started the van.

You know I'm not real, right? As in, I don't actually live in your head? These are your own thoughts.

I know, Leo. I'm not fucking insane.

He turned the radio up so loudly and so quickly, that the speakers vibrated. But Leo's voice was still clear as a bell.

Then you really need to work on your self-confidence, Arly. Like fucking pronto.

22

......

The **Glass** Lake auditorium was unrecognisable from the hall Christine had sat in at the start of the week for the Parents' Information Night. Gone were the orderly rows of seats, the tables topped with tablecloths and carefully arranged finger-food platters, and the parents dressed in suits and autumnal coats. When Christine entered the hall now, just before 1 p.m. on Thursday, she was greeted by colourful pandemonium.

A large group of children stood on the stage, half of them dressed in orange and the other half decked out in blue, but all committing to their chosen colour from the bobble at the top of their hats down to the toes of their socks. Beverley Franklin stood in front of the coordinated children. She had her back to Christine, but it was clear she was reading them the riot act.

Amelia Franklin was standing off to the side of the stage, holding her long blonde ponytail aloft as Maeve pulled at the back of her sky-blue 'Dorothy' dress. A measuring tape and several yards of ribbon hung around Maeve's neck and Christine was relieved that this, at least, had worked out for her easily stressed middle child.

About two dozen more students were milling around the main hall, under the supervision of Mr Cafferty and a couple of other teachers. The students sported a mixture of fantastical costume and

Glass Lake uniform. One child, presumably the tinman, was having large sheets of silver cardboard attached to his body by a woman in her sixties who wore a bright pink kaftan and who herself looked like she could play one of Oz's good witches. Seamus McGrath, the school caretaker, was taping mesh to a tall, wire structure that was already identifiable as a tornado.

Lorna Lick-Arse Farrell was the only other parent present. She was dressed all in black, save for a coffee-coloured wraparound cardigan, and she was holding some sort of stick, which she periodically banged on the ground, adding to the cacophony of noise and making the small circle of students gathered before her leap with fright. Woody Whitehead was among them, dressed in his uniform but with whiskers painted on to his face.

Derek had pitched this article as 'on-the-ground reporting'. 'Our Glass Lake correspondent embeds herself in the trenches of rehearsals and reports on what's *really* going on,' he'd said in the action movie trailer voice he used to spice up rudimentary stories. Christine had written several such pieces in her time with the *Southern Gazette* and knew that the key was to mention as many students as possible, so they could use plenty of photographs of them dressed in adorable costumes.

She pulled her notebook from her handbag and jotted down a few quick observations. She was trying to remember the name of the boy playing the tinman when she felt a tug on her jacket.

A small girl in orange leggings, sweatshirt and woolly hat was standing at her side.

'Director Franklin says you're to wait in the stalls.'

Christine looked up to the stage and waved at Beverley, but she was already turning back to the blue and orange children.

'Wait where?'

'In the stalls,' repeated the child-sized satsuma. 'That's what you call the seats in the auditorium. Director Franklin says she'll be with you as soon as she solves the problem of mass ineptitude.' She paused. 'Do you know what that means?'

'Not a clue.'

The satsuma nodded. 'She also says you're late.'

'Only slightly,' Christine shouted after the girl, who was running back towards the stage. 'I had some cat trouble!'

Christine had been due to arrive at the hall half an hour ago, but she'd finally seen an opportunity to retrieve Porcupine. The three Maguire children had been watching Mrs Rodgers' house from the front-room window for the past week, noting her movements in the notebook Christine had left on the sill and, besides her Tidy Town meetings on Mondays, the one constant was her late-morning walk. The cat thief left the house in a pair of Asics runners every day at 11.30 a.m. She returned between 12.22 and 12.37 and stopped to detangle her beloved roses before disappearing inside. That gave Christine fifty minutes to get in and out of number one Seaview Terrace, cat in tow.

'We are not breaking into our neighbour's home,' Conor had said when she ran the plan past him last night.

'Of course we're not.' Christine had already considered this option. But a few surveys of the perimeter (thank you, Brian) suggested Mrs Rodgers never left so much as the bathroom window ajar. 'We're going to use a key.'

Father Brendan O'Shea, who lived at number twelve, had a key to all Seaview Terrace homes in case of emergencies. Christine was going to call to him, explain that Porcupine had got trapped in their

197

neighbour's home, that they had tried phoning the elderly woman to no avail, and that they were now very worried about her safety. The cat being only an afterthought.

Conor had been against it. 'Porcupine has changed.'

'He has not changed, Conor. He's just had his fur dyed.'

'It was more than that. It was in his eyes. It was like he didn't know me.' Her husband shivered. 'Or didn't want to know me.'

In the end, none of it mattered anyway. After a good five minutes knocking on his door, Christine had gone around the back to try the small shrine Fr O'Shea had built in his garden – the previous owners had installed a goldfish pond; it had only taken a woman's head to convert the water fountain into Our Holy Mother – where she was spotted by his next-door neighbour. Fr O'Shea had left for Medjugorje the day before. There'd been another sighting on Apparition Hill, apparently. 'Says he won't be back until the Virgin Mary shows herself,' relayed the neighbour. 'Or until Ryanair close the Bosnia route in late November. Whichever comes first.'

Now, Christine headed for the small cluster of plastic chairs in the centre of the auditorium where the tinman was having bonus bits of tinfoil wrapped around his forearms. Lorna was leaning on her stick, watching her, and Christine smiled over.

Conor reckoned she should give up – 'The kids don't even mention Porcupine any more' – but it wasn't about the stupid animal, it was about right and wrong, and Christine would find another way into that house, even if it was through the goddam cat-flap.

She took a seat and watched as the tinman wobbled off awkwardly, tripping slightly on his new shin guards.

'That'll help get him into character anyway,' she said to the older woman in the bright kaftan who'd been helping with his costume.

'He probably should have been cast as the lion, poor child. Seems to have a lot of fears. The flying monkeys are giving him nightmares, and his mother came in with him this morning to see if Beverley could eliminate the bit where he kills a swarm of bees by having them bounce against his armour.' The white-haired woman pulled a bottle of something mud-coloured from her bag and took a swig. 'There are no actual bees, of course, just sound effects, but that didn't seem to make a difference.'

'I don't remember a swarm of bees.'

'Oh, it's in the original book. You better get that right, or my daughter will be very cross,' she said, nodding at Christine's notebook. 'It's *The Wonderful Wizard of Oz*, like the book, not *The Wizard of Oz*, which is the movie. You don't want to make that mistake, trust me. I got a twenty-minute lecture on the subtle but important differences on the drive here. I assume you're the local journalist?'

'Christine Maguire, hi. I'm basically here to write a very long picture caption. The more kids we can feature, the more family members guilted into buying a copy.'

'Frances Tandon,' said the woman, extending a hand. 'I'm Beverley's mother – and Dorothy's grandmother.' She held out the bottle to Christine. 'Kombucha?'

'No, thank you.' It looked like what you might find at the bottom of Beverley's kitchen fishpond. 'I actually met you once, about thirty years ago. Beverley and I were in the same class here, and I was at your house working on a school project.'

'Were you?' said Frances, amazed. 'That must have been a first,

199

and a last. I don't remember Beverley ever bringing friends home. I'm afraid my daughter has always been rather embarrassed by her family – and me, in particular.'

Her tone was breezy but Christine glanced around for a change of subject. Maeve and Amelia were gone from the stage, and Lorna Farrell appeared to have broken her stick in two.

'Rehearsals seem to be in full swing,' she said. 'Are they going well?'

'Oh, I'm sure they are. If you want a job done properly, put Beverley in charge. I'm not sure where she got her determination from. I've never had an ounce of it,' said Frances cheerfully. 'Though there does seem to have been some crossed wires with the Munchkins. Half of them have turned up as Oompa Loompas.'

....

Three of the Oompa Loompas were now crying, and another (one of Claire Keating's boys) was trying to make the case for how the Wizard of Oz was Willy Wonka's father based on a 'thread' he'd read on the internet. Beverley was ignoring the boy, who she'd long suspected had an attention deficit disorder, but he kept talking.

'... and the Munchkins actually showed Willy Wonka how to grow magic sweets, especially lollipops, because they have a lollipop guild, and so Oompa Loompas and Munchkins are basically the same thing, and if you watch the film backwards ...'

Another boy, who was at least dressed in blue, kept suggesting ways in which he could enhance his role. He had been doing character development at home with his mother and, having watched the Judy Garland film and spotted a Munchkin mayor, had turned up to today's rehearsals with a gold chain around his neck.

'We're basing our production on the book, where there is no mayor,' said Beverley. 'You're a Munchkin, James. You don't need any more development than that.'

'But why do we have to be blue?' asked a fifth-classer who'd gone as far as painting her face orange.

'Because you're Munchkins.'

'Can I at least keep the hat?' said one of the orange snifflers. 'My granny knit this hat.'

'But who says Munchkins can't be orange?' The face-painter.

'Me. And L. Frank Baum. And no, you can't keep the hat. Maybe your granny will knit you another one.'

'Who's Frank Bum?'

'*Baum*. He's the author.'

'But my granny's dead.'

'The author of Willy Wonka or the Wizard of Oz?'

'Of *The Wonderful Wizard of Oz*! And there's no such book as Willy— It doesn't matter. I say it. All right? Me. I say Munchkins must be blue and I'm in charge.' Beverley took a deep breath. 'Okay?'

The children nodded slowly.

A hand went up.

'Yes?'

'Maybe I could sing a song explaining *why* Munchkins are blue?'

'No, James. No extra songs! No gold chain! No conspiracy theories about fictional characters' parentage! No orange costume pieces, made by the living or the dead! None of it. You all wear blue, sing "Ding Dong the Witch Is Dead" and that's it. You got it?'

Even the Keating twin stopped babbling now. The other brother's lip started to quiver. She couldn't tell which one he was, since the boys had identical haircuts and (incorrect) costumes.

Jesus, don't let them all start crying.

'I know this is stressful,' said Beverley, more calmly. She was in danger of having to get up on stage and sing 'Ding Dong the Witch Is Dead' herself. 'But show business always is. You all know I used to be a professional actress, yes?'

The children nodded glumly.

'So, trust me. We're nearly there. One week to go.' A *week*, and they still couldn't get their colours straight! She did her best to smile. 'But we need to keep going, because currently we are behind schedule.'

It wasn't just the schedule that had her stressed. It was the presence of numerous unwanted people at rehearsals, namely Tamara Watson's son, who had been given a chorus role as a flying monkey; her own mother, who was allowed to attend on condition that she not tell Beverley to take it easy, breathe, or anything similarly dismissive; and Christine Maguire, who had been sent to write about rehearsals, and who was half an hour late.

She felt marginally bad that she had arguably planted a seed that may or may not have people suspecting Maeve Maguire was the girl involved in the sexting episode. But she didn't have time for such frivolities as remorse. They were halfway through rehearsal time and had yet to run a single scene.

'We need to do the arrival to Oz scene, pronto.' She looked around her. 'Amelia?' Her daughter was standing alone in the wings. 'Over here, now. And where's Ciara Murphy? James, go down there and get Ciara Murphy.'

'But I don't want to miss any notes!'

Beverley took a deep breath. 'Oh, for God's sake ... Ciara! Ciara Murphy!'

Fiona Murphy's daughter emerged from the chorus of flying monkeys currently getting the 'fame costs' speech from Lorna.

'Yes, Director Franklin?' she said, running towards the stage.

'You're now the Wicked Witch of the West, congratulations.'

The girl gasped, pushed her hands to her chest and started to bounce manically.

'Yes, yes, well done. Alison O'Hagan has come down with tonsillitis. That's the reason you've been promoted, got it? Ciara!'

The girl stopped bouncing.

'If your mother asks, that's why you got the part, no other reason.' Beverley loathed herself for giving in to blackmail. But what was she to do? She could not have the whole town whispering about her, saying she'd been fired (She had quit!) and casting doubt on her enviable marriage. And she had not been fired! *That* was the most important thing.

'Yes, Director Franklin.'

'Good. Now, up on stage, let's go. Gordon, get her a script.'

Gordon was Beverley's PA. He had crippling stage fright that meant he couldn't even cut it as a cornstalk. But he was a whiz with a spreadsheet.

As a script was found and Ciara came around the side of the stage to the stairs, Beverley cast a cold eye over the auditorium. Her mother was talking to Christine, which was not something she needed right now. God knows what Frances was saying, and to a journalist.

'Got the script.'

Beverley took the stapled pages from the boy. 'Page seventeen,' she said, throwing it to Ciara. 'Gordon, who else do we need for this scene?'

The kid checked his notes. 'Munchkins, Dorothy, Wicked Witch of the West.'

'Check, check, check. Props?'

'The Cyclone. Silver shoes. The broom.'

'You,' she said to another of the Munchkins, 'go down there and tell Caretaker Seamus I want to speak to him. The shoes we have, and ...' She rotated to where her assistant director was psyching up a new batch of supporting cast with her talk of sweat payments. 'Lorna! Lorna! We need the broom! Now!'

But as the Laker made her way to the stage, Beverley could see that the Wicked Witch's broomstick, which Seamus had made especially, was snapped in half.

'For God's sake, Lorna. I told you to stop hammering the thing off the floor. What are we going to use now?'

'It was shoddy craftsmanship. I was going to get a replacement from the storage closet ...'

'Well, go on, so. What are you waiting for?'

'It's locked.'

Beverley put a hand to her chest and swallowed. This was not good for her heartburn.

'You called,' said Seamus, appearing at the foot of the stage. She ignored the caretaker's tone. Here was another person who struggled to comprehend primary colours.

'Seamus, do you have a key for the storage closet?'

'Not currently,' he said. 'But Principal Patterson does.'

Beverley turned back to the children, picking an Oompa Loompa at random. 'Go and ask Principal Patterson for the key to the storage closet. Tell her we need a broom as a matter of urgency.' There wouldn't be any Munchkins left to greet Dorothy at this rate. 'Go on. Go!'

The girl ran off, the bobble of her orange hat bouncing.

'Was that it?' asked Seamus, as Ciara started mumbling her new lines to herself. Out of the corner of her eye, she saw the ambitious Munchkin whip the gold chain out again and throw it around his neck.

'No,' said Beverley. 'I want to talk to you about *that*.' She pointed at the set design Seamus had been working on. 'We have a problem.'

'With the tornado?'

'Exactly. I did not ask for a tornado.'

'You did. It's in the script. It's what carries Dorothy to Oz.'

Beverley shook her head. 'Gordon?'

'According to *The Wonderful Wizard of Oz*, by L. Frank Baum, published in 1900, Dorothy is carried from Kansas to Oz by a cyclone.' Her sidekick looked up from his notes.

'A cyclone,' agreed Beverley.

'They're the same thing,' said Seamus.

'Gordon?'

The boy flicked to the next page. 'A tornado is a collection of strong winds that spiral around a central point, creating a funnel shape. A cyclone rotates around a centre of low pressure. They move slower than tornados and are generally accompanied by rain.' He looked up at Beverley. 'Technically, if we're setting the musical in Cork as opposed to Kansas, it should really be a hurricane. They're more common along the North Atlantic Ocean.'

'Gordon,' warned Beverley, 'what did we agree?'

'No unsolicited opinions. Sorry, Director Franklin. Won't happen again.'

They both regarded Seamus.

The caretaker sighed loudly.

'Can you talk to the kids about the sets? They're meant to be in charge. I'm only supposed to be helping out.'

Beverley spotted the sixth-class teacher heading for the double doors at the rear of the auditorium. 'Eh, Mr Cafferty! Mr Cafferty!' The newest staff member turned back towards her. 'Seamus,' she said, before the caretaker could slink off, 'can you please take another look at the Yellow Brick Road? I appreciate you've gone over it, and there have been some improvements, but it still looks gold at best.'

'Yes, Beverley?' said Mr Cafferty, approaching the stage. He smiled at the caretaker, but the older man ignored him as he sighed again and headed back to his tornado.

'Have you fixed the lion's movements yet? Lorna said he was still creeping about the stage like a burglar last time she ran scenes with him.'

'I'm trying,' said the teacher. 'But it's proving difficult. Woody's ... he's not that open to instruction, at least not from me. Maybe you'd have a better shot at talking to him yourself?'

'I don't talk to Woody Whitehead.'

'Excuse me?'

'Gordon?'

'Director Franklin does not talk to Woody Whitehead,' the boy confirmed.

'Why not?'

'I just don't.'

'But he's playing the lion. That's a lead role. I don't see how that could work.'

'Lorna!' called Beverley. The assistant director scurried over to join her. It had taken thirty-five years, but she'd finally found something useful for the woman to do. 'Go and tell Woody he needs to start stomping on the stage. If he needs more details, Gordon here has an animal information sheet. But tell him to think clubfoot, not twinkle-toes.'

'Right you are,' said Lorna. 'Oh, and Bev,' she lowered her voice, 'did you see who's here? Christine Maguire! *Maeve Maguire's* mother!' Lorna's eyes widened. Her whole face was brimming with implied meaning, but Beverley pretended not to hear.

'And I'll need him up here in about half an hour; we'll be rehearsing the lion's arrival after this. So, you'll need to be up here too, in case I have any further notes to relay to him.' Beverley swivelled back to her assembled leads and clapped her hands. 'Okay, ensemble, let's take this from the top. Dorothy to the left; Munchkins in the middle; and Wicked Witch of the West to the right. Lights, camera—'

'Beverley?' Ciara Murphy was raising her hand. 'I mean, Director Franklin?'

The girl was cut out of her mother. On stage two minutes and already acting like she had a God-given right to be here.

'Do you think we could drop the "wicked"? It stigmatises women. And it goes against the school's bullying policy as regards name-calling.'

Beverley clamped her teeth together so aggressively that she bit her tongue.

'So, okay? The Witch of the West? It's just "wicked" ...' The girl scrunched up her face. 'It might impact my self-esteem.'

....

Lorna Farrell delivered the instructions to Woody Whitehead; gave him a brief, and highly accurate interpretation of a lion walking on two feet; and granted him permission to go to the bathroom. Then she scurried over to where Christine Maguire and Beverley's mother were sitting.

While she wasn't happy any child had been subject to such terrible parenting that she'd resorted to sending naked photos of herself out into the world, she wasn't entirely distraught that the girl involved was Christine's daughter. She was assistant director (an important role!) and she did not take kindly to this glorified copywriter going over her head to Beverley to get her daughter onto the musical. She'd never liked Christine. She'd always suspected she'd started that god-awful Lick-Arse nickname, which continued to plague her to this day. It was particularly hurtful because it wasn't at all true.

'What are you ladies gossiping about?' she said, pulling a third chair up beside them.

'We're not gossiping,' replied Christine, just as Frances said, 'The school's new sex education classes.'

'They start today,' said Lorna, who'd always had great gossip timing. 'I was going to see if I could track down the doctor, actually, and find out what exactly he's teaching. I don't know if you've heard, Frances, but he's quite controversial. What do you think of him, Christine?'

'I don't know much about him.'

'Mmm,' said Lorna. Then she took a deep breath and went for it. 'I heard Woody Whitehead was the boy who sent the nudes.'

'Who told you that?' said both women at the same time. Frances sounded curious, but Christine was livid.

'So, it's true?'

'No comment,' said Christine.

'It doesn't really matter who it was,' said Frances. 'It's great all the kids will get these classes.'

'I think it's too young,' said Lorna, not taking her eyes off Christine. 'Just because two children were sexually deviant, the rest of the class shouldn't be stripped of their innocence. If the girl's parents want these classes, they should organise to have them privately.'

Christine gave a hollow laugh. 'The girl's parents did not want these classes. I can tell you that for nothing. It was not their idea.'

Lorna's face erupted. 'And how do you know that?'

Christine was suddenly flustered.

'You interviewed the mother, didn't you?' coaxed Frances. 'For an article. That's how you know ... I presume?'

'Yes, exactly. That's it. I interviewed the mother under the promise of anonymity, so I can't say another thing about it.'

But Lorna didn't need her to. She had all the confirmation she needed. It was blatantly obvious.

Woody Whitehead and Maeve Maguire.

Lorna removed her phone from the black bumbag she had tied around her waist and discreetly fired off a few correspondences.

23
• • • • • •

'**R**ehearsals can be a tad noisy,' said Nuala Patterson as she led Dr O'Sullivan down the corridor, past the auditorium. She did not throw her head around the door; the longer she could avoid Beverley, the better.

The woman had already called by her office that morning. She wanted to make it clear that she remained 'deeply unhappy' with Nuala's decision to lecture the parents and toss a couple of vague sex ed sessions at the children instead of eliminating the root of the problem: Woody Whitehead.

'They'll be done with rehearsals before two, and then you should have forty-five minutes for your first session. There'll be more time tomorrow. Is half an hour enough for you to set up now? You'll have the classroom to yourself. The whole of sixth class and Mr Cafferty are in the hall.'

'That's fine. I'm all ready to go – except for this,' said Dr O'Sullivan, swinging the black metal box he was carrying in his left hand.

The doctor – a second cousin on her mother's side that she only ever met at funerals – had arrived at the school early because he needed some help welding a hinge on the container.

'Seamus will sort that out for you in no time.'

The doctor nodded.

'His office is just down here.'

'Great.'

Nuala slowed as they passed the younger classes. Mrs Walsh was winding down the Junior Infants with a bit of afternoon story time and Nuala recognised the cover without being close enough to read the title. *Run with the Wind*. Leo had loved that book.

'What's the box for, can I ask?'

'Anonymity,' said the doctor, switching the heavy-looking item from one hand to another. 'It allows the children to ask things or tell me things in the strictest confidence. Sometimes the presence of their peers makes them too embarrassed to speak, so instead, they can write it down and stick it in here.'

There was no mention of that on the departmental curriculum, but it was a clever idea. Still, she'd probably neglect to mention it if Lorna Farrell cornered her again in the schoolyard.

They rounded the final corridor corner.

'How's your son, that was in the accident? My mother told me he was in Dublin?'

'Leo,' said Nuala, the name sounding strange. How long since she'd spoken it aloud? 'Yes. He's been discharged from rehab there, but he still has regular sessions.'

'You must miss him.'

'Yes,' she said, relieved to be placing a hand on the door to Seamus's workshop. 'Well, here we are.' She peered in the window and the growing light-headedness escalated. There was no sign of Seamus. Only Arlo Whitehead, hunched over a table, reading some sort of letter. 'Seamus must still be in the auditorium,' she said, taking a step away from the door. 'But Arlo will look after you.

211

And he'll show you to the sixth-class room afterwards.' She took another step back. 'I've a million and one things to do, so I'll leave you to it.'

'Okay,' said the doctor.

'I'll speak to you after.'

Then she turned and left. But instead of heading back to her office, Nuala made her way through the next available fire exit.

She stood outside for a full five minutes, waiting for the cold wind to blow the unsettled feeling away. When her fingertips started to go numb, she curled them into balls and went back indoors.

....

It took Arlo twelve minutes to fix the hinges on the large black box.

It helped that the doctor hadn't sat there watching him. He seemed to get the message when Arlo offered him the choice of two plumbing manuals to read, and instead walked around the workroom looking at the various kids' drawings of Seamus that adorned the wall. Arlo's personal favourite was the one of the grey-haired caretaker playing Xbox while standing on a surfboard.

Arlo had been staring at his dad's letter since Seamus left for 'five minutes' to check on rehearsals. That was an hour ago. He was relieved to have something to do. He tightened the screws on the other hinge while he was at it. No point doing a half-arsed job.

Arlo led the doctor down the corridor towards Mr Cafferty's classroom. Sixth-class students had been sitting in the same corner of Glass Lake since he was a student.

The corridor was clear except for Mr Cafferty and a student, who appeared to be arguing. Except it wasn't any student, it was—

'Woody?'

His little brother turned, whipping his arm down by his side, and the teacher looked up.

'What's going on?' asked Arlo.

'Hi, there. I'm Mr Cafferty,' said the teacher, smiling broadly as he held out a hand.

'Arlo Whitehead,' he said, shaking it. 'I'm Woody's brother.'

'Dr Cian O'Sullivan.'

'Of course,' said Mr Cafferty. 'I enjoyed your talk on Monday. I'm delighted you'll be speaking to the students.'

Arlo looked at his brother, but he was busy glaring at his feet. 'Aren't you supposed to be at rehearsals in the hall? Woody?'

'Your brother was a little mixed up about where he should be,' said Mr Cafferty. 'I came back to the classroom to get something and found him out here. He must have got confused about the timetable. Was that it, Woody? I'd say it was.'

'I was going to the toilet,' mumbled the boy, avoiding eye contact with all three adults.

'Well, on you go,' said the teacher, watching Woody slouch off in the direction of the bathroom.

Arlo watched him go too. 'I was just showing the doctor to your classroom,' he said.

'Yes, yes, go on in,' enthused Mr Cafferty. 'There's a staff toilet right next door, and the kitchen is just to the left around that corner. I've to get back to the hall – I'm helping with movement, and the tinman is having some issues with staying on stage – but go ahead and make yourself at home.'

....

'He asked if he could go to the bathroom and I said yes. But that was twenty minutes ago.'

'So, where is he?' One cast member, that's all Beverley had asked Lorna to look after. She just had to keep an eye on one student while Beverley looked after the remaining thirty or so, and she couldn't even manage that. 'We need Woody. I can hardly do the Dorothy, Scarecrow and Tinman meet Lion scene without the lion, now can I?'

Lorna was pulling a watery-eyed expression not dissimilar to the one the Oompa Loompas had threatened her with earlier. 'I could go and look for him,' she said. 'He can't have gone too far ...'

'No, forget it. Forget it. We'll do something else.'

The Arrival to Oz scene remained on hold while she waited for word on a replacement broom, but they were running out of time and they needed to perform something so Christine Maguire could write about it. This was their second-best scene, and a central piece to the story, but Woody Whitehead was, of course, nowhere to be found. How Principal Patterson couldn't see that the boy did not deserve to be a Glass Lake student was beyond her.

'Gordon, what other scenes are in reasonable shape?'

Beverley's PA frowned as he read down through the list. 'Dorothy and Scarecrow meet Tinman, maybe?'

'No Munchkins in that one, right?'

'Right.'

'Fine. Dorothy and Scarecrow meet Tinman, it is. You three ready?' Beverley turned to her daughter, who really did look radiant in blue, and the two male students.

'Yes, Director Franklin,' they said.

'You okay, Henry?'

The tinman nodded nervously.

'The armour on my left arm is a bit loose. What if the bees attack me and it comes off?'

'We're not doing the bee scene yet. And, as I told you, they're not real bees, it's just going to be sound effects, and you pretending, okay?'

'Maybe the bees could attack Scarecrow instead?'

'No way,' said the boy playing Scarecrow. 'I'm allergic.'

'Again: they are not real bees. So nobody needs to worry. But let's get your costume fixed, Henry. Where's Shona Martin?' Beverley asked Lorna, as she searched the room for their head of costume.

'Shona's out sick today.'

'Right. Who else is doing costumes?'

'Maeve Maguire.'

'Maeve!' Beverley looked around the stage and then out into the auditorium. 'Maeve! Maeve Maguire! Has anyone seen Maeve?'

Lorna gasped. 'Woody *and* Maeve missing?' She lowered her voice slightly. 'You were so right, Beverley. First photos, now this ...'

'I never said anything about Maeve Maguire,' hissed Beverley.

'No.' Lorna nodded solemnly. 'Of course you didn't. Mum's the word.'

An orange child ran back into the hall and up on to the stage.

'There are no Munchkins in this scene,' said Beverley. 'Please clear the stage.'

'You sent me to get the key to the storage cupboard off Principal Patterson,' said the little girl, panting slightly in her woollen hat.

'Oh, right. You can give it to Lorna.'

'I couldn't find Principal Patterson. She wasn't in her office. I ran down all the corridors but there was no sign of her.'

Beverley did not have time for this. She needed a broom. 'Where's Seamus?'

'He left a few minutes ago,' said Gordon, checking his watch. 'Eight minutes ago.'

'You,' she said to the out-of-breath Oompa Loompa. 'Go down to Caretaker Seamus's office and tell him we need access to the storage cupboard. He must have a bolt cutter or something. What are you waiting for? We don't have all day!' The girl took a big gulp of air, spun around, and sped off again. 'Will you go and get Christine please, Lorna? Tell her we're ready to go if she'd like to watch.'

'Roger that.'

Lorna ploughed off towards the back of the hall and Beverley took a minute to gather herself. She threw a glance in the direction of her mother, who had a group of sixth-classers in stitches. As always with Frances, Beverley did not want to know.

Just then, Woody appeared through the main doors.

'There he is,' muttered Beverley. 'Gordon?'

The boy nodded. 'I'll go and get him.'

'That bloody woman,' said Seamus, bustling back into his workroom and throwing tools down on the floor inside the door. 'I build her an entire cornfield, travel the length and breadth of the country collecting glass for her Emerald City, and what do I get? A fecking lecture on weather phenomena. Stick on the kettle and crack open the emergency Jaffa Cakes, before my blood pressure really takes off.'

'I heard the racket all right,' said Arlo, flicking the switch.

'It's not the kids. You've no idea how much I love those kids. It's the parents.' Seamus considered this. 'Occasionally the teachers, but mostly the parents.'

Arlo took the only two mugs from the draining board of the small kitchen unit and threw in teabags. Then he pulled the jumbo packet of biscuits from under the sink.

'You know what Principal Patterson says? She says the Glass Lake parents make her wish she was principal of an orphanage.' Seamus chuckled. 'You can imagine what *Director Franklin* would have to say if she heard that.'

Arlo pretended to study the row of old baseball cards Seamus had framed and hung above the sink. They were all of the same guy in a striped uniform and New York Yankees cap. Mostly, they managed to get through the day without mentioning Nuala.

'Which of the teachers don't you like?' he asked, carrying the mugs from the counter to the worktable.

'Thanks, son. Hmm? Ah, they're grand, mostly. I'm just giving out. Ignore me.'

Arlo went back for the biscuits and then sat himself on the stool opposite Seamus.

'Mr Cafferty? You were giving out about him last week.'

'Arra, he's just a bit up in your business. I can't stand people like that. Does Woody like him?' The way the caretaker's eyes flickered up from his cup threw Arlo, and he thought back to his brief encounter with Woody and Mr Cafferty in the corridor earlier.

'I don't know,' he admitted.

Seamus dunked a Jaffa Cake into his tea. When he'd caught the soggy biscuit in his mouth and swallowed, he said: 'Didn't you want to ask me something about tomorrow?'

'Oh, yeah,' said Arlo, as casually as he could muster. 'I might need the day off. You said you weren't sure if you'd need me, so I thought it would be okay.' Half of him hoped Seamus wouldn't allow it, that he'd suddenly have too much work on and need his help. 'I was thinking about visiting my dad, you see, and I have jobs on most days; but tomorrow is pretty much free and there are visitor hours in the afternoon ... Would that be okay? If it's not, it's fine. I'm not even sure if I will go. It's just ... It was just an idea.'

Seamus went to say something but a knock on the door cut him short. 'That's grand, son. No bother,' he said, as the door pushed open and a small child dressed head-to-toe in orange appeared in the office.

'Caretaker Seamus?' said the girl, panting. Arlo wondered what role she was playing. Part of the rainbow, maybe?

'Director Franklin said—'

'No.'

The child blinked. She tried again. 'She said to ask if you can—'

'No,' repeated Seamus.

'To ask if you can come back and—'

'No, no, no.'

'But—'

'Sorry, Amy, but no. I am not going back there. I am on my tea break now, and then I have a mountain of work to get through. You tell Director Franklin that if she wants to clear out the gutters at the back of the building, then fine, I'll go and see to her sets.'

Orange Amy looked doubtful. 'I don't think she'd want to do that.'

Was there a rainbow in *The Wizard of Oz*, or was that just the song?

'No,' agreed Seamus. 'Nor do I.'

'But we need a broom from the storage closet, and we can't find the key. She said you might have some sort of cutter to break the padlock.'

Seamus took a loud, long slurp of his tea.

Orange Amy didn't budge.

'Please, Caretaker Seamus. Us Munchkins are already on thin ice. If I go back again without the key, she might get rid of us altogether.'

'Are Munchkins orange?' asked Arlo, who wasn't sure if he'd ever seen the film, or just a few stills.

But suddenly Orange Amy's big eyes were filling with tears and Seamus was pushing himself up from his seat to pat the girl gently on the shoulder. 'Shhh, now. It's all right, Amy petal. Arlo will go and help. Won't you, Arlo?'

'I'm not sure if I'd really be wanted there … I think I'm better out of sight.'

'Principal Patterson will be nowhere near rehearsals. She's far too clever for that,' said Seamus, offering the girl a Jaffa Cake.

But it wasn't just Principal Patterson Arlo was avoiding. Director Franklin was Beverley Franklin, and Arlo's success rate with her remained at zero. He'd decided he was better off focusing all his efforts on Ella's dad.

'Go on down and sort it out, Arlo. It's a cheap warded lock. I've some picks and a tension wrench somewhere in the filing cabinet if you need them, but you should be able to jimmy the thing open. Okay, Amy, you're okay. It's going to be all right. Here. Have another biscuit.'

....

Beverley had sent the girl to get Seamus McGrath, not Arlo bloody Whitehead. She would have demoted her to a flying monkey there and then, only the last scene, the one they'd performed for Christine Maguire and the wider readership of the *Southern Gazette*, had gone very well, so she was feeling generous.

'Come on, then,' she said to the lanky teenager who remained incapable of eye contact. 'Let's go, let's go. Christine – you can come too. We'll walk and talk.' She led the pair of them to the storage closet beside where her mother was seated. Lorna Farrell, who never needed an invitation to ride Beverley's coattails, was clipping at their heels. 'Where were we?'

'You were talking about your own acting background,' said Christine.

'Ah yes. Well, I'm sure you know the basics. A few high-profile adverts, a prominent role in *Cork Life*, a couple of theatre gigs – do you want to stop while you take this down?'

'I'm fine.'

'But then, you know, I had kids, and family won out. So, it's great to be able to get back to my roots, to tap into that creative energy again. And of course, I still have some contacts in the business, so I just made a few calls, sent in some footage of Amelia, and boom: TV cameras in Cooney. I see a lot of what I had in Amelia. She was the only choice, really, to play Dorothy. I've built the production around her.' They came to a stop at the storage door. 'This is the lock. What are you going to do about it?'

Arlo stepped forward and tilted the silver padlock in different directions. He pulled down sharply on it. Nothing happened. He gave it two more strong tugs.

'Is that what your expertise gets us – some brute force?'

'Give the boy a moment, Beverley,' said Frances, who was smiling kindly at him. Her mother's ability to irritate her was incredible. It was like she had a sixth sense for the people Beverley most disliked and made it her business to be nicest to them.

Arlo's face was now such a shade that he could have been an Oompa Loompa. He gave the lock another pull.

Beverley sighed. 'Right. Well, it seems we'll be doing the broom scene without a broom. Wonderful. Lorna, tell the children we're going to use an old-fashioned thing called imagination.'

The teenager inspected the keyhole again. 'Has anyone got a hairpin or a paperclip?'

Beverley rolled her eyes. 'We're not the Famous Five.'

'Oh, I loved those books!' gushed Lorna. 'And there are five of us here. Bagsy George.'

'No, Lorna. I do the casting around here, and you're clearly Timmy the dog.'

'I have a hairclip,' said Christine, pulling a brown slide from the back of her head and handing it to Arlo. 'Are you going to pick the lock?'

'I'm going to try.' He started to bend the clip out of shape. 'Do you mind?'

Christine shook her head, her eyes following Arlo's hands.

Of course the boy knew how to pick a lock, thought Beverley. He'd probably learned it from his father.

Once he had the clip in an L-shape, he shoved one end into the keyhole and started to push it in all directions.

Fifteen or so seconds passed, and nothing happened.

'Time to admit defeat, I think,' said Beverley.

'You need a plan, crumpet,' said Frances, stepping closer to the boy. 'It's a very male approach to just shove the thing in there, poke around and hope for the best. Believe me, I've seen it a lot.'

Dear God, let her mother not tell Arlo what she was referring to.

Frances took the straightened pin from the boy and gently laid it flat on his palm.

'What you need, Arlo' – how did her mother know his name? – 'is to go in there with intent and respect. Think of the padlock as a sacred place, somewhere that should be cherished and worshipped. Know what sensation you wish to achieve and keep that in your mind's eye.' Frances nodded encouragingly. 'Give it another try.'

The boy reinserted the pin.

'Start with some gentle circles – smaller, then larger – that's it, now vary the pressure ...'

'I'm not great when people are watching me,' Arlo mumbled, his face glowing.

'No,' agreed Frances. 'Most people aren't. Although I don't mind it myself ...' She shook her arms out and wriggled her fingers. 'Just reject the shame, reject the judgement, focus on the pleasure that will come with reaching your goal ...'

'You've a very soothing voice, Frances,' said Christine. 'I should get you to record meditation tapes for my daughter.'

'Yes, Maeve!' said Lorna, far too excitedly. 'Have you seen Maeve? We couldn't find her earlier.'

'Couldn't you?' Christine looked around the hall with mild concern.

Lorna's face was pinched. 'Yes. It was around the same time Woody went missing. That's a coincidence, isn't it?'

'Is it?'

'Don't mind her,' said Beverley, throwing daggers in Lorna's direction. 'Nobody's missing. Maeve's around here somewhere. And look. There's Woody over there.'

A sudden click and the bolt came away from the lock.

'Hurrah!' shouted Lorna.

Arlo grinned.

Frances joined her hands together and bowed slightly. 'Bliss.'

'Very impressive,' said Christine. 'Have you done that before?'

'Once or twice,' said Arlo, his face starting to cool now. 'It's not that hard.'

'Not once you know how,' added Frances.

'All right, Mother. You can go back to your seat now,' said Beverley, who did not think they should be praising the boy for being a dab hand at breaking and entering. She grabbed a brush from the cupboard. Lorna and Frances moved away but Christine was still watching the teenage boy with fascination.

'You wouldn't have a business card, would you, Arlo?' asked Christine, inspecting the hairpin that he'd returned to her. 'I might have a bit of work for you.'

....

Maeve Maguire finally stood and stretched out her legs. Her thighs were throbbing. She'd been crouched under Mr Cafferty's desk for something close to forever. She'd leapt under the table when she heard the teacher's voice in the corridor – talking to Woody – and she'd been about to crawl back out when the classroom door opened. She could only see the bottom half of the man who entered (she knew it was a man because of his big shoes and legs) but it wasn't Mr Cafferty because he wasn't humming. Mr Cafferty was always humming. This man was carrying a big black box, which he left on the ground. Then he'd started writing things on the whiteboard. He made that squeaky noise with the marker and more than once Maeve almost shrieked. Then he'd spent forever flicking through a notebook. She couldn't see what he was doing, only hear the pages. She might have fallen asleep with the boredom, if she hadn't been so uncomfortable.

And now he was gone. She had to get out of here quick. She'd been missing from rehearsals for ages and the man could return any minute. Or Director Franklin might come looking for her. Or Mr Cafferty. Or God – even her mom.

She wasn't mad at Woody for not turning up. She'd heard him getting stopped in the corridor. She was worried about him.

She grabbed what she'd come for, stuffed it in her bag and legged it towards the door.

25
• • • • •

Arlo came to an abrupt stop at the lights. He'd just missed them, again. All the lights were against him this afternoon. How was it four o'clock already? Time kept disappearing, while the commitments kept multiplying. He'd managed to move the only two jobs he had scheduled for tomorrow to today and Seamus had let him go early so he could get them done.

I don't see how you're going to get everything done, especially now your Sugar Mama wants you to come and see her too.

He had been in the school car park, climbing into his van, when a text message came through from Fiona Murphy requesting that he call to her house today. She said it was an emergency.

She's not my Sugar Mama, Leo, so will you please fuck off.

It's her you should tell to fuck off, boy. She calls, you come running. You're a wimp. I don't care how many extra twenties she leaves on the nightstand; you don't have time for this today.

I'm not going to leave her with a leaking sink, am I? Anyway, I'm not going running. I told her it would be tonight.

Right on cue, his phone beeped. He glanced over to where it lay on the passenger seat. One new message from Fiona Murphy.

| This evening is perfect xx

A horn beeped and Arlo looked up to see the lights had gone green. He took his foot off the brake and the van lurched forward.

'Don't say it, Leo, don't fucking say it,' he said, out loud, in the van, well aware as always that he was talking only to himself.

Say what, Arly? That if it can wait several hours it doesn't sound like much of an emergency? I wouldn't dream of it. Now come on, we've places to be; move that gearstick down to fourth.

....

Frances observed her daughter, standing at the marble kitchen counter with a beetroot, some fancy lettuce and an open recipe book. She saw Beverley as she was now but also all the versions that had come before. A profound loneliness emanated from her daughter's past selves and she felt sad for how easily they had been discarded.

She was in Cooney because her daughter needed her. Beverley would scorn the idea but, as her mother, Frances knew it intuitively. She had been sitting at her kitchen table last Thursday, as the sun set on her birthday, and it came to her as clear as day: she must go to Cooney. And the urge had still been there the following morning, when the special brownies had worn off.

Her daughter's face was dark as she chopped the vegetables.

They'd been talking about Glass Lake's refusal to expel Woody Whitehead. Again. Frances had spoken to Amelia that evening and she seemed fine; no lasting damage appeared to have been done.

'You think I'm ridiculous,' said Beverley. 'You think I'm over the top. I'm uptight. Go on, just say it.' Beverley's hand went to her chin, where the make-up was starting to wear away and two angry inflamed pimples were breaking through.

'I love you to distraction, *a stór*. That's why I'm here.'

'That boy should not be in Glass Lake. Glass Lake means something and that's not the sort of behaviour it accepts. You don't know Glass Lake. That's why you don't understand.'

'I understand what that school means to you. I know you credit it with all the things people usually credit to their parents. And I'm sorry you were unhappy with my mothering, but it wasn't a coincidence you were sent there,' she said, taking the first batch of chopped beetroot and laying it out on the roasting tray. 'I took that job in Cooney *because* I wanted you to go there. And since you're determined to resent me, I might as well say this now too: I do not believe you are upset with a twelve-year-old boy. At least, not as upset as you think you are. You're annoyed at Malachy. And maybe yourself. You're embarrassed, and you've never dealt well with embarrassment. But nobody expects you to be perfect. You're good enough.'

'You think I'm good ... *enough?*'

'Well now, you've taken my words and given them an entirely different meaning. That's not how I said it.'

'People loved me,' declared her daughter, banging down the knife. 'Everyone else wanted to know about life on set – which actors were bitchy, who was nice – but you never asked. You weren't proud of me.'

'I am immensely proud of you. You're so self-sufficient and capable. They're traits I've been working on for years and they come so effortlessly to you. But you being on television didn't make me any prouder. All I ever wanted was for you to be happy. And I don't think acting made you happy. I certainly don't think that window of fame did. You weren't in it for the right reasons, *a stór*. One

227

day soon, you'll be dead, and it will no longer matter what anyone thought of you. Having people think you're better than them doesn't make you better than them. And no matter what happens, you will always know that and so it will never truly feel good. All that'll matter is that you were impressed by yourself. That you did what you believed was right, that you loved your children, that you cared for those who were vulnerable, that you were the best version of yourself. You're always trying to prove yourself and you're trapped in this image you've created. You're good enough, Beverley, you always were.'

Frances took a deep inhale.

Beverley picked up the knife and resumed chopping. When the beetroot was done, she started on the fancy lettuce.

Whenever Frances started to think she knew her daughter inside out, she reminded herself that there were two goldfish swimming around the floor of what was an otherwise perfect white cube. Beverley still had the ability to surprise.

'I know I'm good enough,' she said, her voice so small it could only have come from her inner child.

It was as much as Frances could ask for.

'Good,' she said, rolling up her sleeves and glancing around the kitchen for a potential source of pots. It was impossible to discern the walls from the cupboards in here. 'What say I make a system-cleansing turmeric grain bowl to go with this? That spice does wonders for the complexion.'

....

Arlo got through the afternoon's work as quickly as he could. He put up shelves for the new woman, Tamara, and he tiled the splashback in Mrs Regan's kitchen without taking a break. When Mrs Regan started talking about how a radiator his dad had installed in her husband's pharmacy was already leaking, he didn't fight it. He just accepted the reduced fee, thanked her politely and left. It was 9 p.m. when he got to Fiona Murphy's house. Depending on the scale of the emergency, he might still have time to see Ella.

Arlo parked the van in Fiona's driveway and took his toolkit from the back. He had a bad feeling that the problem with her sink lay with the water supply line. He'd replaced the drain, examined the pipes, tightened the nuts and bolts. He'd even redone the putty last time he was out. But a leak in the water supply line was a much bigger problem. If that was why she kept having difficulties, he'd be here all night – and even then, there was a good chance it would be beyond his expertise.

When Fiona opened the door, she was dressed, as she sometimes was, in a long silk dressing gown. It was wrapped tightly around her, but it still parted at the bottom and Arlo could see nothing but leg. He crossed the threshold, already blushing and already annoyed at himself.

'I'm sorry I couldn't come sooner,' he said, following her through to the kitchen. Her feet were bare, and he thought for the first time that he should offer to take off his grubby work boots. Maybe this was one of those houses where people didn't wear shoes.

'Not at all,' said Fiona. 'I hope I didn't tear you away from anything important. You weren't on another job, were you?'

'All finished for the day now.'

'Well, that's even worse. Am I interrupting your evening plans? You were probably going to meet someone, go out. It is a Thursday, after all. I know that's the new Friday.'

'No plans,' he said politely. 'Nowhere to go. Nobody to meet.'

'I find that hard to believe,' she said in that sing-song way that made him think she was teasing him. 'You don't have a girlfriend?'

Fiona was friends with Ella's mother. 'Nope,' he said.

'No one?'

'No girlfriend.'

Fiona grinned. 'Good.'

Arlo got down on his hunkers and opened the toolbox. 'I was thinking the problem with the sink might actually be in the supply line,' he said, glancing up, only for his eyeline to be level with the split in her dressing gown. 'I'll have to take up a bit of the skirting to have a look,' he continued, head back in the box. 'Even then it might be hard to say for sure, but if I can't sort it, I have the number for a plumber who owes me a favour and—'

'Oh Arlo, darling. The sink's fine. You did a wonderful job on it last time.'

He blew air up into his face and removed his head from the box. 'Right. Okay, well that's good.' He stood, taking a step back from Fiona and trying not to think about what was or was not under her gown.

'It is,' she said, smiling. 'You always do a wonderful job.'

He did his best to return the smile, but he was starting to get that constricting feeling in his chest. 'So what's, em, what's the emergency?'

Fiona leaned back slightly, her arms reaching behind her so they gripped the edge of the kitchen table. This caused her chest to push against her dressing gown and he was embarrassed to find himself light-headed. He didn't like her. He knew he didn't. So why was he dizzy?

'It's about Woody,' she said.

'Woody? My brother Woody?'

'I'd be surprised if there was another Woody in Cork, wouldn't you? Let alone in Cooney.' She turned around briefly and picked up a phone from the kitchen table. Her phone, Arlo knew, had a Little Miss Fiona cover, but this one had a shiny yellow back plastered with stickers. 'Ciara's at her father's house tonight. He doesn't usually have her on school nights, but I thought it would be better if we could talk about this privately. Where is it?'

She frowned at the screen of her daughter's phone and Arlo felt like every resident of Cooney had their hands around his lungs and they were squeezing at once.

'I heard Woody was the boy involved in the sexting scandal up at the school.'

She made it sound off-hand but of course it wasn't. He said nothing. He couldn't. He just stood there, and she went back to the phone.

'There's been a bit of chatter about it, you probably won't be surprised to hear. I swear Cooney was built on sand and gossip. And petitions. If you went back through the annals, I doubt you'd find any acts about the founding of this town, just a whole load of rumours passed around the various high kings and monks of Ireland.' She looked up again. 'Woody Whitehead and Maeve Maguire. It's only ever a matter of time before the word gets out, isn't it?'

Arlo could not place that name. Maeve Maguire. Fiona said nothing about Amelia Franklin. If they only had the details half right, maybe they weren't so sure. If nobody knew for certain, maybe they'd be reluctant to spread it around.

He could feel Leo pushing to deliver some smart-alecky comeback to that, but he refused to let him in.

'That's not,' he began. 'It's not … That's not right.'

'Look, don't worry, you don't have to say anything about it. I didn't ask you here to catch you out. We're friends. Right?'

She was a customer and he was an employee. He couldn't even bring himself to use her first name.

He nodded.

'Good,' she said, still smiling. 'Which is why I thought you should see this.' She held out the phone. 'I check Ciara's phone every week. Usually it's a cursory check. But after Monday's meeting at the school, and then I heard some things, well, about your brother, at coffee this morning, I thought I should do a deeper dive. I found this in her deleted images. I'm not sure when it was sent exactly but it was saved on …'

He was no longer listening. So much of his attention was trained on the image on the screen that he was barely in the room any more.

'Arlo?'

Fiona's voice was muffled and at a distance. The only thing he heard was the throbbing in his ears.

'Arlo? Arlo?'

He looked up from the screen to where Fiona's mouth and nose were suddenly too large for her head. They were starting to pulsate.

'That is Woody, right?'

The more he looked at them, the more her features no longer seemed to belong to her face. They were coming apart, like the Picasso poster that hung in Ella's bedroom.

'I thought so,' she said, nodding, as he realised he was doing the same. 'I couldn't quite remember what he looked like but the boy in the photo just looked so like your dad and like you.' Fiona laughed. 'His face, I mean. I couldn't speak to the rest.'

'What are you ...? What will you do with this?'

'Oh,' said Fiona, as if it hadn't occurred to her that she might do more with this naked photograph of his little brother than show it to Arlo. 'Well, I'll be talking to Ciara again. She insists it was unsolicited' – Fiona rolled her eyes – 'but I find it hard to believe she didn't send anything in response. She has a bit of a crush on your brother, you know. I think a lot of the girls do. I haven't shown it to her father yet, though I really should. It's just that with him being in the shop all day and trading as much in gossip as meat, I might as well take out an advert in the *Southern Gazette*. The whole town would know by lunchtime tomorrow. I don't really mind people knowing – you know me, I'm an open book – but for you and your family ...' She made a pained expression. 'You've already been through so much. And then, of course, Butcher has such a temper, he'd be up making a show of himself at your door or screaming at your poor mother in the bank. And I wouldn't want that. It's always the mothers who get the blame.'

'So don't tell him.' Arlo's voice squeaked, making it sound more like a question than an order.

Fiona scrunched the lower half of her face in more pained confusion. 'Oh, but I have to. He is her father.' She took the phone back and put it on the table. 'I'd have thought Woody would be more careful, after what happened with Maeve Maguire, and all the attention and drama that brought.' She took a step closer and placed a hand on Arlo's arm. 'I'm sure he's not a *bad* kid, no matter what people say. And I hardly see how this is your mother's fault, or even your father's.'

233

Arlo's head was spinning. He knew the room wasn't swaying, but he couldn't seem to get that through to his inner ear, or wherever it was that controlled his balance. He had been breaking his back trying to turn around the Whiteheads' reputation. He was exhausted from it. His face ached with the constant smiling. It always felt like one step forward, two steps back, but he was still trying. If this got out, that Woody was sending naked photos to multiple girls, they'd be driven out of town with pitchforks.

'Please don't tell him. Please.'

Arlo moved his hands so he was holding her right one in the space between them. There was a flash of surprise, but she didn't pull back.

What was wrong with Woody that he would do this? The parting line of his father's letter swam in his head. *Look after your mother and your brother.* He'd said the same thing the day he was taken away.

He squeezed her hand and implored her: 'Please don't. Please. Just don't say anything, Mrs Murphy – Fiona, Fiona, sorry, Fiona. Don't tell your husband. I'll do anything.'

'My ex-husband.'

'Your ex-husband.' Arlo was nodding too quickly, the dizziness getting worse. This must be what it felt like to float in space, and suddenly have your helmet disappear. 'Don't tell your ex-husband. Please, Fiona. Please.'

'Oh, Arlo, sweetheart. Hush now. It's okay.'

'I'll do whatever you want up here for free for a whole year. I'll clear out your back garden. And I'll talk to Woody. I'll make sure it never happens again, not with Ciara or anyone. But please don't tell anyone. It ... It would kill my mom.'

Fiona's brows nudged ever so slightly closer. He was finding it difficult to look her in the eye; everything on her face seemed too big, almost grotesque, and the more he looked at it, the more stressed he felt.

'I am a sucker for a man who loves his mother,' she said. 'Butcher hated his mother – she is an absolute weapon, but still – that should have been enough to send me flying for the hills.'

'Please,' he said again. 'Please don't say anything.'

'Well ...' Fiona stared into the middle distance over his shoulder, her left hand coming up to join the right so they were clasped around Arlo's. Only where his grasp had been beseeching, hers was gentle. 'I suppose we are friends.'

'Yes,' he replied quickly, his heart pounding. 'Yes, we are.'

'And I wouldn't want you to start getting a hard time in Cooney. I do like you ...'

'And I like you.' He spoke quickly, barely registering that she had taken a step closer and was now moving her fingers ever so slightly against his.

'Do you?' She was in his face. Her nose about three inches from his mouth. She tilted her head up slowly, and it was only at that point that the strangeness of their set-up – standing so close together, holding hands – hit him. She wasn't going to ... Surely she wouldn't—

And then her lips were on his. They pushed his apart and something hard jabbed to get in. It shook him from his daze. Was that Mrs Murphy's *tongue*?

'I'm sorry, no,' he said quickly, as he put his hands on her shoulders and stepped back. 'I have a girlfriend. I'm sorry I said I didn't, but I do.'

A flash in her eyes, an emotion he couldn't quite identify.

'You – you're an attractive woman, Mrs Murphy, Fiona, and maybe if I was older, and didn't have a girlfriend ...'

There was that look again.

For a moment, nobody spoke.

'I was only joking, Arlo,' she said, suddenly breezy, as she returned to her default expression of being in on a private joke. 'You're the one taking it seriously.'

'Right, okay, sorry.'

He was confused, embarrassed, and not sure how the kiss could have been a joke, but fully trusting he was the one who'd misread the situation.

'Sorry,' he said again.

'I suppose you should go see your girlfriend, so.'

'Yes,' he said gratefully. 'Please don't tell anyone.'

'About what?' she asked. 'About Woody, or about our little frisson?'

Arlo had meant about his girlfriend but faced with this choice he wanted to say both. He didn't know what a frisson was, but he was pretty sure whatever had passed between them wasn't it. 'About Woody,' he said, picking a priority.

'I won't.'

He exhaled heavily. 'Thank you, Fiona. Thank you so much.' He picked up his toolbox and felt for the keys in his pocket. 'And I'm sorry for the misunderstanding, if I gave you the impression that I liked you – not that I don't like you, I do like you, but I mean like *that* ...'

Her lips tightened. 'It's fine, Arlo,' she said coolly. 'You really need to stop making such a big deal out of it.'

Ella Belle 9.30 p.m.

Hey. You still planning to call over tonight? My granny might be meditating in the back garden so try not to scare her. X

Ella Belle 11.02 p.m.

It's 11 now so I'm gonna take it you're not calling. I hope you're not working too hard. Good luck tomorrow. Give me a call on the drive to the prison if you want. X

26

......

ABERSTOWN GARDA STATION

I **'m going** out to see the wife,' announced Sergeant Whelan.

'Do you want me to come?' said Joey, hands on his belt once again. 'Or I could go instead?' He pictured himself motoring out to Cooney, making a key discovery and speeding back out to the station with the siren blaring.

Whelan shook his head. 'You've got a second round of interviews to type up. I'm just going to check in. She doesn't appear to have many friends in town. I don't know if anyone is keeping an eye on her.' He pushed himself up, laboriously, and pulled on his jacket. 'The poor woman. Your husband goes to work one day and never comes home. I doubt she thought much harm could come to him. It's got to be one of the safest places to work, doesn't it? A primary school. My eldest is studying to be a teacher and when I think about how he wanted to enter the guards, I'm constantly relieved. Schools, I used to think; nothing all that bad can happen at a school.'

'But his drowning may not have anything to do with the school.'

'Which is another reason I'm going to speak to the wife,' said Whelan, heading for the exit. 'Maybe something has occurred to her – someone with a grudge, or even a reason for him to have been out there. For now, his workplace is just the place he was supposed to be at the very moment that he lost his life.'

'So you don't think there's a connection?'

'That's for us to find out,' replied his boss, one foot out the door. 'I'm hoping we will know, one way or another, today.'

....

Beverley Franklin, parent

I spoke to him the day before. He was helping with the musical - most of the staff were. It was just about that, work stuff. I didn't get the impression he was worried about anything. There was no sense that something bad was about to happen. Is it possible he was having problems at home? Men aren't always the best at addressing their personal issues.

Orla Smith, parent

I'm not as, shall we say, involved as some of the other parents. So I can't exactly say I knew him. Most of my Glass Lake interactions are with my own children's teachers. He seemed nice, though. Are you treating the fall as suspicious? I can't imagine anyone having it in for him.

Ms Cunningham, teacher

It's not the norm to give out progress reports, no. I heard Mr Cafferty was doing it and I told him it wasn't a good idea. You agree to one,

and next thing you know you're doing twenty. He
said he didn't mind. He was really trying with
the parents. Because he was new, I suppose, and
because of the discipline issues. I share a
classroom wall with him, and the truth is they'd
been going on a while. He was doing his best,
but the students just don't want to listen.

27
· · · · · ·

Most of the Glass Lake teachers had a 'yard coat', a heavy-duty jacket worn only when it was their turn to do break-time supervision. The rest of the time, the bulky garments lived in their classrooms. There was no reason yard coats had to be ugly – there were jackets that were both warm and stylish – and Frank Cafferty refused to give in to this trend. His yard coat was a cream trench with tartan lining that Jess had bought him for their second wedding anniversary. He thought of it as his geezer coat.

When the bell went for lunch on Friday afternoon, the sixth-class students leapt from their desks, grabbed their school gaberdines and lined up by the door; it was the one time of day they did what they were supposed to without Frank having to ask, or more often beg. He removed his own coat from where it hung behind his desk. He was on yard duty today.

'Okay, okay, nice and quietly, please,' he called, as the students hopped from one foot to the other, waiting to be set free. Things would be better after lunch, he told himself; they'd settle down once they'd burnt off some energy. 'James,' he said to the child at the top of the line, 'you're going to lead everyone out, all right?'

The tall boy grew taller as he absorbed the temporary responsibility.

A wave of laughter rose behind him and Frank turned, embarrassed to find himself willing it to be aimed at another student, rather than him.

Before he could ask what was so amusing – something he always tried to do in an equally amused voice that suggested he was already in on the joke, so they couldn't turn it on him – Ethan Morton was raising a hand.

'Teacher, what's a ped-oh?'

The sniggering students, mainly boys, laughed louder.

'It's not a ped-oh, you dope,' said one of them. 'It's a pee-do.'

Ethan didn't look any more enlightened. 'What's a pedo?'

'That's not a suitable discussion for right now,' said Frank, the words catching in his throat. 'Right now, we're going out to the yard.'

'Is it a bad word?' asked another student.

'A pedo is someone who fancies children, isn't it, Teacher?'

At the start of the year, he would have engaged them in conversation. But he had learned that the students weren't always asking innocent questions. Often, they were messing with him. He searched the line for the usual suspects, but none of them were laughing. Even Woody was expressionless.

'It's short for paedophile,' said Amelia Franklin. 'That's in the dictionary. It's the same as pedo.'

'I don't want to hear the word again, please,' said Frank. The one time of day he felt any semblance of control over the class and it was slipping through his fingers. 'If you want to know the definition, ask your parents, or check your dictionaries. But I don't want the word used again in this classroom.'

Frank refused to let his mind wander. The students were just testing him, as they always did. The prank calls had subsided – that had been a coincidence too. He made a mental note to phone the parents of the boys who had asked. It was generally best if such things were explained at home. He glanced down the line to Woody, but the boy was messing with the zip on his coat.

'But, Teacher, you're the one using the word.'

He ignored this nonsensical statement and went to open the door. They were forever last out at break-times, often for reasons like this. The more effort Frank made, the worse they seemed to get.

'Yeah, Teacher,' said someone else. 'If you don't like the word, then why is it written on the back of your coat?'

....

Ella Belle 12.13 p.m.
WhatsApp says you haven't read any of these?? U ok? Don't be nervous about today! He's your dad and you've got the moral high ground! I. Love. You. X

....

Lorna Farrell was just contorting herself into the Half Moon Pose, when Fiona came jogging into the studio. She bowed her apologies to Paul, the hot yoga instructor, and Paul smiled as he bowed in return.

'You're late,' whispered Lorna, who was never late for anything. Today, as with most days, she had helped to lay out the yoga mats. She joined her hands together above her head and stretched to the left.

Fiona took the free mat beside her and began to warm up.

'Thought I'd give you a few minutes before I came in and stole Hot Paul's attention.'

Lorna ignored this comment. He was called Hot Paul because he instructed his class in a room heated to above 40 degrees, and because he was attractive. But she had Bill. Who was a *councillor*. And nothing was hotter than power. When Lorna's gaze followed Paul around the room, it was only in search of praise.

'You never turned up last night,' she whispered, as the class stretched out their arms and lowered themselves onto their hunkers. 'I saved you a mat and everything.'

'I told you I mightn't make it.'

'Yes, I know. But you never said for sure, or why. Had you a date?'

'Of sorts.'

Paul passed them now. 'Good, Lorna. Very good.'

She beamed.

He straightened Fiona's arms slightly and moved on.

'Did it go well?' she asked, feeling more generous now. 'Who was it with?'

Fiona tipped her nose as she brought her arms out straight in front of her.

Lorna glanced at her friend, causing her own Awkward Pose to sway. 'Since when are you shy about that stuff? Usually you're singing it from the rooftops.' She gasped, coming down from her tippytoes with a thud. 'Was it *Butcher*?'

Fiona made a face.

'The banker from London?'

'That's long over.'

'Maybe it didn't go well, and that's why you don't want to tell me,' said Lorna, as they crossed all their limbs down into the Eagle Pose.

'Of course it went well,' shot back Fiona. 'I'm just saying it wasn't the banker.'

Lorna made an 'Mm-hmm' sound as she struggled to hold the final step of the pose. It was like vertical twister.

And then, because she could not stand to have her allure questioned, Fiona added: 'If you must know, I've traded him in for a much younger model.'

....

Ella Belle 12.48 p.m.

Are you pissed off with me? Is it about yesterday morning? I'm sorry if I didn't come across as supportive of your decision. I think it's great you're visiting your dad. I think you're great. Please write back.

....

A girl in the front row raised her hand, giving Nuala Patterson a moment's hope that this wouldn't be a drawn-out, painful process.

But alas, the girl had not put her hand up to confess.

'Maybe that word was already there when Teacher bought the coat, but he didn't notice because the shop didn't have one of those mirrors where you can see your back?'

'Thank you, Shona, but Mr Cafferty is perfectly capable of looking in mirrors.'

This drew giggles from the rest of the class and Nuala chanced a glance at Frank Cafferty, who was sitting quietly at his desk, arms wrapped tightly around himself.

Despite her foreboding presence at the top of the room, there was a giddy energy in the class. The children snuck furtive glances at each other and grinned. Ciara Murphy turned her head to the side and nodded vigorously at Ethan Morton. It was, she recognised, an impression of Mr Cafferty.

These were not students who respected their teacher. How had she not noticed? She was slipping this year, and Glass Lake standards were going down with her. *Pedo*. It was such a nasty word, and not one she often heard students use, even in hushed voices. This story was already as good as going around the parent WhatsApp groups and there would be those who, for no reason but their own enjoyment, would speculate on whether there was something to the accusation. It was the sort of rumour that could kill a career. She felt a deep swell of sympathy for the man, and a hard flash of anger at the students sitting before her.

'That's enough,' she shouted, relieving Ethan Morton of his effort to stem the giggles. Ethan, Ciara and every other student looked at her. 'That is absolutely enough. In Glass Lake, we show respect to our teachers and to each other. We do not laugh at anyone. Do you understand?'

The room was silent.

'I have all day,' she said, by which she meant she had forty minutes before the final bell went and she was legally required to send them home. 'And I can wait as long as you can. We'll stay here all night if we have to.'

The suggestion was so ludicrous, she was surprised nobody laughed.

Her eyes roamed the room, looking for a guilty face. A small movement caught her attention. Woody Whitehead was shaking his head at Maeve Maguire, who was seated beside him.

'Maeve?' she said, as the girl gave a start. 'Have you anything to tell me?'

'No, Principal Patterson.'

Another flicker of action, and her gaze moved to the desk right in front of her.

'Amelia? How about you?'

'No, Principal Patterson,' said the pretty girl, as her neighbour smiled.

'What's so funny now, Ciara?'

The child stopped giggling and looked straight ahead.

Nuala paced in front of the whiteboard as the students sat staring at their desks or out the window or into space. In her twenty-two years at the helm, Nuala had dealt with countless incidents of bullying and many horrible words scrawled across bags and coats and even shoes, but none of those items had ever belonged to a teacher. Had Mr Cafferty been too nice? Too soft?

Time passed and nobody spoke. So settled in the silence were the children that when Ethan Morton knocked a pen on to the ground, several of them jumped.

Nuala decided to go for broke. 'As I'm sure you know, we have CCTV cameras in this classroom.' She pointed to the ceiling. The students turned to look at the high-tech sprinkler that hung a foot from the fire alarm. 'And if I do not get a confession in the next five minutes, we will be checking that, and I can guarantee you the punishment will be much more severe.'

Again, they exchanged glances. There was less smirking this time. Several of them looked worried. Perhaps this was a story worth rolling out more generally, like the threat of Santa's omnipresent elves.

The students shifted in their seats and murmurs of a disagreement rose from Woody and Maeve.

'Maeve?' said Nuala. 'Something to say?'

The girl's voice quivered. But it was Woody who finally spoke.

'Say that again, Woody? I didn't hear you.'

....

> Ella Belle 1.55 p.m.
> I know you're probably in there now, but I'd really like to talk to you. Maybe it's a problem with your phone. If not, can you ring me back when you get a chance? XXX

....

Lorna was trying to figure out what sort of coffee would feel like a treat but not completely undo all the good work done during hot yoga. She burnt off an estimated 500 calories during a session and did six sessions a week. She needed to lose 42,000 calories in order to drop a dress size before December. She tried to hold these numbers in her head while she counted backwards to when she first bought a 'bundle' of Hot Paul classes.

'I only drink Americanos,' said Fiona, who'd already ordered hers. 'If I don't know what the other stuff tastes like, then I can't lust after it.'

Lorna found it impossible to do maths and maintain a conversation, so she ordered the same. She would console herself with a generous dollop of full-fat milk.

'Is that the woman Beverley used to work with?' she half-whispered, as they collected their beverages from the end of the counter.

Fiona followed her gaze to the window seat. 'It is. Tamara Watson. You know I found her a house? Nice woman. Let's go and say hello.'

Lorna wanted to talk to Fiona alone, to grill her about this new mystery man. She was being uncharacteristically coy. But before she could object, they were heading towards the small circular table where the woman was reading a magazine and enjoying one of the Strand's legendary flapjacks. This cheered Lorna up slightly. Perhaps she'd offer them a piece.

'Tamara? Hi.'

She looked up from her magazine. 'Fiona! How are you? I've been meaning to call you.'

'Tamara Watson, this is Lorna Farrell. Lorna, this is Tamara.'

'We met briefly at the parents' night, hi. I love your dress,' said Lorna, who liked to start every new acquaintance with a compliment.

'Thank you,' replied Tamara, sitting up straight and closing over the magazine. She had an enviable figure. The breasts of a twenty-year-old.

If Lorna got to know her better, she'd ask who did her work.

'Fiona, I wanted to thank you for recommending that handyman. Arlo? I find flat-pack furniture more painful than childbirth, but he put my bookcases together in record time yesterday evening. He even managed to get a few extra shelves up. He's amazing.'

Lorna did not agree with hiring Arlo Whitehead. She was with Beverley on this entirely and would never let the lad set foot in her house. Charlie Whitehead was the reason the Roches had moved away, which was the reason Cooney GAA had been relegated at the quarter finals. As far as any right-minded resident was concerned, hiring a Whitehead was a betrayal of the town.

'I wanted him to do my son's desk too, but he'd another job to get to – at nine on a Thursday night,' Tamara continued. 'He must be in demand.'

Bill did, very occasionally, get Arlo to do jobs in the garden, but that was entirely different; he never came *inside*.

'That was me, I'm afraid,' said Fiona. 'I took him away from you.'

'Last night?'

Fiona nodded, dipping her chin slightly as she brought her coffee cup up.

'Well, it's fine,' said Tamara. 'He was busy today too, but he's coming back to finish the job next week.'

It took Lorna a moment, but eventually she caught up.

'Wait. Last night?' She turned to Fiona. 'Last night when you should have been at yoga? I thought you said you didn't make it because—' Her friend's eyes were trained on the white lid of her disposable cup. 'Oh my God. Oh. My. God! Is *Arlo Whitehead* the younger man?'

Fiona shook her head as she pulled her fingers across her mouth. 'My lips are sealed.'

·······················

Ella Belle 2.45 p.m.
Okay, I'm kind of worried now. I'm going to try you on email

28
• • • • • •

Arlo had been sitting outside the prison for forty minutes. His visitor timeslot was for 3 p.m. If he didn't get out of the van soon, he was going to miss it. He looked in the rear-view mirror and told himself to take three slow breaths. Things must have been bad because even Leo was trying to help.

Inhale ... Exhale ... Inhale ... Exhale ...

Where did you learn that?

Just shut up and breathe.

This vat of guilt sat on the bed of his stomach and every time he tried to identify its origin – neglect of Woody? Betrayal of Ella? Betrayal of his father? – another possibility popped into his head.

His phone beeped.

Four missed calls, eight new messages, and now, an email notification.

He unlocked his phone, careful not to click into WhatsApp. Until he figured out how to explain himself, he couldn't let Ella know he had read them.

Is this the first email I've sent you since school? Weird. I think there's something up with your phone. Or at least I'm hoping that's the problem. I can't get through to you.

Is everything okay? Have you seen your dad yet?

Even if you're annoyed at me over something, will you just get in touch to say you're okay? It's stupid I know, but I'm worried.

So, get in touch – by phone or email or like messenger owl. Whatever!

El x

The vat threatened to overflow.

Arlo needed to explain to Ella, in person, what had happened with Fiona Murphy. He was supposed to call to her last night, but for some reason he couldn't do it. He'd gone straight home and had a long shower. *She* kissed *him*. He hadn't started anything; he hadn't done anything wrong. He didn't even like her! He had taken her hand first, but that was different, he hadn't done it in a ... in a *sexual* way. Maybe Fiona thought he had? He'd been trying to save Woody. But the way she teased him, the way she smiled ... Had it been his fault?

He couldn't bring himself to respond to Ella, to make casual chitchat, until he'd explained what had happened. He needed to be honest with her; it didn't feel good otherwise. He would go straight from the prison to her house. She'd understand why he hadn't replied then, and hopefully she'd admire him for not being a fraud.

It was five to three now. He had to get out of the van.

Out on the tarmac, he checked the pits of his shirt for sweat stains and fixed the tie that he'd last worn to Mike Roche's funeral. He followed the signs out of the car park, turning left to the visitors' entrance of the modern, white building. He pushed his way through the glass doors into a waiting area and presented himself at the reception desk. The guard took his details, checked his driver's licence, and gave him a sheet of paper. He asked him to empty his pockets and pointed him towards a locker where he could leave his phone and keys. He made a joke about young lads not liking to be parted from their phones, but Arlo had never been happier to see the thing go. He placed his boots into a plastic tray and walked quickly through the full-body scanner. He was given a once-over with a hand-held device, and then again with another. 'It's like the airport,' he said nervously.

One of them smiled. 'It's looking for drugs.'

Around the next corner was a big dog that sniffed at his trousers and boots. And even though he knew he wasn't carrying any drugs, had never carried any drugs, he could feel the sweat forming on his brow.

A different guard led him down a tiled corridor, past cameras and thick doors. It had the same smell as his secondary school, that peculiar mix of must and chemical cleaners. The guard stopped at a small desk and pushed open a heavy cream door.

'Here we are now, the family room.'

Whatever Arlo had expected, it wasn't this.

The room was bright and airy, with a large colourful mural painted on to three of the walls. There were boxes filled with toys and a play kitchen, which was missing one of its hobs but otherwise in good nick. The fourth wall was taken over by a fortified Perspex hut, where two guards sat, laughing at something. That bit was more what he'd had in mind.

One other group was already waiting: a woman and her two young sons. They sat on low green chairs at a matching children's table.

The guard nodded him towards a similar set-up, only red, then waved to the two men in the little hut and left. The chair was so low that Arlo's knees almost came up to his face. When nobody was looking, he brought his head down and sniffed both armpits then straightened his tie again. He'd had the whole morning to think about it, and he hadn't a clue what he was going to say.

The youngest son in the other group took a tentative step towards the kitchen, but his mom shook her head. His elder brother went and brought him back, catching Arlo's eye and nodding solemnly. He nodded back. They were both just sons, waiting on their fathers.

Then the door opened, and two more prison guards appeared, accompanied by his dad.

'That's him,' said Charlie Whitehead to one of the men. 'That's my son.'

He said it with such pride, such admiration, that Arlo instantly pinked, but he also grinned.

Before he could ask if touching was allowed, his dad was across the room, engulfing him in a bear hug. 'Oh, I have missed you,' he said in his big, deep, reassuring voice, the words slightly muffled against Arlo's ear. 'I have missed you something awful.' He pulled back, looked at his son. Arlo did his best to arrange his awkward face, but Charlie was already reaching for him again. This time the hug was tighter, longer. Arlo felt a tingle in his throat. He was relieved when his father let go. A second longer and he'd have erupted into tears.

'Come on,' said Charlie, pulling him back down on to the bright red plastic chairs. 'I asked for the family room. You're probably a bit old for all of this but it's the nicest room, and you'll always be my little boy. And' – Charlie brought his head forward to rest on his right knee – 'these seats come with built-in chin rests; handy, eh?'

Arlo laughed. It was pathetic how comforting his father's presence was, even though he was visiting him in a medium-security facility where he had power over absolutely nothing.

All possible conversation topics vanished from his head. 'How ... how are you?'

'I'm a lot better for seeing you. Thanks for coming. I know it can't be easy to see your dad in a place like this.'

Arlo shook his head. 'Nah,' he said, clumsily, awkwardly. He didn't want his dad thanking him. 'I'm sorry I didn't come sooner. I know I should have. I meant to. I just ...'

The door opened again, and another prisoner was brought in. This man had none of the bonhomie or presence of his dad. He walked over to what was presumably his wife and children. He shook the boys' hands, even though the eldest couldn't have been more than eight.

'So, tell me all the news,' said Charlie, rubbing his hands together. 'How are you? How's the business going? Your mom said you were working all hours. Although that was a while ago now. Is it still going well? Tell me everything. I want to hear it all.'

He noticed now that his father's hair was parted to one side, slicked down with gel or wax. This display of effort increased the pressure.

Arlo told him about work, doing his best to match his dad's energy as he spoke. He omitted all tales of the less courteous clients and the complaints about Charlie's previous supposedly shoddy work, instead discussing the details of certain jobs and asking for advice on others.

'The van's been acting up,' he said. 'Just the last few days. It goes to give out just before I bring it to a stop.'

'Could be the brake pads. Have you had them looked at recently? I don't think I had them changed in a while. Yeah, could be that.'

'Okay, I'll have it looked at. Thanks.'

'Bring it to Dodger's place, tell him you're my son.'

Arlo nodded. Dodger had called to their house three weeks after his dad was sent away and said that if they didn't pay the €400 Charlie owed him, he'd take the wheels off the van himself. 'I'll do that. Thanks.'

'He'll see you right.'

Charlie smiled. So Arlo did too.

'How's Woody?'

'Good,' he said automatically. 'He's fully transitioned into moody teenager and spends most of his time playing computer games in his room, but he's in the musical this year, so he's not a total hermit.'

'Woody's in the musical? Good boy, Woody. That's great. And is he still hanging out with his friends? Ethan and James?'

'I don't think they're in the house as much,' Arlo said, struggling to recall when he'd last seen his brother hanging around with either boy, or anyone else. 'There was the incident in the school with the photos, but I think that's going to blow over. Mom's probably told you all that already.'

Charlie shook his head. 'I haven't spoken to your mom in a while.'

'Oh.' His face started to heat up. 'It's nothing to worry about. He was sending photos to another girl in his class – and she was sending them to him – but it's all fine.'

'You're looking after it?'

'Yeah,' said Arlo, still feeling hot. 'I'm sorting it.'

Charlie nodded. 'Good. How is your mom? Is she seeing her friends?'

'I think she sees some people from work ...' Arlo wasn't going to tell his dad that the only person his mother ever mentioned was her boss, George. If he were the one in jail and someone told him that about Ella and Leo, he would drive himself crazy thinking about it.

'And how about you?'

'Oh, I'm good, great, grand.'

'Have you heard from Leo?'

'I ... no. I haven't heard from him. I don't think I will.'

'That's understandable.'

'Yeah,' said Arlo breathlessly.

'And are you hanging out with anyone else?'

'Why are you so concerned about who we're seeing?'

Charlie shrugged. 'I guess I just want to know youse have support. So, are you? Anyone else from school? A *girlfriend*?'

He looked at his grinning dad in shock. How could he tell? Arlo felt a fresh wave of guilt that he should be embarking on the great love affair of his life while his dad sat in jail, married to a woman who could barely find the will to say something good about him, never mind take his calls.

'Nobody serious,' he said eventually.

'Playing the field? That's my boy. It's the only way to have it when you're young.'

'Yeah.' Another breathless scoff.

'Ten minutes, folks,' called one of the guards, sticking his head out from the hatch.

Arlo wanted to tell his dad all about Ella and her perfect face and how smart she was and how funny. He wanted to get his advice on

Fiona Murphy. His father would put it in perspective. He'd tell Arlo he had nothing to feel guilty about, and Arlo would believe him. Even on the worst night of their lives, when Arlo could do nothing but sob, he'd had a plan.

'I'm really sorry you're in here,' he said, suddenly, keeping his gaze on his father's hands, which had always been so solid and manly. His own fingers were long and thin and devoid of hair.

'It's not your fault, Arlo,' replied his dad calmly.

'Except that it is. We both know that it is.'

29
· · · · · ·

Beverley Franklin had to read the message twice. In her quest to be first with news, Lorna had a habit of getting things arseways. But this, bizarrely, made a lot of sense.

'What is it?' said her mother, who was hunkered down on the kitchen floor, watching the goldfish chase each other. Ella was sitting on the opposite side of the kitchen island to Beverley, a chicken sandwich in front of her. Her daughter had been glued to her phone since dinner the night before. She'd skipped her morning lecture, again, supposedly to spend time with her grandmother, but she'd barely looked up from the screen. They were having lunch late because it had taken this long to coax Ella around to eating. Although she'd yet to have a bite.

'A friend, she's done something ridiculous,' said Beverley, before waving a hand. 'It doesn't matter. You don't know her.'

'You can't say "ridiculous" and then not tell us. You've got our attention now, hasn't she, Ella?'

'Mm.'

Frances puckered her lips and blew a kiss to the fish, before standing and returning to the island.

Beverley hadn't meant to put a mini aquarium in the middle of her kitchen, *obviously*. She'd written 'fishbone', indicating the

259

zigzag pattern she wanted for the marble, but the moronic builder had read 'fishbowl'. She'd have made him rip the thing out, only Malachy had wanted her to hire an interior designer from day one, so she had to pretend two stinky, slimy creatures in the middle of her pristine kitchen was exactly what she'd been dreaming of all along.

'Well, you have my attention anyway,' said Frances, retaking her seat. 'Come on, tell us.'

She was trying to make more of an effort with her mother, now that she knew the trip was finite – she was leaving Monday morning – and dinner last night – just her, her mother and the girls – hadn't been completely awful.

'Fiona Murphy,' she said eventually. 'She was at the Strand café yesterday, lots of cheap charm bracelets and more mismatched gold around her neck. "Friend" isn't actually the right term. She's a Laker, and a particularly silly one.'

'Yes, the woman who ran after us when we were leaving to ask if her daughter could have a solo in the musical. She has quite an aggressive aura, I have to say. Green and tan. You don't often see that.'

'That's her.' Fiona was still trying to leverage whatever sordid details she knew about Beverley's pivot away from Southern Pharmaceuticals, but Ciara Murphy hadn't a note in her head and Beverley would not allow the musical to suffer. 'She's quite an aggressive person generally. She used to be married to one of the butchers in town. He's the same. But that ended a couple of years ago. She's had a few relationships, if you could call them that. Anyway, now it seems she's got a new man. Well, a new boy would be more accurate. She's making a fool of herself.'

'Nothing wrong with a younger lover,' said Frances, a glint in her eye that Beverley chose to ignore.

'It's not just his age,' she said, rereading the message for a third time. 'He's not the sort of person you want in your life full stop. His dad was the one who killed that boy out on Reilly's Pass in February, and his brother was the one soliciting photographs from Amelia.'

Well, there you go. Miracles were possible. Ella had finally looked up from her phone.

'Arlo Whitehead,' Beverley extrapolated for the benefit of her mother. 'You know, the boy you tantric-ed into opening the storage closet at Glass Lake. He does a lot of work for Fiona, out at her house. It seems that's not all he does for her.'

'No,' said Ella softly.

'Of course,' said Beverley. 'He was in your class. Sorry, darling, this probably isn't appropriate conversation. I don't think it's a relationship or anything. But yes, they seem to have had some sort of *liaison* last night. Fiona could never keep something like that to herself, much as we might like her to. But knowing her, it will all be over before ...'

Ella climbed down from her stool and left the room.

'...we know it.' Beverley sighed. 'Don't say goodbye or anything, darling.'

'Beverley,' said Frances.

'What? I've given up understanding that girl's moods.'

'Arlo Whitehead?'

'Yes.' Beverley paused. 'Why? Do you know something more about him?'

'Do you not?'

Beverley frowned. 'Is this a cosmic thing? Had he a pink aura or something?'

'Beverley.'

'*What?*'

'Arlo Whitehead is the love of your daughter's life. He's been sneaking in and out of your house for months.'

'*Excuse me, what?*' said Beverley, in a voice so high-pitched she sounded like Lorna Farrell. 'No.'

'Yes.'

'There's no way. No way. You're getting mixed up.'

'Beverley.' Her mother laid a hand on hers. 'I've been here less than two days and I've seen him. How have you not?'

....

'It's not that bad in here. The food is pretty good, and my cellmate used to be a roadie for the Stones. Or at least that's what he says – he's not the kind of man you challenge. Either way, he's got good stories.' Charlie flashed him the grin that had once made him so popular with the women of Cooney. 'You really don't need to feel bad for me, Arlo.'

They might be in the family room, but he was not a child. Prison was always bad. That was the whole point of it. 'I see it happening in slow motion,' he said. 'I've heard people say that, in films and stuff, but I never really believed it, that you could actually see a memory that clearly, but I do. Now it happens when I'm drifting off to sleep, or when I'm driving and my mind is empty. It jumps back in. And I hear Leo's voice in my head. Sometimes I think I'm going crazy.'

'I know,' said Charlie, legs pulled back into him on the low plastic chair. 'I see it too.'

Arlo shook his head. 'No, but I see the road. The rain splattering on the tarmac, bouncing off the bonnet, the wipers on Mom's Volvo going ninety and getting nowhere. The music is playing and the chorus has just cut in – I can *hear* it, Dad, and the "Welcome to Cooney" sign is up ahead, and I see all this in one micro-second, and then in the next we're gone, the car is swerving off the road and there's nothing I can do. I know this terrible thing is happening, but I can't stop it. I can't get a firm grasp on the steering wheel. It's too late. It's all dark grass and sky. Even when I'm lying in bed at night, I feel my body turning.'

His dad was nodding. He'd been nodding the whole time, and Arlo felt himself getting annoyed.

'I know,' said Charlie. 'It happens to me too, especially when I'm falling asleep. I hear the wheels skidding. I see Mike flying up against the side of the car. It's okay.'

'But it's not the same!'

'Why isn't it?'

He leaned in, even though the guards weren't remotely interested in their conversation. 'Because we didn't have the same view, Dad. You weren't even sitting in the front seat.'

'Arlo.'

The tingle in his throat and nose again. He swallowed it down. 'You were in the back. You weren't the one driving, so just for a second stop pretending you were and let me take some responsibility.'

'Arlo,' he repeated more softly. 'I was driving. We agreed that on the night. I was driving.' He dipped his head down to catch his son's eyes.

To Arlo's horror, tears started trickling down his cheeks. 'I shouldn't have got drunk.'

His dad laughed. 'None of us should.'

'It was my responsibility and I fucked up. I'm so sorry, Dad. I'm so sorry you're in here. It's my fault. It's all my fault. I should have told you we'd all been drinking, that Mike had snuck some in.' He rubbed at his face with the back of his hand. He couldn't bring himself to look around the room. 'I lied to you and I ruined your life and I'm so fucking sorry.'

When he managed to look up, his dad was shaking his head. Gently, kindly. He was looking at him with unabashed love and Arlo was jealous of his ability to express emotions and still be a man. Arlo was capable of neither.

The guards were making moves now and the other prisoner had said goodbye to his family.

He hoped he hadn't shaken the boys' hands again. He hoped he'd given them a hug.

'Arlo?'

'No, don't say something nice. I know you're going to say something nice.'

'Arlo?'

'No.'

'Arlo?'

He looked at his dad and he felt the guards moving and suddenly he was frightened. This was all about to be over. His dad was going to go and Arlo would be right back where he deserved, all alone, scrambling to rescue something from a mess entirely of his own making.

'I love you.'

'Dad,' he pleaded.

'I look at photos of you in here sometimes and I get a fright. I think, Jesus, am I having a heart attack? That's how strong the feeling is. It's like my heart physically lurches forward, trying to get closer to the image of you. I love you and I feel it so keenly that I'd happily die of it. I'd be fucking honoured, actually.'

Arlo laughed in spite of himself, snot threatening to escape now too. He bit the inside of his cheek and blew air up into his eyes.

'It doesn't matter who was driving, Arlo. It was still my fault. I was the adult and I was drunk. You were all underage.'

'You shouldn't have to cover—'

'Shhh!'

'Come on now, Charlie, time to finish up.'

'No bother, Steve. Just saying goodbye to the young lad. Did I tell you he was a musician?'

'Is that right?' said the guard, whose nose hovered in front of his face, just as Fiona's had done last night. 'What do you play, son?'

Arlo had to look away.

'The bass,' said Charlie. 'He's very good.'

He could barely play three consecutive cords when his dad went away and he'd probably gotten worse since.

'Very good,' echoed the guard, shifting his weight. 'Right, so.'

Charlie stood, and Arlo did the same.

His dad engulfed him in a final embrace. This time Arlo hugged him back. Charlie's voice was at his ear again, muffled and insistent. 'You look after Woody and your mother. Let me do the rest.'

....

Nuala Patterson hadn't spoken a word to Connie Whitehead for more than eight months and now she'd had to phone her twice in as many weeks. As soon as Nuala explained why she was calling, Connie was overcome with concern.

'Are you sure it was Woody? I don't think I've ever heard him utter that word. The teacher's jumper? No, his jacket. When did this happen? And you're sure it was him?'

They made an appointment for Connie to come and see her on Monday and then Nuala hung up. She was tired. She had spoken to Leo for the first time in weeks last night. He'd finally agreed to take her call, and he had been worse than she feared: bitter and angry and completely incapable of counting his blessings. Three times, he'd reminded her he was in a wheelchair, as if it excused everything else. If she was any sort of mother, she'd drive to Dublin and give Leo a good talking-to, remind him how other people's lives had ended up – or just ended. But she wasn't a good mother. She was a coward. And he knew that, which only made his anger towards her worse.

The last bell rang, and the students left the building. She powered off her laptop and gathered up several files to tackle over the weekend, though in her heart-of-hearts she knew she'd be returning on Monday with the same folders unopened.

She was just lacing up her runners when there was a knock on her door.

'Oh, Cian, hello.'

'Do you have a moment?' asked the doctor, who was carrying a couple of sheets of paper in one hand and his black box in the other.

'Of course, come in,' she said, hurriedly looping a knot and standing. 'Oh, shoot. I was meant to come and fix up with you, wasn't I? I completely forgot. I have your payment here.' She rustled through the loose pages on her desk until she found the envelope Mairead had labelled 'Dr O'Sullivan'. 'Thank you so much, again, for doing this. We're very appreciative. How was your second session? Fruitful?' She leaned forward and removed a couple of the pages that had spilled from her desk on to the chair on the far side. 'Do you want to sit?'

'I'm fine,' he said, placing the box on the seat instead.

'Did that work?' asked Nuala. 'Did they tell you all their secrets?'

'Yes.'

'Well, good.'

'That's why I'm here.'

She frowned.

'This afternoon I spoke to the class about the dangers of putting images online or sending them to someone else. Not explicitly about sexting but generally about privacy and how they might think they're sending a photo to one person, but they can never be sure of that. The focus is really on feeling comfortable and keeping themselves safe and happy.'

'Okay ...'

'I asked if they had ever shared material that they wouldn't like to get out into the wider world. Nobody put their hand up. That's pretty common among pre-pubescent and pubescent children, particularly in a mixed class.'

Nuala nodded. She had no idea where this was going, but she knew she wouldn't like it.

'So, I invited them to use the box. It worked well yesterday for any questions they had. I asked them to write down whatever they would like to tell me on this subject and to put it in the box. I'd marked the corners of the slips of paper, so I knew who they were coming from. I didn't get to look at the slips until the class was over. And now I'm thinking I should do a third session.'

'Oh, well, I'm not sure we have the funds, but I can check ... Why, though? What did they say?'

'Maeve wasn't the only girl who sent Woody a nude photograph.'

Nuala blew air out through her lips. She'd had enough of Woody Whitehead for one day. For one lifetime.

'Let me guess ... Ciara Murphy?'

He looked down at his sheets of paper. 'Yes.'

Nuala nodded. This was all she needed. 'Thanks for letting me know. I'll call her parents.'

'Any other guesses, or shall I just tell you?'

'How do you mean?'

'Several girls said they sent him naked photos of themselves.'

Nuala frowned. 'How many is several?'

The doctor looked at the piece of paper again, which she now saw was a list.

'Three? *Four?* I refuse to guess more than four ...'

'Seven.'

'*Seven?*'

'And three others received photos of him but didn't send any in return.'

'Ten students! He sent nudes to *ten female students*? Jesus Christ. That must be some sort of record. There can't be more than fifteen girls in the whole class.'

'Fourteen.'

'Fuck. Fuck! Sorry, Cian.'

The man shook his head. 'It is worrying behaviour.'

That was a lot of parents to phone. And as soon as she did, they'd be ramming on her door, be that at school or at home. Could she put that off to Monday morning? She could certainly do her best.

Ten, though. *Ten.* Was there something wrong with the boy? A chill ran through Nuala. When the Lakers found out about this, there would be war. There was no way Beverley Franklin would let it go now.

Woody Whitehead. Of all the students. Would she never be free of that family?

'Are you sure they were all from Woody?'

The doctor nodded. 'Every single one.'

30
· · · · · ·

Joey had finally finished typing up the entire day's statements and was reading back over them. He kept hoping the pathology office would call with their initial findings and, in the sergeant's absence, it would be up to him to handle it. But the phone hadn't rung since Whelan headed off to see the wife.

He finished one transcript and began reading over the next. Halfway down the page, he noticed something. He flicked back a few files and saw the same thing again. Different witnesses referring to different instances, but they were both making the same point. He allowed himself a dramatic gasp, then jumped to his feet. He hiked his trousers up so far that he gave himself a mild wedgy. Ignoring the pain, he lunged across the table for the phone.

'What is it?' barked Whelan, answering on the squad car's Bluetooth system after the first ring.

'Sorry to disturb you, sir, but I'm just after noticing something and I think it could be important.'

'Spit it out, Delaney. I'm about to go into the house.'

'A couple of our witnesses mentioned there being animosity between our man and another Glass Lake employee. Seems there was a bit of bad blood, though I'm not sure why.'

Down the line, Joey heard the muffled sound of wind and the low beep of the squad car being locked from the outside.

'Is that worth investigating?'

'How the bloody hell would I know?'

'Sir?'

'Call them in, Delaney!'

'So, I have permission to conduct supplementary questioning?'

'Yes, you have ... Jesus wept. Just get to the bottom of it and leave me alone!'

The line went dead but Joey felt only triumph. Finally, he had a lead.

....

Christine Maguire, parent

If you'd told me a few days ago that I'd be in here speaking to you about something terrible happening to someone from Glass Lake, I'd have put money on Woody Whitehead. Isn't that awful? He's only a child. But try telling that to the Lakers. I presume you heard what happened at the school on Monday? Absolute anarchy. You'd have a real whodunnit on your hands if Woody was the subject of your investigation, because the suspect list would be long, and the Lakers would be top of it.

Lorna Farrell, parent

It's a blessing he doesn't have children. I'm not saying being a parent always makes you a

better person, but let's be honest: it would
make his death more tragic. I saw him earlier
in the day, talking to Nuala Patterson down by
Cooney Pier. It looked like they were arguing,
which I thought was strange. I gave the horn a
little toot to say, 'hello', and I saw Nuala see
me, but she didn't so much as wave. That's the
only bit that wasn't suspicious. The woman has
always been doggedly rude.

Nuala Patterson, principal
We were discussing school business, all entirely
mundane. So mundane, in fact, that I can barely
remember a word of it. Lorna Farrell told you
that, didn't she? She still hasn't forgiven me
for what happened at Glass Lake on Monday.

31
......

'Lights, *a stór*! Lights!' Frances cried from the passenger seat. Beverley Franklin brought the Range Rover to a sudden stop, causing her body to strain against the seatbelt and the burning sensation to return to her chest.

The traffic control had never flashed orange. It had gone from green to red with absolutely no warning. She could have sworn it.

Frances exhaled just as her suitcase rolled on to its side on the back seat and tumbled down on to the floor.

'Good thing I put my vagina in the boot,' she said cheerfully.

The students of her three-day tantric workshop had been so invigorated by Frances' teachings ('Invigorated' was her mother's word) that they'd clubbed together and bought her a large glass sculpture shaped like a vagina. Frances said it was abstract, but there was nothing abstract about the raw flesh tones or the wide, open slit. It was hand blown, which surprisingly was not more innuendo but an actual term for how the glass was moulded. Frances offered to leave it with her daughter as a thank-you for her hospitality – 'You could put it on the hall table, throw your keys into it' – but Beverley had packed it up this morning

273

and left it by the front door with the rest of her mother's things.

'I must get Bill Farrell to check these traffic lights,' she muttered. If there was something wrong with the colour filter, it would need to be fixed. Cooney did not want another traffic accident.

The lights went green and she started the engine again. 'Isn't it amazing, how one family, or really one boy, can wreak so much havoc and cause so much destruction in one town?'

'Oh, now. You're not talking about Arlo Whitehead again, are you?'

'It's Monday. That means it's three days since Ella stepped foot out of her bedroom.'

'It's not quite that bad. She has used the toilet, and she came down to say goodbye to me this morning ...'

'She's miserable. And it's all that gigolo's fault. Fiona Murphy's the same age as his mother, for Christ's sake!'

'It's hard to stand by when your daughter's in pain, I know. And it's hard to offer help and have it rejected at every turn. But at least Ella knows she's hurting, and that is the first step to healing. Now you said you were going to leave it alone.'

Beverley had said no such thing. She had no choice but to leave Ella alone. Her daughter had locked herself away after Friday's accidental revelation about her cheating boyfriend.

Boyfriend! The word wailed in her head. How could Ella have a *boyfriend* and Beverley not know? They used to tell each other everything. She was hurt and bewildered by her daughter keeping the relationship secret, and maybe a little disappointed – a Whitehead! Of all people! – but she wasn't angry at her. That was reserved entirely for the gangly lothario.

'Lights, Beverley!' Frances screamed, as the car came to another sudden stop, the suitcase bouncing about in the back. 'Sweet heavens above!'

'I'm going around to his house after I drop you to the station,' she said, as her mother groaned.

'Beverley, no. He probably won't be there.'

'Well then, I'll talk to his mother. When we're done discussing Arlo, we'll move on to her other depraved son. So many daughters to exploit; so little time.' She brought her right hand to her chest. 'You don't have any Rennie on you, do you?'

'You know I only use home remedies, crumpet.'

'Well, have you any hocus-pocus potions for heartburn?'

'Afraid not.'

Beverley straightened her back. Righting her posture helped. 'I'll drop you at the station, swing by Regan's Chemist, and then it's on to the Whiteheads for a little *tête à tête*.'

'Ella won't thank you for it.'

Beverley lived in constant fear of losing her daughters, of one day waking up to find they no longer wanted to have anything to do with her. It wasn't just a fear, it was an expectation. This was why she'd wanted to have several children – to increase her chances of being loved. Malachy had dismissed the idea entirely. Franklins had two children, no more no less. He said large families were trashy, which meant Beverley was trashy, although she'd known that already.

'I can't get my head around her stubbornness sometimes,' she said, turning on to Station Road. 'Amelia is so much easier; she's a lot more like me.'

Frances laughed and Beverley, who felt exposed enough already, threw her a look.

'I'm sorry, *a stór*. I'm not laughing at you; it's just the idea that you're more like Amelia than Ella.'

'I am. Ella's so headstrong, it's impossible to tell her anything.'

'I agree,' said Frances, the smile audible. 'I haven't met a teenager as single-minded since you turned thirteen.'

The train station came into view. Her mother would take a commuter train into the city, and then on to Dublin. Beverley had bought her a first-class ticket, only for her mother to remind her she had the travel pass.

'I was listening to an item on the radio the other day,' said Frances. 'They had this doctor on and she was very interesting.'

'A real doctor?'

'Yes.'

'A medical one?'

'Yes, of course a medical one. I'm not about to give you a report on tribal cures from the depths of the Amazon rain forest.'

Beverley shrugged as she turned her head from side to side, looking for a parking space. 'I never know with you.'

'Anyway, she was talking about eating disorders in older people, particularly women. You won't fit in there.'

'Yes, I know.'

'This doctor was saying how there's been a huge increase in diagnoses among over thirty-fives in the past decade. While teenage rates are pretty constant, older demographics have seen a surge. They can't be sure if these women are developing eating disorders for the first time, or if they're flaring up again after years of being dormant, or if maybe they were active all along but the women are finally seeking help.' She felt her mother's eyes on her. She kept her own trained on the parking lot. 'Traumatic life events can trigger them. You know, divorces, or deaths, or even a marital infidelity.'

She stalled the car again, closer to the station. It would be a bit of a squeeze, but she'd manage it. She started to reverse slightly.

'Crumpet, you might get the car in, but you won't get me out. I don't know if you've noticed, but I need a bit of wiggle room.'

Beverley drove on.

'What really surprised me was that eating disorders are more dangerous when you're older. Did you know that? You don't have the reserve of nutrients and the bone density you have in your youth, and your heart finds it more difficult to cope with the weight loss.'

'I haven't lost any weight, Mother,' said Beverley. 'I've been exactly the same weight for the past eight years.' Nine stone, two pounds. It was annoying that she had stalled so close to a nice round number, but it refused to go any lower. It would happily climb, of course, not that she'd let it.

'I didn't say you had,' replied her mother. The breezy innocence made her want to throw Frances and her collection of ornamental reproductive parts out of the car. 'And actually, weight loss isn't a huge symptom in older people. The metabolism starts to stall.'

Finally. Two empty spaces side by side. Beverley pulled in.

'Things like bad teeth, acne, indigestion, even heartburn' – Frances allowed the word to linger – 'they are all far more common.'

Beverley turned off the engine. She wanted to round on her mother and tell her that, actually, she had it wrong; Beverley *had* slipped, yes, but she was past it. She hadn't made herself sick since she'd frightened herself in the Glass Lake bathrooms. And she would have been telling the truth, if they'd had this exchange a few hours ago. But she'd slept so badly last night – she couldn't stop thinking about Ella, no doubt lying face down in her pillow, sobbing over that useless creature – that she'd been exhausted this morning and couldn't stop eating. She'd had Bran Flakes, then toast, then yoghurt, then more toast. Malachy, who'd begrudgingly skipped his morning run to wave off Frances, had wanted to know why Ella hadn't been at dinner the night before and why she wasn't appearing for breakfast. Beverley didn't know what to say. If she told Malachy, it would be her fault. She was at home every day – how had she not noticed a highly undesirable suitor breaking in and stealing their daughter's heart? Instead, she ran upstairs to get her car keys for the school drop-off. Only they were already in her bag. She locked herself in their en suite. She was anxious and twitchy and uncomfortably full; she barely had to do more than lean forward.

She searched her handbag now for the printout of the train ticket. Her phone was aglow. Forty-two new WhatsApp messages, which was some feat given she'd checked her mobile before they left the house. Something must have happened. 'Here you go,' she said.

Her mother didn't take the ticket. She reached past it and covered Beverley's hands, the pudgy skin instantly making hers clammy.

Beverley's father had made her see her mother through his eyes and she hated him for that. What was harder to admit was that she also resented her mother. If she'd lost the weight, everything would have been better. If she'd got thinner, he would have stopped. Why couldn't she have just done that? Hadn't she cared about them enough?

'If you need me, *a stór*, you just call, and I'll come running.'

Beverley pulled her hands free. 'Isn't that a song?'

'The way you feel about your girls, that you'd kill to protect them, that's how I feel about you. And I'm proud of you, always and for ever.'

Beverley cleared her throat. She would pick up some lozenges at the pharmacy too. 'Take the ticket before you forget it. I've paid for the upgrade, so you might as well use it. I'll help with your luggage. I'll carry the ... box up to the platform.'

She crossed the car park, glancing around for who might be watching the unlikely duo of Beverley Franklin and the obese woman wearing a sarong, and instantly hating herself for it.

'Thanks, Mam,' she said, when they were in the small waiting area and she'd placed the bubble-wrapped sculpture at Frances' feet.

'For what?'

For being a role model, she wanted to say. But she couldn't bring herself to do it. She dreaded sounding foolish. 'For telling me about Ella and Arlo,' she said. 'Thank you. It's important information to have.'

....

Christine Maguire's phone was hopping. News of what Lorna Farrell was calling a 'Glass Lake s*x scandal' was spreading through the social networks like wildfire. Even a WhatsApp group for a school tour three years ago had come alive.

Christine was at Cooney Nursing Home, attempting to report on West Cork's oldest citizen turning 106.

'I think you left your torch on, pet,' said the birthday girl.

'Hmm? Oh, no. No, that's just...' She reached into her handbag and turned the phone over, so the screen was faced down. 'Anyway, I think I've got everything I need.'

She'd gathered all her quotes and badgered the woman for her top tips on living longer, as per Derek's request. ('Old people are depressing! At least get me a list!')

'You must stay for cake. It's low sugar, given half of us could keel over from diabetes at any moment, but it's still good, I promise.' The woman wiggled her eyebrows, so her birthday crown tipped slightly to the left. 'It's Black Forest Gateau.'

Christine smiled. It was always Black Forest Gateau. 'How could I say no? Happy birthday again, Muriel.'

She could hang on a few minutes but then she had to get home to Maeve, who was off sick today. As she waited for a care assistant to slice up the cake, she scrolled her way through the onslaught of facts, gossip and everything in between.

Principal Patterson had contacted several sixth-class parents this morning to tell them their children had also been exchanging nudes with Woody Whitehead. With so many informed, any hope of keeping his name private was gone. Christine had phoned the school on her way to the nursing home and the secretary assured her Maeve was not one of them. But something was up with her daughter. Maeve's sick days were always caused by worries that wormed their way so far into her anxious body they made her physically ill.

Someone shook the man at the keyboard awake and he guided the group in a boisterous rendition of 'Happy Birthday'. Christine clicked her phone shut and dutifully joined in.

'*For she's a jolly good fellow ...! For she's a jolly good fellow ...!*'

They applauded the blowing-out of the candles. It took six goes, but Muriel got there in the end.

Christine ate her slice of cake quickly, then she headed for her car. She had to check on Maeve and, after that, she had Operation Liberation to oversee.

....

By the time Beverley had left the train station, called to the pharmacy, and made her way across town to the Whiteheads' house, she had 213 WhatsApp messages and six missed calls, mostly from Lorna. The couple of messages she'd caught flashing up on the screen suggested there was some sort of meet-up this afternoon. She couldn't make it anyway. Her mother's visit meant she was behind on Sneaky Sweets orders. Whatever it was about would have to wait. She couldn't afford to lose her nerve.

Out of the Range Rover and up the path she went. There were two 'For Sale' signs pitched in the small lawn at the front of the house. She'd heard people were doing that. She'd never had reason to drive out this side of town herself, but she believed a few other parents had made an exception.

The door opened before Beverley had a chance to ring the bell. The startled look on Connie Whitehead's face meant it had already been the correct decision to call.

'I'm here to speak to your son.'

'Oh, well, I'm afraid he's at school, and I was just heading up there ...' The woman switched her car keys from her right hand to her left.

'Not that son. The other one.'

The woman glanced behind her. From inside the house, there was the sound of someone coming down the stairs.

'Have you seen my tools?' asked a male voice.

Then Arlo appeared in the doorway.

'Mrs Franklin.' He wiped his hands on his trousers. 'Hello.'

'Beverley is here to see you,' said Connie, giving him a meaningful look. 'But I was just saying I've to get up to the school and that you have a job to get to.' She turned back to Beverley. 'I'm giving him a lift, you see. His van is on the blink. Maybe you could call back another time ...'

'It's fine, Mom,' said the teenager, taking hold of the door frame. 'Go on. You can't be late. I'll take my bike.'

'With all your tools?'

'It's fine.'

Connie looked from Arlo to Beverley before conceding. 'Your toolbox is under the kitchen table,' she said, heading down the path. 'Nice to see you, Beverley.' She looked back at them as she climbed into a car that, according to the licence plate, was older than Amelia.

'The brakes are acting up on my van. I'm having it serviced.'

He said it as if she'd asked – as if she cared. 'Heard from my daughter lately?'

His mouth opened, then shut. Open, shut. Open, shut. 'I don't ... I'm not sure ...'

'I know all about you creeping into my house at all hours, without my say-so. That's trespassing. Did you know that? I could have you arrested.'

'I didn't ... It wasn't ...' He was the colour of one of her tomatoffees (trademark pending). What had Ella seen in him?

'How could you do this to her? Do you know how wonderful Ella is? How lucky you were to get to spend any time with her? You ... You lanky string of piss.' Beverley never cursed, at least not beyond the confines of her own home. It felt wonderful. 'And Fiona Murphy?' She thought of her daughter's pale perfect skin and of the crêpe texture of Fiona's sun-bedded chest. Why were men allowed to exist? 'Have you no respect for yourself? She's heartbroken, you know. She's barely left her room. You're just some cheap cliché gardener, tending to the lawns and sexual desires of his old customers. Just like your father.'

Beverley eyeballed the boy, daring him. It felt good to be defending something she really, deeply cared about. Was this what her mother meant when she said that ultimately all that mattered was that she did what she believed was right?

'Did Mrs Murphy say something happened?' the boy said finally. 'Is that what Ella thinks? Is that why she's ignoring me?' His face was flaming red. Did he really expect her to fall for the innocent act?

Two cars drove past. One of them pulled in a few doors down. With nothing to fan the flames, her fire began to die.

'Stay away from my family and my house. And tell your brother to do the same.' She turned on her heels, before pivoting back. 'You're a plague, you Whiteheads. A plague on this whole town!'

She barrelled back down the path, zipping up her fitted jacket, fob pointed at the car. Safely inside, she watched Arlo reappear from the house in a jacket, carrying a toolbox. He paused in front of the 'For Sale' signs. Then he reefed them out of the grass and flung them over the side gate into their backyard.

Beverley unlocked her phone and started to go through the messages. As she scrolled back to the start – 264 messages! – she watched Arlo throw his leg over an old Raleigh and precariously balance the toolbox on the handlebars. He kicked off and freewheeled down the hill and out of the estate.

There were nine different threads, but they all said the same thing.

'Zut alors,' whispered Beverley as she took in the details.

This afternoon's get-together was happening at the school. Only it wasn't a meet-up they were planning at all. It was a full-on riot.

32
······

Arlo cycled as fast as he could across town. The toolbox jangled on his handlebars, and Beverley's rage rang in his ears. He'd put so much effort into her not finding out about him and Ella, but now he found himself in a situation where that was the least terrible bit.

He'd felt oddly buoyed after visiting his dad and had texted Ella from the prison car park to apologise for not responding and to say he was on his way back to her to explain. He'd never felt so much like he was driving home. When he got to Cooney, he had a reply. All it said was: Don't call. Despite follow-up messages, voice notes and even phone calls, that was the last he'd heard from her. He though she was mad at him for ignoring her messages; now he knew it was much worse.

Flying down Main Street, he checked the clock over Regan's Chemist. Christine Maguire had been very precise about time when she hired him, and it would take twice as long on the bike. But when would he get a chance to contact Ella? He needed to tell her that whatever she'd heard was wrong. Nothing had happened between him and Mrs Murphy. The increased speed kept his mind from spiralling. Every time he imagined a scenario in which Fiona Murphy had somehow told Ella an exaggerated version of events, the wind bellowed in his ears.

When he made it to Seaview Terrace, Christine and a girl he took to be her daughter were waiting outside. He climbed off his bike and they led him back down the street.

'As I said on the phone, our cat is trapped, and we need you to get him out,' said the Glass Lake mother, coming to a halt at a very well-maintained garden.

He tried to keep his thoughts on the job. 'Your roses are lovely.'

'Oh, this isn't our garden. Our house is up there.' Christine pointed back the way they'd come. 'This is our neighbour's house. A sweet old woman who has gone away on holidays – to visit a dying relative, I believe – and our cat has got trapped in her home.'

'When did this happen?' he asked, swiping at the sweat along his hairline.

'When was it, Maeve?'

The girl looked up at her mother in mild terror.

Christine tapped her chin. 'Let me see now ...'

'You phoned me on Saturday.'

'That's right,' said Christine. 'It was Saturday. Porcupine has been trapped in there since Saturday.'

Arlo ran the back of his hand along his brow as he looked up at the house. When he was done with this job, he would send Ella another text. But this time he would make it clear that there had been a huge misunderstanding. 'How did the cat get in there?'

'How does Porcupine get anywhere?' mused Christine. 'He roams the street, calling into neighbours. Nobody minds, we're a close little terrace. I guess he just got stuck in this one. Porcupine's a free spirit, isn't he, Maeve?'

Maeve Maguire. He knew the name.

'Okay, well, Mrs Maguire, I thought I was here to get him out of a shed or a storage unit or something. Was that not what you said on the phone?'

Christine stuck out her bottom lip and frowned. 'No, I don't think so.'

'I couldn't break into this house, even if I wanted to. I'm sorry.' She looked at him blankly.

'This is a pin and tumbler,' he explained, pointing to their neighbour's door. 'It's a totally different kind of lock. I'd need a tension wrench, at the very least, and probably a rake. I don't have those tools with me.'

'So, where are they?'

'Well, there's a lock pick kit up at the school, but—'

'Perfect. We'll wait.' The woman checked her wristwatch. 'We have an hour until she ... until I have to leave for work, I mean. That's enough time to get up to Glass Lake and back.' She smiled. 'You go, and Maeve and I will wait here.'

'I don't—'

'And I'll pay you double for the effort.'

'Mrs Maguire, I really can't afford to get into any trouble. And to be honest, I don't feel comfortable about breaking into someone else's home.'

'I completely understand, but you wouldn't get into any trouble, I promise. If it wasn't for Mrs Rodgers' dying sister – did I mention she was dying? – I'd phone her myself and ask her to come back. I know she'd be heartbroken to think a cat was wasting away, starving to death, in her home. Ask anyone. She's a real animal lover.'

He looked at the house again. The curtains were open and the lights off, which told him precisely nothing. There was no car in the driveway but maybe the resident didn't drive or was just away for the day. It seemed unlikely a Glass Lake parent would want to break into a neighbour's home for immoral reasons, but he really didn't want to get caught up in criminal behaviour. He had enough to contend with as it was.

'Look! Look! There he is!' Maeve ran to the front-room window.

Arlo moved closer to the house, still reluctant to touch it – though he'd already noted there was no alarm – and peered in through the glass to see a rotund cat with the strangest fur colouring padding into the sitting room. In the middle of the rug, he lay on his side, and started licking his paws.

'He doesn't look like he's starving to death.'

'Oh, he is,' said Christine. 'See? He's so hungry he's considering eating himself. Cats do that, you know. Self-cannibalism.'

Maeve moved her face closer to the window. 'Pssh,' she hissed. 'Pssh, pssh, pssh.' But the animal just rolled on to his other side.

'You should have seen him before, honestly. He's wasting away.'

Maeve turned from the window, so the two of them were looking at him.

'I don't have my van,' he said, remembering his trump card. 'It'd take too long to get up to Glass Lake and back again on the bike.'

'No problem,' said Christine. 'I'll drive you. It won't take ten minutes to get there, especially at this time.'

He was working hard to put obstacles in their path, but she was equally determined to remove them.

'Please, Arlo, we really are desperate.'

He was out of excuses. 'All right. All right, let's go.'

He fired off a message to Ella as soon as he was in the passenger seat, and they drove to the school with the radio doing most of the talking.

The car turned on to the tree-lined avenue that led to Glass Lake. 'When we get to the school, Maeve, you'll wait in the car, all right?' said Christine. 'She's supposed to be off sick today, though as you can see, she's not exhibiting many symptoms of illness.'

She brought the car to an early stop. The parking spaces reserved for visitors' cars were full, and about a dozen adults were standing on the grassy verge in front of the school. They were wrapped in jackets and scarves and a few of them were brandishing signs.

'What are they ...?'

Christine trailed off. One of the protestors turned to the side, his banner rotating with him. It said: NO SEXTS AT OUR SCHOOL.

'Is this about Woody?' Arlo said, rubbing condensation from the window. 'Is it to do with the jacket?' Their mom had been called up to the school this morning to talk to Principal Patterson about Woody graffitiing a teacher's coat.

'I'd wager it's got more to do with the nudes,' said Christine, veering the car to the right as she gave the protestors a wide berth and headed for the back of the school.

'From a couple of weeks ago?'

Christine frowned. 'Didn't you hear anything today?'

'No.'

She glanced into the back seat and lowered her voice. 'Woody's been accused of exchanging nudes with other students. Principal Patterson phoned the parents this morning. We'll park up by the pool. You have an access card, right?'

That's why the 'For Sale' signs had reappeared this morning after a month's reprieve. People were back to wanting them gone, because now they thought Charlie's youngest son was some sort of sexual deviant. Was his mother here yet? He'd forgotten to look for

288

her car. He twisted against the seatbelt. Had she seen this?

'Arlo?'

'Yes?'

'Have you got an access card?'

'Yes, I have one.'

They pulled in between Frank Cafferty's Skoda and Principal Patterson's BMW. Christine pushed open her door and, somehow, he followed.

Though they were on the other side of the building, they could easily hear the chants.

'*What do we want, what do we know?*' cried a woman who must have had a megaphone.

The crowd sang back: '*Woody Whitehead must go!*'

Arlo rested a hand on the roof of the car.

'Come on,' said Christine, her voice suddenly soft as she took him by the arm. 'We'll go in the back way and avoid the crazies.'

....

Nuala Patterson walked Connie Whitehead out to the entrance of the school. She did not enjoy spending time in the woman's company, but she was a professional. She'd made it clear that Woody was being punished for the graffiti incident and not the sexting, which was technically not the school's business – although she didn't know how much longer she could maintain that line. It was certainly starting to affect school life. Woody was to be suspended for a week, starting tomorrow, and he would be removed from the musical.

'He'll miss *The Wizard of Oz*. He's been working so hard on it,' said Connie, breaking the hypnotic sound of Nuala's work shoes clip-clopping along the corridor.

'He'll be all right, I'm sure,' she replied, pushing her way through the first set of double doors, and then the ones that led outside.

When she thought of the photo fallout as affecting school life, she meant the sheer number of students now implicated. Foolishly, she'd forgotten about the parents.

'What do we want, what do we know?' Lorna Farrell was shouting into some sort of control panel, the amplified words blaring from a megaphone in her other hand.

'Woody Whitehead must go!' replied a crowd of ten or so other parents.

A father at the rear held up a banner that said NO SEXTS AT OUR SCHOOL, while someone else had a placard calling for LESS LETCHING, MORE LEARNING.

There wasn't a bad situation that Glass Lake parents couldn't somehow make worse.

'Sorry, Principal Patterson,' said Mairead, jogging up behind her. 'I was in the staffroom making a cup of coffee. I just saw them now. What do you want me to do?'

The crowd had caught sight of Connie Whitehead and was now aiming the chants at her.

'Marnie Farrell, say her name!' yelled Lorna.

'Marnie Farrell! Marnie Farrell!' came the reply.

'Ciara Murphy, say her name!'

'Ciara Murphy! Ciara Murphy!'

Nuala could barely believe it. They were going through the list of female students who'd sent explicit photographs of themselves. When Nuala had contacted the parents of the implicated students this morning, she'd asked them to respect the children's privacy. And now they were literally shouting their names through a megaphone.

'Tanya D'Arcy, say her name!'

Nuala turned to Mairead. 'Take Mrs Whitehead back to my office,' she said. 'And then ask Seamus to roll out the power hose.'

....

If Frank Cafferty could just get Woody to listen, they would sort this whole mess out. He only wanted the best for the boy. He cared about him. Couldn't he see that? There was no reason to be acting out in class and destroying his teacher's possessions.

He had taken Woody out of the classroom for a moment so he could explain this. But the child kept turning his head away. He couldn't get him to understand.

'Fuck you,' muttered the boy.

'Woody! You can't speak to me like that. I'm still your teacher!'

Behind him, there was a loud sound of metal clattering to the floor.

Frank jumped.

Seamus McGrath appeared from one of the storage rooms, wheeling a coiled-up hose behind him.

'Seamus ... hi, hello.'

But Seamus just stared at him.

The same thought as always crossed his mind. The caretaker knew.

But no, of course not.

How could he?

Woody took the opportunity to disappear back into the classroom. Frank tried and failed to swallow. Seamus kept staring.

'I was just talking to the boy and—'

'I know what you are,' said the caretaker.

Frank did some version of a smile, as if Seamus had just made a mild-mannered joke, then he too vanished back into the classroom.

....

Lorna Farrell watched Connie Whitehead retreat and felt a rush of victory. She'd been worried she wouldn't have what it took to lead the crowd but, if she did say so herself, she was doing a stellar job.

'*Whose children?!*' she shouted into the voice box, as Principal Patterson stepped out onto the lawn and folded her arms.

Lorna would have folded her own arms, if either had been free. Instead, she held the megaphone higher.

'Our children!' the crowd replied.

That was right. They were here on behalf of their children and as parents, as guardians, they would not be intimidated.

'*Whose children?*' she yelled into the voice box again.

'Our children!'

Lorna had assumed Beverley would take control of the rally, as she did everything. But she hadn't responded to any of this morning's WhatsApp messages. Bill was the one who'd encouraged her to step up, to become leader of this movement. If her husband was going to be mayor one day, she was going to be first lady, and she wanted to be one who used her powers for good. Like Michelle Obama. Lorna was a great admirer of Michelle Obama.

She wasn't glad her daughter had got caught up in this mess, absolutely not, but it did strengthen her right to lead. Plus, they had the megaphone left over from Bill's election campaign.

'*Children's lives ...*'

'Matter!' came the response.

'*Children's lives ...*'

'Matter!'

As well as being a fan of the Obamas, Lorna bought all her soap from a woman in Aberstown who was one-quarter Asian (not that Lorna saw colour), so she was sure the Black Lives Matter movement wouldn't mind her borrowing a few chants. They were very catchy.

'Hey!'

Before she could stop it, Principal Patterson was reefing the megaphone off her, causing the cord to detach from the voice box she was still holding in her left hand.

'We will not be intimidated, Nuala! We will not be silenced!'

'We will not be intimidated, Nuala! We will not be silenced!' echoed the group.

Lorna hadn't meant it as a chant, but good to know they could continue without amplification. It felt particularly defiant to have so many parents referring to Principal Patterson as 'Nuala'.

'Enough,' said the principal. 'What do you all think you're doing? Not only are you in breach of some serious data protection, but you are violating the privacy of a collection of minors.'

'We're their parents,' asserted someone behind Lorna.

'Some of you are. Moira Gaffney – your son is only in Junior Infants; and Gerry Regan, you haven't had a child at Glass Lake in half a decade.'

Gerry let his NO SEXTS AT OUR SCHOOL sign drop slightly. If you needed someone to get involved, you could always count on the pharmacist. He was a great man for a petition or a planning application objection.

'Those of you who are parents of affected students, I have already invited you to come here this afternoon to talk to me, and I expect to see you at those prearranged meetings. But this is not talking. I'm asking you to please leave the school premises. Seamus is due to water the grass, and I would hate for any of you to get wet.'

The school caretaker appeared behind Principal Patterson wheeling a heavy hose reel. He began to unravel it.

'We're parents,' Lorna shot back, 'and we deserve to have a say in the welfare of our children. We were patient. We tried your workshops idea. We went to your information night. I heard that doctor is your cousin, by the way.'

'Second cousin once-removed,' said the principal coldly.

'Mmm.' Lorna paused. Did she dare? 'It's interesting that the Lakers fundraised money for you to spend in the best interest of the school and you spent it on a family member.'

'I hired the best—'

'We did some workshops and they didn't work,' Lorna interrupted. Megaphone or no megaphone, she would be heard! 'The following week, we find out we have a s-e-x pest in our midst. And, according to my daughter, a lewd graffiti artist too. Who knows what will be next? We want the boy gone.'

The crowd cheered and she couldn't fight the smile. This was how the British queen must feel every time she stepped out on to her balcony.

Nuala Patterson looked at her with unmasked irritation.

'This is a place of learning. We have several hundred children here trying to get on with their lessons, in silence. If you want to form a lynch mob, I suggest you take your nooses elsewhere.'

As an opponent to slavery – she had been first to sign Claire Keating's petition to get it removed from the history curriculum – not to mention her well-known Obama admiration – she had organised the bus to Dublin the time Barack came to visit – Lorna found the racially charged comparison pointed and insulting.

'For now, as I said, we have grass to keep alive. Good to go, Seamus?'

The caretaker was gripping the mouth of the hose in both hands.

Reluctantly, the crowd began to disperse. There was some chatter about heading over to the Strand. Gerry had a copy of the 'Ban Articulated Vehicles in Cooney' petition saved to his laptop; he could rework the template.

'You're on my list, Nuala Patterson,' said Lorna, narrowing her eyes as the principal took a step back into the porch. 'And I'll tell you this – it is *not* my homemade thank-you card list.'

33
· · · · · ·

'This is different,' Christine explained to her perpetually concerned daughter as they waved farewell to Arlo.

After the teenager got Mrs Rodgers' front door open, he'd offered to stick around, but she told him there was no need and he hadn't argued. He'd headed off on his bike with an expression not dissimilar to Maeve's.

'How is it different?' asked the girl, still standing on their neighbour's porch.

Christine, who was just beyond the threshold, didn't know if she should keep trying to coax Maeve in, or concentrate on coaxing Porcupine out. They had very little time before their neighbour returned from the Tidy Towns committee meeting and the loud clock in the woman's hallway – which she now realised had pictures of cats where there are usually numbers – was not helping.

'We're not robbers because we're not stealing anything,' she said decisively. 'We're just taking back what is already ours.'

'But we're still breaking and entering.'

'No,' said Christine, shaking her head slowly, waiting for a rebuttal to reveal itself. 'We didn't *break* anything. Entering, maybe. But not *breaking* and entering.'

'Why can't we just wait for Mrs Rodgers to come home?'

'Because she might stop us.'

'How?'

Christine threw her arms up in the air. 'I don't know, Maeve. She might wrestle us to the floor.'

The child was doubtful. 'If Caroline's too old for wrestling, then Mrs Rodgers is definitely too old.'

'Or she might phone the guards on us. Who knows? All I know is we need to find this cat.'

'My tummy doesn't feel good.'

'I know, but it'll feel a lot better when we're home and Porcupine is lying across it, purring away. Now, you can wait there if you like, but I'm going in.'

Mrs Rodgers' hallway was shadowy and smelled faintly of dust balls. The sitting room, where they had seen Porcupine earlier, had a similar odour and was just as dark. She turned on the light.

'Porcupine,' she called. 'Here, kitty, kitty. Here, Porcupine. Here, kitty, kitty. Come on, Maeve! Give me a hand!'

'He's there,' said her daughter, appearing in the living-room doorway.

'Where?'

'By the fireplace. See?'

Christine walked over to the cat, who was at least fifty per cent larger than the last time she'd seen him up close. What had the woman been feeding him? She reached down just as Porcupine pushed himself up and arched his back. He remained as unenamoured of Christine, his rescuer, as ever.

'You pick him up and we'll get out of here.'

'*Me?*'

'It's okay, we're not doing anything wrong. If anyone did a bad thing here, it's Mrs Rodgers. Now, come on, pick him up.'

Her daughter took a step forward. Christine glanced out the window, but her view of the road was obscured by the rose bushes.

She reached out and gently inched her daughter forward until she bent down and scooped up the cat. He purred contentedly. Christine exhaled.

She steered Maeve and the animal out the front door, softly closing it behind them. She pushed against the door, but it didn't budge. No sign of tampering.

'Hang on ...' She held a hand up to her daughter as she jogged down the garden path and threw glances up and down Seaview Terrace. 'Okay, let's go. Let's go, let's go, let's go!'

She ushered her daughter down the garden path and up the road as if this was a hijack situation and she was shepherding the hostages to safety. Which, in a way, she was. 'Keep going. Don't look back. Do not look back,' she said, as she did just that. The road remained clear. A few cars whizzed past the bottom, but none turned up.

When they made it to their own garden, she pulled the key from her shirt pocket and got the door open in double time.

'Mission complete!' she cried, leaning down to kiss her daughter's head and even ruffle Porcupine's hideous fur. 'First thing we're doing is getting that dye out. What sort of psycho ... Maeve? Are you okay?'

Her daughter's eyes were big and pained, and the left one was twitching again.

'I did a bad thing.'

Christine crouched down and brushed her hair back from her face. 'No, you didn't. Honestly, love! You did a very good, a very brave thing. You rescued Porcupine.'

Maeve shook her head. 'I mean before.'

Christine nodded. It might take a while for Maeve to tell them what was up, but the confession always came. 'Is this about why you couldn't go to school today? Because you did a bad thing and you felt too bad, in your tummy?'

Maeve nodded.

'Is it to do with Woody?'

She nodded again, and Christine felt a plunge in her own stomach.

'But it's not photos. I never took any photos.'

'Okay,' she said, head already spinning as the euphoria of being a feline emancipator evaporated. 'Why don't we just start at the start?'

....

Frank Cafferty stared at the blinking cursor on the blank Word document. He had never written a letter of resignation before and wasn't sure where to start.

He hadn't had the chance to resign from his last school. As soon as parents started to complain, he was placed on sick leave, and never taken off it. He'd had two blissful years there before a father confronted him in the playground. Frank had been collecting the cones after PE; he hadn't been expecting it at all.

'I know about you,' the man had said, spat really, head jutting out as his hands bunched into fists.

Frank played dumb.

When the same man approached him at his home, he acted outraged and insulted. He threatened to sue for slander.

'You shouldn't be working with children,' the father shouted, as Frank shut the front door on his tirade.

Then notes started to appear under his windscreen wipers, each one nastier than the last. He'd ignored them all, until the final one. It contained that same four-letter word, as crude in writing as when uttered.

Pedo.

That's when he'd started to get scared.

School management didn't say why they were placing him on leave, just that parents had raised concerns and it was for the best. Frank had agreed in a bid to shut off any further questions. After a few weeks, he started looking for a job in a bigger town.

He had hoped it would be different in Cooney. He had promised Jess it would be. But he couldn't change who he was. The best he could do was keep it to himself, until the rest of the world became more open-minded.

Everyone on the chat forums said he was playing with fire opting for a job that involved working with children. He couldn't help it. He loved being around them too much. But he was done with teaching now, that was it. He was going back to tech.

'Are you sure about this, Frank?' said Jess, appearing in the doorway behind him. 'You didn't do anything wrong.' It sounded more like a plea than a statement of fact. Was he imagining that? He hoped so.

'We'll move to Dublin, start afresh,' he said, with trademark enthusiasm. He'd be a better husband there, a better person, a better version of himself.

....

'I got Mr Cafferty's coat from the classroom last Thursday when I was supposed to be at rehearsals, and I gave it to Woody. We were supposed to get it together but he got stopped in the corridor so I put it in my bag and brought it back to the hall and gave it to Woody and he wrote the bad word on it and now Woody will probably be thrown out of school for ever and ever.'

'Well, I don't think that's going to happen,' said Christine, who hadn't had a chance to fully catch up on the latest WhatsApp goings-on, but the word seemed to be that Woody was suspended for a week.

'It's all my fault.'

'What you did wasn't *good*, but it wasn't that bad either. You didn't have anything to do with writing on the coat, right?'

Maeve shook her head.

'Good.'

'But I did call Mr Cafferty's phone lots of times and hang up without saying anything.'

'*What?* Maeve!'

'I know. I'm sorry.'

'You prank called your teacher! How? You don't even have a phone!'

'I used Dad's phone, when you were both asleep or when you were out. And then I deleted the calls because I didn't want Dad to see and get cross.'

'Where would you even get a teacher's number?'

'Woody gave it to me.'

'Where did he get it? I don't ... Why would you do all that?'

'Because Woody is my friend.'

'So?'

'Woody needs to make Mr Cafferty quit. He needs to make him leave the school and go away and never come back.'

'Why does Woody need to make your teacher quit?'

Maeve shrugged, turning her attention to Porcupine, the absolution of the confession already having an effect. It was amazing how quickly children recovered, while their parents were left reeling. 'I don't know why he wants to make Mr Cafferty quit,' said the eleven-year-old, tickling the cat gently. 'He just does.'

34

. . . . . .

There **was** one more set of quick breaths before Tuesday morning's class was dismissed, but Beverley rolled up her mat, bowed to Paul and quickly left the overheated studio. Usually, after a hot yoga session, she went straight to the bathroom and drenched her face with cold water, waterboarding her pores into submission. But today she lingered by the reception desk.

She'd spotted the pamphlet numerous times, its purple border peeping out from the array of literature on everything from smear tests to resistance training to food supplements. This was the first time she'd considered taking one.

'Beverley.'

Her hand flew two leaflets to the left and she plucked a page at random. Fiona Murphy had left the studio too, red-faced and sweating in a hot-pink Adidas sports bra that was at least a decade too young for her. Fiona threw the gold chain of her Chanel purse across her chest, like one of the tackier Kardashians.

'I'm with you,' she said, still breathing heavily. 'Any excuse to wrap things up early.' Her eyes tracked down. 'Never too soon to be making plans.'

Beverley looked at the brochure in her hand, an advertorial leaflet for a new eco-cemetery in east Cork. She stuffed it back into the display. 'What do you want, Fiona?'

'Just checking in. You've been quiet on WhatsApp. And you didn't sign Lorna's petition for Woody Whitehead's expulsion. Fair enough, I didn't sign it either. It's amazing Cooney hasn't been submerged into the Atlantic with the weight of all these petitions.' She pulled at the strap of her bag. 'So, how are you? How's the musical? I heard Woody's gone. That's quite the mess they've left you in. The lion, wow. Tough role to replace.'

'We'll manage.'

The rest of the class flowed out of the studio now, chatting and fanning their hands in front of their faces. Beverley waited for Fiona to stand to one side, then she did the same.

'I was thinking this might be a chance for Ciara to move up a bit. You remember we were looking for a bigger role for her?'

'And we found one. She's the Wicked Witch of the West.'

'The Witch of the West,' she corrected.

'I have to go now, Fiona. I need to get ice water on my face before it sucks up all these awful toxins.'

Fiona pursed her lips. Beverley felt the twitch, but she didn't blink.

'Now that the lion is available, I was thinking Ciara could move up again,' she said, readjusting her gold chain. 'I was also thinking that since Amelia has the perfect hair to play a lion – all yellowy and coarse – she'd be better suited to that role, while Ciara would work perfectly as Dorothy. Her hair is so fine, it looks great in pigtails, and she knows most of the lines.'

'*In-croy-able*,' said Beverley, throwing her head back and laughing, though what she really wanted to do was smack this pathetic cradle-snatcher hard on her inflamed cheeks. 'I think the heat might have gone to your head.'

'You just need a minute to think it over.'

'I really don't.'

Fiona frowned, or tried to. 'I think you're forgetting what I know, Beverley.'

Beverley stood straighter and relaxed her shoulders. She was always an inch taller after yoga and she used it to her advantage. Fiona didn't balk.

'I was actually out at Tamara's house this morning,' she continued, 'and she was talking about Malachy, your Malachy, of all people. It seems she knows him, too. Which I didn't realise. Did you realise?'

Beverley had had enough. 'And I heard about you and Arlo Whitehead.'

Fiona smiled modestly, flapping a hand, as if batting away a compliment.

'He's a child, Fiona.'

The woman rolled her eyes. 'He's eighteen.'

'You should be ashamed of yourself.'

'Oh, come on,' she scoffed. 'Anyway, it's got nothing to do with you. Worry about your own relationship. And let's not get off subject here. Ciara is playing Dorothy. Or else.'

Two regulars from the class passed them and Beverley cracked a smile.

When they were gone, she moved closer. This time, Fiona's chin betrayed her. She tried to point it upwards, but there was a hint of a tremor.

Beverley thought of Ella sobbing through the ceiling; of all the untouched trays of food that had sat outside her door; of how deathly lonely it felt to be betrayed. If Beverley could get

305

away with it, she'd have pulled that bag strap up and wrapped it around Fiona's neck.

'If you utter one word about my family or me, I'll tell everyone about you and that *child*.'

The woman shrugged. 'He's eighteen, and he's hot.'

'I'll tell Ciara.'

Fiona's eyes narrowed, or tried to.

Beverley, who paid twice as much for her Botox, widened her own.

'You wouldn't dare.'

'And Butcher.'

Fiona looked worried now.

'I'm not sure how he'd feel about his ex-wife taking up with a teenager, but I guess we'll find out. Do you remember that time he thought Mr Peoples had the hots for you? Arlo will have a lot more to worry about than a pig's head on his car bonnet.'

'It's not true, okay?' Fiona hissed, looking over her shoulder. 'We kissed, just about, but he – I mean, I was just about to stop it, but he chickened out first. Not that I was actually going to *do* anything. It was just sort of a joke. Nothing happened.'

'That's not what I heard. That's not what everyone is saying.'

Fiona sighed. 'I can't help it if people are obsessed with my love life. They're trying to live vicariously through me. But I never actually said anything happened; Lorna Farrell heard what she wanted and ran with it.'

'And you didn't think to correct her?'

The woman shrugged.

Beverley could imagine exactly how it had gone down: the teenager shunning Fiona's advances and, not taking this slight well, her allowing everyone to think something had happened between them. It was pathetic, but it was very Fiona.

'Goodbye, Fiona,' she said coldly. 'I really can't allow my pores to suck up any more of *this*.' She looked her straight in the eye. The woman inhaled loudly but said nothing. Then she turned on her heels and walked to the exit.

Beverley headed for the bathroom. If she didn't get water on her face stat, her skin would get even worse. But first, she leaned back and grabbed the *Recovering from Eating Disorders* pamphlet.

....

Mrs Rodgers had waited patiently by the back door for almost twenty-four hours. She'd arrived home from her Tidy Towns committee meeting yesterday afternoon to find the house empty. She'd thought Albert had been suitably fattened so he could no longer fit through the cat flap, but she must have been mistaken. She had the back door wide open now and she was sitting on a low stool ready to greet him, but still he didn't return.

She didn't know how Albert would have coped last night. He'd never been out alone in the dark. Come to think of it, he had never been out alone. She'd done a thorough tour of the house, checking every window, and giving the front and back doors a good once-over. Of course, her mind had sprung to the neglectful family up the street, but there was no way they could have got in to steal her cat.

A thought occurred to her. The only other person with a key to her home was Father O'Shea. As far as she knew, he was still in Medjugorje, hunting for the spectre of Our Lady. Still, it was worth a shot.

To her surprise, he answered on the third ring.

'Blessings upon you, Father Brendan O'Shea speaking.'

'Oh, hello, Father, it's Rita Rodgers, from number one. I wasn't expecting you to be home.'

'Hello, Mrs Rodgers. Yes, I flew in last night. Turned out it wasn't the Blessed Mother up on the hill at all, just some kids playing a practical joke, Protestants probably. So, I said I'd get back before All Saints' Day.'

'I'm sorry you had a wasted trip.'

'Not at all. Didn't I get a beautiful new halo in the apparitions' gift shop? Fits perfectly on my Blessed Mother shrine and phenomenal wattage. You must call and see her, Mrs Rodgers. She'd bring the most lapsed believer to his knees.'

'Sounds lovely.'

'What can I do you for? Another few prayers over an animal grave?' The priest chuckled, but when she didn't immediately correct him, he grew sombre. 'Oh, I am sorry, Mrs Rodgers, don't tell me you've lost another cat? Of all the bad luck. How many is that that have gone and died on you this year?'

'Still just the three, Father. And I don't know what happens; I feed them so well.'

'You need to stop adopting such hopeless cases.'

'That must be it,' she said gravely. 'But no, no funeral required today. I'm calling about the spare key to my house. I wanted to check you still have it. Nobody has come looking for it?'

'Not that I know of, but as I said, I was away until last night. Hang on just a tick and I'll check.'

'Thank you, Father.'

As she waited for the priest to pull out the old tea tin where he kept the keys, Mrs Rodgers gazed out onto her vibrant rose bushes. While every other garden on Seaview Terrace was muted in the autumn months, hers retained colour. She never bothered with coffins. At least that way their lives had not been in vain. Their lovely, overfed bodies were the greatest fertiliser her plants had ever known.

'Still there, Mrs Rodgers?'

'I am, Father.'

'Well, so are the keys. I've got yours right here.' The soft jangle travelled down the receiver.

'Okay, Father, thank you for checking. I'll see you at mass on Sunday.'

'By the grace of God,' said Fr O'Shea, in what was more Irish pessimism than religious blessing.

Mrs Rodgers walked out into her back garden and looked up in the direction of the Maguires' home. If Albert was there, could it be that he'd gone of his own volition? When she thought about all their evenings, eating meat and cheese boards in front of marathon runs of *The Chase* – well, it was almost too much to bear.

....

'Two minutes. Literally, two minutes and then you get the fuck out of my house, boy.'

Ella wrapped her arms tightly across her chest as she stood in the middle of her bedroom. She'd never cursed at him before, not in a serious way. He stayed where he was, right inside her door, arms hanging uselessly by his side. He didn't dare go any further. He was so glad to see her, even if she refused to look at him, even if he'd just risked being shot as she snuck him up the stairs. Ella's father had inherited a military collection of guns, and you could just tell Beverley would have a killer aim.

'Thanks for seeing me. I really appreciate it,' he said, like she was a doctor who'd fitted him in for an early check-up.

'One minute, forty-five seconds.'

She'd finally answered one of his calls. He'd promised it wasn't about him. He needed to talk to her about Woody. He was worried, and there was nobody else.

'You're not wearing your A and E necklace.' He looked around the room, deciding that if he could see it, if it was still here, then all hope was not lost. He scanned the bedposts, the hooks above her desk, but nothing. 'It's not what you think with Mrs Murphy, Fiona, your mom's friend. I barely kissed her – I mean, I didn't kiss her at all. She kissed me, but barely. And I didn't kiss her back. I couldn't. It was barely a second and then I pushed her off.'

'One and a half minutes.'

'I should have messaged you back straight away, I know, but I wanted to tell you about it and I was just trying to figure out how, and then I had to visit my dad and there was all this stuff with Woody, and then your mom came to my house' – her eyes widened at this, but he ploughed on; he didn't want to miss his one chance to explain – 'and she seemed to think something more had happened, like maybe we slept together or something mental like that, but I don't know where she got that idea, because I would never, I could never ...'

Sweet Jesus, Arly, do not cry.

Leo's voice righted him. He hadn't heard from him in days.

'I wouldn't even have let her get that close, if it wasn't for Woody. She knew he'd been sexting other girls in the class and I wanted her to keep it to herself. I mean, it's too late now because everybody knows, but that's the only reason I let her, even for a second ...'

Eyes cold, she didn't budge.

'I'm so sorry, Ella.'

'You promised you were here to talk about Woody.'

'I am.'

'Well, if you don't start talking about him, I'm going to open that door and scream down to my parents that there's a boy in my bedroom – a *Whitehead* boy.'

The scorn hit him in the chest, and it was worse than people phoning their house and telling them to move, worse even than being spat at on the street. He wanted to sink into the carpet and disappear.

'Did you hear about the pictures? About all the other girls, not just Amelia? Woody was exchanging nudes with all these girls in his class. I mean, I know you and me sent ...' She was looking at him now, but it was not a regard he welcomed. He cleared his throat. 'But he's twelve, and so many girls. That's not normal, is it? And he's always on his own, in his room, playing computer games. Why wasn't I more alarmed by that? My dad asked me to look after him and I'm fucking up, Ella. I am fucking everything up.'

There was silence, and he thought she was going to leave it there, his desperation hanging in the air.

'Talk to him.'

'I don't know how.'

'Of course you do. You're close.'

Arlo shook his head.

'You said he was the most important person in your life.'

'When did I say that?'

'In your fifth-year religion essay. You said you knew him better than anyone else.'

He blushed at the memory of that essay being read aloud in school. He couldn't believe she remembered. 'Not any more. I've been avoiding him for months – I've been avoiding everything and everyone in my house. What am I supposed to do? Just waltz into his bedroom now and ask him why he's become some sort of weird sex fiend?'

'I wouldn't phrase it like that but yeah, basically.'

'I can't. I know it's pathetic, but just thinking about it makes me want to die of embarrassment. I can't do it. I'm too much of a wimp.'

'You're not a wimp, Arlo,' she said reluctantly, her arms loosening slightly. She sighed. 'Look, what you need to do is channel Bev. Whenever I have to do something I don't want to do, I just pretend I'm my mother. She sees the thing that needs to be done, and she does it. She can be rude, but she gets shit done. And she does it straight away. She says you should start the day with the task you least want to do and, loath as I am to ever take her advice, it's a pretty good philosophy.'

'So, talk to Woody in the morning?'

'Not just any morning; tomorrow morning. If it wasn't so late, I'd say go home and do it now, but yeah, first thing in the morning. Now get out of my house.'

35

· · · · · ·

Arlo knocked on the bedroom door and waited. It was barely 7 a.m. and already the low rumble of gunfire and general warfare emanated from the other side. He knocked again. Then he let himself in.

His little brother was in his pyjamas, sitting in his usual position, on the carpet with his back against the foot of the bed, eyes focused on the lifelike military forces doing battle on the Whiteheads' old TV set. He leaned slightly to the right, pressing down hard on the controller, and furrowed his brow.

'I don't think you're supposed to be playing games this early.'

'I'm not allowed to play them before school,' corrected Woody, leaning forward now. 'But I'm not going to school today. I'm off all week.'

'You're not off. You're suspended.'

'Yeah, I know.'

'Well, it's a bit different.'

The boy made no further sound until something exploded on the screen, the muted colours reverberated, and the action stopped. 'That's so sly! I almost had him!'

'Can I talk to you for a minute?'

'Yeah, I just have one more life left and then ...'

The screen burst into motion again, text appearing at the top as the man in camouflage began to jog. Arlo could feel his insides tensing. It would be too easy to turn and leave, to say he'd be back into him later.

He walked across the room, so he was standing to the side of the old television. 'Now, Woody.'

'It'll only take two secs—'

'Now!'

His brother looked up at him, mouth slightly open. This was not a dynamic they were used to. Even when they had been closer, he had always been Woody's ally, not his disciplinarian. Arlo wasn't a father figure; he was a big brother.

Woody hit a button on the remote and the whole screen went dark.

Arlo pushed some of the clothes, including the Glass Lake uniform, from the armchair in the corner of the room and sat. Woody scrambled up on to the bed, his legs tucked under him.

'Is – is everything okay? Did something bad happen? Is it you? Is it Mom?'

'No, it's you, Woody. I want to talk about you. Okay?'

Arlo was stalling, trying to figure out how to address the matter. He tried to imagine what his father would say, but all he could hear was Charlie Whitehead's instruction, that Arlo look after his mother and brother. This was his responsibility. He couldn't channel his father any more than he could channel Beverley Franklin.

'I want to talk about the photos of the girls in your class and the graffiti on your teacher's coat. I don't understand why you would do those things. It doesn't make sense to me.'

Woody regarded him blankly.

'Why did you do them?'

'I just did.'

'You just did? That's it? No greater reason than, 'cause I felt like it.'

'Not really.' Woody picked up the controller and turned it around in his hands before tossing it aside again.

'You just really wanted to see the other kids in your class naked, your friends?'

Woody cringed.

'You wanted to see them all naked?'

'No,' said his brother.

'Well, that's what you got. Do you fancy them? I didn't even think you were into girls yet. And now apparently you're into them all.'

'I'm not.' Woody's face started to go that familiar shade of red.

'Well, why else would you send them a nude of yourself and ask them to send one back?'

'Stop.'

'What? I'm just asking a question. And why would you write something so cruel on your teacher's jacket? Do you even know what "pedo" means?'

'Yes.'

'Well, why would you write it, then? Do you think it's true? Did your teacher do something to someone that he shouldn't have? Did someone say something?'

'Stop.'

'I just don't understand. And I have to say I'm worried. I am. How could I not be? This isn't the kind of person I thought you were.'

'Don't be worried,' said Woody, starting to look worried himself.

'I can't help it. It's been a shit year, for all of us, but you're not making it easier. I'm ashamed, to be honest. It's hard for me in this town, for all of us, and you're not making it easier.'

'I'm sorry.'

'I thought you were a kind boy.'

'I am.'

'So then why did you do it? You're better than this.'

Woody's eyes were wide. He blinked and Arlo waited, but no explanation was forthcoming.

'Why did you do it?'

'I didn't want to.'

'So then why did you?'

'I had to.'

'Woody,' he chastised.

'I did. She told me to.'

'Who did? Who's she? Amelia Franklin?'

'No, not Amelia. Ruth.'

'Who's Ruth?'

'This woman I do missions with sometimes. On the PlayStation.'

'But who is she? How do you know her?'

'I just know her from the games. She told me to send a photo of myself to the girls in my class and to get them to send me one in return. I didn't want to, but she made me. I said they wouldn't do it, but she said they would. She said they liked me. I didn't even look at the photos, not really. They made me feel bad. I just sent them to her.'

'Sent them to her how?'

'By email.'

'So, you have her email?'

Woody picked up the remote and the screen came alive. He manoeuvred his way into the settings with the controller. 'There. That's it.'

Arlo stood up from the chair to get a better look at the screen:

| BabeRuth_66@eircom.net

'That's how I know her name's Ruth.' The boy shrugged. 'And I guess she's a babe.'

When Arlo didn't respond immediately, Woody took it as him being out of complaints. 'See?' he said, happier now. 'It's not actually a big deal. The pictures weren't even for me. So, you don't need to worry.'

'This is a big deal. A huge deal. A stranger asked you for naked photos of your friends and you sent them to him?'

'Her. It's a girl. Her name is Ruth.'

'Babe Ruth isn't a girl, he's ...' Arlo shook his head. It didn't matter. He couldn't even remember what sport Babe Ruth was famous for, but he was fairly sure he was dead.

'And it's not a real person,' enthused Woody. 'It's just someone on the internet.'

'Of course it's a real person!' Arlo's mind was racing, trying to piece it together. There was something familiar about this. *Babe Ruth* ... 'Why would you do it? Why would you do something so irresponsible and dangerous just because some stranger asked you to?'

The relief left his brother's face.

'Woody?'

'I can't tell you.'

'What do you mean you can't tell me. Of course you can.'

He shook his head.

'Tell me right now, Woody.'

But the head just kept turning.

'All right, grand. I'll just go call Mom and get her to turn around. She's probably not at work yet. You can tell her.'

'No, don't tell Mom!'

Arlo had no intention of telling their mother. She wouldn't know what to do with this information. She wouldn't be able to handle it. There was a good chance it would break her.

'If you don't want to tell Mom, then you better tell me.'

Woody winced. 'You'll get mad.'

'I won't,' he said, convincing neither of them.

'I really don't want to ...'

'And I really don't care.'

Woody groaned. 'Babe Ruth said that if I didn't get the photos and send them on, she'd tell the police who was really driving the night Mike died. She'd tell them it wasn't Dad and that he was just covering ... for you.' Woody looked up at his brother, eyes cartoon wide again.

Arlo felt dizzy.

'I did it for you,' clarified Woody.

'Please don't say that.' *Please don't let that be true.*

'Babe Ruth said you'd go to jail, and so would Mom for perversing the course of justice ...'

'Perverting,' Arlo corrected, pointlessly.

'And then I'd be on my own and I'd probably be put into care and I really don't want that. I don't want you or Mom or anyone else to go to jail. I don't want to be on my own.'

'You won't be, Woody. Why would you believe what some crazy

person on the internet says? Why would you believe there was anything to what they were saying?'

'Because I know it's true. I heard you all talking the morning after the crash. I was getting ready for school and I was at the top of the stairs and you didn't know I was listening, but I was. I heard you arguing with Dad. You were begging him to tell the truth, that it wasn't fair for him to go to jail for someone else's mistakes, for your fucked-up judgement – sorry for cursing, but that's what you said – and Dad said he was confessing and that was the end of it. I heard it all.'

The frantic energy had pushed Woody further along the mattress, inch by inch, and he was now perched on the edge of the bed.

'But how would *they* know that?' Arlo turned his attention back to the computer screen, where the email address shone in white. Only five living people knew that Charlie Whitehead had gone to jail for an offence he hadn't committed, and none of those people would breathe a word about it. 'How could some stranger possibly know what happened that night?'

Unless they weren't a stranger.

Arlo worked his way through the five people who knew the truth: him, his Dad, Leo—

Six.

His former best friend's voice rang in his ears.

What are you on about, boy?

Six people know what happened on Reilly's Pass. It's six now. You're forgetting about little Woody here. He doesn't have all the facts, but he has enough.

He wouldn't tell anyone.

Eh, I know he's your little bro and all, but he sent those images

319

of children across the internet without a second's thought. I think it might possibly be a question worth asking.

His brother was still perched on the edge of the bed, watching him.

'Woody, did you tell anyone else about what you heard me and Dad discussing the morning after the crash? That Dad wasn't the one driving that night?'

'No.'

So then how? Had someone just taken a lucky guess? It would still have to be someone who knew Woody, who knew about the crash, that he was vulnerable—

'I only told one person, and that doesn't count because they're a responsible adult.'

Arlo looked at his brother, whose face contained none of the confidence of his voice. 'Who?' he asked.

'He said he wouldn't tell anyone. It was when Dad went to jail and I was extra upset. I was in school, waiting for Mom to collect me, but it was one of the days she forgot, and I might have been crying, maybe, and he asked what was wrong, and I told him. I didn't want you to go to jail, Arlo. He was really nice about it and he said he wouldn't tell anyone. He was a responsible adult. In fifth class we did this thing about stranger danger, and the teacher said if we were worried, about anything, we should identify a responsible adult to tell.'

'Who was it, Woody?'

His brother looked at him and swallowed. Arlo felt a dull thud in his stomach.

'Was it your teacher?' he asked.

Woody winced.

'Was it Mr Cafferty?'

'No,' said the boy, his still-forming Adam's apple quivering. 'And anyway, Babe Ruth definitely isn't Mr Cafferty using a fake name, if that's what you're thinking, because this person hates Mr Cafferty.'

'What? How do you know that?'

'They made me do all that stuff about the coat and being mean to Mr Cafferty and getting the other kids to be mean too, like Maeve making prank phone calls ...'

Arlo hadn't a clue what his brother was on about.

'Babe Ruth said I had to send on the photos and I had to make Mr Cafferty quit his job, or else they'd tell everyone about the crash and you and Mom would go to jail and I'd be to blame. I felt bad about the pictures because they're my friends and—'

'Woody!'

'What?'

'Who was the person at Glass Lake that you told about the car crash?'

Woody blinked, so far forward on the bed now that he had to hold on to the edges to stop himself falling onto the floor. And suddenly, Arlo realised.

All those drawings on Seamus's workshop walls, several of him playing games consoles, because the caretaker bonded with the kids over a love of Xbox and PlayStation, and the baseball cards framed around his kitchenette, all depicting images of the same man, dressed in stripes and wearing a baseball cap.

He remembered then what sport Babe Ruth had played.

'It was Caretaker Seamus,' said Woody, just as Arlo could have said the same thing. 'I told Caretaker Seamus about the crash.'

....

Supplementary questioning, conducted by Garda Joey Delaney

Frank Cafferty, teacher

I was at the school all day yesterday. I was doing some additional movement work with some of the kids after classes, and that ran right into all the parents arriving. I never left the building.

Garda Joey Delaney

I heard you handed in a letter of resignation yesterday. Is that true?

Cafferty

You heard about that? Already? Jesus, I'm used to living in towns where people talk, but here, you all have access to so much information. Yes, I gave a letter of resignation to Principal Patterson yesterday morning and she asked me to take the week to reconsider.

Delaney

Why did you resign? You haven't been in the job long.

Cafferty

Personal reasons.

Delaney

Did it have anything to do with Seamus McGrath? A couple of witnesses have suggested there was animosity between you two.

Cafferty

It wasn't to do with Seamus. Well, maybe a little bit, I'm not sure, but no. It was personal. Is it relevant?

Delaney

Potentially.

Cafferty

It was … I'm … Well, if you must know, I'm gay. I don't tend to shout it from the rooftops, but if it's really relevant … My husband, Jess, would say I'm ashamed of my sexuality. That's not true; I just don't always feel the need to correct people if they make assumptions that aren't entirely accurate. It's not like I call him 'my wife' but Jess is a unisex name, you know, and if people think one thing, what do I care? I'm not ashamed of myself, or of him, but when you've been a teacher in a tiny country school that feels like it's stuck in the 1950s … Did you know that over 80 per cent of LGBT teachers in Ireland keep their sexuality a secret? That's an official statistic. I'm in a few online support forums and even there, most of us use pseudonyms. People think things have changed in Ireland, and maybe they have in the big cities, but not everywhere, and definitely not at my last school. It was only about 200 miles from here, but it was decades away too. I was practically chased out when the parents found out I was married to a man. I thought Glass Lake would be different, but similar things started happening. I was getting prank phone calls and one of the students wrote 'pedo' on my coat and, not to sound too millennial about it, but it was fairly triggering. So, I decided to leave. I mean, I'm reassessing that now. Jess thinks I should stay and Principal Patterson wants me to, which is nice, and the phone calls have stopped, and Woody, the kid who wrote on my coat, sent me a really lovely apology note, which I received this morning. That was great because we did get on well, at the beginning. I don't know what happened there. And I really do love my job, the kids are great. So anyway, we'll see.

Delaney

And what was the connection to Seamus McGrath? You said it had something to do with him.

Cafferty

No, I said maybe it did. I don't know, and I have zero proof. But I got a feeling off him

… that he didn't like me, I guess. The first
time we met, it was fine, but then one day I
was queuing behind him in Regan's Chemist, to
print out some photos. They have one of those
booths where you connect your phone and it will
print out whichever images you select. Seamus
was using the machine and I was waiting. I
was looking through my phone; I wasn't looking
over his shoulder or anything. But when he was
done, I looked up, and he was glaring at me.
He snapped at me for standing so close, even
though I was metres behind. Ever since then,
he's been cold with me. He's made it clear
he's not comfortable with my sexuality. I know
you're supposed to be the bigger person and rise
above bigotry, but have you ever tried it? It's
exhausting.

Delaney

Did you argue about this?

Cafferty

No, never.

Delaney

Did you argue about anything else?

Cafferty

Not at all. It was clear he didn't like me, but
I never challenged him on it. I hadn't a thing
to do with his drowning. He was a bigot and

paranoid - what photos could possibly have been
that frickin' private? - but I am sorry he's
dead. It must be very hard on his family.

36

......

ONE DAY EARLIER

B**everley had** delivered the second wake-up call of the morning and now had her laptop and tablet out side by side on the kitchen's central island as she waited for Amelia to appear downstairs. She was comparing two near identical, and pointedly negative, Facebook reviews for Sneaky Sweets. The timing of the reviews – shortly after yesterday's yoga class – and their personal nature had her suspecting Fiona Murphy.

Amelia's footsteps on the stairs told her she did not need to disturb herself to answer the door. It was probably the DPD man. Beverley was a staunch supporter of shopping local, but if Gerry Regan refused to stock non-comedogenic facial cleanser, she didn't see what choice she had.

She added her phone to the tech hub and began scrolling through old WhatsApp messages to see if her fellow Laker had form on using the word 'omnishambles'.

'Mum!'

Still scrolling, Beverley slid off the stool. All the child had to do was sign for the package.

'Mum!' Amelia called again when she was halfway across the kitchen. 'Arlo Whitehead is at the door!'

Beverley paused, then powered ahead, cutting the kitchen-to-front-door journey time to what might be expected in a basic semi-d. She yanked the door away from her daughter. She could barely believe it, but there he was, standing on her doorstep with that eyesore of a van back up and running and blighting their driveway. He may not have been a complete gigolo after all, but he was still a Whitehead.

'Are you lost?'

'No,' he began.

'Or have you suffered a concussion? That's the only reason I can think for why you would be knocking on my door.'

'Mrs Franklin—'

'Ella isn't here, if that's what you're after.'

'I'm here to see you.'

Beverley hooted. 'You are not. And if you don't leave now, I'll phone my husband.' An empty threat, of course. Malachy would tell her to take the boy in from the doorstep and stop making a scene.

'Mrs Franklin, could I just talk to you for a couple of minutes? Please.' The teenager glanced down at Amelia, who was watching the exchange like she was umpiring a particularly embarrassing tennis match. 'Just you, if that would be okay.'

He was paler than usual, none of his rosiness, and he was looking her in the eye – something she wasn't sure he'd done before. Against her better judgement, she opened the door a fraction more.

'Go into the kitchen and get some breakfast, Amelia.'

She waited until her daughter had crossed the foyer and disappeared through the door on the far side. Then, reluctantly, she took a half-step backwards. Arlo stepped inside.

'Shoes off. Actually, no,' she said, as he bent down to undo the laces. 'Keep them on.' She believed Fiona when she said the

328

whole thing with Arlo had been one of her fabrications, but that didn't change the fact that Ella was barely sleeping. She'd heard her daughter pottering around on the top floor last night, and this morning she had left for university about an hour earlier than usual. This lad had the gall to think he was good enough for Ella – and then he had the audacity to break her heart. There was something far too intimate about him walking around their home in socks. 'You can step into the drawing room. It's this way,' she said, veering him to the left. 'Although, what am I saying? You could probably give me a tour of my own house at this stage.'

She closed the door behind him, checking before she did so that Amelia had not reappeared from the kitchen.

'So, what is it?' she said, positioning herself in the centre of the room. She didn't invite the teenager to sit. He wouldn't be staying.

'I'm not sure where to start ...'

'I've got ten minutes before I drop Amelia to school, so you'd better figure it out.'

'It's about the photos Amelia and the other girls sent to Woody – except they weren't sending them to Woody, not really ...' And then he told her the worst thing she had heard in a long time. He talked quickly and clumsily, falling over certain words and abandoning sentences only to start them again, but he got the details out.

'Seamus McGrath?' she echoed.

'Yes,' he said uncertainly, and she realised she was a few sentences behind him.

She nodded and he continued. He told her how the school caretaker had come to contact Woody, that he had blackmailed him with some unspecified threat, and made the child send on all the photos of the girls. Seamus McGrath was looking at those

329

photos. Seamus McGrath was looking at a naked photo of her beautiful, ambitious, confident daughter. Seamus McGrath, the school caretaker, a man well into his fifties, had all those photos.

The teenager explained how he didn't know what to do, how he was technically an adult but didn't feel like one, and how Ella had told him that Beverley always knew what to do. His dad had been like that, he said, but since he wasn't around any more, he'd come to her. He thought Beverley was the kind of person he needed. He knew she wasn't his biggest fan, but Glass Lake was important to her and obviously Amelia was important to her and maybe she'd know what to do.

'Do you know what to do?'

'I just have to think ...' she replied, though instinctively she knew exactly what to do. She would get in her car and drive around Cooney in circles until she saw Seamus McGrath crossing the road on Main Street or pulling into the hardware shop down by the pier, then she would mount the pavement and run him over. Or perhaps she would wait until he was at the top of a ladder, fixing the spotlights on the auditorium stage, and she would charge across the stage and topple the thing, sending him crashing to his death. The details were vague, but the outcome was clear: she would kill him.

'I thought about going to the guards but they're not big fans of our family. A lot of them are in the GAA club and they weren't too happy when Mike Roche Senior moved away. Anyway, it would be too hard to prove. It's just an email address – how can I prove that Seamus was the one operating it? Even though I know he was. Maybe we could get a confession? What do you think about that? Mrs Franklin? Do you think we could get him to confess?'

'I'm thinking ...'

It was not the photo she had walked in on Amelia taking that she saw in her mind's eye, but rather the framed one in the living room, the one of Amelia in her school uniform, her navy stockings pulled right up to the hem of her skirt, and grinning so widely you could see her missing tooth. Seamus McGrath had taken that.

Arlo ran through their various options, but none fit the bill. There was nothing for it but to get rid of the depraved man. It was almost serene, this visceral realisation. She'd gone from nought to ready to kill in a matter of seconds, and she was fine with it. She knew now that this was what her mother was talking about. This was the defining point in her life, the one she would recollect on her death bed and know she had done what was right, the one where she was led by love for her children and a desire to protect the vulnerable.

'Mrs Franklin?'

'Yes,' she replied in that same sharp, defensive tone she used when they were at a Lakers meeting and Claire caught her daydreaming.

'What ... what should I do?'

'You'll leave it to me.'

Arlo nodded, waiting for her to say more.

'It's Wednesday now so ... today. I'm at the school this evening. It's the last night of preparations before opening night tomorrow.'

'I'll be there too,' said Arlo. 'It's my last few hours' work with Glass Lake. Seamus has me helping with lights and some other bits. Will we talk to him then? But there'll be a lot of other people around. Maybe it'd be better to confront him somewhere more private? If we want to get a confession? But then I don't know where. He's not at the school today. He's out collecting some final set pieces. I'm not sure where he is exactly ...'

'This evening at Glass Lake will be fine,' declared Beverley.

Amelia was in danger of being late for school, and she had a lot to organise. 'I'll see you then, Arlo.' She stood from her stool and walked the teenager to the door. 'We'll keep this between ourselves, all right? It's only another few hours, and it won't help to tell anyone else. Is that—' She peered out the glass panel, but she had imagined the sound of her daughter's hand-me-down banger pulling up. 'So, we're agreed? We'll keep it between us?'

So used was she to getting her own way that Beverley took this to be a closed matter. Nobody else was to know. She didn't notice that the teenager hadn't responded; she didn't know that Arlo had one other confidant in mind.

37

......

Joey had felt sure today would bring a development, maybe even a resolution, but there was fifteen minutes left in his shift and he was no closer to understanding why Seamus McGrath had ended up in the River Gorm than he had been this morning. He'd chased his one lead and it had led to nothing. Frank Cafferty had been at the school all yesterday and he'd been surrounded by witnesses the whole time. What had he expected? That the mild-mannered teacher had pushed the unremarkable janitor to his death because they hadn't gotten on particularly well?

The clock above the station exit ticked loudly and Joey watched the second hand make its journey around the face. The sergeant still wasn't back from visiting Miriam McGrath and Joey had done every scrap of work he could think to do. He was just reaching for the pen jar – a few biros were wearing the wrong colour lids – when the phone rang. Joey dived for it.

'Aberstown Station,' he said breathlessly, just as the double doors pushed open and Whelan lumbered in from the cold.

'This is Sergeant Mulhern. Is Sergeant Whelan about?'

'He's ...'

333

Whelan was about two feet from him now, slowly removing his hat and reaching up to the coat stand.

'I'll just check ... Can I tell him what it's about?'

'News on Seamus McGrath.'

Joey's heart soared, then sank. Couldn't this man have called two minutes earlier? Or couldn't his sergeant have stopped for another sandwich?

'Are you phoning from pathology?'

'Forensics. Is the sergeant about or not?'

Reluctantly, Joey held out the receiver. 'A call from forensics, sir. News on Seamus.'

His boss took the phone. 'Sergeant James Whelan,' he said, lowering himself into the chair.

The younger guard tried to hear what was being said down the line. But all he got was the creak of the sergeant's battered chair as he rotated it towards the desk.

'And they've done a thorough search?' said Whelan, after an eternity of listening. He swung the chair again, so he now had his back to Joey. 'No, I understand. Yes, I agree. Not what you'd want, but still. That does seem to settle the matter.'

38
• • • • •

THE EVENING BEFORE

On her third visit in almost as many weeks, Christine Maguire found the Glass Lake auditorium to be in a whole new state of disarray. It was the evening before opening night – officially the worst time of year to find yourself in the place – and the parents were frantically charging about the hall just as their children had done a week ago. Claire Keating's husband was arguing with Mr Peoples, the choirmaster, while banging something out on the piano, and Beverley was lecturing several sheepish-looking parents on the stage. They may not have been dressed head to toe in the same colour, but the scene was oddly familiar.

She glanced around the auditorium, but there was no sign of Connie Whitehead. She had been feeling uneasy since Maeve's confession on Monday afternoon and while she wanted to make her daughter own up to the prank phone calls and apologise, she also couldn't help thinking about the why of it all. What had Mr Cafferty done that Woody was so eager to get rid of him? She didn't want to add to Connie's hardship, potentially over nothing, but it would be irresponsible to not at least voice her concerns to an adult member of the Whitehead family. She had been hoping to mention it to her, in a semi-casual way, this evening.

There was a roster board in the middle of the hall, but there was no sign of Connie's name. Christina found her own name and headed over to Mrs Walsh. Glass Lake's oldest staff member was standing before six towering stacks of plastic chairs and two towering mothers.

'If you could just start to place some of these in rows ...' the Junior Infants' teacher was saying, in what was clearly not her first plea.

'I'm not putting out a single chair until someone gives me a good reason why my son can't be the Munchkin mayor.'

'My God, woman. There is no Munchkin mayor,' snapped Lorna Farrell. 'Beverley made it clear that this production is based on the book, not the film. There is no mayor in the book.'

'I do not see the harm in letting my son wear a gold chain on stage,' said the other woman, ignoring Lorna and beseeching Mrs Walsh. 'We ordered it especially, paid for fast-track delivery and everything, and we've been doing character development for weeks now. He's sitting on the floor at dinner time because, as a Munchkin, he's too short to make it on to the seats, and he's dreaming about chairing council meetings. The child is committed!'

'Sounds more like he should be committed,' muttered Lorna.

'Ladies, please, we need to get these chairs out and in rows,' begged Mrs Walsh. 'I'd lift them myself if it wasn't for my trapped nerves. Christine, dear! Hello! Could you start putting out the chairs ...? Please?'

'Of course, Mrs Walsh,' she said, pulling a plastic seat from the top of the pile. She placed it down beside her and gave the auditorium another quick search. 'Has anyone seen Connie Whitehead?'

'Thank you, Christine, but the row actually starts at the other—'

'Connie Whitehead doesn't volunteer,' scoffed Lorna. 'Especially not now her son has been kicked out of the musical.'

'So she's not coming?'

'The chairs, ladies, please!'

Christina took a chair from a separate pile and started a row going in the other direction. She had about five of them lined up when the double doors opened at the back of the hall and Arlo appeared, looking slightly frazzled.

He was an adult, technically – and speaking to him about it was better than nothing.

Mrs Walsh blocked her path. 'Don't go.'

'I'll just be a minute. I'll be back.'

'If you go, they'll go. Please. I can't put the chairs out myself. My back can't handle it.' The teacher looked up at her imploringly.

'I ...'

The double doors opened again, and she glanced over in time to see Arlo disappearing back out into the corridor. Beverley was down off the stage and hot on his heels. Whatever set design drama she wanted him for could wait until Christine had had a quick word.

'I'm sorry, Mrs Walsh, I really am. I'll be right back,' she called as she jogged off across the hall, side-stepping an argument about camera positions as she made her way out into the corridor.

'Arlo!' she called.

The teenager, who was halfway down the corridor, stopped. Beverley also turned. Then, Beverley started moving again, pulling the teenager with her. This was not a pairing Christine had expected. Just that afternoon, when she called to Butcher Murphy's to get some lamb, she heard that Arlo and Ella Franklin had been secretly dating for months and that Beverley had just found out. So, unless Beverley was leading the teenager somewhere to do away with him ...

She ran to catch up with them. 'Can I speak to you for a minute, Arlo?'

'Is it about your cat?'

'Hmm? Oh no, that's all fine. It's about Woody, actually, and my daughter ...'

'Photos?'

'No ...'

'Come on,' said Beverley, pulling the teenager again. 'We haven't time.'

'This is actually quite important, Beverley. If I could speak to Arlo in private for a minute ...'

'And what we're doing is actually quite important too. Come on,' she said again.

'Can I find you later, Mrs Maguire?' the teenager said, turning so he was walking backwards away from her.

'This isn't really the sort of thing that can wait,' she said, following them.

'I'm sorry, but we are in the middle of something.'

'Maeve has been prank phoning Mr Cafferty,' she said, annoyed that she'd been given no option but to have this conversation in front of Beverley. 'She's been doing it at Woody's behest. She said Woody was trying to get Mr Cafferty to quit his job.'

'Please, Mrs Maguire, could we talk about this later?'

'Don't you think that's worrying? That your brother would want his teacher to quit his job that badly? I mean, what could he possibly have done?'

She couldn't be sure, but she was pretty sure Beverley rolled her eyes.

'Arlo!'

The teenager stopped again. 'I'm really sorry Maeve got caught up in this. It won't happen again.'

'I'm not worried about Maeve. I'm telling you because of Woody. You don't seem concerned. Would I be better speaking with your mother?'

'No, don't do that!' Arlo glanced at Beverley. What was going on with these two? 'I already knew about the calls. I only found out this morning, and I am sorry Maeve was involved, but it's not what you think, and ... we're taking care of it.'

'That's enough,' muttered Beverley, as they came to a halt outside Caretaker Seamus's workroom.

'I have to go,' he said apologetically. 'But thank you for letting me know. And you don't need to worry. Thank you but—'

'Ready?' asked Beverley, hand on the knob. Then she pushed the door and disappeared inside.

'Sorry,' said Arlo again. 'Thanks for the heads-up.'

And he, too, was gone.

Christine looked back down the corridor, then peered through the small window in the workroom door, but there was some sort of translucent paper stuck to the other side and she couldn't see in. She felt a wave of irritation at the entitled way Beverley was commanding the teenager and (in spite of her commitment to never becoming too interested in Glass Lake goings-on) an itching curiosity to know what exactly this unlikely duo were up to.

She might not be up for writing sensationalist news stories, but she was still a journalist. It was her job – no, her *duty* – to be nosy.

'Feck it,' she said under her breath, and she pushed the workroom door open.

....

'Where is he? Where's Seamus?'

Beverley had stormed through the door, all guns blazing, ready for an almighty showdown with the Glass Lake caretaker.

Instead, she was faced with the Glass Lake principal.

'What are you doing here?'

Nuala Patterson barely blinked. 'This is my school, Beverley.'

The door opened behind Beverley, and the principal's face changed. It didn't make sense – because it was Arlo Whitehead who had entered the room – but she could have sworn it softened.

'Where's Seamus?' the teenager demanded, coming to a stop between her and the principal. Whatever about the tone Beverly had used, Nuala wasn't going to accept *that* from a Whitehead.

But when the principal spoke, she sounded apologetic. 'He's not here,' she said. 'I already spoke to him.'

'But we agreed.'

'I know. I'm sorry, Arlo. But I didn't want you getting mixed up in anything else. I took it upon myself. I've dealt with Seamus.'

'What does that mean?'

'He won't be coming back,' said Nuala.

Even though Beverley had been on the verge of murdering the man this morning, she felt a shiver run down her spine. This whole bizarre situation had gone up a notch. Arlo had told someone else about what was going on, despite her ordering him not to. And he'd told Nuala, of all people. Since when did these two speak to each

340

other, let alone in courteous, apologetic tones? Nuala was talking like she was the one who owed Arlo something.

Beverley looked at the teenager, waiting for him to ask some of the many, obvious, follow-up questions. When he did not, she took it upon herself to interrupt this bizarrely cosy chat.

'Okay,' she said, raising a hand, like she was back in school, 'someone needs to fill me in on what's going on here – and quickly.'

'Yeah,' said a voice from behind her, and she spun around to find that Christine Maguire had followed them into the room. 'I was about to say the same thing.'

39
······

Nuala Patterson's mind had been racing for several hours now. From the moment Arlo had appeared in her office earlier today, she had felt like she was floating outside her own body.

Seamus McGrath. The Glass Lake caretaker. *Her* caretaker. The man she had hired and trusted with so many jobs at the school. Seamus who opened the school in the morning and locked it at night, who fixed everything that needed fixing, who built the sets for the annual musical and took the class photos. Glass Lake was Nuala's school, it was her responsibility, and she had taken her eye off the ball. Had she been so distracted by her personal dramas that she hadn't realised what a perverted man was working under her roof?

There was a chance, she had told herself when Arlo had left her office under the false promise that she would sit tight until that evening, that he had got it wrong.

She held out hope as she checked the staff location planner, told Mairead she had to head into town on urgent business, and drove down to the hardware shop on Cooney Pier. It was possible, she told herself as she tapped on the steering wheel, waiting for the caretaker to appear, that Arlo had put two and two together and come up with the most unsavoury number.

But in her heart of hearts, something about it rang true.

Seamus's van pulled in about three cars down and Nuala hopped out. The caretaker had just shut his own door when he clocked the principal heading towards him. He was carrying a large empty paint tin and splattered crowbar.

'Everything all right?'

'I need to speak to you.'

Seamus kept his eyes on her as he locked the van. 'Beverley finally signed off on a yellow-enough yellow for the brick road, so I'm just picking up another couple of tins for the final coat.' She must have looked how she felt because the man stuffed his keys into his pockets and, face sombre, stepped away from the road and into the narrow laneway between the hardware shop and the credit union. He placed the crowbar and tin at his feet. 'Everything all right, Nuala?' he asked again.

Her plan had been to tell him what was alleged and to ask if it was true. But now that she was here, and she was regarding him in a whole new light, she abandoned that tack, and went instead with foregone conclusion.

She told the caretaker that she knew what had been going on. She made it sound like several concrete sources had come to her, as opposed to one uncertain teenager, and she put forward the extrapolations as facts. They knew he had been messaging Woody and befriending him under a pseudonym; they knew he had blackmailed the child; they knew he had instructed him to pose nude and to use that image to solicit similar photos from the female students in his class; and they knew the photos were being sent on to Seamus for God knows what purpose.

'Who told you that?'

'Like I said, several people.'

A woman with a buggy passed about five feet from them and Seamus turned away from the road. 'Was it Frank Cafferty?'

'I'm not naming names, Seamus.'

The caretaker's temper flared. 'It was, wasn't it? You can't believe him. He's a fairy, Nuala. Did you know that about him?'

Nuala had been hoping for speechless shock, extreme outrage, dogged denial. Even a threat to sue her for slander would have been welcome. If his aim was to come across as innocent, his focus was in the wrong place.

'He might think he saw me printing out certain photos, but he's wrong,' Seamus continued, his face red. 'He was too far away. He couldn't have seen anything. He's let his imagination run away with him. That lot often do. It's for the best he's leaving, if he's going to spread such awful rumours as that.'

'Mr Cafferty never told me anything.' The sixth-class teacher had handed in his resignation that morning but she had yet to accept it. 'Though I do also know you were instructing the boy to make his life difficult. I believe you gave Woody the teacher's mobile phone number. And you told him to write "pedo" on his coat.'

'I never – I – I never ...' Seamus's foot started tapping the damp concrete. He took another couple of glances over his shoulder. 'Prove it,' he said suddenly, defiantly. 'Do you have proof?'

Not 'You don't have proof' or 'You couldn't possibly have proof because it's not true' but 'Do you have proof?'. A self-incriminating question.

'I stopped by your workroom before coming here. I was looking at your framed cards over the kitchen counter.'

'My baseball card collection. So?'

'Babe Ruth,' she all but spat, finding it difficult to look at the man that she had thought was an ally at least, but often a friend. She'd never noticed the cards before and wouldn't have if Arlo hadn't mentioned them. 'I trusted you. I gave you a job and I confided in you. I would have trusted you with anything at this school. Our students, Seamus? It's ...' She flinched. 'You disgust me.'

His foot stopped tapping. His body slumped. His whole demeanour changed.

'I'm sorry. I'm really sorry. I didn't mean to hurt anyone. I didn't hurt anyone. I never touched Woody or any other child. It was all harmless, a sort of joke.'

'A joke? Naked images of our students are a *joke*?'

'No, not a joke. But they weren't ... I wasn't ... I didn't do anything with them. They were only for my use. I printed them off and that was it. I'm rubbish with technology. I didn't upload them to the internet or anything like that. I just ... There's something wrong with me, I can't help it, I know it's not right, but—'

'Enough!' she spat. Even the idea of the photos made her feel physically ill. She did not need to know what went through Seamus's mind when he looked at them. 'You're gone, Seamus.'

'Please, Nuala, no; you can't fire me. I love this job. What would you do without me? Who would build the sets? Opening night is tomorrow and—'

'Of course you're fired! That's the least of it. I'm going to the guards.'

All anger gone from him now, his face drained to white. 'No.'

'Yes.'

'No, no, no, please, please, don't do that. Don't tell anyone. My wife – she wouldn't – it would kill her, and my sister ... I couldn't handle it – all our neighbours, my friends. Oh God. You can't ...'

'I trusted you – with my school, with my students!'

'No, no. I'll ... You can't. Please. My wife has a bad heart, you know that. She couldn't ... The neighbours. She couldn't stand them all talking. I couldn't stand it. You know this place, everyone would know, and they wouldn't even care about the truth, I'd never be allowed to explain my side!'

A heat began to rise. The flames started in her diaphragm and whooshed into her chest, her shoulders, up into her head. Her gaze fell on the items at Seamus's feet. It would be so simple to lift up the crowbar, to swing for the man in his flummoxed, panicked state and send it flying on to the side of his head.

'Please, Nuala. It would kill me.'

She felt her hand relinquishing her waist, reaching down. It was not something she would have thought herself capable of, but now it seemed perfectly reasonable. None of us know the extent of our abilities, until we are pushed to the limit.

....

'Jesus Christ, Nuala! I was tempted to kill him myself this morning but come on – what were you thinking?!'

'Oh relax, Beverley,' the principal snapped. 'I didn't bludgeon the bastard! I just contemplated it. I'm only telling you what I was thinking, not what I did.'

'Well, it sounded very convincing from where I was standing.'

'So, what did you do?' asked Arlo, keen to bring this whole thing to a conclusion and get out of here. Nuala had put some sort of baking paper over the small window in the door, but any parent or teacher could easily walk in on them, looking for Seamus to help with some staging issue. Christine Maguire was still standing against the back wall. They'd given her a summary of what was going on and she looked mildly ill. Already far too many people knew. Now they'd thrown a journalist into the mix.

He returned his attention to the woman he'd once thought of as a sort of second mother and asked, yet again: 'Where is Seamus?'

'He's gone to the guards,' replied Nuala. 'I told him I was going to Aberstown Station and he begged me to let him do it.'

'So he's gone by himself? You just took his word for it?' came a voice, Christine's, from the back of the room. 'What if he makes a run for it?'

'He won't.'

'Because he's such an upstanding, trustworthy member of society?'

'Where would he go? And even if he did do a legger, what then? He knows I'd go to the guards and they'd find him eventually.'

'Why are we getting the police involved?' demanded Beverley. 'If the police know, there'll be a full investigation and then everyone in town will know where the children's naked photos really ended up. What good is that going to do anyone?'

'Of course the police have to know,' said Christine.

'Easy for you to say,' Beverley shot back. 'Your daughter wasn't caught up in this thing. How do you think Amelia is going to feel when she finds out the image she thought she was sending to a boy in her class was actually going to a near sixty-year-old man who she thought was an adult she could trust? She'll be scarred for life!'

'If there was another way, I'd have taken it,' began Nuala.

'Of course there was another way!'

'What were you planning to do, Beverley? Hmm? Kill him?'

'I was going to record a confession,' the woman retorted, waving her phone at the principal, 'and use it as blackmail. I was going to run him out of town and ensure he never came back.'

'Oh yes. So just make him someone else's problem?'

'Rather that than it being our children's problem.'

Arlo wasn't particularly thrilled about the guards getting involved either – he didn't want Woody to know who he'd really been sending the photos to and, once they knew his brother was being blackmailed, they'd want to know what information 'Babe Ruth' had on Woody and his family. None of them wanted the investigation into the crash resurfacing.

'When did he say he was going to the guards?' he asked.

'Right after I spoke to him,' said Nuala. 'Around two p.m., I'd say. I watched him jump in his van and go.'

They all glanced towards the clock.

'And have you heard from the guards yet?' asked Christine.

'No,' conceded Nuala. 'But I'm sure I will ...'

Beverley guffawed.

And then, right on cue, the unmistakable wail of a siren began to gather in the distance.

40
· · · · · ·

'**N**uala.'

Sergeant Whelan was striding down the corridor, hat hanging from his left hand, and his shirt its usual amount of crumpled.

She raised her hand in greeting, turning once to check the others had obeyed her request and were staying put in the workroom. Of course, there was a good chance Sergeant Whelan would want to inspect the workroom, lest it contained some sort of evidence.

'I'm here to see if the school might have a phone number on record. One for Miriam McGrath.'

'Miriam,' repeated Nuala. It made sense they'd want to speak to the wife, but surely Seamus could have given them that. 'Seamus's Miriam?'

The sergeant nodded. 'We swung by the house but she's not in.'

'Doesn't Seamus have a number for her?'

He gave her a peculiar look then he dropped his eyes and fed the rim of his hat through his hands. 'I'm afraid Seamus is the reason we're looking to contact her.'

Nuala nodded, not quite getting what the problem was. If Seamus was in custody then surely they could just ask for the number, or take his phone and retrieve it if he wouldn't oblige.

'I'm sorry to be the bearer of tragic news, Nuala, I know you two were close, but Seamus is dead. His body has just been taken out of the Gorm.'

'His ... He's *dead*?'

The sergeant nodded. 'We've just come from the scene. Pathology are working on an initial assessment now, but his car was spotted out near the bridge on the edge of town about 4 p.m. He must have gone in then ...'

Nuala's head was shaking, while Sergeant Whelan's was nodding. 'Was it ...?' she began.

'We don't know what happened. We're investigating. Foul play looks unlikely and it's possible he fell, it is windy this evening, but it wouldn't be that easy to fall ...' He caught her eye in a way that confirmed the guard's suspicion but didn't force him to speak ill of the dead. It was a lot more noble to have fallen than to have jumped.

Nuala thought back on her conversation with Seamus, on how sure he'd been that he should go to the station alone, and how incapable he'd been of accepting a reality in which he would be known as the man who had done such a terrible thing.

'I should clear the school,' she said, thinking aloud.

'It's not strictly necessary ...'

'We won't be doing the musical now. We can hardly open a show the day after the set builder has died, can we?'

'I suppose not.'

'I'll get you that number from my office,' she said, as she turned and started walking, the sergeant following after her. She glanced in through the double-door windows as they passed the auditorium. 'Then I'll send them all home.'

'You don't have any idea why he might have done this to himself, do you?'

Nuala paused at her office door. This was the moment. This was the point at which she should tell the gardaí exactly what she had been planning to tell them a few hours earlier – she should tell them the very things Seamus had promised to relay before he took the easy way out. But she thought of the others in the workroom, about what it would do to Woody, and the other children, and all their families. What good would it do them to know where their photographs had really ended up? What purpose could it possibly serve now that the person who needed to be punished was no more? What would be the benefit in punishing everyone else instead?

'If he did do it,' the sergeant added. 'Hypothetically.'

'Not an idea,' she said, holding the sergeant's gaze so firmly she almost believed herself. 'I am as shocked as it is possible to be.'

41

······

'**T**hat was Sergeant Mick Mulhern from Cork City forensics,' said Whelan, having hung up the receiver and studied it for a good three seconds.

Joey nodded, hands instinctively going to his belt and hoisting it up.

'He was calling about our DOA ...'

'Yes, Sergeant,' replied Joey, desperate for any information he didn't already have.

'... Seamus McGrath.'

Joey waited.

The sergeant sighed.

Joey waited some more.

'Yah.'

He was doing it on purpose.

Joey forced his hands away from his belt and did his best to look relaxed. *Tell me, don't tell, it's all the same to me.*

He had barely finished thinking this mantra when he was opening his mouth to beg for information. But the sergeant got in just ahead.

'They found a suicide note, in the car. They're sending it through to us now.'

Joey clamped his mouth shut. His hands flew back to his belt. He was ready for action.

'It's short. Addressed to his wife and scrawled on the back of a discarded envelope which, judging by the footprints, had been sitting on the floor of his car for a while. It was the only thing he had to hand, I suppose, but that suggests it wasn't premeditated; that he hadn't gotten up that morning intending to take his own life.'

'What did the note say?'

'I'm sorry to leave you. Please forgive me. I didn't mean any harm.'

'That's it?'

'That's it.' The sergeant made a sound somewhere between a sigh and a growl. 'Didn't mean any harm ... in topping himself? Scant comfort that'll be to his missis, all alone in that house now. She's the nervy type, you know. Doesn't seem to have much of a life, no real friends, doesn't even appear to have full access to their bank accounts. When I was out there today, she told me he couldn't swim.'

'Oh,' said Joey.

'Never learned. She bought him lessons when they first got married, but he didn't go. Too proud, I suppose.'

'So that's why he threw himself in the river? He knew he'd have no way out?'

'Suppose so,' said the sergeant, groaning as he stood from the chair again. 'I guess I'm heading back out to Cooney, amn't I? I'd almost rather be telling her he was pushed. You'd be less likely to take that personally. Can you hang on a few more minutes until Corrigan comes on shift?'

Joey nodded as his superior removed his hat and coat from the stand once again.

'And Delaney?'

'Yes, sir?'

'Put your last few minutes to good use.'

'Yes, Sergeant. Whatever you need.'

'Get a screwdriver from the back office and put another notch in your belt. All day those goddam trousers have been falling down.'

....

Arlo Whitehead, temporary employee

I was working with Seamus for the past couple of weeks. I didn't notice anything out of the ordinary. I can't think of a single reason he might have jumped, or a reason he might have been pushed. He was a very popular man. As far as I know, nobody had a bad word to say about him. Has anyone said a bad word about him?

Beverley Franklin, parent

The last thing he said to me? Mmm ... Oh, yes. He apologised for messing up the paint on the Yellow Brick Road so many times. That was it. He said I was right, and he was wrong and that the colour hadn't been correct, but now it was. I thanked him for the apology and for all his work. We parted on excellent terms.

Christine Maguire, parent

I went looking for him in his workshop yesterday evening, yes. It was for an article I was planning to write on the musical. But he wasn't there. A few people were looking for him. Which just shows you how valued a member of our community he was. Drownings are so tragic. Poor Seamus. It couldn't have happened to a nicer man.

42
· · · · ·

Christine Maguire piled costume fabric into her boot as the wind continued to howl. The parents had all left the hall on Principal Patterson's instruction and, around her, they were clambering into their own cars. She saw Beverley approaching from a couple of metres away.

'Don't you think that was strange?'

The wind caught the tail of a roll of blue satin and she grabbed it just before it went sailing out of the boot and across the car park.

'I think I made it clear I thought it was all very strange,' replied Christine.

'It was the best possible outcome,' said Beverley matter-of-factly. 'That barbarian is no more, and my daughter doesn't have to be subjected to police interrogation and neighbourhood gossip over something that was entirely not her fault. It's always the victims that suffer. At least this way, justice was still served.'

Christine continued to stack the material, doing her best to keep it apart from Conor's mucky hiking boots that had been living in the boot for several months.

'Anyway. I'm talking about Arlo and Nuala Patterson,' said Beverley, lowering her voice. Orla and Rodney Smith were heading for the car beside Christine's.

'Can't wait for the show tomorrow!' enthused Orla.

'We've been watching the film in preparation,' added Rodney.

Nuala had sent the parents home, but she hadn't told them why. Only the few who'd been present in the workroom knew about Seamus's death and that there would be no show tomorrow, or at all. Beverley nearly had a fit when Nuala told them the plan – 'The TV producers are already in town!' – but even she accepted there was no way around it.

'It's not based on the film, you ignorami,' she muttered now after the Smiths shut their doors and started their car.

Christine slammed the boot. She was jealous of the Smiths. She was jealous of everyone who had already left this car park and who hadn't been bound for life to Beverley Franklin over a deeply uncomfortable secret.

The sound of the boot shutting focused the other woman's attention. 'Don't you think it's strange that Arlo and Nuala, of all people, were in cahoots?' said Beverley. 'They usually go out of their way to ignore each other. And you couldn't blame Nuala for that. Imagine your child was in a horrific accident and you have to risk meeting the people associated with it every time you walk down the street?'

'What's your point, Beverley?'

'Why did Arlo go to Nuala for help? And why did Nuala give it so readily?'

'I don't know,' admitted Christine. As surprised as she'd been to see Beverley and Arlo chatting civilly, she'd been even more taken aback to find Nuala apologising to the boy. There were rumours out of Aberstown Garda Station after the crash, inconsistencies in the forensics reports, heavy suggestions Charlie hadn't really been

357

driving that night, that he was covering for his son. They were only ever rumours, nothing she could report. But still, if there was even a possibility that Arlo had been the one to injure her son, how could Nuala be so civil to him?

'I can't think of a single reason for it,' mused Beverley, as Christine opened the driver's side of her car. 'It just doesn't make any sense.'

....

'Everything looks perfect,' said Arlo, as he and Nuala stood at the back of the auditorium, surveying the impeccably straight rows of chairs, and the picture-perfect cornfield that occupied the entire stage. There was bunting streamed around the perimeters of the hall, and a huge banner hung from the vast ceiling: *The Wonderful Wizard of Oz.*

'It really does,' agreed Nuala, her hand hovering over the light switches a moment longer. Everything was ready to go for opening night. 'Pity we won't get to put any of it to use.'

She brought her fingers down and the hall plunged into darkness.

He kept pace as they made their way down the corridor, their footsteps echoing softly. The faint murmur of the last few stragglers travelled in from the car park. They were the last to leave. He pushed his way through the side foyer and out into the blustery night. He held the door for the principal.

'Thank you,' he said, as Nuala turned back to lock the door and the tails of her coat whipped around her.

'You don't need to thank me.'

He wanted to say that he missed talking to her, but embarrassment stopped him. It hadn't even been a year, but he felt so much older, too old for those kinds of declarations. Everything was different now.

The wind whooshed around them and Nuala squinted against it, pulling her personal keys from her pocket now and clamping her fist around them. 'I owe your family,' she said, catching the hem of her coat. 'I told you I'd never forget that. I'm just glad to have the chance to start paying you back.'

43

......

Mike was the one who snuck in the alcohol.
Mike was always chancing his arm, and he was a demon for the drink. He had his dad's spirits cabinet watered down to nothing. Luckily for his son, Mike Roche Senior still treated his body the way he had when he played GAA. But some day he would open the mahogany sideboard in his study and wonder why his eighteen-year-old bourbon-barrelled Jameson was now the colour of well-hydrated piss.

When Charlie got chatting to someone at the bar before the gig started, Mike pulled his two friends up from their seats. 'Come on,' he said. 'We're going to the jacks.'

'I'm not going to the jacks with you,' said Leo, shaking him off.

Mike winked at Leo. 'I've got something that'll make it worth your while,' he said, whipping one side of his jacket open to reveal a brief glimpse of a Sprite bottle containing a liquid too dark to be Sprite.

'Where'd you get that?'

'Big Mikey's stash, of course.'

'Your auld fella has nothing worth taking any more,' said Leo. 'We're just drinking our own diluted muck at this stage.'

Mike rolled his eyes. 'It's a new bottle, *Leonardo*. Gerry Regan wants his son on the senior team; he dropped this into my dad during the week to sweeten the deal.'

'I've seen Ralph Regan trip over his feet walking down Main Street,' said Arlo sceptically. 'He hasn't a chance of making the team.'

'A total no-hoper,' agreed Mike, patting his breast pocket. 'So, you know this stuff has got to be good.'

There was one other lad in the bathroom, using the urinal. Mike nodded at him – 'A very good evening to you, sir' – then he pulled his friends into the last stall after him.

'I'm not going to bum fuck you, Leo,' said Mike, catching the look on his friend's face. 'And I'll do my best to restrain myself with Arlo, too. He's got a girlfriend now, so I suppose that means he's taken.'

'Arlo hasn't got a girlfriend,' scoffed Leo. 'Unless you're talking about his right hand.'

'She's a secret,' said Mike, climbing up on to the toilet cistern as the other two squeezed in and stood with their backs against opposite stall walls.

'You don't have a girlfriend, do you?' said Leo. The tight quarters meant his face was about ten inches from Arlo's. 'Who?'

'Nobody. I don't have a girlfriend.'

'Your fucking face, Arly, it's on fire,' he laughed. 'Who is she? Do I know her? Of course I know her. Is it someone from school? Rachel Grogan? Kathy Fleming? Who?'

Mike took a generous swig of the whiskey before proffering it forward. 'Gentlemen?'

Arlo shook his head. 'I'm driving, remember?'

'Why won't you tell me who she is?'

The bathroom stall was too small to look anywhere but at his friend. 'It's nobody.'

Leo turned to Mike, who was taking a second swig. 'Do you know who she is? Is it someone from school?'

Mike stopped swirling the whiskey around his mouth and swallowed. Then he gave a wide, mischievous grin and nodded.

Arlo threw him a look and mouthed, *Shut up*.

'I don't know any more than that, though,' said Mike. 'Now, does anyone else want this or am I going to get wasted on my own? Leo, here.'

Leo took the bottle, then he held it out to Arlo. 'You have it. You've something to celebrate.'

'Thanks, but I have to drive us home.'

'I'll do it. I'm a better driver than you, anyway.'

'You're not insured on the car,' said Arlo, eyeing the bottle. He felt giddy with the excitement of his secret romance and the fact that he was about to watch one of his favourite artists play live with his two best friends and his dad.

'Do you think Charlie'll give a fuck?'

They all knew the answer to that.

'All right, cheers,' said Arlo, taking the bottle. Leo wouldn't be offering him anything if he knew his mystery girlfriend was Ella Franklin. But as it was, he was looking at Arlo in a way he never did, with something approaching respect.

Arlo brought the bottle to his mouth and threw it back.

Leo liked Ella. Everyone at school knew that. They'd kissed once and Leo said they were taking things slow, but that was about two years ago. They'd been friends since they were kids, though less so lately. Arlo also liked her, a lot. But he didn't do anything about it because Leo was his best friend and he'd made his intentions clear, and also because, as Leo liked to remind him, he was a wimp. Then one day, about a month ago, she caught up with him after school. She walked in the wrong direction, in the rain, just so she could talk to him. That was when she told him she liked him too.

The three of them left the jacks and headed back out to the venue. Arlo felt like he was sailing above the crowd. He hadn't had that much to drink but, as Leo liked to tell everyone, he was a lightweight.

Donovan appeared on stage and they dumped their belongings where they'd been sitting. Arlo waved to his dad at the bar, who lifted his pint in reply. Then they squeezed their way to the front. This was going to be one of the greatest nights of his life. Arlo loved his friends and he loved his dad and it was all very new but fuck it he loved Ella Belle Franklin too.

After the third song, the music stopped and Donovan told a funny story about a misunderstanding with a local taxi driver.

Arlo pulled out his phone.

'Checking for a message from your mystery girlfriend?' said Leo, looking over his shoulder.

'No,' lied Arlo, for once grateful that there was none. 'Just checking the time.'

Mike swooned into them: 'Oh Arlo, I miss you, will you come over and massage me?'

'Massage?' laughed Leo, as Arlo joined in. Mike was always fun, but drunk Mike, when Arlo was also drunk, was the best buzz.

'Oh yes, Ella,' Mike continued. 'I'll be over as soon as the night allows. Leave a light on for me and I will climb the drainpipes of your mansion ... Wait, do mansions have drainpipes?'

Nobody answered his question. Leo looked at Arlo like he might lunge for him, but then the music started again, and the crowd carried them all forward.

'I meant to tell you,' Arlo shouted over the guitar, but Leo turned and pushed a path away from them through the crowd.

'Fuck,' said Arlo, as Mike began to jump and sing along again.

'*Ba baa ba-ba-ba!*'

When the gig was over, Arlo and Mike met Charlie back at their original seats. It was a few minutes before Leo appeared. He approached the group and handed Mike his jacket.

'I was wondering where that was.'

'All right, let's go,' said Charlie, pulling on his own coat. 'Jesus, but it's great to have my own personal designated driver now.' His face was flush from the drink as he winked at his son.

'Actually, Dad, I'm not gonna ...' Arlo looked to his friend, trying to confirm if he was still willing to cover for him and drive home.

'Arlo has had a bit to drink, Mr Whitehead,' said Leo loudly. He never called Charlie 'Mr Whitehead'.

'Really?'

'Yes, he and Mike drank quite a lot of whiskey.'

'Fuck, Arlo. Seriously? I don't mind you drinking but how are we going to get home?'

'I'll drive us,' said Leo, still talking in that weird, studied way.

'Are you sure?'

Leo nodded. 'Absolutely.'

They hurried to the car, Charlie walking in front with his head bowed against the rain. Arlo tried to speak to Leo, but his friend wasn't interested.

'Another one for the road, Arlo?' said Mike, reaching into his breast pocket.

'I'm grand.' Now that things had turned sour the alcohol was making him feel ill. He'd been so excited about the gig that he'd barely touched his dinner.

'All the more for— What the fuck?' Mike turned the empty bottle upside down then right way up. 'I had about a third of this left.' He patted his other pockets, as though the liquid might just be sitting in one of them. 'Leo? Did you fucking drink this?'

Leo kept walking and kept looking ahead. He had a hood, but he didn't bother to pull it up. 'My best friend just told me he stole my girlfriend, so yeah, I needed a drink.'

'She's not your girlfriend,' said Arlo.

'Not any more she's not.'

'But did you have to drink it all?' whined Mike.

'She was never your girlfriend. She told me the kiss was a mistake.'

'Oh, she told you, did she? Did you have lots of lovely little chats? Did she tell you that she let me put my hand on her tits?'

'Fuck off, Leo,' said Arlo, banging against his friend.

'No, you fuck off,' he shouted, grabbing Arlo's arm and twisting it back.

'Ow! Fucking ow!'

'Oi! Lads!' Charlie was jogging back to them, his feet sending a gentle spray up onto the cuffs of his jeans. He looked between them. 'Ah, Jesus! Have youse *all* been drinking?'

'I haven't,' said Leo, the stoic tone and raindrops hanging at his fringe really adding to the martyrdom.

Arlo and Mike exchanged a look but neither of them said anything. Arlo climbed obediently into the passenger seat of his mother's ancient Volvo as Leo positioned the driver's chair and side mirror to his liking.

His dad talked about the gig for a while, but Mike was the only one responding, so he soon gave up. He was dozing in the seat behind Arlo by the time they left the city.

They were about twenty minutes from home and Arlo was just starting to relax when Leo suddenly declared 'Music!' and lifted himself from the driver's seat so he could retrieve his phone from his pocket.

'I'll do it, I'll play something,' said Arlo, pulling out his own phone, relieved to see both Leo's hands back on the steering wheel.

Then the rain got heavier.

Arlo's eyes flicked nervously between playlists and the road. He suddenly felt very sober. He wished he was the one driving.

'No Guthrie,' said Leo, as the first chords of 'Dust Bowl Blues' filled the car.

'You're annoyed at me, don't take it out on Guthrie.'

'I'm the one driving and I'm the one you fucked over, so I pick the music.'

'I was going to tell you. I know you like Ella—'

'I don't like her,' said Leo automatically. 'She likes me. She's just using you.'

'What would she be using me for? This car?'

'You're like a practice boyfriend. That's actually exactly what you are. Someone she won't mind messing things up with. You're not threatening. You'll let her do whatever she wants once she goes out with you. It's embarrassing really.'

'That doesn't even make sense,' said Arlo, his tone neutral, though he could feel himself going red.

'You keep telling yourself that.' Leo leaned forward as Woody Guthrie sang on.

'You're being childish now. Slow down.'

Leo sat back, then leaned forward again, foot down, accelerator tearing.

'Stop, Leo. It's too wet for messing. It's too dark.'

'You're a wimp, Arly, a pathetic weasel. Do you know that? You're pathetic.'

'Fuck off.'

'Like a little limp dog or something. How could you think she likes you? You're a fucking wimp. You're deluded. How could you even—'

'Slow down!'

But it was too late. They were coming around the last bend, right at the 'Welcome to Cooney' sign, when the car started to skid out of control. Leo tried to get a grip on the steering wheel, but the thing kept sliding back in the other direction. The car slipped and skated, turning so quickly that it was almost facing fully in the opposite direction by the time it left the road and headed on to the mucky verge. Arlo reached over to grab control – his mom's steering wheel was loose, unlike the one in the van; he should have told Leo that – but he couldn't get a grasp on it. He was sent banging into the passenger door, then thrown forward, wincing as the seatbelt tightened against his chest. The car should have slowed on the grass, but there was a slope, followed by a ledge, and the grass was so wet. The car picked up speed as it fell then tumbled and flew full force into one of Cooney's 200-year-old oak trees.

Next thing Arlo knew it was morning and his dad was calling him for school. 'Five minutes,' he said, turning on to his side. Only he couldn't turn. Something was restraining him. Reluctantly he opened his eyes and saw that he was not in his bed.

'Just hang on, okay? I'm going to open the door.'

Arlo turned the only way he could, towards Leo. His friend was breathing fast, muttering something to himself. He turned further again, wincing at the pain in his shoulder, and saw Mike. How was he still asleep? The windows were smashed and the rain was coming in. How much had his friend drunk that he could snooze through that? And who uses a tree trunk as a pillow?

Slowly, then quickly, Arlo got his bearings. His dad opened the passenger door and pulled him out of the car.

'Dad, Dad! Mike! Stop, I'm all right.' He pushed his dad off. 'Mike is ... We need to get Mike!'

He moved his hands down over his body. A pain in his chest and at the side of his head, but otherwise he was all right.

'Come on, quick! Dad!'

'Stop, Arlo.'

'What? No. Come on!'

'It's too late, Arlo.'

'I can't feel my legs! I can't feel my legs!'

'It's okay, Leo, we'll get you out now,' said Charlie, moving around to the driver's side and reefing the door open.

'Am I moving my feet? Can you look, Charlie? Can you see? There, now, am I moving them?'

Charlie looked down under the steering wheel, then over at Arlo. 'It's too dark, Leo.' But it wasn't dark. The dashboard was lit up and Arlo had a perfect view from the passenger side. The only part of his friend that was moving was his face.

'Take me out,' shouted Leo, his breathing fast again. 'Take me out of here.'

'Hang on, I'm just ...' Charlie trailed off. He was drenched. His hair had flopped forward into a sort of modish fringe and the rain was hitting his face.

Arlo was scared. He couldn't deal with this. He needed his dad to tell him what to do.

'Am I going to go to jail? I am, amn't I? Fuck. Oh God. My mom is going to kill me.' Leo was whimpering now. 'I was drinking, Charlie. I'm sorry I lied, but I was drinking and now I'm going to go to jail. Where's Mike?' Leo strained his head up to look in the rear-view mirror. 'Is Mike still there? Is he okay? He's not ... Charlie! Arlo! Did I kill Mike? Oh fuck, tell me. Did I? I can't—' But the rest of it was lost to incontrollable sobbing.

Arlo was crying now too. He couldn't decipher the snot and the tears from the rain, but he could feel the stinging in his eyes.

'Okay, everyone, listen.' His dad was back in adult mode and Arlo felt himself calming slightly. 'We're going to move you, Leo, okay? But not out of the car.'

Leo whimpered.

'Listen, just listen. We're going to move you into the passenger seat.'

'What? Why?'

'Because I was driving, all right? I was driving us home and I lost control of the car and we crashed.'

'Dad, no, you—'

'Shhh!' Charlie gave him a look that made Arlo feel about four years old. 'I was driving. Leo was in the passenger seat and Arlo, you were sitting behind him, okay? Okay? Repeat that, please.'

'Y-you were driving. I was ... I was in the passenger seat,' said Leo, starting to sob again. 'And Arlo was sitting behind me.'

'Good. Okay. I'm going to call an ambulance and then we're going to move you.'

44
······

The doctors had told Nuala what to expect but when she walked into the hospital room and saw her only child shrouded in wires and tubes and imposing machines, she faltered for the first time since her phone had rung four hours earlier.

'Leo,' said her husband Martin, skirting around his frozen wife to move to their son's side. 'How do you feel? Are you in pain? What can we do?'

'Am I moving my legs? Nobody will tell me for sure, but I don't think I'm moving my legs.'

'You need to take it easy now. Don't be pushing yourself to move anything until the doctor asks you to.'

'I'm sorry, Dad. I'm so sorry.'

Her son's blubbering helped Nuala to rediscover her sense of purpose. She crossed the room to stand beside her husband, only now appreciating that she was still in her slippers and pyjama bottoms. How had Martin found the time and wherewithal to get dressed?

'Don't get upset, Leo,' she said. 'You don't need to be sorry for anything.'

'What if I never walk again? What if I can't ...?'

'Shh. It's okay, it'll be okay.'

'Is Mike dead?'

'We're not sure but … we think so,' said Martin, as Nuala reached out for her son's hand. The doctor said Leo had suffered a spinal injury. The first surgery suggested it was incomplete, but they'd need to go back in and examine it again. He had also fractured his left tibia and broken three ribs. But he was still alive. The gratitude almost knocked her to the floor.

'We love you,' she said, careful not to squeeze his hand too tight.

'I was driving,' he whimpered, looking at her as if he couldn't quite believe what was coming out of his mouth.

'No, Charlie Whitehead was.'

'Charlie's taking the blame. He told them it was him. But it was me. And I was drinking. I don't know what to do, Mom. I'm scared. I'm proper scared. What should I do?'

Her son threw his eyes in her direction but the apparatus around his neck and shoulders prevented his head from moving. Just a few days ago, she'd thought it would be good for Leo if something happened to take the wind out of his sails. He was a cocky young fellow. Not that it was unwarranted – he was academically gifted, good at sports, handsome and popular – but it was unbecoming. He could be cruel about his friends without giving it a second's thought. Arrogance was not a flattering trait and certainly not one she had encouraged.

But she'd been thinking of him getting turned down by a girl or dropped from the football team, something like that. She hadn't wanted her son to learn a lesson that he would have to keep learning for the rest of his life.

'What should I do?' he asked again.

'You should tell the—'

But Martin cut in. 'You should do what Charlie said,' he whispered, moving closer to the bed as he looked at the door. 'He was the adult. What was he thinking letting you drink? And what was he thinking letting you get behind the steering wheel? He was probably drunk too, knowing Charlie. Was he? Was he drunk?'

Leo nodded, still whimpering.

'Well, there you are then,' said Martin, as if the whole matter had now been put to bed.

'Mom?'

Nuala felt, as she often did, outnumbered. Leo's personality was closer to Martin's than her own. She knew what her son would do, just as she knew what her husband would do, but still she asked: 'What do you want to do?'

'I don't want to go to jail.'

'And you won't,' decreed Martin, doing a great job of implying he was a legal expert as opposed to a taxation one. 'Not a chance.'

An hour later, Nuala and Martin were gently ushered out of the hospital so Leo could get some rest. There would be another surgery and tests later that day. For it was a new day now. The six o'clock morning news came on the radio as they drove out of the hospital car park.

'Can we really allow Leo to let someone else take the blame?'

'It was Charlie's idea,' said Martin. 'And what's the alternative? Leo goes to jail for a decision he made when he was a teenager? He's probably going to be in a wheelchair for the rest of his life. Don't you think that's sufficient punishment? Charlie was in charge. Either way, he'd probably end up in prison.'

'So why don't we just let the courts decide? At least that way, Leo will have a clear conscience.' She said Leo, but she meant herself. She did all the guilt wrangling in this family.

'I'm not putting Leo through some circus trial, no way. It'd destroy him. It'd destroy us.'

Nuala let her head fall back against the headrest. The rain had stopped, but the roads remained wet. The sound of tyres on water used to make her feel safe and warm inside the car. Now, it made her shiver.

She instructed Martin to drive out to the crash site, where he stayed in the car while she clambered down the muddy slope, past the young guard who was minding the crime scene until forensics arrived. She observed the place where Leo had lost the use of his legs and killed his friend, and questioned if she was the sort of woman who could sacrifice another family to save her son.

Then she climbed back up to the car and told Martin to take her to the Whiteheads' house.

....

Arlo was discharged in the early hours. He'd suffered minor lung contusions, a fractured rib and a head injury. The doctor wanted to keep the lungs and head under observation for twenty-four hours, but when Arlo learned his dad was leaving, he wanted to go too. Charlie's injuries were worse, but nothing could stand between him and the police station. They'd made an appointment for him to come in that afternoon with a solicitor.

Charlie didn't tell his wife the truth. He had been insistent; nobody but him and Arlo and Leo were to know what had happened. As far as Connie was concerned, her husband had been driving the car that killed Mike and seriously injured Leo. They weren't home

374

from the hospital long when the doorbell went. It was Mr and Mrs Patterson.

'Oh, hello,' said Leo, taken aback. ' Come in. Were you looking for ...?'

'Your dad. Is he home?'

Arlo wanted to rescind the offer, but he'd already stood to the side and Principal Patterson had one foot through the door. They stopped in the hallway. Mr Patterson removed his coat, but his wife was wrapping hers tighter. Her slippers left a trail of muck on the carpet.

'Nuala, Martin.' Charlie appeared from the kitchen holding a tea towel. 'I'm so sorry. I'm ... I don't know what to say.' The distress on his dad's face was such that for a second Arlo was convinced he had been driving. But then his own face probably didn't look much different. They were all responsible in their own way.

'If you want to swing for me, do.' Charlie held his arms out like he was going for a group hug. 'I deserve it.'

Arlo cringed. His dad was mad for grand declarations. His mom said this all the time. 'King of the big gesture, but no follow-through.' Although what was taking the rap for manslaughter, if not follow-through?

'We know you weren't driving, Charlie,' said Principal Patterson.

'I was.'

'No, you weren't. Leo told us.'

Charlie gave a half-laugh. 'I don't know why Leo would say that because it's not true, is it, Arlo? Have the doctors looked at his head? Might he have concussion?'

She looked at Arlo. 'Is it true, Arlo? Was your dad driving?'

He didn't know what to say.

375

What was the right answer? How was he supposed to know? He could feel the tears prickling at his eyes. He hadn't slept in more than twenty-four hours. He couldn't do this.

Charlie ushered them all into the living room and closed the door.

'Please let me do this,' he said quietly. 'The accident was my fault.'

He looked at Martin who held up his hands. 'You won't get any disagreement from me. My son is a child. You're an adult. Shame on you.'

'How is Leo? How are his legs?'

Neither of them said anything.

'I don't want him to suffer any more. I will not be able to live with myself if you do not let me do this. Please, I am begging you. It was my fault.'

'Agreed,' said Mr Patterson.

'I don't know how I'm going to accept this,' said his wife quietly. 'If you go to prison, how will I look at your family?'

'Don't,' said Charlie, as if it were the simplest thing in the world, as if they lived in New York City or London or even Dublin, not the small, intimate village of Cooney, West Cork. 'People would think it strange if you were to talk to them. From now on, you hate me, and you want nothing to do with us. It's the only thing that would make sense. You won't want to look at us anyway. We'll be a reminder.'

Arlo glanced at Principal Patterson, waiting for her to say this was not true. She liked him; he knew she did. They got on great. But she didn't look at him. She hadn't, he realised, since she'd come into the house.

It was easier this way. They were all carrying guilt. They all felt responsible. They hadn't the capacity to take on anyone else's.

She nodded, and her husband placed a hand in her lap, grateful for her acquiescence.

'But I owe you,' she said. 'I owe all of you. And I won't forget that. I promise.'

EPILOGUE

· · · · · · · · · · · · · · · ·

THREE MONTHS AFTER THE DROWNING

Nuala Patterson had found it surprisingly easy to go along with the whole charade. She had declined to speak at the funeral (a refusal everyone presumed was because she found Seamus's death too upsetting), made sympathetic sounds when fellow mourners said how desperately sad it was, and silently cheered as his body was lowered into the ground.

The initial pathology report had confirmed death by drowning, no signs of foul play. There would be a coroner's court hearing in a few months' time as a matter of procedure, but the cause of death, combined with the suicide note and Miriam McGrath's testimony that her husband could not swim, meant the finding was a foregone conclusion.

She'd lied to the gardaí when they asked if she'd any idea why her colleague might have taken his own life, and she hadn't lost any sleep over it. It was for the greater good of the children involved. With Seamus gone, they would have been the focus of the inevitable scandal.

The whole ordeal had made her less judgemental of her own son. Letting Charlie Whitehead take the rap for the crash had never sat well with her. She hadn't said this explicitly, but her husband and

Leo could tell. They felt she was judging them, and maybe she was. It just wasn't the sort of person she'd wanted her son to be. But she also hadn't wanted him to go to jail.

When Leo and Martin first left for Leo's therapy in Dublin, there was vague talk of her following. But once they got there, the subject never came up again. She couldn't make her peace with Charlie going to jail and it had been easier to avoid the whole situation. Then it was too late. Leo was so angry about what had happened to him, and completely incapable of seeing his own role in it. Speaking to his mother, who he was convinced had disowned him, only made things worse. And then the divorce papers arrived.

But the whole business with Seamus had made her more understanding, and more willing to compromise. We do what we think is best and then we live with that decision. So, who was she to judge anyone else?

She'd been to visit Leo and his father three times this month. She even spent a couple of nights there over Christmas. She was making progress, she thought, drawing him out of himself, helping him to realise the world was not closed to him, and that feeling sorry for himself was not the best use of his time. She brought the divorce papers with her every time she went to Dublin, but they were still sitting right where they always were – on the back seat of her car. She hadn't been asked for them yet anyway.

It was shortly after eight o'clock on a Monday morning and she was on her way to the school. She'd got back late from Dublin last night, but she had plenty of energy. She was through the worst of the menopause, thank God. (That might also have something to do with her increased tolerance for other people, family included.) They'd had to hire a new caretaker at the school, and the Whiteheads had moved into the city, but otherwise things continued as normal. Mr Cafferty had agreed to stay – she'd told him she couldn't go into details, but that she'd got to the root of the problem and it wouldn't happen again.

Arlo had left Cooney before his mother and brother. He relocated to the city not long before Christmas, with Ella Franklin of all people. Apparently, they'd been an item for a while now. She remembered Ella from school. A fine girl, despite her mother. Nuala was delighted for them. She was still so fond of Arlo. It did her heart good to know that he was happy.

....

It was 27 January – exactly three weeks since everyone else on their street had taken down their decorations, and yet a wreath still hung on Arlo and Ella's front door and a Christmas tree sat dying in their tiny living-room-cum-kitchen.

'I like it,' said Ella, feet up on the table as she shovelled cornflakes into her mouth before legging it to her first lecture. 'This is my first home of my own and I want to do things my way.'

'Our way, you mean.'

'Sure.'

'It's starting to smell.'

'And Woody likes it,' she countered. 'Isn't he staying tonight? Just imagine the look on his cute little face when he arrives to find the tree and all the festive magic is gone.'

Arlo sighed. 'Well, when are we going to take them down?'

'February,' she said decisively, throwing her feet back on to the floor and placing her bowl in the sink. 'Just in time for Valentine's Day. I've got my eye on some great 3D hearts in the two-euro shop.'

She scooped her bag up from the floor and kissed him on the mouth. Already the milk tasted sour, and he liked it. 'Gotta go.'

He walked to the door and kissed her again. She waltzed up the street, turned at the halfway point, and waved. In the end, Beverley had been his unexpected knight in shining armour, telling her daughter the truth about how nothing had happened between him and Fiona Murphy, and inadvertently saving a relationship she'd rather not have saved.

His first job wasn't for another hour. He returned to the kitchen and washed the breakfast things. He needed to decide what he was going to cook tonight. Woody was coming over after school.

Days after Arlo told his family that he was moving into Cork city several months earlier than intended, his mom decided to do the same. A fresh start for all of them. Nuala Patterson had helped to get Woody into a good primary school for the last few months of sixth class and, in September, he would be moving up to secondary. Arlo was delighted; it had relieved his guilt about abandoning them, and it meant he still got to see his little brother several times a week.

Arlo often cooked for him now, something he never used to do. He loved eating with him, and chatting to him, and staying up late playing computer games together. They were as close as they used to be, and Arlo grinned every time he realised that.

Tonight, he would make macaroni and cheese, Woody's favourite. His mom was coming for dinner too. She wouldn't care what he made, she was just happy when they were all together.

She thought his new home was cute.

Though she might not be so taken by the browning Christmas tree.

....

The woman making her way along the aisle slowed as she came to Beverley's table. Beverley had assumed that once the train was moving, she'd be free from the possibility of strangers wanting to squash their bodies up against hers.

She pointed to the two electronic names above the seats: Beverley Franklin, Ella Franklin.

'These are both taken,' she said, before the woman got any ideas. 'My daughter's just in the bathroom.'

When the woman shuffled on, she returned her handbag to 'Ella's' seat.

Her daughter was not in the bathroom, or anywhere else on this train. She was probably sitting in a lecture hall or crammed into that tiny shed of a place she and Arlo Whitehead now called home. But if Beverley was going to get public transport, she'd be damned if she was going to spend the journey wedged in beside a potential psychopath. So she'd booked both seats. It was the logical solution.

She'd been to Ella's house twice now, and while it would not be to her liking – who gets a real tree, let alone still has it up in late January? – she was happy her daughter was happy. More importantly, she was happy she was talking to her. They hadn't had anything worse than a disagreement since she moved out. Maybe absence really does make the heart grow fonder. Or maybe it was easier for Ella to be civil to her mother when she wasn't trying to keep a lover squirrelled away on the top floor of their home. She'd still rather her daughter was dating someone with more prospects than Arlo Whitehead but, after the whole business with Seamus and the photos, she had a newfound respect for the boy. She felt confident, at least, that he'd do all he could to protect her daughter.

Her phone buzzed and she pulled it from her handbag.

'Did you make the train?'

'Of course I made the train, Mother. I'm sitting here now.'

'Wonderful, *a stór*, just wonderful!'

'Are you all right? You sound a bit out of it.'

'No, no,' said Frances, wind chimes jangling somewhere in the background. 'I'm just getting everything ready for your visit. My lovely neighbours heard you were coming and they dropped around a few brownies for the occasion. Isn't that lovely? I may have started on one, but I promise there'll be lots here for you. You know, if you wanted to stay until Thursday, I'm running a beginners' workshop and I think you'd really—'

'I have to be back by Thursday, I told you. The camera crew is coming to film Amelia.'

'Of course, of course. Dorothy finally goes to Oz!'

The musical had been cancelled after Seamus's death, but a few weeks later *The Big Children's Talent Show* got in touch to say they'd still like to feature Amelia, maybe with a solo performance of 'Over the Rainbow'. Naturally, the other Lakers were already clandestinely complaining about nepotism, but their daughters couldn't carry a note between them, and she had little time for shameless jealousy.

'I'm going now, Mother. I'll get a taxi from the station and I'll see you shortly,' said Beverley, pulling a newspaper out of her bag. 'I have the *Southern Gazette* to read.'

Fiona Murphy's estate agency business had appeared on the latest tax defaulters' list – and Beverley hadn't read a single newspaper article so many times since her own heyday in the acting limelight.

....

Christine was working on an article about Bill Farrell's official mayoral bid. His wife was running his campaign and she had Christine bombarded with press releases. If she didn't write something soon, Lorna's accusations of political prejudice would start to have merit. But she didn't care how many times the woman quoted them, she would not be likening Bill to Barack Obama or, and this was a journalistic principle she was willing to go to jail for, Lorna to Michelle.

'Do you think something bad will ever happen again?' asked Derek, despondently, from a desk across the room.

'I don't know, boss.'

Her editor sighed.

A real-life, legitimate mystery had finally happened in Cooney and it had been solved – in so much as a suicide note could solve anything – before he could even get an issue of the paper out of it. The pathologist's report had brought an end to any remaining speculation or conspiracy theories. Derek hadn't felt this short-changed since Charlie Whitehead confessed to dangerous driving causing death, doing him out of a trial.

He was a good newspaper man, but he was not the most sensitive of humans.

'Someone has to be up to *something*,' he beseeched, continuing to make his way through the local phonebook. An 'O'Sullivan' had been added to Interpol's 'Most Wanted' list the previous week and he was cross-referencing the name. For all his news hack cynicism, Derek remained an optimist.

'Post,' declared Amanda, appearing at the entrance to the office. She dumped three envelopes on their boss's desk.

'Hope!' declared Derek, greedily ripping open the first envelope.

'Another bloody complaint about all the Keating twins' photos ...'
He balled that one up and threw it in the bin. The next one, he
waved above his head. 'This is for you.'

Christine walked over to collect the latest Bill Farrell for Mayor
missive.

'Our last shot ...' he said, rubbing the final A4 envelope between
his hands like a man about to roll the dice at a high-stakes craps
table. 'Come on, compromising photographs of a high-ranking
official ...'

He tore the top from the envelope and pulled the single
photocopied sheet from within. It was, at least, a photograph.

'Another missing cat! Who do these people think we are? We
might be desperate, but we'll never be *that* desperate. I spent
seventeen months embedded with a notorious crime gang, and the
subsequent six under garda protection. I do not report on missing
bloody cats!'

The two journalists leaned over their boss's shoulder to look at
the flyer. 'Dr Tickles,' read Amanda. 'Cute.'

Derek slammed the page down on his desk and stormed out of
the office. 'I'm going for a smoke! Call me when someone gets shot!'

Christine dedicated another forty minutes to putting some shape
on the Bill Farrell article, then she grabbed her car keys and bag.
Amanda had already left, and Derek was back at his desk, poring
over the phonebook.

He looked up as she pulled on her coat.

'Didn't you say something terrible happened to *your* cat?' he
asked hopefully. 'Someone stole him or crucified him or something?'

'Our cat was abducted, yes, but just temporarily. All is well now,
and he is safe at home.'

385

'Oh,' sighed Derek. 'Great news.'

'See you tomorrow, boss.'

He waved a hand distractedly in her direction as she disappeared out the door and down the stairs.

It had taken a while to get the last of the dye out of Porcupine's fur but once they'd achieved it, he had settled back in easily. The children were more besotted with him than before and, with the musical scrapped, Maeve's bedroom noticeboard had returned to being a shrine solely dedicated to the unworthy creature. Even Mrs Rodgers had eventually stopped lingering at their garden gate.

Personally, Christine would be delighted if nothing bad, or even exciting, ever happened in Cooney, ever again. Come back endless petitions and parental tiffs, all is forgiven! She'd seen Principal Patterson and Beverley a few times since the showdown in the Glass Lake workroom, but she hadn't said more to them than a few words. Word around town was the Whiteheads had moved to the city – and Arlo was now sharing a house with Ella Franklin. Good for him.

She turned the car up Seaview Terrace, slowing as she passed Mrs Rodgers' house – a habit she had yet to get out of. The older woman was sitting on her stoop, wrapped up against the January chill in a bulky coat, oversized hat and furry hand muff.

Only, it wasn't a hand muff.

'Is that ...?'

Christine brought the car to a near stop.

Sitting on Mrs Rodgers' lap, blocking her hands from view, was another cat. The woman smiled brightly as she stood from the step. With some trepidation, Christine rolled down the window. The cat had light ginger fur and a crude white stripe running down the centre of its forehead. It was identical to the animal from this afternoon's missing poster ... except for the white streak and about three extra pounds.

'Hello, Christine,' the woman shouted over. 'Have you met Terence? He's my cat. I've had him a long time now.'

Christine looked from the animal formerly known as Dr Tickles to her deranged neighbour. She opened her mouth but the words would not come. The animal stood on all fours and stretched. Unable to tear her eyes away, she felt for the window control.

'Lovely to see you, dear,' called Mrs Rodgers, as the cat nuzzled down to sleep and the window eventually, thankfully, shut.

ACKNOWLEDGEMENTS

This was the first book I wrote after becoming a mother – and the first I wrote during a pandemic – so a lot of the process is a blur. But I must thank some of the people who helped me through it.

I wrote the first draft of *It Could Never Happen Here* in my parents' house – which is ten minutes from my own. Covid-19 had just struck and my son was six months old and at home with his father while I headed off up the road to my childhood home to get a few hours' writing in before breastfeeding called me back again. I was avoiding contact with my parents, bringing my own teacup and water bottle, and all childcare was off the table. It was a mad time.

As things relaxed slightly, my dad started to make me coffee and deliver it to the bedroom where I was writing. It was always served in the same Seamus Heaney mug – which has the word 'Inspiration' on it. I hope it had the desired effect, Dad. And thank you, too, for never asking how the writing was going. This book is dedicated to you.

My mam, a retired primary school deputy principal, inadvertently provided the initial spark for the book. She has given me so many ideas at this stage that she is likely owed a royalty. I am also grateful for the lockdown baking spurt she went through while I was writing in her house. Warm scones went very well with the Heaney coffee.

I'd like to be able to thank my son, but honestly, he was a terrible sleeper throughout the first draft of this and so not of much direct assistance. I do love you though, Ruan, dearly, and I am so very glad you exist. Thanks are, however, due to my partner Colm, who often got up to settle him during the night and was the parent most likely to rise with him in the morning.

To Sarah Hodgson, my editor, thank you for your care, patience and understanding. And to everyone else at Corvus who helps with my novels – I will avoid the temptation to list names, in case I forget anyone, but know that the work is appreciated. A huge thank you to my agents – Liz Parker at Verve, and Sarah Lutyens at Lutyens & Rubinstein – for being invested in the book at every stage. I am very grateful.

And finally, to you, the reader. With every book I write, I grow more appreciative of the people who read them. Without you, these words wouldn't exist. I hope you enjoyed it. (Or if you are one of those people who skims the acknowledgements first – that you will enjoy it.) Thank you, thank you.

D1385564

ALL ABOUT TROPICAL FISH

ACKNOWLEDGMENTS

This book would not have been started but for the encouragement and enthusiasm of my wife, and certainly would never have been finished had it not been for the unceasing hard work and help given me by Miss Jean Christie.

I wish to express my thanks to my co-author Geoffrey Gerard and his wife for all their help, and to Mrs C. Gale for typing and corrections.

To Brian Barratt all praise for his patience and skill in producing the majority of the photographs. I am indebted to the Zoological Society of London for permission to photograph the following species: *Cæcobarbus geertsi, Hemichromis bimaculatus, Hippocampus brevirostris, Leporinus fasciatus, Malapterurus electricus, Pterois volitans,* and *Serrasalmus spilopleura*; also to Dr E. Trewavas, of the British Museum (Natural History: Fishes), for help in identifying some of the rarer species. To the following thanks are due for the loan of specimens: Mr H. Axelrod, New York, *Monodactylus sebæ, Pelmatochromis guntheri*; Mr R. Chandler, Cambridge, *Jordanella floridæ* (and for help in chemistry); Mr K. Fawcett, Reigate, Veil-tail Angel; Mr A. Gale, Dulwich, *Mollienisia velifera*; Mrs G. Hollis, Wandsworth, *Epalzeorhynchos kallopterus*; Mr J. Hunter, Maidenhead, *Æquidens curviceps*; Wing-Commander L. Lynn, Courtrai, *Heniochus acuminatus*; Mr R. Mealand, Putney, *Hydrocotyle vulgaris, Naias microdon, Samolus floribundus,* and *Saururus cernus*; Mr P. Phillips, Tottenham, *Tilapia mossambica*; Mrs K. Robertshaw, Edgware, *Aphyosemion sjoestedti*; Mr H. Russell-Holland, Totteridge, *Barbus vittatus*; Mr R. Skipper, Hendon, *Symphysodon discus*; Mrs I. Smith, Kingsbury, *Telmatherina ladigesi*; Mr E. Smykala, Friern Barnet, *Rasbora kalachroma*; Mr C. Stoker, Sutton, *Barilius christi, Cichlasoma biocellatum, Herichthys cyanoguttatus, Metynnis schreitmelleri,* and *Phenacogrammus interruptus.*

Acknowledgments are also due to Mr R. Clegg, Haslemere Museum, for photographs of water insects, to Mr L. Perkins, Dulwich, for photographs of *Abudefduf uniocellatus, Amphiprion bicinctus, Angelichthys ciliaris, Chætodon vagabundus, Dascyllus aruanus, Dascyllus trimaculatus, Gymnotus carapo,* and *Holocanthus annularis,* and to Mr W. Pitt, Walton-on-Thames, for photographs of *Mesogonistius chætodon* and *Polycentrus schomburgki.*

That this book should ever have been published is entirely due to Miss Juliet Piggott, and to her I give my sincere thanks. Lastly I must express my appreciation to my publishers for the kindness and consideration shown to me throughout.

DEREK McINERNY

Ewhurst
1958

ALL ABOUT
TROPICAL FISH

by

DEREK McINERNY
of McLynn's Aquarium Ewhurst, and

GEOFFREY GERARD F.R.S.E.

with a foreword by

H. F. VINALL

*With over 100 illustrations in colour and
200 illustrations in monochrome, photographed
by Brian Barratt, of PACE, Sidcup, and line
diagrams in the text*

**Leonard Yaffie
Casa Nana
46 Herriet Street
Glasgow
G41 2JY**

GEORGE G. HARRAP & CO. LTD
LONDON TORONTO WELLINGTON SYDNEY

To

W/Cmdr L. A. LYNN, D.S.O. and bar, D.F.C.

THE ORIGINAL PARTNER IN
McLYNN'S AQUARIUM

First published in Great Britain 1958
by GEORGE G. HARRAP & CO. LTD
182 High Holborn, London, W.C.1

Reprinted: 1960; 1962

© *Derek McInerny and Geoffrey Gerard* 1958

Made and printed in Great Britain by Jarrold & Sons Ltd, Norwich

FOREWORD

by

H. F. VINALL, F.Z.S.

LATE CURATOR, THE AQUARIUM,
THE ZOOLOGICAL SOCIETY
OF LONDON

and holder of the Society's Silver and Bronze medals

DURING MY FIFTY-FOUR YEARS WITH THE ZOOLOGICAL SOCIETY OF LONDON, thirty years of which were devoted to the practical study of tropical fish, both sea- and fresh-water, many books have been written about this absorbing subject, and world-wide hobby. However much one studies fish, it is always possible to learn many new and exciting things, so that every new book by a knowledgable and discerning writer adds something to the sum-total of knowledge.

Mr McInerny is a colleague of long standing for whom I have the greatest respect: a Fellow of the Zoological Society of London, and a man who has dedicated many years to the practical study and breeding of fish at his specialist-built breeding-station at Ewhurst, in Surrey. His ideas and theories are therefore related to practice, and can be relied upon.

This book covers the whole field of aquaria, and will be invaluable for anyone interested in keeping fish. It is written in non-technical language, and explains not only what to do, but why—which is the important thing. The beginner—or the expert, for that matter—may learn much from it.

The coloured illustrations are superb, the colours being accurate for fish in healthy condition.

Altogether, I am happy to recommend this book, and I trust that it will, besides interesting the initiated, also induce many to begin the absorbing hobby of fish-keeping.

CONTENTS

CHAPTER	PAGE
Scientific Names	13
Useful Information	13
Introduction	15
1. *The Aquarium*	19
2. *Siting and Setting up an Aquarium*	27
3. *Some Important Rules*	34
4. *Water and its Components*	41
5. *Miscellaneous Apparatus*	49
6. *Fish-foods and Feeding*	62
7. *Snails*	77
8. *Fish Enemies*	82
9. *Diseases*	87
10. *Kindnesses and Cruelties*	94
11. *Plants for Beauty and Utility*	97
12. *Fishes in General*	128
13. *Live-bearing Fishes*	135

CHAPTER	PAGE
14. *Oviparous or Egg-laying Fishes*	158
15. *Cyprinidæ*	162
16. *Rasborinæ*	198
17. *Characidæ*	221
18. *Cyprinodontidæ*	278
19. *Cobitidæ*	312
20. *Mastacembelidæ*	324
21. *Siluroidea*	327
22. *Anabantidæ*	362
23. *Channidæ*	391
24. *Nandidæ*	394
25. *Cichlidæ*	398
26. *Knife Fishes*	436
27. *Gobioidea*	438
28. *Ambassidæ*	447
29. *Atherinidæ*	450
30. *Centrarchidæ*	454
31. *Tropical Marines*	464

Leonard Yaffle
Casa Nana
46 Herriet Street
Glasgow
G41 2JY

INDEX

All scientific names marked with an * are those of plants; names
not so marked are those of fishes or other animals.

Abudefduf uniocellatus, 469
Acanthodoras spinosissimus, 351
Acanthophthalmus semicinctus, 313
Acanthophthalmus species, 314
Acanthopsis choirorhynchos, 315
Acorus intermedia, 98
pusillus, 98
Advantages of tropicals, 15
Æquidens curviceps, 401
latifrons, 402
maronii, 403
portalegrensis, 404
Aeration, artificial, 35
by air-stones or diffusers, 59
drawbacks, 36
function, 35
pumps, 58
African knife fish, 437
Air-lift tube, 60
Alestopetersius caudalis, 222
Algæ, 37
Amazon Sword, 108
Ambassidæ, 447
Ambassis buroensis, 447
lala, 448
Ambulia, 115
American pond snail, 80
Amphiprion bicinctus, 470
ephipreus, 470
percula, 471
Ampullaria cuprina, 77
Anabantidæ, 362
Anabas testudineus, 365
Angel fish, 418
sexing, 420
Angelichthys ciliaris, 472
Anguillula silusiæ, 67
Anoptichthys jordani, 223
Anostomus anostomus, 225
Anubias lanceolata, 98
Aphyocharax rubripinnis, 226
Aphyosemion australe, 279
bivittatum, 281
cæruleum, 282
calabaricus, 284
cognatum, 285
gardneri, 286
petersi, 287
shoutedeni, 288
sjoestedti, 289
splendopleuris, 291

Apistogramma agassizi, 425
ornatipinnis, 426
pertense, 427
ramirezi, 428
Aplocheilus blockii, 292
dayi, 293
lineatus, 294
panchax, 295
Aponogeton fenestralis, 98
foliaceus, 99
ulvaceus, 99
undulatum, 100
Aquaria, accessibility, 28
capacity, 14
community, 33
construction, 20
cost, 16
filling, 31
glazing, 21
heating, 22
height, 27
introducing fishes, 33
lighting, 24
maintenance, 16
ornaments, 30
scavengers, 312, 327
settling period, 32
siting and setting up, 27
size, 19, 27
species, 33
stands, 26
types, 19
water, 46
weight, 27
Arched catfish, 330
Archer fish, 463
Argentine pearl, 302
Argulus, 82
Artemia salina, 66
Artificial insemination, 96
Astronotus ocellatus, 405
Atherinidæ, 450
Aureomycin, 90
Australian rainbow, 450
dark-striped, 451
Australian red snail, 79
Azolla caroliniana, 100

Bacopa amplexicaulis, 101
caroliniana, 101
Bacteria, discouragement, 38
multiplication, 40, 48
Badis badis, 394
Bagridæ, 341
Balanteocheilus melanopterus, 189

Barbs, spawning the, 159
Barbus, 162
bimaculatus, 163
binotatus, 164
conchonius, 165
cumingi, 166
dorsalis, 167
everetti, 168
fasciatus, 169
filamentosus, 170
gelius, 171
hexazona, 173
lateristriga, 174
lineomaculatus, 175
nigrofasciatus, 176
oligolepis, 178
partipentazona, 179
schuberti, 180
schwanenfeldi, 181
semifasciolatus, 182
stoliczkanus, 183
tetrazona, 184
ticto, 185
titteya, 186
vittatus, 187
Barilius christi, 190
Barred Panchax, 297
pencil fish, 271
Battery jars, 19
Beacon fish, 239
Belgian flag, 251
Belontia signata, 366
Betta picta, 367
splendens, 369
Black angel, 419
-banded cichlid, 410
-line tetra, 257
ruby barb, 176
shark, 193
-tailed pencil fish, 270
wedge tetra, 240
widow, 236
Bladderwort, 86
Bleeding heart tetra, 245
Blind barb, 188
cave tetra, 223
Blood fins, 226
Blood worms, 75
Blue acara, 402
angel, 419
angel (marine), 478
Botia, 321
damsel, 479
eyes, 305
gourami, 386
gulare, 282

7

Blue Limia, 146
  lyre-tail, 284
  Panchax, 295
  -throated Aphyosemion, 289
Blushing Rasbora, 212
Botia almorhæ, 318
  horæ, 319
  lucas bahi, 319
  macracantha, 320
  modesta, 321
  strigata, 322
Botias, 317
Brachydanio albolineatus, 214
  nigrofasciatus, 215
  rerio, 215
Brachygobius doriæ, 441
  sua, 442
  xanthozonus, 442
Brackish-water fishes, 456
Brass tetra, 243
Brine shrimps, 66
Broad-finned mollie, 149
Bronze catfish, 329
Bubble-nest-builders, breeding the, 362
Bubble-nest-building catfish, 345
Buckets, enamel, 51
Bulinus australianus, 79
Bullying, 94
Bumble-bee catfish, 343
  goby, 442
Butterfly fish, 472

★Cabomba aquatica, 101
  ★caroliniana, 101
  ★rosæfolia, 102
Cæcobarbus geertsi, 188
Callichthyidæ, 345
Callichthys, breeding the, 345
  callichthys, 345
  species, 347
Carbon dioxide, 35
Cardinal tetra, 247
Carnegiella strigata, 227
Centrarchidæ, 454
★Ceratophyllum demersum, 102
★Ceratopteris deltoides, 102
  ★pteridoides, 103
  ★thalictroides, 104
Chætodon vagabundus, 472
Chain-sword, 110
Chanda wolffii, 449
Channa orientalis, 392
Channel rubber, 55
Channidæ, 391
Characidæ, 221
Characins, spawning the, 159
Cheirodon axelrodi, 247
Chequer barb, 178
Cherry barb, 186
Chilodus punctatus, 229
Chocolate gourami, 380

Chondrococcus, 90
Cichlasoma biocellatum, 406
  festivum, 407
  meeki, 409
  nigrofasciatus, 410
  severum, 411
Cichlidæ, 398
Cichlids, breeding the dwarf, 400
  large, 398
  medium, 399
Cleanliness and balance, 39
Climbing perch, 365
Cloudy damsel, 474
Clown barb, 168
  fish, 471
  loach, 320
  Rasbora, 205
Cobitidæ, 312
Colisa fasciata, 371
  labiosa, 372
  lalia, 374
Colombian ramshorn, 80
Comb-tail, 366
Congo glass catfish, 358
Copeina arnoldi, 230
  guttata, 231
Coral, cleaning, 467
Coral fishes, 464
  aquaria for, 465
  diseases, 468
  feeding, 466
  purchasing, 467
Corals, various, 465
Corydoras, 327
  breeding and sexing the, 328
  aeneus, 329
  arcuatus, 330
  auratus, 331
  brevirostris, 332
  elegans, 333
  hastatus, 334
  julii, 335
  melanistius, 336
  multipunctatus, 337
  myersi, 338
  paleatus, 339
  reticulatus, 340
Corynopoma riisei, 232
Cover glasses, 26
Cream Botia, 319
Croaking gourami, 390
Crustacea, 81, 464
★Cryptocoryne beckettii, 104
  ★bulosus, 105
  ★ciliata, 105
  ★cordata, 106
  ★griffithii, 106
  ★harteliana, 106
  ★longicauda, 107
  ★nevillii, 107
  ★willisii, 107
Crystalwort, 122
Ctenobrycon spilurus, 233

Cuming's barb, 166
Cupid cichlid, 414
Cyclops, 72
Cynolebias bellottii, 302
  nigripinnis, 303
Cyprinidæ, 162
Cyprinodontidæ, 278

Danio malabaricus, 216
Danios, 212
  breeding, 213
  protecting eggs of, 213
Daphnia, 71
  catching, 71
  dried, 72
Dark Clown fish, 470
Dascyllus aruanus, 473
  carneus, 474
  trimaculatus, 475
Dermogenys pusillus, 140
Dip-tubes, 51
Diseases, 87
Diving beetle, 82
Doradidæ, 350
Dormitator maculatus, 439
Dragon fish, 480
Dragonfly larvæ, 85
Dropsy, 91
Duckweed, 115
Dwarf catfish, 334
  cichlids, 425
  gourami, 374
  Panchax, 292
  rainbow cichlid, 434
Dytiscus marginalis, 82

EARTHWORMS, 68
★Echinodorus intermedius, 108
  ★kala, 109
  ★martii, 109
  ★radicans, 109
  ★rangeri, 110
  ★tenellus, 110
★Egeria densa (Elodea densa), 110
Egg-droppers, breeding the, 159
Egg-laying fishes, 158
Egg-laying tooth-carps, 278
  breeding the, 278
Egyptian mouth-breeder, 429
★Eichhornia crassipes, 110
Elassoma evergladei, 455
Electric catfish, 357
Electricity, 22
  consumption, 25
Elegant catfish, 333
  Rasbora, 202
★Eleocharis acicularis, 111
Eleotridæ, 438
★Elodea canadensis, 111
  ★crispa, 112
Enchytræus albidus, 68

Epalzeorhynchos kallopterus, 196
   siamensis, 197
Ephipicharax orbicularis, 234
Epicyrtus microlepis, 235
Epiplatys chaperi, 296
   fasciolatus, 294
   macrostigma, 298
   sexfasciatus, 299
Esomus, 218
   danricus, 218
   malayensis, 219
Etropiella debauwi, 358
Etroplus maculatus, 412
   suratensis, 413
Euflavine, 91
Eye-infections, 92

FEATHER-FIN TETRA, 242
Feeding, 39
   rings, 54
Festive cichlid, 407
Filament barb, 170
Filters, 60
Fire Rasbora, 211
Fire-mouth cichlid, 409
Fish enemies, 82
Fish-foods and feeding, 62
Fishes, anatomy, 128
   colouration, 132
   external covering, 128
   fins, 128
   in general, 128
   lateral line, 132
   reproductory methods, 134
   swim-bladder, 133
Flag fish, 304
Flame fish, 248
Floating fern, 102
Flukes, 91
Flying barb, 218
   fox (fish), 196
★Fontinalis antipyretica, 112
   ★gracilis, 112
Foods, animal, 64
   cultured, 65
   dried, 63
   fresh, tinned, or frozen, 64
   hormone, 63
   other, 76
   pond, 69
   vegetable, 64
Forceps, 52
Fouling, 39
Four-leafed clover, 117
Fresh-water puffer, 461
Fungus, 90

Gambusia affinis, 142
Gasteropelicus levis, 228
Genus, 128
Geophagus cupido, 414
   jurupari, 415
Ghost fish, 359

Giant Danio, 216
Gilded Panchax, 301
Girardinus metallicus, 143
Glarydichthys falcatus, 143
Glass characin, 235
   fish, 448
   jars, 49
   pipes, 58
Glass worms, 74
Glowlight Rasbora, 208
Glowlight tetra, 249
Gobiidæ, 440
Gobioidea, 438
Gobius vaimosa balteati, 443
Gold-line catfish, 331
Gold-lipped mackerel, 190
Golden barb, 180
   lyre-tail, 288
   medaka, 306
   Panchax, 300
Gonopodium, 135
Gravid spot, 135
Green acara, 404
   kissing gourami, 377
   Panchax, 299
   water roses, 125
Grindal worms, 68
Guppy, 146
Gymnocorymbus ternetzi, 236
Gymnotidæ, 436
Gymnotus carapo, 436
Gyrinocheilidæ, 322
Gyrinocheilus aymonieri, 323
Gyrodactylus, 91

HAIR-GRASS, 111
Half-banded barb, 182
Half-beak, 140
Haplochromis multicolor, 429
Haplosternum littorale, 348
   maculatum, 349
   species, 350
Hardness, comparison of, 45
   degrees of, 46
   testing for, 44, 45
Harlequin, 203
Hasemania marginata, 237
Headstander, 229
Heating, electrical, 22, 23
   gas, 24
   oil, 24
   space, 24
Helastoma rudolphi, 375
   temmincki, 377
Hemichromis bimaculatus, 416
Hemigrammus caudovittatus, 238
   nanus, 237
   ocellifer, 239
   pulcher, 240
   rhodostomus, 241
   unilineatus, 242
Hemirhamphidæ, 139
Hemirhamphus pogonognathus, 141

Heniochus acuminatus, 476
Herichthys cyanoguttatus, 417
Heterandria formosa, 144
★Heteranthera zosteræfolia, 112
Hippocampus brevirostris, 477
Holacanthus annularis, 478
Hornwort, 102
Hump-backed Limia, 148
Hydra, 83
   destruction, 83
★Hydrocotyle vulgaris, 113
Hydrogen, 34
★Hygrophila polysperma, 113
   ★stricta, 114
Hyphessobrycon bifasciatus, 243
   callistus minor, 244
   callistus rubrastigma, 245
   callistus serpæ, 246
   cardinalis, 247
   flammeus, 248
   gracilis, 249
   heterorhabdus, 251
   innesi, 252
   pulchripinnis, 255
   rosaceus, 256
   scholzei, 257
Hypopomus artedi, 437

Ichthyophthirius multifiliis, 87
Important rules, 34
Indian ferns, 103, 104
Infusoria, 65
   snails, 77
Insecticides, 86

JACK DEMPSEY, 406
Japanese live-bearing snail, 80
Jewel cichlid, 416
Jordanella floridæ, 304

KEYHOLE CICHLID, 403
Killing fishes, 95
Kindnesses and cruelties, 94
Kissing gourami, 375
Knife fish, 437
   fishes, 436
Kryptopterus bicirrhis, 359
Kuhli loach, 313

Labeo bicolor, 192
   chrysophekadion, 193
   erythrurus, 195
Labeos, 191
Labyrinth fishes, 362
   breeding the, 362
Lace gourami, 382
Large spiny eel, 324
   upside-down catfish, 361
Laubuca laubuca, 217
Lebistes reticulatus, 145
Leeches, 85
Leiocassis siamensis, 341

Lemna gibba, 115
Lemon tetra, 255
Leopard catfish, 335
Leporinus fasciatus, 258
friderici, 259
striatus, 260
Light, functions of, 37
hoods, 25
Lighting, artificial, 24
natural, 24, 37
Limia melanogaster, 146
nigrofasciata, 148
Limnæa auricularia, 79
stagnalis, 79
Limnophila sessiliflora, 115
Lined Leporinus, 260
Live-bearers, broods, 136
cannibalism, 136
cross-mating, 137
delivery of young, 136
feeding young, 138
gestation period, 136
growth of fry, 138
hybrid, 137
mating, 135
removal of female, 137
selective breeding, 137
sexing, 138
trapping, 137
Live-bearing fishes, 135
tooth-carps, 142
Lizard's tail, 126
Long-snouted barb, 167
Loricaria parva, 353
Loricariidæ, 352
Ludwigia mulerttii, 116
Lyre-tail, 279

Macropodus cupanus dayi, 377
opercularis, 379
Macuilamia rotundifolia, 117
Malapteruridæ, 357
Malapterurus electricus, 357
Malayan angel, 456
snail, 80
Marbled cichlid, 405
hatchet, 227
Marine aquaria, community, 467
lighting, 467
scavengers, 467
temperature, 466
Marisa rotula, 80
Marsilea quadrifolia, 117
Mastacembelidæ, 324
Mastacembelus circumcinctus, 324
pancalus, 325
Medicine chest, 92
Melania tuberculata, 80
Melanotænia mccullochi, 450
nigrans, 451
Mercurochrome, 89
Merry widow, 153
Mesogonistius chætodon, 454

Methylene blue for white spot, 88
for preventing disease, 87
for preventing egg fungus, 329
Metynnis schreitmulleri, 261
Micranthemum orbiculatum, 117
Microglanis parahybæ, 343
Microworms, 67
Midnight mollie, 152
Minerals, 41
Miniature barb, 171
goby, 441
Rasbora, 210
Minor tetra, 244
Miscellaneous apparatus, 49
Mænkhausia pittieri, 262
sancta filomennæ, 263
Mogurnda mogurnda, 440
Mollienisia latipinna, 149
sphenops, 150
velifera, 151
Monodactylus argenteus, 456
sebæ, 457
Moonlight gourami, 384
Mosaic catfish, 340
Mosquito fish, 144
larvæ, 75
Mottled catfish, 339
sucking catfish, 354
Mouth fungus, 90
Mouth-breeding Betta, 367
Mud skipper, 446
Mulm, 40
Mussels, freshwater, 81
Myriophyllum braziliense, 119
hippuroides, 118
proserpinacoides, 119
verticillatum, 119
Mystus vittatus, 342

Naias microdon, 120
Nandidæ, 394
Nannacara anomala, 431
Nannachromis nudiceps, 432
Nannæthiops unitæniatus, 264
Nannostomus anomalus, 265
marginatus, 266
trifasciatus, 267
Neolebias ansorgi, 268
Neon tetra, 252
breeding, 252
disease, 253
Nepa cinerea, 85
Nets, 49
nylon filtering, 50
Nitella gracilis, 120
Noemacheilus species, 316
Notonecta, 85
Notopteridæ, 437
Nuphars and *Nymphæas,* 121
Nylon mops, 56

ODONATA, 85
Œdema, 91
Oodinium limneticum, 89
Orange chromide, 412
-throated Panchax, 296
Ornate dwarf cichlid, 426
Oryzias javanicus, 305
latipes, 306
Otocinclus affinis, 354
vittatus, 355
Ova, 134
Over-crowding, 95
Over-feeding, 39
Oviparous, or egg-laying, fishes, 158
Ovoviviparous fishes, 134
Oxygen, 34

Pachypanchax playfairii, 300
Panchax group, 292
breeding the, 292
Panchax homomolotus, 301
Paper-shell snail, 79
Paradise fish, 379
Parasites, 82
Pearl Danio, 214
Pelmatochromis guntheri, 433
kribensis, 434
Penguins (fish), 276
Peplis diandra, 122
Periophthalmidæ, 446
Periophthalmus koelreuteri, 446
Persian carpet, 440
Peruvian long-fin, 307
pH, adjusting, 42
definition, 41
testing for, 42
Phallichthys amates, 153
Phenacogrammus interruptus, 269
Physa fontinalis, 80
Pigment, 133
Pimelodella gracilis, 344
Pimelodidæ, 343
Pipe-fish, 459
Piranha, 275
Pistia stratiotes, 122
Planaria worms, 86
Planorbis corneus, 80
Plant pots, 53
Planting sticks, 53
Plants, functions, 38
method of planting, 31
suitable aquarium, 97
Plastics, 19
Platy, 156
Plecostomus plecostomus, 356
Plistophera, 253
Plumatella repens, 86
Pœciliidæ, 142
Pœcilobrycon auratus, 270
espei, 271
harrisonii, 272
unifasciatus, 273

Polycentropsis abbreviata, 396
Polycentrus schomburgki, 397
Polythene bags, 95
Pomacentrus cæruleus, 479
Pompadour, 422
Pond-snail, 79
Poor man's angel, 454
Potassium permanganate, 82
Pristella riddlei, 274
Psettus argenteus, 456
Pterois volitans, 480
Pterolebias peruensis, 307
Pterophyllum altum, 421
    eimekei, 418
    scalare, 421
Puffer fish, 461
Pumps, 58
Puntius, 162
Putty (aquarium cement), 21
Pygmy sunfish, 455

QUEEN ANGEL FISH, 472
Quinine hydrochloride, 89

RAMSHORN SNAIL, 80
Rasbora borapetensis, 198
    daniconius, 199
    dorsiocellata, 200
    einthoveni, 201
    elegans, 202
    heteromorpha, 203
    kalochroma, 205
    maculata, 206
    pauciperforata, 208
    species, 212
    trilineata, 209
    urophthalmus, 210
    vaterifloris, 211
Rasboras, 198
Rasborinæ, 198
Red-finned shark, 195
    -nosed tetra, 241
    -tailed black shark, 192
    pencil fish, 273
    tetra, 238
Rhino-horn goby, 443
*Riccia fluitans, 122
Rivulus, 308
    breeding the, 308
    cylindraceus, 308
    hartii, 310
    strigatus, 311
Rocks and rockwork, 29
Rosy barb, 165
    tetra, 256
Rotifers, 69
Rubber suction cups, 55

SADDLE-BACK, 90
*Sagittaria lorata, 122
    *microfolia, 122
    *natans, 124
    *sinensis, 124
Sail-finned mollie, 151
Salmon discus, 234
Salt treatments, 89, 90

*Salvinia braziliensis, 124
*Samolus floribundus, 125
Sand, grades of, 28
    pocket in, 29
    silver, 465
    washing, 28
Sand-hoppers, 76
Saprolegnia, 90
*Saururus cernus, 126
Scaring, 95
Scat, 458
Scatophagus argus, 458
Scissor-tail, 209
Scrapers, 52
Sea-anemones, 467
Sea-horse, 477
Sea-water, artificial, 465
    density, 466
    dissolves some metals, 465
    evaporation, 466
    hydrometer, 466
Seaweeds, 467
Sediment, 38
Serpæ tetra, 246
Serrasalmus spilopleura, 275
Sheepshead acara, 401
Short-finned mollie, 150
Siamese fighting fish, 369
Siluridæ, 357
Siluroidea, 327
Silver chromide, 413
    hatchet, 228
    mercury preparation, 90
    tetra, 233
    tips, 237
Siphon tube, 50
Six-zoned barb, 173
Skin eruptions, 92
Slim half-beak, 141
Snails, 77
Snake head, 392
Snakeskin gourami, 385
Sodium amytal, 95
Spanner barb, 174
Sparkling gourami, 388
    Panchax, 291
Spawning the egg-droppers, 159
Spear-tailed paradise, 377
Species, 128
Spermatozoa, 134
Sphærichthys osphromenoides, 380
Spiny eel, 325
Spotted barb, 175
    catfish, 337
    Danio, 215
    Leporinus, 259
    lyre-tail, 285
    Panchax, 298
    Rasbora, 206
    sleeper, 439
Stigmatagobius   sadanundio, 444
    species, 445

Striped Anostomus, 225
    barb, 169
    Botia, 322
    damsel, 473
    gourami, 371
    knife fish, 436
    Leporinus, 258
Sucking catfish, 355
Sudden vibrations, 94
Sunlight, 38
Surface area per fish, 35
Sword-tail characin, 232
Swordtails, 154
Symphysodon discus, 422
Syngnathidæ, 458
Syngnathus species, 459
*Synnema triflorum, 126
Synodontidæ, 359
Synodontis nigriventris, 360
    shoutedeni, 361

TALKING CATFISH, 351
Tanichthys albonubes, 220
Teleosteans, 128
Telmatherina ladigesi, 452
Temperature, adjusting, 32
    sudden changes of, 94
    variation, 36
Terramycin, 89
Tetraodon fluviatilis, 461
    species, 461
Tetraodontidæ, 460
Texas cichlid, 417
Thayeria sanctæ mariæ, 276
Therapon jarbua, 460
Theraponidæ, 460
Thermometers, 55
Thermostats, 22
Thick-lipped gourami, 372
Three-spot damsel, 475
Tiger barb, 184
Tilapia mossambica, 424
Tinfoil barb, 181
Titration, 45
Toxotes jaculator, 463
Toxotidæ, 462
Transporting fishes, 95
Traps for egg-layers, 213
    for live-bearers, 57
Trichogaster leeri, 382
    microlepis, 384
    pectoralis, 385
    trichopterus, 386
Trichopsis pumilis, 388
    vittatus, 390
Tropical marines, 464
    diseases of, 468
Tuberculosis, 92
Tubifex, 73
Two-spot barb, 163

UPSIDE-DOWN CATFISH, 360
*Utricularia major, 86
    *minor, 86

*_Vallisneria gigas_, 126
   *_spiralis_, 127
   *_torta_, 127
Velvet disease, 89
" Vitrolite," 20
   bar for spawning, 408
Viviparous fishes, 134
Viviparus malleatus, 80

WANKLYN TEST, 44
Wasp goby, 441
Water, 40
   brown, 47
   cloudy, 48
   distilled, 47
   green, 47
   hardness of, 43

   peaty, 44
   pond, 47
   rain, 47
   softening, 43
   well, 47
Water boatman, 85
Water hyacinth, 110
Water lettuce, 122
Water scorpion, 85
Water tiger, 82
Water wisteria, 126
Whip-tail Loricaria, 353
White cloud mountain
   minnow, 220
White spot, 87
   cures, 88
   symptoms, 88

White worms, 68
Wimple fish, 476
Winged Danio, 217
Worms, blood, 75
   earth, 68
   glass, 74
   Grindal, 68
   micro, 67
   Tubifex, 73
   white, 68

X-RAY FISH, 274
Xenomystus nigri, 437
Xiphophorus helleri, 154
   maculatus, 156

ZEBRA DANIO, 215

SCIENTIFIC NAMES

♂   ♀

This denotes the   This denotes the
male   female

Many aquarists prefer to call fishes by their popular names, and consider that the use of scientific titles is an affectation. This is a mistaken idea, as in the long run it is much simpler, frequently it is shorter, and mistakes are avoided. Furthermore, the scientific name once learned is no more difficult to use than two or three common ones which are sometimes misleading. For instance, *Labeo bicolor* signifies the Red-tailed Black Shark. Again, as previously stated, there is the advantage that the genus, coming in the nomenclature before the species, gives an immediate indication that the fish in question will in all probability prefer the same conditions and breed in a similar manner to others of the same genus.

Unfortunately, in the light of present-day reclassification many of the old scientific names are constantly changing. It is therefore impossible to keep absolutely up-to-date. Even so, the original scientific name is still less vague than popular terms which vary from country to country.

USEFUL INFORMATION

1 imperial gallon of water weighs 10 lb.
1 imperial gallon=4·55 litres of water.
1 United States gallon of water weighs 8·34 lb.
1 United States gallon = 0·83 imperial gallon.
                            = 3·8 litres of water.
1 litre of water   = 0·22 imperial gallon.
                            = 0·264 United States gallon.
                            = 0·0353 cubic foot.
                            = 2·2 lb.
1 cubic centimetre of water weighs 1 gramme = 1 millilitre (ml.).
1 litre = 1000 cubic centimetres.

To find the capacity of a tank in gallons

Multiply length in feet by breadth in feet by height in feet. The result is the capacity in cubic feet.

Since 1 cubic foot of water = 62·3 lb., the total weight of water in the tank = capacity in cubic feet × 62·3 lb.

Then the number of imperial gallons in the tank is obtained by dividing the total weight of water by 10 (1 gallon of water weighs 10 lb.).

The number of United States gallons is obtained by dividing the total weight of water by 8·34 (1 U.S. gallon weighs 8·34 lb.).

Examples. A tank measures 20″ × 10″ × 10″. What is its cubic capacity, what is the weight of water it holds, and how many gallons does this represent? Give results in both imperial and United States units.

$$\text{Capacity of tank} = \frac{20}{12} \times \frac{10}{12} \times \frac{10}{12} = 1\cdot16 \text{ cubic feet approximately.}$$

$$\text{Weight of water} = \frac{20}{12} \times \frac{10}{12} \times \frac{10}{12} \times 62\cdot3 \text{ lb.} = 72\cdot27 \text{ lb. approximately.}$$

$$\text{Imperial gallons} = \frac{72\cdot27}{10} = 7\cdot23 \text{ gallons approximately.}$$

$$\text{United States gallons} = \frac{72\cdot27}{8\cdot34} = 8\cdot67 \text{ gallons approximately.}$$

To find surface area of a tank multiply length by breadth. Allow each fish 12 square inches of surface area. Therefore a tank 24″ × 12″ has a surface area of 288 square inches: allowing 12 square inches per fish, it will hold 24 fishes.

Temperature scales

To convert Fahrenheit to Centigrade: subtract 32, then multiply result by $\frac{5}{9}$.

To convert Centigrade to Fahrenheit: multiply by $\frac{9}{5}$ and add 32.

Apothecaries' Weight

1 grain = 0·065 gramme.
15·4 grains = 1 gramme.

INTRODUCTION

THE REMARKABLE INCREASE IN THE NUMBER OF AQUARISTS (THE GENERAL term for those who keep fishes) shows the growing popularity of a hobby which transcends national frontiers and provides a common interest among men and women all over the world. Why is it that in so many homes there are to be found aquaria, and that of these the major proportion are tropical?

Advantages of Tropicals

In comparison with cold-water fishes, most tropicals are smaller, more dainty, and more colourful. They are accustomed to warmish water, which naturally contains less dissolved oxygen, so they need less of this gas. The warmth speeds up metabolism, making them more active than cold-water fishes. This has the advantage that in a given-sized tank more tropicals can be kept than cold-water species.

Interior Decoration

Once an illuminated aquarium has been installed, it becomes the focal point of the room. It is a fascinating sight to watch the brilliantly coloured exotic fishes weaving in and out among the rocks and aquatic plants. There is something intriguing in this living picture which gives a glimpse of the mysteries of the underwater world, and brings nature right into the home.

Expression of Individuality

There are many ways in which a tank can be set up; no two aquaria are likely to be identical. Some people prefer to keep fish of one species only; others like diversity, and their tank may harbour fishes from many parts of the world. But, whatever form the aquarium may take, the arranging of the various plants, with their different types of foliage and varying shades of green, and the placing of the rocks in position, gives plenty of opportunity for artistic expression.

Educational Value

Another aspect of an aquarium is its educational value. The study of the habits of fishes and their methods of breeding is both interesting and instructive. The owner soon begins to differentiate between one genus and another, and learns about their methods of reproduction. Some fishes give birth to live young; others produce eggs. But, since most tropicals breed frequently, the aquarist who keeps some live-bearers is bound sooner or later to have the opportunity of seeing the mating and eventual birth of some of these species in his aquarium. With the aid of a small breeding tank he can watch the spawning, hatching, and development of egg-layers. Moreover, the simple manner in which fishes mate affords a natural method of introducing children to the ways of Nature.

Finally, it might be mentioned here that, both for children and for adults, looking after, and having regard for, dumb creatures helps to develop a good trait in the human character. Where larger pets are out of the question, fishes may help to compensate for their lack. Strange as it may seem, even fishes soon learn to recognize their owner and treat him as a friend, coming fearlessly to his hand at feeding-time. In some hospitals, particularly those for children, fish tanks in the wards have proved to be most beneficial, as they create an interest and help to take the mind off pain.

Economy of Space and Freedom from Restrictions

A great advantage of the tropical aquarium lies in its economy of space. With 2 or 3 cubic feet one can keep 30 to 60 fishes; this means that even the smallest room can accommodate the fascinating hobby. Again, on owning an aquarium there are no restrictions such as apply in some blocks of flats, where dogs and other animals are prohibited on grounds of noise. Nobody is likely to complain of the aquarist, with his tank of silently swimming fishes.

Initial Cost and Maintenance

What does it cost? Here is a fundamental question asked by everyone who wishes to keep an aquarium. Fortunately, the tank and equipment is not an unduly expensive piece of apparatus; the handy amateur who is prepared to do his own glazing can minimize the drain on his pocket. Rocks and water cost practically nothing; the common plants are inexpensive; fishes can be purchased from about a shilling or 15 cents upward; heating and lighting costs are reasonable, as in a tropical tank the water is only lukewarm. Maintenance is low; if properly kept all that is necessary is an occasional scraping of the front glass, and perhaps siphoning away a small amount of sediment and topping up with water. These operations require only a few minutes, and involve no expenditure. The skilful aquarist can organize the feeding so that it costs practically nothing. With experience it is possible to breed certain fish whose sale not only will recover the annual expenditure on the aquarium but may even show a profit.

Social Aspect

The aquarist will soon find that his hobby is helping him to make a widening circle of friends whose interests coincide with his own. Almost certainly his enthusiasm will inspire other people to follow his example and become aquarists. Moreover, we must not forget to mention that in many parts of the country there are fish clubs where newcomers are welcomed. Here for a very moderate subscription a member can attend periodical meetings, join in discussions, see films, and hear talks on various aspects of his hobby. The clubs organize shows, and perhaps the aquarist will win a coveted prize. The club brings him into touch with those who are more experienced fish-keepers than himself; this gives him opportunities of gaining valuable information which will help him to avoid making mistakes. In many countries there are fish magazines; these link together enthusiasts the world over. Through correspondence in the columns aquarists get in touch with one another, and friendships are formed. Contacts such as these contribute something towards building up a better understanding among men, and thereby help to establish peace and good-will.

CHAPTER I

THE AQUARIUM

THE FIRST THING TO BEAR IN MIND IS THAT THE AQUARIUM SHOULD BE AS large as space and money will allow; the greater the volume of water the more stable will be the temperature, and the water will not foul so quickly. Again, sooner or later most aquarists wish to expand their hobby; the man who initially installs a large tank can extend without additional expense on equipment.

A vital point is that the surface area of the water exposed to the air should, for reasons given later (see p. 35), be as large as possible. To achieve this the tank should be long, and the width be at least as great as the height.

TYPES OF AQUARIA

Metal Framework

The best aquarium is made with sheets of glass which are held in a metal framework. This is usually constructed of pieces of angle iron or stainless steel which are welded together at the corners; leakage between the glass and metal is prevented by putty or aquarium cement.

Stainless steel has the advantage of being rustproof and very durable. Since it is not essential to paint this material, it can be kept bright and clean by an occasional rub over with a piece of cloth.

Battery Jars

This type of aquarium is useful for emergency purposes, but is not to be recommended as a permanency. All-glass aquaria are cast in one piece, and a crack, however small, may suddenly expand and cause a flood. This not only results in a loss of fishes, but also necessitates the buying of a new tank, as it is impossible to repair the old one. Moreover, when looking through the walls of this type of aquarium there is distortion, which adversely affects one's view of the fishes. Similar disadvantages apply to fish globes or bowls. Battery jars suffer from the additional limitation that their height is usually much greater than the length or width. This means that, relative to the volume of water, the surface area is small, so oxygenation is restricted.

Plastics

With the ever-expanding applications of plastics, it is not surprising to find that, particularly in America, plastic materials have in some instances been used to replace glass for aquaria. The synthetic product has the advantage of being unbreakable, but some plastic materials are soft enough for the surface to become scratched; this in time will mar the transparency.

"*Vitrolite*"

This glass-like material is available in many different colours, and some very pleasing effects can be obtained by applying it to the sides or the back of the aquarium. Moreover, being opaque, "Vitrolite" will hide the wall and any unsightly wires or other apparatus behind the aquarium. In cases where the tank has to be placed with its back to the window, "Vitrolite" can be used to cut down the light, and prevent the fishes from being silhouetted against a colourless background.

As will be explained later, a long panel of this material is ideal for breeding angel fish and festivum cichlids, as these fishes like to deposit their eggs on it.

Wood

For æsthetic reasons it may be desirable for the framework of the aquarium to be made of wood rather than metal. A wooden framework, however, is not very satisfactory, as it is porous, and will warp if there is dampness. A way of counteracting this disadvantage is to employ a framework of metal faced with wood, which can be polished or stained to harmonize with the furnishing of the room.

CONSTRUCTING AN AQUARIUM
(36″ × 15″ × 15″)

Making one's own tank is not really difficult, but requires a little skill and great accuracy, while in these days few people have sufficient time to spare on constructing an article that may be purchased quite reasonably. Moreover, a bought tank that leaks would be exchanged by the vendor, while an amateur aquarium-builder may break the glass, or find that his home-made tank leaks when completed, and waste more time and money in the end.

Framework

However, for those keen enough to try it is best to buy a stout, undistorted frame of $\frac{1}{8}$″ angle-iron, making sure all the corners are welded in true right angles.

Glass

Five pieces of glass $\frac{1}{4}$″ thick may be cut or purchased, but accurate measurements here are essential. If a $\frac{1}{4}$″-thick slate base—which is preferable—is used, then only 4 pieces of glass are necessary.

The authors recommend that the base be inserted last, as this ensures that all four walls are locked in position against the framework. Quarter-inch plate glass is necessary for the front panel, but a little money can be saved if ¼″ cast glass be used for the back, base, and sides; however, vision is thereby restricted.

The front and back panels should be glazed in first (if cast glass is used the smooth face must be on the inside of the aquarium). These are cut to the outside measurements of the tank less ½″ all round to allow for the thickness of the framework and the putty.

A tank 36″ long by 15″ high would require front and back panels of glass 35½″ × 14½″. The two side panels fitting between front and back panels would need to be 14″ long by 14½″ high. Similarly the base, whether slate or glass, fitting inside all four walls would be 35″ × 14″.

Putty (Aquarium cement)

About 14 lb. of any good putty bound by linseed oil will serve, but this must be of the correct workable consistency. It is better purchased in air-tight tins than loose, as it lasts longer should there be delay before it is used.

Generally new putty is far too wet and sticky, and as soon as it is worked one's hands become completely gummed up. If this happens place large lumps of the putty between sheets of newspaper and tread on it; when it is uncovered it will be seen that much of the linseed oil has been squeezed out and absorbed by the paper. Repeat the process again and again with clean paper, until when rolled in the hands the putty stays in a pliable lump, leaving the palms of the hands perfectly clean.

In the event of purchased putty being too hard it may be softened to the right workable state by kneading into it a few drops of pure linseed oil.

Glazing

Place the aquarium frame, back downward, on newspaper laid out on the floor, fill the whole right angle of the framework with putty (see Fig. 1), place the glass over it in the correct position, and allow it to fall gently on to the putty. Now with the palms of the hands flat press it down evenly all round the edges—do not force it—then tip the frame on to its base, and, with a putty knife point forward, cut off the excess putty which has been squeezed out. If this putty is of the right consistency it will fall cleanly away in long strips, and may be used again. Once more tilt the tank over, and press the glass home a little more. Repeat this operation until it is evenly embedded with ⅛″ thickness of putty showing all round.

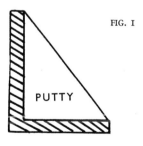

FIG. 1

PUTTY

SECTION OF ANGLE IRON
FILLED WITH PUTTY

Turn the tank upside down, so that it now lies on its face, and insert the front glass. Do not fear the back glass suspended above will fall out; if the putty is of the right consistency mentioned all will be well. Treat all four walls in the same way.

The sides may not fit in at first, but will do so if inserted on a slight slope, making sure that the lower end is towards the front panel (Fig. 2)

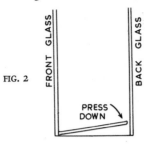

FIG. 2

—then, as it is eased into position, any scratches made will be on the back panel only. When inserting these side glasses putty will be forced out as usual, but also by the front and back panels, as they are farther embedded. Never force any glass, remove surplus putty squeezed out, and then more pressure may be applied safely.

Finally insert the base, and follow the same procedure. If the base is inserted first pressure on the edges of the glass walls is more difficult, as all the work has to be done through the one top opening, often at arm's length. Putting it in last enables one to move to the opposite side of the tank and apply pressure through both top and base openings.

METHODS OF HEATING

The average aquarist with one or two tanks will employ simple heating equipment operating on electricity, gas, or paraffin (kerosene). But the professional breeder may use space heating dependent on one of the above sources of heat, or he may employ a boiler fired with solid fuel or diesel oil.

Electricity

Many aquarists start their hobby with a tank of cold-water fish, and because they are unaware of the simplicity of heating installations they are reluctant to go in for tropicals. There are, however, many reasonably priced electric heaters which are reliable and efficient. A thermostat is employed to maintain the temperature of the water at a fairly even value.

Electric Heaters

We shall not consider how to make electric heaters and thermostats, as they are usually cheaper to buy than to construct. Also, most bought apparatus is guaranteed by the manufacturers to give satisfactory service for a period. Here we merely state that the usual form of heater consists of a length of wire wound on a suitable support. The whole is contained in a heat-resisting glass tube sealed by a rubber cork, through which the two lead-in wires pass. The heater is placed horizontally on the sand at the bottom of the tank, and lies in a position half-way along the back of the aquarium.

Thermostats

There are various types of thermostat. Most operate on the expansion and contraction of a bimetal strip with different coefficients of expansion.

This strip forms a curve on heating; on cooling it straightens out, thus making and breaking the electric circuit. To avoid arcing at the contacts —with the resulting pitting of the metal, and radio interference—a magnet is employed to bring about a snap action. The temperature is controlled within certain limits by means of a set-screw. This screw should be readily accessible. The thermostat is connected in series with one lead from the heater in the manner shown in Fig. 3.

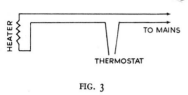

FIG. 3

It is then held vertically in a special clip, placed in one of the back corners of the tank. We prefer the heater and thermostat to be spaced well apart, so that the latter responds to the average temperature of the water, rather than to the warm currents rising in the vicinity of the heater. In America many thermostats and heaters are constructed together in one unit.

Heater attached to a Slate Base

A very satisfactory method of heating can be employed if the tank is provided with a base of $\frac{1}{4}''$ slate instead of glass. Two holes are bored through the slate; into each of these is fixed a hollow casing which projects upward into the tank. The heater is screwed from below into one of these casings, and into the other goes the thermostat. When either component needs repair it can easily be removed from the casing and a spare unit inserted. With all electrical installations it is highly desirable to keep spare heaters and a thermostat ready for immediate use should the need arise.

Consumption

For the benefit of those aquarists who are unfamiliar with the principles of electricity, and imagine that heating a fish tank must be very expensive, we will touch on the question of cost. A 100-watt heater consumes the same current as a 100-watt lamp. Should the latter be burning continuously, it will consume one unit of electricity in ten hours, whereas a one-bar electric fire of one-kilowatt loading would consume the same amount of electricity in one hour. But an aquarium heater thermostatically controlled, and of sufficient capacity for the size of tank, is very unlikely to remain in circuit for hours at a stretch; it will cut in and out as the temperature of the water falls and rises, thereby decreasing consumption.

Where central heating is installed in the house, the wattage of the aquarium heater can, of course, be reduced.

A Precaution

It is vital where water abounds that electrical installations be efficiently earthed to prevent a dangerous shock.

Gas

A gas-operated heater and thermostat can be purchased, but the equipment is rather bulky and costly. In small fish houses situated in a garden the most usual method of gas heating is to install a number of small burners underneath the tanks. But an efficient baffle must be arranged over the naked flames, otherwise the direct heat will crack the base of the tanks.

Paraffin (Kerosene)

Small paraffin oil-lamps similar to those used in chicken brooders serve for aquarium heating, but the base of the tanks must be protected from the naked flame. It is a good plan to mount the tanks on small legs, so that the heaters can be accommodated underneath. Paraffin is reasonably cheap, but it has the disadvantage of causing an unpleasant smell. If it is used extensively in a small fish house it is advisable periodically to cleanse the surface of the water in the tanks, as this is liable to become coated with a greasy film which may prevent oxygen entering the water. To do this lay newspaper on the water surface, leave for a second or two, and then strip off.

Larger Installations

When a large number of tanks are housed in a room or in a separate building, some form of space heating is more economical than individual units. To obtain the greatest efficiency it is essential that the walls be heat-insulated, so as to avoid unnecessary losses of thermal units. Space heating may be performed electrically by means of tubular heaters or convectors.

Another system makes use of hot water circulating in pipes, heat being generated by a boiler fired with solid fuel, gas, or diesel oil. Aquarists who have not had much experience in space heating are advised to consult a heating engineer, who can estimate the capacity of the equipment needed.

Lighting

An essential factor in keeping an aquarium is light. Not only is it required to enable the fish to be seen, and to enhance the beauty of the tank, but it is essential to stimulate plant growth and bring about photosynthesis (formation of carbohydrates in presence of light). For the large breeder, with his tanks housed under a glass roof in a special building, natural lighting will be adequate. The average amateur has to supplement daylight by artificial means. During the summer months—particularly if the rays of the sun penetrate the tank—artificial light must be reduced.

Practically all small aquaria are lit by electricity. Specially shaped hoods are used to house the lamps; the colours of the fish show up better when the light strikes them from the same side as the viewer takes up his position. It is not good practice to have the light shining from behind the fish, as this tends to silhouette them, and detracts considerably from their beauty. Figs. 4 (*A*) and (*B*) show two types of hood which light the

A   B

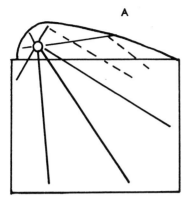 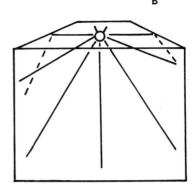

LIGHT DIRECTED AND
REFLECTED BACKWARD   FIG. 4

whole aquarium from above. With (*A*) the light is mostly directed back-ward, and this shows off the fish better.

It will be found that under an all-over hood moisture condenses, so to ensure that this drips back into the tank the hood should be provided with an inner lip, as shown. Any electric wiring inside the hood should be protected against condensation.

In order to distribute the light as evenly as possible over the length of the tank it is better to employ, say, four 15-watt units spread out under the hood, rather than a single 60-watt bulb at the centre. Lamps may be either clear or pearl, the latter giving a softer light. Strip lights and fluores-cent units give a good distribution of light, and the latter have the advan-tage of being more economical than ordinary bulbs in the consumption of electricity. The disadvantage of a fluorescent installation is initial cost, as in addition to the luminous tubes certain auxiliary apparatus is employed.

Before ending this section on lighting, we must remind the aquarist that artificial light produces heat, and this must be taken into consideration.

Consumption

As a very rough guide, a tank 3 ft. long by 1 ft. by 1 ft., thickly planted and receiving no daylight whatsoever, will need two 30-watt strip light lamps burning for about 8 hours per day. If strong daylight enters the tank the above period must be reduced. No artificial illumination what-soever will be needed if overhead sunlight enters the tank.

It is preferable to burn a low-powered lamp for ten hours than, say, one of twice the capacity which can be switched on for only half the time. The lower intensity of the light is more pleasant for the aquarist, and gives less glare to try the eyes of the fishes.

It is also suggested that during darkness the room light is switched on some minutes before the lamps over the aquarium are lit, so that the fish can adjust themselves to the light. Similarly, the aquarium light should be turned off first, and the room one later.

Not only is this practice a kindness, but it may save the aquarist expense, since startled and blinded fish may injure themselves against rocks or the walls of the aquarium in their dash for cover, damaging themselves sometimes fatally.

COVER GLASSES

Where all-over hoods are not used it is essential to employ cover glasses, as many tropical fishes jump; without a protective lid they may leap out of the water and be lost. Unfortunately, cover glasses just placed flat on the top of the aquarium collect condensation; drops of water run off and cause damage to furniture and carpets when the cover plates are removed.

To avoid these troubles a cover plate should be held on the incline just inside the frame of the aquarium; condensation then runs down the slope and drips back into the tank, and the frame is kept dry. Various clips are obtainable to hold the cover glass at the correct angle.

STANDS

When there is no suitable piece of furniture of just the right height on which to place the tank an angle iron stand can be purchased. Although this is not beautiful, it is at least strong and rigid, and if money is not the main consideration ornate stands in wrought iron, chromium plate, or bronze may be obtained. To improve the appearance of the stand some ingenious aquarists cover it with plywood, and make doors in the front. This useful cupboard can serve to house fish foods and equipment. A cheaper screen is to hang a curtain from wire stretchers.

An important point to bear in mind is that most stands have sharp feet, which will cut the carpet and even dig into floor-boards. To prevent this damage rubber, plastic, or wooden discs may be placed underneath the metal feet.

If the aquarist is having a stand made it is a good idea to have three tiers of angle iron running horizontally round the structure; one at the top, one near the bottom, and one in the middle. The tank is supported by the top members; the bottom and middle ones strengthen the stand and serve as supports for boards. These provide two useful shelves which may serve for holding equipment or even a small breeding tank.

CHAPTER II

SITING AND SETTING UP AN AQUARIUM

Weight

As an aquarium once set up is heavy and difficult to move, it will pay to give careful consideration to determine the best site so as to avoid having to undertake a difficult removal.

Bearing in mind that a cubic foot of water weighs approximately 62·5 lb., the water in a tank 36″ × 12″ × 12″ will weigh about 188 lb. To this must be added the weight of the tank, sand, rocks, etc., and the stand, so we arrive at a total of about 2 cwt., which is not an easy load to move about the room. From what has been said it will be appreciated that the aquarium should stand on a strong floor, which is well supported with substantial joists.

Size and Shape of Tank

As far as the fishes are concerned, a good shape of tank is the one referred to above. But it may not be convenient to hold rigidly to these dimensions, as the aquarist may wish the aquarium to occupy a special site in the room, such as a narrow mantelpiece or a particular cabinet. Size and shape, therefore, will depend on local conditions.

Height

This is not easy to determine, as it is difficult to be able to see straight into the front of an aquarium from both the standing and sitting positions. If the tank is situated in a hall it will need to be placed sufficiently high to avoid undue stooping. On the other hand, in a living-room where people are mostly seated a convenient height of stand is 3 ft., and this will be the height of the bottom of the tank.

Windows and Power Plugs

As has been previously mentioned, it is a bad plan to place an aquarium with its back to a window. A tank standing at right angles to the window will get the benefit of some natural light, and thus save artificial illumination, which otherwise would be necessary. A good north light is preferable to a window facing south, where much direct sunlight will enter the tank and cause green water.

When artificial light is to be the sole means of illumination even a dark corner is quite suitable, and here one may be guided mostly by accessibility to power plugs, or electric outlets. It is advisable to use as short a cable as possible, and it is best to have the tank circuit connected to a plug point or outlet used entirely for the aquarium so as to avoid inadvertent switching on and off.

Accessibility for Feeding and Cleaning

The tank should be placed so that it is easy to raise the lighting hood for feeding. There should be enough space in front to enable the aquarist to move about comfortably with jugs, jars, buckets, and siphon tubing.

Splashing and Spilling

Where there is water even the most careful aquarist will occasionally spill some, and it is unwise to place the tank on a highly polished or valuable piece of furniture. Even cloths laid down for protection sometimes become soaked, and can cause trouble.

SETTING UP AN AQUARIUM

Any new aquarium should first be given a thorough test to ensure that it is water-tight.

If after twelve hours there are no leaks it may be emptied and placed in its final position. Should the test reveal a very small leak it is possible that this will seal itself, as the weight of water tends to bed down the glass on to the putty. A large leak, however, must be repaired, or, if the tank has been purchased, it must be exchanged for one that is sound.

Now all is ready to set up the aquarium; for this work we shall require various items such as sand, rocks, etc. These will be dealt with in order.

Sand

Sand should be purchased with care, but most pet stores sell the right material. It should be of the nature of fine gravel or flint, and not contain too much limestone or other minerals soluble in water. Too coarse a sand allows particles of food to fall into the crevices and give rise to decomposition, bacteria, and fouling of the water. On the other hand, too fine a material, such as silver sand or sea-shore sand, packs too tightly to allow the roots of the plants to spread and flourish. The most suitable is called in Britain 1/16th grade; it is about the size of the average pinhead. The amount required is approximately 12 lb. per square foot of aquarium base.

Washing Sand

The sand must be washed thoroughly; it is surprising how much dirt can be removed. The method is as follows:

Half fill an enamel bucket with sand, place it in the sink, and fill up with tepid water. With one hand dig right down to the bottom of the bucket and stir every grain of sand for two or three minutes. Now gently pour off the dirty water. Do this ten or twelve times until the water poured off is quite clean. Dump the cleansed sand in the aquarium and repeat the process until sufficient is obtained to cover the whole base at an even slope. This should be from $2\frac{1}{2}''$ at the back to $1''$ in the front.

It is advisable at this stage to leave a small pocket in the centre front of the tank. This depression can be made by building a semicircular retaining wall of rocks which hold back the sand and leave a sump. Here the sediment will collect, and can easily be siphoned away.

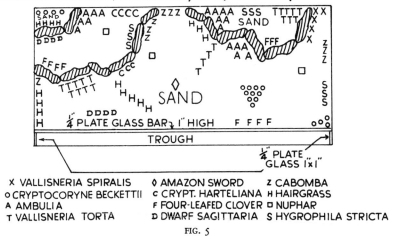

X VALLISNERIA SPIRALIS	◊ AMAZON SWORD z CABOMBA
o CRYPTOCORYNE BECKETTII	c CRYPT. HARTELIANA H HAIRGRASS
A AMBULIA	F FOUR-LEAFED CLOVER □ NUPHAR
T VALLISNERIA TORTA	D DWARF SAGITTARIA S HYGROPHILA STRICTA

FIG. 5

Another way of achieving the same object is to hold the sand away from the front of the tank by a long strip of $\frac{1}{4}''$ glass, $1''$ wide (Fig. 5). This runs the entire length of the front of the aquarium, and is prevented from falling forward by placing in each front corner of the tank, flush with the side glasses, two small $1'' \times 1''$ squares of $\frac{1}{4}''$ glass. Now we have a long trough into which sediment collects, and where it can be siphoned away. All sharp edges of glass must be filed down to prevent the fishes cutting themselves.

Rocks and Rock-work

Well-designed and carefully laid out rock-work can enhance the appearance of the aquarium. It is important that the right kind of rock be chosen: natural water-worn stone is best. Flint, or other rock free from lime, is satisfactory, but artificial objects and lumps of coloured glass are not to be recommended. As the rock-work in many aquaria is badly arranged, it is worth while to consider briefly the technique of rock setting.

The method of haphazardly placing large clumps of rock has serious objections. Rarely is the appearance natural, and the fishes tend to stay out of view behind the rocks much of the time. Sediment, uneaten food, and even a dead fish can lodge behind a stone, decompose, and brew trouble for the aquarist.

A better method is to set up the rock-work in a series of steps. This is done by building an irregular line of rocks standing on end and embedded into the sand near the front. The entire area behind is filled with sand level with the top of the rocks, which should lean slightly backward to increase the stability. Now about 4" behind the front step a second irregular line of rocks is built, raising the level another 4″ or 5″; the space behind is filled with sand as before. There are now three levels (Fig. 6). If the work is done properly only the front face of the rocks will be seen, and there will be nowhere for dead fishes or sediment to lodge. When the three levels are planted a background of green plants stretches from top to bottom of the aquarium. On each layer the tops of the plants just reach to the bottom of those behind. With the exception of a few low ones in front, this system does away with the old idea that no short plants can be used at the back of the aquarium; see Fig. 6.

FIG. 6

The tiers need not stretch the full width of the tank. Some aquarists may prefer two tiers, one in each back corner, leaving the centre back low; others may like to see a single tier with the summit at the centre of the back of the aquarium descending towards the sides. In either case, tall growing plants are used in the deeper parts. There will be small crevices through which the sand tends to pour, and these must be dammed up with rock fragments. The artistically minded aquarist has plenty of scope to create a most beautiful effect, and when the fish are introduced they prefer to swim in the foreground, and the undulating background is most natural and pleasing.

Ornaments

On the market there are miscellaneous coloured ornaments such as reclining mermaids, castles, treasure caskets filled with jewels, sunken ships, divers, starfish, etc. For those who like these, and perhaps in a children's nursery, they may add colour and amusement. But surely there is nothing more attractive than a natural under-water setting where the colours of the fish mingle with the various shades of the plants and the tints of the rocks? If the aquarist aims at giving the effect of having swum under water and literally scooped up, complete as it stood, a section of the river's edge, the aquarium will appear natural and beautiful.

Filling the Aquarium with Water

Generally speaking, an aquarium may be safely set up with ordinary tap-water. Once the rock and sand work has been completed, all is ready to fill the tank. To pour water from a jug in a haphazard manner is courting trouble, as the pains which have been taken in building up the interior of the aquarium will probably be wasted. It is quite likely that the artistic setting will collapse; also, despite the careful washing of the sand, innumerable floating particles will appear and cause a cloudy effect.

A good way to fill the aquarium is as follows: on the sand near the front place a saucer, and on this sit a clean jam-jar. Then, aiming carefully, slowly pour water of approximately 78°F. from a jug into the jam-jar. This fills rapidly, spills into the saucer (which breaks the fall), and trickles over the edge. Continue to pour gently until the saucer is covered, after which the pouring can be more rapid, as the curved lip of the saucer directs the stream of water upward, and not a grain of sand need be disturbed. The tank is filled to within 2″ of the top, and the water will be quite clear. All is now ready for planting.

Plants

Plants are described fully under the chapter of that heading. Here we are concerned only with the method of planting. The main object to bear in mind is to form an attractive background, leaving ample space in front where the fishes can swim unhampered, and be seen. The tall, grassy type is best planted at intervals in rows, whereas the feathery ones look better when they are bunched into small clumps, which makes them appear like branching bushes.

Method of Planting

If the plants have roots hold the tip of the bunch of roots between the thumb and second finger and rest them on the sand. Now with the first finger push the upper part of the roots (where they join the stem) half an inch into the sand. Without moving this finger, scrape with the thumb and second finger some sand over any uncovered portion of the roots. Fig. 7 overleaf shows the method. The roots now lie horizontally just under the sand, and are firmly held down.

When putting in rootless plants in bunches the method explained above is repeated, but this time the lower ends of the stems are placed together and treated exactly as if they were roots.

Some authorities advise aquarists to carry out their planting when the tank is only half full of water, but this method has disadvantages. The

FIG. 7

leaves of the plants tend to lie flat on the surface of the water, and so obscure the view of the roots. In addition, the foliage is liable to catch on the aquarist's hand, which when withdrawn from the water pulls the plants out of the sand.

Once the planting is completed top up the aquarium by pouring the additional water from a jug into one's hand, cupped beneath the surface so as to break the fall and avoid a disturbance. It is important that the water surface should be right up to the lower edge of the top angle iron of the tank, so that looking from the front the water surface cannot be seen, and the viewer gets the impression that there is no water in the aquarium. If the level is allowed to fall below the top angle iron the tank looks like a container holding water.

Settling Period

No doubt the beginner will be anxious to see fishes swimming around in his tank, but before stocking the aquarium it is advisable to allow a settling period. This permits the water to age a little, and gives time for particles in suspension to settle. Furthermore—and this is the most important factor—a settling period allows the new plants to anchor their roots, and to get a hold before they are subjected to the buffeting of the fishes.

Temperature

For the aquarist who is going in for tropicals the settling period provides an excellent opportunity to adjust the temperature which is to be maintained in the tank. Install, as previously described, the heater and thermostat, and switch on. Watch the thermometer now and then. If it ranges between 74° and 78° F. all is well, but should the temperature vary much above or below this the thermostat must be adjusted accordingly. Remember that without fishes in the tank the water is static, and likely to be warmer at the top than at the bottom, so before reading the thermometer stir gently. Later this will be done automatically by the fishes.

Introducing the Fishes

Assuming that from five to seven days have elapsed since planting, the aquarium should now be crystal-clear and the plants showing signs of growth. All is now ready for the great moment when the inhabitants take possession of their home. But here is a word of caution to the budding aquarist: until he has gained some experience, he will find it better to keep a few of the cheaper fishes. Many enthusiasts, through expensive initial losses, have become disheartened and given up; if only they had gained a little knowledge first, aquarium-keeping might have become a great interest.

When purchasing fishes it is essential to be quite certain that they come from a reliable source, and are free from disease. Good-quality stock may be a little more expensive, but is well worth the initial outlay. When buying fishes, look for an air of well-being, liveliness, well-spread fins, plump stomachs, with no signs of sluggishness, drooping fins, or fungus anywhere on the body.

On arriving home net the fishes into a few half-filled jam-jars containing the water in which they arrived, and allow the jars to float in the tank. In half an hour the temperatures inside and outside the jars will be equalized, but the quality of the water may be different. For this reason it is advisable not to tip the fishes straight into the tank, but first to dip the jars so as to allow the tank water to enter slowly. Continue the mixing process of allowing the water to flow in and out of the jars for a few minutes, finally tipping the fishes into the tank.

Community Tanks

This expression is commonly used when several species of fish are housed together in one tank. For the aquarist wishing to have a number of fishes of different shape and colour, and intending to use the aquarium purely for decoration and interest, the community tank is perhaps the best type of aquarium to keep. Remember that some species prefer to swim about at different depths. This means that to fill the aquarium evenly it is necessary to have some fishes that normally swim in the top strata of water, others that prefer the middle strata, and some that are at home in the deepest water. It must be borne in mind that not all species will live together peacefully in a community tank; size is usually the governing factor, but where an exception arises it will be mentioned.

Those who own several aquaria and intend to breed may prefer to have only one species to one tank. Certain fishes have the habit of swimming in shoals, and undoubtedly these seem to be happier and look better than when kept with others.

CHAPTER III

SOME IMPORTANT RULES

IN FISH-KEEPING RIGID RULES ARE FEW. EXCEPT FOR THE ESSENTIALS, QUITE a wide latitude is permissible. One aquarist following a certain line is successful and believes his theory to be correct, expounding it to everyone he meets. Another aquarist, holding views which are practically the opposite, meets with equal success, and is convinced that *he* is right. The fact is that fishes are adaptable, and in time become acclimatized to the prevailing conditions. Nevertheless, certain rules must be observed, otherwise failure is inevitable. Below are listed vital factors which no aquarist may ignore for long.

(i) Oxygen and other gases.
(ii) Temperature variations.
(iii) Light and its functions.
(iv) Plants and their actions.
(v) The influence of animal life.
(vi) Feeding and fouling.
(vii) Cleanliness and balance.

Each of the above will be dealt with under a separate heading.

(i) OXYGEN AND OTHER GASES

Just as human beings require to breathe, so do fishes; their gills, like our lungs, extract oxygen, and this vital gas is distributed through their entire system by the blood-stream. Remember, therefore, that the fishes do not merely aerate their gills: they need oxygen throughout their whole body.

The lungs of a man standing still extract enough oxygen to supply all parts of the body. But when he starts to run more oxygen is required to feed the muscles in operation. If he continues to run the demand for oxygen increases, until finally a stage is reached where the muscles require a greater supply of the gas than the lungs can furnish to the blood-stream. At this point he is forced to stop or slow down, otherwise he will collapse. In the same way fishes, which are practically continuously on the move (thereby using their muscles), must have an adequate supply of oxygen. Starve them of this, and they will become sluggish, lack the energy to move about, be unable to eat or digest their food, become liable to disease, and will collapse. From the foregoing it will be appreciated that oxygen is of supreme importance.

Water is a compound of two gases—hydrogen and oxygen—and normally holds in addition dissolved oxygen and other gases; it is this dissolved oxygen that fishes breathe. Clearly, they can only extract the gas as long as it is present in the water. Oxygen from the air can be absorbed only at the surface of the water, where this comes in contact with the atmosphere. If, therefore, the surface area is small the intake of oxygen is also small; a large surface area will allow a more rapid absorption of oxygen. Nevertheless, there is a saturation point beyond which water will not absorb more oxygen. Normally, the proportion of dissolved oxygen is not very high: roughly it can be taken at 5·8 parts per million, at 78° F.

Now, what happens when the fishes are introduced? Immediately they start to consume the dissolved oxygen in the water; at the same time the water replenishes its supply from the air above. As long as oxygen is replaced as fast as it is consumed by the fishes all will be well. But once the demand exceeds the supply, either by the fishes growing bigger and requiring more oxygen, or through a greater number having been introduced, troubles begin. As a rough guide, allow six square inches of surface area per inch of tropical fish; this applies at a temperature of approximately 77° F. It should, however, be borne in mind that with an increase of the temperature of the water there is a decrease of oxygen.

Unfortunately for the aquarist, although water can contain only a small amount of oxygen, it is able to hold a higher proportion of carbon dioxide—and fishes exhale carbon dioxide. This gas is given off at the surface of the water; the process is, therefore, the reverse of the absorption of oxygen. Once again, if the surface area is small the discharge of carbon dioxide is restricted; the excess builds up in the water, taking up space that otherwise would have held oxygen.

The escape of carbon dioxide is just as important as the absorption of oxygen: bad conditions will still result if the tank is too crowded. This is because the fishes are exhaling carbon dioxide into the water faster than it can escape from the surface.

To find the area in square inches of the surface of a tank, multiply length by breadth—for instance, a tank measuring 24 inches long by 12 inches wide is 24 × 12 = 288 square inches.

Apart from oxygen and carbon dioxide, water may absorb other gases, such as carbon monoxide given off by slow-combustion stoves. Fumes from petroleum products and paint also may be taken in with harmful effects. For these reasons it is advisable to keep the aquarium in a clean, healthy atmosphere.

Artificial Aeration

With the use of an air pump, artificial aeration can be installed in the aquarium. In a healthy tank, contrary to the popular belief, very little oxygen is absorbed by the water direct from the rising bubbles; nevertheless, artificial aeration permits the aquarist to keep 50 per cent. more fishes than he would otherwise be able to maintain in his tank. This increase is because the rising stream of bubbles creates a circulation in the water; as a result of this process the water at the bottom of the aquarium containing much carbon dioxide moves round and up to the surface.

Here the unwanted gas escapes into the atmosphere, and is immediately replaced by oxygen from the air. The circulating water, now recharged with oxygen, moves round and down to the bottom of the aquarium, so that in the end the whole body of water contains oxygen. Without this artificial aeration there is a tendency for the water to form a double stratum with oxygen above and carbon dioxide below.

Here we must add a word of warning. Most aquarists employing artificial aeration are sooner or later tempted to increase unduly the fish population in their tanks. Since the water is adequately oxygenated throughout, all goes well at first. But it is too much to expect that any pump will operate continuously, year in and year out, without a break-down. Should this occur when the aquarist is absent, the fishes will soon be affected by lack of oxygen and an excess of carbon dioxide. These unhealthy conditions will result in serious losses.

There is a further drawback to aeration. In tanks which have a considerable depth of sediment this moves slowly towards the point where the bubbles rise. The sediment is then carried upward and distributed throughout the upper strata of water, from whence it sinks slowly, covering the plants with dirt and spoiling their fresh appearance.

(ii) TEMPERATURE VARIATIONS

Most tropical fishes can withstand a fairly large variation in temperature, provided the increase or decrease is gradual and does not go to extremes. In nature the fluctuation can be very considerable; for instance, in India the temperature of a natural pool containing 'Panchax' lineatus was found to be 66°F. at 10 P.M., and 109°F. in the afternoon. But it is not wise to take these liberties under artificial conditions. Here the extremes should be 68°F. to 90°F.; this range may allow a margin of safety for some species.

It is advisable to keep the average tropical fish at 78°F.; this means that with a reliable thermostat the temperature will fluctuate between 76°F. and 80°F. Some authorities recommend a lower temperature, but the authors disagree on the grounds that their fishes, kept within the above temperature range, are more lively, have a greater intensity of colour, eat better, grow quicker, and breed sooner than they would under lower temperature conditions. True, the speeding up of the fishes' metabolism may shorten their life by a week or two, but since the average fish lives two to three years, the curtailing of life by a relatively small span is unimportant, especially as we have avoided sluggishness and drabness of colour.

A sudden change of temperature either way causes discomfort to fishes. If they are suddenly introduced into cooler water considerable harm may be done; a chill can bring about a loss of resistance and make them susceptible to disease. A slight increase of temperature is unlikely to cause trouble, but a decrease must be avoided. When changing fishes from one container to another equalize the temperatures by the method explained on p. 33.

(iii) LIGHT AND ITS FUNCTIONS

Reference was made on p. 24 to light purely as a means of enhancing the beauty of a tank. But light has a much more important rôle to play than this; it is a fundamental factor in the life-cycle of animal and vegetable matter. Without light most life would cease; this applies in an aquarium just as much as anywhere else.

Light is essential to plants, enabling them, through the process of photosynthesis, to absorb carbon dioxide, which they break down into sugar and starches for food. It is through the action of light that the plant is able to breathe, feed, and reproduce. Under strong illumination plants give off oxygen; sometimes when there is a surplus of this gas it can be seen in the form of tiny bubbles rising from the leaves to the surface of the water. At the same time the plant is absorbing carbon dioxide from the water, but this action is not visible. During the hours of darkness the process is reversed, the plant extracting oxygen from the water and giving off carbon dioxide.

From the foregoing it will be seen that plants need light for their existence; if there is insufficient they will die. Too much light will cause green cells to develop until there are millions which can be seen collectively in the form of a green haze. If excess light continues, the cells form chains (blanket and thread algæ) suspended in the water, or they attach themselves to rocks, plants, or the sides of the aquarium, on which they grow as a fur. Some cells cling together and form a mat of dark green algæ, smothering leaves, rocks, sand, etc.; others may collect in a slimy mass near the surface of the water. While a small amount of algæ is good as vegetable food, too much becomes unruly, unsightly, and can be harmful.

Strange as it may seem, plants can die from a lack of light resulting from over-illumination of the tank. The explanation is that the excess amount of light immediately causes algæ to grow on the plants, forming a dark green or almost black covering over each leaf. So thick is the growth that light cannot penetrate it; as a result the smothered plant-leaves beneath become pale and weak. This process is seen if, say, a tin or a piece of wood is left for several days on a patch of grass. When the object is removed the grass underneath will be found to be weak and of a pale yellow tint compared with its surroundings. The black-green algæ clinging to the leaf of a plant can be peeled off, when it will appear like a strip of leather. The effect can be further illustrated if one imagines a woman removing a black suede glove from a pale hand.

The correct illumination of an aquarium is a major factor in keeping it clean and clear. Just the right amount of light maintains the plants growing healthily, but leaves nothing over for the formation of algæ cells; as a result it should not be necessary to have to scrape green deposits off the walls of the aquarium.

For an illustration, let us suppose that x watts burning for ten hours will supply the needs of 100 plants. Now, if the number of plants be halved there will be a surplus of light, and nature will quickly see that this is utilized by growing algæ. On the other hand, if we have 200 plants they will have to share the x watts available; each plant will now receive approximately half the illumination it really needs, and growth will suffer accordingly. If one must err it is far safer to have an excess of plants rather than a deficit.

Having referred to the effects of light on plants, we will now consider its importance to the fishes themselves, and to certain other forms of aquatic life. In the first place, fishes, with the exception of the naturally blind species, require light to enable them to find their way about and search for food. Development and growth are influenced by light, which has a stimulating effect, causing the fishes to swim around, and exercise themselves; and it helps their bodies to perform the natural functions. Fishes kept in a tank receiving some direct sunlight will benefit from Vitamin D. This vitamin, being an antibiotic, builds up resistance to disease.

Strong light destroys bacteria, and this naturally helps to keep the tank healthy and prevent fouling. In cases where the sand has become polluted and blackened by bacteria it need not be discarded, but should be taken out, washed thoroughly (see p. 28) to remove suspended matter, and then spread out thinly on a tray or ground-sheet, and allowed to stand for several hours in bright sunlight. This treatment will destroy the bacteria, and the light will bleach the sand, so that it regains its natural colour and can be returned with safety to the aquarium.

(iv) PLANTS AND THEIR ACTIONS

As has been already mentioned (p. 37), plants play a vital rôle in an aquarium.

They take in some carbon dioxide and give off a little oxygen; by absorbing light they discourage the growth of algæ; the roots feed on and absorb sediment from the bottom of the tank (see p. 40). If there are sufficient plants to absorb all the sediment being formed they assist the aquarist by relieving him of the necessity to siphon off the excess. Where there are insufficient plants, there is generally an excess of sediment.

Besides beauty, plants also provide shade and a natural setting for fishes, and may induce spawning; their foliage serves as supports for the eggs deposited by some species, and affords protection for the hatching fry. Even when larger fishes are concerned, plants act as a refuge for sick or bullied individuals, and for persistently pursued females. In some cases pieces of plant are bitten off by the fishes and used as nesting material.

An aquarium should contain as many plants as possible. Generally speaking, most tanks are under-planted. A thickly planted aquarium gives less trouble, it is much easier to maintain in a perfectly clear condition, and the fishes are usually healthier. If the planting is done correctly (see p. 31) there need be no fear that the fishes will not be seen.

(v) THE INFLUENCE OF ANIMAL LIFE

In an aquarium all forms of animal life require oxygen to breathe. By exhaling carbon dioxide they affect the nature of the water, tending to change the pH (hydrogen ion content), which in turn increases the acidity. Moreover, the droppings contain organic matter, and this also affects the composition of the water. Not only fishes, but snails, Daphnia, mussels, etcetera, can create overcrowded conditions, by lowering the oxygen content and increasing the carbon dioxide in the water.

Another factor to bear in mind is the effect of a dead creature. Although a single dead body, even if uneaten by the other inhabitants of the aquarium, may not cause much trouble, a number can quickly foul the water due to mass decomposition; this applies especially to snails and Daphnia.

(vi) FEEDING AND FOULING

The commonest cause of trouble in an aquarium is due to over-feeding. Overfed fishes become bloated, lazy, and unhealthy; uneaten food which drops to the bottom of the tank decomposes, and sets up a chain of undesirable reactions. Fortunately, tropical fishes do not need large quantities of food. They are, when circumstances make it necessary, capable of existing without being fed for several days. This is because they are able to live on nourishment stored up in their bodies. It is much safer to underfeed slightly than to over-feed grossly; the latter causes fouling, which leads to far more trouble. Fouling, if allowed to persist, will necessitate the changing of the water, cleansing of the sand, replacement of plants and fishes.

If the aquarist has to be away for a period not exceeding fourteen days, and has no friend sufficiently experienced in feeding aquarium fishes, it is better to leave them unfed. For a period exceeding fourteen days, an inexperienced friend should be left small portions of dried food screwed up in tiny pieces of tissue paper. These can be laid out in a row, and instructions left that not more than one packet be fed to the fishes every other day. As a further safeguard hide away all other food, or the temptation to a kindly but inexpert assistant is often to augment the rations, which undoubtedly he will consider far too meagre.

(vii) CLEANLINESS AND BALANCE

The water in an aquarium kept under natural conditions should be clean, clear, and practically odourless; it should not need changing, as the life-cycle and bacterial activity are functioning naturally, and should not be interfered with. Any interruption will disturb the cycle, and there will need to be a period before readjustment is established again. Cleanliness is natural to the healthy aquarium, just as it is in nature. But if through over-feeding, over-stocking with fishes, under-planting, or some other cause, dirt, foulness, and bacteria are created in excess much trouble and even disease may result.

There are aquarists who claim that a dirty aquarium is healthy. The authors do not agree. True, due to plant-leaves dying and fishes excreting waste products in an aquarium, a sediment inevitably appears. It is generally called mulm, and a little is to be found even in the cleanest tank. Mulm, however, is natural and harmless; it is a factor in the life-cycle. Since the roots of plants feed to a certain extent on mulm, it is gradually drawn down below the surface of the sand; a little, therefore, is good. But if the aquarist has too many fishes, or insufficient plants in his tank, an unnatural excess of mulm will result; this should be siphoned off occasionally, though, better still, the cause of its formation should be rectified.

Although an excess of mulm may be unsightly, it rarely causes trouble. Rotting food, decaying plants, dead fishes, and decomposing snails cause bacteria and innumerable troubles. A clean aquarium is a healthy aquarium.

CHAPTER IV

WATER AND ITS COMPONENTS

WATER, AS PREVIOUSLY MENTIONED, IS A COMPOUND OF TWO GASES, hydrogen and oxygen, in the proportion of two volumes of hydrogen to one volume of oxygen. Water has great solvent powers, and, owing to this, perfectly pure water is not found in nature. The purest natural form is rain-water, but even this while falling from the clouds dissolves gases and impurities present in the atmosphere. Moreover, on reaching the earth the rain starts to dissolve various minerals with which it comes in contact.

MINERALS

Depending on the nature of the ground through which water percolates is the minerals held in solution. These vary considerably: for instance, in moorland districts where peat prevails the water will contain dissolved acids. In places where there are considerable deposits of chalk the water will be alkaline. The alkalinity or acidity of the water is expressed in terms of what is known as the hydrogen ion concentration (symbol, pH).

pH HYDROGEN ION CONCENTRATION

To understand fully about pH one would need to be a chemist. But for the aquarist it is only necessary to appreciate that by the theory of ionic dissociation an acid when dissolved in water does not exist entirely as molecules. Some of the molecules are dissociated into (a) positively charged hydrogen ions (H+) and (b) negatively charged hydroxyl ions (OH−).

The acid properties of a solution are entirely due to the hydrogen ions, and the degree of acidity expressed by the concentration of these. Sörensen introduced the symbol pH to denote the hydrogen ion exponent, and drew up a scale. This scale was graduated from the strongest acid solution pH 0·0 up to the strongest alkaline solution pH 14·0. Distilled water, being neither acid nor alkaline, is midway on the scale, and therefore has a pH value of 7·0. It follows that, the more acid the solution, the lower is the pH.[1] Conversely, the greater the alkalinity of the solution the higher the pH. Some species of tropical fish come from water which is naturally slightly acid or slightly alkaline, and do better in an aquarium where the water approximates to the pH of their natural habitat. For the aquarist who wishes to breed certain species it is advisable to determine the pH of the water he intends to use, and adjust if necessary.

[1] It must be remembered that the pH grading *varies inversely* as the H concentration. The pH is, in fact, the log of the reciprocal of the H ion concentration.

TESTING FOR pH

To obtain the correct pH value it is advisable to carry out certain tests, three of which are referred to below:

Indicator Papers

These papers are obtainable in the form of small booklets, and can be purchased from manufacturing chemists. The material is available in a number of ranges, depending on the particular scale of pH values required. From the aquarist's point of view, short-range papers varying from pH 6·0 to pH 7·8 are the most suitable, as they cover the entire range from slightly acid, through neutral, to slightly alkaline. With each booklet there should be a chart; this takes the form of a band of various colours, each marked with the relevant pH reading.

When one of the papers is dipped into the water the paper will change colour, and when this is compared with the corresponding colour on the chart the pH reading will be obtained. Litmus paper serves as only a rough guide for ascertaining the pH.

Bromothymol Blue Method

This is a more accurate method, but necessitates a slightly greater outlay. The complete equipment consists of ten sealed test-tubes each containing, say, 12 c.c. of buffered solution. This solution is coloured differently in the various tubes, which are marked with the corresponding pH values. These rise from 6·0 to 7·8 in steps of 0·2—*i.e.*, 6·2, 6·4, 6·6, etc. In addition, there is a bottle of bromothymol blue, a dropper bearing a mark indicating 1 c.c., and an open-ended test-tube marked at 12 c.c. To find the pH of a sample of water, proceed as follows:

Into the open-ended test-tube drop 1 c.c. of bromothymol blue, and then fill up to the 12 c.c. mark with the water to be tested. Shake gently, when the colour will change and can be matched with one of the sealed test-tubes of the same colour, from which the pH reading can be obtained. Another range of tubes can be purchased to cover readings from 5·0 to 6·0. Here chloro-phenol red is used instead of bromothymol blue, and this range will apply to a few species preferring extra low pH values.

Electrical Method

This is the most accurate method, but the equipment required is costly, and is beyond the pocket of the average aquarist. Also, absolute accuracy with regard to pH is unnecessary where fishes are concerned.

ADJUSTING pH

When altering the pH value of water strong acids such as sulphuric acid, or alkalis like caustic soda, should never be used. Weak acids or alkalis may, however, be employed. The most usual of these are sodium bicarbonate and sodium acid phosphate; the former will make the water more alkaline, the latter will tend to increase the acidity. Such changes must always be made slowly.

Most aquarists pass through a phase where pH is the all-important factor in their minds; sometimes it becomes an obsession. All success or failure in breeding is, in their opinion, entirely due to the pH value. They add strong acids or alkalis to the water in order to obtain the correct hydrogen ion concentration, only to find that by the next day the water has reverted to its original state. Again they readjust it, until finally the tank contains an excess of chemicals. As a result the water becomes unfit for breeding purposes.

Small quantities of acids or alkalis are sufficient to alter greatly the pH. Even the carbon dioxide in the air above the tank has an appreciable effect. Unless certain precautions are taken to buffer the solution it is difficult to maintain a definite pH value for any length of time. The majority of fishes adapt themselves to the prevailing conditions, and will breed. There are, however, a few problem species which definitely require a low pH value and very soft water before success can be achieved.

HARDNESS OF WATER

Hardness can be of two kinds, temporary or permanent. The temporary is that which is removed by boiling, when substances such as calcium bicarbonate and magnesium bicarbonate are decomposed. Permanent hardness is that which cannot be removed by boiling, and is chiefly due to calcium and magnesium sulphates and chlorides.

SOFTENING WATER

Temporary hardness can be removed by the following methods:

(i) By boiling the water, since this process decomposes the bicarbonate present; carbon dioxide passes off as gas, and the monocarbonates are left suspended in an insoluble and inert form.

(ii) By decomposing the bicarbonates with any alkali soluble in water, lime being generally used.

(iii) By passing the water through a porous mass of zeolite. This sodium alumino-silicate gives up its sodium in exchange for an equal amount of lime or magnesia in the water.

Permanent hardness can be removed from water by:

(i) Distillation—*i.e.*, boiling the water and condensing the steam. This method is the only one for fully purifying water rich in soluble sodium or potassium salts, such as sea-water.

(ii) By the addition of a soluble carbonate, such as sodium carbonate (soda). Any soluble calcium or magnesium salts present in the water are then precipitated.

The domestic water-softener is a relatively expensive piece of apparatus, and the average aquarist is hardly justified in purchasing the equipment merely to facilitate his hobby.

Peaty water

Generally speaking, tap-water is slightly alkaline and moderately hard. It is only in a few peaty districts that the water is inclined to be acid and very soft. For breeding the problem fishes, such as neons, glowlights and Aphyosemions, the softness of the water is quite as important a factor as the pH. All of these fishes come from areas where the water has been found to be very soft, the hardness being between 1 and 20 parts per million as $CaCO_3$ (calcium carbonate), and a pH of 5·0 to 6·6. Such water is of a clear brownish colour, and is practically free from bacteria, which are harmful to fish eggs.

Experience has shown that rain-water passed through a peat filter or, better still, rain-water that has stood for some time in a glass container with a few inches of peat fibre or moss at the bottom, becomes brown in colour and very soft. Such water is ideal for use in breeding the problem fishes.

Aquarists wishing to breed the more difficult species should keep at hand a supply of soft brown peaty water. To obtain this, proceed as follows. In a darkish place fill a spare aquarium or glass container with clean rain-water, and throw into this broken-up peat (usually sold by seedsmen). The peat will float, so add sufficient to form a two-inch layer. In 10 to 20 days the peat will become water-logged and sink. Once it has all sunk the water will be clear and clean but tinted brown. In towns where clear rain-water is not available, boiled tap-water may be used.

TESTING FOR HARDNESS

The simplest test is the standard soap solution method (Wanklyn test). The equipment is obtainable from manufacturing chemists, and consists of a tin of soap solution, a graduated pipette or a 1 c.c. eye-dropper, a graduated beaker of 70 c.c. capacity, and a shaker bottle with a glass stopper. The test is made as follows. With the beaker, 70 c.c.'s of the water to be tested are measured and poured into the shaker bottle. To this is added with the eye-dropper or graduated pipette 1 c.c. of the soap solution. The bottle is stoppered and shaken vigorously. If the water is hard no lather will appear, but a cloudy solution of soap curd will be formed. A further 1 c.c. of soap solution is added, and the bottle reshaken. The procedure is repeated until a copious lather persists for five minutes above a clear solution. Every 1 c.c. of soap solution added represents one degree of hardness. For example, if 10 c.c.'s of soap solution are necessary, the hardness is 10 degrees, as $CaCO_3$.

Some of the problem fishes require less than 1 degree of hardness, so it will be realized that the above test is not accurate enough. A more exact method is to express hardness in parts per million as $CaCO_3$. This enables us to cover a range from 0 (very soft) to 300 (very hard). It is done by titration.

Hardness Titrating Test

This test is simple to operate. The equipment and solutions cost about £3, or $8·50, and are obtainable from manufacturing chemists. The requirements are as follows:

A large flask or bottle with a glass stopper.
A burette with glass tap graduated for 20 c.c.'s.
A stand to hold the burette in a vertical position.
A pipette graduated to 50 c.c.'s.
An eye-dropper holding $\frac{1}{2}$ c.c.
A small shaker flask with a narrow neck.
A small bottle of concentrated volumetric hardness titrating solution.
A small bottle of hardness indicator.
A small bottle of hardness buffer solution.
A litre of distilled water.

First the concentrated volumetric solution is poured into the 1 litre of distilled water. This makes the hardness titrating solution, which should be stored in the large flask or bottle for future use.

Titrating (Schwarzenbach method). To find the hardness of any water the procedure is as follows:

With the pipette 50 c.c.'s of the water to be tested are emptied into the shaker flask. To this should be added with the eye-dropper $\frac{1}{2}$ c.c. of hardness buffer solution. Next, one or two drops of hardness indicator are added to the liquid in the shaker flask, which, when agitated, will turn the solution pink. Now the burette is clipped into the stand and filled up to the zero mark with hardness titrating solution. The shaker flask is then held below the burette, and by turning the tap the titrating solution is allowed to drip slowly into the flask. After each drop the flask is shaken, and the pink-coloured solution therein is watched. At some stage in these proceedings the liquid in the shaker flask will suddenly turn a blackish-green. As soon as this occurs the test is over.

As each drop of hardness titrating solution leaves the burette the column of liquid drops. Immediately the colour change occurs an accurate reading of the surface of the solution in the burette is taken. Let it be assumed that 4·3 c.c.'s of hardness titrating solution has been used. This figure is multiplied by 20, and the resulting product gives the parts per million of $CaCO_3$ (calcium carbonate). In this example the hardness is 86 parts per million, showing that the water is moderately soft. The amount of titrating solution used is multiplied by 20 because we started by taking 50 c.c.'s of water to test, but this was only 1/20th of a litre, on which the test is based.

COMPARISON OF HARDNESS

In Britain, America, and Germany hardness of water is calculated in degrees, or the amount of salts dissolved in the water, expressed in parts per million. Clark's scale is used in Britain and America, and:

1 degree of hardness=14·3 parts per million as $CaCO_3$ (calcium carbonate).

In Germany:

1 German degree, written (DH)=17·9 parts per million as CaO (calcium oxide).

The two differ; one refers to calcium carbonate, the other to calcium oxide, but when both are compared under their atomic weights, as follows:

Element	Chemical Formula	Atomic Weight
Calcium	Ca	40
Carbon	C	12
Oxygen	O	16

$$CaCO_3 = 40+12+3(16) = 100$$
$$CaO = 40+16 = 56$$

then 1 (DH) is only 0·56 of an English degree. Thus, when German aquarists state that the hardness of the water for breeding a certain fish should be 6 (DH), to us it should be only 3·3 degrees in our Clark's scale—*i.e.*, $\dfrac{6 \times 56}{100} = 3·36$.

The Germans, noted for their Teutonic thoroughness, number among them some of the finest fish-breeders in the world, and these, together with their compatriots who have emigrated to the U.S.A., obviously still express hardness in (DH), and now many aquarist magazines printed in America use the same foreign terms.

In this book all the hardness readings under the breeding requirements of the species are expressed in parts per million as $CaCO_3$, and testing can be done as explained under Titrating.

However, conversion is easily done by multiplying the (DH) figures by $\dfrac{56}{100}$ to obtain English degrees, or, conversely, the English figures by $\dfrac{100}{56}$ to obtain the (DH).

NATURE OF THE WATER USED IN AN AQUARIUM

Earlier we pointed out that tap-water in many localities is quite suitable for most fishes. In some districts, however, the Water Boards chlorinate heavily, and this may cause the aquarist trouble. Generally speaking, the chlorine content can be reduced by drawing water from the tap and allowing it to stand for several hours in the open air.

Distilled water

This is unnatural: it is generally too pure, and lacks the minute organisms present in ordinary water that give it life. Distilled water can be used occasionally with advantage in a breeding tank, but under ordinary conditions the cost is not justified, and the water in any case would soon become contaminated in the tank.

Well water

Some aquarists are fortunate enough to have a well on the premises. If the water is free from sewage pollution it can be used in an aquarium. Well water usually contains a wealth of minerals, and is generally crystal clear.

Rain-water

This is the most natural water. In country districts where the air is pure the rain-water will be practically neutral, but in industrial areas smoke and fumes are present in the atmosphere, and some of these will be absorbed, making the rain-water slightly acid.

Rain-water is best collected in a wooden butt, an iron bath, or any receptacle of glass, china, or enamel, but a galvanized container should be avoided. It will be found that the water is cleaner and purer if one waits at least a quarter of an hour after the start of a shower before starting collecting, as initially a considerable amount of dirt and dust from the air and on roofs is washed down.

Pond water

Water taken from most natural ponds is excellent, provided it is carefully filtered to eliminate harmful pests such as dangerous larvæ and undesirable organisms.

It is surprising how a small change of any water, providing it is good, will stimulate the fishes in an aquarium. They appear to enjoy it as much as human beings enjoy a change of air. As will be shown later, it is often advantageous to mix a quantity of rain-water into a breeding tank, as this freshening up may excite and stimulate the fishes.

Green water

It was explained earlier (see p. 37) that clear water will turn green from excessive light or lack of plants. From what has been said before, the cure is to cut down the light, or to increase the number of plants.

Brown water

This occurs naturally when the catchment area draining into the reservoirs is of a peaty nature. The same effect is produced if a peat filter is employed. Peaty water has a yellowish to brown tint, is clear, and is usually good; it impedes the multiplication of bacteria.

If, however, the clear water in an aquarium turns brown it may be harmful. The cause is usually insufficient light, when the vegetable life starts to die and decay and bacteria begin to multiply. Over-feeding may be another cause, where once again the surplus food is encouraging millions of bacteria to breed. The cure for brown water is to increase the plants, and to maintain their development by giving more light. Discourage bacteria by taking care not to over-feed the fishes. In addition it will be beneficial to give artificial aeration to dissipate undesirable gases in the water.

Cloudy water

The water in most aquaria when newly set up, although initially clear, may turn a cloudy grey after a few days. This is a natural process which takes place as the cycle of life adjusts itself. But when equilibrium is reached the water will begin to clear and should remain so, unless the aquarist interferes too much with the natural processes going on in the tank. Should cloudy conditions persist they are generally caused by over-crowding, excessive feeding, a large production of bacteria, or minute vegetable cells.

Cloudy water, therefore, may be the initial stage of either green water or brown water, as yet insufficiently developed to determine the ultimate colour. After a few days the reproduction of the organisms becomes so great that in the mass they colour the water. This will be brown if caused by bacteria, or green if by vegetable matter.

CHAPTER V

MISCELLANEOUS APPARATUS

NUMEROUS PIECES OF EQUIPMENT ARE AVAILABLE TO AQUARISTS; SOME ARE good, many are unnecessary, and the beginner is recommended to wait until he finds a certain item essential. The handyman may be able to construct something which will meet his own requirements. We find that some of the simplest apparatus is the most satisfactory.

Glass jars

The first and most useful articles are a selection of glass jars—*i.e.*, jam-jars, sweet jars, preserving jars. When a single fish is being examined closely ordinary jam-jars are needed; they are also useful for transferring fishes from one tank to another, particularly when temperatures are different, and require time to equalize. For sorting fry a larger container, such as a sweet jar, is useful: a spawning can be netted into it, from which the larger specimens can be extracted. Lastly, the wide-necked jar with a screw-on lid serves as a good transporter for carrying fishes for short distances, say to or from a shop or show.

Nets

It is advisable for the aquarist to possess several different-shaped nets. They can be purchased in most pet stores, or made at home.

For catching nets nylon mesh is recommended, as it lasts much longer than muslin, does not become slimy, or deteriorate so soon through becoming alternately wet and dry. A small round one that will fit inside a jam-jar is essential. The frame should be made of fine-gauge wire, as this is easily bendable and will accommodate any curve or arc. Two stout-framed, medium-sized nets approximately 6″ square are ideal for catching most fishes in the average aquarium; there should be a kink in the neck of the frame (see Fig. 8), so that it fits tightly against the front

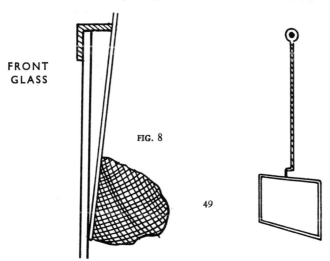

FRONT
GLASS

FIG. 8

49

glass of the aquarium. It is important to remember that the bag should be made as deep as it is wide, as this facilitates catching.

Once a fish is ensnared it will make every endeavour to escape, and if the net is shallow it is extremely difficult to keep the fish confined in the small space available and bring it to the surface of the water. With a deep net the captive can be driven into the back of the bag and lifted out easily. Furthermore, once withdrawn from the tank it is simple enough to place one's hand underneath and fold the fingers round the captive, entirely enclosing it. Held in this position, one can turn the net inside out and drop the fish into a narrow-necked jar. With a shallow net the most one can do is to spread the hand over the top of the net and hope that the fish does not jump between one's fingers. There still remains the difficult operation of getting the fish into a jar.

Fine Nylon Net for Filtering

In addition to nets used for catching fishes, the authors have found that two other types of net are invaluable. Both are employed as strainers and have the bag made of fine nylon similar to that used for making shirts or blouses; the smaller net, approximately 3″ diameter, fits over the mouth of a 2-lb. jam-jar, and is most useful for straining newly hatched brine shrimps.

The larger should be made in a rectangular shape approximately 8″ × 8″: it should have a minimum depth of 8″, and a handle about 10″ long. The frame must be constructed of heavy-gauge wire, which will need to be bent into shape by using a vice or a strong pair of pliers. Since the net will be called upon to hold a heavy weight of water, the frame must be robust enough to remain rigid. When siphoning mulm from a tank the net will be found an extremely useful article. Placed across the top of an enamel bucket, the end of the siphon tube can be put inside the net, which will strain the water as it passes through. The aquarist may be surprised at its efficiency.

Siphon tube

This is an essential article for removing mulm from tanks, and for emptying an aquarium. Generally speaking, a piece of rubber tubing about 6 feet long with an internal diameter of $\frac{1}{4}″$ is ideal. The tubing should be long enough to reach from the bottom of the tank over the top rim, down to the floor, and up to the aquarist's waist. This will ensure a rapid and powerful discharge. By pinching the tube the flow of the water can be controlled, or stopped immediately should a fish approach the danger zone too closely.

Some aquarists complain that sucking, in order to start the siphon working, invariably gives them a mouthful of water. This is because the siphon tube is too short. With a long tube the water rises over the rim of the tank and descends to the floor, often with a distinctive thud; but before it reaches the mouth the tube is pinched, and the end placed in a bucket. For those who prefer a more rigid end to the siphon it is only necessary to insert a length of strong celluloid tubing into one end of the rubber tube.

Enamel bucket

At least one 2-gallon enamel bucket used solely for the aquarist's purpose is essential. It is required when siphoning from the tank, or for sterilizing nets in boiling water.

It should never be used for household tasks.

Dip tube

A dip tube is useful for picking out of the aquarium one or two odd bits of food that remain uneaten. The small amount of water withdrawn would hardly justify the use of a siphon.

Any piece of glass tubing will act as a dip tube. Hold the tube vertically, and place a finger over the upper end to prevent the escape of air. The tube can now be introduced into the aquarium and located so that the open end is immediately over the particle to be extracted. This will be flushed into the tube as soon as the finger is withdrawn from the top end. To prevent the unwanted matter from re-entering the tank the finger is reinstated and the tube is raised sufficiently to allow another finger to seal the lower end, when the tube can be withdrawn.

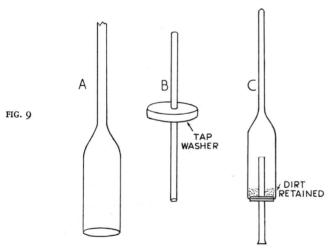

FIG. 9

A more elaborate type of dip tube is shown in Fig. 9. It consists of a glass tube *A*, with an enlarged end. Into this is inserted *B*. This is merely a short glass tube passing tightly through a tap washer which fits closely into the mouth of *A*. The method of use is the same as before, but due to the greater volume of the tube more water can be sucked up, and the particles which have been extracted are trapped in the pocket. Before the dip tube needs emptying it can be used to collect several separate particles in different zones of the tank. Cleaning is easy, as the tube can be dismantled.

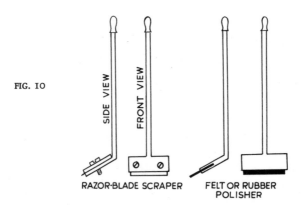

FIG. 10

SIDE VIEW   FRONT VIEW

RAZOR-BLADE SCRAPER   FELT OR RUBBER
POLISHER

Scrapers

A scraper (see Fig. 10) for removing algæ from the walls of the aquarium is another cheap, yet useful, piece of equipment. Essentially a scraper is a long rod bent to an angle of 45 degrees at the bottom to which is attached a razor blade, a strip of rubber, or a piece of felt. When applied to the inside face of the tank and moved up and down the scraper either scrapes or polishes the glass. The razor-blade type usually has two holes in the fitting and two screws to secure the blade. The rubber and felt types are provided with a slot which firmly grips the material.

Forceps

Forceps can hardly be regarded as being essential, although they have their uses at times. In a marine tank they are perhaps of more use than in

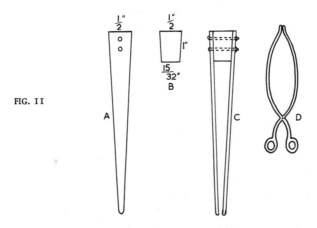

FIG. 11

the ordinary fresh-water aquarium. This is because relatively static animals such as anemones need to be fed by placing the food within reach of their tentacles. There are two types of forceps, one made of wood, the other of metal. The former can easily be made at home, and are probably the most satisfactory. The method of construction is as follows. Cut two pieces of three-ply or other flexible wood, 12″ long and $\frac{1}{2}$″ wide at one end, tapering to $\frac{1}{8}$″ wide at the other end (Fig. 11). Next, make a small wooden block about 1″ long, $\frac{1}{2}$″ square at one end, tapering slightly at the other end, as shown at B. Now with two small bolts secure the three pieces together as shown at C. If properly constructed the pointed ends of the pincers should remain slightly apart; owing to springiness these can now be pinched together by a slight pressure, enabling small objects to be picked up and released at will.

The metal type illustrated at D are in the shape of scissors, and can be purchased at most pet stores. Metal forceps do not have the advantage of springing open of their own accord as do the wooden type referred to above.

Planting sticks

Planting sticks occasionally have their uses. For example, they serve when it is desired to plant a single stem in the centre of a bunch of similar stems; also the sticks are useful when planting in awkward positions, such as between two rocks where it is impossible to reach with the hand. Otherwise it is preferable to insert plants with the fingers, which are less likely to shear off or damage the roots.

A planting stick can be made out of a thin strip of wood or metal approximately 15″ long, $\frac{1}{4}$″ wide, and $\frac{1}{8}$″ thick. At one end a V-shaped notch is cut out to guide the plant into position.

Plant-pots and trays

Some aquarists prefer to have a few special show plants in pots (Fig. 12). If used, the pots are best made of unglazed earthenware with a few small holes round the base to allow root growth to penetrate through, and so prevent cramping. Where possible the whole pot should be buried beneath the sand in the aquarium to hide its unnatural and unsightly appearance. The few advantages of using pots are:

(i) They can be removed from one position to another in the tank, or they may be transferred to another aquarium without seriously interrupting the plants' root growth.

(ii) A special medium such as loam or clay, which the plant may prefer, can be used in the lower part of the pot, the upper stratum being sand.

**SPECIAL PLANT IN POT WHICH IS
BURIED OUT OF SIGHT UNDER THE SAND**
(Note growth of roots through holes)

FIG. 12

Feeding rings

Feeding rings (Fig. 13*A*) are not essential, although some aquarists advocate their use. Generally they are constructed of plastic or glass tubing in the form of a square or a circle. They float on the water and serve to limit the spread of dried food. Fishes get accustomed to these rings, and come readily to the appointed place at feeding-time, though the larger species tend to get the greater share more easily than when the food is not confined to one area.

The aquarist who persistently indulges in the harmful practice of over-feeding his fishes with dried food may find a feeding ring to be an

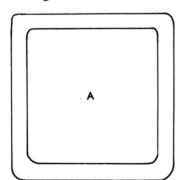
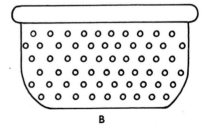

FIG. 13

advantage. All particles of uneaten food fall directly below the ring, and so limit any blackening of the sand to one area. When, therefore, it is necessary to siphon out and cleanse the sand, only a relatively small amount needs to be dealt with.

Fig. 13B shows another type of feeding ring, sometimes used when feeding with enchytræ. The ring is usually made of plastic in the form of a well-perforated basin with a large rim. The basin floats with the perforations below the surface of the water. When a small mass of worms is dropped into it they break up and gradually wriggle through the holes, giving all the fishes an opportunity of getting a few worms each. Without the basket the worms tend to cling together in small masses, thereby giving the larger fishes the opportunity of grabbing whole mouthfuls at the expense of the smaller inhabitants of the aquarium.

Rubber suction cups

A few cheap suction cups are worth stocking, as they have many uses. Applied to the inside of the tank, they may be used to anchor feeding rings, thermometers, heaters, thermostats, aerator and filter tubes. If it becomes necessary to partition off a section of the aquarium with a sheet of glass, suction cups serve to retain the glass division in position.

Thermometers

A good thermometer, preferably one that floats in a vertical position, is an essential item. It should be located in an unobtrusive position, but one in which it can be easily read. Mercury thermometers, though costing a little more than the alcohol type, are generally more accurate, and worth the extra money. Most are dual calibrated for Fahrenheit and Centigrade. When purchasing one of these instruments it is advisable to verify the accuracy by comparing the readings of several. Should some of these disagree, choose one which corresponds with the majority. Another type of thermometer possesses a circular dial about 1¼″ diameter, and a pointer which moves like the hand of a clock round the scale. These unobtrusive instruments adhere by means of a suction cup to the glass of the aquarium.

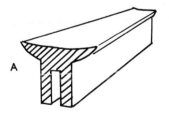
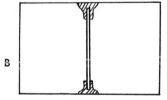

A
B

FIG. 14

Channel rubber

For the more advanced aquarist who raises fry from egg-laying fishes, a few feet of channel rubber is invaluable. This material enables a tank to be tightly partitioned so that the babies cannot pass into the neighbouring compartment. Without channel rubber it is almost impossible to divide a tank so that fry can be segregated satisfactorily. Fig. 14*A* shows a section through a piece of channel rubber. It will be seen that there is a slot to receive the glass, and the slightly concave outer face permits it to be pressed flat against the walls of the aquarium; it is the flexibility of the rubber that makes the tight joint. Fig. 14*B* illustrates a tank partitioned by a sheet of glass secured each side by channel rubber as seen from above.

Nylon mops

These mops can be made easily at home, and are excellent for spawning many of the problem fishes, in otherwise bare tanks containing peaty water. The mops can be sterilized by boiling and used time and time again.

Skeins of pure nylon are cut into lengths roughly 10″ long. With one of the threads tie the strands in the middle, then fold over double, and tie again near the bend, to form bushy mops. See Fig. 15.

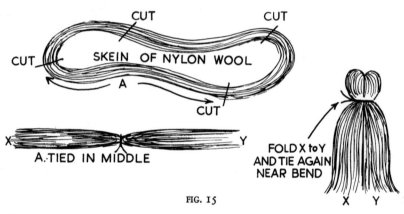

CUT   CUT

CUT   SKEIN OF NYLON WOOL

A

CUT

X   Y

A. TIED IN MIDDLE

FOLD X to Y AND TIE AGAIN NEAR BEND

X   Y

FIG. 15

Traps

Most beginners start with live-bearing fishes, and are immensely thrilled when the first batch of young is born. Their joy, however, does not last long, as most of the babies are gobbled up by other fishes. Even though the mother may be isolated by herself in a separate container before she has her young, she is not averse to eating them after they are born. This unpleasant characteristic also sets a problem for the commercial breeder, whose aim is to get the maximum number of fry from several females.

To prevent the females from satisfying their appetite at the expense of their young, traps are used. A trap is a device that can be suspended in a separate breeding tank, confining the mother but permitting the young to escape from her by swimming through small holes to safety. Most traps on the market are made of plastic, and are provided with holes or slots (see Fig. 16, *A* and *B*) in the base through which the fry pass. Usually these traps are too small to allow the female or females adequate freedom,

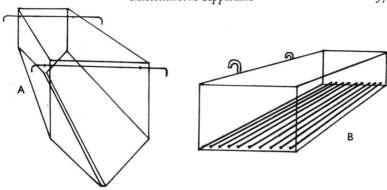

PLASTIC BREEDING TRAPS

FIG. 16

and the holes or slots in the base of the trap provide insufficient exits for the babies. Fig. 16*A* shows a plastic trap with a single opening at the base, while *B* illustrates a plastic box with a row of holes running along the bottom of the ends into which are inserted glass or plastic bars.

A much better trap (*C*) can be made quite cheaply at home from fine stainless steel wire gauze with a mesh of approximately $\frac{1}{8}''$. Cut one piece of this material 12″ square, and two pieces 5″ × 6″. Turn over all projecting ends to make smooth edges. Roll the large piece into a semicircle to form a long trough, and by means of wire attach the two ends as shown in photograph. All that is now required is to push two lengths of wire through the mesh at each end of the trough and bend over the extremities of this wire to fit the tank in which the trap is to operate. The trap will then be suspended with its top rim just above the surface of the water.

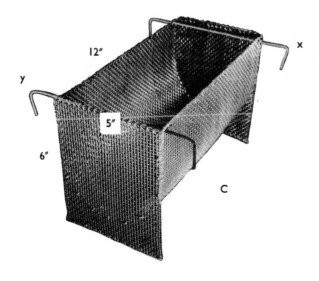

Alternatively, in a very shallow tank the trap will stand on its two square ends which act as legs. In a trap of this size several females can be placed with safety; babies can escape with ease in any direction.

It may be thought that, since the babies are able to get out of the trap so easily, they will just as readily re-enter. Undoubtedly a few do this, but the majority realize by instinct that danger abounds and stay outside until they are strong enough to dart about and evade capture. At first the females may try to snap at the fry they see swimming outside the trap, but quickly realize that such attempts are futile. Later, if a few fry re-enter the trap the females still seem to consider them beyond reach, and do not molest them. By this time, however, the babies are strong enough to dart through the mesh should such a quick exit become necessary.

Commercial breeders will find that they are able to remove from the trap females that have given birth, and substitute others about to have young. It will be appreciated, therefore, that large traps may be in use for prolonged periods. Here is one final word of advice that applies to all traps: keep all plants, whether of the rooted or floating variety, *outside* the trap, since fry instinctively make for the nearest cover.

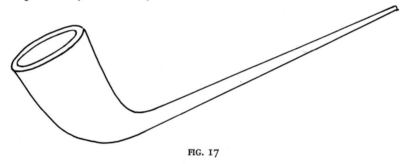

FIG. 17

Glass pipes

On the market there are glass pipes (Fig. 17) of various sizes for catching young fry. Pipes have the advantage that fry can be picked out of an aquarium with less likelihood of damage than when a net is used. Unless, however, the aquarist has had considerable experience of using a pipe, he will find it a difficult tool to manage. Another point to bear in mind is that very small fry should not be moved unless it is essential to do so.

Having covered some of the more essential and easily constructed equipment, we now come to certain apparatus which the average aquarist will be unable to construct at home.

Pumps

There are many types of electrically operated pumps available. Some are dependent on a flexible rubber diaphragm which operates like a bellows; others employ pistons in cylinders. There is one pump with a long vertical cylinder in which a steel plunger falls under its own weight;

at the end of the stroke contacts are made to energize a solenoid, and the resulting magnetism lifts the plunger. Another type of pump is operated hydraulically, and requires running water. For commercial use power-driven compressors which start and stop automatically through a pressure switch are used to charge air bottles which operate at high pressure.

When buying a pump it is well to remember that some of these machines are noisy, and should be heard in operation before purchasing. It is also important to bear in mind that as time goes on extension aerators may be added. The pump should therefore be of adequate power to meet increased loading. Finally, choose if possible a machine covered by the maker's guarantee.

Diffusers, or Air-stones

To obtain the maximum effect from artificial aeration it is best to have a thick column of fine bubbles rising to the surface rather than a chain of large single ones. To create this effect diffusers are used.

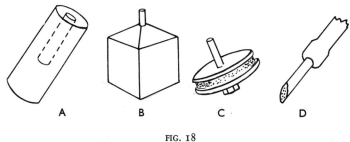

A   B   C   D

FIG. 18

Fig. 18 shows four types of diffuser. *A* is made of porous stone and is shaped like a small log with a hole in one end into which is inserted a short length of celluloid tube to receive the air-line from the pump. *B* shows a similar pumice-stone diffuser of a different shape, and one which is provided with a piece of celluloid tube cemented in. A metal-type diffuser is illustrated at *C*. It consists of two metal discs screwed together with a piece of felt sandwiched between. A short pipe rises from the centre of the upper disc. Air passes through the felt, and the size of bubbles can be adjusted by varying the pressure between the two metal discs.

Although these three diffusers are inexpensive, they all eventually become clogged. *A* and *B* can be baked in an oven to shrink the particles clogging the pores, while *C* can be fitted with a new piece of felt.

For the commercial breeder, however, hundreds of diffusers may be required, and their total cost will be considerable. The authors have found that an inexpensive and satisfactory diffuser can be made out of a length of ordinary cane used for basket-work. 12 ft. will cost only a shilling or two—say 25 cents. The cane is the correct diameter to fit the standard aerator tubing, and when cut in $\frac{3}{4}''$ lengths will make nearly 200 satisfactory diffusers. To improve the action the end of the diffuser is cut obliquely as shown in Fig. 18*D*. After many months the short pieces of cane rot, but it is only a matter of seconds to cut them off with a razor blade and insert a replacement.

Air-lift

This is a tube, usually of plastic, with a longish stem. The top curves over and ends in a spout, as shown in Fig. 19. About 2" from the bottom is inserted an air inlet in the form of a short length of tubing which is sealed into position. When the air-lift is stood vertically in the tank water enters the bottom of the stem and rises to the normal level. Rubber tubing connects the air inlet to the pump, and the rising bubbles lift the water sufficiently to discharge it from the spout.

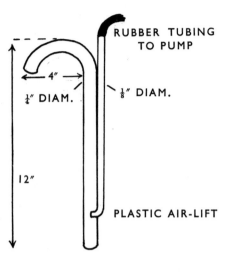

RUBBER TUBING
TO PUMP

4″

¼″ DIAM.

⅛″ DIAM.

12″

PLASTIC AIR-LIFT

FIG. 19

Filters

There are two types of filter. One of these, known as an interior filter, operates from inside the tank; the other is the exterior type, and is attached to the outside of the aquarium.

Internal filters (Fig. 20 *A*) usually take the form of a small three-cornered basket held in position just above the surface of the water in the tank. The basket contains layers of cotton or glass wool and activated charcoal. The wool picks up small particles, and can be replaced when dirty. Gases

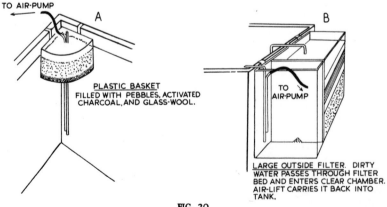

TO AIR-PUMP

A

PLASTIC BASKET
FILLED WITH PEBBLES, ACTIVATED
CHARCOAL, AND GLASS-WOOL.

B

TO
AIR-PUMP

LARGE OUTSIDE FILTER. DIRTY
WATER PASSES THROUGH FILTER
BED AND ENTERS CLEAR CHAMBER.
AIR-LIFT CARRIES IT BACK INTO
TANK.

FIG. 20

are absorbed by the charcoal, which is broken up into small pieces in order to present as many surfaces as possible, and thereby accelerate the action. Now, if an air lift is used water can be drawn from the bottom of the aquarium and spilled into the basket through which it filters. The activated charcoal will eventually become ineffective, but can be reconditioned by baking in an oven. This drives off the absorbed gases, and the charcoal is fit for re-use.

An external filter can be a much larger piece of equipment, and, due to its dimensions, the efficiency is greatly increased. Small external filters can be made from glass battery jars in the following manner. A piece of 2″ diameter celluloid tubing is cut to correspond with the height of the jar. Perforations are made round the base of the tube, which is stood up in the centre of the jar. The jar is now filled to a depth of 3″ with clean gravel. Above this is placed a 3″ layer of activated charcoal. Finally a top layer of silver sand or glass wool is added to within 2″ of the top of the jar; an air-lift is placed down the celluloid tube so that the spout discharges back into the tank. The filter is then stood close to the side of the aquarium so that the top of the jar is just above the water surface in the tank. A separate piece of celluloid tubing runs from the bottom of the tank and curves over the top of the frame into the filter jar. Once this tube is completely filled with water it will act as a siphon, and the water running over will percolate through the layers in the filter, enter the perforated centre tube, and rise to the surface level. When the air line is attached to the air-lift the rising bubbles carry the water up the air-lift and back into the tank. This circulation persists as long as the air supply continues.

Fig. 20B shows a large and efficient filter, having glass sides fitted into an angle-iron frame like that of an aquarium, and provided with two hooks so that it may hang from the top of the tank. A sheet of glass divides the filter vertically into two compartments, one of which is much smaller than the other. A small V-shaped notch is cut out of the bottom of the glass dividing wall, to permit the passage of water. The smaller compartment of the filter is left empty, while the larger compartment contains the layers of filter material previously referred to. Water from the aquarium siphons into the filter bed through the pipe shown in the figure, and after passing through the layers flows via the V-shaped notch into the clear compartment. From here it is returned to the aquarium by means of an air-lift. This type of filter is suitable for use with a marine aquarium.

A new type of filter, made of plastic, is now on the market. These operate beneath the sand.

CHAPTER VI

FISH-FOODS AND FEEDING

FISH, LIKE HUMAN BEINGS, IF THEY ARE TO REMAIN IN PERFECT HEALTH require a balanced diet. This must include proteins, carbohydrates, fats, minerals, and vitamins. Since some aquarists find these terms confusing, a brief explanation may be helpful.

Proteins

These are the body-building foods, and serve to replace worn-out tissues. Just as a stove consumes fuel, and ultimately will go out unless replenished, so is the body continually consuming itself and requiring replacements to make good the loss. Animal proteins are found in meat, liver, kidney, chicken, fish, eggs, and cheese. In addition, there are vegetable proteins in certain leguminous foods such as peas, beans, and lentils.

Carbohydrates

These are the energy-giving foods, and serve to produce warmth in the body. Included under this heading are bread, biscuit meal, oatmeal, and other starchy foods. Sugar is a carbohydrate.

Fats

Fats and oils help to produce energy and warmth; they also feed the nerves. Fats and oils are stored up as a reserve supply of food on which the body can draw in times of shortage. They are found in meat, milk, fish, cheese, and some vegetable foods.

Minerals

In most foods there are present minerals—salts of calcium, phosphorus, iron, etc.; their chief functions are to develop bones and teeth, to ensure the healthy working of the nervous system, circulation, muscles, and certain glands.

Vitamins

These serve to promote health and prevent disease. They are present in animal fats and oils, in fresh fruit and vegetables, and in wheat germ.

Balanced diet

Since the body requires different kinds of food to fulfil different functions, it will be appreciated that a normal healthy diet must contain some items from each of the aforementioned groups. As far as aquarists are concerned, fish food may be classified under four main headings:

62

(i) Dried foods.
(ii) Fresh, tinned, or frozen foods.
(iii) Cultured foods.
(iv) Pond foods.

(i) DRIED FOODS

There are many brands of dried fish-food on the market, obtainable in jars, cartons, or plastic boxes. A first-class product should contain a balance of the various kinds of food previously referred to. There are important advantages of dried food. Due to its high concentration, a little will last for a relatively long period. This food is readily obtainable, and most can be stored for a considerable time without deterioration.

Dried food acts as an excellent form of roughage for keeping the bowels open, and the authors recommend that where fish are fed twice daily one of these meals should consist of a good dried food.

If, however, too much be given at a time it remains uneaten and sinks to the bottom. Here, due to its colour and fineness, it becomes invisible against the sand, and is difficult to siphon away. The particles of food then work their way down through the sand until they are out of reach to all fishes, even including the scavenging species which will dig below the surface of the sand for their meals. Once they sink too deep decomposition may set in, causing harmful bacteria, fungus, and so forth. If over-feeding continues the bacteria multiply rapidly; foul gases are generated, and the sand turns black. The roots of plants near by soon become affected, and instead of being strong, healthy, and white, turn black, soggy, and rotten. The plants themselves begin to die, and cease their functions of absorbing mulm on which the roots normally feed.

A state of affairs has now arisen where bad gases from the decomposing matter and the carbon dioxide given off by the fishes begins to build up in the water and drive oxygen out at the surface. If this unhealthy process continues the concentration of bad gas, which at first was a mere stratum along the bottom, soon expands upward—first two or three inches, later six or seven inches—until finally it reaches the surface. At this stage all the water in the tank is depleted of oxygen and over-charged with unwanted gas, causing the fishes to suffocate. Any remaining alive will be found swimming just below the surface at an angle of about 30 degrees, with their tails down and mouths up. They are not searching for more food but struggling to obtain the vital oxygen from the atmosphere.

From the foregoing it will be clear that over-feeding with any type of food is dangerous, but, generally speaking, it is more easily done with dried foods than with fresh ones. In either case the sand will blacken; this will necessitate its removal and cleansing, and in addition there will be the trouble and expense of replacing the rotting plants.

Hormones

In recent years experiments have been carried out to produce dried foods containing hormones for special purposes such as increasing normal growth or retarding growth; sex stimulation to induce breeding, ovum-production, the attempted increase of the proportion of male or female births in a spawn, colour intensity, and mutation. These experiments are still in their early stages, and research continues. The aquarist, however, should verify the claims of certain of the products offered before accepting them as being infallible. Moreover, he should have some knowledge of what he is doing, as irresponsible use of these foods is dangerous.

(ii) FRESH, TINNED, OR FROZEN FOODS

No matter how good any dried food may be, fishes, like human beings, need a change.

Fresh foods can be either vegetable or animal. First, we will consider the vegetable. These give the fishes minerals and vitamins.

Algæ

As previously explained, algæ are a natural vegetable growth; they are present in most aquaria, as they grow in water through the action of light. Many species of fish enjoy algæ, and will keep them cropped and under control provided excessive light does not produce them in exorbitant amounts. Where no algæ are present the fishes will require alternative vegetable matter. In the summer this may consist of finely shredded fresh lettuce-leaves or duckweed, and in the winter chopped cooked spinach or tinned spinach, sieved well. Practically any green vegetable matter can be given in small quantities, if finely chopped.

Animal foods

These include shrimp, prawn, crayfish, lobster, crab, white fishes, roe, lean meat, particularly heart, liver, kidney, also cheese and hard-boiled yolk of egg. Many of these foods are to be found in every home. All are equally good whether fresh, tinned, or frozen, though the latter must be thawed out.

Fish, meat, and offal require scraping or chopping, and may be served raw or cooked; most are easier to chop fine when cooked. Cod roe is highly nutritious yet cheap; it is best boiled for 20 minutes, and the outer skin peeled off. The remainder is broken into small pieces for large fishes, or if rubbed between the fingers it will sink as single eggs, and is ideal for fry and the smaller species.

Hard-boiled yolk of egg, squeezed through a piece of muslin and shaken under water, produces a cloud of minute particles perfect for newly hatched fry, but must be fed sparingly, or it will soon foul the water. Hard-boiled egg yolk pushed through a very fine sieve and served on the point of a knife does not disintegrate into a cloud, and may be given to most fishes.

Ordinary Cheddar cheese finely chopped or grated is also appreciated occasionally.

Most of the above foods are greedily taken, but should too much be given they will not decompose for 24 hours, and by that time very little remains. A few uneaten pieces may sometimes be seen developing a fungus growth, but these cannot sink into the sand, and are easily removed with a dip tube.

(iii) CULTURED FOODS

Having purchased an initial supply, the following foods may be cultured, and, with a minimum of trouble, provide a permanent form of nourishment.

Infusoria

This is a general term for various groups of minute organisms such as Paramecium which, under certain conditions, live and multiply in water. Infusoria are suitable for feeding to newly hatched fry. The spores of many infusoria are airborne, so the resulting organisms may be found in most water which has been standing exposed to the air. When the spores come in contact with water containing suitable feeding matter they grow and multiply; some merely by a process of division.

Infusoria may be found in ponds, butts, or even in a flower vase which has contained stems for several days. Unless, however, the source of supply is abundant it will be necessary to make a culture in order to obtain adequate quantities for raising a batch of fish fry. A limited culture may be developed by boiling chopped hay in water for about 20 minutes, and straining the liquid into jam-jars. These may be either infected with an initial supply of infusoria, or the jars may be exposed to the atmosphere until they become infected. Another method is to dry lettuce-leaves for a short period in an oven, and then crumble them, and sprinkle them into jam-jars containing water. Some people employ banana skins, potato peelings, or fresh lettuce-leaves. Since a good batch of fry is capable of consuming three 2-lb. jam-jars of infusoria per day, it will be appreciated that fresh cultures must be made in rotation every few days to replenish the supply.

To-day it is possible to purchase various proprietary products which contain or produce infusoria, so those aquarists who do not desire to go to the trouble of culturing infusoria are able to obtain some by these modern methods.

For the commercial breeder requiring a permanent supply of infusoria perhaps the best and easiest method is to keep a large number of Ampullaria snails in a battery of bare tanks. Lettuce-leaves are fed to the snails daily. The more snails the thicker the infusoria produced. The snails should breed and replenish themselves, thereby ensuring a permanent source of infusoria. The snails live in water at a temperature of approximately 78° F., so when feeding infusoria to fry it is only necessary to take a jam-jar full of water from the culture tanks and empty it into the tank containing the fry. As the water-level in the snail tank drops it is replenished with clean, fresh water of the same temperature. The next day the second snail tank is used, and so on. By the time the last tank has been reached the first one is again thick with infusoria.

In addition to lettuce, Ampullaria snails will eat dandelion leaves,

Savoy cabbage, and spinach. But the nature of the culture of infusoria obtained depends largely on the kind of food given to the snails, since it is their droppings that form the culture medium. The aquarist anxious to obtain a particular type of infusoria must experiment by giving the snails different kinds of food, and examining the resulting organisms under a microscope.

It is important to bear in mind that all cultures of infusoria poured into tanks of fry must be at aquarium temperature. If one of the jar methods is employed the infusoria will have to be warmed up. In the event of no separate heating being available the jars of infusoria should be floated in the aquarium for some time before being tipped out. Better still is to culture infusoria at a temperature of 78° F. It not only multiplies quicker, but is warm enough to add direct to a breeding tank.

Brine shrimps (*Artemia salina*)

These small crustacea make an excellent food for feeding to many of the larger fry. Unfortunately, they are expensive, and a little trouble is required to prepare them. The two main types of brine shrimps used by aquarists come from California and from the Great Salt Lake. The tiny brown eggs, looking like black pepper, are collected, dried, and distributed all over the world. Although they may have been dried for some years, it is remarkable to find that if they be placed in a brine solution of the right temperature they will hatch in 24–36 hours.

The method is as follows. Fill battery jars or other glass containers with, say, half a gallon of tap-water. Add to this 2½ tablespoons of ordinary block salt. The temperature should be maintained at 78° F. Once the salt has dissolved sprinkle in a level saltspoonful of the eggs, which will float on the surface. In approximately 30 hours nearly all the eggs should have hatched, and the small shrimps, bright pink in colour, will be hopping about near the bottom of the jar. Strong aeration increases the percentage of hatching. A thin rubber siphon tube can now be inserted deep into the container, and the shrimps drawn off. These are strained through a nylon net placed over another jar; afterwards the water that has passed through is returned to the hatchery. When siphoning try to avoid sucking up unhatched eggs or egg-shells. The mass of newly hatched shrimps in the nylon net can be fed to the fry with the point of a penknife.

An alternative method, which some aquarists prefer, is as follows. A shallow rectangular dish is divided approximately in half by a thin wall of wood which fits tightly at the sides, but a space of about ⅛″ is allowed to remain between the lower edge of the wood and the bottom of the dish. The brine-shrimp eggs are placed in the rear half of the dish, which is now covered with a sheet of cardboard to keep it in semi-darkness. When the shrimps have hatched they make their way under the wooden division and reach the light end of the dish. From here they are siphoned off as before, and, if care is taken to ensure that the surface of the water is not allowed to drop below the wooden division, few if any egg-shells will pass into the front compartment. The salt water in the hatchery may be used a number of times before losing its strength or becoming foul. But as soon as the percentage of eggs hatching out falls the containers must be cleansed and refilled with clean salt water.

Newly hatched brine shrimp is an excellent food for the slightly larger fry, and can be fed as first food to fry of angel fish and other cichlids, as well as the larger barbs. The smaller fry require infusoria initially, but as soon as they are large enough to eat brine shrimp it should be given to them. It will soon be evident if the shrimps are being swallowed, as their pink colour will show through the distended walls of the stomach of the fry. Here there is one word of warning: brine shrimps, though an excellent food, must not be served exclusively for long periods, since their intense salinity adversely affects the fishes, which may die after three weeks of this saline diet.

Microworms (*Anguillula silusiæ*)

Working up the scale, we next come to microworms. This is the term applied by aquarists to the tiny nematode worms known commonly as 'eels' or 'eelworms.' These minute worms are whitish in colour, and may be cultured easily. They make an excellent food for very small fishes, particularly the species that grub about near the bottom of the aquarium, being ideal for baby fishes such as Corydoras, dwarf cichlids, etc. The tiny worms sink slowly to the bottom of the tank, and although during this descent some are eaten, by far the greater number reach the sand. Since they do not swim, microworms are not ideal for the fry of angels and similar fishes, which normally feed in mid-water.

Culturing microworms. First acquire a few shallow dishes about 4″ in diameter and 1″ deep, preferably of a material with a rough surface. Into some of these containers place about one tablespoonful of cooked porridge, which has cooled, and been mixed with cold milk to a creamy consistency. Infect the centre of each container with about a saltspoonful of microworms; cover with a sheet of glass, and keep in the dark at a temperature of 70°–75° F. If there is no dark place where the cultures may be housed cover them with a black cloth. Now the microworms begin to multiply, and in about a week to ten days they will have become so numerous and overcrowded that they require more room. As a result the tiny worms swarm up the sides of the containers; this, however, they cannot do unless the surface is rough enough to grip. The worms are removed by wiping a finger round the sides of the dish; they may then be deposited into several tanks by momentarily inserting the finger into the water. Do not over-feed.

The culture will continue to increase and maintain itself in strength for about a week, after which it will deteriorate and the worms will decrease in number. Before this stage is reached more dishes must be brought into use. New porridge is placed in them and infected by taking a saltspoonful of worms from the old culture. As before, these will take a week to multiply and be thick enough to use. In order to maintain a continual supply it is necessary to employ three sets of culture in different stages of development.

Like sets of underclothing, one on, one in the wash, and one in the airing cupboard, so we need in micro cultures No. 1 set ripening, No. 2 in use during its peak, and No. 3 set deteriorating, ready to be washed up and cleaned in time to become No. 1 set again.

Grindal worms

This is another white worm—named after Frau Grindal, who discovered them—considerably larger than the microworm, growing to a length of $\frac{1}{8}''$ to $\frac{1}{4}''$. They make excellent food for all the smaller tropical fishes. Grindal worms are too fatty to be used exclusively, and, although eaten greedily at first, they may become monotonous after a time.

Grindal worm culture. Make a few small wooden boxes approximately 7″ long by 5″ wide by 1½″ deep, fill with a well-moistened mixture of peat, soil, and leaf-mould, to within ¼″ of the top. Place the culture in the centre of the boxes and feed by sprinkling over them a dessert-spoonful of dry baby-cereal food. Now cut a piece of glass, preferably with one corner nicked out, to fit inside the box. Keep the boxes dark, and stand in a *warm* place, approximately 75° F. After a few days the worms should have multiplied and consumed the food. Lift the glass, and with a razor blade collect the worms, afterwards re-feed the remainder and store as before. They will continue indefinitely, provided they are fed regularly, kept moist, and maintained at the correct temperature. Occasionally dig up the soil to keep it well aerated.

Enchytræus albidus

Known to aquarists as white worms, this excellent food is useful for all fishes. Being larger than Grindal worms, yet always having young ones among them, they are taken by all fishes, large and small. Enchytræ are particularly useful for feeding to those species of fish which will touch nothing but living food. This applies particularly to fishes such as Mastacembelus, which have very small mouths, but are able to suck in these worms end on.

Similar to Grindal worms, enchytræ are somewhat fatty, and should not be used exclusively. They are cultured in exactly the same way as Grindal worms, except that they differ in not liking warmth, so should be kept at a temperature of 50°–60° F.

Earthworms

The common garden worm is, surprisingly, one of the finest foods for fishes. It is of great nutritive value, and seems to have almost everything in its favour. The great disadvantage is that the worms have to be cut up to a suitable size. Most fishes, even the coral species, are attracted by the earthworms, though they cannot normally come across it under natural conditions. The smaller pink worms up to 1″ long are eaten whole by medium-sized fishes. Large fishes, like cichlids, will take worms up to 5″ long and keep returning for more. But for the small tropicals, chopping or mincing is inevitable.

Since earthworms are such an excellent and appetizing food for fishes, and common enough throughout the world, it is surprising that they are not used more often. City dwellers and those living in flats who cannot dig up worms in the garden can usually purchase them from pet stores, or find them when on a trip in the country. They may even be cultured in an old sink filled with soil and leaf-mould, provided they are fed with household scraps such as vegetable peelings, stale bread, and so forth, and kept damp and cool.

When feeding fishes with worms collect them in a jam-jar, wash them free of mud, and place them on a board to be chopped finely with a very sharp razor blade. Since worms contain an appreciable amount of soil, the resulting mince is rather muddy and may cloud the tank if put in before cleansing. So scrape the mince from the board into a fine muslin net, hold under a running tap, and shake well. Now wash the board, and by reversing the net drop the clean mince on to the clean board; serve to the fishes on the point of the razor blade. The net will still contain mud and slime, but if this is allowed to dry it will rub off easily, and the net be ready for further use. There is no finer food for putting body on to fishes than garden worms, and it cannot be equalled for getting breeding stock into prime condition before spawning.

Crushed snails

Sooner or later most aquarists find they have an unwanted culture of snails infesting their tanks, which has to be netted out and thrown away. Instead of discarding the snails, they can be crushed with the bottom of a jam-jar on a thick piece of glass and fed to the fishes, who will gobble them up except for the small bits of shell. When these become too numerous they can be siphoned off.

(iv) POND FOODS

The foods to be covered in the following pages are found in ponds. Throughout most of the year supplies can be caught if the aquarist is prepared to go to a little trouble in making nets, and is lucky enough to discover a good hunting-place which is not over-fished by other enthusiastic aquarists. Too wide a publicizing of the merits of the pond will soon result in it being denuded. On the other hand, it is not always advisable to be too mean about sharing a pond with a few others, since a reasonable removal keeps the pond life from becoming over-crowded.

These live foods have purposely been considered last, for they are generally regarded to be of such importance that the other excellent foods referred to earlier in this chapter are often ignored.

Rotifers

These are minute animals, slightly larger than infusoria, and are generally found in ponds. The commoner rotifers include *Brachionus rubens* and *Hydatina senta*. Under very favourable conditions they are so

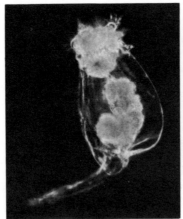

Rotifer

Daphnia

Glass worm

Cyclops

Gnat larva

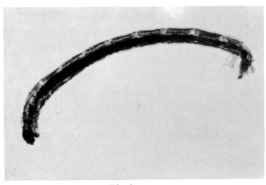

Blood worm

amassed that they will appear to colour the water. They are not easy to culture, so the aquarist is dependent mainly on finding and catching them. For this purpose a net of very fine material, such as nylon, is suitable. It should be about 6″ in diameter at the mouth, 2 ft. long, and tapering to a blunt point.

This type of net may be used in shallow water where most rotifers are to be found. To prevent larger organisms from entering the net, a piece of fine nylon gauze should be clipped over the mouth to act as a strainer. Rotifers carried home in jars can be strained through nylon, and served to the fishes on the point of a knife.

Daphnia

There are many species of Daphnia, the commonest, probably, being *Daphnia pulex*, but for food purposes we need not differentiate between them. The colour of Daphnia in the mass varies in shades of grey to green and brown to red, according to the nature of their diet. They are usually found in shallow farm ponds, particularly those which are frequented by ducks, geese, cattle, or other livestock whose droppings create organic matter which encourages the life of animal and vegetable cellular organisms upon which the Daphnia feed. Daphnia may also be found at waterworks where large, shallow filter beds are exposed to sunlight and depend on the growth of algæ to assist the filtration of the water; and, because of the abundance of algæ, Daphnia soon appear and multiply rapidly. Similarly, the cleaner filter beds at sewage works frequently provide a good crop.

These little crustacea, distantly related to crabs, are of a similar form, having a hard outer shell enclosing a soft interior which contains the nutriment; the shell acts merely as roughage, with little or no food value. For this reason Daphnia is not the perfect food which many aquarists believe it to be. Nevertheless, it is a natural live food, and its hopping motion in the water attracts the eye of a fish and gives it the urge to pursue its prey. Furthermore, fishes which are inclined to refuse food may be tempted to eat Daphnia. The Daphnia may be sifted through fine muslin nets; the smaller crustacea passing through are good for young fry. Not only do these get exercise in pursuing their food, but, Daphnia being aquatic creatures, they will live in the tank and not die before all the fry have satisfied their hunger. City dwellers unable to catch their own Daphnia can usually purchase them from pet stores during the summer months, but the price is high for the relatively small amount obtained.

Catching Daphnia. Assuming that the aquarist has found a pond of the type already mentioned, although no Daphnia may be visible he is advised to investigate, since there may well be Daphnia near the bottom. The equipment required consists of a muslin net about 12″ deep, stitched to a frame roughly a foot in diameter. The shape of the bag thus formed should resemble a bowl rather than a pointed cone, since any Daphnia caught in the latter may be crushed as the net is drawn through the water, and most will be found to be dead on arrival home. The net is attached to a handle as long as can be wielded conveniently and, if it is to be carried in a car, it should be made in sections which can be connected together. The only other piece of equipment required is a can with a large surface area to allow plenty of oxygen to contact the water in which the Daphnia will be transported.

After having filled the can with pond water, all is ready to start operations. Reaching out as far as possible into the pond to avoid the shallows, insert the net sideways, and take care not to submerge it completely. Now start weaving the net in a figure of eight about a dozen times. Haul it in, and, provided one has not fished too deeply and Daphnia are present, it will contain no mud but a solid mass of Daphnia, either green or red in colour. Tip the contents into the can, where the Daphnia will hop about with their normal swimming motion. Catch only sufficient for the immediate needs, as most of that taken will not live longer than a day or two, after which it is unfit for food. To catch more Daphnia than necessary is a pure waste; it is far better to leave the remainder to breed naturally, and to return for further supplies as required.

Daphnia are most prolific in the late spring and early summer, when the increased daylight encourages the growth of algæ. Although some Daphnia are to be found during the winter, the majority of the last batch of eggs laid by the females in the autumn remain dormant much longer than the normal hatching period, thus enabling them to weather the winter, when their food is short.

Attempts have been made to breed Daphnia in tubs and baths, and, although a few can be produced, nothing like enough can be obtained artificially, and the attempts at culturing are certainly not worth the bother. A word of warning: in sweeping for Daphnia in a natural pond sooner or later some harmful creatures will be picked up with the catch. Some of these, including water tigers and dragonfly larvæ, are referred to in Chapter VIII. The larger enemies can be seen and removed, but the smaller pests such as Hydra, particularly when contracted, are inconspicuous, and therefore cannot be eliminated. For this reason it is advisable to make a rule that Daphnia is never fed to breeding fish which have been put into a breeding tank to spawn. If by mischance a crop of Hydra is introduced into the tank they will devour greedily any fry in their initial swimming stages. The wise breeder will also exclude Daphnia in tanks containing fry until the young fish are large enough not to fall prey to Hydra.

Dried Daphnia. Much of this is offered for sale, but a large proportion of the nutriment has been driven off in the drying process, leaving behind little other than dried shells or husks of practically no food value. But, as previously explained, when mixed as an ingredient of dried food dried Daphnia supplies excellent roughage.

Cyclops

These little crustacea get their name from the Greek giant Cyclops (since they have only one eye, which is situated in the centre of the forehead).

They are found with Daphnia, as they live and feed under the same conditions. As a fish-food Cyclops are good; they are rather smaller than Daphnia, and are usually greyish-green in colour. The females can often be seen carrying two clusters of eggs near the end of the body, which increases their bulk and makes them look rather different creatures from the males. If anything, Cyclops appear to be more hardy than Daphnia, and in the colder months are often obtainable in larger quantities than Daphnia.

Some aquarists believe that Cyclops will attach themselves to very young fry and devour them, but the authors have never had grounds to think this to be true, and in any case where a good spawn of fry is being raised the merits of Cyclops as a food easily outweigh any alleged demerits. When sifting a catch from a Daphnia pond through a muslin net into a tank containing small fry many Cyclops will pass through as well. The fry appear to prefer the Daphnia, since they usually go for these first. This preference may be due to the ability of the Cyclops to dart about at considerably higher speeds than Daphnia, making them more difficult to catch. Having eaten the Daphnia, the fry next turn their attention to the Cyclops. These, if not too numerous, and allowed to remain uneaten, will live in most tanks far better and longer than Daphnia. Finally, we must repeat the warning given with regard to introducing enemies into breeding tanks.

Tubifex worms

These are thin, dull reddish worms varying in length from $\frac{1}{2}''$ to $2''$, or even more. They are sometimes found in the filthiest of farm ponds, those which are virtually sumps of liquid manure draining from adjacent buildings. Large quantities of Tubifex live where sewage is discharged into a tidal estuary or river. The worms bury their heads in the sludge and leave their tails waving in the shallow water above. But at the slightest movement they contract their bodies and disappear from sight. To collect the worms it is necessary to haul in a quantity of sludge in a net or bucket. The substance is then washed through fine nylon or butter muslin until most of the dirt has been removed, leaving behind a mass of the worms. Most of the Tubifex sold in pet shops is sent by rail by individuals who undertake the cold and unpleasant task of collecting the worms.

Once the worms are purchased from a pet shop it is advisable first to wash them, and then to feed them to the fishes as soon as possible; any Tubifex remaining over should be put in a dish or trough, and placed under a tap where a slight trickle of water is allowed to flow over them continually. The receptacle will eventually overflow, so must be stood in a sink. In this running water the worms will live longer, but, having nothing to eat, many will die. The dead ones turn greyish in colour, and to eliminate them the mass should be stirred before feeding to the fishes, in order that the dead and decomposing worms may be washed away in the overflow.

From what has been said it will be appreciated that Tubifex live and eat in most unhygienic surroundings. For this reason the authors do not favour this form of fish food, and prefer *never to use it*. Not only can many forms of harmful bacteria be introduced into an aquarium when feeding the fishes on imperfectly cleansed Tubifex, but the worms themselves, having lived on filth, seem to bring out boils on some fishes. These appear as a reddish bump, which bursts in due course.

For some time there have been rumours that Tubifex worms may continue to live in the intestines of a fish, and bore their way through various organs, thus bringing about the death of the host. The authors have never been able to establish this as a fact, and consider that it is most improbable. Nevertheless, if Tubifex is fed to fishes, it should be chopped with a razor blade, as some of the worms are so long that they will entwine themselves in a fish's gills and cause discomfort, even death. If the aquarist decides to feed his pets with Tubifex it is advisable to do so sparingly, as they quickly sink to the bottom and bury their heads in the sand. Although the tails oscillate in the water, the approach of a fish looking for a meal makes the worms contract immediately and disappear into the sand. It is true that such fishes as Corydoras, which rout in the top layers of the sand, are able to extract a few of the worms; but when many worms are present a great number will die, decompose, and tend to foul the tank. Some Tubifex well-established in a tank live on matter which has penetrated the sand; they make a most unsightly spectacle of waving red fronds, impossible to dislodge unless the whole tank is dismantled and the sand thoroughly cleansed before re-setting.

Glass worms

These transparent creatures—known also as 'phantom larvæ'—are the larvæ of the gnat Chaoborus, and measure about $\frac{1}{4}''$ to $\frac{1}{2}''$ in length. They are found in natural ponds, and are caught in a net in the same manner as Daphnia. For fishes large enough to eat them, glass 'worms' make an excellent diet, and have the advantage that they survive for a considerable time in the aquarium. They are often found in small ponds overhung by trees and not necessarily frequented by domestic animals. It would appear that the larvæ subsist on vegetable matter such as decaying leaves. One great advantage of this larva is that it can be caught in the winter months, even if one has to break the ice to reach it; and at this season Daphnia and Cyclops are almost impossible to obtain.

Glass worms are too large to be fed to small fry; in fact, the reverse is the case. Being equipped with a sharp hook on their heads, glass worms can ensnare very small fry and devour them. Bigger fishes enjoy the worms, and delight in the chase after their prey. From a motionless position in mid-water the worms, noticing the approach of a fish, coil themselves into a spring, then with a jerk they dart away an inch or two and finally come to rest, relying upon their immobility and transparency for protection.

Blood worms

These are the larvæ of Chironomus midges, and are deep blood-red in colour, the body being formed of numerous segments. They are an excellent food, containing a high proportion of hæmoglobin, which is easily digested and beneficial to the system. It is highly desirable to serve this diet at least once a week to all fishes capable of masticating these rather thick 'worms.' Unfortunately, however, the worms are not available throughout the year, and even when obtainable are difficult to find in large quantities.

Blood worms are usually found in old water-butts and small pools containing decaying vegetable matter, algæ, and rotting wood. Where the water is old but clear the worms are not dangerous or harmful.

Mosquito larvæ

The mosquito lays its eggs on stagnant water. These develop into the larvæ, which, although living in water, still depend upon air to breathe. The respiratory organs are situated at the tail end of the larvæ, which must frequently wriggle their way to the surface of the water, and, while hanging head downward, extend their breathing tubes to the air. Equipped with large eyes, they are quick to see the slightest movement or passing shadow above the water. At the least disturbance the larvæ will dive to the bottom and remain there until danger is past. They are provided with formidable pincers to catch their prey, and are able to grab newly hatched fry. For this reason the larvæ must be fed only to fishes which are large enough to be immune from attack.

Mosquito larvæ are seasonal, appearing in water-butts, old cans, or anywhere where there is stagnant water; a static pond may produce great numbers. To catch them a large, long-handled net is required. Make a stealthy approach, plunge the net into the water, and with a quick scooping action collect all those which have come up to breathe. The remainder will dive to the bottom, and there is nothing to do but to wait until they reappear to breathe, imagining that the danger has passed. Then another swift action with the net will trap more. During the waiting period the net must not be allowed to cause disturbing ripples by dripping into the water, and the catcher must stand still and not make the least movement likely to throw a shadow on the pool. An aquarist who falls a victim to mosquito bites has the double satisfaction of knowing that every mosquito larva swallowed by his fishes is not only benefiting his pets but indirectly himself, since it is one that will not develop and bite him.

Gnat larvæ are very similar to those of the mosquito, but smaller. Some may be sifted through fine nylon mesh and fed to smaller fishes. Since both gnat and mosquito larvæ breathe air, they do not quickly deoxygenate the water in the aquarium, so quite large quantities may be fed at one time. But there are limits, and it is well to remember that those not eaten by the fishes can hatch out and escape into the room.

Sandhoppers

Those aquarists living near the sea may find under boulders on the shore small crustacea commonly known as sandhoppers. When discovered they leap about, but quite a number can be picked up and placed in a jar of sea-water. On arriving home these can be caught or strained through a net and fed to medium-sized fishes, who seem to enjoy the change. Sandhoppers, of course, make an excellent food for many of the marine coral fishes, who pounce on all they can see, the remainder living quite happily in the crevices of the coral until they venture out.

Other foods

There are numerous other creatures—mayfly grubs, young tadpoles, and so forth, which will serve as fish-food. It is quite impossible to list them all here, but if a source of supply is available to any aquarist it is advisable to try a small amount initially and see how the fishes react. Most natural foods will be found to be satisfactory, but care should be taken to avoid introducing dirt, harmful bacteria, or other fish enemies.

CHAPTER VII

SNAILS

MOST BEGINNERS THINK THAT SNAILS ARE ESSENTIAL AS SCAVENGERS, AND purchase, at quite a high price, a few red ramshorns only to find that after a day or two these have been attacked by the fishes, who nip their antennæ every time they are extended, finally killing them or forcing them to remain inside their shells until they starve to death. It is a remarkable fact that if one desires to keep snails they are frequently killed off, but when not wanted they usually multiply profusely and become a pest.

Alkaline water is necessary for most snails, as they require certain minerals to maintain their shells in condition. In soft water containing little or no calcium the shells may become brittle and even disintegrate.

A few colourful snails in a community tank may be decorative, and they certainly will dispose of some uneaten food and some algæ. They will not, however, eat fish excreta; on the contrary, they will add their own to that already in the tank. Snails are therefore of no great advantage in an aquarium where the fishes are not over-fed; in fact, a little extra food will have to be provided to enable the snails to live.

Should they survive they are likely to become too numerous, and to compete with the fishes for oxygen and food. Periodically, therefore, it will be essential to remove and dispose of most of the snail population. Another disadvantage is that any dead snails are unsightly and detrimental. Some not only eat algæ, but devour plant leaves as well, puncturing them all over, and often biting right through the stems, which float to the surface of the water and rot.

The aquarist who wishes to breed fishes will find that most snails are a definite nuisance. Although a breeding tank is set up with washed sand, rinsed plants, and clean water, it is impossible to remove every tiny snail smaller than a pin's head. Worse still, a few eggs adhering to the under-side of plant leaves hatch surprisingly quickly, and the young snails devour any fish eggs they can find.

In spite of what has been said above, there are a few species of snails which are a boon to the fish-breeder, notably *Limnœa stagnalis* and the Ampullarias.

Ampullaria cuprina (apple snail)

To the fish-breeder this snail has great advantages. There are, however, four distinct species of Ampullarias. Three of these are ravenous plant-eaters, and should be kept out of planted aquaria. All are sometimes known as 'infusoria snails,' as when kept in unplanted tanks and fed on lettuce-leaves their droppings create ideal conditions for the production of infusoria, the first food for newly hatched minute fry. Water from the

Ampullaria cuprina   Limnœa stagnalis
Planorbis corneus   Physa fontinalis   Melania tuberculata

Ampullaria tank is poured into the one occupied by the free-swimming fry, but in doing so a baby snail will also occasionally be transferred. This will not matter if only *Ampullaria cuprina* are kept, but if any of the other three species be inadvertently introduced they will wreak havoc with the growing plants. It is therefore necessary for the aquarist to be able to identify the species.

A. canaliculator has a raised spiral coming to a point, and a deep groove is formed between the coils. *A. cuprina* has a raised spiral and a slight groove. *A. gigas* is the largest of all fresh-water snails. Its salient features are a low spiral which is not very pointed, and a deep groove. Finally, a low spiral with only a slight groove characterizes *A. paludosa*.

Ampullarias have four horns and are equipped with an extendable breathing tube which they stretch upward to the surface of the water, and with a pumping action breathe in sufficient air to last them for some time while submerged. These snails are not bisexual, so to breed them it is necessary to have a male and a female. It is possible to sex Ampullarias even when they are closed up, since the operculum (the trap-door with which they close the mouth of the shell) of the female is slightly concave, whereas that of the male is slightly convex. In breeding, the male, which is usually the smaller, climbs over the back of the female a little to the right of the head and inserts a long, thick muscular organ, whitish in colour, into the vent under her shell. During this act the snails are locked together, and should not be forcibly parted or injury may result.

When laying eggs the females climb up the walls of the aquarium and out of the water, where they hang motionless. The bright pink eggs emerge from under the shell and pass singly along a groove outside her body to become attached to the glass. A steady stream of eggs moves upward and sticks to the mass now forming on the walls of the tank, until the cluster resembles a large raspberry. This hatches in approximately three to four weeks, providing it does not fall into the water or become too dry. When sufficient snails are kept egg-laying is profuse, and without special care sufficient will hatch to keep the species going. Should an abundance be required for stocking or selling, the clumps of eggs should be carefully removed from the glass with a razor blade. They are then placed on a glass platform stood on two jam-jars in a small tank. This is then filled with water until it reaches the platform. The water is kept at 78°F., and to ensure the correct humidity the tank is covered by a sheet of glass.

On hatching, the baby snails make their way into the water and search for food. *A. cuprina* has an enormous appetite, and must be fed regularly with the leaves of lettuce, dandelion, or Savoy cabbage. Ampullarias will not stand foul conditions, so their home must be given a thorough clean-out, dead snails removed, and the tank re-filled with clean water at least once a month.

Bulinus australianus (*Australian red*)

This snail, which comes from the Southern Hemisphere, has a pretty yellowish-red shell. The spiral twists in the opposite direction to that of the Physa snail. *B. australianus* is a prolific breeder; it is rather larger than Physa, but similar in shape.

Limnœa auricularia (*paper shell*)

Occasionally seen in aquaria, this rather pretty snail has short horns. The shell is yellowish, marked with dark blotches. *L. auricularia*, coming from northern Europe, can withstand fairly low temperatures. It dislikes heat, so is not really suitable for use in tropical tanks.

Limnœa stagnalis (*common pond snail*)

This is found in most ponds, natural or artificial. The snails are greyish in colour, with sharp spiral cone shells about $1\frac{1}{2}''$ long when full grown. They breed profusely, laying a mass of eggs encased in a glutinous jelly usually in the form of an elongated oval about $1''$ in length. Development of the young snails can be observed. When first hatched they are slightly smaller than a pin's head; they are voracious, and will eat animal or vegetable matter. They have the great advantage to the fish-breeder that they will devour Hydra with relish. It is unwise to bring the snails straight from a cool pond and place them direct into a tropical tank, but if warmed up gradually they will stand the change.

Should a breeding tank containing fry be found to have Hydra in it a dozen *L. stagnalis* will quickly clear the pests, and not harm the fry. The aquarist can watch the snails devouring Hydra attached to the front panel of the aquarium; they are sucked into the snail's mouth, whose scythe-like tongue slices the pest clean off the glass. The snails perform this feat much quicker and better than the generally recommended blue gourami, which is not only more costly to obtain but has to be kept very hungry before it will oblige, sometimes inefficiently. Care, however, must be exercised to control the snails. They should be removed after clearing the Hydra, and kept in a spare jar until required again.

Marisa rotula (Colombian ramshorn)

This snail is rarely seen in British aquaria, but may be more popular in America. It has a smart flat-spiralled shell lined longitudinally with alternate stripes of dull yellow and brown. The antennæ are long, and the foot is of a mauvish colour. *M. rotula* reaches a diameter of $1\frac{1}{2}''$. This snail has the drawback of nibbling plants.

Melania tuberculata (Malayan snail)

These small live-bearing snails rarely exceed $\frac{3}{4}''$ in length, and have long, sharp-coned shells. They have two advantages: in the first place, Malayans scavenge deep into the sand, which is thereby kept loose. Secondly, they reach uneaten food inaccessible to other snails. During daylight Malayans hide beneath the sand. At night, however, the aquarist may experience quite a shock to find hundreds of them swarming all over the walls of the tank. Because of their nocturnal habits they are difficult to eliminate. When over-abundant probably the best method is to remove the sand, scald, and then sift, to remove the larger shells.

Physa fontinalis (American pond snail)

Common in ponds, these small snails rarely exceed $\frac{1}{3}''$ in length. They are nearly black in colour, extremely hardy, and have very tough shells which discourage fishes from eating them. They breed quickly, and soon become a pest, especially in breeding tanks. Once in an aquarium they are difficult to eradicate. Their excessive excretion covers the sand with unsightly black droppings. These snails are not to be recommended for the aquarium.

Planorbis corneus (ramshorn snails)

The shells take the form of flat spirals, like the mainspring of a watch. They are generally black; but there is a pretty red variety. Ramshorns are the snails usually seen in tropical aquaria. Red ones may add a little colour to a community tank, but have virtually no other advantage. In breeding tanks they are a nuisance, as they consume fish eggs and eat much of the food fed to the fishes. The snails breed profusely throughout the year, laying eggs enclosed in small globules of yellow-tinted jelly.

Viviparus malleatus (Japanese live-bearing snail)

This gives birth to fully formed young snails, and does not lay eggs. The snail is quite a large one, and may be confused with the Ampullarias, but the spiral of *V. malleatus* is much more raised, and the shell is wider than it is high. This snail is not bisexual, so for breeding male and female are necessary. Sex may be distinguished, as the male has a shorter and a curved right antennæ in comparison with the female. After mating the young hatch inside the mother's shell, and emerge about the size of small pearls. It does not like high temperatures, and is not altogether happy in a tropical tank. A great advantage is that it is not a plant-eater.

FRESH-WATER MUSSELS AND CRUSTACEA

Some aquarists occasionally keep fresh-water mussels, small fresh-water crayfish, and fresh-water shrimps. Usually, none of these survive at tropical temperatures; mussels die, and, being fairly large, quickly foul the water; crayfish with their large claws can catch fishes, and so be dangerous; fresh-water shrimps are usually eaten.

In marine tanks it is possible to keep small crabs, shrimps, and prawns, which are good scavengers, but often fall prey to the fishes. Crabs that survive may become too large and dangerous, and eventually will have to be returned to the sea. If any of these crustacea are collected from a cold sea-shore they will stand the temperature of the tropical marine aquarium if gradually acclimatized to warmer conditions.

CHAPTER VIII

FISH ENEMIES

THE AQUARIST WHO CATCHES HIS OWN LIVE FOODS FROM PONDS MAY occasionally come across enemies. A few of these are large enough to be seen easily, caught, and removed. Those which are practically invisible can be dealt with by other means. Below the commoner enemies are listed, their characteristics described, and methods of eliminating them explained.

Minute parasites

There are numerous minute aquatic parasites. When introduced into an aquarium which is somewhat dirty the conditions are favourable to permit these to breed. So dense may they become that the top strata of water may appear greyish or a cloudy brown. Thousands will attach themselves to the fishes, causing discomfort, and even covering the scales with greyish-brown patches. Should the gills of a fish become encrusted death may follow. An aquarium which has become infested with parasites may be cleared as follows. Dissolve some crystals of permanganate of potash in a jam-jar, and pour some of the solution into the tank until the water is a mauvish-pink. Cover the tank with a large cloth to keep it dark, as light soon oxidizes the potassium solution, destroying its effect. In a few hours all the offending parasites will be dead, and sink to the bottom of the tank, from where they may be siphoned off.

Care must be taken not to colour the tank water too deeply, as too strong a dose will kill the fishes. If the fishes show signs of distress, staying up at the surface, change some of the water, to dilute the strength of the dose.

Argulus (fish lice)

This parasite—which is not a louse but a crustacean—attaches itself to fishes, and can be seen with the naked eye. The lice may be killed as follows: a solution of potassium permanganate is made up in the proportion of one grain to five gallons of water in the aquarium. The solution is then poured into the tank.

Dytiscus marginalis (water tiger)

Both the beetle and the larvæ are extremely dangerous; the former is large, and can be seen and removed. The larva varies in length from $\frac{1}{2}''$ to $2''$ or more; it is long, slender, and greenish-yellow in colour; the tail end is equipped with breathing apparatus; from the head project formidable pincers. It must surface occasionally, tail up, to breathe, but can remain submerged for longish periods, and then it is most dangerous. A voracious creature, it will pounce on anything it can grab and suck the victim's juices. Water tigers will attack small to medium-sized fishes, and once the prey is seized it is unlikely to escape. These enemies abound in most natural ponds, and are frequently collected with Daphnia. As a safeguard it is advisable to net some Daphnia from the can and tip them into an enamel basin containing clear water. The tigers can then be picked out before the Daphnia is fed to the fishes.

Hydra

So called after the mythological many-headed monster which, when decapitated, sprouted new heads. This pest is well named. When contracted it is as small as Daphnia, and is hardly visible. It attaches itself to plants, rocks, sand, or the sides of the aquarium. Nevertheless, Hydra can move about by bending over its trunk, extending and gripping with the tips of its tentacles, and then transferring its sucker foot to a new position, repeating the action for further progress. Stretching its trunk to a length of about $\frac{1}{4}"$, it unfurls numerous long tentacles which wave in all directions in search of prey. When magnified each tentacle resembles that of an octopus and bears rows of circular sucking discs equipped with stinging cells, with which the Hydra can grasp its victim, at the same time stinging and paralysing it. The tentacle is then drawn to the mouth and the food swallowed. Nevertheless, while this operation is taking place the other tentacles are actively searching for more prey. It is possible for a Hydra to ensnare several victims simultaneously.

The Hydra reproduces itself by budding from the stem; the process is similar to a side shoot branching from the trunk of a tree. If the creature is cut or broken into pieces each of these will develop into a new Hydra. Hydra are harmless to fishes over $\frac{1}{4}"$ in length, but deadly to newly hatched fry of the egg-laying species of tropicals; Hydra in a breeding tank can clear a spawn of hundreds of fish in a few days. The pests are usually introduced with Daphnia or Cyclops; sometimes they come in attached to plants. For this reason breeding tanks should be set up with plants that have been thoroughly washed, and soaked in salt water. On no account should the fish put out to breed be fed on Daphnia.

When an aquarium becomes infested with Hydra they may be killed as follows:

(i) Add 1 teaspoonful of vinegar to every 2 gallons of water in the tank. The dose may be increased slightly if the treatment does not prove to be 100 per cent. effective. A little vinegar will not harm the fishes.

(ii) Another good method is to introduce into the tank a number of *L. stagnalis* snails, which will soon devour the Hydra. If the snails are taken from a cold pond they must be warmed up slowly to aquarium temperature. The snails should not be used in a breeding tank until the spawn has hatched; though they will not harm the minute fry, they will devour fish eggs.

(iii) Perhaps the best method of all is to pass a weak electrical current through the water. To do this take a 4-volt battery of the type used in a

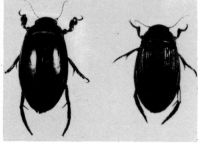

Water Boatman

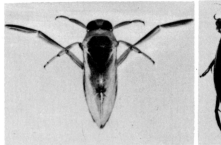

Diving Beetles

Fish Louse

Water Tiger

Hydra

Water Scorpion

Planaria Worm

Fresh-water Leech

lantern torch, two pieces of insulated wire, and two pennies or bits of copper about $1\frac{1}{2}''$ square. Bare the ends of both wires sufficiently to attach them to the pennies. The other two ends are connected one to each terminal of the battery. Place the pennies in the water at the opposite ends of the tank. In about 4 hours the current passing through the water will kill the Hydra, which may be seen dropping to the bottom. The electricity seems to have no effect whatever on minute fry even as small as dwarf gouramis.

Leeches

In an aquarium these unpleasant creatures are more unsightly than dangerous. When contracted small ones are about twice the size of a pin's head, and attach themselves firmly to any object. By stretching their bodies, gripping with their jaws, and then drawing forward their hind-quarters they can move about. Generally they are too slow to catch fishes, but if the tank becomes infested with leeches they can drop on to a victim and suck its blood. Leeches may be introduced inadvertently into the aquarium on plants, but this may be avoided by alternately dipping the plants in warm and then in cold water. After this treatment they should be left soaking for half an hour in a gallon of water to which has been added two level tablespoonfuls of salt.

When feeding Daphnia to the fishes, a few leeches may get into the tank, but they should be removed immediately.

Nepa cinerea (water scorpion)

This bug may be recognized by its scorpion-like front legs and the pointed tail; this consists of two grooved rods which serve as breathing tubes. It abounds in most ponds, but if introduced into an aquarium can be seen, and should be removed.

Notonecta (water boatman)

This insect is often seen skimming over the surface of ponds, using its large rear legs as oars. It is approximately $\frac{1}{2}''$ long by $\frac{1}{8}''$ broad when full grown, so is large enough to be seen and removed. The water boatman is harmless to all but very small fishes, which it may seize in its front legs and attack with its beak. Large fishes will eat the bug.

Odonata (dragonfly larvæ)

Like the dragonfly they will develop into, these thick, large-eyed larvæ have enormous jaws. These are covered by a mask, which is in effect an enlarged lower lip. The larva is able to thrust its jaws forward, thereby extending its long pincers. From a motionless position it grasps the unwary prey. Dragonfly larvæ usually live near the bottom of most ponds. The creatures are not so frequently caught as water tigers, as these are more active in the upper strata of water.

Planaria worms

Grey to brownish in colour, these flat worms are about $\frac{1}{4}''$ long, and some have a diamond-shaped head. They may be seen on the plants and on the glass sides of the aquarium, often congregating just under the surface of the water. When a mass appear adhering to the glass they can be wiped off with a cloth. Planaria worms will eat spawn and very small fry, but seem to be harmless to bigger fishes. Treat as for leeches.

Plumatella repens

These are small creatures rather like miniature Hydra, except that the trunk is much shorter and the tentacles are less numerous and more feathery. *Plumatella repens* increase by sending out runners or side shoots from the base of the trunk; if left alone they will form long brown threads in all directions. The creatures are not large enough to be of much danger, but they may be able to catch a few of the smallest fry. It is mostly the minute organisms in the water, such as infusoria, that are eaten by *Plumatella repens*, therefore probably their worst feature is to consume some of the food for the fry.

Utricularia major and Utricularia minor (Bladderwort and Lesser Bladderwort)

The aquatic plant *Utricularia major* takes the form of a mass of slender filaments bearing numerous small sacs. These bladders engulf minute forms of aquatic life, on which the plant feeds. Bladderwort is of a pretty shade of green, and is used for decorative purposes in some aquaria. It is harmless, except in breeding tanks, where it will engulf and digest some newly hatched fry of egg-laying fishes.

A smaller species (*Utricularia minor*, or lesser bladderwort) is similar, but, the bladders being much smaller, the plant has long been considered safe for all except minute organisms. It is frequently used for spawning purposes, particularly for some of the pencil fishes which produce extremely small fry. There is no doubt that lesser bladderwort can and does engulf some of these baby fishes, but the majority escape.

Other enemies

The undermentioned usually concern outdoor pools, but are referred to here in case some are introduced as additional pets to an indoor aquarium. Frogs, terrapins, and water snakes should not be kept with fishes. In the outdoor pool there is the added danger of fish-eating birds such as herons and kingfishers. Cats, otters, snakes, and alligators are enemies which will eat fishes.

Insecticides

Many of the living enemies of fishes are obvious, but few aquarists realize the danger of modern insecticides. Various washes and sprays used on trees or indoor plants if allowed to contaminate the water in pond or aquarium can quickly prove fatal, D.D.T. being particularly deadly.

CHAPTER IX

DISEASES

FORTUNATELY, TROPICAL FISHES DO NOT SUFFER FROM MANY DISEASES. THIS is particularly true in well-kept, clean aquaria. Nearly all diseases are introduced from outside, and this generally occurs when adding new fishes, without subjecting them to an adequate period of quarantine. Less frequently, the trouble can be traced to the addition of plants which have not undergone a thorough cleansing.

To prevent diseases every aquarist should have a quarantine tank, and all new fishes, without exception, should be isolated in it for at least ten days before they are permitted to enter the set-up and planted aquarium. During the period of isolation it is as well to add one level teaspoonful of salt, and 5 drops of 5 per cent. aqueous solution of methylene blue, to each gallon of water in the quarantine tank. Then should the fishes develop disease it will be confined to the newcomers who are already undergoing treatment.

Large-scale breeders and all aquarists' shops should have one pair of nets allocated to each tank, and used in no others. If the owner can rely on his assistants, he can save the cost of many nets by using one pair and sterilizing these in boiling water every time before moving to a different tank. This will make certain that no disease is spread from one tank to another.

Below are described most of the diseases encountered. Even those which are very infrequently met are mentioned, so that, should they appear, the aquarist will know how to overcome them.

Ichthyophthirius multifiliis (white spot)

This is considered first, because it is the most common. Although it is the bane of some aquarists, it is not nearly so bad as is generally supposed. Perhaps its worst characteristic is being exceedingly infectious—so much so that a net dipped even momentarily into infected water can transfer the parasite elsewhere. Few aquarists realize that, when food is distributed from a plate to several aquaria, the disease is quickly spread should the fingers be dipped into the infected water and allowed to touch the food which is then fed into other tanks.

White spot is caused by a minute protozoon which burrows under the scales of the fish and feeds on its host. At this stage the parasite forms a small swelling, which appears as a white spot about the size of a pin-hole; it is most likely to show first of all on the tail fin. This develops for about three or four days and finally drops off, leaving the fish quite clear. The aquarist may have the mistaken idea that the disease has cleared up. Actually the most dangerous time has arrived, as the encysted protozoon, much too small to be seen in the sand, bursts open. Hundreds of young parasites emerge from it and swim about searching for a host on which to fasten themselves. Many fail in their search, but sufficient reach their goal, which means that in a few days most of the fishes will be showing spots. Since each cyst is able to release over 1000 spores, it will not be long before white spots literally cover every fish in the tank; their vitality is lowered progressively; the gills become infected; and shortly the fishes will die.

It has always been supposed that fishes subjected to a chilling will invariably develop white spot, but this is not necessarily true. It is also thought that the spores of the disease are always present in water, and thus a chilled fish with its resistance lowered will inevitably be attacked. How the parasite is able to survive without attaching itself to a host is unexplained, and in the authors' opinion the theory is illogical. Fishes do get chilled, but often do not develop white spot. If, however, a diseased fish is introduced into an aquarium containing healthy stock, none of which have been subjected to the slightest chill, in ninety-nine cases out of a hundred white spot will spread to all. Then if all the fishes are removed from the tank, and the water is left untreated from a week to ten days, the parasites will starve to death. Introduce clean fishes and white spot will rarely reappear.

Symptoms. The very first sign of suspected white spot may well be shown by the fishes trying to scratch themselves, or to knock off the parasites by suddenly brushing up against a plant, rock, or other object. The aquarist should therefore keep his eyes open continually for such behaviour. If one or two fishes only occasionally perform in this manner there is no need to worry, but if one fish is persistently scraping, and later several others start acting in the same manner, beware! It may mean that a few parasites are burrowing beneath the scales of the fishes and setting up an irritation. Now for a few days keep a sharp outlook for the appearance of white spots on the fishes' tails.

Cure. It is practically impossible to attack the protozoon embedded in the fish without harming the host. But there is no need to try, as it must fall and drop to the bottom of the tank. When the cysts burst and release the baby parasites their most vulnerable stage has arrived; now they are not difficult to destroy. The best method is to remove the fishes into an unplanted tank. Pour into this tank a 5 per cent. aqueous solution of methylene blue, until the water is coloured an inky blue-black. Do not be frightened at the apparent strength of the solution. It will do absolutely no harm, and will cure white spot in 8 to 10 days without having to raise the temperature or do anything else. After this period has elapsed the fishes may be netted and returned to their own tank, where they will be found to be in excellent condition. A nervous aquarist who uses only sufficient methylene blue to make the water a pale blue colour will not succeed in curing white spot.

Methylene blue is a dye and a mild disinfectant; it is cheap, and is obtainable from most chemists. Even a strong solution will not harm the scaled fishes like small neon tetras and so forth, up to large barbs, but strong methylene blue should not be used for the scaleless fishes, such as Botias and Acanthophthalmus. The dye penetrates the skin and poisons them. For the scaleless species only 2 drops of 5 per cent. methylene blue per gallon should be used. The treatment may have to be repeated every 5 days for 3 weeks. A quicker treatment for scaleless fishes is quinine hydrochloride, used at a strength of one grain per gallon of water.

Not every aquarist has a spare tank into which he can transfer his fishes. In this case he must treat them with strong methylene blue where they are. The dye may be detrimental to some of the plants but the robust ones will be quite unaffected; a few delicate ones, such as *Vallisneria torta*, will suffer a little, but most will recover later. After 10 days half the water in the aquarium may be changed, siphoning where possible from the bottom of the tank to remove tinted sediment. A week later more water may be changed. When it has reached a pale blue tint further changes are unnecessary, as the remainder will fade away in time.

Another treatment is a 2 per cent. solution of mercurochrome, using 5 drops to 1 gallon of water. But if this is employed more than once on the same fish it may suffer from mercurial poisoning. With young fishes it may have a stunting effect on growth.

Some aquarists prefer to use additional heat as a cure for white spot, raising the temperature to between 90° and 95° F. for a few days. But if Corydoras are kept they are uncomfortable under these abnormal conditions, and may die. Again, if all the parasites have not been eliminated the trouble may recur when the temperature is lowered to normal.

Finally, some aquarists are turning to terramycin, using one 500 mg. tablet for each gallon of water. The authors have employed this with varying success, but still prefer methylene blue, as being safer and more certain.

Oodinium limneticum (velvet disease)

This in some ways is similar to white spot, and can be mistaken for the former by an inexperienced aquarist. The spots are very much smaller, and are yellow to brown in colour. They quickly coat the fish over its back, so that when it is seen in a head-on position it looks as though it has been dusted with a sun-tan face powder. The edges of the fins, particularly the tail, appear ragged as they are attacked, and the fishes occasionally rub themselves against objects, but not with the vigour seen with white spot. If untreated the fins are eaten away, vitality is lowered, the gills become infected and swollen, the fish gives up all activity, and finally dies. The disease seems to attack mostly young or half-grown fishes, and all those in the tank quickly become infected.

The remedy is simple. Merely add 1 ounce of sea-salt crystals to each gallon of water, and the disease should be cured in 2 or 3 days. If not, on the third day add an additional ounce of salt per gallon. The cure is more rapid if the fishes are treated in an unplanted tank. Moreover, plants will not stand strong salt solution. Methylene blue will not cure velvet disease.

Saprolegnia (fungus)

Tropical fishes are not attacked by fungus nearly so often as their cold-water cousins. This is because fungus prefers lower temperatures. Nevertheless, the disease does appear on raw wounds, particularly after a fish has been badly mauled by another. The spores of fungus are present in most water, but the natural mucus covering on a fish is sufficient to protect it from attack. If, however, damage to the mucus permits the spores to reach the flesh of the fish, then they will develop and spread. The first sign is a few short white hairs protruding from the infected spot. They quickly lengthen and spread over a larger area, and the fish swims with difficulty, exhibiting a miniature hairy growth attached to it.

Only the affected fish needs treatment. It should be gently wiped with a soft cloth dipped in a strong salt solution. As an additional safeguard the patient may be placed in a large sweet jar half full of water to which has been added a tablespoonful of salt. The jar can now be floated back into the tank. The fish, thus protected, remains immune from bullying, yet individual treatment continues. Rarely, if ever, does fungus attack all the fishes in an aquarium. If, however, the trouble is not confined to wounded fishes it may be that the natural mucus on the bodies of the others is being destroyed, making them prone to fungus attack. A chill may cause this to happen. In this case add sea-salt crystals to the aquarium in the proportion of one heaped teaspoonful per gallon of water, and raise the temperature slightly.

Chondrococcus (mouth fungus)

This is a rare but highly infectious and contagious disease, usually introduced from imported fishes. The victim shows a whitish fungus round the lips, which rot away. Sometimes a rotted strip of lip, attached only at one end, will move in and out of the mouth as the fish breathes. Unless the affected fish is of considerable value, it should be killed before this fatal disease attacks the other occupants of the tank. Should it be desired to keep the fish, and in case the infection has already been passed on, the following treatment is advised, but is not always 100 per cent. effective.

Swab the lips with a soft cloth dipped in strong salt solution, and keep the patient isolated in a jar containing strong salt water. Later try swabbing the lips with a 5 per cent. silver-mercury preparation. More recent research has shown that aureomycin in the proportion of 0·05 gram per gallon of water is effective.

Saddle-back

This is another parasitic disease, which is highly contagious and infectious. It occurs usually on newly imported fishes. Saddle-back appears first of all as a whitish patch on the upper part of the caudal peduncle, just in front of the tail fin; this quickly spreads forward along the back of the fish. The infected part becomes completely paralysed; the whitish area previously referred to is, in fact, dead flesh. The fish is unable through paralysis to move the affected part of the body, and is prevented from making the usual waving motions which propel it forward; it tends to float with the tail higher than the head. Within 24 hours the infected parts disintegrate, leaving half a fish, usually the forward part, struggling to swim. Death follows very soon. The parasites spread quickly and infect all the other fishes in the tank. Furthermore, those which are as yet uninfected tend to bite at the diseased parts of the sick fish. This results in the infection being transferred to the mouth of the attacker.

The best treatment is salt, but it must be used at a high degree of concentration to wipe out the disease before it destroys all the fishes. The whole tank must be treated at a strength of three ounces of sea-salt crystals per gallon of water. At this strength it will be detrimental to plants, but in any case newly imported fishes should be quarantined in an unplanted tank. The salt treatment should be gradually increased daily until all signs of the disease disappear. Even so, the aquarist must expect during the early days of treatment more fishes to become infected and die, before the upper hand can be gained.

Gyrodactylus (flukes)

There are numerous small parasites that lodge in the gills of fishes. The resulting irritation tends to cause the membrane to swell and fill with lymph, thereby making it difficult for the fish to extract the oxygen from the water. This in effect brings about the death of the fish by drowning. Aquarists usually call any such troubles by the name of flukes. The affected fish frequently dash aimlessly across the aquarium. They may shoot up to the surface, writhing and twisting as they fall back through the water, sometimes turning over and over with their bodies bent in a crescent shape. The fish is suffocating, and needs immediate attention. Other fishes in the tank will soon be infected unless the parasites are destroyed.

Fortunately, most of these gill infections respond rapidly to the following treatment. "Euflavine" tablets (one tablet = 1·75 grains, or 0·113 gram) are dissolved in the proportion of 1 tablet per 20 gallons, ½ tablet per 10 gallons, and so on. These orange-coloured tablets, or fractions of them, should be crushed and dissolved in a cupful of water, and then the solution poured into the tank. It will turn the water a fluorescent yellowish-green. Usually this treatment produces a complete cure within 24 hours, though in severe cases 36 hours may be necessary. True, the fish on the point of dying may not recover, but the others are saved, and the disease halted. The fluorescent tint in the water is rather persistent, and after a few days can be reduced by changing half the water. "Euflavine" is harmless to plants if used at the strength stated above for a shortish period.

Œdema (dropsy)

This is not an epidemic, but occurs in individual fish, though some species, such as Bettas, gouramis, Molliensia, and some of the Hyphesso-brycons, seem more prone to it.

The symptoms of the disease are that the fish gets grossly bloated, and the scales which normally lie flat over the body become splayed outward. The excess fluid in the body tends to buoy up the fish, causing it difficulty in swimming in the normal way.

There is no known cure, but sometimes the disease responds temporarily to the following treatment: the patient is placed in shallow water to which has been added salt in the proportion of one ounce of sea-salt crystals per gallon of water. Even this is unlikely to prolong the fish's life for more than a month or two.

Eye infections

These are generally caused by bruising, and should be gently dabbed with a soft paint-brush dipped in 5 per cent. silver-mercury preparation ("Protargol").

Tuberculosis (consumption)

Malnutrition and over-crowding are the main causes of consumption in fishes, as in human beings. It is best avoided by feeding a balanced diet, and providing adequate housing, with plenty of light and air per fish in the tank. Little can be done for those fishes which are hollow-bellied, and so wasted that the head appears out of proportion to the under-nourished body. Young fishes in the initial stages of the disease may be saved if given more healthy conditions and better nutrition. The aquarist who continually loses fishes from tuberculosis is himself largely to blame. Sometimes a whole tankful of fishes get thin and waste away. If the aquarium is clean and not over-crowded this is not tuberculosis but more often caused by a gill infection. Dose as for Gyrodactylus.

Skin eruptions

Occasionally certain fishes suffer from boils which swell up on the body as a reddish lump. These in time may burst, and a whitish mucus exude from them. It would appear that they are caused by a blood infection. When a boil has burst it should be swabbed with a soft cloth dipped in a weak solution of potassium permanganate.

The authors have found that in nearly every case where boils are persistently recurring Tubifex is fed regularly. It would seem that the worms house bacteria, and when eaten by the fishes set up a disorder in the blood. Boils certainly seem to cease after a time if Tubifex is abandoned. If the sources of food are of doubtful cleanliness (see Tubifex worms, p. 73) a change should be made to a cleaner diet, say chopped shrimp, boiled cod-roe, etc.

MEDICINE CHEST

In spite of quarantining newly purchased fishes, and maintaining the aquarium in a good clean condition, slip-ups occur, and disease may break out. It is therefore advisable for every aquarist to keep a few common remedies. Of these he should have:

1 bottle of 5 per cent. aqueous solution methylene blue, complete
   with eye dropper.
1 small bottle of 2 per cent. solution of mercurochrome.
10 packets each containing one grain of quinine hydrochloride.
5 tablets of "Euflavine," each 1·75 grains.
3 (500 mg.) tablets of animal formula terramycin.
15 grains of potassium permanganate.
1 packet of sea-salt crystals.

The above should be kept in a box which is light-proof, in order to prevent deterioration. They will be available to cure most common ailments
which may break out in the aquarist's tank or in those of his friends.

CHAPTER X

KINDNESSES AND CRUELTIES

IT IS NOT ASSUMED THAT ANY AQUARIST IS DELIBERATELY CRUEL, BUT HE may not realize some of the small things which cause terror and discomfort to fishes.

Blinding

Fishes have no eyelids, so the switching on of powerful lighting does not give the eyes time to adjust themselves to the changed conditions. Illumination, therefore, should be gradual, and the room lights turned on several minutes before the lamps over the aquarium are lit up.

Sudden vibrations

Like all other vertebrate animals, fishes are equipped with a nervous system. They also possess a most wonderful organ called the lateral line. This runs from head to tail on each side of the body, and picks up vibrations which pass through the water, just as a wireless aerial receives signals out of the ether. Any disturbance will pass a shock wave through the water, and will be felt by the fishes. Suppose, for example, a heavy object be dropped on the floor, or an ignorant person raps his knuckles on the aquarium, or an aeroplane breaks through the sound barrier: in each case shock waves will pass through the water and strike the sensitive lateral line. This will make the fishes jump, and cause nervousness. Some fishes even dash madly for cover, and injure themselves against a solid object. Tapping the glass is particularly stupid, for it always achieves the opposite result to that which is desired. Instead of bringing the fishes into the foreground, they hide behind objects in the background.

Quick temperature changes

Fishes can stand quite a wide range of temperature variation, and have to do this in nature, but it is always gradual, either up or down. They should not be subjected to any sudden temperature change.

Bullying

Bullies abound in the fish world, as they do elsewhere. It is natural for a large fish to regard a smaller one as a meal. To avoid trouble the aquarist should not mix fishes differing considerably in size. Even when uniformly matched, one fish may develop into a bully; a watch must therefore be kept, and the aggressor either disposed of or taught a lesson. The latter may sometimes be achieved by placing the bully when possible into a tank of large fishes, who soon relieve him of his superiority complex.

Over-crowding

Restriction of movement is not the only result of over-crowding; it also brings about lack of oxygen, dirt, and finally causes tuberculosis. This form of cruelty is in some ways the worst, because of its lingering nature.

Over-feeding or starving are unkindnesses in the same category.

Scaring

Few aquarists realize the terror instilled into their pets by unskilled catching. Chasing a fish round and round the aquarium until it is utterly exhausted is cruel and unnecessary. It is usually caused by the aquarist endeavouring to catch the fish with one shallow net. His repeated failures exasperate him, particularly if choice plants are uprooted in the process. His temper makes his efforts even more wild and less fruitful. If he would use two deep nets, and move them very gently, the required fish can be guided to the front glass and hemmed in on both sides, sometimes quite unaware of what is taking place. Furthermore, not a single plant is disturbed. Again, certain kinds of fishes such as Panchax normally rest just under the surface of the water; here the easiest way to catch them is to move a net slowly underneath, and raise it only when the fish is centrally above the net. Fishes which swim in shoals, such as Danios, are best caught with two nets slightly below the surface with the opening upward; the shoal is driven by one net into the other, when many are captured at once.

Transportation

When carrying fishes from one place to another the container must not be over-crowded. It should have a large surface area, and sufficient external wrapping to maintain the temperature. Those fortunate enough to possess a large vacuum flask will find it ideal for moderate distances.

If fishes have to be transported far by air, use is made of polythene bags containing sufficient water. Any air in the bag is squeezed out and immediately replaced by pure oxygen from a cylinder, the neck of the bag being twisted, then doubled over and tied securely. It is then packed in containers which are adequately heat-insulated, and stowed in heated compartments on board the plane. Sodium amytal is sometimes used to anæsthetize the fishes which then, in a quiescent condition, require less oxygen. This means either that more fishes can be safely packed in the bag, or, alternatively, the given amount of oxygen will last over a longer period, since it is used up more slowly. All travelling containers should be thoroughly cleansed before re-use.

Killing

Unpleasant as killing may be, it is the kindest thing to do when a fish is beyond hope, particularly when it is no longer able to defend itself against attack. Some aquarists dispose of fish down the lavatory basin; this method is extremely cruel, as death is slow and lingering. Others drop them into boiling water; though a better method than the former, they are scalded momentarily before death. The ideal method is to drop the fish into a quart of water containing $\frac{1}{4}$ grain of sodium amytal, when the creature is painlessly anæsthetized. While still insensible it is picked out of the solution, and smashed with full force on to the floor. If no anæsthetic is available hurling on the ground is quick and effective.

Artificial insemination

This form of reproduction is possible, and frequently done by experts with fish such as trout. It should not, however, be undertaken by the inexperienced with tropical fishes. Internal damage usually occurs, and nearly always results in the death of the female egg-laying fish; and inevitably with a female live-bearer, as it has to undergo a Cæsarean operation.

CHAPTER XI

PLANTS FOR BEAUTY AND UTILITY

PLANTS ARE ESSENTIAL IN ANY PERMANENT FRESH-WATER AQUARIUM WHERE beauty and the well-being of the fishes is concerned. The different shades of green or red and the diverse forms of foliage not only add greatly to the attractiveness of the under-water scene, but create the conditions which are natural to the fishes. Plants afford refuge and shade, and often provide places for spawning. Besides all these advantages, plants absorb carbon dioxide, give off oxygen, and feed to a large extent on the mulm at the bottom of the aquarium. These processes are fully explained in Chapter III, p. 37.

Plants vary greatly in their habit of growth; some remain short, others grow tall, bushy, or straight. A few float at the surface. All help the aquarist to decorate his tank. Below are listed most of the common species seen in the majority of aquaria. In addition, some rarer ones are described. Nevertheless, new plants are continually being introduced, and it is impossible to cover every specimen suitable for an aquarium. In this chapter plants are considered in alphabetical order; their methods of growth and reproduction are described, and any special requirements stated.

Acorus intermedia   *Acorus pusillus*

ACORUS INTERMEDIA

These little plants are not true aquatics, but marginals. They do not like high temperatures, but if acclimatized slowly will hold their own in a tropical tank. Growth is slow. *A. intermedia* has stiff, sword-like leaves, $\frac{1}{4}''$ wide at the base, which taper to a point, usually reaching a length of 6–7″. The foliage grows from one point on a rhizome. This sends down thick, stout roots, and occasionally produces next to the parent a young plant which may be severed with a sharp knife and transplanted.

ACORUS PUSILLUS

Similar to the foregoing, but the leaves are thinner and shorter, reaching a height of only 3″. Propagation as for *A. intermedia*.

Anubias lanceolata   *Aponogeton ulvaceus*

ANUBIAS LANCEOLATA

A favourite aquarium plant from French Guiana, it prefers soft water, and makes a good centre-piece in small tanks. The stout leaves, lanceolate in shape, are borne on stems which shoot from a root stock. Foliage is darkish green, and attains a length of $5'' \times \frac{3}{4}''$. *A. lanceolata* is a slow grower. Propagation is from small offshoots which spring from the root stock.

APONOGETON FENESTRALIS

The famous Madagascar lace plant, of which there are several species varying in colour and size. It is called the Lace Plant because the leaves are merely a network of veins which run lengthwise and crosswise in a lattice formation—hence the name *fenestralis*, from the Latin *fenestra*, a window. Most of the specimens on sale are imported from Madagascar. Since the plant requires very soft acid water for growing, and is difficult to propagate, it remains scarce, fetching a high price. Some other species of lace plants are not truly aquatic, and fare poorly in an aquarium, usually dying after a few months. These, if planted in a half tub and rooted in 4″ of earth covered by a 2″ layer of sand, can grow to a height of 2 ft., sending their leaves well clear of the water. Some of these leaves will grow 18″ long by 4″ wide.

If the aquarist is fortunate enough to obtain one of the aquatic species it will, with care, live in the aquarium. Contrary to the old contention that the plant should be grown in semi-darkness, we find that it likes a fair amount of light. But the lattice-work of the leaves must not be allowed to become choked with algæ, which will weave themselves in and out of the veins and be difficult to remove. Snails eat some algæ, but may destroy the leaves; it is better to use fishes such as Mollienisia or Otocinclus to consume the algæ.

Though the leaves look most fragile, they are in reality tough and fibrous; under good conditions new ones appear every day or so, as long, thin filaments. These grow, widening as well as lengthening, and usually attain 10″ in length by 1½″ in width. When several leaves of this size are flourishing the plant is superb, and should be left alone: it abhors being moved. For this reason it may be preferable to plant the bulb in a shallow pot containing soil below and sand above. When flourishing the plant will flower, but propagation from seed is difficult, Occasionally the bulb will sprout a side-shoot, forming a baby plant. When this has attained a length of 3″ or 4″ it can be separated from the parent and grown on its own.

APONOGETON FOLIACEUS

Similar to the foregoing in most respects, except that the prominent network of veins is closed with a thin membrane. This plant is rarely exported from Madagascar.

APONOGETON ULVACEUS

Naturally a marginal plant, as the Latin name (*ulva*, sedge) implies. It will grow in an aquarium, where it develops into a show specimen. The plant does well in soft water of 1 foot depth, and requires plenty of space and light in which to spread its large, graceful, pale green, almost transparent leaves. These grow from longish stalks, and attain 6″ in length by 1½″ in width; they have undulating edges, and the veining runs lengthwise. The plant has a delicate texture, and the leaves are easily torn or damaged. The stems can be bruised and broken if handled roughly.

Growing from a bulb, *A. ulvaceus* sends up aerial runners which flower; it also produces young plants at intervals along its length. Occasionally the bulb will spring a side-shoot which may be divided off when large enough. When grown in natural daylight *A. ulvaceus* dies down in the winter, but shoots out again in the spring. During the annual cycle three different leaf formations are developed.

Aponogeton undulatum   *Bacopa caroliniana*

APONOGETON UNDULATUM

A showy plant, and a little stronger than *A. ulvaceus*. It prefers slightly acid water, but is not too sensitive about this. Probably it is the commonest of the Aponogetons, though still remaining relatively scarce. Growing from a bulb, the long, thin leaves, carried on slender stalks, end in a fine point; they may reach a length of 10″, though they rarely exceed $\frac{3}{4}$″ in width. The edges are closely undulated, giving the appearance of a continuous ripple. The plant likes a depth of 12–15″, but does not spread quite as widely as *A. ulvaceus*.

Aerial stems are sent upward prolifically, and these terminate in a spike of pale mauve flowers which rise above the water surface. The bloom may be trained through a corner of the cover glass and enclosed in an upturned jam-jar; it will then continue to grow in the moist, warm atmosphere inside the jar until the flower-head reaches as much as 4″ in length. The flowers produce pollen, and if this is distributed with a very soft brush seeds will develop. When these are about $\frac{1}{8}$″ in diameter the aerial runner should be cut off and the whole piece suspended over a small tank containing sand and water. The seeds ripen, burst, and release minute plants with tiny roots. Great care must be taken to anchor these into the sand where they will grow. They should not be moved, neither must boisterous fishes be put in the tank, as they will bruise or uproot the seedlings. Well-grown ones in due course will produce bulbs.

AZOLLA CAROLINIANA

Essentially this is a floating plant. Each small piece looks like an enlarged snowflake bearing minute leaves. These vary in colour from bright green to rusty red, depending on the amount of light received. Under suitable conditions the plant spreads rapidly; it will form a compact covering on the surface of the water, and provide excellent shade. If allowed to become too thick it may prevent the light from reaching plants below, and so cause them to suffer. Green water, if caused by excessive top light, can be effectively checked by Azolla. Unfortunately, it rarely makes a sufficient depth of growth to provide a spawning ground or a refuge for small fishes.

BACOPA AMPLEXICAULIS

This is different from most plants in its growth and appearance, but makes a pleasant change. It is a bright green, and the small, round leaves, orbicular in shape, are carried on short stalks $\frac{1}{4}''$ long from a central stem. The plant will grow to a height of 12" or more, the top leaves pointing in an upward direction. Half-way down the stem the leaves spread horizontally, while lower down they tend to droop.

B. amplexicaulis is a slow grower. The stems may be cut in half and the upper part replanted. Under a good light this portion slowly roots itself. The original stem will sprout again below the cut. The plant is tall and narrow; it looks better if several stems are bunched together.

BACOPA CAROLINIANA

Very similar to the aforementioned, but the leaves are slightly longer and more pointed. The plant is perhaps a little hardier, and is more apt to send out side-shoots.

CABOMBA AQUATICA

One of the finest of aquarium plants. This is one of several related species, all of which have the same form of growth. The leaves, like open fans, are supported on short stalks. These appear opposite each other from a central stem at intervals of $1\frac{1}{4}''$. The next pair of leaves is set at right angles to those below. When in a situation to its liking Cabomba bears magnificent heads, sometimes measuring $1\frac{1}{2}$–2" in diameter. If these grow towards the viewer they present rosettes of vivid green, not easily forgotten. The plant prefers slightly acid water and a good illumination. Under these conditions it remains bushy and colourful. In alkaline water and under too strong a light the growth of the stems is forced, and these tend to become pale and spindly.

Stems may grow several feet in length, trailing back and forth across the surface of the water. Long stalks may be cut, and look best if planted in bunches, where they soon root. The decapitated stems quickly shoot new heads. The plant is ideal for spawning egg-laying fishes.

CABOMBA CAROLINIANA

Similar to the foregoing, but the foliage is denser, the pairs of leaves appearing every $\frac{1}{2}''$ up the stem, and the fronds of each fan are more tightly packed.

Cabomba	Cabomba	Ceratophyllum
caroliniana	aquatica	demersum

CABOMBA ROSÆFOLIA

An uncommon reddish species.

CERATOPHYLLUM DEMERSUM (Hornwort)

A common plant which abounds over most of Europe and North America, but there is also a tropical variety which comes from India. All varieties are rootless and bushy, consisting of long stems bearing side-branches. The leaves are short, thin spikes, sharp and harsh to the touch. The general colour is a darkish green. Under strong light this rootless plant is a profuse grower, spreading in all directions under the surface of the water. *C. demersum* is useful for spawning the Mastacembelus species, who like to rest supported in the fronds, and deposit their eggs in the prickly thickets.

CERATOPTERIS DELTOIDES (Floating Fern)

A useful floating plant. The leaves, ovate in shape, grow radially from a bunch of roots which hang submerged in the water. The leaves attain a length of 6″ and a breadth of 2″, and are carried on short stems which have a spongy core. In strong light numerous baby plants appear at the edges of the leaves. The young plants, when large enough, float off and grow independently. So prolific is the growth that the water surface soon becomes densely packed, and in the crush some of the leaves are forced out of the water. Unless thinned out, *C. deltoides* will cut out all

Ceratopteris deltoides   *Pistia stratiotes*

overhead light. It is an excellent plant for combating green water. Many of the bubble-nest-building fishes like to make their nests under the leaves.

Ceratopteris pteridoides   *Ceratopteris thalictroides*

CERATOPTERIS PTERIDOIDES (Broad-leafed Indian Fern)

An excellent aquarium plant, not particular as to water, though when fully mature it needs a large tank. It grows to a height of 15″ and spreads as much as one foot in diameter. These dimensions need not deter the aquarist with a small aquarium, since young plants can be accommodated easily.

C. pteridoides is light green in colour, and looks a typical fern. It is composed of many stalks and numerous fronds. Near the base of each stalk the fronds appear as separate leaves, but higher up the stems these are joined together as one irregular-edged leaf. The somewhat hairy roots of the plant are comparatively small. The leaf stems are crisp externally but have a spongy interior; if bent they will kink and rot away, but are quickly replaced by new ones which appear with their tips curled up like a shepherd's crook, but unfurl as they grow.

From the stems young plants are produced in great quantity, and they soon develop their own roots; if left undisturbed many will grow quite large while still attached to the parent. Others get knocked off and float to the surface, where they will form a dense mat. As soon as any of these are large enough to handle they may be rooted in the sand. By this time the parent plant may have grown too big for the tank, and become very buoyant, so that the short, shallow roots can no longer anchor it down. It can now be removed without any trouble or disturbance to the sand, and be replaced by one of the larger youngsters.

The Indian fern in its various stages of development has many uses. Being such a quick grower, it has no equal for clearing green water. Medium-sized plants, if bunched together and planted in a breeding tank, make a good spawning place for egg-layers. A handful of young ferns left floating are ideal for spawning those bubble-nest-building fishes which combine leaves and bubbles. A carpet of young ferns rooted in a breeding tank will hide the spawn of fishes like Danios, who are liable to devour all the eggs they can find. Finally, young plants left floating at the surface make an excellent cover for baby live-bearers and provide good shade from strong light.

CERATOPTERIS THALICTROIDES (Fine-leafed Indian Fern)

This is another good aquarium plant. It is similar in every respect to the broad-leafed species, except that the leaves are smaller and the fronds more divided. The stalks are more easily seen through the tracery of its foliage.

CRYPTOCORYNE BECKETTII

The smallest of the Cryptocorynes at present used by aquarists. The leaves, lanceolate in shape, are a light green shade. The upper surface is smooth, and usually convex in form. Each leaf has a 1″ stem which grows from a root stock. Development is slow. After about a year the whole plant may be lifted and divided for propagation purposes. Occasionally small runners from the parent grow outward for an inch or two, and these may be cut off and transplanted.

The plant rarely exceeds 3″ in height, and then only under strong light, with the leaves growing in a nearly vertical direction. Under subdued illumination, which it prefers, the height may not exceed $1\frac{1}{2}$″, and the leaves may fall into a more horizontal position. *C. beckettii* is used more for compactness than utility. It is suitable for growing in the front of the aquarium.

Cryptocoryne beckettii

Cryptocoryne bulosus

CRYPTOCORYNE BULOSUS

Just introduced by the authors from Thailand, this species (which prefers more light than most Cryptocorynes) is rare, but will surely become very popular. At first glance it resembles *Aponogeton undulatum*. Springing from long stalks, the leaves have a length of 10″, and are $\frac{1}{2}$″ wide, tapering to a point. They are of a bright green, and intensely crinkled. The stem continues right through the leaf to the tip, and the translucent foliage reflects the light as it strikes the shiny, crinkled surface. Growth is slow, but occasional runners spread over the sand. Each produces a new plant, which can be cut off and transplanted when 3″ high.

Cryptocoryne ciliata

Cryptocoryne cordata

CRYPTOCORYNE CILIATA

This is the giant of the genus. When young its pale green pointed leaves resemble *Anubias lanceolata*. As it grows the stems lengthen to 9–10″, and the large oval leaves may measure as much as 8″ × $3\frac{1}{2}$″. These are a pale green, the veining being clearly visible. This is a superb plant; it is expensive, and is uncommon.

CRYPTOCORYNE CORDATA

Until recently this was the most popular of all the Asiatic Crypto-corynes. It grows to a height of 6″ or 7″ and bears numerous leaves, 4″ long by ¾″ wide; these are olive green on top and pink to rusty red underneath. The colour of the under side varies greatly according to the amount of light received. When this is subdued—which the plant prefers —the leaves are more luxuriant, and the under sides deeper in colour. Under powerful illumination the upper sides of the leaves tend to be more yellow, while the lower faces are pale. The foliage is tough, and those species of tropicals that devour plants rarely chew *C. cordata*. Like most of the genus, it is very slow-growing, but may be lifted after 12 months, when small subsidiary plants can be divided from the parent. Once established, quite a thicket can be grown, and will live for years.

CRYPTOCORYNE GRIFFITHII

This plant reaches a height of 12″. The long leaf-stems grow 6″ or 7″ high to bear large, glossy, dark green leaves, 3″ long by 1½″ wide, some-what oval in shape, with a pointed tip. Here and there the under side of the leaf bears brownish-pink dots or blotches. The plant likes subdued light, and should not be disturbed once established.

Under ideal conditions it will flower, sending up a long, trumpet-shaped bloom terminating in a pennant-like tongue. Inside is a long cream-coloured spadix. The spathe is yellowish-green externally, the interior varying from pink to bright red. Once flowering begins a dozen or more blooms may follow each other during the season. The plant is a slow grower, but does send out three or four runners a year. These may be cut off and transplanted when about 3″ high. *C. griffithii* makes a decorative background or centre plant.

CRYPTOCORYNE HARTELIANA

First introduced into Britain by the authors just after the Second World War, the plant has proved to be the best Cryptocoryne to date. The dark green leaves, 6″ long by 1″ wide, are striped longitudinally, with veining of a paler shade. The under side is a vivid bright purple which shines like satin. Under subdued illumination the tints of the leaves are intensified. The under sides become so rich in colour that it is a pity these are mostly hidden from view. Under most conditions *C. harteliana* is a prolific and rapid grower, sending out an array of runners in all directions. If left undisturbed they rapidly cover a large area of sand so thickly that a veritable forest may quickly spring up. The great mass of young plants vie with each other for nourishment. In their struggle they become dwarfed, and their leaves spread horizontally in a dense mat about 2″ above the sand. If any of these struggling youngsters are moved and given greater space they will quickly attain mature size, indicating that no permanent harm has been done.

Cryptocoryne harteliana

A single *C. harteliana* will grow to a height of 12″ and a width of 8″, the long stems being robust enough to support the leaves at a graceful angle, without drooping. Individual mature plants create an excellent centrepiece for the aquarium, or a few specimens spaced along the rear of the tank make a delightful background. Smaller runners, if bunched in the foreground of the tank, will form a dense carpet. Few fishes molest this tough Cryptocoryne. Moreover, being a heavy feeder, the numerous roots absorb quantities of mulm.

CRYPTOCORYNE LONGICAUDA

A recent introduction, this plant has a bright future. Being somewhat like a bigger edition of *C. griffithii*, it bears large, deep green leaves, approximately 4″ long by 2″ wide, on long, rigid stems. Its erect habit of growth makes it ideal as a show-piece. Reproduction is by runners. Like most Cryptocorynes, it is not a rapid grower, but will last for several years.

CRYPTOCORYNE NEVILLII

Pale green in colour, the leaves are long, narrow, and smooth. They grow on stalks about 2″ long. Growth is slow, and therefore its main use is decoration. Propagation is by runners.

CRYPTOCORYNE WILLISII

The brownish-green leaves, 4″ long by ¼″ wide, have wavy edges, and the under sides show red veining. They grow from long, slender stalks which emanate from a root stock. Part of this often emerges from the sand, and forms a kind of trunk from which side-buds, as well as roots, appear. Eventually this trunk grows several inches tall, making the plant

Cryptocoryne willisii

Echinodorus radicans

appear to have pushed itself out of the sand. The top part may be pinched off and, providing some of the aerial roots are attached, may be replanted. The lower half will sprout side-shoots. *C. willisii* is not a prolific grower, nor is it extremely robust. Nevertheless, it is decorative, and somewhat dainty.

Echinodorus intermedius

ECHINODORUS INTERMEDIUS (Amazon Sword Plant)

Here is a magnificent aquarium plant, providing one has sufficient room to house it. When mature it will reach a height of 20″, and spread out to a diameter of 18″. It bears numerous pale green translucent leaves.

Each leaf, growing from a 4″ stem, will reach a length of 14″ by 1¼″ in width. They are usually carried loftily, and do not droop languidly. When rolled between thumb and forefinger the square-sided stems feel like a match-stick. Unfortunately, they are rather brittle, and if severely knocked or bent will kink, and afterwards rot away.

E. intermedius in perfect condition is a truly gorgeous sight, but so often it is marred by torn and broken leaves which tend to turn brown. Grown in soft water, under a good light, the plant throws up from the crown long, flat-sided runners, which grow upward and travel a foot or more just below the surface of the water. At intervals along these runners there are joints, from which young plants appear complete with leaves and small roots; these may be cut off and transplanted when large enough. Because of the numerous large leaves, the Amazon Sword Plant is excellent for combating green water.

ECHINODORUS KALA

This unusual plant is the giant of the family, reaching a height of 2 ft. or more. Where there is insufficient depth of water, the foliage rises well above the surface. The large, thick, oval leaves, 8″ long by 3″ wide, are of a glossy medium green, with lighter veining running longitudinally; each is carried on a stout stem ¼″ thick and up to 14″ in length. The stems emanate from a crown just above the sand. Long, powerful roots spreading a foot or more in all directions anchor the plant firmly in position. Under a good light growth is rapid. Since no runners appear, it is likely that propagation is by seed from the flower stems which are held high above the water. During the winter months the foliage dies down, but growth is resumed in the spring. *E. kala* is only suitable for large, deep aquaria.

ECHINODORUS MARTII

A plant similar to *E. intermedius*, but with broader leaves which are undulated.

ECHINODORUS RADICANS

Here is a beautiful member of the genus, but somewhat difficult to describe, as it has three types of foliage. When young the leaves are rather transparent; they are broad, but taper to a point. Later they develop even longer stalks with floating foliage; finally these stand above the water. In summer the plant is most attractive, but dies down during the winter months. Reproduction is by runners carrying young plants. *E. radicans* also sends up a stalk which bears white flowers. These if pollinated produce seeds, which may be planted to form new specimens.

Once established *E. radicans* should be left alone, as the somewhat tender leaves are easily bruised and damaged by buffeting. Snails ruin the plant by biting holes in its leaves. It is definitely a plant of beauty rather than utility.

ECHINODORUS RANGERI (Broad-leafed Amazon Sword Plant)

A beautiful, showy aquarium plant, which will make a magnificent centrepiece, but needs a fair amount of space. It has broader leaves than *E. intermedius*, but is in all other respects similar.

Echinodorus tenellus

ECHINODORUS TENELLUS (Chain Sword)

This attractive plant resembles most of the Swords, but does not grow so large, being happy in a depth of 10″ of water. Propagation is by runners, which grow from the crown and spread outward along the sand. A young plant appears, but long before it has grown to full size the same runner has travelled on and produced four or five more youngsters, each becoming progressively smaller as the extremity of the runner is reached. Leaving a portion of runner on either side, the plantlets may be cut and transplanted in exactly the same way as for *E. intermedius*.

EGERIA DENSA

This plant, under the name of *Elodea densa*, is very common. The foliage is a darkish green, and forms dense whorls springing from a central stem. Under a strong light it will grow as much as 1″ per day, becoming rather too long and straggly. Stems should be cut back and planted in bunches, when they root easily. Because of its rapid growth a mass of *E. densa* will often prevent the formation of algæ, and help to clear green water.

The plant is illustrated on p. 116.

EICHHORNIA CRASSIPES (Water Hyacinth)

A showy floating plant, though rather large for the average aquarium. The bright green, oval-shaped, spongy leaves rise above the surface from bulbous stems which give the necessary buoyancy. Under suitable conditions the plant bears a head of pale lavender flowers, somewhat like a small hyacinth—hence the common name. Beneath the surface of the water *E. crassipes* sends down a jungle of fine, hairy roots; these are useful for catching adhesive fish-eggs, and make an excellent hiding-place for newly hatched fry. Propagation is by floating runners.

Eleocharis acicularis

ELEOCHARIS ACICULARIS (Hair-grass)

A dainty plant which is a delightful shade of green, and consists of hair-like stems growing to a height of 3–4″. In good light hair-grass sends out numerous runners. Sometimes it divides half-way up the stems, where young plants are formed; these too will send runners downward to reach the sand.

When amassed in a breeding tank Eleocharis is excellent for protecting the spawn of non-adhesive egg-layers. The falling ova drop between the fronds out of reach of the parent fish. Similarly, a mass of hair-grass makes a perfect retreat for young fishes. Unfortunately, it is inclined to die away in winter, especially in fish houses with glass roofs where day-light provides the only illumination.

ELODEA CANADENSIS

Not truly a tropical plant, it is found in natural ponds throughout the temperate regions of North America and Europe. It adapts itself to tropical tanks, but the heat and light force growth so much that it becomes long, straggly, brittle, and tends to be a nuisance. If cut back and planted in bunches it serves for decoration, a hide-out for young fishes, and a good clearer of green water. Another use not generally known is that a large bunch tied loosely with raffia and floated into hard water seems to absorb some of the salts, thereby reducing a certain amount of the hardness.

Elodea crispa   *Elodea canadensis*

ELODEA CRISPA

Another member of the genus, but it has a harsher foliage which grows in tight whorls. Each leaf curls downward and inward so that its tip touches the leaf below. Otherwise the general remarks relating to the genus apply here.

FONTINALIS ANTIPYRETICA

This plant, like the Elodeas, is not recommended for tropical tanks. Its tiny leaves grow from branching stems, which resemble some forms of coral. Being less bushy than *F. gracilis*, it is not even useful for spawning fishes. The plant does not like warm water, and soon dies.

FONTINALIS GRACILIS

Though sometimes seen in aquaria, it rarely lasts long, since its natural habitat is in cool running water, where it attaches itself to stones. Being very finely leaved, and having the stems massed together, the plant looks ideal for use with spawning fishes, and is often sold for this purpose, but it soon loses its dark green leaves and dies off. The minute foliage sheds, and makes quite a mess to clear up. As there are so many more suitable plants, *F. gracilis* is hardly worth buying for warm-water aquaria.

HETERANTHERA ZOSTERÆFOLIA

Not widely used in Britain, mainly on account of its spindly appearance. The plant is attractive because of its delicate form. The tall stems bear small, thin leaves which are pale green in colour; these are stalkless, and grow alternately right and left at $\frac{1}{2}''$ intervals horizontally up the stem. *Heteranthera* can be made to look denser if several stems are planted

Hydrocotyle vulgaris

Heteranthera zosteræfolia

together. It is hardly bushy or robust enough to be used as a spawning or refuge plant. Propagated easily from cuttings.

HYDROCOTYLE VULGARIS

A queer little plant, which unfortunately is not very robust. It is of such a distinctive appearance that it makes a pleasing change in the front of an aquarium. A creeping runner travels along the top of the sand, anchoring itself here and there with short roots. Slender stems, about 1″ apart, grow vertically upward. Each of these bears a single round, flat leaf with an indented border. These circular leaves are pale green and dip slightly in the centre where they join the stalk. Propagation is by division.

HYGROPHILA POLYSPERMA

Wing-Commander L. A. Lynn, to whom this book is dedicated, introduced this excellent plant to Britain in 1945. In a pool near Madras he found *H. polysperma* growing wild, so he brought home some cuttings which he handed to the authors to try out in a tropical aquarium. Thrive it certainly did, and soon many tanks were well stocked with it. Some months later the plant was imported from America, and from both stocks it has now become an established favourite in Britain.

H. polysperma is an excellent grower in neutral water, bearing many pairs of bright green leaves. These grow direct from a central stem, and have no stalks. Under good light the leaves attain a length of 3″ by ¾″ wide, and are lanceolate in shape. When illumination is poor the leaves are smaller. The stems grow quickly, and send out aerial roots. Cuttings root very easily, and if several stems are planted together in a bunch the effect is very pleasing. *H. polysperma* has the advantage of being shallow-rooted; this allows bushy clumps to be transplanted here and there with very little disturbance to the sand. Sufficient clumps will prevent green water. Short, thick bunches are good for use in breeding tanks. The plant is highly recommended for use in all tropical aquaria.

Hygrophila polysperma   *Hygrophila stricta*

HYGROPHILA STRICTA

This plant was introduced by the authors from Thailand in 1955. Already it has become a firm favourite in Britain, and is spreading rapidly.

The plant has a central stem which is thick, strong, and rigid. The leaves, lanceolate in shape, are a beautiful glossy bright green, and attain a length of 5″ by 1¼″ wide; they grow in pairs opposite each other on short stalks. If the plant is left undisturbed it will grow right out of the water. The leaves then become a darker green with a coppery tinge. Small flowers, mauve in colour, resembling miniature antirrhinums, appear in the joints between stem and leaf stalks. If the plant be decapitated, and the top part pushed into the sand, it soon produces a bunch of strong, hairy roots which anchor firmly. This continues to grow in a single column; but the decapitated portion will throw out numerous branches and form a thick tree-like growth, reaching a height of 18″, and spreading out to a diameter of 10″. This will make a magnificent centrepiece. *H. stricta* is a prolific grower, and so easily propagated that even a single leaf nipped off and pushed into the sand will root and start a new plant. One drawback is that snails and some larger fishes seem to enjoy eating the leaves, and so destroy the plant.

LEMNA GIBBA (Duckweed)

Found on most ponds, this miniature-leaved bright green plant and its smaller cousin *L. minor* (lesser duckweed), float at the surface of the water in summer and bear minute submerged roots. In the autumn the plants sink to the bottom and remain inert until the following spring, when they start new growth. Duckweed is usually introduced into the aquarium with pond food, and rapidly spreads over the surface, becoming a pest and shutting off much of the overhead light, but most of the growth can be skimmed off with a net and thrown away, or better still, fed to larger barbs, who will obligingly eat every bit. A rarer species, *L. trisulca*, is similar, but the edges of the leaves are serrated.

Limnophila sessiliflora

LIMNOPHILA SESSILIFLORA (Ambulia)

An excellent importation from India, Ambulia has become very popular. It is a lovely pale green colour, and presents a feathery growth. The leaves radiate from a central stem, making circular fans, which get closer together as they near the top of the plant—this crowns each stalk with a beautiful bunched head. Ambulia requires a fair amount of light, and grows ideally in soft water of a depth of 12″. Rooting should take place in sand which is free of lime. Looking best if planted in bunches of seven or eight strands, the stems splay outward gracefully, and are stiff enough not to droop in an untidy manner. When grown in quantity Ambulia is one of the better plants for counteracting green water.

Aerial roots appear from long stems and sometimes anchor themselves in the sand; from any piece thus layered a new plant will grow. Otherwise propagation is by cuttings. The decapitated stems will bring forth new heads.

Being feathery for catching eggs, and soft enough for the fishes to push in among the fronds, the plant is ideal for spawning many of the egg-laying fishes. If the stalks of Ambulia are crushed between the fingers the sap will be found to give off a pungent odour.

Ludwigia mulerttii   *Egeria densa*

LUDWIGIA MULERTTII

This South American species is the best of the Ludwigias, all of which are really bog plants. Even when growing under congenial conditions in an aquarium, Ludwigia prefers to rise above the surface of the water, and may trail over the top rim of the tank, and cascade down the outside. It is an attractive plant, bearing shiny darkish green obovate leaves, the under sides of which are a beautiful pinkish-brown, sometimes being quite rosy. Unfortunately, the central stems are inclined to twist and droop, giving a straggly appearance when several stems are bunched. Moreover, it does not thrive everywhere. Sometimes the leaves rot and drop off, the plant finally succumbing altogether.

Propagation is by cuttings. In comparison with *Hygrophila polysperma* it is not such a good grower, is less robust, and does not hold itself in such a stately manner. There is a red form which, if its tints remain, adds colour to the aquarium; but usually when this plant is removed from its native home its leaves revert to green.

MACUILAMIA ROTUNDIFOLIA

As its name implies, this plant has round leaves. These grow from a central stem. *M. rotundifolia* is rather like a larger-leafed edition of Bacopa. The foliage is a bright green, and somewhat thick. Propagation is by cuttings.

Macuilamia rotundifolia

Marsilea quadrifolia

MARSILEA QUADRIFOLIA (Australian Four-leafed Clover)

An aquatic plant that resembles field clover. The small, round leaves, dark green in colour, are carried on thin stems about 2″ high. When in alkaline water the plant spreads rapidly by sending out runners, frequently in a straight line. These give the appearance of a line of posts. Each stem is rooted at the bottom, and if the runners are severed here and there a section of five or six stems, still joined together, may be transplanted. If given too much light the plant stems become so long and straggly that they reach the water surface.

MICRANTHEMUM ORBICULATUM

Very like, but not to be confused with, Lysimachia (Creeping Jenny) which rarely survives long as an under-water aquatic. *M. orbiculatum* has small, oval-shaped, pale green leaves, which grow on short stalks carried

Micranthemum orbiculatum

on the main slender stem. Aerial roots are profuse, and if cuttings are made and placed together, the plant may be grown in dainty clusters.

MYRIOPHYLLUM BRAZILIENSE

The water milfoils supply the aquarist with many species of superb aquarium plants. They are perhaps the most widely used of all in breeding tanks, especially with the smaller egg-laying species. All have long stems from which a profusion of hair-like fronds grow radially. These fronds are in themselves divided, and each bears smaller fronds along its length. Some species attain a height of 2 ft. or more, and end in thick, clustered heads. Nearly all the milfoils are a bright green, but one or two kinds are a coppery red. *M. braziliense* is typical of the genus, and may be readily identified because the heads at the top of each stem close up at dusk. Propagated from cuttings which quickly take root in the sand.

MYRIOPHYLLUM HIPPUROIDES

A fine, dainty plant of bushy growth and pale green in colour. The branched fronds grow opposite each other from a central stem; they are rather widely spaced apart, giving a less heavy appearance than other species of Myriophyllum. Best planted in bunches, it does not seem to collect so much thread algæ or harbour such quantities of mulm as other members of this group. Propagation is by cuttings, and under good conditions growth is fairly rapid. *M. hippuroides* is an excellent spawning plant.

| *Myriophyllum* | *Myriophyllum* | *Myriophyllum* |
| *proserpinacoides* | *hippuroides* | *verticillatum* |

MYRIOPHYLLUM PROSERPINACOIDES (Parrot's Feather)

This species is not particularly suited to the aquarium, and is more of a bog plant. In a tank the stems will grow out of the water, trail over the top, and hang down outside. It is a very pale green, the leaves growing in dense whorls round the stem. The plant produces white flowers. Propagation may be made from cuttings.

MYRIOPHYLLUM VERTICILLATUM

Being both useful and beautiful, this is the most popular feathery plant used in the aquarium. Up the entire length of the stem dark green fronds radiate thickly, and these terminate in a small, but showy, head. To look its best several stems should be planted together, when the feathery mass appear to be branches of one bushy plant.

The fine fronds of this plant make it ideal as a spawning medium. Most egg-laying fishes delight in quivering side by side as they push their way through the silky texture of the foliage. The shining eggs deposited in a clump are easily seen, as the network of leaves supports masses of spawn.

Myriophyllum has two drawbacks. In the first place, many algæ are apt to adhere or entwine themselves tenaciously round the fronds, and are difficult to remove without doing damage. Secondly, where an aquarium contains much mulm, this is stirred up if an aerator is used. The sediment then settles and sticks to the foliage, clogging it with

Naias microdon

unsightly dirt. The green stems become brownish, and, if not cleaned, the coating will cut off the light rays. The lack of illumination will make the plant brittle, so that it tends to disintegrate, and may even die.

There is a red variety, *M. heterophyllum*, but unfortunately it often reverts to green when removed from its natural habitat. If the foliage can be kept red it makes a beautiful contrast to other green plants in the aquarium. Like all the milfoils, propagation is by cuttings.

NAIAS MICRODON

A dainty pale green fronded plant with many side-shoots from the main stem. The spear-shaped leaves form cluster-like heads at the extremities of each branch. It prefers a good light, and will grow either planted or floating, being prolific in either case. Long stems cut in half and bunched together in the sand form a bushy growth. This plant is very similar in shape to *Peplis diandra*, but is not so brittle, and its leaves are perhaps paler and thinner.

NITELLA GRACILIS

This useful plant, though common in America, has yet to be widely adopted by British aquarists. It is a rapid grower, especially in alkaline water receiving good light. The pale green fronds sprout sparsely from the central stem, forming a very open network. The plant is somewhat harsh to the touch, and is brittle. Any pieces broken off grow independently without roots. For spawning purposes it can be left to develop a mass of growth at the surface of the water, or several strands can be anchored in the sand to form a bush.

Nymphæa species

NUPHARS and NYMPHÆAS

There are numerous cold-water Nuphars and tropical Nymphæas sold to aquarists as aquarium plants. Most of these are unsuitable for tropical aquaria, the former on account of their preference for cooler water, the latter because they require too much space. Nuphars can sometimes be acclimatized and look decorative. From a stout rhizome pale green stems shoot out and bear heart-shaped leaves of a bright green. In good light growth is rapid. But this often results in the leaves climbing to the surface, only long stalks being seen through the front glass of the tank. Under poor light the leaves tend to rot round the edges, and are often attacked by a virus which punctures the foliage with many small holes; these enlarge as the perimeter rots away.

Occasionally side-shoots appear on the rhizome, which by now has grown long, stout roots. If the side-shoots are cut off and transplanted many will rot from their open wound. To prevent this trouble the severed shoots should be tied with a piece of string and suspended from the top of the tank. The leaves should remain under water, but the cut rhizome is kept exposed to the air. Oxidation takes place, the cut portion turning brown and becoming sealed. When hardened the cutting may be planted in the sand.

PEPLIS DIANDRA

Frequently misnamed *Didiplis diandra*, it comes from North America, particularly Texas and Missouri. It is very brittle and weak, and not such a good aquarium plant as *Naias microdon* (see p. 120) which it strongly resembles.

PISTIA STRATIOTES (Water Lettuce)

Possibly the prettiest of the floating plants, appearing like a miniature velvety cabbage lettuce. The spongy, fluted leaves stand above the water, and are covered with fine, silky hairs. The plant produces numerous floating runners; these, under a good light and in a moisture-ladened atmosphere, multiply quickly. Beneath the surface bunches of hairy roots make an ideal spawning ground for fish such as *Aphyosemion australe*; the growth also creates a refuge for newly hatched fry.

This plant is illustrated on p. 103.

RICCIA FLUITANS (Crystalwort)

The fronds of this rootless plant are a very bright green; they grow in all directions, and each section is shaped like the letter Y. Crystalwort must have plenty of light; then growth is so prolific that it forms a dense mat, sometimes 2" or 3" in depth, at the surface of the water.

Because of its rapid growth the plant is a good oxygenator, becoming literally filled with silver bubbles of this life-supporting gas. The mass of fronds can easily be broken up and transferred to other tanks.

Unfortunately, Riccia has two drawbacks. Firstly, it becomes so much entangled with bladderwort and thread algæ that it is impossible entirely to remove these from the fronds. Secondly, without artificial illumination the foliage tends to die off in the winter, and is difficult to keep going from one year to another. For breeding purposes the plant is ideal for all egg-layers that spawn near the surface. Furthermore, bubble-nest-building fishes that use plants to bind their bubble nest together utilize crystalwort.

SAGITTARIA LORATA

An attractive member of this hardy genus. The grassy, emerald green leaves are thickish in section, and narrow. The foliage, growing from a crown, is carried nearly vertically for two-thirds of its length, then curves outward in a graceful arc. The plant is an exceptionally good grower, under most conditions. Propagation is by runners, and is so prolific that a considerable mass of youngsters will soon develop. Cut runners transplant easily.

SAGITTARIA MICROFOLIA

This diminutive plant grows numerous short, sword-like leaves, $\frac{1}{8}"$ wide and up to 2" in length. These shoot upward and outward from a crown. Given a fair amount of light, and placed with smaller fishes who will not continually uproot it, numerous runners are sent out, and soon create a miniature bright green lawn in the front of the aquarium. The runners often form a chain of plants; these can be severed and transplanted elsewhere, for they have surprisingly good roots in relation to their size. When *S. microfolia* thoroughly carpets a breeding tank it makes an excellent refuge for non-adhesive fish eggs which the parents would otherwise devour.

Sagittaria lorata

Sagittaria natans   *Sagittaria microfolia*

Sagittaria sinensis

SAGITTARIA NATANS

Of all the Sagittarias, this is the most common, not only because it grows almost anywhere, but also on account of its average height, which suits most aquaria. The grassy leaves grow to a length of 8″ to 10″, and are about ¼″ wide. They are darkish green in colour, and are thick and tough. If they are closely examined very thin grains will be seen running across the leaves. *S. natans* will send out several runners which soon form a dense thicket. Few fishes attack its leaves, and therefore once established it will last a long time and multiply.

SAGITTARIA SINENSIS (Giant Sagittaria)

This is the largest member of this excellent genus of aquarium plants. All are hardy enough to stand acid, neutral, or alkaline water, and grow in either good or poor light. Nature, it would seem, has supplied Sagittarias in stock sizes to suit all aquaria, large or small. Even in a single tank they provide the aquarist with beautiful greenery ranging from small in the front, medium in the middle, to tall at the back. *S. sinensis* has broad, thick leaves which splay gracefully upward and outward. Propagation is by runners.

SALVINIA BRAZILIENSIS

A floating plant which grows in short lengths, each of which consists of a stem with a row of small leaves on either side. A larger species, *S. natans*, has bigger and thicker leaves. In both species the foliage is hairy and varies in colour from medium green to brownish-red. There are short roots. Development is rapid under strong light, and soon the surface of the water is carpeted. Such growth helps to combat green water; otherwise the plant is of little use.

Samolus floribundus

SAMOLUS FLORIBUNDUS (Green Water Roses)

Quite an attractive pale green plant, though more like a young lettuce than a rose. When growth is short the top view resembles a rosette. The leaves sprout from a crown and gradually broaden up their length to a round end. It prefers a medium light and not too high a temperature; even so, it develops slowly. Reproduction is from young plants which grow up through the centre of the rosette. These should be carefully separated and replanted.

Saururus cernus

SAURURUS CERNUS (Lizard's Tail)

This attractive plant does well in tropical tanks with a medium light. It is sometimes nicknamed "Mouse Ears," though "Red Squirrel's Ears" would be more appropriate, as each leaf ends in a point. Stems bearing single leaves rise from the root stock. These may be divided and replanted.

Synnema triflorum

SYNNEMA TRIFLORUM (Water Wisteria)

A recent introduction, this plant has quickly gained favour. Pale green leaves on short stalks grow from a central stem. The foliage at first is oval in shape, with a slightly serrated edge. However, as it ages the leaves split into fronds, not unlike those of *Ceratopteris thalictroides*, but carried horizontally. The full development of the plant is not yet known by the authors; very probably it will flower above water. Propagation at present is mainly by cuttings, or the aerial roots on the stem often layer the plant naturally.

VALLISNERIA GIGAS

All members of the genus are grassy-leaved plants growing from a crown. Beginners sometimes confuse Vallisneria with Sagittaria. The leaves of Vallisneria are not so thick in section. They are more ribbon-like, have a more delicate appearance, and are more translucent. If they are examined closely faint grains are seen running longitudinally through the foliage. Each leaf has a wide central band which is edged on either side by a narrower one.

V. gigas, as the name implies, is the giant of the family, and is rather too large for the home aquarium. It bears leaves $1\frac{1}{4}''$ wide by 5 or 6 feet in length, and makes an effective background in huge tanks such as those seen in public aquaria. The plant does not like a great heat.

VALLISNERIA SPIRALIS

Well deserves its reputation of being one of the best aquarium plants. The tall, narrow, pale green leaves, $\frac{1}{4}''$ in width, reach a length of 18" to 3 ft., and will trail over the surface of the water if the depth is insufficient. *V. spiralis* likes plenty of light, when it sends out numerous shallow-rooted runners. These soon make a perfect background of graceful growth. Propagation may also be from seeds, the female sending up long, thread-like, spiral flower stems. It is from these that the plant derives its name.

Vallisneria torta   *Vallisneria spiralis*

VALLISNERIA TORTA

Although fairly common, this is one of the most beautiful grass-like plants. From a crown a cluster of broad ribbon-like leaves of a brilliant green grow to a height of 12". These are gracefully twisted to form a spiral growth. Contrary to general belief, the plant does not like excessively strong light. Under these conditions the foliage grows pale and spindly, eventually becoming so weak that it fades away altogether. Under medium illumination the leaves remain a deep green and will be $\frac{1}{2}''$ wide, the three longitudinal veining bands becoming very pronounced.

Propagation is by runners; these often extend into a chain of plants. *V. torta* is somewhat crisp, and the leaves will crack across if bent too sharply. It is often alleged that Vallisneria and Sagittaria are allergic to each other and will not grow in the same tank. The authors, however, are not convinced that this is true, for clumps of both of these plants do well together in some tanks, yet not in others. It would seem that conditions are the governing factor. Sagittaria will thrive in a weak light or a strong light, whereas Vallisneria abhors extremes in either direction.

CHAPTER XII

FISHES IN GENERAL

FOR A MUCH LONGER PERIOD THAN MAN FISHES HAVE BEEN IN EXISTENCE. Even so, many of the primitive ones are extinct, and only a few super orders exist to-day. Of these the largest are called Teleosteans; it is to this super order that all the fishes in this book belong.

The super orders are divided into orders, sub-orders, divisions, families, genera, and species. In this volume we will cover only the families, genera, and species, since certain families of fishes have similar bone construction, and so afford a convenient method of classification. To know the genus is helpful, because the majority of species of a given genus conform to a similar breeding pattern. Though there are exceptions, nine times out of ten the standard breeding procedure will prove successful. In every case the species will be stated, since all aquarists will wish to identify the individual fishes they possess.

Throughout the book the common signs ♂ denoting the male and ♀ the female will be employed.

It appears to the authors that the average hobbyist will not wish to go too deeply into the extremely complicated study of ichthyology. But those wishing to do so are referred to the *Cambridge Natural History: Fishes*. This excellent work covers classification, anatomy, organs, and senses.

External covering

Externally most fishes are covered with fine skin, scales, or bony plates. These scales and plates overlap rather like tiles on a roof, the anterior covering the posterior, and forming a complete shield which also presents a streamlined surface to the water. The scales are covered with a protective mucus.

The fins

Usually there are seven fins. Three of these are single (dorsal, anal, and caudal); the remaining four are in two pairs (one pair of pectorals and one pair of ventrals). Some species have the dorsal split into two separate parts, while others possess a small adipose fin situated on the back between the dorsal and the caudal (Fig. 21). A few fishes have dorsal, caudal, and ventral fins united into one continuous median fin. The various fins and their functions will now be briefly considered.

The dorsal fin stands up on the fish's back, and may be in one piece or divided into two separate parts. When divided the front portion is called the anterior dorsal, the rear section the posterior dorsal. The front rays, whether single or double, are usually hard and spiny; those in the rear are

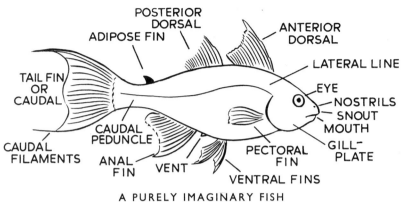

POSTERIOR DORSAL
ADIPOSE FIN
ANTERIOR DORSAL
LATERAL LINE
TAIL FIN OR CAUDAL
EYE
NOSTRILS
SNOUT
MOUTH
CAUDAL PEDUNCLE
GILL-PLATE
CAUDAL FILAMENTS
ANAL FIN
VENT
PECTORAL FIN
VENTRAL FINS

A PURELY IMAGINARY FISH

FIG. 21

soft. The dorsal fin or fins act as a stabilizer, and keep the fish in an upright position when cutting through the water.

The pectoral fins are to be found on each side of the body, behind and just below the gills. The pectorals correspond to human arms, or the fore-legs of an animal. In a few species these fins are used as fore-legs, enabling the fish to crawl forward in an irregular manner. The pectorals are used mainly for balance and in swimming upward and downward. These movements are performed by inclining the angle of the leading and trailing edges. This means that when moving forward the water pressure bears against the pectorals, as does the wind against the wings of a bird or an aeroplane, giving lift or dive as required. When paddling the fish moves the pectoral fins forward by flattening them horizontally, like feathering an oar. They are brought back vertically, thereby reacting at a maximum against the water. Moreover, to minimize resistance, these fins are somewhat compressed on the forward stroke, but they are expanded to obtain a greater effect when moving backward.

Another use of the pectorals is seen when a stationary fish desires to turn. The fins are again employed like oars. By moving one forward and the other backward, the fish can pivot on its own axis. Lastly, the pectorals are used as a brake when the fish is slowing down and stopping. This action corresponds to holding a paddle rigidly below the water surface when halting a canoe.

Beneath the fish project the second pair of fins, known as the pelvic or ventral fins. These correspond to the hind-legs of an animal, and some species of fishes use the ventrals to cling to and move along flat surfaces. Generally, however, they act as stabilizers, performing a similar function to the anti-roll devices now fitted to each side of the hull of many ships. If one ventral fin is cut off, a fish is unable to swim in an upright position, and may roll over and even turn upside down. A few species use the ventrals as a form of basket for the temporary carrying of eggs.

Behind the ventrals is the anal fin. This acts as a keel to keep the fish in an upright position, and helps to steer it straight when gliding ahead.

The forward rays are often hard and spiny, the remainder being soft. In the live-bearing species the anal fin of males undergoes a change. Originally it is fan-shaped like that of a female, but in males at puberty the front rays get thicker and form a pencil-like appendage known as the gonopodium. Normally this is carried with the tip pointing backward, but can be moved at will either sideways or forward. When breeding the gonopodium is pointed forward and the tip inserted into the vent of the female. Spermatozoa are injected, and the ova are fertilized inside the female's body. This subject is dealt with more fully in the chapter on live-bearing fishes (Chapter XIII).

Finally, we come to the caudal or tail fin. This is the principal means of locomotion, and acts as a rudder for turning. Beautifully streamlined, the caudal is a perfect instrument for under-water propulsion and navigation.

Propulsion

Man's nearest approach to a fish's caudal fin is a propeller, which, though effective, is nothing like so efficient. The rotating blades of the propeller create a pressure which drives the ship forward. Nevertheless, a resistance is set up in front of the propeller which lowers efficiency. Moreover, the spinning blades cause the water to move backward in a spiral. This means that the propeller is pushing on water spiralling in the same direction as the blades; but the push would be greater if the water were turning in the opposite direction. If one stirs water in a bucket at first a resistance will be felt, but as the water gains speed the back pressure falls to practically nil. Now reverse the motion, and the resistance will be found to be very great. The tail fin of a fish operates on this principle. It is continually pushing against water moving in the opposite direction to the movement of the fin (Fig. 22).

It may be thought that in swinging from side to side the tail must also encounter a back pressure, but this is not the case, as will be seen in Fig. 22.

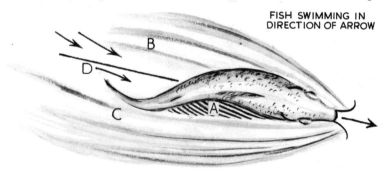

FISH SWIMMING IN DIRECTION OF ARROW

CAUDAL PEDUNCLE OF BODY MOVING FORWARD MEETS LITTLE RESISTANCE BECAUSE OF SLIPSTREAM (A). POWERFUL STROKE OF TAIL FROM B TO C DRIVES FISH FORWARD. AFTERWARDS WATER AT D TENDS TO RUSH IN, GIVING ADDED IMPETUS.

FIG. 22

The slight curve made by the fish's body shown in the shaded portion permits most of the slipstream of the water to pass by when the tail is curved as shown, and no back pressure is encountered. Furthermore, when in this position the rays of the fin are closed, making it narrower. At the same time the upper or lower edge is inclined so that the fin may cut with a minimum resistance through the water. And what is more, the forward movement of the fish would cause a vacuum to form behind it, were it not for the water rushing in to fill the void. This water, flowing in behind the fish, actually provides a forward impetus.

Now the tail is about to begin the powerful backward stroke. First, the inclined fin is straightened, and the rays are spread out to make as large a surface as possible. It is then thrust backward against the incoming water. This action produces the maximum force to propel the fish forward. At the same time the curve of the body is straightened, and the fish speeds like an arrow with negligible resistance. This process is repeated as the tail moves from side to side.

So great is the impetus of this action that one stroke of the tail can propel a fish, not only many times its own length, but frequently enables it to leave the water and travel many yards through the air. The so-called flying fish does not use its pectoral fins as air-beating wings. They are merely employed to prolong the glide.

Eyes

The eyes are generally large, and so placed that the fish is able to see in all directions. Fishes have no eyelids, and vision is acute. Some of the mud skippers have eyes perched on the top of their heads. In Anableps, the Four-eyed Fish, the retina is of double formation, so that the lower pair has an all-round under-water view, while the top pair covers aerial vision. A few species which have lived in subterranean streams where there is no light have no eyes, as these organs would be useless.

Nostrils

Between the eyes and the mouth are situated the nostrils. These enable the fish to smell within a limited range—sharks and piranhas soon gather on the scent of blood—and, like human beings, the nasal organs help to provide the sense of taste, which accounts for some particles of food being eaten, while others are rejected.

Mouth

Most fishes have large mouths, often equipped with sharp teeth for gripping and biting, though mastication of food is usually performed by bony plates in the throat. Some species have sucker lips to enable them to cling to leaves, or rocks, and browse on algal growth. Besides eating, the mouth is used to draw in water, which is passed through the gills.

Gills

These highly complicated organs, equipped internally with fine capillary tubes, extract the oxygen from the water and pass it into the blood-stream. Some fishes possess a labyrinth situated above and behind the roof of the mouth. The species which are endowed with this organ rise to the surface of the water, take a mouthful of air from the atmosphere, and store a certain amount of oxygen in the labyrinth.

A few species are equipped to take a mouthful of air from above the surface of the water, which is then passed through the intestines. These, being lined with many capillaries, are able to extract the oxygen, the unwanted gases being expelled through the anus. The gills are covered by the operculum, or gill-plate, for protection.

Anus

Behind the ventral fins is the anus, through which waste products are discharged. In some species immediately behind the anus is the cloaca, or terminus of the urinary and genital ducts.

Lateral line

Running along each side of the fish is the lateral line. This may be seen on most fishes, and looks as though it had been scratched with a pin. The lateral line is not always straight from gill-plate to caudal peduncle. In some species it takes an upward curve behind the gills, descending again to finish straight through the caudal peduncle. In other species the line will take a downward arc behind the gills.

The lateral line consists of canals which contain sense organs developed in the epidermis. These pick up sound waves travelling through the water and, it is thought, enable fishes to recognize their own species by the frequency of the waves received. Different wave lengths may give warnings of enemies. In some cases vibrations are also passed to the swim-bladder, which acts as an auxiliary hearing organ.

Colour

There are special pigment-containing cells, called chromatophores, in a fish's skin. These cells are capable of expansion and contraction. This is shown very diagrammatically in Fig. 23. If several chromatophores in close proximity begin to expand colour spreads. Suppose all the chromatophores in this part are red; then a red patch will develop. But where the

CELL CONTAINING   FULLY
PIGMENT CONTRACTED   EXPANDING   EXPANDED

CHROMATOPHORE, GREATLY ENLARGED

FIG. 23

cells are differently coloured a mixture or blending produces another hue. Similarly, when the cells contract a red patch on the fish may shrink into a few brown spots or bars.

Light acting on the visual organs often brings about an expansion or contraction of the colour cells, thus enabling a fish to match its surroundings. Emotions transmitted through the nervous system also affect the colour cells, accounting for brilliant hues at courting time. Fear usually results in a shrinkage of the cells, and a corresponding loss of colour. Finally, age and health affect the chromatophores, and are responsible for brilliance, or lack of it.

Another factor of importance regarding coloration is that fishes possess a peculiar reflective tissue. This tissue contains iridocytes formed of guanin, a product of waste excretion. It is deposited in granules in the skin and muscles. Iridocytes are opaque, and highly reflective. Light striking the tissue is reflected back and split up into prismatic colours. This accounts for the brilliant iridescence displayed by most fishes.

Although both chromatophores and iridocytes are present, where chromatophores are plentiful iridocytes are scarce, and vice versa. Chromatophores are abundant on the head, back, and upper sides of most fishes. It is here that pigmented coloration is seen. But on the lower sides and belly, chromatophores are scanty and iridocytes abound. Here there is little pigment; what one sees is reflected light split into one or more of the colours of the spectrum. Thus the silvery belly of a fish may shine pink when viewed from one position, yet look pale blue if seen from a different angle.

Internal organs

Internally fishes have a nervous system and the usual organs, such as heart, liver, kidneys, intestines, but to go fully into all these is beyond the scope of this book. A brief reference, however, will be made to the swim-bladder and ova.

Swim-bladder

The function of the swim-bladder is to render the fish, bulk for bulk, of the same weight as the water which it displaces. This enables equilibrium to be reached, so that the fish floats without effort at different levels. On rising or sinking it is subjected to an increase or decrease of hydrostatic pressure, bringing about an expansion or contraction of the volume of gas in the swim-bladder. To counteract this, gas is either absorbed from the swim-bladder, or more gas is secreted into it.

Ova

There are two types of ova—pelagic, which float, and demersal, which are larger, heavier, and always tend to sink. The outer membrane may be viscid and adhesive, in which case these eggs stick to rocks or plants, and do not always fall to the bottom. The eggs of some fishes are equipped at one end with several fibres, so that when deposited they stick and hang.

When fanned by the parents they wave up and down like seaweed swaying in the tide.

Each ovum has a minute nucleus surrounded by a small mass of protoplasm and a large quantity of yolk, the whole being enveloped in protective membranes. Near the nucleus the egg membranes are perforated by a small aperture. This is so minute that only a single spermatozoon can enter at a time.

When spawning the female discharges her eggs, and the male ejects thousands of spermatozoa into the surrounding water. The majority of these die, since only one is necessary to fertilize each egg. Nevertheless, thousands of spermatozoa are necessary to ensure that one shall find its way through the minute opening of the ovum.

When the head of the sperm penetrates the nucleus the egg is fertilized and undergoes a change; the cells divide and development is initiated. The embryo in the egg lives on the yolk. After emerging, nourishment is provided by the remaining yolk contained in a sac attached to the fry. When this is fully absorbed the baby fish is strong enough to go in search of food.

METHODS OF REPRODUCTION

Fishes have three main methods of reproduction:

(i) Oviparous—*i.e.*, producing young by means of eggs expelled from the body.
(ii) Ovoviviparous, or the production of young by eggs which hatch within the body itself, not nourished by the mother.
(iii) Viviparous, the giving birth to live young, nourished by the mother.

The oviparous species may be subdivided into five categories:

(i) Fishes which scatter non-adhesive eggs.
(ii) Species which drop or attach semi-adhesive eggs.
(iii) Bubble-nest builders (Anabantidæ).
(iv) Those which carefully deposit and tend their eggs (*e.g.*, Cichlidæ).
(v) Mouth breeders—*i.e.*, fishes which after laying eggs pick them up and hatch them in the mouth, eventually expelling free-swimming fry (Cichlidæ, and some Anabantidæ also).

Each of the foregoing will be dealt with in the relevant chapters. The keen aquarist will wish not only to keep fishes, but also to achieve success in breeding. With this object in view, at the beginning of each section we will give the general characteristics relating to a family; individual features will be specified under the appropriate species. Most details of breeding which appear in the following chapters are from the authors' practical experiences. It has not, however, been possible to possess and breed every fish suitable for aquaria. For this reason are included a few authentic accounts of breeding achieved by personal friends who have been successful. These special cases are stated. In certain instances suggested methods of breeding are based on probabilities.

CHAPTER XIII

LIVE-BEARING FISHES

SINCE MOST BEGINNERS IN THE TROPICAL FISH HOBBY START WITH LIVE-bearers, these will be dealt with first. The species are distinguished from the egg-layers in that at puberty the anal fin of the male live-bearer becomes thickened and rod-like, the organ being called a gonopodium. This is normally pointed backward, but can be moved at will sideways and forward. When mating the tip is inserted into the vent of the female; spermatozoa are injected, and the eggs fertilized.

The female has the normal-shaped anal fin. Slightly forward of this, inside her body, appears a dark area known as the gravid spot. It is, in fact, equivalent to the womb, but, unlike mammals, the egg is not attached to the mother's body and fed by her direct. Each egg contains an embryo, and is well furnished with nutritive elements on which it feeds during development.

As the eggs incubate the eyes of the fry are sometimes visible through the thin walls of the gravid spot. To accommodate the developing eggs the mother's body expands, becoming deeper and broader. A few days before delivery she develops a bulge below the gills, her outline becoming fairly square in this region, while the gravid spot has enlarged its area. When the young are perfectly formed they lie in a semicircular position and are delivered, usually tail first, one at a time over a period of hours. On birth the fry fall a few inches through the water, but quickly straighten out and, if strong enough, make for cover among the plants. If these are not near by the fry sink to the bottom and take refuge in the sand, mulm, or whatever other cover there may be. They lie motionless for a short time while gathering strength.

The majority of live-bearers are born about $\frac{1}{4}''$ long, and all their fins are formed in the normal shape. They are not only much larger than the newly hatched young of egg-layers, but are also capable of swimming and looking for food and protection. Most newly born live-bearers are large enough not to require infusoria as first food. In a few hours after birth they will take brine shrimp and sifted Daphnia.

Mating

The males are persistent drivers, so mating occurs frequently. Where a few live-bearers of the same species are kept breeding is inevitable. Any male will serve any female of the same species, so that the parents do not pair off. Neither is there a prolonged courtship; the males merely seize any opportunity afforded them, though the females rarely, if ever, make advances.

For the benefit of beginners who are anxious to know whether their specimens are breeding the answer, nine times out of ten, is 'yes.' If any particular male is observed, sooner or later he will be seen darting around a female, his fins spread and quivering. Then, advancing from behind, he will momentarily bring his gonopodium to a forward or sideways position and insert it into the vent of the female. Often the resulting thrust tips her slightly off balance, so that her tail end is tilted upward.

Gestation

The period of gestation depends considerably on temperature, and on the species concerned. Moreover, since mating occurs so often, it is difficult to give the exact number of days from fertilization to birth. Generally speaking, it is about 30 to 35 days at a temperature of 76°F. Experience will be the best guide as to the probable date of birth, but the size of the female and the squareness of her body under the chin give some indication.

Delivery

From the foregoing it will be seen that there is no reliable indication of imminent delivery, so the beginner is advised to remove the female to a separate breeding tank long before she is expected to give birth. It is only necessary to transfer her, the male having completed his function some time before. Furthermore, it is dangerous to handle or disturb a female on the point of delivery. Such a move can cause premature birth, and the young may be born with part of the yolk sac on which they feed not fully absorbed. This frequently causes the death of the fry. Although giving premature birth does not appear to harm the female, the natural cycle has been curtailed, and this can do her no good.

Size of brood

From 8 to 30 or 40 fry may be expected from a young female; medium-sized ones may produce 50 to 100; large fishes can bear from 100 to 250.

Cannibalism

Most fishes large enough to eat others often attempt to do so. This applies equally to the mother, as she is not averse to devouring her brood. In a thickly planted breeding tank a lone female may not be able to find and eat all her own young; some will escape among the plants. To save most of her brood she should be put into a large trap so designed that the fry can easily escape. (See Trapping, opposite.)

Later Broods

Female live-bearers may produce three or four, sometimes five, consecutive broods from the original mating. Each family is delivered after a lapse of the normal gestation period.

Selective Breeding

If the aquarist desires to produce young live-bearers from a particular male and female he should select a young female while she is still in the virgin state, and isolate her until large enough to mate with the chosen male. As a result she will produce several consecutive broods from this one mating. Had the female been previously mated she might bear a number of families as a result of being served once by a male. Although after her first delivery she may be placed alone with a special male, there is no certainty that her next brood will be from this masculine partner; they could be a second family from the original mating. A female may be allowed to produce her succession of broods; then, if after an interval of at least another month she has delivered no more young, it would be safe to serve her by a selected male.

Cross-mating

Many beginners are under the impression that if they keep in a community tank a pair of red platys, a pair of blue platys, and a pair of tuxedo platys, each male will mate with his own coloured female. But this, of course, is not the case. Any male of a species will serve any female of the same species, irrespective of colour. Thus if the breeder wishes to produce pure red platys none of his female reds must ever be allowed to come in contact with any other coloured males.

Hybrids

It is possible to produce hybrids intentionally or by accident. Usually the male and female of two different species are brought together, having never seen one of their own kind before. Nevertheless, mating does not always take place, and even though it may occur, young are not necessarily produced. Moreover, often these hybrids are sterile like mules. It is, however, possible to produce new coloured platys by applying Mendel's laws of inheritance. But to go into genetics here would take up too much space, and those aquarists keen on this subject will find plenty of books devoted to it. Here we must point out that it is quite impossible to cross a live-bearer with an egg-layer. Often a strange fish appears in an aquarium and the owner is convinced that it is such a cross. But, of course, it must be that the newcomer has hatched from an egg which has been introduced into the tank on a plant or in a net.

Trapping

To save as many young as possible the expectant female should be transferred in a jam-jar and placed into a trap in a separate breeding tank. This tank should be moderately shallow, and well planted. To allow the female ample room for free movement the trap should be capacious— say 8″ long by 4″ wide. It should be suspended so that the depth of water inside is about 4″. The advantage in keeping the water shallow is twofold. Firstly, the hydrostatic pressure is low; secondly, the young have to fall only a few inches to reach safety. Where floating plants are also used these should be placed outside the trap, as the fry tend to hide in the foliage. If this is inside their refuge is insecure.

Removal of female

After giving birth to her brood the female will be quite slim, and the gravid spot considerably shrunken. She may now be removed from the breeding tank, and returned to her normal quarters. She will most likely be hungry, and is sure to be pestered by the males. For these reasons if a spare aquarium is available she will appreciate a short resting period. Unless it is desired to house another female about to deliver young, the trap may also be taken out. It is important to remember that the breeding tank has a limited capacity. If over-crowded with young fishes they will not grow rapidly; on the contrary, too many may result in considerable losses.

Feeding young live-bearers

As these fishes are fairly large at birth, feeding is no problem. They will take fine powdered dried foods, brine shrimp, Cyclops, and sifted Daphnia. Only small amounts should be fed. Feeding little and often is better than a large meal once a day. The fry have small stomachs, and cannot hold much. On the other hand, because of their limited capacity the amount eaten does not last long, and replenishment is frequently necessary. A tiny pinch of dried food, as much as will go on the end of a match-stick, should be fed three times a day or, alternatively, a teaspoonful of sifted Daphnia or Cyclops twice daily, since these crustacea hop about in the water where they can easily be seen and caught by the fry. Furthermore, most will be devoured, and the risk of fouling the tank is minimized. To sift Daphnia they are netted from the can in a fine muslin net, which is then suspended in the fry tank for a few minutes. Only the finest Daphnia will pass through the mesh; the bigger ones remaining in the net can be fed to larger fishes in another aquarium.

Growth of fry

Given normal healthy conditions and correct feeding, the fry should double their length in a month. By then there will be signs of sex development in some cases. When line breeding to bring out a certain characteristic the sexes should be segregated as soon as possible in order that, say, a virgin daughter may later be mated back to her father. Likewise, the choicest son can be crossed back to his mother.

The baby fishes may be returned to the community tank only when they are large enough not to be eaten by the bigger occupants. This may mean sorting the babies into two sizes, the smaller ones being put back in the breeding tank. It is often surprising to find that many of the smaller fry, suspected of being runts, now put on rapid growth. This is because they have more room and are able to receive their full share of the food which was previously grabbed by their larger brothers and sisters.

Sexing and sex changing

It is often thought that once young fishes begin to sex they cease to grow. This is not necessarily so. Nevertheless, those which are the last to develop the gonopodium often become the biggest. The aquarist should give adequate food and space in order to promote early growth.

Some cases are on record of females which, after bearing young, have developed into males. This has now been stated to be impossible.

HEMIRHAMPHIDÆ

These quaint little fishes (known as the Half-beaks), of which there are many species, all come from the Far East. They have tubular bodies and a long, protruding lower jaw. The upper jaw is pointed, but usually extends only about half the length of the lower. The jaws are rigid, but can be broken and snapped off when fighting, or if the fish hits a solid object head on when travelling at speed. Careless handling may also damage this magnificent feature. Many of the species come from coastal areas; some inhabit brackish water, others live in fresh.

These fishes have been used by natives for fighting, wagers being placed on the outcome. Two males will often spar and interlock their jaws, writhing and twisting in an endeavour to throw the opponent off balance, tire him out, or even break his jaws. Frequently no damage is done, as the loser quits the ring before the knock-out blow. Hemirhamphidæ are not generally aggressive, though they will snap up and swallow young fry. Females when giving birth are very cannibalistic. They should therefore be trapped or placed in thickly planted aquaria containing feathery foliage, as well as a good layer of floating plants such as Riccia.

DERMOGENYS PUSILLUS

Half-beak

INDIA, BURMA, THAILAND, INDONESIA   ♂ 2½″ ♀ 3″

COMMUNITY   DIET: MOSQUITO LARVÆ, DAPHNIA, ENCHYTRÆ,
                             FLOATING DRIED FOOD

SWIMS: UPPER HALF OF TANK

This is the most commonly imported species, and is slightly smaller and chubbier than most. In comparison with other members of the family the lower jaw is shorter; often it is carried at a slightly drooping angle.

The addition of one teaspoonful of salt per gallon of water seems to be appreciated.

The body is a silver-grey, the sides being paler and the belly nearly white, though prismatic light produces tints of blue or green. Such colouring may serve as camouflage, because the species prefers to lie immediately below the water surface.

At first glance the males and females look alike, but the anal fin on the male is split. The forward portion is slightly thickened, and serves as a gonopodium, though the rear part of this fin is rounded. Males have a bright red patch in the lower front part of the dorsal fin, a red streak in the lower jaw, and black tips to the ventral fins.

BREEDING. Tank: 24″ × 8″ × 8″. pH: 7·2–7·4. Hardness: 150–180 p.p.m. Temperature: 78° F. Produces live young. Method: trap female. Young: 20–50. Free-swimming: at birth. Food 1st week: brine shrimp, Cyclops. 2nd week: sifted Daphnia, fine dried food.

The females are very inclined to eat their young, so the mothers should be trapped in shallow water near the surface. Otherwise, a female may give birth and immediately turn round and snap up the baby before it has fallen an inch. Young are delivered over a period of days.

HEMIRHAMPHUS POGONOGNATHUS

Slim Half-beak

INDIA, BURMA, THAILAND, INDONESIA   ♂ 2½″ ♀ 3½″

COMMUNITY   DIET: SMALL LIVE FOOD, DRIED FOOD

SWIMS: UPPER HALF OF TANK

This Half-beak, in comparison with the last-mentioned, has a longer and straighter lower jaw, the tip of which ends in a flattened nodule. The body is longer and slimmer and has more colour.

There is a silvery blue sheen on the sides with three bluish dashes between the gill-plates and the anal fin. The dorsal, caudal, and ventral fins have their edges tinted with reddish-orange, which varies in intensity according to the mood of the fish and the background against which it is seen.

The males are generally smaller and slimmer than the females. Sex can be ascertained from the shape of the anal fin.

Except when scared, the fish prefers to lie just under the surface of the water, making quick darts for any tasty morsel which catches its eye.

BREEDING. *Tank: 24″×8″×8″. pH: 7·0-7·2. Hardness: 120-160 p.p.m. Temperature: 78° F. Produces live young. Method: trap female. Young: 20–50. Free-swimming: at birth. Food 1st week: brine shrimp, Cyclops. 2nd week: sifted Daphnia, fine dried food.*

Females of this species are not so inclined to eat their own young; these are delivered over a period of days.

PŒCILIIDÆ

Most members of this family are the live-bearing tooth carps. The majority of these come from the south of North America, Mexico, the West Indies, Venezuela, Colombia, Guiana, Ecuador, and Brazil. The family is very adaptable to aquarium life. The majority are hardy, of medium size, easily bred, and will eat most foods. Furthermore, these fishes do not require excessive space or heat; generally they are not aggressive. The foregoing notes on live-bearers relate in the main to the Pœciliids.

GAMBUSIA AFFINIS

VIRGINIA, FLORIDA   ♂ 1½″ ♀ 2¼″

NON-COMMUNITY   DIET: ALL FOODS   SWIMS: MID-WATER

This live-bearer has had its heyday. Due to its unpleasant habit of nipping the fins of other fishes, it lost its chances of remaining popular. It likes live food, especially mosquito larvæ, and for this reason the fish have been exported to malaria-infested countries to eat the larvæ of the pest. When live food is absent Gambusia attacks small fishes, and has the effrontery to nip some species larger than itself.

The body colour is mainly grey, dusted with black spots and blotches. A few specimens are so thickly marked that they are almost black. These, being the more highly prized, are sometimes sold as a distinct species, *Gambusia holbrookii*, although they are really the same. A few almost black males are found in nature; it is from these that most of the best stocks are bred.

The male is considerably smaller than the female.

BREEDING. *Tank: 24″ × 8″ × 8″. pH: 7·0–7·2. Hardness: 150–180 p.p.m. Temperature: 78° F. Produces live young. Method: trap female. Young: 20–50. Free-swimming: at birth. Food 1st week: brine shrimp, Grindal worms. 2nd week: sifted Daphnia, dried food.*

More young escape if the female is trapped, and removed after delivering her brood.

GIRARDINUS METALLICUS

WEST INDIES ♂ 1½″ ♀ 2½″

COMMUNITY DIET: ALL FOODS SWIMS: UPPER HALF OF TANK

Although this fish is quite attractive, and is peaceful and hardy, it does not seem to be universally popular, and is not often stocked by dealers in Britain. The gonopodium is long and bent over slightly at the tip.

Both sexes have a metallic sheen, hence the name. The sides are covered with short light-coloured bars; greenish dots mark the gill-plates. At the base of the posterior end of the dorsal fin there is a black spot.

The gonopodium of the male determines sex.

BREEDING. *Tank: 24″ × 8″ × 8″. pH: 7·0–7·2. Hardness: 120–180 p.p.m. Temperature: 78° F. Produces live young. Method: trap female. Young: 20–40. Free-swimming: at birth. Food 1st week: infusoria and brine shrimp. 2nd week: dried food, microworms.*

GLARYDICHTHYS FALCATUS

CUBA ♂ 1½″ ♀ 2″

COMMUNITY DIET: ALL FOODS SWIMS: UPPER HALF OF TANK

A pleasant, peaceful little fish which will withstand most conditions, and is ideal in a community tank.

The overall colour is pale gold set off by an intensely bright blue iris to the eye.

Males are considerably smaller than females, but make up for loss of stature by possessing great stamina. They constantly court the females, which develop a large gravid spot when pregnant.

BREEDING. *Tank: 24″ × 8″ × 8″. pH: 7·0–7·2. Hardness: 120–180 p.p.m. Temperature: 78° F. Produces live young. Method: trap female. Young: 20–50. Free-swimming: at birth. Food 1st week: infusoria, brine shrimp. 2nd week: microworms, dried food.*

HETERANDRIA FORMOSA

Mosquito Fish

VIRGINIA TO FLORIDA   ♂ ¾″   ♀ 1¼″

COMMUNITY   DIET: ALL FOODS   SWIMS: ALL DEPTHS

The smallest of the live-bearers, these little fish should be kept on their own or with other small species. They are lively, active, and attractive. Unfortunately, however, they are too small for the average community tank. Here the larger inhabitants bully and buffet them, forcing them to take refuge in plant thickets or dark corners of the tank where they are not seen and their lively disposition is lost. The species will withstand a temperature range of from 60° to 90° F. if gradual.

The general colour is olive to brown on the top half, the belly being white. A dark brown line runs from the tip of the nose to the base of the tail. Above this, thin vertical black bars cross the body. The one subdued splash of colour is a red spot above a black one in the dorsal fin.

Males show long gonopodiums in comparison to their size.

BREEDING: Tank: 24″ × 8″ × 8″ or smaller. pH: 7·0–7·4. Hardness: 120–150 p.p.m. Temperature: 76° F. Produces live young. Method: young delivered over a period. Young: 10–25. Free-swimming: at birth. Food 1st week: infusoria, brine shrimp. 2nd week: microworms, fine dried food.

Females deliver live young over a period of days. If the tank is well planted, and contains a layer of Riccia at the surface, the population will increase rapidly, as only hungry parents will eat their fry.

LEBISTES RETICULATUS

Green-lace Guppy · Scarf-tail Guppy

Veil-tail Guppy · Sword-tail Guppy

Guppy

VENEZUELA, GUIANA · ♂ 1¼″ ♀ 1¾″

COMMUNITY · DIET: ALL FOODS · SWIMS: ALL DEPTHS

The attractive guppies are known throughout the world by nearly everyone, whether aquarists or not. They have become so commonplace and inexpensive that they are not generally treated with the respect due to such magnificent fish. Were they rare, and their cost ten times as great, they would be highly prized, for no two males are identical in colour and markings. Even the ordinary guppy is a lively, colourful, hardy little fish, and is generally the first species kept by beginners.

In spite of unsuitable treatment due to inexperience, the guppy not only survives but reproduces regularly. Later, when the aquarist has acquired some skill, he begins to ignore the beauty of this fish, and treats him mainly as a guinea-pig. For example, when ascertaining if certain water is suitable for fishes, often guppies are thrown in for observation. They have been subjected to various conditions such as excessively high or low temperatures, and extremes of acidity and alkalinity. Again, guppies are used for tests of endurance when there is a lack of oxygen. Frequently the fish are purposely infected with diseases so that new drugs may be tried out on them. More often than not these happy little fish withstand all these experiments, and yet when returned to normal conditions will produce lively youngsters none the worse for the ill-treatment of the parents.

It is practically impossible to state accurately the colour or pattern of the present-day guppy: all are beautiful. Several types are shown in our colour plates. A few specialists devote much time to line breeding various types. Among these there are recognized Sword-tail, Double Swords, Lyre-tails, Scarf-tails, Veil-tails, Laced Guppies, Red, Green, Gold, Chain, Bird's-Eye, and numerous others. Not only do some breeders produce new types, but achieve great success in establishing definite colour patterns and markings. Such super guppies still demand a high price, and rightly so. The breeder's knowledge and patience have to be devoted over many generations. The majority of fish produced have to be thrown out, and only a select few retained to advance a step further towards the aim in view. But, once established, the buyer with no further trouble can reproduce many of the particular type, before non-selective breeding causes the strain to revert.

The males, though smaller, are the more colourful, and constantly show off to the stately females. The latter are generally grey, though some have been developed with colour in the tail fin. Many breeders are devoting their time to producing an all-coloured female, but as yet this has not been achieved.

BREEDING. *Tank: 24″ × 8″ × 8″. pH: 6·8–7·4. Hardness: 100–180 p.p.m. Temperature: 78° F. Produces live young. Method: thickly planted tank or traps. Young: 20–70. Free-swimming: at birth. Food 1st week: infusoria and brine shrimp. 2nd week: microworms, dried food.*

Guppies are prolific breeders, and the young grow rapidly; as many as four generations may be raised in a year. This gives specialist breeders the opportunity of selecting suitable specimens for producing new strains.

LIMIA MELANOGASTER

♂

♀

Blue Limia

JAMAICA ♂ 1¾″ ♀ 2″

COMMUNITY DIET: ALL FOODS SWIMS: ALL DEPTHS

Many experienced aquarists do not know this fish. Somehow it has been overlooked; because it is not often asked for, few dealers stock it. Yet when seen under good lighting it is one of the prettiest live-bearers. It has a lively disposition, and is suitable for most community tanks, provided these are not stocked with large fishes which may be bullies.

Bright blue is a colour not common among fresh-water tropicals. This fish, however, is generously spangled with shining scales of rich royal blue on an olive background. The females, though not quite as bright as the males, are none the less attractive, and the large gravid spot is also tinted with dark blue. Males in perfect condition are beautiful. The blue spangles are set off by yellow crescents in the dorsal and tail fins, the outer edge of each being bordered with black. The base of the dorsal in both sexes is blue-black, and four or five short vertical black bars cross the hind portion of the body.

BREEDING. *Tank: 24″ × 8″ × 8″. pH: 7·0–7·4. Hardness: 120–180 p.p.m. Temperature: 75° F. Produces live young. Method: trap female. Young: 10–25. Free-swimming: at birth. Food 1st week: infusoria, brine shrimp. 2nd week: microworms, fine dried food.*

Males are persistent courters, and sometimes show tremendous pace when chasing females. Nevertheless, the species is not prolific, broods being small. Several females may be trapped together.

LIMIA NIGROFASCIATA

♀

♂

Hump-backed Limia

WEST INDIES   ♂ 2″   ♀ 2¼″

COMMUNITY   DIET: ALL FOODS   SWIMS: ALL DEPTHS

Here is another very popular Limia. It is robust, hardy, and not aggressive and is somewhat chunkier than the foregoing. With age the males develop a splendid dorsal fin on an arched back. This feature accounts for their popular name, though they are also known as striped Limias.

The overall body colour is old gold striped with many thin black bars. The fins of the female are tinged with yellow. The dorsal of the male is black-laced with a yellow crescent across the middle, and his tail is black-edged.

BREEDING. *Tank: 24″ × 8″ × 8″. pH: 7·0–7·2. Hardness: 120–150 p.p.m. Temperature: 78° F. Produces live young. Method: trap female. Young: 10–25. Free-swimming: at birth. Food 1st week: infusoria and brine shrimp. 2nd week: microworms, dried food.*

Females produce small broods, and are very inclined to eat their own young, so it is advisable to use a trap. If this is large enough several females can be placed in it together. It has been observed that deep-bodied females which look likely to give immediate birth are in reality far from this state. Only when they become square in profile under the chin are they about to deliver young.

MOLLIENISIA LATIPINNA

Broad-finned Mollie

S.E. STATES OF U.S.A.   ♂ $3\frac{1}{2}''$ ♀ $3\frac{1}{2}''$

COMMUNITY   DIET: ALL FOODS   SWIMS: MID-WATER

The main feature of this fish is the magnificent dorsal fin seen on good specimens. Unfortunately to-day the majority of mollies, like some modern women, seem to be shorn of their crowning glory. In Britain super-finned mollies are rare, so the price is high. The dorsal fin on a good male will extend from the back of the neck to the beginning of the caudal peduncle, and will stand $1\frac{1}{4}''$ high in front to $\frac{3}{4}''$ at the rear.

The colour is hard to describe, though the general appearance is metallic green splashed liberally with yellow. Here and there on the body blue highlights show up, but they are more prominent in the upper and lower portions of the tail. A few half-bars, more like blotches, appear on the lower sides of the fish. Several fine brownish stripes of a rather zig-zag pattern traverse the body horizontally from gill-plate to caudal peduncle.

Males are generally slightly larger than females, and when courting put on a magnificent display, expanding the caudal and dorsal fins until it would seem that they must split. At this time male colours are at their height, and shine like burnished metal. Usually the best and biggest males are those which grow to a good size before developing their gonopodium.

Mollies are constant feeders, and it is advisable to provide small but frequent meals. Dried food is readily taken, particularly that which floats. Since the lower lip protrudes slightly beyond the upper one, the mouth opens towards the water surface. The fish like to swim with their lips at surface level and suck in quantities of floating dried food. They also enjoy a vegetable diet, and are constantly nibbling at algæ growing on the plants and walls of the aquarium. Plant food is a real need to them, and must be available at all times. Mollies come from warm, alkaline water, and do better in aquaria where the pH is 7·2 to 7·6 and the temperature 78°–82° F. A small quantity of salt in the water is beneficial.

BREEDING. Tank: 30″ × 15″ × 15″. pH: 7·4. Hardness: 150–180 p.p.m. Temperature: 80° F. Produces live young. Method: large, well-planted tank. Young: 30–70. Free-swimming: at birth. Food 1st week: brine shrimp and Cyclops. 2nd week: fine dried food, sifted Daphnia.

Breeding habits are similar to other live-bearers, but once gravid the females resent handling or any change from one tank to another. Where possible the male should be removed. If the females have to be transferred it must be done very early in the gestation period. Otherwise premature birth may occur. As a result she may waste away, and not return to her former condition.

MOLLIENISIA SPHENOPS

Short-finned Mollie

SOUTHERN U.S.A. TO VENEZUELA   ♂ 3″   ♀ 3½″

COMMUNITY   DIET : ALL FOODS   SWIMS : ALL DEPTHS

This is the short-finned mollie more often seen. The dorsal fin, in comparison with that of *M. latipinna*, is small, being neither so long nor so high.

The common variety is olive to green, but by line breeding various other types have been fixed. Notable among these are the Perma black and Liberty. The former have been developed from wild sports, and bred until they have become a velvety black all over. They should produce jet-black young which retain their colour, and should not become speckled as they grow. The best of these have completely black eyes, but some others still have a lighter-coloured iris. The Liberty variety has a bluish tinge along the back, the dorsal and caudal fins being an attractive red and yellow.

When feathery plants such as Myriophyllum become coated with algæ the best method of cleansing is to put the bunch into a tank containing mollies. These fish will eat every scrap of algæ, and yet not damage the fine fronds of the plant.

Sex is determined by the gonopodium of the male.

BREEDING. *Tank: 24" × 8" × 8". pH: 7·4. Hardness: 150–180 p.p.m. Temperature: 80° F. Produces live young. Method: large, well-planted tank. Young: 30–70. Free-swimming: at birth. Food 1st week: brine shrimp and Cyclops. 2nd week: fine dried food, sifted Daphnia.*

For further details see *M. latipinna.*

MOLLIENISIA VELIFERA

$\male$

Sail-finned Mollie

YUCATAN, MEXICO $\male$ 4½" $\female$ 4½"

COMMUNITY   DIET: ALL FOODS   SWIMS: MID–WATER

Known as the sail-finned mollie, this king of live-bearers is indeed rare. It is the largest of the mollies, and has a dorsal fin which is unrivalled by any other fish of the same size. This enormous fin may be as high as $1\frac{1}{2}''$, and has 17 to 18 rays, whereas *M. latipinna* usually has 14 or 15.

The colour of the two species is similar. *M. velifera* reproduces young with large dorsal fins. *M. latipinna* sometimes fails to pass on this feature to its offspring. Most of the finest specimens come from stock raised in outdoor pools. It is doubtful whether specimens reared in tanks will ever attain the size and finnage of the outdoor fish.

Females lack the huge sail-fin.

BREEDING. *Tank: 30" × 15" × 15". pH: 7·4. Hardness: 150–180 p.p.m. Temperature: 80° F. Produces live young. Method: large, well-planted tank. Young 20–50. Free-swimming: at birth. Food 1st week: brine shrimp and Cyclops. 2nd week: dried food, sifted Daphnia.*

Details as for *M. latipinna.*

MIDNIGHT MOLLIES

Sometimes known as black sail-fin mollies, they are not a separate species as is generally believed. Originally most were produced by crossing the *velifera* or *latipinna* to black *sphenops*. The resulting babies bore larger dorsal fins and had black speckled bodies. Further line breeding with the blackest specimens finally produced the all-black body and the large dorsal. Nevertheless, throwbacks occur, and many beginners are disappointed when an expensive pair fail to produce many Sail-finned Perma blacks. Owing to the original crossing, some of the young may be born black or mottled; many as they grow become more mottled and remain so. A very few turn jet-black all over and grow to a large size. It is from these that further line breeding continues.

In the males of the choicest specimens the huge black dorsal fin is bordered along the upper edge with orange gold. Unfortunately, mollies soon become in-bred, and the progeny tend to get smaller and smaller with each generation. Before this occurs it is advisable to introduce new blood, but this must come from good stock if first-class features are to be maintained. Like *M. velifera*, the largest sail-fins are bred and reared in warm outdoor pools; few tank-raised specimens ever attain great size, or the magnificent dorsal fin.

PHALLICHTHYS AMATES

♀

♂

Merry Widow

GUATEMALA, HONDURAS   ♂ 1½″   ♀ 2″

COMMUNITY   DIET: ALL FOODS   SWIMS: UPPER HALF OF TANK

A merry, lively fish, hardy, and ideally suited to community life. The male has a striking dorsal fin which he carries upright and well spread at all times. This fin has an outer border of white immediately below which runs a black crescent. A smaller and less colourful crescent appears in the middle of the fin.

The body colour is an olive-grey becoming more golden on the under side. There is, however, on the flanks a bluish-green sheen which is intensified on the gill plates and below the mouth. Numerous faint black bars appear on the sides of the male.

In relation to his size, the gonopodium is long. Females are larger than males.

BREEDING. *Tank: 24″ × 8″ × 8″. pH: 7·0–7·2. Hardness: 120–150 p.p.m. Temperature: 78° F. Produces live young. Method: well-planted tank or trap. Young: 10–30. Free-swimming: at birth. Food 1st week: infusoria, brine shrimp. 2nd week: microworms, dried food.*

The species is a prolific breeder. If kept well fed they are not inclined to eat their young.

XIPHOPHORUS HELLERII

Gold Swordtail

Green Swordtails

Albino Swordtail

Red-eyed Red Swordtail

Swordtails

MEXICO		♂ 4½″ ♀ 3½″
COMMUNITY	DIET: ALL FOODS	SWIMS: ALL DEPTHS

All the swordtails are hardy, prolific, inexpensive fish, and many books recommend them as an essential species to most beginners. The authors hold the opposite view, because the average beginner rarely starts off with a large tank, and Swordtails grow big. Many of them turn spiteful, and a rogue male frequently becomes a downright bully, constantly chasing and worrying his smaller companions. Realizing that most of the fishes in his community tank are unhappy, the beginner is apt to feel that this is due to his mismanagement. Often gaining the impression that tropicals are too difficult to keep, he may give up in despair and dispose of his tank. Had he removed the swordtails the serenity of the aquarium would have been restored quickly, and possibly the aquarist would have become a life-member of the fold.

Nevertheless, swordtails when kept in large aquaria with biggish fishes are attractive and colourful. The most striking feature is the magnificent sword-like extension formed by the lower rays of the caudal fin in the males. This sword is purely for adornment, and is never used as a weapon; indeed, it is far too flexible even to penetrate a piece of tissue paper.

Through line breeding the common Green Sword has now been developed into several distinct colour varieties. These include Red, Red-eyed Red, Albino, Black, Berlin, Gold, Red-wag, etc. Our colour plate shows four examples. Each will breed true to type if not crossed with any other. *Xiphophorus hellerii* are so common and well known, and bred in so many colour varieties, that a full description of each will not be given.

Excluding the length of the sword, males and females are approximately the same size.

Like the mollies, the mouth of the swordtail is inclined upward, and is well equipped for taking in floating dried food, which it seems to enjoy. Even so, these fish have no objection to scavenging head downward on the bottom of the tank. Between feeding-times swordtails are constantly pecking algæ from the plants and the sides of the aquarium.

When not eating, males are either chasing other fishes or courting a female of their own species. While paying homage to his lady the male shows to the greatest advantage. Adorning himself in his best colours, and with fins stretched to full extent, he darts around her. Often during these antics the male will shoot backward two or three times his own length. This feat must be performed with the pectoral fins, though no doubt his sword helps him to cut through the water when in reverse.

BREEDING. *Tank: 30"×15"×15". pH: 7·0–7·4. Hardness: 120–180 p.p.m. Temperature: 78° F. Produces live young. Method: well-planted tank or trap. Young: 20–200. Free-swimming: at birth. Food 1st week: brine shrimp, fine dried food. 2nd week: Cyclops, microworms.*

Swordtails are prolific. A large female may produce a brood of 250 at one time. The young are born about ¼" long. They are robust and easy to rear. In order to obtain large specimens it is necessary to give plenty of food, warmth, and space, so that the fish can grow as much as possible before the males develop a gonopodium, and later the start of the sword-tail.

XIPHOPHORUS MACULATUS

♀

Yellow Wagtail Platy

Red Platy

♀

Blue Platy

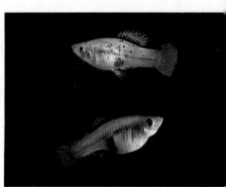

Platy Variatus

Platys

S. MEXICO   ♂ 2″   ♀ 2½″

COMMUNITY   DIET: ALL FOODS   SWIMS: ALL DEPTHS

Previously known as *Platypœcilus maculatus*, and commonly called platys, this species forms one of the most colourful and pleasant live-bearers known to aquarists. In comparison with *X. hellerii*, the fish is shorter in body, has a more chunky appearance, carries no sword, and is not aggressive.

The species provides the aquarist with the most numerous colour varieties of live-bearers. These include Red, Gold, Blue, Black, Tuxedo, Berlin, Variegated, Red-wag, Yellow-wag, Sunset, Bleeding Heart, Festival, Moons, etc. Still more varieties are well on their way to being established. In view of the diversity of colour, no attempt will be made to describe any particular fish. Our plate shows four distinct varieties. All have been developed by line breeding from the original moon fish, so named because of the dark crescent which appears in the tail fin next to the caudal peduncle. But in most of the modern varieties the black crescent has either been eliminated or the colour has been so modified that it blends in the overall hue and becomes unnoticeable. In each variety both sexes are similarly coloured, though males are frequently a little brighter and often slightly smaller.

Platys have a cheerful disposition and are not shy. They sport their gay colours at all depths, and frequent the unplanted front portion of the aquarium. They enjoy nibbling at algæ, and spend much time bumping their lips on the side of the tank in their efforts to dislodge this vegetable food.

BREEDING. Tank: 24″ × 8″ × 8″. pH: 7·0–7·2. Hardness: 100–150 p.p.m. Temperature: 78° F. Produces live young. Method: well-planted tank or trap. Young: 10–75. Free-swimming: at birth. Food 1st week: infusoria, brine shrimp. 2nd week: fine dried food, microworms.

All platys are prolific breeders, bearing about 10 to 75 young at each brood. These remain unmolested in the majority of cases, but an occasional female has cannibalistic tendencies. The young are hardy, and grow quickly, thereby lending themselves for line breeding.

CHAPTER XIV

OVIPAROUS OR EGG-LAYING FISHES

WE NOW COME TO THE NUMEROUS SPECIES OF TROPICAL FISHES WHICH ARE oviparous, or egg-layers. Under this category come all the remaining species in the book. Not all behave in the same manner: some scatter non-adhesive eggs and, save for eating as many as possible, take no more interest in them. Others drop semi-adhesive eggs. Several build bubble-nests, and generally the males tend the eggs and ward off enemies. Certain species carefully place and fan their eggs, male and female guarding the young. Finally, there are those which lay eggs and after fertilization take them up and incubate them in their mouths. Each type will be covered separately under the appropriate families.

Because the newly hatched fry of many of the egg-laying fishes are so minute, and need special care and microscopic food, many beginners—and for that matter more experienced aquarists—are reluctant to try their hand at breeding them. It is well-nigh impossible to go wrong with live-bearers. No aquarist, except those who line breed, feels that he has achieved much until he has raised some of the beautiful egg-laying species. Once having done so, however, his confidence is raised, and he is spurred on to tackle the more difficult ones.

The authors feel that many aquarists are deterred from becoming breeders by the fear of failure resulting from lack of knowledge. They imagine that such a venture is bound to be beyond their capabilities. But every expert had to make a start, and this comforting thought should help to encourage those who aspire to become skilled breeders. Unlike the pioneers who had nothing to guide them, the breeder of to-day can reconstruct the conditions which have proved successful in the past, and thereby follow the path already partially cleared in front of him.

It is the object of this book not only to describe the various species for recognition, but also to assist those aquarists who would like to breed the fishes of their choice. Nearly all breeding methods described in the following pages are from the authors' first-hand experience, and have proved successful. It is hoped that the information given will be helpful, and enable the reader to achieve his object.

Many of the egg-layers are easy to breed. Providing they are mature enough, in superb condition, and given a clean and properly planted tank, they will usually spawn within 24 hours. Some species require special soft water with a low pH value before they can be induced to spawn. Even so, these conditions can be created. A few fishes respond with artificial aids such as flower-pots, "Vitrolite" bars, etc. These are readily obtainable, and are inexpensive.

Since the newly hatched fry are so small, microscopic live food has to be provided, and to be plentiful by the time the fry hatch out. It must, therefore, be started well in advance. And it is the provision of this food which deters many aquarists from breeding egg-layers. Producing microscopic food, however, is not as difficult as may be imagined. If the instructions given in this book are followed the problem can be surmounted.

With oviparous fishes it is preferable to house males and females in separate tanks. This segregation allows the females to become full of roe. Where males are present they may drive the females, who may frequently scatter a few eggs, thereby remaining slim. Such eggs, of course, have no chance of hatching, since they are immediately eaten by the other fishes in the tank. When a chosen pair are deliberately placed in a breeding tank the male, not having seen a female for some time, is all the more excited and anxious to start the courtship.

It is essential to have a separate breeding tank for each species. There are, however, occasions when two males and three females of one species may be placed together in a breeding tank and a greater number of fertilized eggs obtained. Other details are mentioned either under the family concerned or the individual species.

Spawning the Egg-droppers (particularly barbs and characins)

It is impossible to give one formula for spawning all the various species of egg-droppers. Some spawn in floating plants, others in rooted thickets, some species spawn over a period of days while others complete the act in a matter of hours. There are eggs which hatch in 24 hours, while others take several days, and some even weeks or months. Beginners are advised to start with the easier fishes first. Many barbs and characins spawn easily and hatch quickly, particularly *Barbus conchonius*, *Barbus nigro-fasciatus*, and *Hyphessobrycon scholzei*, so with these in mind we give a typical example to show the procedure likely to prove successful.

For most barbs and characins a breeding tank approximately 24″ long by 8″ wide by 8″ high should be set up as follows. On the bottom is placed a 1″ layer of well-washed fine sand. Now the tank should be filled with clean water (two-thirds rain, one-third tap) giving a pH of approximately 6·8 and a hardness of 100 p.p.m. Temperature 78°–80° F. Numerous short, well-washed plants should be inserted in the sand. Near each end there should be a clump of Myriophyllum, Ambulia, or Cabomba standing higher than the rest of the foliage. This arrangement allows free swimming space in the middle section of the aquarium.

Assuming that the sexes have been kept in separate tanks, a deep-bodied female should be selected. Besides being deep, her belly when seen from the front should resemble a broad letter U, not a V. The best-coloured male should be chosen as mate, and the two placed in the breeding tank in the afternoon about an hour before sunset. This gives them time to become acquainted with each other and settle down in their new surroundings before darkness falls. With the dawn the pair should no longer feel strange, and as the light increases the male will start to court his mate.

His colour heightens, and with fully spread fins he shows off his beauty, which the female rarely ignores. He will butt her with his nose and generally excite her. She will respond by intensifying her colour, extending her fins, and nudging and nosing him. Now and again she may coyly swim away but the male, as intended, will follow closely in order not to lose her. When she is completely worked up she may even chase after the male. Excitement grows until the pair, cavorting in the clear space in the centre of the tank, work their way towards one of the bushy clumps of plants at either end. Now, side by side, the couple tremble together, the female expelling a few eggs, and the male discharging his sperms. The eggs, oval in form as they leave her body, absorb the sperm-laden water and swell to a spherical shape. Thus fertilized, they fall among the feathery fronds of the plants.

The breeding pair continue to spawn until the female has expelled all her eggs, which may take an hour or two, or sometimes more. She is then very thin, and the male likewise considerably leaner. The excitement being over, their attention turns to food, and both parents may start looking for eggs to eat. If the aquarist is present, he should remove both fish and place male and female separately to recuperate from their exertions. After a good feed and a rest, the male may be returned to the original male tank and the female to her former quarters.

If the aquarist has not been up early enough to witness the spawning, he should at least be about before all the eggs are eaten. His first move is to approach the tank stealthily and see how the couple are behaving. If spawning, they should be left alone and inspected again later. On the other hand, should the fish not be spasmodically trembling together the female should be scrutinized, and should she appear much slimmer the two fish should be removed forthwith. Afterwards, with a magnifying glass, some eggs may be observed among the plant fronds. If about fifty eggs are visible the spawn is likely to be three times this figure, as many more eggs will have dropped out of sight among the plants, while others have nestled between the grains of sand and are hidden from view.

Many beginners ask what fish eggs look like, and no doubt it helps when one knows what one is looking for. Eggs are about the size of a pin's head, and the colour is that of clear celluloid. They should not be confused with air bubbles, which, though of the same size, shine like silver. On close examination each circular egg will be seen to have a smaller nucleus inside, though this is not always central. Some eggs may turn opaque white. These may be infertile and eventually become covered with fungus; ignore them, they will not affect the rest. The remainder start to develop, usually within 12 hours, when the eyes of the embryo may be seen. Later, the unhatched fry may be observed making an occasional jerky turn inside the egg.

The following morning, 24 hours after spawning has occurred, minute babies may be found hanging from the under sides of plant leaves or on the walls of the aquarium. These fry with black eyes appear like splinters of clear glass, and can sometimes only be seen as the light shines through their bodies. Each is hanging perpendicularly with the head uppermost. They remain in this position for nearly 24 hours, occasionally shifting a fraction of an inch. During this time they feed on the egg-sac forming their bellies. After absorbing the nourishment provided, the fry have gained a little strength. They drop through the water and struggle upward again, to hang beneath the foliage. In a short while some may be seen darting here and there and coming to rest under a horizontal plant leaf. At this stage they are extremly difficult to see, and many a brood has been lost as the aquarist, believing that all have died and disappeared, clears out the tank. Actually the fry are merely taking cover, for in the wild state many would be gobbled up if they carelessly flaunted themselves in mid-water.

Once free-swimming, the babies need food, and since they are too frightened and too weak to go far in search of it, infusoria must be plentiful enough to come to them. If Ampullaria snails are not permanently kept cultures of infusoria should have been started several days previously, and by now be thick. Two 2-lb. jam-jars will be required daily, one in the morning, the other in the afternoon. Most beginners starve their fry, and lose large numbers.

Through pouring in two jam-jars of infusoria daily, naturally the water-level in the tank rises until it is necessary to siphon some off. To prevent fry being sucked up the tube a fine nylon bag should be used as a strainer. This should be placed in the tank, and the siphon end held inside the bag. By spreading the fingers the bag is kept away from the siphon.

After a week the babies will have grown big enough to take newly hatched brine shrimp, so this should be available when required. About ten days later microworms may be given, and when the young fish have reached a length of $\frac{1}{4}''$ sifted Daphnia, Cyclops, and fine dried food should be served.

So far we have assumed that the selected pair have spawned quickly and the eggs hatched, but this is not always the case. If spawning has not occurred within three days it is generally useless to keep the male and female together longer. Usually the disappointed male becomes bad-tempered and bites, buffets, or injures the female. The aquarist should be on the look-out for this during the three days, and the fish separated before harm is done. Should the female still be fat and full of roe, another male may be tried. But generally it pays to change both fish for another pair. Breeders that do not spawn on the first morning may require food; this, however, must not be allowed to contaminate the sand or the water. Daphnia or other pond foods should not be fed, as these may also introduce into the tank Hydra which will devour most of the fry that hatch later. It is far better to feed a few small pieces of shrimp or prawn, which cannot cause trouble. Any uneaten particles are easily removed. The tank must be clean and free of snails before further breeding attempts are made. Should all the eggs turn white and fungus, the reason is most probably bacteria. Try again with cleaner water. Rarely are the parents sterile, though repeated failures may prove this to be the case.

CHAPTER XV

CYPRINIDÆ

THIS IS ONE OF THE LARGEST OF ALL FISH FAMILIES IN THE WORLD. IT inhabits most of Europe, Asia, Africa, and North America. The fishes vary in size from a few inches to several feet; the larger ones are used for food in many lands. But it is the smaller species that are of interest to aquarists. Most of the carps have barbels, small appendages which hang from the lower lips like miniature whiskers. They do not have teeth, but grind their food with bony plates in the throat. One method of identification is that they do not possess an adipose fin.

BARBUS (? PUNTIUS)

Certain aquarium inhabitants gain temporary favour, only to lose it again shortly after. The barbs, however, have always been popular, and will remain so. This is because they are highly coloured, generally peaceful, not shy, keep their fins well spread, breed readily, and are very adaptable to aquarium life. The majority have large, shiny scales which often give the appearance of enclosing the body in a fine network. Moreover, they come in two sizes; the smaller ones averaging 2″ in length are happy in moderate-sized tanks; the large fish of 3″ upward are best in bigger homes.

Barbs like warmth and plenty of light. They are happy at temperatures from 75° to 85°F., and prefer slightly acid water with a pH value of 6·8. Space and oxygen are important considerations. Barbs will not stand crowding, so if ample surface area is not available they must have artificial aeration. Never should more than two barbs be carried a long distance in a jam-jar: they will most likely suffocate. After any exertion, such as breeding, it is important to make sure that the exhausted parents are given plenty of space and oxygen, or death may result.

Breeding

The spawn of most barbs hatches in 24 hours. With species of 2″ and upward the fry, as soon as free-swimming, are large enough to be fed brine shrimp as first food. The newly hatched babies of species under 2″ should be fed with infusoria. For further information see Spawning the Egg-droppers, p. 159.

BARBUS BIMACULATUS

♂   ♀

Two-spot Barb

CEYLON   ♂ 2¼″ ♀ 2¾″

COMMUNITY   DIET: ALL FOODS   SWIMS: LOWER HALF OF TANK

A recent introduction from Ceylon, this attractive little barb has quickly gained popularity. In shape it is long and slender. It is of lively disposition, but a little shy. It spends most of its time swimming around the base of plants and scavenging in the sand.

A broad pink band traverses the sides from nose to tail. Above this is another of bright green. The back is olive, the belly silvery. Two small but intense black spots are prominent, one at the base of the dorsal fin, the other at the root of the tail.

The pink band on males is more pronounced, and they are slimmer than females.

BREEDING. *Tank: 24″ × 8″ × 8″. pH: 6·8. Hardness: 80–100 p.p.m. Temperature: 80° F. Spawns: in plant thickets. Method: standard for barbs. Eggs: 75–120. Hatch: in 48 hours. Fry hang on: 1 day. Free-swimming: 4th day. Food 1st week: infusoria. 2nd week: brine shrimp, microworms.*

The pair behave like other barbs, but remain near the bottom of the tank. Eggs are usually deposited in the lower fronds of plant clumps.

BARBUS BINOTATUS

MALAYA, THAILAND   ♂ 4″   ♀ 5″

COMMUNITY, WITH LARGER FISHES   DIET: ALL FOODS

SWIMS: LOWER HALF OF TANK

Though not aggressive, this is one of the larger barbs, and is inclined to buffet smaller fishes out of the way.

The main colour is silver-grey, a dark blotch appearing on the back just below the first rays of the dorsal fin. Another elongated spot lies horizontally in the caudal peduncle. The eyes are golden brown.

Any food, particularly duckweed, is eaten.

Females are larger and deeper-bellied than males.

BREEDING. *Tank: 30″ × 15″ × 15″. pH: 6·8. Hardness: 80–100 p.p.m. Temperature: 80° F. Spawns: in plant thickets. Method: standard for barbs. Eggs: 200–500. Hatch: in 48 hours. Fry hang on: 2 days. Free-swimming: 5th day. Food 1st week: brine shrimp. 2nd week: fine dried food, microworms.*

The parents are inclined to eat their eggs, and should be removed immediately spawning ceases. The young have numerous spots in the rear portion of the body, mostly along the lateral line. These spots fade with growth.

BARBUS CONCHONIUS

Rosy Barb

INDIA

♂ 3″ ♀ 3¼″

COMMUNITY   DIET: ALL FOODS   SWIMS: ALL DEPTHS

Probably the commonest of all the barbs kept in aquaria. The male when in colour is truly gorgeous. Below the lateral line the body is a rich red; above it is bright green. The dorsal, anal, and ventral fins become solid black in fine specimens, though poorer ones are often only edged with black. There is a black diamond in the rear portion of the body in both sexes. The female is a golden olive colour and her fins lack the black of the male, who is often slightly smaller.

First indications of sex in young fish is that the males develop a black area in the dorsal fin. Strange as it may seem, males show their best colours when kept together. Now and then they perform a circular dance. Head to tail, they gyrate round and round until the viewer becomes giddy from watching them. During this spin the fins are fully extended, and their colouring is superb. When placed with a female in a breeding tank spawning will take place; but the male rarely adorns himself in the colours produced when two males perform their strange dance.

BREEDING. *Tank: 24″ × 8″ × 8″. pH: 6·8. Hardness: 120–150 p.p.m. Temperature: 80° F. Spawns: in plant thickets. Method: standard for barbs. Eggs: 200–250. Hatch: in 24 hours. Fry hang on: 1 day. Free-swimming: 3rd day. Food 1st week: brine shrimp. 2nd week: microworms, fine dried food.*

This barb is one of the easiest to breed, and is specially recommended to beginners. See Spawning the Egg-droppers, p. 159.

BARBUS CUMINGI

♀

♂

Cuming's Barb

CEYLON   ♂ 2″   ♀ 2″

COMMUNITY   DIET: ALL FOODS   SWIMS: LOWER HALF OF TANK

One of the smaller barbs ideally suited to life in a community tank. It is peaceful, colourful, and breedable, thus making it one of the most popular species in the family. When in slightly acid water the fins are carried in an erect manner and are always well spread, giving the impression that the fish is healthy, vigorous, and happy.

As will be seen from our plate, the male is more colourful, and slimmer. In good specimens the female's dorsal is orange-yellow with black markings. Many poor males are seen which have clear fins. Sexing is not easy until the fish are nearly breeding size.

BREEDING. *Tank: 24″ × 8″ × 8″. pH: 6·8. Hardness: 120–150 p.p.m. Temperature: 80° F. Spawns: in plant thickets. Method: standard for barbs. Eggs: 100–150. Hatch: in 24 hours. Fry hang on: 1 day. Free-swimming: 3rd day. Food 1st week: infusoria. 2nd week: brine shrimp.*

BARBUS DORSALIS

♀

♂

Long-snouted Barb

CEYLON

COMMUNITY, WITH LARGE FISHES

SWIMS : LOWER HALF OF TANK

♂ 3½″ ♀ 4″

DIET : ALL FOODS

Although not one of the brilliant barbs, and little known, this fish is quite attractive. It is a recent introduction, and is said to grow large. Whether this will occur in captivity has yet to be discovered; certainly the size of those kept by the authors remain within bounds, and growth does not appear to be rapid.

The edges of the scales are darkish, giving the body the appearance of being covered by fine network. The back and sides are brownish; the belly is silvery. The outstanding mark is an elongated spot in the base of the dorsal fin. The fins of the male are reddish-brown, while those of the female are brown. The mouth is set lower than in most barbs; the lips are alternately extended and contracted as the fish grubs about on the sand. When scavenging it swims with the head tilted downward. Our specimens have not reached maturity, so no attempts at breeding have yet been made.

BREEDING. In all probability the procedure is similar to B. everetti.

BARBUS EVERETTI

♀

♂

Clown Barb

MALAYA, BORNEO   ♂ 4½″   ♀ 5½″

COMMUNITY, WITH LARGE FISHES   DIET: ALL FOODS

SWIMS: LOWER HALF OF TANK

This is another of the larger barbs, and is extremely colourful. Growth is rapid, and soon a large tank is required. If the fish remained smaller it would be more popular. When many are kept together they have the bad habit of chewing the more tender plants. This means that their home becomes bereft of all but Cryptocorynes. These, being slow-growing plants, are unable to consume all the mulm formed; neither can they compete with algæ. As a result the water turns green and, unless continually siphoned off, the bottom of the tank is covered with mulm. Clown barbs are rather timid; when frightened their quick movements and large size soon stir up the sediment, causing the tank to become so clouded that the fish are rarely seen.

Our colour plate shows a breeding pair.

Sexing is difficult until the fish are mature. Then the male is slimmer than the female, and the red in his fins is more intense. When not frightened the fish will swim in the upper portion of the tank. They are not aggressive, but on account of their bulk should be kept with species of a similar size. Like other large barbs, they are wonderful dustbins for unwanted duckweed, which they devour with relish.

BREEDING. *Tank: 30″×15″×15″. pH: 6·6–6·8. Hardness: 50–80 p.p.m. Temperature: 80° F. Spawns: in plant thickets. Method: standard for barbs. Eggs: 2000–3000.*

Hatch: in 48 hours. Fry hang on: 2 days. Free-swimming: 5th day. Food 1st week: infusoria. 2nd week: brine shrimp, microworms.

If the female is really fat, and the pair have previously been kept apart, spawning may start in 15 minutes, so it is advisable to put these fish out to breed in the early afternoon. The male drives the female vigorously. Pushing his flank close to hers, the pair press together, then with a flick of their tails they shoot apart. Tiny eggs are expelled and fertilized. Little of the spawn remains on the plants. Being non-adhesive, it falls through the foliage and nestles out of view between the grains of sand. In about 2 hours the spawning is over. It is important to remove both fish as soon as they start picking up mouthfuls of sand from which they sift and swallow the eggs. If the parents are removed at once the fry, which hatch in 36 to 48 hours, may number as many as 2000. But if the adults are left in for as little as an hour after spawning they may consume nearly every egg, and only 20 or so fry may hatch. For such large fish the babies are minute.

BARBUS FASCIATUS

♀

♂

Striped Barb

BORNEO, SUMATRA, MALAYA		♂ 4″ ♀ 4½″
COMMUNITY	DIET: ALL FOODS	SWIMS: MID-WATER

A not so common or colourful species. Nevertheless, this barb has a peaceful disposition, and an attractiveness all of its own. The nose is more pointed than in most barbs, and, what is more, the bars run horizontally. These are composed of lines of black dots. The main colour of the body is silver.

Females are deeper-bodied, and have fins slightly smaller than the males. They will spawn when 2″ long.

BREEDING. *Tank: 24″ × 8″ × 8″. pH: 6·6–6·8. Hardness: 100–120 p.p.m. Temperature: 80° F. Spawns: in plant thickets. Method: standard for barbs. Eggs: 100–200. Hatch: in 24 hours. Fry hang on: 1 day. Free-swimming: 3rd day. Food 1st week: infusoria. 2nd week: brine shrimp, microworms.*

BARBUS FILAMENTOSUS

♂

Filament Barb

CEYLON   ♂ 5″   ♀ 4½″

COMMUNITY, WITH LARGER FISHES   DIET: ALL FOODS   SWIMS: MID-WATER

A newish introduction, this fish was originally imported in 1953 as *Barbus machechola*. But the specimens grown by the authors left no doubt that it was in fact *Barbus filamentosus*, since the adult males developed dorsal fins in which the rays produced streaming filaments, hence the name.

When very young the fry have little colour, although they bear black spots. But when three months old they become most attractive. The belly and sides are silver; the back is golden. A black bar passes from the nape of the neck forward through the eye. A large vertical black blob or bar shows in the middle of the body, and a large black spot of diamond shape appears in the forward portion of the caudal peduncle. It is, however, the fins that add the striking colours, the dorsal being solid red at the base and faintly black above. The tips of the forward rays are greyish-white. The tail fin has an intense red splash followed by a black one in the upper and lower lobes. On reaching maturity the bars and coloured blotches fade out completely, but the large spot in the caudal peduncle remains permanent. In males the dorsal fin retains the greyish-white tip and the rays extend into long filaments.

The fish is streamlined and a swift swimmer. When being caught it will speed through the water, leap from the surface, and travel several yards before landing. The species is excellent for clearing unwanted duckweed.

Females do not grow the long filaments in the dorsal fin.

BREEDING. *Tank: 30″×15″×15″. pH: 6·8. Hardness: 100–120 p.p.m. Temperature: 80° F. Spawns: in plant thickets. Method: standard for barbs. Eggs: 800–1200. Hatch: in 48 hours. Fry hang on: 2 days. Free-swimming: 5th day. Food 1st week: infusoria. 2nd week: brine shrimp, microworms.*

The breeding tank should be filled with rain-water and be thickly planted. The following morning the pair will spawn in the normal manner of barbs. Immediately afterwards they should be removed. The fry grow quickly, and soon will eat sifted Daphnia and dried food.

BARBUS GELIUS

Miniature Barb

INDIA   ♂ 1¼″   ♀ 1½″

COMMUNITY   DIET: ALL FOODS   SWIMS: LOWER HALF OF TANK

To date this is the smallest barb kept in aquaria. Owing to the diminutive size, and lack of bright colours, it misses the popularity it deserves, for it is a game little fish, and is quite prepared to look after itself, even with companions twice its size. This does not mean that it is in the least aggressive, but merely that it will not be pushed into the background. It likes to be in the forefront of the aquarium, and to have its share of the food. When driven off it repeatedly returns until finally the aggressors, becoming tired of chasing away such a determined little fish, allow it to remain unmolested.

The upper sides and back of the body are bright gold, the belly silver-white. The shades are deeper in the males, and the rear portion of the body from below the dorsal fin to caudal peduncle is a rich red gold.

The female is slightly larger, and her belly is deeper and rounder. She lacks the deep red gold possessed by the male.

BREEDING. Tank: 24″ × 8″ × 8″. pH: 6·8. Hardness: 100–120 p.p.m. Temperature: 80° F. Spawns: in plant thickets. Method: standard for barbs. Eggs: 50–100. Hatch: in 24 hours. Fry hang on: 1 day. Free-swimming: 3rd day. Food 1st week: infusoria. 2nd week: brine shrimp, microworms.

For spawning pure rain-water is best. The tank must be thickly planted, since the parents are liable to eat the eggs, which are large relative to the size of the fish. When a little spawn is seen among the plants the parents should be removed; if this is done in time 70 to 100 fry may be expected to hatch out.

BARBUS HEXAZONA

♀

♂

Six-zoned Barb

SUMATRA, MALAYA		♂ 2″ ♀ 2¼″
COMMUNITY	DIET: ALL FOODS	SWIMS: MID-WATER

This is one of the prettiest barbs, but somewhat rare in Britain and America. Although prolific in Malaya, the species travels badly. Rarely more than 10 per cent. survive the journey, and total loss so frequently results that many importers now avoid the species. Once settled in an aquarium and cured of Ichthyophthirius, to which it is very subject, the fish live happily. The species is somewhat shy, and often remains hidden among the plants at the back of the tank.

BREEDING. Though the authors have not bred this fish, they understand from Continental breeders that it prefers clean rain-water. The species is difficult to induce to spawn, and rather prone to eating its eggs. These problems keep the species in short supply, and at a fairly high price.

BARBUS LATERISTRIGA

♂

♀

Spanner Barb

MALAYA, SUMATRA, BORNEO, THAILAND   ♂ $5\frac{1}{2}''$ ♀ $6''$

COMMUNITY, WITH LARGER FISHES   DIET: ALL FOODS

SWIMS: LOWER HALF OF TANK

This is perhaps the largest barb kept by aquarists. Due to its size, and lack of bright colours, it is not among the most popular. In Britain it is called the spanner barb; in America the 'T' barb.

The main colour of the body is silver-grey, the forward portion being crossed by two vertical bars, while the rear bears a long horizontal line. Though distinct in the young, these bars fade with age, and become less clear-cut.

The fish normally cruises slowly around, but when attempts are made to catch it can show a surprising turn of speed.

In adult specimens the female is rounder and deeper-bellied.

BREEDING. *Tank: 30″ × 15″ × 15″. pH: 6·6–6·8. Hardness: 50–80 p.p.m. Tempera-ture: 80° F. Spawns: in plant thickets. Method: standard for barbs. Eggs: 800–1200. Hatch: in 48 hours. Fry hang on: 2 days. Free-swimming: 5th day. Food 1st week: infusoria. 2nd week: brine shrimp, microworms.*

The breeding habits are similar to those of the Clown Barb.

BARBUS LINEOMACULATUS

♀

♂

Spotted Barb

CONGO ♂ 1¾″ ♀ 2″

COMMUNITY DIET: ALL FOODS SWIMS: LOWER HALF OF TANK

Similar in size and shape to *B. bimaculatus*, this newly imported barb is interesting, though not highly coloured.

The back is olive, the sides greyish-brown, the belly white. From gill-plate to tail a single line of dots, spaced equally apart, give the fish its name. It is somewhat shy, and spends most of its time grubbing about the surface of the sand, under low plant leaves.

BREEDING. *Tank: 24″ × 8″ × 8″. pH: 6·6–6·8. Hardness: 80–100 p.p.m. Temperature: 82° F. Spawns: in plant thickets. Method: standard for barbs. Eggs: 70–100. Hatch: in 48 hours. Fry hang on: 1 day. Free-swimming: 4th day. Food 1st week: infusoria. 2nd week: brine shrimp, microworms.*

The breeding habits closely resemble those of *B. bimaculatus*.

BARBUS NIGROFASCIATUS

Black Ruby Barb

CEYLON   ♂ 2½″   ♀ 2¾″

COMMUNITY   DIET: ALL FOODS   SWIMS: MID–WATER

With the possible exception of *B. conchonius* this barb is the commonest seen in aquaria. No wonder, as it is one of the most beautiful, and easy to breed and feed; also it is hardy, peaceful, and of ideal size.

The female is silvery. Four broad black bands cross the body vertically, the centre one sometimes being so wide that it becomes a broad blotch. Her dorsal, ventral, and anal fins are black on the inner portions, but the edges are clear. The male, out of colour, is similar to the female, except that his dorsal, ventral, and anal fins are solid black right to the edges. But when in full colour he is hardly recognizable as the same fish. Now the whole rear portion of his body and all his fins turn jet-black, the bars disappearing. His front half, however, turns a complete strawberry red, and, with fins spread to splitting point, he literally sparkles like some exotic gem. Males more frequently don their party dress if kept together and apart from females. On occasions the males perform the spiral dance described under *B. conchonius*. At such times their coloration is at its best, and few exotic fish can surpass them.

BREEDING. *Tank: 24″×8″×8″. pH: 6·8. Hardness: 120–150 p.p.m. Temperature: 80° F. Spawns: in plant thickets. Method: standard for barbs. Eggs: 100–150. Hatch: in 24 hours. Fry hang on: 1 day. Free-swimming: 3rd day. Food 1st week: infusoria, brine shrimp. 2nd week: fine dried food, microworms.*

One of the easiest egg-layers to breed. If a good pair which have been kept apart are placed in a breeding tank in the late afternoon, they rarely fail to spawn the following morning. For breeding two-thirds rain-water and one-third tap-water is best. Though not difficult to rear, the fry grow rather slowly, and often stick when about $\frac{1}{2}″$ long, suddenly shooting ahead again. They can be sexed when quite young, since the dorsal fin of the males is black throughout, whereas this fin in young females is not black on the outer edge.

BARBUS OLIGOLEPIS

♀

♂

♂

Chequer Barb

SUMATRA   ♂ 1½″   ♀ 1¾″

COMMUNITY   DIET: ALL FOODS   SWIMS: LOWER HALF OF TANK

Here we have one of the most colourful of the smaller barbs. Hardy and peaceful, it is an excellent fish for beginners, though somewhat shy until well at home. It derives its popular name from the colouring of the central scales, which produce a chequer pattern from gill-plate to tail.

The males have bright orange fins, all of which are edged with a thin black border. The colour is more intense when in breeding condition. The female's fins are yellow, and the black border is absent save on the dorsal. Her back is golden, whereas the male's is more orange.

The species always carry their fins erect. Should these drop the fish is unhappy or suffering from some disease.

BREEDING. *Tank: 24″ × 8″ × 8″. pH: 6·8. Hardness: 120–150 p.p.m. Temperature: 80° F. Spawns: in plant thickets. Method: standard for barbs. Eggs: 75–100. Hatch: in 24 hours. Fry hang on: 1 day. Free-swimming: 3rd day. Food 1st week: infusoria. 2nd week: brine shrimp, microworms.*

Spawning usually occurs in or around the lower stems of bunched plants, and consequently the eggs are more difficult to see. The parents are very inclined to eat these. If the female is obviously slimmer and pecking about the sand, both parents should be removed.

BARBUS PARTIPENTAZONA

MALAYA, THAILAND

♂ 1¾″ ♀ 2″

COMMUNITY   DIET: ALL FOODS   SWIMS: MID-WATER

This attractive little fish was popular before the Second World War, but has lost its place to the more colourful *B. tetrazona*.

The silverish body is divided by five vertical bars, though all of these do not cross the fish completely. The first bar travels from the nape of the neck forward through the eye; the second, often incomplete, runs from in front of the dorsal across the belly; the third bar passes through the middle portion of the dorsal fin and just into the upper part of the back; the fourth bar crosses from well behind the dorsal to the ventral fin; the final bar is at the caudal peduncle. There is a bright red streak in the dorsal fin. Faint red also appears in the ventrals and upper and lower edges of the tail.

Male and female are similar, though the red in the males is brighter.

BREEDING. *Tank: 24″×8″×8″. pH: 6·8. Hardness: 100–120 p.p.m. Temperature: 80° F. Spawns: in plant thickets. Method: standard for barbs. Eggs: 100–150. Hatch: in 24 hours. Fry hang on: 1 day. Free-swimming: 3rd day. Food 1st week: infusoria. 2nd week: brine shrimp, microworms.*

The fish is as easy to breed as *B. nigrofasciatus.*

BARBUS SCHUBERTI

♀

♂

Golden Barb

S. CHINA   ♂ 2½″   ♀ 3″

COMMUNITY   DIET: ALL FOODS   SWIMS: LOWER HALF OF TANK

As a complete contrast, this medium-sized barb is a bright golden-yellow, and said by some to be a colour variety of *B. semifasciolatus*. All the fins except the pectorals are brick red. Males are slightly smaller than females, and can be identified immediately by a row of black spots which run horizontally from the gill-plate to the caudal peduncle. Females are deeper-bodied; they lack the row of black dots, though they have a few odd spots here and there on the upper portion of the back.

BREEDING. Tank: 24″ × 8″ × 8″. pH: 6·6–6·8. Hardness: 80–120 p.p.m. Temperature: 80° F. Spawns: in plant thickets. Method: standard for barbs. Eggs: 150–200. Hatch: in 24 hours. Fry hang on: 1 day. Free-swimming: 3rd day. Food 1st week: infusoria. 2nd week: brine shrimp, microworms.

Pure rain-water is required. Sometimes the fish are difficult to induce to spawn, mainly because the males are not in condition. At breeding-time he develops a red coloration which stretches from the belly to the anal fin, and it is useless to attempt spawning until this adornment is apparent.

BARBUS SCHWANENFELDII

♀

♂

THAILAND   *Tinfoil Barb*   ♂ 6″   ♀ 6″

COMMUNITY, ONLY WITH LARGE FISHES   DIET : ALL FOODS   SWIMS : MID-WATER

This new barb was introduced into Britain by the authors in 1955 through the aid of a pilot in Pan-American Airways who described the fish, which he saw in Bangkok. The species travelled well. Owing to the minute scales, which resemble burnished silver, it was immediately nick-named the Tinfoil Barb by the wife of one of the authors. This title has since become established. Unfortunately, the specimens have grown so large that the fish is unlikely to be very popular except in public aquaria.

The outline of the body is diamond-shaped, and, unlike most barbs, which are rounded in section, this one is flat with compressed sides like the angel fish. All the fins are large, and its streamlining makes the fish a fast mover. It prefers to swim in shoals. The species is excellent at clearing duckweed. When this is not available the fish is inclined to devour the more tender plants.

In young specimens the outer edges of the ventrals, the anal, and the tail fin are red. But when maturity is reached these fins become red throughout. The pectorals are pale yellow. The dorsal is dark grey on the outer portion and orange on the inner. The upper and lower edges of the tail are also dark grey. The top half of the eye is orange.

BREEDING. So far the authors' specimens show no indication of sex. It is thought that, although 6″ long, they are still too small to breed.

BARBUS SEMIFASCIOLATUS

Half-banded Barb

S. CHINA   ♂ 3″   ♀ 3½″

COMMUNITY   DIET: ALL FOODS   SWIMS: LOWER HALF OF TANK

Here is another of the larger barbs which has lost popularity mainly because of its size and lack of gaudy coloration.

Generally the body is greenish-gold slashed with numerous thin black bars which are irregular in length. The fins are pale orange. Recently imported specimens from Singapore may restore the species to favour, since the body colour is much more intense, and all the fins are broadly bordered with rusty red, making quite a showy fish. The same effect has been produced when ordinary dull tank-bred specimens were fed with colour-mutation hormone foods.

Males are slimmer than females, and the latter are rather the larger.

BREEDING. *Tank: 24″×8″×8″. pH: 6·8–7·0. Hardness: 120–150 p.p.m. Temperature: 80° F. Spawns: in plant thickets. Method: standard for barbs. Eggs: 150–200. Hatch: in 24 hours. Fry hang on: 1 day. Free-swimming: 3rd day. Food 1st week: infusoria. 2nd week: brine shrimp, microworms.*

The species is one of the easiest to breed, though they are very prone to eating their eggs. A good deep female should be chosen; but this should be done only when one of the males shows reddish colouring on the lower part of the body similar to that described under *Barbus schuberti*.

BARBUS STOLICZKANUS

♀

♂

INDIA, CEYLON   ♂ 2¼″   ♀ 2½″

COMMUNITY   DIET: ALL FOODS   SWIMS: MID-WATER

There is some doubt as to the true identification of this species. Certain authorities consider it to be *Barbus ticto*. It is a colourful, peaceful fish, and does well in aquaria. It has a sprightly bearing and keeps its fins well spread.

The dorsal fin of the male bears a black crescent near its base. This is surmounted by an intense red arc, which is set off with a thin black border on the outer edge.

All the fins of the female are pale yellow, and she is deeper in the belly.

BREEDING. *Tank: 24″ × 8″ × 8″. pH: 6·8–7·0. Hardness: 100–120 p.p.m. Temperature: 80° F. Spawns: in plant thickets. Method: standard for barbs. Eggs: 150–200. Hatch: in 24 hours. Fry hang on: 1 day. Free-swimming: 3rd day. Food 1st week: infusoria, brine shrimp. 2nd week: fine dried food, microworms.*

The species is easy to spawn and raise.

BARBUS TETRAZONA

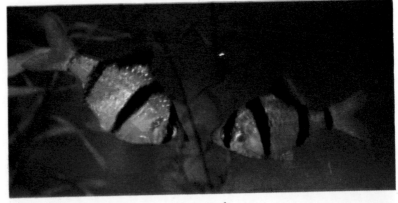

♀   ♂

Tiger Barb

SUMATRA, BORNEO, THAILAND   ♂ 2"   ♀ 2¼"

COMMUNITY   DIET: ALL FOODS   SWIMS: MID-WATER

Probably the most striking and colourful of all the barbs, but it has one serious drawback: some males become aggressive. In bad cases these bullies will not only make life intolerable for other barbs but, having killed them off, will set about adult angel fish. By constantly pecking the fins and body they will turn a show fish into a ragged, unhappy list-less specimen which, unless protected, will give up the ghost. Luckily, not all tiger barbs are so bad. The bullies should be eliminated, and breeding confined to the more docile members so that the vicious trait is less likely to be perpetuated. The fish has a lively disposition, and always keeps its fins erect and well spread. When resting the body is often inclined nose downward.

Four broad black bands, evenly spaced, cross the fish vertically. In some lights these bands reflect a deep bottle green. The pectoral and ventral fins are bright red. The dorsal is red beyond the black bar. The anal fin is bordered with red, and intense red streaks appear in the upper and lower lobes of the tail.

In males all the red markings are more intense, and when in breeding condition they have a red snout. The female is larger than the male, and much deeper in the belly.

BREEDING. *Tank: 24"×8"×8". pH: 6·8. Hardness: 80–120 p.p.m. Temperature: 80° F. Spawns: in plant thickets. Method: standard for barbs. Eggs: 150–200. Hatch: in 24 hours. Fry hang on: 1 day. Free-swimming: 3rd day. Food 1st week: brine shrimp. 2nd week: microworms.*

The species breeds readily in pure rain-water. Parents should be re-moved immediately after spawning to prevent egg-eating. They should then be rested separately, and given space, or aeration, or death may occasionally occur from exhaustion.

BARBUS TICTO

CEYLON

♂ 2″ ♀ 2″

COMMUNITY   DIET: ALL FOODS   SWIMS: LOWER HALF OF TANK

As will be seen from the plate, this barb is very different from *B. stoliczkanus*, and it is surprising that they are so often confused.

The males in their native habitat are said to be bright red, but in aquaria they often only show a diffused pinkish red band along the sides and the fins are clear. The shoulder spot is small, and in the caudal peduncle there is a black dot immediately followed by a black dash. The females are rather drab.

BREEDING. Tank: 24″×8″×8″. pH: 6·8. Hardness: 80–120 p.p.m. Temperature: 80° F. Spawns: in plant thickets. Method: standard for barbs. Eggs: 100–150. Hatch: in 24 hours. Fry hang on: 1 day. Free-swimming: 3rd day. Food 1st week: infusoria. 2nd week: brine shrimp, microworms.

BARBUS TITTEYA

♂   ♀

Cherry Barb

CEYLON   ♂ 2″   ♀ 2¼″

COMMUNITY   **DIET: ALL FOODS**   **SWIMS: LOWER HALF OF TANK**

One of the smaller barbs which is attractive, peaceful, and popular. It is hardy, easy to keep, and fairly long-lived.

When not in breeding garb male and female are somewhat similar. Both have a pale brown body and an intense dark brown line which runs from tip of snout to base of tail. Above this is a pale golden stripe. The fins of the female are nearly clear, while those of the male have a brownish tint which is intensified on the edges. When he shows off, however, he is beautiful. The whole body becomes a reddish mahogany, the centre line disappearing altogether, and a bluish tinge adorns the back in some lights. At such times the male spreads all his fins, which look like little round fans stretched to splitting-point. These become deep mahogany veering to copper. This is well illustrated in our colour plate.

Two males often perform the circular dance described under *B. conchonius*, and then show their finest array.

BREEDING. Tank: 24″ × 8″ × 8″. pH: 6·6-6·8. Hardness: 50-100 p.p.m. Temperature: 80° F. Spawns: in plant thickets. Method: standard for barbs. Eggs: 100-150. Hatch: in 24 hours. Fry hang on: 1 day. Free-swimming: 3rd day. Food 1st week: infusoria. 2nd week: brine shrimp.

The species is not difficult to breed in rain-water. But the parents are avid egg-eaters. As soon as they cease spawning and start to search for eggs they should be removed.

BARBUS VITTATUS

♀

♂

INDIA, CEYLON   ♂ 1¾″ ♀ 2″

COMMUNITY   DIET: ALL FOODS   SWIMS: LOWER HALF OF TANK

Perhaps the hardiest of all the barbs, this little fellow makes up in longevity what he lacks in brilliance. Once settled down in an aquarium he is likely to be a friend for many years, eight or nine being by no means unusual.

The body-colour is silverish below, shading from olive green on the sides to brownish on the back. An arching green line is sometimes seen in the upper flanks, starting just behind the gill-plate and ending at the base of the tail. The fins are pale yellow. In the lower half of the dorsal there is an oblique dark stripe; this surmounts a triangle of orange which may be seen in the bottom front rays.

Adorning the sides are a few dark spots; a larger one appears in the caudal peduncle, and another just above the vent.

The male is slightly smaller than the female; his orange triangle is somewhat deeper in colour.

BREEDING. Tank: 24″ × 8″ × 8″. pH: 6·8–7·0. Hardness: 120–150 p.p.m. Temperature: 80°F. Spawns: in plant thickets. Method: standard for barbs. Eggs: 100–120. Hatch: in 24 hours. Fry hang on: 1 day. Free-swimming: 3rd day. Food 1st week: infusoria. 2nd week: brine shrimp.

Breeding is not difficult. Water conditions need not be exact. A good pair will spawn for six or seven years, long after many other barbs have lived, loved, and died.

CÆCOBARBUS GEERTSI

Blind Barb

CONGO   ♂ 3″   ♀ 3¼″

COMMUNITY   DIET: ALL FOODS   SWIMS: MID-WATER

Here we have one of the blind fishes, of which there are several. This one has only recently been imported, and is not generally known to aquarists. Though without eyes, it rarely bumps into any object or plant. Presumably radiations emitted by this fish are reflected back and picked up by the sensitive lateral line. The nervous system sends a message to the brain, and so permits evasive action to be taken. In shape *C. geertsi* is long and slender, with a rather pointed head.

Like many other blind species which live in permanent darkness, colour (which helps other fishes to camouflage themselves) has slowly been lost. The Blind Barb is a pale cream all over, the fins being almost clear. The gill-plates are transparent, and the pink membranes beneath show through.

Females are deeper-bodied, and slightly larger, than males.

BREEDING. So far there is no record of this fish having been bred in captivity.

BALANTEOCHEILUS MELANOPTERUS

♂

THAILAND   ♂ 5″   ♀ 5″

COMMUNITY, WITH LARGER FISHES   DIET: ALL FOODS   SWIMS: MID-WATER

Here is an attractive species belonging to the genus Balanteocheilus, which also comes under the family Cyprinidæ. It has been so much admired that it is worth including in this book, as it undoubtedly has a future. The species is periodically abundant in Thailand, but being as yet relatively unknown among aquarists, the demand is insufficient to encourage capture in its native haunts. This state of affairs will quickly change should its popularity increase. The fish is slim and streamlined; it has large, graceful fins which at all times it keeps well spread and erect. This gives it a pleasing appearance, and an air of well-being. It is a fast swimmer, extremely active, and if frightened will sometimes leap several feet out of the water. *B. melanopterus* is not aggressive, but should be kept with species of similar size. It lives happily in an aquarium with a pH of 7·4.

The body is silver all over. The fins are orange-yellow, and are vividly set off, since each is surrounded by a black border nearly $\frac{1}{8}$″ thick.

BREEDING. So far insufficient specimens have been received to establish the breeding procedure.

BARILIUS CHRISTI

♂

♀

Gold-lipped Mackerel

BELGIAN CONGO   ♂ 4½″   ♀ 5″

COMMUNITY, WITH LARGER FISHES   DIET: ALL FOODS

SWIMS: UPPER HALF OF TANK

Still belonging to the family Cyprinidæ, one species of the genus Barilius is shown.

This is a fairly recent introduction, but in a short time has gained considerable popularity. The body is long and slim; the mouth is large. Since it is an extremely fast swimmer it should not be placed with small fishes, but with species of its own size. Then it is not aggressive.

The body colour is silver, the back is bluish-green, the flanks are barred with numerous thin, blue-black, vertical stripes. The lips are a shining gold. The fish prefers neutral water, pH 7·0, and though liking plenty of live food may be taught to take the dried product.

So far as is known, *B. christi* has not been bred in captivity.

LABEOS

Within the last few years some interesting fishes belonging to the family Cyprinidæ have been imported from Thailand. We shall first deal with the genus Labeo.

Labeos come from India, Burma, Thailand, Cambodia, Laos, and Indonesia. These fishes have long, cylindrical bodies with large fins. The head is somewhat pointed, the snout bearing pairs of barbels. The mouth is round and appears to have lips, hence the name Labeo. These fishes do well in aquaria in slightly alkaline water, eating most foods, but also partaking of algæ, which they browse off leaves and rocks. Often they turn upside down in their efforts to reach this vegetable matter growing in nearly inaccessible places.

LABEO BICOLOR

♀

♂

Red-tailed Black Shark

THAILAND   ♂ 4½"   ♀ 4½"

COMMUNITY, WITH LARGER FISHES   DIET: ALL FOODS AND ALGÆ

SWIMS: LOWER HALF OF TANK

First introduced into Britain by the authors in 1953, the fish caused quite a sensation. Similarly, the first exports sent to America a few months later also created a stir. Though nicknamed a shark, this attractive fish is not shark-like in habits. The popular name refers to the graceful lines and the large, triangular dorsal fin which, as in some sharks, is tipped with white. The body and fins are a velvety jet-black; the tail is bright red. Two pairs of short barbels protrude from the upper lips.

Male and female are similar, though the red in her tail is less intense, and the enamel white tip in her dorsal is slightly more pronounced. Her body is also fuller. Happiest in alkaline water with a pH value of 7·4, the fish is not shy, and performs delightful antics in the front part of the aquarium, often coming to rest on the sand. On occasion it will roll over on to its side for a more comfortable rest. This habit sometimes gives the owner a fright, for generally this attitude in other species foreshadows death. But not so here. After a few moments the fish swims off gaily. The lips protrude and form a sucker mouth with which to clean algæ off plant leaves and the glass sides of the tank. To reach this delicacy on the under sides of leaves the fish often turns upside down. The snout is rounded and equipped with short barbels; these act as feelers to assist when scavenging along the bottom in search of food. Occasionally *L. bicolor* makes a dart at its companions and chases them a short distance, but this is more a playful habit, and rarely if ever is any harm done.

BREEDING. As far as is known, *L. bicolor* has not been bred in captivity. Nevertheless, a pair was put into a 30″ × 12″ × 12″ planted breeding tank, containing a flower-pot which had the bottom knocked out and was laid on its side. It was observed that the pair repeatedly entered this pot and trembled side by side in an upside-down position, waggling their tails in an exaggerated manner, but no eggs were seen.

LABEO CHRYSOPHEKADION

Black Shark

INDONESIA, THAILAND   ♂ 10″ ♀ 10″

COMMUNITY, WITH LARGER FISHES   DIET: ALL FOODS AND ALGÆ

SWIMS: LOWER HALF OF TANK

This was the first of the Labeos to be imported from the Far East, and was received many years ago. Once fabulously expensive and highly prized, it is no longer in such demand, having been superseded by *L. bicolor.*

The scales of *L. chrysophekadion* are clearly visible, each containing a pinkish spot in the middle which becomes more apparent in specimens of 6″ and upward. The fish is large, slightly aggressive, and not a jet velvety black; these are the main factors which account for it taking second place to its red-tailed cousin.

There appear to be two distinct species that are termed 'Black Shark.' One, with a name derived from the Greek word *chrysos*, meaning gold, is said to develop a golden tail with age. This has not been observed by the authors, who presumably possess the other species. Their specimens, received at 3″ in length, have grown to 10″, but they still retain a black tail which shows no sign of changing colour.

The fish is somewhat shy, and frequents the back of the tank, lying on the sand behind the plants. It does not behave in the attractive manner of *L. bicolor*, which seems to enjoy showing itself off in the foreground of the aquarium.

Although *L. chrysophekadion* eats algæ, it rarely crops this vegetable food from the leaves of plants, seeming to prefer scraped algæ that has settled on the floor of the tank. The fish is a bottom feeder, and its two pairs of barbels no doubt assist it in feeling for food. Large specimens develop an extra bunch of barbels below the chin, giving the appearance of a distinct beard.

BREEDING. So far we have not heard of this species being bred in captivity.

LABEO ERYTHRURUS

Red-finned Shark

THAILAND   ♂ 4½″   ♀ 4½″

COMMUNITY, WITH LARGER FISHES   DIET: ALL FOODS AND ALGÆ

SWIMS: LOWER HALF OF TANK

Though not black, this is another attractive member of the family. It is slightly different in shape from the two previously mentioned species. The head is more pointed, and the mouth is not situated so far underneath.

The red-finned shark has large, beautiful fins and a streamlined body. It is a fast swimmer, and occasionally, without vicious intention, makes playful darts at other fishes. Like the rest of the family, *L. erythrurus* is found in alkaline water with a pH value of 7·4.

The general body colour is bluish-grey. All the fins are bright red. A dark line runs from the snout through the eye to the edge of the gill-plate, and a dark spot adorns the base of the tail. Male and female are similar, though she is slightly deeper-bellied.

The fish is not shy, and will take any food, being particularly fond of chopped shrimp. Vegetable matter is enjoyed, and plant leaves continually searched for algæ.

BREEDING. The species has not been bred in captivity, though it was observed that inside a flower-pot a pair behaved in a similar manner to *L. bicolor.*

EPALZEORHYNCHOS KALLOPTERUS

Flying Fox

SUMATRA. BORNEO, THAILAND ♂ 4½″ ♀ 4½″

COMMUNITY, WITH MEDIUM-SIZED FISHES DIET: ALL FOODS

SWIMS: LOWER HALF OF TANK

This fish is a fairly recent importation, and belongs to the sub-family Garrinæ, which in turn comes under the family Cyprinidæ. It is a long-bodied fish, a swift swimmer and a fairly good scavenger. At times it will nibble algæ from leaves.

The colour is black and silver, and most striking. The top of the back is black; a thin silver line runs from above the eye across the body to the top half of the caudal peduncle. Beneath this a broad black band runs from the tip of the nose and passes through the eye. It traverses the whole length of the body and ends in the fork of the tail. Below this band from mouth to tail the fish is silver. The outer portions of the dorsal, ventral, and anal fins carry black blotches, but the tips are silver-white.

Females are slightly deeper-bodied than males, but have the same colour and markings.

BREEDING. We have not heard of this fish having been bred in captivity.

EPALZEORHYNCHOS SIAMENSIS

♀

THAILAND   ♂ 5½″ ♀ 5½″

COMMUNITY, WITH LARGER FISHES   DIET : ALL FOODS

SWIMS : LOWER HALF OF TANK

Here we have a rare fish which is seldom imported.

The mouth is prehensile. From the corners a pair of drooping barbels hang, and two shortish ones protrude forward from the upper lip. Like Labeos, the circular-shaped lips are used as suckers for cleaning algæ from leaves, and for extracting particles of food from sandy or muddy river beds.

The overall body colour is golden, the fins being rather more orange. The dorsal and caudal fins are large, and the first rays in these are tinged with red. A pronounced black line runs from the lips to the fork of the tail. *E. siamensis* grows large, but is quite peaceful, though occasionally it makes a playful dart at other fishes without doing harm.

Male and female are the same size, though her fins are paler in colour and her belly is rather deeper and rounder.

BREEDING. Although a pair have been placed in a 30″× 15″× 15″ tank, and have been seen chasing about actively, no eggs have been observed. But the female was so much slimmer that it would seem spawning had taken place at night and the eggs been devoured before daybreak.

CHAPTER XVI

RASBORINÆ

RASBORAS

STILL UNDER THE FAMILY CYPRINIDAE, WE COME TO THE SUB-FAMILY Rasborinæ. Dealing first with the genus Rasbora, there are many species. The fishes differ so greatly in appearance and size that it is hard to believe that all belong to the same genus. The majority are long and slender, but a few are short and deep-bodied. Most of the larger ones are rather dull, but the smaller species are colourful, and firm favourites.

Rasboras do well in aquaria, particularly if the water is soft and slightly acid, with a pH of 6·6.

Unfortunately, the larger and less popular Rasboras are easier to breed than their smaller cousins, which are in greater demand. Since the methods of spawning differ, breeding habits will be given under the various species.

RASBORA BORAPETENSIS

THAILAND ♂ 1½″ ♀ 1¾″

COMMUNITY · · · DIET : ALL FOODS · · · SWIMS : MID-WATER

This is one of the smaller Rasboras of elongated shape, and has only recently been imported. Though not brilliant, the fish is colourful. The body is a golden grey. A black stripe bordered above by gold runs from the gill-plate to the base of the tail. The dorsal, ventral, and anal fins are tinged with red.

The female is longer than the male; her belly is rounder and deeper.

BREEDING. To date our specimens, although living happily in aquaria, have shown no inclination to breed. There has not yet been time to experiment and discover the conditions required.

RASBORA DANICONIUS

INDIA, CEYLON   ♂ 3½″ ♀ 4″

COMMUNITY, WITH LARGER FISHES   DIET: ALL FOODS   SWIMS: MID-WATER

Here is a medium to large Rasbora of the typical elongated shape.

The body is silver. Running from the gill-plate to the caudal peduncle is a thin black line bordered on each side by one of gold. The back is over-cast with olive brown. The fins are slightly tinted yellow.

The female usually grows a little larger than her mate, and is fuller in the belly.

BREEDING. Tank: 30″×15″×15″. pH: 6·8–7·0. Hardness: 100–120 p.p.m. Temperature: 80° F. Spawns: just above sand. Method: see text. Eggs: 300–500. Hatch: in 3 days. Fry hang on: 2 days. Free-swimming: 6th day. Food 1st week: brine shrimp. 2nd week: fine dried food, microworms.

For breeding the tank should be filled with rain-water, and thickly planted with feathery clumps. The fish chase each other swiftly; when they come into contact eggs are discharged; these are fertilized among the plants. On other occasions the fish will wriggle side by side just above the sand, with their noses in a corner of the aquarium. Large eggs are expelled and fertilized. The parents set up such a current in the water that the spawn is carried across the tank, and builds up in a mound against the glass at the opposite end. After spawning parents should be removed before they can devour their eggs.

RASBORA DORSIOCELLATA

♂

♀ ♀

♀

SUMATRA, MALAYA		♂ 1½″ ♀ 1¾″
COMMUNITY	DIET: ALL FOODS	SWIMS: MID-WATER

Of fairly recent importation, this little Rasbora is hardy, peaceful, and active.

Though lacking in bright colours, it makes up for loss of brilliance by other prominent features. A green highlight adorns the lower half of the eye, and slants across the body, ending just in front of the anal fin. Another highlight of gold appears horizontally in the caudal peduncle. A large black spot in the dorsal fin contrasts with a white splash immediately below.

Male and female are alike, except that she grows larger; when she is mature her belly is much rounder and deeper.

BREEDING. Tank: 24″ × 8″ × 8″. pH: 5·4–6·0. Hardness: 5–20 p.p.m. Temperature: 80° F. Spawns: in plant thickets or nylon mops. Method: standard for egg-droppers. Eggs: 50–100. Hatch: in 48 hours. Fry hang on: 2 days. Free-swimming: 5th day. Food 1st week: infusoria. 2nd week: infusoria, brine shrimp.

The fish will spawn among plants in brown peaty water which is extremely soft and has a very low pH. But the authors get better results by using nylon mops placed in a bare tank containing only 4″ of water.

RASBORA EINTHOVENI

♂

♀

MALAYA, SUMATRA   ♂ $3\frac{1}{2}''$ ♀ $3\frac{3}{4}''$

COMMUNITY, WITH LARGER FISHES   DIET: ALL FOODS   SWIMS: MID-WATER

The species illustrated here, being long-bodied and slender, is typical of some of the larger Rasboras.

They prefer slightly acid water, and when settled down swim idly in the middle of the aquarium. But they can show a surprising turn of speed when attempts are made to catch them.

Like many species of the family, *R. einthoveni* is not brilliantly coloured, neither are the fins outstanding. The general colour of the body is a greyish-olive. A black line runs from the tip of the lower lip through the eye right through to the base of the tail. The line is not quite straight, but dips slightly in the middle. The fins are tinged with pale yellow, which is more rust-coloured in the male, who also in some lights carries a mauvish sheen here and there on the back.

The female is a little larger and deeper-bellied than the male.

BREEDING. Tank: 30″ × 15″ × 15″. pH: 6·8. Hardness: 80–120 p.p.m. Temperature: 80°F. Spawns: in plant thickets. Method: standard for egg-droppers. Eggs: 500–600. Hatch: in 3 days. Fry hang on: 2 days. Free-swimming: 6th day. Food 1st week: brine shrimp. 2nd week: Cyclops, microworms.

The tank should be thickly planted and the adults should be removed when spawning is completed. Some of the eggs turn white, presumably because unfertilized, but from the enormous quantity laid sufficient hatch to produce several hundred fry.

RASBORA ELEGANS

Elegant Rasbora

MALAYA, SUMATRA ♂ 4″ ♀ 4½″

COMMUNITY, WITH LARGER FISHES DIET: ALL FOODS

SWIMS: UPPER HALF OF TANK

This is one of the largest of the Rasboras kept in aquaria. The name is rather misleading, as the fish is not particularly elegant. Though not aggressive, when mature *R. elegans* should be kept with larger fishes.

The overall body colour is a silver-grey. A black rectangle adorns the centre of each side, and a dark spot lies at the base of the tail. These blotches lose their crispness as the fish grows. Above the anal fin there is an oblique black line.

The female exceeds the male in length, and her belly is deeper.

BREEDING. *Tank: 30″ × 15″ × 15″. pH: 6·6. Hardness: 100–120 p.p.m. Temperature: 80° F. Spawns: in plant thickets. Method: standard for egg-droppers. Eggs: 500–600. Hatch: in 2 days. Fry hang on: 2 days. Free-swimming: 5th day. Food 1st week: brine shrimp. 2nd week: Cyclops, microworms.*

In spite of being prolific in their natural habitat, the fish do not spawn readily in captivity. Large specimens occasionally tremble together in plant thickets and discharge numerous clear eggs. The parents should be removed after spawning, as they are inclined to eat the eggs.

RASBORA HETEROMORPHA

Harlequins

MALAYA, SUMATRA ♂ 1¾″ ♀ 1¾″

COMMUNITY   DIET: ALL FOODS   SWIMS: UPPER HALF OF TANK

This little beauty differs so greatly in shape from the elongated members of the group that the inexperienced aquarist may be excused in thinking that *R. heteromorpha* belongs to another genus. Since the advent of air travel harlequins are imported in thousands, 500 travelling quite comfortably in a plastic bag a foot in diameter, containing 1½ gallons of water, and blown up with pure oxygen. Few die, but in spite of the constant demand the source of supply is not depleted. They literally swarm in numerous pools in Malaya.

Our colour plate shows the fish in their normal hues, but at breeding-time these are intensified, and there is more suffused pink over the body.

Male and female are the same size, but the sexes are easily distinguished. Males are much redder in the dorsal and tail fins, also in the caudal peduncle region. The female is more golden, and when full of roe her belly is deeper than that of her mate. It is surprising that so many aquarists are under the impression that the fish are unsexable. Many people consider that the corner of the black triangle nearest the belly is more pointed and extends farther forward in males. This does occur sometimes, but is an unreliable guide to distinguish sex. The males are always redder; in our plate they will be seen as the leading fish, the one above in the third place, and the last one in the shoal.

When seen in a well-planted tank, containing peaty acid water, the fish are at their best, and present a beautiful and impressive sight.

BREEDING. Tank: 24"×8"×8". pH: 5·0–6·4. Hardness: 10–50 p.p.m. Temperature: 80° F. Spawns: adhesive eggs. Method: eggs deposited under plant leaves. Eggs: 50–70. Hatch: in 24 hours. Fry hang on: 1 day. Free-swimming: 3rd day. Food 1st week: infusoria. 2nd week: brine shrimp.

Breeding is not easy, but possible, given the right conditions. The tank should be filled with rain-water that has stood on peat for a week or two. This water should be a deep brown, and very soft. The tank should be planted with Cryptocorynes. A well-coloured male and the roundest, fattest female should be selected. In a day or two the male will make short darts at his mate and, with fins well spread, show himself off. Soon she responds to his attentions. After a time she will swim to a leaf and turn upside down under it. The male follows, and curves himself against her. They tremble together, while the eggs are laid and fertilized under the leaf, to which they adhere. This behaviour is repeated at short intervals for an hour or two, after which the parents should be removed, otherwise they may eat any eggs they can find.

Harlequins are sometimes bred communally, using two males and four females. But should only one pair start spawning the remaining fish are apt to devour the eggs. Occasionally the authors have witnessed a couple of these fish, not in an upside-down position, trembling together in a thicket of fine-leaved plants. Later eggs have been observed caught in the foliage. It would seem, therefore, that the upside-down spawning position is not always used.

RASBORA KALOCHROMA

♀

♂

Clown Rasbora

MALAYA   ♂ 3″   ♀ 3″

COMMUNITY   DIET: ALL FOODS   SWIMS: MID-WATER

As will be seen from the photograph, this is an attractive Rasbora. It has only recently been received from Singapore in a consignment of other fishes. It is peaceful, and, because of its long, slender shape, is a fast swimmer. The fish seems happy in captivity.

The body is suffused with red. A blue-black spot appears on the flanks a little behind the gill-plates. A larger block of the same colour adorns the forward portion of the caudal peduncle. The fins are red, but the ventrals and anal fin of the male are tipped with black.

BREEDING. Our specimens are still too young to spawn, but eventually attempts will be made in soft brown water, using nylon mops to catch the eggs.

RASBORA MACULATA

♀

♂

Spotted Rasbora

MALAYA   ♂ 7/8″   ♀ 1″

COMMUNITY, WITH SMALL FISHES   DIET: ALL FOODS   SWIMS: MID-WATER

Until recently the smallest of all Rasboras, this pretty little fish is
imported in hundreds. But frequently it fails to survive the journey.

The overall colour is reddish mahogany, and a large black spot adorns
the forward part of the body. The dorsal fin is red; the forward rays are
tipped top and bottom with black spots. A further small spot is found at
the base of the tail, and another on the upper portion of the anal fin. In
males there is a spot on the body above the anal fin, but females show two
spots here. These features enable the sexes to be distinguished when quite
young. At maturity, however, the male is a richer red and generally more
colourful than his mate; she is somewhat rounder in the region of the
belly.

BREEDING. Tank: 10″ × 5″ × 5″. pH: 5·4–6·0. Hardness: 5–20 p.p.m. Tempera-
ture: 80° F. Spawns: in plant thickets or nylon mops. Method: male locks female in
caudal grip. Eggs: 50–100. Hatch: in 48 hours. Fry hang on: 2 days. Free-swimming:
5th day. Food 1st week: infusoria. 2nd week: infusoria, brine shrimp.

The species may be spawned in a very small tank containing soft brown
peaty water, and planted with one or two clumps of Myriophyllum. But
recently the authors have found it less trouble to place a pair in a glass
battery jar, roughly 8″ long by 5″ wide, filled with very soft brown peaty
water to a depth of 4″. In this place two nylon mops which have been
sterilized in boiling water. The male soon starts driving the female, and,

coming side by side, he presses her into the foliage or mops, though sometimes this action takes place above the plants or mops. Then, quivering
together, the male locks the hinder portion of his body—*i.e.*, his tail
and most of the caudal peduncle area—over and round the same part of
the female. Immediately eggs are discharged and fertilized, dropping into
the plants or mops. The procedure is repeated for an hour or more, after
which the parents should be removed. The small, slightly amber eggs are
not easy to see. Neither are the tiny fry until free-swimming. They grow
quickly, and are ¼″ long in 3 weeks.

RASBORA PAUCIPERFORATA

♂

♀

Glowlight Rasbora

MALAYA, SUMATRA   ♂ 2½″   ♀ 2¾″

COMMUNITY   DIET: ALL FOODS   SWIMS: MID-WATER

Seldom imported in quantity, this smallish Rasbora when kept under ideal conditions rivals the neon tetras for brilliance. It is peaceful, quite hardy, and likes to swim in shoals, though frequently remaining motionless in one spot. If kept in a community tank it must only be housed with small fishes. To see *R. pauciperforata* at its best a few should be placed in a special aquarium containing soft brown peaty water. The tank should be thickly planted with Cryptocorynes against a dark background, the whole lit from above with the light rays projected backward.

The brownish body is adorned by a fiery red stripe, edged below by one of black, and above by a thin one of gold. So brilliant is the red line that it literally seems to draw the eyes of the observer.

Sexing can only be told by the fuller belly of the mature female.

BREEDING. *Tank: 24″ × 8″ × 8″. pH: 6·0–6·6. Hardness: 70–90 p.p.m. Temperature: 76° F. Spawns: in plant thickets. Method: male and female tremble side by side. Eggs: 200–300. Hatch: in 48 hours. Fry hang on: 3 days. Free-swimming: 6th day. Food 1st week: infusoria. 2nd week: brine shrimp.*

The authors have not succeeded with this difficult to breed fish. But success has been achieved by Mr and Mrs Robertshaw, of Hendon, who provided the following particulars. A small tank with a bottom layer of peat was filled with rain-water. Unplanted Cryptocoryne roots and cuttings were placed so thickly in the aquarium that there was no swimming space left. It was then allowed to stand for 3 to 4 weeks. After this period fish were introduced on the off-chance of spawning: they started doing so the next day. Male and female could be seen trembling together, though no eggs were observed. The parents were removed in the evening. A week later fry were seen swimming. 250 youngsters were raised. The parents were stated to be three years old.

RASBORA TRILINEATA

Scissor-tails

MALAYA, SUMATRA, BORNEO, THAILAND ♂ 3″ ♀ 3″

COMMUNITY   DIET: ALL FOODS   SWIMS: MID–WATER

A firm favourite, this semi-transparent fish is light and dainty. In the wild it is said to grow to 8″ or 9″, but the aquarium specimens rarely reach more than a third of this length.

From the gill-plate to the base of the tail there runs a thin black line; the forward portion of this is sometimes less distinct than the rear half, which has a thin, greenish-gold upper border. Another thin black line appears just above the anal fin. The back is a golden-green. All the fins are golden. But the tail is different; in fact, it is the most striking feature. The upper and lower lobes each contain an oblique black patch. This is bordered on either side by a yellow one which is fainter on the outside. As the fish swims the tail opens and closes, and the markings draw attention to the scissor-like action—hence the popular name.

Females are a little longer and deeper-bodied than males.

BREEDING. *Tank: 24″×8″×8″. pH: 6·0–6·8. Hardness: 30–80 p.p.m. Temperature: 80°F. Spawns: in plant thickets. Method: standard for barbs. Eggs: 1000–1500. Hatch: in 36 hours. Fry hang on: 2 days. Free-swimming: 4th day. Food 1st week: infusoria. 2nd week: brine shrimp, microworms.*

The species will spawn when only 2″ long. The tank should be filled with rain-water, and in the middle contain short plants, small Indian ferns serving well. At each end a clump of feathery foliage is provided. The fish should spawn the following morning, after which the parents should be removed.

There is a colour variety of this fish. It is called the Golden Scissor-tail, as the caudal fin is more yellow.

RASBORA UROPHTHALMUS

Miniature Rasbora

MALAYA ♂ ¾″ ♀ ¾″

COMMUNITY, WITH SMALL FISHES   DIET: ALL FOODS   SWIMS: MID-WATER

This tiny Rasbora has only recently been imported from Singapore. Like most fishes from this area, it prefers brown peaty water. It is so small that it vies with *R. maculata* for the distinction of being the smallest species of the genus.

When kept under these conditions this otherwise drab little fish assumes a quiet coloration. The back is reddish-brown, the belly bluish-silver. A blue-black line, edged above with gold, runs the length of the sides from gill-plate to tail, and ends in a spot of the same colour; hence the name *urophthalmus* (literally, 'tail-eye').

Females are rounder and deeper-bellied than males.

BREEDING. Tank: 12″ × 8″ × 8″. pH: 5·6–6·4. Hardness: 25–75 p.p.m. Temperature: 80° F. Spawns: in plant thickets. Method: standard for barbs. Eggs: 50–70. Hatch: in 48 hours. Fry hang on: 2 days. Free-swimming: 5th day. Food 1st week: infusoria. 2nd week: infusoria, brine shrimp.

Originally having no information on the breeding of this species, the authors, knowing it to be a Rasbora, applied the technique required by most of these fishes. This proved to be successful (which shows the advantage of knowing the generic name). The tank was filled with soft brown peaty water, the bottom being covered with a half-inch layer of sieved peat that had become waterlogged. Two young Indian ferns with their roots held down by a small piece of slate were used as spawning plants. The male began to follow the female and drive her gently. The pair came together in the plant fronds, trembled side by side, and minute eggs were seen falling. The parents were removed, and young were observed hanging on 48 hours later.

RASBORA VATERIFLORIS

♂

♀

♂

Fire Rasbora

CEYLON   ♂ $1\frac{1}{4}''$ ♀ $1\frac{1}{2}''$

COMMUNITY   DIET: ALL FOODS   SWIMS: UPPER HALF·OF TANK

A recent introduction, this fish first appeared in Britain in 1955. In size and shape it resembles *R. heteromorpha*, but *R. vaterifloris* is more translucent and delicate-looking. The dorsal and anal fins are slightly longer, more pointed, and have a graceful backward curve.

This is no black triangle on the sides of this fish. The back is bluish-grey, the sides silvery. The whole body is overcast with reddish amber, being richer in the caudal region. All the fins are reddish amber, except the tail, which carries this colour only in the lower lobe, the upper one being clear.

In comparison with the male, the female is slightly deeper in the body. She is a little smaller and paler, being more amber in hue.

BREEDING. So far the authors have not succeeded in breeding this fish, nor have they heard of any other aquarists who have achieved success. But it would seem that the procedure may well follow that of *R. heteromorpha*.

RASBORA SPECIES

♀

♂

Blushing Rasbora

MALAYA   ♂ 1¾"   ♀ 2"

COMMUNITY   DIET: ALL FOODS   SWIMS: MID-WATER

So far unidentified, this small and slender fish has recently arrived from Singapore among a consignment of harlequins, and thus prefers slightly acid water. The main colour of the body is silver with a suspicion of bluish-pink as an overlay—hence the nickname given by the authors. The eyes are black; the fins are clear except for a black spot near the tip of the forward rays in the anal fin.

Both sexes look alike, but the female when full of roe is slightly deeper bodied.

BREEDING. As yet they have not been bred in captivity.

DANIOS

Belonging to the same family Cyprinidæ, and coming under the sub-family Rasborinæ, are the following minnow-like fishes which come from India, Ceylon, Indonesia, and Thailand. The larger species are called Danios, the smaller members being Brachydanios (from the Greek *brachys*, meaning short). All are swift, streamlined fishes which scatter non-adhesive eggs in shallow water among plant thickets. They do well in ordinary aquarium conditions, preferring neutral water. They delight in swimming in shoals in the upper part of the tank, and usually are not scary.

Danios will take any food of suitable size, dried, fresh, or live.

Breeding

All are prolific breeders, but avid egg-eaters. For spawning a suitable-sized tank would be the standard 24″× 8″× 8″. The bottom should be covered with clean, coarse gravel, and very thickly planted with the feathery-type plants and young Indian ferns. It should be filled with water of a pH value of 7·0 to a depth of 3″ or 4″. Like all other egg-laying fishes, breeding-sized males should be kept in a separate tank from females. In the late afternoon the deepest- and roundest-bellied female is selected and placed in the tank with a suitable male. The pair rarely fail to spawn next morning, but unless the aquarist is up early the parents will eat many eggs. If the female looks slimmer both fish should be removed at once. The eggs, no larger than a pin-head, are difficult to see, since they are non-adhesive, and drop through the plants into the crevices of the gravel. At a temperature of 78° F. they take 3 or 4 days, or even longer, to hatch, and many a good spawning has been thrown out by beginners who are usually informed that the hatching period is 24 hours. Failing to see any young, they clear the tank or put out another pair. Either the eggs are discarded or the new fish devour the young as they hatch.

After hatching the fry may be seen hanging from plant leaves or on the glass sides of the aquarium. They are so small that they require infusoria as first food. Growth, however, is rapid, and soon larger nourishment can be given. The babies should reach 1″ in length in about 8 weeks.

Protecting the eggs

Some aquarists favour the use of traps in unplanted tanks. The traps permit the eggs to fall through slots or openings which are small enough to prevent the passage of the parents. These traps take various forms. Some are merely clean pebbles or glass marbles in layers at the bottom of the tank. But occasionally one of the spawning fish manages to wriggle down and get stuck, so perhaps a fine wire or nylon mesh, $\frac{1}{8}$″, cut to fit the tank, is better. The trap is lowered on to two pieces of slate, one at each end of the aquarium, so that it is raised about 1″ off the bottom. Care must be taken to ensure that the parents cannot squeeze down between ill-fitting sides. Another advantage of mesh is that some plant-stalks can be inserted through the gauze and stand upright. This arrangement makes the fish feel more at home than in a bare tank. Some aquarists construct a large trap, having a base of glass or plastic bars, the whole being immersed in the breeding tank. But very often with these methods a high proportion of the eggs fungus and fail to hatch. In view of this, perhaps a clean, well-planted tank is the best in the end.

BRACHYDANIO ALBOLINEATUS

Pearl Danio

SUMATRA, BURMA, THAILAND   ♂ 2"   ♀ 2¼"

COMMUNITY   DIET: ALL FOODS   SWIMS: UPPER HALF OF TANK

This is the pearl danio, though there seem to be two types. They are hardy, not timid, and peaceful. One, the gold danio, has a yellowish tone over the body, and in our view is not so attractive as the mother-of-pearl variety, which has a pinky-bluish hue. In both types there is a translucent sheen of various colours depending on the angle of the reflected light. *B. albolineatus* grows slightly larger than the other two species in the plate. Like all Danios, they are fast swimmers, and prefer to move in shoals.

Males are considerably slimmer and slightly shorter than females. A shoal of pearl danios in good daylight, particularly against a background of dark plants, is extremely beautiful.

BREEDING. *Tank: 24" × 8" × 8". pH: 7·0–7·2. Hardness: 100–150 p.p.m. Temperature: 78° F. Spawns: in plant thickets. Method: standard for Danios. Eggs: 200–300. Hatch: in 4 days. Fry hang on: 2 days. Free-swimming: 7th day. Food 1st week: infusoria. 2nd week: infusoria, brine shrimp.*

Easy to breed, following standard for Danios.

BRACHYDANIO NIGROFASCIATUS

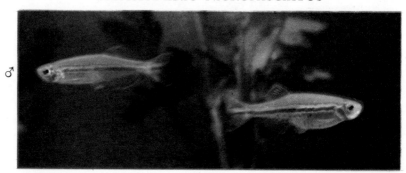

BRACHYDANIO NIGROFASCIATUS

Spotted Danio

BURMA, INDIA   ♂ 1¼″   ♀ 1½″

COMMUNITY   DIET: ALL FOODS   SWIMS: UPPER HALF OF TANK

This little fish is often erroneously called *B. analipunctatus*, which refers to the spotted anal fin. Males are considerably slimmer than females, and, with the exception that it is more difficult to induce to spawn, all the points previously mentioned under Danios apply here.

BRACHYDANIO RERIO

♀

♂

Zebra Danio

INDIA   ♂ 1½″   ♀ 1¾″

COMMUNITY   DIET: ALL FOODS   SWIMS: UPPER HALF OF TANK

One of the most popular of all aquarium fishes. It is adaptable, peaceful, active, easily fed, and breeds prolifically. The fish is usually recommended to those making their first attempts at spawning the egg-layers. This advice, however, is not endorsed by the authors, as the eggs take several days to hatch, and the fry are so small that they require infusoria. *Barbus nigrofasciatus* or *Hyphessobrycon scholzei* should be much easier for beginners.

The first impression of this fish would seem to denote a colour pattern of blue and silver stripes running horizontally from the gill-plate to the end of the tail. But on closer examination it will be found that the males are really blue and gold.

Breeding fish are very often trapped in shallow water to prevent the spawn from being eaten.

DANIO MALABARICUS

♂

♀

Giant Danio

INDIA   ♂ 4″ ♀ 4¼″

COMMUNITY, WITH LARGER FISHES   DIET: ALL FOODS

SWIMS: UPPER HALF OF TANK

This is the largest of the Danios, and for many years an old favourite with those aquarists having big tanks. It is an active, showy fish, fairly peaceful, and hardy.

It is a very fast swimmer, and quite difficult to catch, sometimes leaping from the water to avoid the net.

Males are much slimmer than females, and the fins are brighter red.

BREEDING. *Tank: 24″ × 8″ × 8″. pH: 7·0–7·2. Hardness: 100–180 p.p.m. Temperature: 80° F. Spawns: in plant thickets. Method: standard for Danios. Eggs: 200–300. Hatch: in 3 days. Fry hang on: 2 days. Free-swimming: 6th day. Food 1st week: infusoria. 2nd week: brine shrimp, microworms.*

Breeding fish are often trapped to prevent spawn being eaten.

LAUBUCA LAUBUCA

♀

♂

Winged Danio

CEYLON   ♂ 3″   ♀ 3¼″

COMMUNITY   DIET: ALL FOODS   SWIMS: UPPER HALF OF TANK

This attractive fish is a recent importation. It has rather beautiful fins, particularly the pectorals and ventrals. The former are large and wing-like, the latter long and pointed, the front rays being elongated with a graceful backward curve. The species is not so active as the giant danio. It swims more slowly, and rests here and there for long spells.

The body colour is mother-of-pearl with a beautiful sheen. A faint stripe made up alternately of pale blue and gold runs from the pectoral fins to the caudal peduncle. Immediately above the end of this stripe is a brilliant golden splash. The fins are yellow with a tinge of orange in the forward portion of the ventrals.

The female is larger and deeper-bodied than the male, but her colouring is the same.

BREEDING. So far the authors have not succeeded in breeding *L. laubuca,* but it would seem that they would follow the standard procedure of Danios.

ESOMUS

These are small, slim fishes recognizable by very long, slender barbels, which curve back from the mouth and reach to the middle of the belly. They have large, wing-like pectoral fins.

ESOMUS DANRICUS

♂

♀

Flying Barb

INDIA, CEYLON		♂ 1¾″ ♀ 2″
COMMUNITY	DIET: ALL FOODS	SWIMS: UPPER HALF OF TANK

The popular name is misleading, for the fish does not belong to the genus Barbus. The nickname refers to the large pectoral fins and the long barbels emanating from the mouth.

These fish like light and warmth; they spend their time gliding about just below the surface of the water.

Extending from the gills to the tail is a black line bordered above by another of gold. The fins are clear.

Males are slightly smaller and slimmer than females, though even she is of a long, slender shape.

BREEDING. Tank: 24″ × 8″ × 8″. pH: 6·6–6·8. Hardness: 80–120 p.p.m. Temperature: 80° F. Spawns: in plant thickets. Method: similar to Danios. Eggs: 100–150. Hatch: in 48 hours. Fry hang on: 2 days. Free-swimming: 5th day. Food 1st week: infusoria. 2nd week: infusoria, brine shrimp.

The species is not difficult to spawn. The male drives the female towards clumps of plants and bumps her gently to excite her. Pale yellow eggs are scattered among the foliage. Once past the hanging-on stage, the fry stay near the bottom of the tank, but when able to swim strongly and have more confidence they take to the clearer water above the plants.

ESOMUS MALAYENSIS

MALAYA   ♂ $1\frac{3}{4}''$ ♀ $2''$

COMMUNITY   DIET: ALL FOODS   SWIMS: UPPER HALF OF TANK

This species, as the name implies, comes from Malaya. The fish has the same long barbels and wing-like pectoral fins as *E. danricus*, but is slightly deeper in the body.

The overall colour is a golden-hued mother-of-pearl with bluish high-lights in the region of the back. It lacks the strong horizontal stripe, but has a dark spot at the base of the tail.

In all other respects the remarks concerning *E. danricus* apply here.

BREEDING. *Tank:* 24"×8"×8". *pH:* 6·6–6·8. *Hardness:* 80–120 p.p.m. *Tempera-ture:* 80° F. *Spawns: in plant thickets. Method: similar to Danios. Eggs: 100–150. Hatch: in 48 hours. Fry hang on: 2 days. Free-swimming: 5th day. Food 1st week: infusoria. 2nd week: infusoria, brine shrimp.*

Breeds as *E. danricus*.

TANICHTHYS ALBONUBES

♂

♀

White Cloud Mountain Minnow

CHINA   ♂ 1¼″   ♀ 1½″

COMMUNITY   DIET: ALL FOODS   SWIMS: UPPER HALF OF TANK

One of the most attractive aquarium fishes, these little beauties will live happily in indoor tanks in cool rooms without any additional heat. Nevertheless, they are more lively and colourful if kept between 75° and 80°F., at which temperature they will breed. The fish are happiest swimming in shoals.

Adults are easy to sex, males being brighter. The females are slightly larger and deeper in the belly; this depth extends as far back as the anal fin. In males the chest may be deep but he tapers off just behind the ventrals. Unfortunately, the glowing green line loses its lustre with age, becoming a creamy green.

BREEDING. Tank: 24″ × 8″ × 8″. pH: 7·0–7·4. Hardness: 100–150 p.p.m. Temperature: 78°F. Spawns: in plant thickets. Method: similar to Danios. Eggs: 100–150. Hatch: in 48 hours. Fry hang on: 1 day. Free-swimming: 4th day. Food 1st week: infusoria. 2nd week: brine shrimp, microworms.

One of the easiest species to breed, but the tank should be thickly planted to prevent the parents eating their eggs.

Commercial breeders often favour spawning these fish communally. This is best done using a thickly planted large shallow tank or an old sink, the surface of the water being covered with a 1″ thick layer of Riccia. Then with an enamel soup-ladle the Riccia is pressed down each morning, and the tiny fry scooped up and transferred to small tanks.

CHAPTER XVII

CHARACIDÆ

A LARGE FAMILY OF FISHES COMING FROM MOST OF SOUTH AMERICA, PANAMA, parts of Mexico, and Texas; also from Central, East, and West Africa. Although belonging to the same order as the carps and catfishes, characins, as they are popularly called, possess teeth and an adipose fin; not the whole family have both these features, but at least one of them is possessed by all members. The fishes vary greatly in size and shape, the smaller ones being generally peaceful and attractive, but some of the larger specimens, particularly the notorious piranha, are very savage, and use their razor-like teeth to slash and devour anything meaty which happens to cross their path.

A few of the medium-sized species are apt to tear and chew up the more tender plants in the aquarium, and occasionally use their teeth to fray the tails of small fishes. Nevertheless, the small species are not only peaceful and good community fishes, but they provide the aquarist with some of the most beautiful inhabitants of the tank. Moreover, they are easily cared for and fed; dried food and any small live food will be taken.

Some are extremely easy to breed; others are difficult. The majority drop semi-adhesive eggs. The standard 24″ × 8″ × 8″ tank is usually adequate, and procedure follows that laid down for spawning egg-droppers (p. 159). The breeding of those species which are exceptions to the rule is described under the individual fish.

ALESTOPETERSIUS CAUDALIS

BELGIAN CONGO   ♂ 2½″   ♀ 3″

COMMUNITY   DIET: LIVE FOOD, MAY BE TRAINED TO TAKE DRIED FOOD

SWIMS: MID-WATER

A recent introduction of great beauty. It is slender in shape, the flanks are somewhat compressed, and, like so many of the West African fishes, the eye is large in comparison with the overall size.

Above the lateral line the body is pale blue, turning to golden along the centre line, and the belly is silver-white. Gold and blue highlights reflect from the scales as the angle of light catches them. The fins are rich yellow-gold, and in males the dorsal is large, with trailing points on the first few rays. These are edged with grey-black. The anal fin is long and pointed, and the tail has a central extension forming a point projecting between the upper and lower lobes. This spike is blue-black in colour. The fins of the female are similar, but she lacks the long points.

BREEDING. Tank: 30″ × 15″ × 15″. pH: 5·6–5·8. Hardness: 20–50 p.p.m. Temperature: 78° F. Spawns: in plant thickets. Method: standard for egg-droppers. Eggs: 50–100. Hatch: in 48 hours. Fry hang on: 2 days. Free-swimming: 5th day. Food 1st week: infusoria, yolk of egg. 2nd week: brine shrimp, microworms.

These fish are difficult to induce to spawn, but will do so on occasions, using soft peaty water in which has been placed a large mat of lesser bladderwort anchored down here and there with well-washed pebbles or pieces of clean slate. Spawning was not observed, but eggs were seen among the plant threads, which hatched in 48–60 hours.

ANOPTICHTHYS JORDANI

♀

♂

Blind Cave Tetra

MEXICO   ♂ 2¾″   ♀ 3″

COMMUNITY   DIET: ALL FOODS   SWIMS: MID-WATER

Here we have a most interesting characin, which is naturally blind. This feature is by no means unique, as there are several species of blind fishes in the world. The majority of aquarists on seeing *A. jordani* for the first time are reluctant to buy it, having the mistaken impression that to keep such a creature is unkind and somewhat repulsive. The authors have no hesitation in saying that it is one of their favourites, and those aquarists who have been persuaded to overcome their prejudice have become equally ardent enthusiasts.

Thousands of years ago these fish were carried by currents into underground caves where little or no light existed; and because sight was of no use in this subterranean home Nature in the course of time ceased to provide these useless organs.

The fish is a brilliant shining silver, the fins being creamy. In large females the first rays of the anal and ventral fins are pink.

A. jordani swims at all depths; even in thickly planted tanks it rarely bumps into the foliage. The fish are equipped with extremely sensitive organs which warn them of obstacles in their path. It is amazing to see how they change direction to avoid plants, rocks, other fishes, and the sides of the tank.

Their blindness is no handicap, for the instant the aquarium cover is raised these docile fish become active and acute; they are first on the food, be this live or dried. Should anything edible be given during the hours of darkness 'blind caves' have a distinct advantage over all fishes with sight. As scavengers *A. jordani* are equally as good as the generally recommended catfishes, but whereas the latter after satisfying themselves frequently disappear among the foliage at the back, remaining hidden until the next meal, blind caves disport themselves at all times in full view in the forefront of the aquarium.

Sexing is easy, as females are much rounder and deeper-bellied than the males.

BREEDING. Tank: 30"×15"×15". pH: 6·8–7·2. Hardness: 120–180 p.p.m. Temperature: 78° F. Spawns: in clear water above plants. Method: scatters semi–adhesive eggs. Eggs: 500–750. Hatch: in 24 hours. Fry hang on: 2 days. Free-swimming: 4th day. Food 1st week: infusoria. 2nd week: brine shrimp, sifted Cyclops.

Large fish breed easily. The tank should be filled with 4/5ths tap-water and 1/5th rain-water. The bottom should be covered with short plants, but two or three clumps of Myriophyllum should be provided. A good male and a very plump female should be placed in the tank shortly before dusk; they will spawn next morning. The pair swim about in the clear water above the plants. Periodically they approach one another head on and, with bodies touching, rapidly revolve round each other. Then, with a slap of their tails, they break apart, and scores of tiny eggs may be seen falling through the water. The process is repeated for about two hours. Occasionally, though not generally, a pair will swim side by side, pressing their bodies in close contact, and again with a slap of their tails they will break apart, showering fertilized eggs into the water. At the end of the spawn the female is so thin that she looks like a male, while he, slimmer to start with, is now so reduced that his lower sides cave in. Moreover, his anal and ventral fins may become streaked with blood, as though the strain had caused internal bleeding. Both parents should now be removed and placed apart, where they can receive peace and good food. In a few days the blood-streaks fade, and the fish return to normal weight. Most of the tiny eggs fall to the sand, disappearing from view; a few get lodged in the clumps of Myriophyllum, and can be seen.

Next day the tiny fry will be noticed hanging from plants and on the glass walls of the aquarium. Once the babies are large enough to eat brine shrimp it should be given. However, this should be fed alternately with other foods, since the saline diet used exclusively for more than 21 days kills the fish. It will be noticed that the fry have eyes, though it would appear that they are sightless, as movements of the hands in front of the tank are unnoticed. After several weeks scale grows over the eyes, which appear to disintegrate, leaving a hollow socket in their place.

ANOSTOMUS ANOSTOMUS

♂

Striped Anostomus

GUIANA ♂ 5″ ♀ 5″

COMMUNITY, WITH LARGER FISHES DIET: ALL FOODS

SWIMS: LOWER HALF OF TANK

An odd fish with a long, cylindrical body, a flattened, pointed head, and large eyes. It moves about slowly with the head inclined downward, but at the slightest disturbance it can speed through the water rapidly.

The body is divided by longitudinal stripes of blue-black and gold. A deep patch of blood-red adorns the forward portion of the dorsal fin, and appears again spreading from the caudal peduncle through the fore-part of the tail. The other fins are clear.

The male is slimmer than the female, and his colours are a little more intense.

BREEDING. So far the fish has not been bred by the authors.

APHYOCHARAX RUBRIPINNIS

♂   ♀

Bloodfins

ARGENTINA   ♂ 1½″   ♀ 1¾″

COMMUNITY   DIET: ALL FOODS   SWIMS: UPPER HALF OF TANK

This little fish has long been an aquarium favourite. It has a lively disposition, keeps its fins well spread, is extremely hardy, and easy to breed.

The streamlined body is a silvery grey-blue. The dorsal, ventrals, anal, and forward portion of the tail fins are bright blood-red, the edges of these fins being clear. The ventrals and anal are tipped with white.

Females are a little larger than males, and when full of roe are much deeper-bodied. Males caught in a fine net sometimes get hooked by a minute spine on the tip of the anal fin. But sexing by this method is unreliable, since this tiny hook does not always catch in the net.

BREEDING. *Tank: 24″ × 8″ × 8″. pH: 7·0–7·2. Hardness: 120–150 p.p.m. Temperature: 78° F. Spawns: in top weed; fish leaps out of water. Method: standard for eggdroppers. Eggs: 100–150. Hatch: in 48 hours. Fry hang on: 1 day. Free-swimming: 4th day. Food 1st week: infusoria. 2nd week: infusoria, brine shrimp.*

For breeding the tank should be filled with fresh tap-water, and very thickly planted with short Indian ferns or other wide-spreading leafy plants. Breeding takes place in the early morning under good light, the pair chasing each other, and finally leaping from the water. Their bodies come into contact above the surface, when numerous eggs are discharged and fertilized. These sink to the bottom and remain hidden among the low foliage. If some Riccia is floating near the surface the fish will sometimes wriggle into it and spawn without leaping from the water, some of the eggs remaining among the green threads. Immediately spawning has finished the pair should be removed, as they are likely to eat every egg they can find. Though bloodfins are easy to spawn, the young are so small that they may be difficult to raise. Some breeders use egg-laying traps, as described on p. 57. Alternatively several pairs may be spawned by the sink method referred to on p. 220.

CARNEGIELLA STRIGATA

♀

♂

Marbled Hatchet

GUIANA		♂ 1½″ ♀ 1¾″
COMMUNITY	DIET: ALL FOODS	SWIMS: UPPER HALF OF TANK

The hatchet fishes, as they are popularly called, are extremely deep-bodied, and their side view resembles an axe-head. They have large, wing-shaped, pectoral fins which are used for skimming about beneath the water surface, also for carrying the fish through the air, into which it leaps when pursued. The span of the pectorals enables the fish to glide for considerable distances; during these flights the deep body serves as a keel to keep an upright position. To prevent these fishes from leaping out of the aquarium a cover glass is essential.

Hatchets are extremely peaceful, but they should be kept on their own or with other small species. Larger fishes are apt to bully them, and shorten their aquarium life.

C. *strigata* is probably the prettiest of the hatchets, and is a most desirable fish in the small aquarium. Unfortunately, it is shy, and tends to hide in the top back corners until confidence is gained. In the right environment it lives well. It is not cheap.

The body is silvery. Dark wavy brown to black bars run diagonally across the flanks, giving a marbled appearance. Gold and green patches are reflected about the head, and behind the pectoral fins.

BREEDING. Breeding has not been achieved by the authors.

GASTEROPELECUS LEVIS

Silver Hatchet

COLOMBIA, VENEZUELA   ♂ 2¼″ ♀ 2½″

COMMUNITY   DIET: ALL FOODS   SWIMS: UPPER HALF OF TANK

This fish is shown here, out of the strict alphabetical order of the chapter, owing to its similarity to *C. strigata*.

It is the largest of the hatchets so far imported, and is moderately hardy provided it is given good conditions. Because of its size it does well with medium-sized fishes in a community tank. Like other hatchets, it can be trained to take dried food.

The body is a glistening silver; the back is olive. A dark blue stripe bordered above and below by silver runs from the pectoral fins to the base of the tail.

Males are usually a little smaller than females, but sexing is difficult.

BREEDING. So far as is known, *G. levis* has not been bred in captivity.

CHILODUS PUNCTATUS

♀

♂

Headstander

GUIANA, AMAZON ♂ 3″ ♀ 3″

COMMUNITY   DIET: ALL FOODS   SWIMS: MID-WATER

This is a somewhat rare but pleasing characin which spends most of its time with its head inclined downward at an angle of about 60 degrees from the horizontal. When not swimming or hovering in this position it is usually pecking small particles of food from the sand, with the body almost vertical. This habit makes it a good scavenger. It seems peaceful with other fishes, but makes short darts at its own brothers and sisters.

The body has a slight greenish sheen, but is covered with horizontal rows of brown spots. A brown line runs from the tip of the pointed snout through the eye to the edge of the gill-plate, and behind this there is a large brown spot. All the fins are clear except the dorsal, which has a dark brown front ray and a large brown patch in the upper foremost portion, the rest of this fin being sprinkled with brown dots.

Females are plumper than males.

BREEDING. *Tank: 24″ × 12″ × 12″. pH: 6·6. Hardness: 50–80 p.p.m. Temperature: 80° F. Spawns: in nylon mops. Method: standard for egg-droppers. Eggs: 150–200. Hatch: in 3 days. Fry hang on: 2 days. Free-swimming: 6th day. Food 1st week: infusoria. 2nd week: infusoria, brine shrimp.*

The species is not easy to induce to spawn, but the pale brown eggs can be seen in the nylon mops. After this both parents should be removed.

COPEINA ARNOLDI

♂

♀

VENEZUELA, GUIANA, BRAZIL   ♂ 2¼″   ♀ 2″

COMMUNITY   DIET: ALL FOODS   SWIMS: MID-WATER

Though not brilliant in colour, this delightful aquarium fish is by no means drab. The finnage on good males is magnificent. The female's fins are shorter, and there is no white spot in the base of her dorsal.

BREEDING. *Tank: 24″ × 8″ × 8″. pH: 6·8–7·0. Hardness: 100–150 p.p.m. Temperature: 80° F. Spawns: above water surface. Method: adhesive eggs stuck to cover glass. Eggs: 50–100. Hatch: in 4 days. Fry wriggling: 1 day. Fry fall into water, becoming free-swimming: 6th day. Food 1st week: infusoria. 2nd week: infusoria, brine shrimp.*

This peaceful species has a unique method of breeding. It lays eggs above the surface of the water, which should be about 1″ to 1½″ below the cover glass. The tank should be moderately thickly stocked with assorted plants, merely to provide peaceful surroundings and afford a possible refuge for the female. A good pair is introduced, and a day later the male, coming alongside, presses his flank against the female and coaxes her to the surface. Suddenly the pair will leap from the water, and with quite a resounding smack hit and cling to the under side of the cover glass. Their damp bodies, having displaced some of the surrounding air, adhere momentarily to the flat surface. Eggs are laid and fertilized on the under surface of the glass; then the pair fall back into the water. The process is repeated several times. The male then drives the female away, and she is best removed. He takes full charge from now on. Periodically he may be seen going to the surface beneath the eggs, then with a vigorous stroke of his tail he will splash up water to keep them moist. Between these damping bouts the male moves away from the eggs, as though not wishing to advertise their presence.

From above the eggs can be seen in little globules of water, and development can be watched. They must not be allowed to fall into the tank before the babies are strong enough to swim. Whenever the cover glass is raised for feeding, or for any other purpose, it must be held dead level. Otherwise the globules of water run down the slope and carry the eggs with them; these may prematurely drop into the tank, or even fall on the floor. When it is necessary to rest the cover glass on anything it is best to place it over two jam-jars so that the eggs on its under surface are not squashed. After a few days the fry can be seen moving in the globules still adhering to the under side of the cover glass. It is now time to remove the male. Later the fry in their struggles cause the globules to drop into the water, when the babies are liberated in the tank to swim freely about.

Occasionally a male is too vigorous when splashing the eggs, and the globules of water become too large and drop into the tank, carrying the developing eggs with them. These the male proceeds to devour. Should this happen, on the next occasion the fish are spawned both parents should be removed, and an air-line with a stone diffuser at its end should be placed in the water below the eggs. The minute rising air bubbles cause a tiny spray of water to be thrown upward; this proves to be sufficient to keep the eggs damp until they hatch.

COPEINA GUTTATA

GUIANA, BRAZIL $\male\ 4''\quad \female\ 3\frac{3}{4}''$

COMMUNITY, WITH LARGER FISHES   DIET: ALL FOODS   SWIMS: MID-WATER

This is a colourful, peaceful fish, but due to its size it is more suitable for large tanks.

The back and sides are pale blue, the belly white. All the fins are pale yellow, bordered by cherry red. The dorsal, however, is lemon-coloured with an oblique black blotch in the forward central portion. This marking is less pronounced in the male, but he has rows of bright red spots along his sides, and his caudal fin has more red in it. He is also slimmer than the female.

BREEDING. *Tank:* $24'' \times 8'' \times 8''$. *pH:* $7 \cdot 0 - 7 \cdot 2$. *Hardness:* $100 - 150$ p.p.m. *Temperature:* $80° F$. *Spawns: on flat surface. Method: adhesive eggs fanned by male. Eggs: 150–250. Hatch: in 48 hours. Free-swimming: 3rd day. Food 1st week: infusoria. 2nd week: infusoria, brine shrimp.*

Breeding is simple. The tank should be filled with equal quantities of rain- and tap-water, and be moderately well-planted. In the centre a clear space should be left, and a flat stone or saucer should be placed on the sand. After courtship the male and female quiver side by side and deposit about 200 fertilized eggs, which adhere to the saucer or stone. Afterwards the male drives the female away, and she should be removed. He now spends all his time fanning the spawn with his pectoral fins to circulate the water round the eggs.

CORYNOPOMA RIISEI

Swordtail Characin

TRINIDAD, VENEZUELA, GUIANA   ♂ 2¾″   ♀ 2½″

COMMUNITY   DIET: ALL FOODS   SWIMS: UPPER HALF OF TANK

This peaceful characin derives its scientific name from the long filament which grows from the gill-plate of the male, and normally lies flat along the sides of the body. Due to the extended rays in the lower lobe of the male's caudal fin, the popular name is swordtail characin.

The body is creamy-coloured with no bright markings, but it is the fins of the male that strike the eye. When fully grown he has, relative to his size, large dorsal, anal, and caudal fins. The dorsal is somewhat kite-shaped, being broader at the top than at the base. The anal is wide, deep, and well-rounded, spreading from the vent to the caudal. His tail has several long rays in the lower lobe; these extend beyond the upper one.

The fins of the female are not spectacular.

BREEDING. Tank: 24″× 8″× 8″. pH: 6·8–7·2. Hardness: 100–150 p.p.m. Temperature: 78° F. Spawns: male and female 1″ apart. Method: eggs deposited on leaf. Eggs: 100–200. Hatch: in 24 hours. Fry hang on: 1 day. Free-swimming: 3rd day. Food 1st week: infusoria. 2nd week: infusoria, brine shrimp.

The species breed readily, though what actually occurs at the mating is uncertain. The tank should be moderately planted. The male soon starts courting by spreading his fins to full extent and joyfully disporting himself in front of his mate. Periodically, at right angles to his body, he holds out the filament of his gill-plate on each side. This is equipped at its extreme end with a spoon-like disc. The pair do not come close together, but swim side by side about $1\frac{1}{4}''$ apart. The male then curves his anal fin towards the female. It is thought that this action directs spermatozoa towards her, for a few seconds later she may be seen depositing eggs on plant leaves. The process is repeated until up to 100 eggs are laid, when the male should be taken out of the tank. The female often transfers the eggs from one leaf to another with her mouth. It is just as well to remove her when the fry are free-swimming.

Some breeders believe that the male ejects spermatozoa into the spoon-like disc at the end of the gill filament and proffers it to the female. It is thought that she takes the sperm into her mouth, spitting it out on to the leaf which she has selected for laying her eggs. She certainly appears to mouth the leaves before depositing her ova. This theory would explain the need for the gill extension possessed by the male. But again, why should the male extend his offside 'corynopoma' as well as the nearside one?

Though somewhat rarer, there is a golden variety of this fish.

CTENOBRYCON SPILURUS

Silver Tetra

GUIANA ♂ $3\frac{1}{2}''$ ♀ $3\frac{1}{2}''$

COMMUNITY, WITH LARGER FISHES   DIET: ALL FOODS   SWIMS: MID-WATER

One of the larger characins, this fish has compressed sides, so that viewed head on it appears less bulky than seen in profile. It has lost much of its popularity, for it is inclined to nip the fins of other fishes. Worse still, it is an inveterate plant-eater, and will quickly ruin a beautifully planted tank. Furthermore, the fish is inclined to remain stationary, head inclined downward, in one of the back corners, refusing to display itself in an attractive manner.

The body is void of bright colours, being silvery all over, with one dark spot in the shoulder region and another at the base of the tail.

The male is slightly smaller than the female. When mature she shows a pinkish tint in the rear portion of the anal fin.

BREEDING. *Tank: 30″×15″×15″. pH: 7·0–7·4. Hardness: 100–150 p.p.m. Temperature: 78° F. Spawns: in plant thickets. Method: standard for egg-droppers. Eggs: 200–300. Hatch: in 48 hours. Fry hang on: 1 day. Free-swimming: 4th day. Food 1st week: infusoria. 2nd week: brine shrimp, sifted Cyclops.*

The species is easy to breed. The tank should be thickly planted at each end with bushy clumps. Spawning takes place in the morning, the pair trembling side by side in the thickets. After spawning the parents should be removed.

EPHIPICHARAX ORBICULARIS

♀

♂

Salmon Discus

WEST AFRICA   ♂ 2½″   ♀ 2¾″

COMMUNITY, WITH LARGER FISHES   DIET: ALL FOODS   SWIMS: MID–WATER

This is a fairly recent introduction, and is in every way far superior to *C. spilurus*. Salmon discus are a better shape, and the fins are more attractive. The fish are not fin-nippers or destroyers of plants. Moreover, they delight in swimming backward and forward across the front of the aquarium, always displaying themselves to view. Though generally hardy, *E. orbicularis* are susceptible to shock. A sudden fright or, when in transit, a bad bump, will cause them to roll over; some recover, but others die.

The body is covered with small, shining silver scales. The gracefully backward-curved dorsal and anal fins are longish and pointed. The first rays in each are black, but are more pronounced in the anal. When in perfect condition both these fins are bordered with a thin black edge.

The female is slightly larger and deeper-chested than the male. When viewed from the front the lower portion of her body is U-shaped, whereas the male is sharper, and more resembles the letter V.

BREEDING. *Tank: 24″×8″×8″. pH: 7·0. Hardness: 100–150 p.p.m. Temperature: 80°F. Spawns: in plant thickets. Method: standard for egg-droppers. Eggs: 150–200. Hatch: in 24 hours. Fry hang on: 1 day. Free-swimming: 3rd day. Food 1st week: infusoria. 2nd week: infusoria, brine shrimp.*

Breeding is not difficult. The tank should be filled half with rain-water and half with tap-water. The pair usually spawn the following morning, after which they should be removed. Eggs may be seen among the plants, but in any case the female is now so slim that it is difficult to distinguish her from the male. The young grow quickly, and reach $\frac{1}{2}''$ in diameter in 4–5 weeks. Fry should be occasionally sorted, as the bigger ones are liable to eat their smaller brethren.

EPICYRTUS MICROLEPIS

Glass Characin

AMAZON, GUIANA $\qquad$ ♂ $3\frac{1}{2}''$ ♀ $3\frac{3}{4}''$

COMMUNITY, WITH LARGER FISHES   DIET: ALL FOODS   SWIMS: MID-WATER

Here we have an attractive, rather transparent fish that is peaceful enough with other species of roughly the same size. Though most of the organs are enclosed in a silvery sac, the swim-bladder can be clearly seen. The position of the head and back suggests deformity, but this appearance is quite natural.

The body is covered with minute silvery scales. One large black spot appears on the side; another, somewhat elongated, is at the base of the tail. Just in front of the forward spot there is a bright splash of green-gold. Also, running along the lateral line, is a thin green-gold stripe, which is reflected in certain lights. As the fish turns away a green-gold hue on the lower portion of the swim-bladder shines through the transparent scales.

The male is slightly smaller and slimmer than the female. When she is full of roe, though laterally compressed, she is thicker in section than the male in the abdominal region.

The fish swim in mid-water, often stopping motionless for periods with their heads tilted downward. They occasionally make a playful dart at each other, but no harm is done.

*BREEDING. Tank: 24″ × 8″ × 8″. pH: 7·0. Hardness: 100–150 p.p.m. Temperature:
80° F. Spawns: in plant thickets. Method: standard for egg-droppers. Eggs: 150–200.
Hatch: in 24 hours. Fry hang on: 1 day. Free-swimming: 3rd day. Food 1st week:
infusoria. 2nd week: infusoria, brine shrimp.*

Adults breed easily in well-planted tanks filled chiefly with tap-water
plus a little rain-water. After spawning parents should be transferred to
another tank. Some fry race ahead of others; these should be removed, or
they will devour the smaller ones.

GYMNOCORYMBUS TERNETZI

♂

♀

Black Widow

PARAGUAY   ♂ 1¾″   ♀ 2¼″

COMMUNITY   DIET: ALL FOODS   SWIMS: MID-WATER

A firm favourite of long standing, this attractive fish is at its best when
young, and if seen in a shoal against a green background. Under these
conditions it resembles a black butterfly. When in health it always carries
its fins erect, and is sprightly in its movements.

The fore-part of the body of a young fish is silvery, with two black
bars running vertically across. The dorsal, large anal, and hind portion
of the body is jet black. With age the fish becomes less sprightly, and the
intense black fades to a dark grey. When stimulated the black reappears.

Many aquarists find it difficult to sex half-grown specimens. But if the
eye is trained to observe only the body of the fish, and to disregard

completely the fins, it will be noticed that the males are more elongated, whereas females are deeper in comparison with their length. When filled with roe females are so bulged that sex is obvious.

BREEDING. *Tank: 24"×8"×8". pH: 6·8–7·0. Hardness: 100–150 p.p.m. Temperature: 78° F. Spawns: in plant thickets. Method: standard for egg-droppers. Eggs: 150–200. Hatch: in 24 hours. Fry hang on: 1 day. Free-swimming: 3rd day. Food 1st week: infusoria. 2nd week: infusoria, brine shrimp.*

Black Widows are one of the easiest characins to breed. The tank should be thickly planted. If a really fat female and a good male are placed together before dusk they should spawn the next morning. The parents should then be removed.

HASEMANIA MARGINATA

♀

♂

Silver Tips

BRAZIL		♂ 1¼″ ♀ 1½″
COMMUNITY	DIET: ALL FOODS	SWIMS: MID-WATER

Now known as *Hemigrammus nanus*, this is an attractive little characin; it is sprightly, not shy, peaceful, and when mature is moderately colourful.

The body and fins of the male are old gold; vivid white tips stand out on the dorsal, ventral, and caudal lobes. A black wedge runs through the caudal peduncle and ends in the fork of the tail; this is adorned above and below by gold patches in the front part of the caudal fin. Females lack the golden hue, and consequently the white tips to the fins are less conspicuous.

BREEDING. *Tank: 24"×8"×8". pH: 6·6–6·8. Hardness: 80–120 p.p.m. Temperature: 78° F. Spawns: in plant thickets. Method: standard for egg-droppers. Eggs: 70–120. Hatch: in 24 hours. Fry hang on: 1 day. Free-swimming: 3rd day. Food 1st week: infusoria. 2nd week: infusoria, brine shrimp.*

HEMIGRAMMUS CAUDOVITTATUS

Red-tailed Tetra

ARGENTINA, URUGUAY   ♂ 3″ ♀ 3½″

COMMUNITY, WITH LARGE FISHES   DIET: ALL FOODS   SWIMS: MID-WATER

This is quite a showy fish of pleasing appearance, although its habits are rather unpleasant. It nibbles most of the aquarium plants, but does not seem to fancy the Cryptocorynes. When *H. caudovittatus* reaches maturity it should be kept in a large tank with other fishes of similar size, as it is liable to chase little ones and nip their tails.

Both sexes are similarly coloured, but the males are slightly brighter. Females are larger and deeper-bellied.

BREEDING. *Tank: 24″ × 8″ × 8″. pH: 6·8–7·0. Hardness: 100–150 p.p.m. Temperature: 78° F. Spawns: in plant thickets. Method: standard for egg-droppers. Eggs: 150–250. Hatch: in 24 hours. Fry hang on: 1 day. Free-swimming: 3rd day. Food 1st week: infusoria. 2nd week: infusoria, brine shrimp.*

One of the easiest characins to breed. A large pair placed in a well-planted tank at dusk rarely fail to spawn next morning. Parents should be removed immediately afterwards.

HEMIGRAMMUS OCELLIFER

♀

♂

Beacon Fish

BRITISH GUIANA, AMAZON   ♂ 2″ ♀ 2¼″

COMMUNITY   DIET: ALL FOODS   SWIMS: MID-WATER

The beacon, or head-and-tail-light fish, derives its popular name from the splash of gold seen in the top half of the eye and the upper portion of the caudal peduncle. Both these splashes are bordered by red below. The fish are best seen in shoals lit from above against a dark background. When kept singly, or in pairs with other species, the head-and-tail-light effect, though still there, is less obvious.

The species is one of the most susceptible to Ichthyophthirius (white spot), and in a community tank is usually the first to show an outbreak of the disease. When purchased from a pet stores these fish should without exception be quarantined in an empty tank for a full ten days, and during this period the water should be tinted with methylene blue.

Males are slimmer than females. Sex can be determined before maturity, since on close examination of the anal fin males show a faint, milky-white bar. This runs across three-quarters of the forward rays of this fin, a little lower than half-way down.

BREEDING. *Tank: 24″×8″×8″. pH: 6·8–7·0. Hardness: 80–120 p.p.m. Temperature: 78° F. Spawns: in plant thickets. Method: standard for egg-droppers. Eggs: 150–200. Hatch: in 24 hours. Fry hang on: 1 day. Free-swimming: 3rd day. Food 1st week: infusoria. 2nd week: infusoria, brine shrimp.*

Mature fish spawn readily. The procedure mentioned under *H. caudovittatus* applies here.

HEMIGRAMMUS PULCHER

Black Wedge Tetra

ECUADOR, COLOMBIA   ♂ $1\frac{1}{2}''$ ♀ $1\frac{3}{4}''$

COMMUNITY   DIET: ALL FOODS   SWIMS: MID-WATER

This chubby little tetra is peaceful and attractive. It should be kept with small fishes, as it is not an active swimmer, preferring to take life quietly and sedately.

Females are deeper-bellied and thicker than males.

BREEDING. *Tank: 24″ × 8″ × 8″. pH: 6·6–6·8. Hardness: 80–100 p.p.m. Temperature: 80° F. Spawns: in plant thickets. Method: standard for egg-droppers. Eggs: 100–150. Hatch: in 24 hours. Fry hang on: 1 day. Free-swimming: 3rd day. Food 1st week: infusoria. 2nd week: infusoria, brine shrimp.*

The species is not easily induced to spawn, but when a good pair do breed they should afterwards be segregated, and not be put back with the others. This facilitates selecting the same breeding pair for subsequent spawns. Such a couple can usually be relied on to produce many broods. Once the babies are free-swimming, they stay near the sand tucked under the lower leaves of plant clumps, making them very difficult to see. Feeding should be continued for at least a fortnight before abandoning hope. By then the young should be visible.

HEMIGRAMMUS RHODOSTOMUS

Red-nosed Tetra

BRAZIL ♂ 1¾″ ♀ 2″

COMMUNITY DIET: ALL FOODS SWIMS: MID-WATER

A long, slender characin, which is peaceful, hardy, and attractive.

The body is silver with a slight tinge of gold. On the flanks there is a thin black line which gradually widens until it reaches the base of the tail. It then narrows again, stretching across the tail, ending in a point. A black bar adorns the upper and lower lobes of the caudal fin. But the most striking feature is the bright red forehead and nose, which gives the fish its popular name.

Males are slimmer, smaller, and slightly brighter than females.

BREEDING. Tank: 24″ × 8″ × 8″. pH: 6·8. Hardness: 50–80 p.p.m. Temperature: 80° F. Spawns: in plant thickets. Method: standard for egg-droppers. Eggs· 150–200. Hatch: in 24 hours. Fry hang on: 1 day. Free-swimming: 3rd day. Food 1st week: infusoria. 2nd week: infusoria, brine shrimp.

Not easily induced to spawn.

HEMIGRAMMUS UNILINEATUS

♀

♂

Feather Fin Tetra

TRINIDAD, GUIANA, AMAZON   ♂ 2″   ♀ 2½″

COMMUNITY   DIET: ALL FOODS   SWIMS: MID-WATER

A pleasing, though not strikingly beautiful, fish of peaceful habits. It resembles *Pristella riddlei*, but is not so colourful. One point in its favour is that it is long-lived.

The body is silver, the back olive. A black blotch appears in the upper portion of the dorsal fin; this is tipped with yellowish-white. The leading edge of the anal fin is yellow, and immediately behind this the second and third rays are black. The tail is rusty red.

Males are slimmer than females. When she is full of roe her bulging sides make sexing obvious.

BREEDING. *Tank: 24″ × 8″ × 8″. pH: 7·0–7·2. Hardness: 100–150 p.p.m. Temperature: 78° F. Spawns: in plant thickets. Method: standard for egg-droppers. Eggs: 200–250. Hatch: in 24 hours. Fry hang on: 1 day. Free-swimming: 3rd day. Food 1st week: infusoria. 2nd week: infusoria, brine shrimp.*

An easy to breed, prolific species. A pair put out overnight should spawn next morning. The parents should then be removed.

HYPHESSOBRYCON BIFASCIATUS

Brass Tetra

S.E. BRAZIL   ♂ 2½″   ♀ 2¾″

COMMUNITY, WITH LARGER FISHES   DIET: ALL FOODS   SWIMS: MID-WATER

This fish is not common in Britain these days, having lost its popularity to more colourful species. It is generally yellowish-silver, but from time to time wild specimens are imported which glow with a brassy gold to bronze colour—hence the popular name. Even these colourful importations fail to produce young of the same hue; this disappointment has no doubt contributed to the fish's fall from esteem.

Males are usually more colourful than females, but she is deeper-bodied. In large specimens the anal fin of the male is wider, and he may develop longer points on his ventrals.

BREEDING. Tank: 30″ × 15″ × 15″. pH: 6·8–7·0. Hardness: 100–120 p.p.m. Temperature: 80° F. Spawns: in plant thickets. Method: standard for egg-droppers. Eggs: 200–300. Hatch: in 24 hours. Fry hang on: 1 day. Free-swimming: 3rd day. Food 1st week: infusoria. 2nd week: infusoria, brine shrimp.

The fish are quite easy to spawn, following standard procedure. The parents should be removed immediately afterwards.

HYPHESSOBRYCON CALLISTUS MINOR

Minor Tetra

BRITISH GUIANA, BRAZIL   ♂ $1\frac{1}{4}''$ ♀ $1\frac{1}{2}''$

COMMUNITY   DIET: ALL FOODS   SWIMS: LOWER HALF OF TANK

There is uncertainty about the correct name of this fish, also of its cousin *H. callistus serpæ*. Some authorities consider *H. minor* and *H. serpæ* are separate species. *H. callistus minor* are chunky, of good disposition, and carry their fins well spread.

Deep red overcasts the sides. A round spot appears on the shoulder. The dorsal fin is black, tipped with white. The anal and ventrals are red, both being tipped with white at the lower points. A thin black line borders the rear edge of the anal fin; the hindermost tip of this is black. The caudal fin is red.

The male is slimmer than the female, and his colouring is more intense.

BREEDING. Tank: 24" × 8" × 8". pH: 6·6. Hardness: 50–80 p.p.m. Temperature: 78° F. Spawns: in plant thickets. Method: standard for egg-droppers. Eggs: 100–150. Hatch: in 24 hours. Fry hang on: 1 day. Free-swimming: 3rd day. Food 1st week: infusoria. 2nd week: infusoria, brine shrimp.

Though some pairs do not spawn readily, others oblige frequently. Once a good couple has been discovered they should be kept where they can be recognized easily, and so used for further breeding.

HYPHESSOBRYCON CALLISTUS RUBRASTIGMA

♀

♂

♂

Bleeding Heart Tetra

AMAZON, GUIANAS   ♂ 2″   ♀ 1¾″

COMMUNITY   DIET: ALL FOODS   SWIMS: LOWER HALF OF TANK

Only a few of these fish have so far reached Britain. At first glance they look like *H. roseaceus*. They are similar in shape, and come from the same area, but the coloration is different, and the fins longer, and grander.

It prefers soft brown peaty water, and when in good condition, with fins spread, the stature and colour are magnificent. In hard water the colour fades, and the black edge to the anal fin vanishes.

BREEDING. Tank: 30″ × 15″ × 15″. pH: 6·0–6·8. Hardness: 50–80 p.p.m. Temperature: 80° F. Spawns: above plant thickets. Method: the pair tremble side by side, dropping eggs. Eggs: 100–150. Hatch: in 48 hours. Fry hang on: 2 days. Free-swimming: 5th day. Food 1st week: infusoria. 2nd week: infusoria, brine shrimp.

Spawning follows the pattern of *H. roseaceus*.

HYPHESSOBRYCON CALLISTUS SERPÆ

♀

♂

Serpæ Tetra

BRAZIL, BRITISH GUIANA   ♂ 1½″   ♀ 1½″

COMMUNITY   DIET: ALL FOODS   SWIMS: LOWER HALF OF TANK

This fish may well be a variety of *H. callistus*, but in Europe, like its cousin *H. minor*, is considered a separate species.

H. minor and *H. serpæ* are very similar in appearance, but the latter is a blacker red over the body, and has a dark vertical stripe on the shoulder; whereas *H. minor* has a redder body colour and only a round spot on the shoulder. In all other respects the two are the same.

Mature females are wider and deeper-bellied than males.

BREEDING. *Tank: 24″ × 8″ × 8″. pH: 6·8. Hardness: 60–100 p.p.m. Temperature: 78° F. Spawns: in plant thickets. Method: standard for egg-droppers. Eggs: 80–120. Hatch: in 24 hours. Fry hang on: 1 day. Free-swimming: 3rd day. Food 1st week: infusoria. 2nd week: infusoria, brine shrimp.*

HYPHESSOBRYCON CARDINALIS

♂

♀

♀

Cardinal Tetra

PERUVIAN AMAZON   ♂ 1⅛″   ♀ 1¼″

COMMUNITY   DIET: ALL FOODS   SWIMS: LOWER HALF OF TANK

Also known as *Cheirodon axelrodi* (after my friend Herbert R. Axelrod, the well-known author of aquarium magazines and books in the United States). The fish's correct name is being decided by the International Commission for Zoological Nomenclature.[1]

A recent discovery, this beautiful fish resembles very closely the neon tetra, but in shape it seems a little longer and slimmer.

Though the colours are similar to the neon, the brilliant blue-green stripe and the deep red area below are not identical. The beginning of the blue stripe on the cardinal covers the whole eye, whereas in neons it adorns only the upper portion. In the cardinal the blue stripe is straighter, and fades out behind and below the adipose fin, whereas in neons it has a definite upward bend in the latter half, and ends on the back just in front of this fin. The red area in the cardinal covers most of the lower flanks and belly as well as the caudal peduncle, while in neons the red area is confined to a broad streak covering only the centre part of the flanks and caudal peduncle. A close study of the colour plates of the two species will show the main differences.

Sexing is difficult, except in adult fish. Then the female is obviously rounder and deeper.

BREEDING. This species requires the identical conditions described under *H. innesi* (neon tetras)—very soft, brown peaty water with a pH 5·6–6·6. They spawn on nylon mops, but are not such ready spawners, or as prolific, as neons.

[1] Since writing the above, but before going to press, the scientific name has been decided in favour of *C. axelrodi*.

HYPHESSOBRYCON FLAMMEUS

♂

♀

Flame Fish

RIO DE JANEIRO   ♂ 1½″   ♀ 1¾″

COMMUNITY   DIET: ALL FOODS   SWIMS: LOWER HALF OF TANK

A firm favourite with most aquarists, this colourful little fish has enjoyed great popularity for years, being known in the United States as the Tetra von Rio. It is somewhat short and dumpy, is very lively, keeps its fins well spread, but is inclined to be shy until it gets used to its home.

Our colour plate shows that the male has redder fins than the female, and the edges of his ventrals and anal are bordered with black.

In a shoal the redder males are easily noticed. Colour, however, is not the only indication of sex; females when full of roe are much deeper and wider in the belly.

BREEDING. *Tank: 24″ × 8″ × 8″. pH: 6·8–7·2. Hardness: 100–120 p.p.m. Temperature: 80° F. Spawns: in plant thickets. Method: standard for egg-droppers. Eggs: 150–200. Hatch: in 24 hours. Fry hang on: 1 day. Free-swimming: 3rd day. Food 1st week: infusoria. 2nd week: infusoria, brine shrimp.*

So simple is this fish to breed that we recommend it to beginners who are spawning egg-layers for the first time. (See Spawning the Egg-droppers, p. 159.)

HYPHESSOBRYCON GRACILIS

♂   ♀

Glowlight Tetra

GUIANA   ♂ 1½″   ♀ 1¾″

COMMUNITY   DIET: ALL FOODS   SWIMS: LOWER HALF OF TANK

It is sometimes unbelievable how different fishes can appear when seen in ideal surroundings, as against being huddled together in a corner of a bare tank, frightened and unhappy. Here we have a case in point. The glowlight can be a drab, colourless fish, or a fiery, startling beauty that glows brilliantly. Seen in soft peaty water in a beautifully planted aquarium, having a dark background and lit from above, a shoal of these little gems is a sight not easily forgotten. This fish is only at its best when on its own or with other small fishes.

The body is translucent; a vivid red stripe runs across the flanks from eye to base of tail. The dorsal has red in the forward part. The other fins are clear, except for white tips.

When young, males may sometimes be identified, as on the anal fin they have the characin hook; this often gets caught up in a fine net. In adult specimens sex is obvious, the females being larger and much deeper-bellied.

BREEDING. *Tank: 24″×8″×8″. pH: 6·0–6·6. Hardness: 10–20 p.p.m. Temperature: 78° F. Spawns: in nylon mops. Method: males and females lock fins and roll over. Eggs: 150–250. Hatch: in 24 hours. Fry hang on: 1 day. Free-swimming: 3rd day. Food 1st week: infusoria, yolk of egg. 2nd week: infusoria, brine shrimp.*

Once considered to be a difficult species to breed, it now presents no problem whatsoever. A bare tank should be thoroughly cleaned, and contain soft brown peaty water with a reading not higher than 20 p.p.m. In it are placed two or three nylon mops which have been sterilized by boiling. A large pair is selected, the female bulging with roe. They are placed in the tank in the late afternoon. Next day, after some love play which takes the form of short darts at each other, male and female come side by side, and lock fins. Then, trembling in close contact, they roll over in or against the nylon mops. Eggs are laid and fertilized, many falling to the bottom of the tank. The parents are removed after spawning is completed. When free-swimming the fry may be given a few feeds with yolk of hard-boiled egg. A tiny portion of this is dropped into the corner of a fine muslin net. This is then dipped into the tank, squeezed with the fingers, and shaken. As a result a cloud of egg yolk disperses into the water. Care must be taken not to overdo this food, as if much remains uneaten it will quickly foul the water. The fry will take fine infusoria, and a week later brine shrimp. After this the young are easy to raise, and grow quickly.

HYPHESSOBRYCON HETERORHABDUS

♂

♀

Belgian Flag

GUIANA, AMAZON		♂ 1½″ ♀ 1¾″
COMMUNITY	DIET: ALL FOODS	SWIMS: MID-WATER

This is another beautiful fish; but it only shows its best colours when happy and in good condition in a well-planted tank containing soft, slightly acid water.

The male is slimmer and slightly smaller than the female.

BREEDING. Tank: 24″×8″×8″. pH: 6·0–6·6. Hardness: 10–20 p.p.m. Temperature: 78° F. Spawns: in nylon mops. Method: standard for egg-droppers. Eggs: 100–150. Hatch: in 48 hours. Fry hang on: 1 day. Free-swimming: 4th day. Food 1st week: infusoria, yolk of egg. 2nd week: infusoria, brine shrimp.

Though the authors have not succeeded with this problem fish, Mr Smykala, of London, the well-known breeder and importer, has bred several generations of them, using the method described under *H. gracilis*. He finds that once reared the young are more prolific than wild specimens.

HYPHESSOBRYCON INNESI

♀

♂

♂

Neon Tetra

PERU, WESTERN BRAZIL   ♂ 1⅛″ ♀ 1¼″

COMMUNITY   DIET: ALL FOODS   SWIMS: LOWER HALF OF TANK

This is regarded by many aquarists as the gem of the tropical world. The neon tetra has been named after William T. Innes, the celebrated author and well-known publisher of many aquarium books and periodicals; and it is fitting that such a universally sought-after fish should bear the name of a man who has done so much to advance the hobby all over the world.

Neons are small, peaceful, extremely perky, and really beautiful fish. Once settled down they are not shy, and, although not aggressive, have the courage to stand up for themselves if the occasion arises.

Females are larger than males. It has been noticed by the authors that when the males are young the upper edge of the red splash starts on the back beneath the front rays of the adipose fin. With females the red begins farther back, just below the posterior rays of this fin. When they are mature the larger, bulging, deep-bodied females are unmistakable.

BREEDING. *Tank:* 24″ × 8″ × 8″. *pH:* 5·6–6·6. *Hardness:* 0–10 p.p.m. *Temperature:* 78° F. *Spawns:* in nylon mops. *Method:* standard for egg-droppers. *Eggs:* 80–150. *Hatch:* in 24 hours. *Fry hang on:* 2 days. *Free-swimming:* 4th day. *Food 1st week:* infusoria, yolk of egg. *2nd week:* infusoria, brine shrimp.

Neons are still considered to be problem fish to breed, and regarding the methods used various rumours are constantly circulated. Most of these purport to come second- or third-hand from German aquarists, and all these methods are most complicated. Some state that the breeding tank must be sterilized with chemicals and then filled with distilled water in which oak-leaves and bark are soaked for a fortnight. Later sterilized plants are introduced, and a pair of fish transferred into the breeding tank with the aid of a dip tube. After all this, if they do not spawn within two days the whole process has to be repeated. Such conditions are not provided in nature. The rumours do not explain how distilled water put into a tank remains free of bacteria for more than a few hours, or how to catch the parents in dip tubes.

In spite of the above, the authors have proved that success can be achieved quite simply. What is more, healthy fish will breed every ten days from the age of 12 weeks upward, provided that the correct conditions are created. These are: (i) perfectly healthy, medium-sized adult fish, free from Plistophera (neon disease); (ii) a clean, bare tank; (iii) very soft brown peaty water with a hardness not exceeding 10 p.p.m., which is practically bacteria-free.

The peaty water is prepared in advance; in fact, the wise aquarist will always keep a tank full at hand. It is best to start with rain-water into which is put several handfuls of peat. When all this has sunk to the bottom the water will be brown, practically free from bacteria, and the hardness will be between o and 10 p.p.m. (see Titrating, p. 45). The pH should be adjusted to come within the range of 5·6 and 6·6, though this need not be exact. The authors have frequently bred neons successfully in water anywhere within the pH range 5·0 to 6·8, but never where the hardness has exceeded 10 p.p.m.

It is only necessary to cleanse the breeding tank thoroughly and dry out with a clean cloth. The peat-water is now poured in to a depth of 4″, and a couple of nylon mops which have been sterilized in boiling water are put in as spawn-receivers. The temperature should be adjusted to 76–78° F., and the tank placed where it will receive only subdued daylight. A female bulging with roe and a good male are put in the tank before dusk. They will probably spawn during the middle of the next morning for two hours. After this the parents should be removed with a net which has been dipped into boiling water. The tank is then covered with paper to exclude strong light.

Neon eggs are not easy to see among the nylon mops, but if a glass-bottomed tank is used many eggs lying on the floor of the tank are clearly visible through the base-glass. Quite a few turn opaque white in a few hours—these must be infertile, for many others remain clear and hatch, thus proving that the water is satisfactory, and not the cause of the trouble.

Provided the conditions are correct, the eggs will hatch in 24 hours, and a few minute fry may be seen hanging from the mops and on the glass walls of the aquarium. If none are visible do not be disappointed, as they are so small and transparent that they are easily overlooked. In a further 36–48 hours a few fry may be seen lying on the glass bottom of the tank or hanging on the side walls. Probably only the eyes (appearing as two black specks) will be noticed. When the paper covering is lifted one or two fry may be seen to dart to the sides, corners, and base of the tank, where they remain motionless. If close watch is kept on the bottom inch of water a few will be observed swimming short distances. They should be fed with the yolk of hard-boiled egg (see *H. gracilis*, p. 249) or fine infusoria. They will take brine shrimp in a few days. The fry show no colour until they are between 3 and 4 weeks old. At this stage the blue line appears on the sides and the eyes. The young, judging by the depth of body, are sexable in 10 weeks, and, as previously stated, will breed when 3 months old.

Plistophera (neon disease), which may be a form of tuberculosis, appears as a white patch on the flanks of the fish. It seems to be more prevalent in imported specimens than on home-bred fish. Although various cures have occasionally been reported, the authors know of no certain remedy, and, since the disease may soon spread to affect other fish, it is usually wiser to kill the infected ones, in order to minimize further contamination.

HYPHESSOBRYCON PULCHRIPINNIS

♀

♂

Lemon Tetra

AMAZON BASIN   ♂ $1\frac{3}{4}''$ ♀ $1\frac{3}{4}''$

COMMUNITY   DIET: ALL FOODS   SWIMS: MID-WATER

This is another charming little tetra, peaceful, pretty, and of average size. It carries its fins jauntily, and likes to swim in the front of the aquarium.

The body is overcast with pale yellow; the upper half of the eye is bright crimson; but it is the yellow streak bordered by black in both the dorsal and anal fins that catches the eye.

The female is much deeper in the belly than the male, and he has slightly brighter colours.

BREEDING. *Tank: 24″ × 8″ × 8″. pH: 6·6. Hardness: 20–50 p.p.m. Temperature: 80° F. Spawns: in nylon mops. Method: standard for egg-droppers. Eggs: 100–150. Hatch: in 24 hours. Fry hang on: 1 day. Free-swimming: 3rd day. Food 1st week: infusoria. 2nd week: infusoria, brine shrimp.*

The species is not difficult to breed (following the procedure described under *H. gracilis*), although individual fish sometimes will not spawn. Once a good pair has been bred they should be segregated from the others, so that they will not be muddled when selecting them again. If the fish do not breed within 3 days it is a waste of time to keep them in the breeding tank. Another pair should be selected, and the originals conditioned further. The parents are not avid egg-eaters, but nevertheless should be removed in case of cannibalism.

HYPHESSOBRYCON ROSACEUS

♂

♀

Rosy Tetra

BRITISH GUIANA, BRAZIL		♂ $1\frac{3}{4}''$ ♀ $1\frac{1}{2}''$
COMMUNITY	DIET: ALL FOODS	SWIMS: MID-WATER

One of the showiest of the characins, it is not always seen at its best. It prefers soft, peaty water, and should be kept on its own or with other small fishes requiring the same conditions. When in the correct environment the fish displays its finest colours, and spreads its fins to full extent. In community tanks it often carries the fins rather limply, and folded.

Sexing presents no difficulty, since the dorsal and anal fins of the male are much longer, and pointed. Moreover, the upper tip of the female's dorsal fin shows a fine edging of red.

BREEDING. *Tank: 30″ × 15″ × 15″. pH: 6·4–6·6. Hardness: 55–85 p.p.m. Temperature: 80° F. Spawns: in clear water above plants. Method: drops eggs into thickets. Eggs: 50–100. Hatch: in 48 hours. Fry hang on: 1 day. Free-swimming: 4th day. Food 1st week: infusoria. 2nd week: infusoria, brine shrimp.*

Conditions must be ideal before the species can be induced to spawn. Although the fish are not large, they will not spawn in a small tank. This must be filled with very soft peaty water to a depth of 10″, and planted with short plants rising no more than 4″ above the sand. Two feathery clumps should be placed one at each end of the tank, and these should not exceed 6″ in height. With fins spread to splitting point, the males make playful darts at the females, and resemble delta-winged aeroplanes in their dives and upward sweeps. The pair will come side by side, and swimming in the clear water above the plants, tremble together, dropping fertilized eggs into the foliage below.

After spawning, the adults should be removed.

HYPHESSOBRYCON SCHOLZEI

♂

♀

Black-line Tetra

LOWER AMAZON   ♂ 2¼″   ♀ 2½″

COMMUNITY   DIET: ALL FOODS   SWIMS: MID-WATER

A popular fish, not by reason of its bright colours, but because it is extremely hardy, and one of the easiest of the egg-layers to breed. *H. scholzei* has a wide temperature range, and is not particular as to exact conditions. It should be kept with medium-sized species, as it may occasionally take sly nips at small fishes' fins.

The body is silvery, the back olive, the eye jet-black. A striking black line runs the length of the sides, ending in a large black spot at the centre of the tail fin. The first rays of the ventrals and anal fin are white.

The female is much deeper-bodied than the male. He sometimes shows a darkish area in the centre of the dorsal, particularly when young.

BREEDING. Tank: 24″×8″×8″. pH: 7·0. Hardness: 100–180 p.p.m. Temperature: 78°F. Spawn: in plant thickets. Method: standard for egg-droppers. Eggs: 100–250. Hatch: in 24 hours. Fry hang on: 1 day. Free-swimming: 3rd day. Food 1st week: infusoria. 2nd week: brine shrimp, microworms.

Black-line tetras are extremely easy and prolific spawners, and are strongly recommended to any beginner attempting to breed egg-layers for the first time. If the procedure detailed on p. 159 is followed it is almost certain spawning will take place next morning. The eggs, the size of a pin-head, are very adhesive, and can be seen in great profusion sticking to most of the plant leaves. Another advantage to the beginner is that these eggs are robust, and hatch in 24 hours.

LEPORINUS FASCIATUS

Striped Leporinus

GUIANA, AMAZON   ♂ 6″   ♀ 8″

COMMUNITY, WITH LARGER FISHES   DIET: ALL FOODS   SWIMS: MID-WATER

This fish is rare in Europe, partly because it is difficult to find and catch in its native haunts, and partly because air routes travelling via Gander, Newfoundland, and thence across the Atlantic result in unusually heavy losses. The fish is elongated in shape, and has a sharp-pointed nose.

When young the general body colour is orange, and five black bars cross the sides vertically. As the body lengthens with age the bars split, one forming two, until the fish has ten altogether. The body colour fades to an ivory yellow. The small adipose fin is black and white, and the anal fin has two bands of black running across it.

The fish has a habit of remaining stationary in mid-water with its head dipped at an angle of 30 degrees below horizontal.

BREEDING. There are no records of this fish having been bred in captivity.

LEPORINUS FRIDERICI

Spotted Leporinus

AMAZON, GUIANA ♂ 6″ ♀ 8″

COMMUNITY, WITH LARGER FISHES   DIET: ALL FOODS   SWIMS: MID-WATER

A recent introduction, this fish is similar in shape to its cousin *L. fasciatus*, and swims with the head tilted down. It will take any food, and is peaceful when not too large.

The body is olive green, but in strong light thin stripes of a brilliant gold appear horizontally from head to tail. The back is marked with numerous short bars that reach to the lateral line, and the sides are adorned with numerous large, round black spots.

When mature the pectorals, ventrals, and anal fins of males develop a reddish tint, and both sexes appear more blotched.

BREEDING. Breeding has so far not been achieved.

LEPORINUS STRIATUS

♀

Lined Leporinus

AMAZON, GUIANA ♂ 6″ ♀ 7″

COMMUNITY, WITH LARGER FISHES DIET: ALL FOODS

SWIMS: LOWER HALF OF TANK

    Another member of the family, this fish, like its relatives, grows too large for the average aquarist. Among bigger fishes it seems to do well, minding its own business, but refusing to be intimidated.

    As will be seen from the photograph, the stripes or lines in this species run horizontally.

BREEDING. As yet we have not heard of this fish being bred in captivity.

METYNNIS SCHREITMULLERI

♀

AMAZON   ♂ 4″ ♀ 4¼″

NON-COMMUNITY   DIET: ALL FOODS   SWIMS: MID-WATER

There are several species of Metynnis: all are disc-shaped, with laterally compressed sides. This is not a species for the average aquarist on account of its bulk and plant-eating habits, but it should be kept with bigger fishes in medium-sized aquaria. Even so, it may nibble the tenderer plants.

The body is silver, the fins are grey. A warm yellow tint appears on the edge of the anal fin. The dorsal is carried upright, and is adorned with several black specks. In its smaller sizes the fish seems peaceful.

BREEDING. This fish has not been bred in captivity.

MŒNKHAUSIA PITTIERI

♂

♀

VENEZUELA   ♂ 2½"   ♀ 2¼"

COMMUNITY   DIET: ALL FOODS   SWIMS: MID-WATER

Though not always available, this is a very desirable fish for those with medium to large community tanks. It is peaceful, and, although not brilliantly coloured, has striking fins which it displays well.

The body is silver-grey with an iridescent pale blue on the lower sides, and small green spots reflect here and there as the light catches them. The upper half of the eye is bright red. But it is the fins which mark this fish out among others: the dorsal and anal are long, wide, and gracefully pointed, being more exaggerated in the male. The female may be told from her fuller and deeper belly, and her shorter fins.

BREEDING. *Tank: 30"×15"×15". pH: 6·8–7·0. Hardness: 80–120 p.p.m. Temperature: 78° F. Spawns: in plant thickets. Method: standard for egg-droppers. Eggs: 100–200. Hatch: in 48 hours. Fry hang on: 2 days. Free-swimming: 5th day. Food 1st week: infusoria, brine shrimp. 2nd week: microworms, fine dried food.*

The species is not one of the easiest to breed, but when spawning does take place many eggs are laid and fertilized in thickets of fine-leaved plants. The eggs are semi-adhesive, and may be seen clearly. The parents should be removed immediately after spawning.

MŒNKHAUSIA SANCTA FILOMENNÆ

♀

♂

BRAZIL, GUIANA   ♂ 3½″   ♀ 4″

COMMUNITY, WITH LARGER FISHES   DIET: ALL FOODS   SWIMS: MID-WATER

This fish—formerly known as *M. oligolepis*—is not brilliantly coloured, and grows rather too large for the average community tank. When fully adult it may bully and kill smaller species.

The body is grey, with large scales; as each of these is edged with black, there is a network pattern over the fish. The upper half of the eye is brilliant red, and a large black spot appears at the root of the tail, and above this, behind the adipose fin, is a gleaming gold patch. The fins are grey, the first ray of the anal being creamy white. When the fish are young the contrast of eye, sides, and tail spot is clear-cut and pleasing, but this tends to fade with age.

Both male and female are deep-bodied, but she is considerably rounder in section.

BREEDING. *Tank: 24″×8″×8″. pH: 6·8–7·4. Hardness: 100–150 p.p.m. Temperature: 78–80° F. Spawns: in plant thickets. Method: standard for egg-droppers. Eggs: 200–400. Hatch: in 48 hours. Fry hang on: 2 days. Free-swimming: 5th day. Food 1st week: infusoria and brine shrimp. 2nd week: microworms, fine dried food.*

The species breeds fairly readily even when 1½″ long, scattering very tiny eggs among bunches of plants, after much chasing. They will spawn for a period of 1½–2 hours, the eggs being seen among the foliage, after which the parents should be removed.

NANNÆTHIOPS UNITÆNIATUS

♀

♂

CENTRAL AFRICA   ♂ 2″   ♀ 2½″

COMMUNITY   DIET: ALL FOODS   SWIMS: MID–WATER

By no means brilliant, this fish is none the less attractive, in a modest way. It is peaceful and quiet, and makes few demands.

The back is dark, but on closer examination proves to be made up of rows of small dark dots; the lower flanks and belly are silver-white. A dividing line of intense black runs through the eye along the sides, and ends just in the caudal fin; this is set off by another line of bright gold immediately above, giving the top half of the eye a golden lid. All fins are clear.

Males are slimmer and smaller than females.

BREEDING. *Tank: 24″ × 8″ × 8″. pH: 6·8–7·0. Hardness: 100–150 p.p.m. Temperature: 78° F. Spawns: in plant thickets. Method: standard for egg-droppers. Eggs: 100–150. Hatch in 48 hours. Fry hang on: 1 day. Free-swimming: 4th day. Food 1st week: infusoria. 2nd week: infusoria, brine shrimp.*

NANNOSTOMUS ANOMALUS

AMAZON BASIN, BRITISH GUIANA   ♂ 1¾″ ♀ 1¾″

COMMUNITY   DIET: ALL FOODS   SWIMS: MID-WATER

Here we have quite a common, but very attractive, aquarium fish. The body is elongated, and tapers at both ends, the nose being particularly pointed. Although shy at first, if kept with smaller species it will soon learn to be unafraid, and come forward to receive its share of food.

Sexing is not difficult, as the male's red ventral fins are tipped with silver-blue. The belly of the female is considerably deeper.

At night, when the aquarium is dark, these fish change colour so completely that they are hard to recognize at once. Then the body bears large dark-brown patches in rectangular blocks along the sides.

BREEDING. *Tank: 24″ × 8″ × 8″, or smaller. pH: 6·2–6·6. Hardness: 50–80 p.p.m. Temperature: 76–78° F. Spawns: in floating plants or peat. Method: eggs deposited over a period of 2 to 4 days. Eggs: 100–200. Hatch: in 48 hours. Fry hang on: 2 days. Free-swimming: 5th day. Food 1st week: infusoria and yolk of egg. 2nd week: brine shrimp, microworms.*

The fish are easy to spawn, requiring only a small tank filled with soft brown peaty water. A little water-logged peat sprinkled over the bottom of the tank will hide any eggs that fall. On the surface place a good-sized patch of lesser bladderwort. If a good pair, consisting of a colourful male and a deep-bodied female, are placed in the tank, probably in a few hours the male will start driving his mate. Both fish tremble side by side in the floating weed, and eggs are deposited freely. If well fed the parents need not be removed, and spawning will continue over several days.

NANNOSTOMUS MARGINATUS

♂

♂

♀

GUIANA   ♂ 1″   ♀ 1¼″

COMMUNITY   DIET: ALL FOODS   SWIMS: ALL DEPTHS

This is the smallest of the Nannostomus known so far, and makes an ideal fish for those aquarists with smaller tanks. It is extremely peaceful, most attractive, lively, not shy once it has settled down, and will take any food. In comparison with *N. anomalus*, the body is shorter, and altogether stubbier.

The female is deeper-bellied than the male.

BREEDING. *Tank: 24″×8″×8″ or smaller. pH: 6·4–6·8. Hardness: 50–80 p.p.m. Temperature: 78–80° F. Spawns: in floating plants. Method: similar to N. anomalus. Eggs: 50–75. Hatch: in 48 hours. Fry hang on: 2 days. Free-swimming: 5th day. Food 1st week: infusoria. 2nd week: infusoria, brine shrimp.*

Eggs are deposited in Riccia or lesser bladderwort. The fry must be fed with very fine infusoria at first, as their mouths are particularly small. When they are about ½″ long the tail fin of the babies is round at its outer edge, but the pointed lobes develop later.

NANNOSTOMUS TRIFASCIATUS

AMAZON, GUIANA   ♂ 1½″   ♀ 1½″
COMMUNITY   DIET: ALL FOODS   SWIMS: ALL DEPTHS

Possibly the prettiest of the three Nannostomus shown in this book, and the rarest in Europe. It is a beautiful little fish, and highly recommended to those who keep small aquaria.

The back is olive, the belly silver. A dark band runs from the tip of the lower lip through the eye to the base of the caudal peduncle. Above this is a broad gold band, and in males this band is further beautified by a line of well-spaced red dots, giving the impression of an ermine robe. The golden band on females lacks the red spots. The dorsal, ventrals, anal, and tail fin are adorned with largish red blotches, the outer edges of all these fins being clear.

BREEDING. *Tank: 24″ × 8″ × 8″, or smaller. pH: 6·6–6·8. Hardness: 60–80 p.p.m. Temperature: 78–80° F. Spawns: in plant thickets, Riccia, etc. Method: similar to N. anomalus. Eggs: 30–70. Hatch: in 48 hours. Fry hang on: 2 days. Free-swimming: 5th day. Food 1st week: infusoria, yolk of egg. 2nd week: infusoria, brine shrimp.*

The fish are not prolific breeders in captivity, but can be induced to spawn, slightly acid water being preferred. The fry are somewhat prone to dropsy, and on occasions the authors have lost a whole batch from this disease when about six weeks old.

NEOLEBIAS ANSORGI

BELGIAN CONGO, W. AFRICA   ♂ 1½″   ♀ 1¾″

COMMUNITY   DIET: ALL FOODS   SWIMS: LOWER HALF OF TANK

Quite a pleasing little fish of subdued colour and quiet nature—in fact, somewhat shy, staying in the background beneath the horizontal leaves of Cryptocorynes.

When in soft peaty water the overall colour is rich mahogany, and green spangles appear as highlights on the sides. The fins are a rusty red, and a broad dark green band runs horizontally from gill-plate to caudal peduncle. This band deepens and fades according to the fish's whim.

Females are deeper-bodied and less brightly coloured.

BREEDING. *Tank: 24″ × 8″ × 8″. pH: 6·4. Hardness: 2–15 p.p.m. Temperature: 78–80° F. Spawns: in plant thickets, Riccia, etc. Method: similar to* Nannostomus. *Eggs: 100–150. Hatch: in 48 hours. Fry hang on: 2 days. Free-swimming: 5th day. Food 1st week: infusoria. 2nd week: brine shrimp, microworms.*

The breeding tank should contain dark brown peaty water, which is very soft, a layer of peat on the bottom, and a good layer of lesser bladderwort floating on the water surface. Leave the pair for 2 or 3 days, and then remove them. Fry may not be observed for a week, but feeding should be continued, nevertheless.

The small fry grow slowly.

PHENACOGRAMMUS INTERRUPTUS

♂ ♀

BELGIAN CONGO ♂ 3″ ♀ 3″

COMMUNITY   DIET: LIVE FOOD, MAY BE TRAINED TO TAKE DRIED FOOD

SWIMS: UPPER HALF OF TANK

Another recent introduction from the Belgian Congo. The fish is peaceful, active, and displays itself well if given a good-sized aquarium in which it can swim freely.

The upper portion of the back is mauvish, and the belly silvery. Along the lateral line is a broad, pale greenish band without defined edges. This band intensifies or fades according to the angle at which the light strikes across the sides of the fish. The fins are mauvish-blue edged with blue-grey, the dorsal is long and pointed, and the tail fin of the male has a protruding central section which tapers to a jagged point. The female has the same colouring, but her dorsal is not so long and pointed, and she lacks the protruding point in the caudal fin.

BREEDING. Tank: 30″×15″×15″. pH: 5·6–5·8. Hardness: 20–50 p.p.m. Temperature: 78° F. Spawns: in plant thickets. Method: standard for egg-droppers. Eggs: 50–100. Hatch: in 48 hours. Fry hang on: 2 days. Free-swimming: 5th day. Food 1st week: infusoria, yolk of egg. 2nd week: brine shrimp, microworms.

In our experience these fish can only be induced to spawn when fully adult. The female becomes distended with roe, and the procedure follows that of *Alestopetersius caudalis*.

PŒCILOBRYCON AURATUS

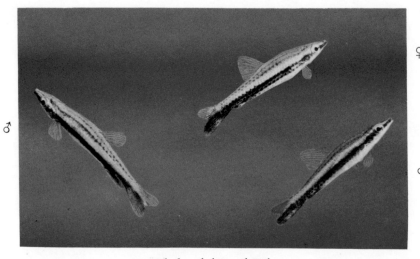

Black-tailed Pencil Fish

GUIANA, AMAZON   ♂ 2″   ♀ 2″

COMMUNITY   DIET: ALL FOODS   SWIMS: UPPER HALF OF TANK

These attractive, slender fish have earned the nickname of pencil fish because of their slim, cylindrical bodies and tapering noses. In Europe this species often goes under the name of *P. eques*. It is harmless but rather shy, and should only be kept with small non-aggressive fishes. *P. auratus* has a habit of sitting still in mid-water with its tail end curved downward at an angle of 20–30 degrees below horizontal, but when disturbed swims or darts off on a level keel.

The body is golden-brown, and a dark stripe runs from the tip of the snout through the eye to the lower lobe of the tail, where it spreads into a black patch. The black band is bordered above by a thin line of gold. The upper lobe of the tail is colourless, and tends to become unnoticed, and this helps to give the impression that the tail end of the fish curves downward. In males the anal fin has a dark red spot in its upper portion.

BREEDING. *Tank: 24″ × 8″ × 8″. pH: 6·6–6·8. Hardness: 80–100 p.p.m. Temperature: 80° F. Spawns: on plant leaves. Method: male fans deposited eggs. Eggs: 50–75. Hatch: in 48 hours. Fry hang on: 1 day. Free-swimming: 4th day. Food 1st week: infusoria. 2nd week: infusoria, brine shrimp.*

Given the right conditions these fish are not difficult to spawn. They prefer soft water, and lay their eggs on the fine curving leaves of *Sagittaria natans*. They do not seem to be prolific, but guard their eggs and occasionally fan them with their pectoral fins; but if the adults are removed the eggs hatch just as well without such attention.

PŒCILOBRYCON ESPEI

♀

♂

Barred Pencil Fish

GUIANA, AMAZON   ♂ 1½″   ♀ 1¾″

COMMUNITY   DIET: ALL FOODS   SWIMS: ALL DEPTHS

A recent discovery, this is a pencil fish of distinction, for the markings on the flanks are vertical. It is quiet and peaceful, though a little shy.

From the pointed snout a faint line of gold runs above the eye along the sides to the caudal peduncle. A short black line passes from the lips through the centre of the eye across the gill-plate. The body is slashed in the lower half by five short, thick, blue-black bars which slant slightly forward at their base. Occasionally pinkish highlights appear in the abdominal region. The fins are clear.

Females are slightly shorter and thicker than males.

BREEDING. *Tank: 24″×8″×8″. pH: 6·2–6·6. Hardness: 5–10 p.p.m. Temperature: 78° F. Spawns: under plant leaves. Method: similar to* Nannostomus. *Eggs: 50–75. Hatch: in 2 days. Fry hang on: 2 days. Free-swimming: 5th day. Food 1st week: infusoria. 2nd week: infusoria, brine shrimp.*

The breeding tank should contain very soft brown peaty water, and have a layer of peat on the bottom. A cutting of *Hygrophila stricta* is anchored to a small piece of thick slate buried in the peat, so that the plant stands upright in the water. The surface is covered with Riccia.

The male, after courting the female, presses her sideward and upward under a leaf, and the two tremble in this position for nearly ten times as long as most fishes employing this interlocking method.

Eventually they break apart, and then eggs may be seen falling into the peat. The process is repeated on and off for a day or two, after which the parents should be removed. The eggs remain hidden in the peat, but on hatching the young fry take refuge in the floating Riccia.

PŒCILOBRYCON HARRISONII

GUIANA, AMAZON   ♂ 2″ ♀ 2″

COMMUNITY   DIET: ALL FOODS   SWIMS: LOWER HALF OF TANK

The fish strongly resembles *P. auratus*, but swims on an even keel.

The back is olive down to a thin dark line which runs from above the eye to below the adipose fin. A broader dark line runs from the tip of the snout through the eye and as far as the fork of the tail. Here it spreads out and covers the upper portion of the lower lobe of this fin. Between these two dark lines is a band of bright gold. The tips of the lips are also gold. Other fins are clear.

The females are slightly deeper-bodied than the males.

BREEDING. *Tank: 24″ × 8″ × 8″. pH: 6·6–6·8. Hardness: 80–100 p.p.m. Temperature: 80° F. Spawns: on plant leaves. Method: male fans deposited eggs. Eggs: 50–75. Hatch: in 48 hours. Fry hang on: 1 day. Free-swimming: 4th day. Food 1st week: infusoria. 2nd week: infusoria, brine shrimp.*

PŒCILOBRYCON UNIFASCIATUS

Red-tailed Pencil Fish

AMAZON, GUIANA   ♂ 2″   ♀ 2″

COMMUNITY   DIET: ALL FOODS   SWIMS: UPPER HALF OF TANK

Even more slender in shape than *P. auratus*, this pencil fish is rare in Europe.

A prominent band of black runs from the tip of the nose to the lower lobe of the tail. Below this are three crescents, red, white, and black, making a striking splash of colour. In all other respects the fish resembles *P. auratus*.

BREEDING. Tank: 24″ × 8″ × 8″. pH: 6·8–7·0. Hardness: 80–100 p.p.m. Temperature: 80° F. Spawns: on plant leaves. Method: deposits adhesive eggs. Eggs: 30–70. Hatch: in 48 hours. Fry hang on: 1 day. Free-swimming: 4th day. Food 1st week: infusoria. Food 2nd week: infusoria, brine shrimp.

PRISTELLA RIDDLEI

♂

♀

X-ray Fish

VENEZUELA, GUIANA   ♂ 1½″ ♀ 2″

COMMUNITY   DIET: ALL FOODS   SWIMS: MID-WATER

Here we have a very popular, sprightly little characin. It swims in a rather jerky fashion, allowing its tail to drop slowly, and then with a flick of its fins the tail is raised again, only to drop slowly once more. When in a shoal the fish swim rapidly back and forth. It is peaceful, keeps its fins well spread, and is very active, but inclined to be shy, and stay in the background.

The popular name, X-ray fish, is only partly appropriate, for, although the swim-bladder can be seen, the stomach and intestines are quite opaque. The hinder portion of the body is only partly transparent.

Males are slimmer and smaller than females, and their colours are more pronounced. The tiny hook on his anal fin often gets caught in a fine mesh net.

There is a golden variety of this fish.

BREEDING. *Tank: 24″ × 8″ × 8″. pH: 6·8–7·2. Hardness: 80–120 p.p.m. Temperature: 78–80° F. Spawns: in plant thickets. Method: standard for egg-droppers. Eggs: 70–150. Hatch: in 24 hours. Fry hang on: 1 day. Free-swimming: 3rd day. Food 1st week: infusoria. 2nd week: infusoria, brine shrimp.*

The fish is one of the easiest characins to breed. The tank is set up according to the standard described under 'Egg-droppers,' and placed where it will receive plenty of light. Fish put out before dusk will spawn next morning, providing it is a bright, sunny day, or the tank is well-lit artificially. After spawning both parents should be removed. Once free-swimming, the fry hide under plant leaves, and are extremely difficult to see. It is not until they are about two weeks old that they take to open water and are noticeable. No doubt many a spawn has been thrown away during this period, the breeder imagining that the fry have perished. Once on to microworms and dried food the young grow rapidly, and start to colour in six weeks.

SERRASALMUS SPILOPLEURA

♂

Piranha

AMAZON, BRITISH GUIANA · ♂ 8″ ♀ 10″

NON-COMMUNITY · DIET: ANIMAL PROTEIN · SWIMS: MID-WATER

One of several species of the renowned piranhas, all of which are rather ugly, bulldog-faced fishes, whose mouths are equipped with formidable razor-sharp teeth which they have no hesitation in using on anything, large or small. Piranhas infest many tributaries of the Amazon, and stories are told of humans being literally stripped to the bone in a few minutes when attacked by large shoals of these predators. It is therefore not a fish for the average aquarist, but one for those who like something out of the ordinary, and which will always make a showpiece on account of its savage reputation.

The body colour is brownish-silver, flecked with dark patches. The fins are grey-brown with black borders, the eye large, and the incurving vicious teeth are clearly seen.

Sexing is uncertain, as they have not been bred in captivity. Attempts at mating usually result in one being killed by the other. The species requires a high protein diet, taking meat, liver, fish, or any other flesh. They will seize and devour any fish, gulping small ones whole, and slashing out large pieces from others even larger than themselves.

THAYERIA SANCTÆMARIÆ

♂

♀

Penguin

AMAZON BASIN

COMMUNITY   DIET: ALL FOODS

♂ $2\frac{1}{2}''$ ♀ $2\frac{3}{4}''$

SWIMS: MID-WATER

This is not a gaudy-coloured fish, but its contrasts of black and silver make it most noticeable in any tank. Generally its habits are good, but occasionally a large specimen will make darts at smaller fishes and nip their tails. Just after the Second World War the authors imported the first specimens into England, and Mrs Muir, late secretary of the Edinburgh Aquarists Society, remarked that they had a resemblance to penguins. Though somewhat far-fetched, the simile was accepted throughout the British Isles, and this popular name has now spread overseas.

This is one of the fishes that sits in the water, slowly dropping its tail; when it has reached an angle of 45 degrees it flicks its fins and brings the tail up to nearly horizontal, before allowing it to drop slowly again. When frightened it can swim with amazing speed, often leaping out of the water.

The back is olive, the lower sides and belly silver. A broad black band traverses the body from the gill-plate down into the lower lobe of the tail.

When adult, females are deeper-bodied and much thicker in the abdominal region than males.

BREEDING. *Tank: 24″ × 8″ × 8″. pH: 6·6–7·2. Hardness: 100–150 p.p.m. Temperature: 78–80° F. Spawns: in plant thickets. Method: standard for egg-droppers. Eggs: 100–150. Hatch: in 48 hours. Fry hang on: 1 day. Free-swimming: 4th day. Food 1st week: infusoria. 2nd week: infusoria, brine shrimp.*

The fish are not easily induced to spawn. Once a pair has bred they should be kept apart from others, so that they can be identified again. The spawning tank is set up to the standard pattern for egg-layers (p. 159), and a pair of fish introduced. The male may start chasing the female the next day or the day after, and when sufficiently excited she will retaliate by chasing him. Finally the pair quiver together in bushy plants and drop adhesive eggs among the foliage. The parents are then removed. The embryo of each egg is jet black, and consequently they show up quite clearly. Infusoria should be poured into the tank twice daily after the eggs have hatched. This should be done even if after a day or so no youngsters can be seen. The fry are adept at hiding themselves, and the slightest movement in front of their tank sends them into cover immediately. However, a slow, stealthy approach often reveals several dozen fry motionless in the water, but on approaching closer they vanish as if by magic. Thus it is advisable to keep feeding for a week or two. At the end of this time the fry will be $\frac{1}{8}''$ long, and unable to hide so easily. They now begin to realize that danger is not inevitable, and gradually they acquire more courage.

This fish has for some time been erroneously called *T. obliqua*, which is seldom seen in Europe. The latter is said to have a longer, more pointed lower lobe to the tail.

CHAPTER XVIII

CYPRINODONTIDÆ

THIS IS A LARGE FAMILY FOUND THROUGHOUT THE SOUTHERN STATES OF the U.S.A., through Panama, over most of north-eastern and central South America, and much of Africa, Persia, India, Indonesia, and Indo-China. They are, in fact, related to the live-bearing tooth carps covered in Chapter XIII, and often called egg-laying tooth carps, killifishes, or top-minnows.

Most are elongated and cylindrical in shape and, as the name implies, have teeth. Although many species come from the equatorial belt, frequently near the coast, they live in well-shaded pools and do not like excessively high temperatures or bright light. They do best between 72° and 76° F. The majority are small, and are rather particular as to water conditions. They are extremely colourful, and prefer acid peaty water for spawning, to which has been added a small amount of salt. Given the right conditions, the majority are not difficult to breed, but in most cases the eggs take from 14 days to several weeks before they hatch. Since the parents spawn over quite a long period, they will still be laying eggs while the first day's spawn is hatching; and as time goes on some of the fry will have grown large enough to devour their newly hatched brethren. Therefore it is advisable to have periodic sortings to keep the babies in age groups, and thus circumvent cannibalism.

Breeding the egg-laying tooth carps

In the majority of cases the breeding tank need not be large, our standard 24″ × 8″ × 8″ being quite suitable for most species. This should be filled with dark brown peaty water, with a pH between 6·0 and 6·6, and a hardness of only 50–75 p.p.m. In addition, a teaspoonful of salt should be added to every 2½ gallons of water used.

The bottom of the tank should be covered with a thin layer of crumbled waterlogged peat, and a good thick mat of lesser bladderwort or Riccia should float on the surface of the water. Alternatively, the tank may be filled to a depth of 1″ with lime-free sand, and then filled with old soft rain-water, planted with a few grassy plants such as Sagittaria, Vallisneria, Cryptocorynes, and one or two bunches of Ambulia or Cabomba. Given these conditions, most species show themselves to be prolific spawners, and the young when hatched are large compared with most egg-layers, the greater number being able to take brine shrimp and sifted Daphnia straight away. They enjoy live foods, but most can be trained to take dried food, which after a time they accept with relish. The fry grow fairly rapidly. When they are half-grown the peaty water in which they are living may gradually be made less acid, and the pH increased, until they are happily conditioned to the average water found in most aquarists' tanks. Any sudden change from acid to alkaline conditions or vice versa will result in a folding of the fins, lack of appetite, lethargy, and, unless corrected, may soon end in death.

APHYOSEMION AUSTRALE

♀

♂

Lyre-tail

FRENCH EQUATORIAL AFRICA		♂ 2¼″ ♀ 2″
COMMUNITY	DIET: ALL FOODS	SWIMS: LOWER HALF OF TANK

One of the most beautiful of the lovely Aphyosemions. It is particular about changes in water conditions, preferring very soft brown peaty water. Any change to harder conditions and increase of pH must be done gradually. The species is peaceful, and will take any food. Oxygen requirements are low, and they will therefore stand considerable crowding, 20 or more living quite happily in a tank 24″ × 8″ × 8″.

The fish often rests in the water with the back curved in a slight crescent, tail down, the pectoral fins oscillating forward and backward as though treading water; but at the slightest movement it will dart a few inches and resume its practically motionless position, with wary eyes seeking the source of danger. When kept under ideal conditions it soon loses all nervousness, and then, with fins spread to splitting point, displays its gorgeous beauty.

Sexing is easy, for the male has all the colour and splendour of finnage. His mate, though graceful in shape, lacks his gaudy hues, and her fins are evenly rounded.

BREEDING. *Tank: 24″ × 8″ × 8″. pH: 6·2–6·8. Hardness: 20–50 p.p.m. Temperature: 74–76° F. One teaspoonful of salt to every 2½ gal. water. Spawns: in floating plants. Method: standard for Aphyosemions. Eggs: 200–300. Hatch: in 12–14 days. Free-swimming: 13th day. Food 1st week: brine shrimp. 2nd week: sifted Daphnia, microworms.*

A small tank, even an all-glass battery jar, is sufficient space to spawn one pair. In a slightly larger tank it is possible to use 2 males and 4 or 5 females together. The water should be old, acid, and brown with peat, and placed where it will receive subdued light. Some peat which has sunk to the bottom of the tank will hide any eggs that fall or are deposited low down. A good layer of lesser bladderwort or Riccia an inch thick should float on the surface of the water.

Males are continuous drivers, and chase the females into either the floating plants or the waterlogged peat that has settled on the bottom. Interlocking fins, the pair tremble side by side and deposit single eggs, the process being repeated many times a day. The parents if well-fed do not eat many eggs, but should be removed on the 12th day, as the first eggs laid will soon be hatching. The same parents may be placed in another breeding tank where spawning is likely to continue. The eggs are large, about the size of a pin's head, and are hard and robust. They may be seen among the plants, and if small portions of the weed are rolled between thumb and forefinger the hard eggs can be felt easily. Even this rolling appears to do them no harm. The eggs in the original tank start to hatch between the 12th and 14th day, according to temperature, and, strange as it may seem, unlike most other egg-layers, the higher the temperature the longer the period of incubation. In 14 or 15 days after the parents have been removed all the eggs will have hatched, but as the last babies appear it must be remembered that the earlier fry may now be about two weeks old, and consequently large enough to eat their younger relations. Any outsize babies should be separated to prevent this cannibalism. The fry grow rapidly, and start to develop colour in 6 to 8 weeks, when sexing is apparent. The original breeders can be moved several times into different breeding tanks before the females cease to spawn; but even then after a short resting period the whole process may be started over again.

APHYOSEMION BIVITTATUM

TROPICAL W. AFRICA ♂ 2″ ♀ 1¾″

COMMUNITY DIET: ALL FOODS

SWIMS: MID-WATER TO UPPER HALF OF TANK

This beautiful fish has longer fins than the foregoing, though the colour is more sombre. It is extremely peaceful, and should be kept only with its own kind or other small fishes. It prefers very soft acid water, and likes plenty of small live food, though it will take dried food as well. Like other Aphyosemions, it has a habit of hovering in the water, making short darts at intervals.

Once again sex is told by colour and finnage, the male having a much longer dorsal and anal fin, and an elongated lyre-shaped tail.

BREEDING. Tank: 24″×8″×8″. pH: 6·2–6·8. Hardness: 20–50 p.p.m. Temperature: 74–76° F. One teaspoonful of salt to every 2½ gal. water. Spawns: in floating plants. Method: standard for Aphyosemions. Eggs: 200–300. Hatch: in 12–14 days. Free-swimming: 13th–15th day. Food 1st week: brine shrimp. 2nd week: sifted Daphnia, microworms.

One or more pairs may be spawned together, the procedure following identically that of *A. australe*.

APHYOSEMION CÆRULEUM

Blue Gulare

TROPICAL W. AFRICA   ♂ $4\frac{1}{2}''$ ♀ $4''$

COMMUNITY, ONLY WHEN YOUNG   DIET: ALL FOODS

SWIMS: LOWER HALF OF TANK

This fish has often been maligned, and considered aggressive. Until full-grown it is usually peaceful, particularly if well-fed, and even when full-grown will not bite at other fishes, but, of course, it will swallow small, slender species not too large for its capacious mouth. However, so will any other fish of similar size, and it is generally the aquarist's fault in attempting to keep fishes of unequal proportions together without due consideration of natural tendencies.

Sexing is obvious, as the male develops larger fins and vivid coloration. The female resembles other Aphyosemions, having a golden body sprinkled with a few spots, and rounded fins.

BREEDING. *Tank: 24″ × 8″ × 8″. pH: 6·2–6·8. Hardness: 20–50 p.p.m. Tempera-ture: 74–76° F. One teaspoonful of salt to every 2½ gal. water. Spawns: at bottom of tank. Method: buries eggs over a period in peat. Eggs: 100–250. Hatch: in 6–13 weeks. Food 1st week: brine shrimp, sifted Daphnia, Grindal worms. 2nd week: small Daphnia, Cyclops, etc.*

The tank need only be half filled with dark brown peaty water, and a good layer 1″ thick of crumbled waterlogged peat should cover the bottom. The tank should be placed in a subdued light, and a pair introduced. The male is an ardent driver, and soon the fish, trembling side by side, lock fins and, raising a cloud of peat, deposit a single egg in the soft fibre, the process being repeated many times a day for several days. After 10 or 12 days the parents should be removed, and the spawning tank left severely alone. According to temperature, the eggs hatch in 6 to 13 weeks. The young fry may be seen after this time, and measure ¼″ in length. They should be fed copiously, and will then grow quickly.

Another method, said to resemble more the natural conditions, is to remove the parents after spawning and gently siphon off the water, leaving the peat just damp. If the tank is covered with a piece of glass the peat dries out slowly. After 8 weeks a small quantity of soft water which abounds with infusoria is poured gently on to the peat.

In nature these fish live in shallow pools, many of which evaporate during the dry season. When the pool becomes completely dry the parents die, but the eggs they have laid sink into the soft mud forming the bottom of the pool. Even though the mud appears to be completely dry, and through shrinkage numerous cracks appear, the warmth and early morning dews create sufficient moisture to keep the eggs at the right humidity, so that the embryo inside never becomes completely dehydrated. Various leaves and decaying water plants settle on the mud, dry out, and partly disintegrate. But with the coming of the rains several weeks later the pools begin to fill with soft rain-water, and the dried leaves and bits of plant produce a most favourable breeding medium for the infusoria (much like the aquarist's method of culturing infusoria in crumbled dried lettuce-leaves). The infusoria are thought to attack the egg-shells (which are once again lying in shallow, soft mud) and, biting through the outer shell, assist in releasing the now fully formed young fish who, on emerging, find ample food among the abundant infusoria. The fry grow rapidly, and later take to mosquito larvæ and other natural foods. They attain full size and breed before the coming of the next dry season, which will end their lives.

APHYOSEMION CALABARICUS

♀

♂

Blue Lyre-tail

TROPICAL W. AFRICA   ♂ 2"   ♀ 2"

COMMUNITY   DIET: ALL FOODS   SWIMS: LOWER HALF OF TANK

This is perhaps the loveliest of all the Aphyosemions, but unfortunately is very rare in Europe. It is practically identical with *A. australe*, except that the body is a beautiful royal blue, and some of the red dots on the sides form vertical bars across the posterior part of the flanks.

The female is fawn in colour, and her fins are clear and rounded.

BREEDING. Tank: 24" × 8" × 8". pH: 6·2–6·8. Hardness: 20–50 p.p.m. Temperature: 74–76° F. One teaspoonful of salt to every 2½ gal. water. Spawns: in peat on bottom of tank. Method: standard for Aphyosemions. Eggs: 200–300. Hatch: in 12–14 days. Free-swimming: 13th–15th day. Food 1st week: brine shrimp. 2nd week: sifted Daphnia, microworms.

Breeding follows the same pattern laid down for *A. australe*, except that the male and female usually tremble side by side in the crumbled peat and lay their eggs at the bottom of the tank.

APHYOSEMION COGNATUM

♀

♂

Spotted Lyre-tail

TROPICAL W. AFRICA   ♂ 2¼″   ♀ 2″

COMMUNITY   DIET: ALL FOODS   SWIMS: LOWER HALF OF TANK

A pretty fish, similar in size and shape to *A. australe*, but the points on the tail are usually shorter, and not quite so lyre-shaped.

The gill-plate and forward portion of the body are adorned with blue, but the fish is so well sprinkled with rows of red dots that its overall colour takes on a reddish mahogany. The pectoral fins are orange; the dorsal and anal are maroon-striped and have a maroon edge; the caudal has the same maroon border, but the upper and lower edges are bluish-white.

The female is liberally sprinkled with red dots, which spread all over her body and into her rounded dorsal, anal, and caudal fins.

BREEDING. *Tank: 24″ × 8″ × 8″. pH: 6·2–6·8. Hardness: 20–50 p.p.m. Temperature: 74–76° F. One teaspoonful of salt to every 2½ gal. water. Spawns: in floating plants or peat. Method: see A. australe. Eggs: 70–150. Hatch: in 12 days. Free-swimming: 13th day. Food 1st week: infusoria. 2nd week: infusoria, brine shrimp.*

The recommended procedure for breeding this species follows exactly that described under *A. australe*.

APHYOSEMION GARDNERI

♂

W. AFRICA   ♂ 2¼″   ♀ 1¾″

COMMUNITY   DIET: ALL FOODS   SWIMS: LOWER HALF OF TANK

Another beautiful Aphyosemion which has a lyre tail. The body is a pale shade of blue crossed by numerous wavy bars of mahogany, turning to deep red, particularly over the gill-plates. The fins are mottled with red spots; they shade from pale yellow to blue. A dark maroon line runs from the base of the caudal peduncle through the tail, dividing off the lower lobe.

Sexing is easy, as the fins of the female are rounded, and she is not so gaudy.

BREEDING. *Tank: 24″ × 8″ × 8″. pH: 6·4–6·8. Hardness: 20–50 p.p.m. Temperature: 74–76° F. One teaspoonful of salt to every 2½ gal. water. Spawns: in floating plants or peat. Method: standard for Aphyosemions. Eggs: 70–150. Hatch: in 12 days. Free-swimming: 13th day. Food 1st week: infusoria. 2nd week: infusoria, brine shrimp.*

Breeding procedure follows that described under *A. australe*.

APHYOSEMION PETERSI

♂

♀

W. AFRICA   ♂ 2¼″   ♀ 2″

COMMUNITY   DIET: ALL FOODS   SWIMS: UPPER HALF OF TANK

This species is not so highly coloured, the body being a fawny-yellow with a few patches of yellow flecked upon it, as well as one short maroon bar lying horizontally a little behind the gill-plate. The flanks are marked with numerous faint, fawn-coloured bars. The anal, ventrals, and lower edge of the tail fin are lemon, the bottom edge of the anal fin having a maroon border.

The female is similarly coloured, though fainter, but all her fins are rounded, and her tail lacks the golden colour at its base.

BREEDING. *Tank: 24″ × 8″ × 8″. pH: 6·2–6·8. Hardness: 20–50 p.p.m. Temperature: 74–76° F. One teaspoonful of salt to every 2½ gal. water. Spawns: in floating plants or peat. Method: standard for Aphyosemions. Eggs: 70–150. Hatch: in 12 days. Free-swimming: 13th day. Food 1st week: infusoria. 2nd week: infusoria, brine shrimp.*

Breeding procedure follows that of *A. australe.*

APHYOSEMION SHOUTEDENI

Golden Lyre-tail

W. AFRICA   ♂ 2"   ♀ 1¾"

COMMUNITY   DIET: ALL FOODS   SWIMS: LOWER HALF OF TANK

Another attractive Aphyosemion, with a greenish-yellow tinge over most of the body, particularly in the hinder-quarters, the forward part being more bluish-green. Like most Aphyosemions, the body is sprinkled with red dots, and these form themselves into oblique lines on the gill-plates. The fins of *A. shoutedeni* are yellowish-green, the dorsal and caudal being edged with maroon.

The female lacks the pointed fins, but bears the same colours, rather less pronounced.

BREEDING. *Tank: 24"×8"×8". pH: 6·2–6·8. Hardness: 20–50 p.p.m. Tempera-ture: 74–76° F. One teaspoonful of salt to every 2½ gal. water. Spawns: in floating plants or peat. Method: standard for Aphyosemions. Eggs: 70–150. Hatch: in 12 days. Free-swimming: 13th day. Food 1st week: infusoria. 2nd week: infusoria, brine shrimp.*

This fish is a prolific breeder, and the procedure given under *A. australe* applies here.

APHYOSEMION SJOESTEDTI

♂

♀

Blue-throated Aphyosemion

TROPICAL W. AFRICA   ♂ 3″   ♀ 2¾″

COMMUNITY, WHEN YOUNG   DIET: ALL FOODS

SWIMS: MIDDLE TO LOWER HALF OF TANK

This is another gorgeous Aphyosemion, but without the typical lyre-tail. It grows rather larger than most Aphyosemions, has a bigger mouth, and rather bulbous gill-plates. In its larger sizes it is apt to swallow small fishes, but is peaceful enough with medium-sized species.

The female is less brightly coloured. All her fins have rounded edges, and are clear except for a few red dots.

BREEDING. *Tank: 24″×8″×8″. pH: 6·4–6·8. Hardness: 20–50 p.p.m. Tempera-ture: 76° F. One teaspoonful of salt to every 2½ gal. water. Spawns: around base of plant thickets. Method: deposits eggs over a period. Eggs: 50–150. Hatch: in 3–5 months. Food 1st week: brine shrimp, microworms. 2nd week: sifted Daphnia, Cyclops.*

A. sjoestedti spawns readily, but the eggs take from 3 to 5 months to hatch. The tank should be filled to a depth of 6″ with old acid water, brown in colour, and a 1″ layer of lime-free sand placed in the bottom. Into this plant bunches of Myriophyllum, Ambulia, or Cabomba. Some floating plants will serve as a refuge for the female, as the males are rather aggressive drivers. After much chasing the pair come together at the base of the clumps of plants and, trembling, with fins locked, deposit their eggs in the foliage just above the sand. Spawning continues over several days. The large eggs are easily seen, and these should be lifted with the aid of a pipette or piece of glass tubing and then placed in shallow petri jars. If not well fed the parents will eat their eggs, so removal of the eggs daily prevents such cannibalism. The shallow petri jars should be floated in a small, bare tank at a temperature of 74° F. As the eggs lie in only $\frac{1}{4}$" of water, they can be examined daily. Any which fungus should be removed, but this should not occur if the water is soft enough, and deeply tinted by peat. In some cases the merest suspicion of methylene blue in the petri jars helps to prevent eggs from fungusing.

After 7 or 8 weeks the embryo can be seen forming inside the egg, the eye showing first. A few more weeks and the young fish may be observed in a curved position moving jerkily now and then inside the shell. Even so, hatching does not occur for a week or two more, but eventually the young fry emerge, and are moderately large. They may now be tipped into a small tank containing very shallow peaty water, and fed on brine shrimp, microworms, and sifted Daphnia. They grow rapidly, and need sorting for size, as the larger ones have no hesitation in eating their smaller brethren.

Reproducing these fish is not easy, but well worth the trouble involved, as they are always scarce and fetch a high price.

APHYOSEMION SPLENDOPLEURIS

TROPICAL W. AFRICA ♂ 2″ ♀ 1¾″

COMMUNITY   DIET: ALL FOODS   SWIMS: UPPER HALF OF TANK

A species very similar to *A. bivittatum*, with superb points on the dorsal and caudal fins. It is very colourful: reddish shading and bluish highlights adorn the flanks. Both male and female bear the same dark brown stripes as *A. bivittatum*, but in the male these are less pronounced, and the anal and caudal fins are yellow. The tips of the tail are bluish-white.

BREEDING. Tank: 24″ × 8″ × 8″. pH: 6·2–6·8. Hardness: 20–50 p.p.m. Temperature: 74–76° F. One teaspoonful of salt to every 2½ gal. water. Spawns: in plant thickets or peat. Method: standard for Aphyosemions. Eggs: 70–150. Hatch: in 12 days. Free-swimming: 13th day. Food 1st week: infusoria. 2nd week: infusoria, brine shrimp.

The procedure follows exactly that for *A. bivittatum*, the species being well worth breeding.

THE PANCHAX GROUP

This group comprises Aplocheilus, Epiplatys, Panchax, and Pachypanchax. They are all from Africa, India, Ceylon, and Indonesia. The body is long and tubular, the jaw large and pointed. They will swallow smaller fishes, and although many are safe in community tanks, because the majority like slightly acid water they are better on their own. Most are excellent jumpers, and it is well to see that their tank is securely covered.

Most of the fishes belonging to this group are extremely colourful, and nearly all swim just under the surface of the water. On the top of the head is a light marking which, though not an eye, is extremely sensitive to light and shade. Any shadow thrown by a moving hand causes the fish to dive for safety. When catching these fishes a net should be held immediately below them, and if this is raised gently they are ensnared before realizing what is happening.

Breeding

They breed easily, laying rather large eggs in floating plants such as Riccia or bladderwort. Spawning continues over several days, the young hatching from the 12th or 14th day onward. The parents if well fed do not usually eat their eggs, but will devour the fry. Therefore the adults should be removed from the spawning tank just before the first eggs hatch—say 12 days after they have been put out to breed. The fry are of medium size, and most will take brine shrimp from the start. Where large spawns occur the babies must be sorted for size, as the larger ones will eat the smallest.

APLOCHEILUS BLOCKII

Dwarf Panchax

INDIA, CEYLON   ♂ 1¾″   ♀ 1½″

COMMUNITY   DIET: ALL FOODS   SWIMS: UPPER HALF OF TANK

A delightful little fish, and the smallest of the Panchax group. It is often known as *Panchax parvus*.

The overall colour is green, the back being darker, but the sides are lit by shining scales of yellowish-green, further adorned by brilliant red dots. The gill-plates are semi-transparent, and the pink-coloured gills show through. The dorsal and anal fins of the male are long and pointed, greenish-yellow in colour, and are edged with orange-red. The tail is diamond-shaped, and, like the other fins, is sprinkled with red dots.

The female is similarly coloured, but her fins are smaller and more rounded. An oblique dark bar crosses the lower portion of her dorsal.

BREEDING. *Tank: 24″ × 8″ × 8″, or smaller. pH: 6·8. Hardness: 80–120 p.p.m. Temperature: 76–78° F. Spawns: in floating plants. Method: deposits eggs over a period of days. Eggs: 50–120. Hatch: in 12–14 days. Food 1st week: infusoria, brine shrimp. 2nd week: brine shrimp, microworms.*

The species is easy to breed and raise. The breeding tank need not be large: one 24″ × 8″ × 8″ will hold 2 males and 3 or 4 females. It should be planted with one or two clumps of Ambulia, and here and there a small Indian fern. The top should be covered with a good mat of lesser bladderwort or a ½″ layer of Riccia. The males constantly drive the females into the floating plants, then, taking a position alongside her and slightly below, he presses her upward against the plants until she is lying practically on her side. One egg is then deposited and fertilized. The process is constantly repeated for several days, after which the parents should be removed. The clear eggs hatch in 10–12 days.

APLOCHEILUS DAYI

♀

♂

CEYLON   ♂ 3¼″   ♀ 3″

COMMUNITY, WITH MEDIUM–SIZED FISHES   DIET : ALL FOODS

SWIMS : UPPER HALF OF TANK

One of the most beautiful of the Panchax group, and rather similar to *A. lineatus.* Although the fish is a good size, and has a large mouth, the authors have found that it is inclined to be bullied by other Panchax even slightly smaller than itself. Our own specimens were then moved to a tank of small fishes, and have behaved themselves and not molested them.

Male and female are very similar in colour, but she is deeper-bellied, and has a black dot at the rear end of the base of the dorsal fin.

BREEDING. *Tank: 24″×8″×8″. pH: 6·6–6·8. Hardness: 80–120 p.p.m. Temperature: 78° F. Spawns: in surface plants. Method: standard for Panchax group. Eggs: 50–150. Hatch: in 10–12 days. Food 1st week: brine shrimp. 2nd week: brine shrimp, sifted Daphnia.*

APLOCHEILUS LINEATUS

Sparkling Panchax

INDIA   ♂ 4″   ♀ 4″

COMMUNITY, WITH LARGER FISHES   DIET: ALL FOODS

SWIMS: JUST BELOW SURFACE

This is one of the most beautiful of the Panchax, also one of the largest. When adult it is not safe with smaller fishes. The mouth is large, and capable of swallowing a full-grown male guppy with ease.

All Panchax have a light spot on the top of the head, but it is much more pronounced on *A. lineatus*. It is, in fact, a rudimentary eye, and although the organ now lacks sight, it still retains enough sensitivity to distinguish light and shade and pass a warning to the brain. A hand placed over the tank will soon show that the fish notices the cutting off of the light rays, and it will dart into cover.

The fins of the female are not so long and pointed, and she shows a dark spot in the lower portion of her dorsal. Her body is frequently more barred in the hind portion.

BREEDING. *Tank: 24″ × 8″ × 8″. pH: 6·6–6·8. Hardness: 80–120 p.p.m. Temperature: 78° F. Spawns: in floating plants. Method: standard for Panchax group. Eggs: 100–150. Hatch: in 10–12 days. Food 1st week: brine shrimp. 2nd week: Cyclops, sifted Daphnia.*

The species is a prolific breeder, and if one male is placed with two or three females they will spawn over several days. If well fed they will not eat their eggs, but after 5 or 6 days, when the females are slim, remove all adults. Hatching over a period, the earlier fry are large enough to swallow their smaller brethren, so sorting is recommended.

APLOCHEILUS PANCHAX

♀

♂

Blue Panchax

INDIA, BURMA, MALAYA, SIAM   ♂ 3″   ♀ 3″

COMMUNITY, WHEN YOUNG   DIET: ALL FOODS

SWIMS: JUST BELOW THE SURFACE

This is a typical Panchax, with a long, cylindrical body, flattened head, and tapering mouth. It is not as highly coloured as others of the group, but is none the less attractive. The species is peaceful if kept among medium-sized fishes, but, as in most Panchax, the mouth is large, enabling them to gulp in small fishes, provided these can be swallowed whole. They do not go in for biting or tearing fins.

The female as shown is similarly coloured, but bears an orange splash above the black mark in the dorsal. She lacks the blue border to her tail, but has a suspicion of red in the upper and lower edges. She has a tiny black dot at the extreme upper end of the caudal peduncle.

BREEDING. Tank: 24″ × 8″ × 8″. pH: 6·6–6·8. Hardness: 80–120 p.p.m. Temperature: 78° F. Spawns: in floating plants. Method: standard for Panchax group. Eggs: 100–150. Hatch: in 10–12 days. Food 1st week: brine shrimp. 2nd week: Cyclops, sifted Daphnia.

EPIPLATYS CHAPERI

Orange-throated Panchax

W. AFRICA   ♂ 2″ ♀ 1¾″

COMMUNITY   DIET: ALL FOODS   SWIMS: UPPER HALF OF TANK

A medium-sized Panchax of good behaviour, and in good condition one of the prettiest. It is not aggressive or dangerous.

The female does not have the sword-like extension to the lower portion of the tail, all her fins being more rounded.

BREEDING. Tank: 24″ × 8″ × 8″. pH: 6·6–6·8. Hardness: 80–120 p.p.m. Temperature: 78° F. Spawns: in floating plants. Method: standard for Panchax group. Eggs: 100–150. Hatch: in 10–12 days. Food 1st week: brine shrimp. 2nd week: Cyclops, sifted Daphnia.

The species is a prolific breeder, and in the above-sized tank it is possible to breed 2 males and 3 or 4 females together. Spawning proceeds over several days, after which the parents should be removed.

EPIPLATYS FASCIOLATUS

♀

♂

Barred Panchax

TROPICAL W. AFRICA   ♂ 3½"   ♀ 3"

COMMUNITY   DIET: ALL FOODS   SWIMS: UPPER HALF OF TANK

This medium-sized species is safe with all but small fishes, and although not brilliantly coloured, the male is readily identified by the bright elongated yellow crescent in the oval tail, all fins being yellow and bordered by black. The upper half of the body is olive, but covered with horizontal rows of small red dots. The belly and caudal peduncle are patterned by short, dark, vertical bars. The female is mostly greenish-grey, her fins being almost clear, but the vertical bars on her flanks are more pronounced.

BREEDING. *Tank: 24" × 8" × 8". pH: 6·6–6·8. Hardness: 80–120 p.p.m. Temperature: 78° F. Spawns: in floating plants. Method: standard for Panchax group. Eggs: 70–100. Hatch: in 10–12 days. Food 1st week: brine shrimp. 2nd week: Cyclops, sifted Daphnia.*

The species spawns readily, but is not so prolific as others of the genus.

EPIPLATYS MACROSTIGMA

♂

♀

Spotted Panchax

TROPICAL W. AFRICA   ♂ 2¼″ ♀ 2″

COMMUNITY   DIET: ALL FOODS   SWIMS: UPPER HALF OF TANK

Another pretty little Panchax, although not as vividly coloured as most; neither is it as common. Like the rest of the family, it prefers old, acid water.

The body is bluish-green on the lower sides, shading to olive-brown towards the back. Numerous deep maroon dots sprinkle the sides and spread into the dorsal, anal, and caudal fins, these fins being bluish-green in colour.

The female does not have such a large anal fin, but this and her ventrals are tipped with bluish-green. She is also deeper-bodied.

BREEDING. *Tank: 24″ × 8″ × 8″. pH: 6·6–6·8. Hardness: 80–120 p.p.m. Temperature: 78° F. Spawns: in floating plants. Method: standard for Panchax group. Eggs: 50–100. Hatch: in 10–12 days. Food 1st week: brine shrimp. 2nd week: Cyclops, sifted Daphnia.*

It breeds like most of the other members of the group, but does not seem so prolific.

EPIPLATYS SEXFASCIATUS

♀

♂

Green Panchax

TROPICAL W. AFRICA   ♂ 3¼″   ♀ 3¼″

COMMUNITY, WITH MEDIUM-SIZED FISHES   DIET: ALL FOODS

SWIMS: UPPER HALF OF TANK

This is one of the larger Panchax, and none too safe with smaller fishes. It lacks the brilliant colouring of *A. lineatus,* which it resembles in size and shape.

The general body colour is dull green, shading to olive on the back. The sides are adorned with numerous dark green bars, vertical near the tail, becoming more diagonal towards the forward portion of the body. The flanks are also peppered with dark spots. The fins of the male are larger and greenish-yellow in colour, and his tail fin is tipped with red. The female's fins are clear to pale yellow.

BREEDING. *Tank: 24″ × 8″ × 8″. pH: 6·6–6·8. Hardness: 80–120 p.p.m. Temperature: 78° F. Spawns: in floating plants. Method: standard for Panchax group. Eggs: 100–150. Hatch: in 10–12 days. Food 1st week: brine shrimp. 2nd week: Cyclops, sifted Daphnia.*

The species is easy to breed, and fairly prolific. The procedure follows precisely that described under *A. lineatus.*

PACHYPANCHAX PLAYFAIRII

♂

♀

Golden Panchax

ZANZIBAR, E. AFRICA   ♂ 3″ ♀ 3″

COMMUNITY, WITH MEDIUM-SIZED FISHES   DIET: ALL FOODS

SWIMS: UPPER HALF OF TANK

This is a most attractive fish, rather more chunky than most Panchax, and the snout is shorter. The scales in larger specimens do not lie absolutely flat. They are inclined to stand slightly on edge, giving the appearance that the fish is suffering from dropsy, but this is a perfectly natural formation, and therefore nothing to worry about. The species is peaceful enough in its smaller sizes, but when large it should be kept with medium-sized fishes.

The fins of the female are clear to pale yellow, except that a dark oblique bar appears in the lower rays of her dorsal. When in breeding condition her belly is greyish and well distended.

BREEDING. Tank: 24″ × 8″ × 8″. pH: 6·6–6·8. Hardness: 80–120 p.p.m. Temperature: 78° F. Spawns: in floating plants. Method: standard for Panchax group. Eggs: 80–150. Hatch: in 10–12 days. Food 1st week: brine shrimp. 2nd week: Cyclops, sifted Daphnia.

The fish are easy to breed, and prolific spawners. They are not so particular about acid water as are most other Panchax. Nevertheless, spawns seem larger and greater in number when the water is on the acid side, and fairly soft. They breed in top weed like other members of the group, and after a few days the parents should be removed to prevent egg-eating.

PANCHAX HOMAMOLOTUS

♂

♀

W. AFRICA   ♂ 2″   ♀ 2¼″

COMMUNITY   DIET: ALL FOODS   SWIMS: UPPER HALF OF TANK

A recent introduction, this beautiful fish should have a great future. It is of medium size, and striking colour, and is peaceful and adaptable.

Our colour plate needs no description, and from it sexing is obvious.

BREEDING. Tank: 24″ × 8″ × 8″. pH: 6·6–6·8. Hardness: 80–120 p.p.m. Temperature: 78° F. Spawns: in floating plants. Method: standard for Panchax group. Eggs: 50–80. Hatch in 10–12 days. Food 1st week: infusoria, brine shrimp. 2nd week: microworms, fine dried food, sifted Cyclops, etc.

The authors obtained a pair of these fish from Belgium in March 1957 and bred them a month later. Though not prolific they present no problem.

[End of Panchax group]

CYNOLEBIAS BELLOTTII

♀

♂

Argentine Pearl

ARGENTINA   ♂ 2″   ♀ 1¾″

COMMUNITY   DIET: LIVE FOOD, MAY BE TRAINED TO TAKE DRIED FOOD

SWIMS: MID-WATER TO LOWER HALF OF TANK

A superb little fish, never common in Europe, partly because it is not easy to breed, requires very soft water, and rarely lives longer than one year. It is peaceful, but males may sometimes become aggressive towards one another when breeding approaches.

The male and female are dissimilar. Her body is olive to yellow in colour, and numerous thin, wavy bars of a brownish shade cross her flanks and appear in her fins.

The male is gorgeous. His back is deep mauve, paling to a lavender-green on the sides. His dorsal and anal fins are not only larger than his mate's, but deep mauvish-green in colour. The tail is lavender-green, and has a maroon-red border. The whole of his body and fins are sprinkled with silver-blue dots, and his flanks are crossed by thin, whitish vertical bars.

BREEDING. *Tank: 24″ × 8″ × 8″, or smaller. pH: 6·0–6·4. Hardness: 10–50 p.p.m. Temperature: 74–78° F. Spawns: in peat or mud. Method: buries eggs over a period. Eggs: 50–75. Hatch: in 12–16 weeks. Food 1st week: infusoria, brine shrimp. 2nd week: brine shrimp, microworms.*

The breeding tank need only be small, and the bottom covered to a depth of 1½″ with waterlogged sieved peat. No plants are necessary. It is filled with very soft brown peaty water and a pair are placed therein during the morning. In a few minutes the male displays his beauty to his mate, and, with fins spread, flutters round and about her head; then suddenly the pair dive side by side into the peat, sometimes disappearing from view. With fins locked, a few eggs are laid, and the fish reappear. Some minutes later, diving once again into the peat, more eggs are laid. At the end of the day the female is quite slim and spawned out. Both parents are now removed. In a day or two the water should be carefully siphoned off, and the peat left just damp. Evaporation slowly takes place, and the peat gradually dries out, but it should be kept at a temperature of 74° F. After 3 or 4 months soft water is gently poured on to the peat, and some infusoria introduced. Providing that all has gone well, the eggs begin to hatch after this very long period of incubation, and the fry must be fed little and often with minute food.

This is one of the species that lives only a year in nature. The pools they inhabit dry out, and the adult fish die off; but the eggs remain in the mud until the rainy season allows them to hatch out some months later. The fry grow and spawn before the drought in the following year.

CYNOLEBIAS NIGRIPINNIS

ARGENTINA   ♂ $1\frac{1}{4}''$ ♀ $1''$

COMMUNITY   DIET: LIVE FOOD, MAY BE TRAINED TO TAKE DRIED FOOD

SWIMS: MID-WATER

Related to the foregoing, this little fish is smaller, and even more beautiful. They are peaceful, but are particular as to conditions, preferring old, acid water tinged brown with peat.

The first impression given by the male is of a starry night in December, for his whole body and fins are a velvety blue-black like the night sky, and he is covered with shining silver-blue spots like a galaxy of stars. His mate is rather more drab, being a brownish-grey, and her sides and fins are patterned by wavy dark bands.

BREEDING. Tank: 12″×8″×8″. pH: 6·0–6·4. Hardness: 10–50 p.p.m. Temperature: 74–78° F. Spawns: in peat or mud. Method: buries eggs over a period. Eggs: 50–75. Hatch: in 12–16 weeks. Food 1st week: infusoria, brine shrimp. 2nd week: brine shrimp, microworms.

The fish is not easy to breed and rear, but the procedure follows exactly that of *C. bellottii*.

JORDANELLA FLORIDÆ

Flag Fish

FLORIDA ♂ 2″ ♀ 2″

COMMUNITY, WHEN SMALL DIET: ALL FOODS

SWIMS: MID-WATER TO LOWER HALF OF TANK

An attractive, rather stumpy-bodied fish, though inclined to be aggressive, especially as spawning-time approaches. It is therefore advisable to keep it with species of similar size. It likes to browse on soft algæ.

The male has longer fins, which are bluish in colour and well sprinkled with red dots. His sides glow with scales of many hues, blue, red, and yellow being equally distributed, and these are separated by thin lines of red. The female is not so colourful. She may be recognized by a black dot preceded by a white fleck in the last rays of her dorsal fin. Both fish have a large black dot in the centre of each side, but this is more clearly seen on the female.

BREEDING. *Tank: 24″ × 8″ × 8″. pH: 7·0–7·2. Hardness: 100–150 p.p.m. Temperature: 76° F. Spawns: in depression in sand. Method: deposits eggs over several days, which male fans. Eggs: 100–150. Hatch: in 6 days. Fry wriggling: 2 days. Free-swimming: 9th day. Food 1st week: brine shrimp, microworms. 2nd week: brine shrimp, Cyclops.*

The fish is easy to breed, and the males are aggressive drivers. The tank should therefore be thickly planted with bunches of feathery plants to afford the females some refuge. The male drives the female towards the base of a clump of plants where side by side they deposit and fertilize their eggs, usually in fanned-out depressions in the sand. The process continues spasmodically over several days, after which the female should be removed. The male now fans the eggs, which hatch in 5–6 days, after which he guards his babies and protects them from attack. The young grow quite quickly, and as soon as they are free-swimming the male should be taken out.

ORYZIAS JAVANICUS

Blue Eyes

MALAYA, JAVA ♂ 1½″ ♀ 1½″

COMMUNITY DIET: ALL FOODS SWIMS: UPPER HALF OF TANK

Rather similar to *Oryzias latipes*, but it has a more pointed nose and the head is flatter on the top, followed by an arching back, giving the appearance of having a dip in the back of the neck. It is peaceful.

The general body colour is silvery-grey, and it has an electric-blue spot above each eye which is very striking. The body is semi-transparent, and the swim-bladder is clearly seen through the fish's sides.

The female is considerably deeper-bodied and wider in the belly.

BREEDING. *Tank: 24″ × 8″ × 8″. pH: 6·8–7·0. Hardness: 50–80 p.p.m. Temperature: 78–80° F. Spawns: in clear water above plants. Method: eggs attached by fine thread, catch on plants. Eggs: 50–100. Hatch: in 8–10 days. Food 1st week: infusoria. 2nd week: infusoria, brine shrimp.*

For breeding procedure see *O. latipes*.

ORYZIAS LATIPES

Golden Medaka

JAVA, MALAYA, CHINA, JAPAN, KOREA ♂ 1½″ ♀ 1½″

COMMUNITY DIET: ALL FOODS SWIMS: UPPER HALF OF TANK

Often known as the rice paddy fish, it is not common in Europe, though it does appear from time to time. Although not striking in appearance, it has a pleasant disposition, is quiet and not aggressive, and is extremely easy to breed.

The general body colour is a light golden-yellow, the fins being slightly paler.

The female may be distinguished by her smaller fins and deeper belly.

BREEDING. *Tank: 24″ × 8″ × 8″. pH: 6·8–7·0. Hardness: 50–80 p.p.m. Temperature: 78–80° F. Spawns: in clear water above plants. Method: eggs attached by fine thread, catch on plants. Eggs: 100–150. Hatch: in 8–10 days. Food 1st week: infusoria. 2nd week: infusoria, brine shrimp.*

The breeding tank should be placed where it will receive good light, and set up with several bunches of feathery plants. Two males and three or four females may be used. The males chase the females over thickets and, trembling side by side, she expels eggs while he fertilizes them. The eggs often appear in little bunches of five or six, and are attached to her vent by a slender thread. Females may often be seen swimming around with the bunches of eggs still attached, but these eventually get brushed off on to the plants. In a day or two numerous bunches may be seen caught in the foliage, mostly near the top of the stems. The parents if well fed do not eat the eggs, and rarely touch the hatching fry.

Some breeders prefer to leave the parents in the original breeding tank for only 5 or 6 days, and then move them to another aquarium, where spawning continues. This method eliminates the chances of the fry being eaten, or being pushed about at feeding-time. As many as 100 fry appear every fortnight. Alternatively, eggs attached to pieces of plant may be floated in battery jars, where they hatch.

PTEROLEBIAS PERUENSIS

Peruvian Longfin

PERU   ♂ 2¾″ ♀ 2½″

COMMUNITY   DIET: ALL FOODS   SWIMS: MID-WATER

Of fairly recent introduction, this is an attractive species. It is one of those fishes which lays its eggs in mud, and during the dry season the parents die off. The eggs lie buried even though the mud may dry out and crack, but with the next rainy season they hatch, and a new generation grows up. Their lives are necessarily short, and because of this, and the length of time required to raise youngsters, the species is unlikely to become cheap. They prefer soft brown peaty water, and although we call them community fish they are better kept on their own; even then, in their constant driving, males may nip the tails of females.

The general colour is fawny-brown with numerous vertical bars crossing the body. In some lights there is a bluish sheen on the gill-plate and a reddish tinge in the tail. The eye is a beautiful blue-green. The pectorals are large, as are also the anal and caudal fins of the male. The dorsal and anal are striped, and the male's large forked tail is peppered with blue dots. The fins of the female are rounded.

BREEDING. *Tank: 24″ × 8″ × 8″. pH: 6·6–6·8. Hardness: 50–80 p.p.m. Temperature: 80° F. Spawns: in plant thickets, or peat. Method: similar to* Aphyosemion cæruleum. *Eggs: 70–120. Hatch: in approximately 3 months. Food 1st week: brine shrimp, Cyclops. 2nd week: sifted Daphnia, Grindal worms.*

A pair will spawn 12–15 eggs per day for a period of two weeks, after which they should be removed. The water in the breeding tank is then siphoned off, and the soggy peat left to dry out. After three months water well charged with infusoria should be gently added, and the fry will appear a few hours later.

RIVULUS

This genus comprises fishes from the West Indies, Venezuela, Guiana, and Eastern Brazil. All have long tubular bodies, and most have a habit of hanging motionless in the water just below the surface plants. But in spite of their immobility they can dart suddenly, and may even jump out of the water—hence the advisability of keeping the tank covered. The tail is often allowed to drop, giving the back an arched outline. The fishes are generally not brightly coloured, but are none the less attractive in somewhat subdued hues. All females carry a spot in the upper portion of the tail base. A few are as colourful as their male counterparts.

The fishes prefer small live food, but may be trained quite quickly to take the dried product. The genus is not safe with small fishes, but is unhappy if kept with ones that are too large and boisterous. Rivulus should be housed with species of their own size who do not disturb their tranquillity.

They breed in much the same way as the Panchax group, spawning among floating plants just beneath the surface. They prefer old, slightly acid water.

RIVULUS CYLINDRACEUS

RIVULUS CYLINDRACEUS

CUBA   ♂ 2″ ♀ 1¾″

COMMUNITY   DIET: ALL FOODS   SWIMS: UPPER HALF OF TANK

Typical of the genus is this species, with a long, cylindrical body.

The male is attractive, though not gaudy. His back is brown to olive. A serrated dark brown line starting on the gill-plates extends well into the tail fin. Just above this line the body is tinged with a greenish sheen. Below the line the belly and throat are yellowish-orange; red and green spots embellish his flanks. His dorsal fin is yellowish-green, the top edged with white. The anal fin is yellowish, with red blotches and dots. The tail is greenish-yellow, with a cloudy black border. The female's fins are pale yellow, and she shows the typical 'Rivulus spot' in the upper rear part of the caudal peduncle.

BREEDING. Tank: 24″×8″×8″. pH: 6·8. Hardness: 80–100 p.p.m. Temperature: 78° F. Spawns: over a period. Method: lays eggs in floating plants. Eggs: 100–150. Hatch: in 10–14 days. Food 1st week: brine shrimp. 2nd week: microworms, sifted Daphnia.

The species is easy to breed, and the males are vigorous drivers. The tank should be filled with old, acid water, and planted thickly with Indian ferns. At the surface there should be a good layer of Riccia or lesser bladderwort. The male drives the female into the floating plants and, placing himself along her side, tilts her over as he presses her upward. One egg is laid and fertilized. The process is repeated at intervals over the next five or six days. During this time the parents should be well fed on chopped frozen shrimp which has been well thawed out. If their appetites are satisfied they are less likely to eat their eggs. After five or six days the parents are removed, the eggs hatching between 10 and 14 days after laying. The young are fairly large, and will take brine shrimp from the outset.

RIVULUS HARTII

VENEZUELA, TRINIDAD   ♂ 3½″ ♀ 3¼″.
COMMUNITY, WITH LARGER FISHES   DIET : ALL FOODS
SWIMS : UPPER HALF OF TANK

This is one of the larger Rivulus, and consequently a little more dangerous than most of the genus. It is a prodigious jumper.

The body is greyish-green with numerous thin horizontal stripes from gill-plate to caudal peduncle. These stripes are formed of red dots. The male's fins are greenish-yellow, sprinkled with red dots. His tail has a border of brownish-black. The female is duller, and the red spots on her sides are less bright. Her fins are clear. The Rivulus spot in her tail is not clearly defined, but can be seen as a dark shading.

BREEDING. *Tank:* 24″ × 8″ × 8″. *pH:* 6·8. *Hardness:* 80–100 p.p.m. *Temperature:* 78° F. *Spawns: over a period. Method: lays eggs in floating plants. Eggs: 100–150. Hatch: in 10–14 days. Food 1st week: brine shrimp. 2nd week: microworms, sifted Daphnia.*

The species is a prolific breeder, but not over-popular. The procedure is identical to that of *R. cylindraceus.*

RIVULUS STRIGATUS

Herring-bone Rivulus

AMAZON, GUIANA ♂ $1\frac{3}{4}''$ ♀ $1\frac{1}{2}''$

COMMUNITY DIET: ALL FOODS SWIMS: UPPER HALF OF TANK

Here we have the smallest and most beautiful of the Rivulus, and the most peaceful. Unfortunately, it is a little timid, and inclined to hide its beauty in the top back corners of the aquarium, lurking under the leaves of floating ferns. It is easily bullied by larger fishes, so should be kept with small species. Old, acid water is preferred, and a slightly higher temperature is needed—say 80°F.

The forward portion of the body and back is brownish and well covered with red spots. The hinder part bears an arrow-head or herring-bone pattern of bright red and beautiful blue-green. The dorsal and anal fins are yellowish-orange tipped with red and sprinkled with red dots and streaks. The tail bears wavy lines of red and blue-green; it is yellowish on the upper and lower edges.

The female carries the same colours, less brightly, and the herring-bone pattern is not so clearly defined. Her Rivulus spot is present, but apt to become merged with the streaks of colour in her tail, and this makes it less obvious.

BREEDING. *Tank: 24"×8"×8". pH: 6·8. Hardness: 80–100 p.p.m. Temperature: 80°F. Spawns: over a period. Method: lays eggs in floating plants. Eggs: 100–150. Hatch: in 10–14 days. Food 1st week: brine shrimp. 2nd week: microworms, sifted Daphnia.*

This species, being shyer and more temperamental, is not quite so easy to induce to spawn, but given peace and quiet the fish will soon settle in their new surroundings and breed. This follows the procedure given under *R. cylindraceus*.

CHAPTER XIX

COBITIDÆ

THIS FAMILY, WHICH INCLUDES THE LOACHES AND BOTIAS, COMES FROM Malaya, Sumatra, Java, Borneo, and Thailand. They are quaint, rather long-bodied fishes, and they are usually to be found at the bottom of pools on the mud, or in some cases beneath it. They therefore provide the aquarist with excellent aquarium scavengers. Most are exceedingly fast swimmers, and their activity is inclined to stir up sediment, and tends to make the water cloudy. To avoid this their aquarium should be kept clean, and occasionally the mulm should be siphoned out of the tank. The majority of this family have barbels for feeling about the bottom in their search for food. They have no teeth in the jaw, and are thus unable to bite other fishes. Generally speaking, they are peaceful, but a few of the Botias chase one another, often making a series of clicking noises during this pursuit. Rarely, however, is any damage done.

Some members of the family are equipped with two bony spikes under the eyes and in front of each gill-plate. The spikes when erected are very sharp; they curve backward and appear formidable weapons, though they seldom seem to be used in aggression. Normally they lie flat and harmlessly against the cheek, where they are inconspicuous. When a Botia is held in a net the large spines are immediately projected at right angles from the face, and are very liable to get hooked into the mesh; sometimes this has to be cut before the fish can be released. When it is necessary to catch Botias a net of plain silk, cotton, or nylon is preferable to one of mesh material.

ACANTHOPHTHALMUS SEMICINCTUS

♂

♂

Kuhli Loach

MALAYA, JAVA, BORNEO, SUMATRA, THAILAND   ♂ 3½″   ♀ 3½″

COMMUNITY   DIET: ALL FOODS   SWIMS: LOWER HALF OF TANK

These are fascinating, snake-like little fishes with long tubular bodies. The popular name covers several distinct species, but is derived from only one, *A. kuhli*. This is because originally all Acanthophthalmus were considered to belong to one species with variable local markings. The fish is an excellent scavenger, but is not easy to catch in a planted aquarium. It is peaceful, and pleasing to watch.

The majority are of a pinkish-grey colour turning to brown on the back; chocolate-brown bars cross the body from top to bottom. In *A. semicinctus* these bars do not reach as far as the belly, but end about half-way down the flanks. Other species have variations in the length, thickness, and shape of these chocolate bars, thus making identification difficult. The dorsal fin is set well back, the last rays ending a little in advance of the first rays of the anal fin.

Sexing is extremely difficult. Occasionally an adult female looks plump.

BREEDING. When the authors have put two fish into a separate breeding tank to spawn they have never done so. But when they are kept in numbers in large tanks breeding takes place, for young ones of various sizes continually appear long after the original number of adults have been removed. What actually takes place has not been witnessed in its entirety, but pairs have been seen with mouths locked together swimming just above the sand before the back glass of their tank. Their behaviour at these times shows frenzied excitement as they writhe with their long bodies close together. Eggs seem to be scattered, but must sink between the grains of sand, for none remain visible. The hatching period is uncertain, but young fish are seen about a fortnight later, though these tend to hide under low-lying leaves or round the base of clumps of plants.

It would appear that the female becomes much plumper when full of roe. Should a pair be seen to be behaving in an erratic manner they had best be placed in a separate breeding tank. This should be moderately well-planted and contain some sieved peat about $\frac{1}{4}''$ thick, covering the sand on which the eggs may settle and be hidden from view. Breeding is a matter of chance, but is worth a try, since any information obtained will help in bringing about more certain conditions.

ACANTHOPHTHALMUS SPECIES

THAILAND   ♂ 3″ ♀ 3″

COMMUNITY   DIET: ALL FOODS   SWIMS: LOWER HALF OF TANK

This is a rare loach which is seldom imported. It may possibly be *A. javanicus.* An excellent scavenger, it is extremely peaceful, easy to feed, but rather shy. The body is long and snake-like, but thicker in section than most other Acanthophthalmus.

The back and head are mauvy-brown, the sides and belly are silver-grey, but in some lights they have a pinkish sheen. The dorsal fin is situated far back; it ends the length of its own base in front of the anal fin.

The female when full of roe becomes twice as thick as the male, and her belly is so distended that it appears grotesque.

BREEDING. The authors have not succeeded in breeding this fish, but in all probability the procedure is the same as for *A. semicinctus.*

ACANTHOPSIS CHOIRORHYNCHOS

THAILAND, INDO-CHINA, INDONESIA   ♂ 6″ ♀ 6″

COMMUNITY   DIET: ALL FOODS   SWIMS: LOWER HALF OF TANK

These quaint fish are not well enough known to have become popular yet. Nevertheless, they have proved themselves to be at home in an aquarium. In spite of their size, they do not seem in the least aggressive; on the contrary, they are very shy. They make excellent scavengers, not only clearing up food which lies on the sand, but burrowing beneath it to forage out any particles which have worked their way between the crevices. Moreover, they keep the sand well loosened, and are amusing to watch. Mouthfuls of sand are taken in, every particle of food is sifted and swallowed, then the cleansed grains are shot backward out of the gills like a miniature sand-blaster.

The eyes are placed well up on the head, so that the fish while resting on the bottom has a clear all-round view.

In its native haunts *A. choirorhynchos* lives in swift-running streams with sandy or gravel bottoms, and its coloration is in keeping with its surroundings. The belly is silverish, the back and sides are sandy-grey. Regularly spaced brown spots appear along the back. A thin line runs from the lips upward to the eye, and thence from the top of the gill-plate to the base of the tail. Equally spaced along this line are brown dots. The fins are clear, except for a few small dots. The mouth, which is undershot, is equipped with short barbels. The spotted sandy colour is such a good camouflage that the fish is quite difficult to see. When disturbed it will dive beneath the sand, remaining buried for long periods, then only raising its eyes sufficiently to reconnoitre.

As yet the species lacks a popular name; but the Pan-American pilot who first brought it to the authors had nicknamed it 'Horse-face.' This undoubtedly fits, in an uncomplimentary manner, since it has a long nose and an elongated jaw.

There is no indication of sex, neither has it been bred.

NOEMACHEILUS SPECIES

INDIA, BURMA, INDONESIA, THAILAND   ♂ 3″   ♀ 3″

COMMUNITY   DIET: ALL FOODS   SWIMS: LOWER HALF OF TANK

This is a large genus with numerous species coming from most of South Asia. All are good scavengers, and peaceful. The body is elongated, and the fishes swim with snake-like movements. They have small mouths which are provided with short barbels enabling them to feel around the sand, mud, or gravel for particles of food.

Generally speaking, these fishes are sandy-grey in colour with brown markings. Some have spots, others bars; yet others are mottled to fit in with the locality in which they are found. In the species illustrated the only splash of colour is a dull red spot at the base of the front rays of the dorsal fin.

Sexing is difficult. Adult females are slightly plumper than males.

BREEDING. *Tank: 24" × 8" × 8". pH: 7·2. Hardness: 120–150 p.p.m. Temperature: 78° F. Spawns: in plant thickets. Method: scatters adhesive eggs. Eggs: 100–150. Hatch: in 36 hours. Fry hang on: 1 day. Free-swimming: 3rd day. Food 1st week: brine shrimp. 2nd week: microworms, sifted Daphnia, fine dried food.*

The authors have bred one species of Noemacheilus. A pair was placed in a well-planted tank, and were observed swimming swiftly side by side over the sand and along the back of the tank. Periodically the pair would rise together to swim over a bunch of short plants, while eggs were being laid and fertilized. After two hours the pair were removed, and numerous largish eggs were seen among bunches of plants and scattered over the sand. Over 100 fry were reared.

BOTIAS

So far there have been five or six species of this genus found in Thailand, and one which inhabits Java. Most Botias are attractively coloured, though quite a few have different markings in different localities. Others appear to develop more vertical stripes with age, thus making true identification somewhat difficult at present. For this reason if during the next few years, with more of these fishes being imported annually, they are reclassified and become known under different names from those which follow, the authors must be excused.

All the Botias are similar in shape, having a somewhat arched appearance over the back, mainly brought about by the sloping shoulders which drop to the head and low, pointed nose. The fishes have short barbels on the lips, assisting them to feel for food when grubbing around the bottom of the tank.

All are equipped with formidable spines which are instantly raised at right angles to the cheeks whenever these fishes are alarmed. They come from rivers where the water is slightly alkaline, pH 7·4. They dislike acid water, which may even cause death. They grow fairly large, and should only be kept with fishes of a similar size. They are very fond of chopped shrimp, chopped garden worm, and boiled cod roe, but will take dried food.

BOTIA ALMORHÆ

THAILAND   ♂ 4½″   ♀ 4¼″

COMMUNITY, WITH LARGER FISHES   DIET: ALL FOODS

SWIMS: LOWER HALF OF TANK

Typical of the Botia shape, this species is not colourful. It is a dull grey all over, and has a large oval-shaped blotch in the caudal peduncle. In males the sides are streaked with numerous faint vertical bars which do not entirely cross the body. The female occasionally shows a few of these bars, but they are less pronounced, and not so numerous. In both sexes the fins are faintly tinged with yellow. The species should be kept only with fishes of similar size.

BREEDING. As far as is known, *B. almorhæ* has not been bred in captivity.

BOTIA HORÆ
Cream Botia

THAILAND   ♂ $2\frac{3}{4}''$ ♀ $3''$

COMMUNITY   DIET: ALL FOODS   SWIMS: LOWER HALF OF TANK

This Botia is not so large as most, and is peaceful with smaller fishes.

The body is a pale cream, the belly white. The tail fin is well sprinkled with dark spots. The most prominent feature for identification, however, is the thin black line which runs from the tip of the snout right over the top of the back, and ends by completely encircling the caudal peduncle. This line is just visible in our illustration of the upper fish, but does not show on the lower one, since it follows the curve of the back.

In males the rear portion of the flanks are crossed by three or four irregular vertical black stripes. The female does occasionally show a few of these bars, but they are much fainter, and usually not more than two or three in number. Sometimes her anal and ventral fins are tipped with bright orange.

BREEDING. As far as is known, the species has not been bred in captivity.

BOTIA LUCAS BAHI

THAILAND   ♂ $5\frac{1}{2}''$ ♀ $5\frac{1}{2}''$

COMMUNITY, WITH LARGER FISHES   DIET: ALL FOODS

SWIMS: LOWER HALF OF TANK

This attractive Botia grows large. It has a habit of excavating a depression in the sand, which it considers its own private domain, and refuses to share with other fishes.

The body is yellowish-green, liberally spotted along the lower half. The back is crossed by numerous vertical bands formed of brown spots. The head and forward portion of the back bear horizontal stripes, again formed by numerous small brown spots. The dorsal fin has a splash of red on the outer edge, sometimes wholly or partly margined with black. No indication of sex has been noted.

BREEDING. As far as is known, this species has not been bred in captivity.

BOTIA MACRACANTHA

Clown Loach

SUMATRA, BORNEO		♂ 4½″ ♀ 4½″
COMMUNITY	DIET: ALL FOODS	SWIMS: LOWER HALF OF TANK

We now come to what is probably the most striking of all the Botias, which, though medium to large in size, is extremely peaceful. It will live happily with fishes like *Barbus tetrazona, Barbus nigrofasciatus,* etc. Unlike the Thailand Botias, it is not unhappy in slightly acid water. Like all the genus, it enjoys chopped shrimp or cod roe, but will quickly learn to take dried food. These fish are very subject to Ichthyophthirius (white spot disease), and most imported specimens develop it shortly after arrival. They should not be treated with deep methylene blue, as, since they are scaleless fish, this dye if used strongly will penetrate the skin and kill the specimens. As the species is generally expensive, the aquarist naturally does not wish to take risks with chemical treatment. Perhaps the safest cure in this case is additional heat, coupled with strong aeration, slowly raising the temperature to 90° F.

The body is a golden yellow, but at times has a tint of orange. Three broad, blue-black bands run obliquely across the flanks.

The colour somewhat resembles *Barbus tetrazona*.

When one of these Botias is placed in a community tank which contains a single male tiger barb the authors have noticed that the barb immediately begins to take an interest in the clown loach, following it about wherever it goes. This would seem to indicate that fishes are able to recognize colour, particularly in those cases where it closely resembles their own. The entirely different shape of the loach does not seem to matter to the tiger barb.

Females are deeper-bellied than males.

BREEDING. Unfortunately, this attractive Botia has so far not been reproduced in captivity.

BOTIA MODESTA

Blue Botia

THAILAND   ♂ 5½″   ♀ 6″

COMMUNITY, WITH LARGER FISHES   DIET: ALL FOODS

SWIMS: LOWER HALF OF TANK

Although of pleasing colour, this Botia grows quite large, and should only be kept with fishes of similar size. Like *B. lucas bahi*, it digs a depression in the sand for private occupation, and will chase away any fishes that try to share its abode. Nevertheless, it is not pugnacious, and does not attack unless provoked; even then it inflicts no bodily harm on its opponent. It will often chase one of its own species, and during the pursuit will make clicking noises, which can be heard quite clearly ten or twenty feet away.

The body is a pale blue all over. A darker blue band crosses the end of the caudal peduncle. The dorsal is a pale blue, all the other fins being golden yellow.

A colour variety sometimes known as *B. pulchripinnis* has a pale green body, and bright red fins and tail. Both are shown in our plate.

Sex is indicated by the bulging belly of the female.

BREEDING. As far as is known, the species has not been bred in captivity.

BOTIA STRIGATA

Striped Botia

THAILAND, SUMATRA ♂ 3″ ♀ 3″

COMMUNITY DIET: ALL FOODS SWIMS: LOWER HALF OF TANK

Shorter and more chunky than its near relations, this Botia does not grow so large, and is peaceful even with quite small fishes.

The body is yellowish, the belly pale cream. The sides are crossed by numerous vertical bars of a chocolate-brown colour tinged with grey. Quite often several thin bars lie so close together that they form a broader band, then there is a space before more thin bars form themselves into a further band. Possibly this marking has a relation to sex. In our illustration the fish on the right is more evenly striped, slightly deeper-bodied, and plumper; it is probably a female. In both sexes all the fins are crossed by curving bars of a chocolate-grey colour. This species does not seem to entrench itself in a depression in the sand as do some other members of the family. One indication of sex may be the more rounded belly of the female.

BREEDING. So far attempts at breeding have not been successful.

GYRINOCHEILIDÆ

At one time these fishes were considered to be members of the family Cobitidæ, but are now classified separately. Only a few species (and one genus) are known, mostly from Thailand. They are remarkable in that they do not breathe like other fishes, which take in water through the mouth and pass it out over the gills. Above the regular branchial opening used for exhaling is a supplementary one for inhaling. They lack pharyngeal teeth. The mouth is provided with sucker lips which have rough folds on the inner surfaces, enabling them to attach themselves firmly to rocks or leaves, even in fast-running streams. Although these fishes have a swim-bladder, it is small and inadequate to work hydrostatically; only by swimming actively are they able to leave the bottom of the stream.

GYRINOCHEILUS AYMONIERI

THAILAND   ♂ 3″   ♀ 3″

COMMUNITY   DIET: ALL FOODS   SWIMS: LOWER HALF OF TANK

Above is shown a species of this interesting genus. It is a queer little fish with a long tubular body; in comparison with its size, the fins are large. These are no doubt provided to overcome the disadvantage of being unable to float by means of the swim-bladder. The under side of the snout forms the upper lip. The fish is shy, and makes quick darts for cover at the slightest sign of danger. These darts carry it a few feet forward, and then it sinks back on to the sand, being unable to remain for long in mid-water. Frequently it attaches itself to plant leaves or the glass walls of the aquarium, adhering firmly by its sucker lips. It feeds mainly on algæ, and therefore is most useful to the aquarist who is bothered by an excess of this vegetable growth. Nevertheless, it will eat dried food which has sunk to the bottom; even small pieces of chopped shrimp and so forth are taken, providing these do not require mastication.

The back and sides are brownish-yellow, paling beneath. A brown line extends from the snout through the eye to the base of the tail. Equidistant along this line, both above and below it, appear blocks of the same colour. The tail is flecked with spots, the other fins being clear. There is no clue to sex.

BREEDING. The fish has not been bred in captivity.

CHAPTER XX

MASTACEMBELIDÆ

THE SPINY EELS ARE FOUND IN THE FAR EAST. SOME SPECIES HAIL FROM INDIA, others from Burma and Thailand. The body, extremely long and thin, is covered with minute scales. It is eel-like in appearance and movement. The head is long and narrow, the snout being sharply pointed with a fleshy proboscis tipped with nostrils; this organ is movable, and is poked in and around the sand in search of food. The fish has a second pair of nostrils more normally situated. The mouth is tiny, with minute teeth in the jaw.

Some species have separate dorsal, anal, and caudal fins. Others have a single median fin, which is all three combined as one. Many Mastacembelidæ grow 9–30" in length. These large ones can swallow small, thin fishes, so are unsuitable in the average aquarium. One species, however, *M. pancalus*, is a desirable novelty.

MASTACEMBELUS CIRCUMCINCTUS

Large Spiny Eel

THAILAND   ♂ 7"   ♀ 7"

COMMUNITY, WITH LARGER FISHES   DIET: LIVE FOOD

SWIMS: LOWER HALF OF TANK

The authors have received some species from Thailand. Although several were identical, others had slightly different markings. Some were without doubt *M. circumcinctus*. All grew 7–8" in length, and were somewhat quarrelsome, while their yellowish-brown bodies bore vertical stripes. Some others were speckled; large brown spots adorned the dorsal fins. They ate the same foods as *M. pancalus*, but, having larger mouths, were able to eat small garden worms, which they seized with relish. Females appeared thicker than males.

BREEDING. Because they were not so trustworthy as the smaller *M. pancalus*, the authors made no attempt to breed the larger species. But, from their similar behaviour, spawning would likely have followed the pattern described under *M. pancalus*.

MASTACEMBELUS PANCALUS

Spiny Eel

MADRAS ♂ 4″ ♀ 4″

COMMUNITY   DIET: SMALL LIVE WORMS   SWIMS: LOWER HALF OF TANK

This is the smallest member of the genus; it is harmless, uncommon, attractive, and breedable. A disadvantage is that it is extremely difficult to catch. When approached it dives into the sand and, as the net gets near, it shoots to another place beneath the sand. When several have to be caught it necessitates removing the plants and taking the sand out in small handfuls until each fish is captured. The species devours Hydra, but it will be seen that to transfer a few to an infested tank means wrecking the aquarium to get them out again. There are less troublesome ways of clearing Hydra (p. 78).

M. pancalus has been much maligned. It is said to hide in the sand with only its head showing, in order to pounce upon and swallow any unwary fish approaching too closely. This is not true. The mouth is so small that it can swallow only white worms, blood worms, glass worms, and Daphnia, as well as a few Hydra. Even these are sucked in lengthwise. The fish soon becomes tame, and at feeding-time will emerge from its hiding-place and take white worms from its owner's fingers. Any worms which fall to the bottom—even those which bury themselves in the sand—are soon searched out by this fish.

The colour is a sandy grey; thin stripes cross the sides vertically. Large dark spots, each encircled with a rim of yellow, adorn the dorsal fin. In this species dorsal, anal, and tail are three separate fins.

Females are distinguishable from males by greater thickness of body.

BREEDING. *Tank: 24″ × 8″ × 8″. pH: 7·0–7·2. Hardness: 150–180 p.p.m. Temperature: 80° F. Spawns: among floating plants. Method: deposits adhesive eggs. Eggs: 50–100. Hatch: in 3 days. Fry hang on: 2 days. Free-swimming: 6th day. Food 1st week: infusoria, brine shrimp. 2nd week: sifted Daphnia, microworms.*

Thanks to Wing-Commander Lynn, the authors can claim to be the first to breed any of this genus in captivity. Lynn was fishing in a small pond in India, and, although he saw many species of fishes, all attempts to catch them with a Daphnia net proved futile, so mosquito netting was placed in the pond and allowed to sink. Waders then crossed the pool from the far bank, and in doing so had to push aside fronds of floating hornwort. On reaching the net it was pulled in as though seining. Various fishes were captured, among them being *M. pancalus*.

The authors tried unsuccessfully to breed these in flower-pots laid on the sand and among bunches of rooted plants. It was only after Lynn explained how these fish were caught that the key to their breeding was realized. Had the fish been in the mud the mosquito netting sinking on top of them would have trapped none. But if they were lurking in the floating hornwort they would, on being disturbed, have dived downward for safety: in this case they plunged into the net.

Since the fish lives and feeds on the bottom, why was it lurking in floating weed? Probably for spawning purposes. To test this theory a breeding tank was set up and covered with a 1″ layer of hornwort. Immediately our specimens swam into it and wriggled together, half supported in the fronds of the plants. Eggs were laid, fertilized, and hatched in 3 days. The young did not have long, pointed snouts; these developed after about a month. The parent fish completely ignored the eggs and fry. Later, for experiment, newly born guppies were placed in the tank, but proved to be too big to be swallowed, and were of no interest to the adult spiny eels.

CHAPTER XXI

SILUROIDEA

AT THE MENTION OF THE WORD CATFISHES (SUB-ORDER SILUROIDEA) THE mind of the average aquarist immediately jumps to the genus Corydoras. But there are, of course, several other catfishes, such as talking catfish, glass catfish, sucking catfish, electric catfish, upside-down catfish, and bubble-nest-building catfish, all of which belong to separate families. However, since Corydoras generally spring to mind first, we will start with these.

CORYDORAS

There are innumerable species of Corydoras, the majority of which come from northern South America. Most are short and chunky in shape, with high, arching backs and flattish bellies. They do not possess scales. Instead their bodies are covered with bony plates which overlap. These are so hard that few fishes are tempted to attack them, and fortunately Corydoras themselves are extremely peaceful. Their lips are equipped with barbels, enabling them to feel about on the bottom in their constant search for food. It is because of this that they have become known as the scavengers of the aquarium. Not only do they eat any food which falls to the sand, but they will dig strenuously between the grains to a depth of half an inch to reach some tit-bit which has settled in a crevice. Neither do they spurn particles of food which are no longer in their first freshness. On the contrary, they seem to enjoy and wax fat upon them.

All Corydoras have an adipose fin, the first ray of which is hard-spined. This feature is also present in the first rays of the pectoral fins and the dorsal fin. They have movable eyes, which periodically roll upward as if they were giving a wink. From time to time they make a quick dash to the surface, gulp a mouthful of air, and dive to the bottom again. The air inhaled is stored in a branchial cavity and used as required.

Nearly all the genus prefer alkaline water and a temperature between 68° and 78°F. They do not like excessive heat, so if any aquarist is considering raising the temperature of his tank to, say, 95°F. in an effort to cure an attack of white spot, it is advisable to remove the Corydoras before doing so. Care, however, should be taken to isolate these, so as not to transfer the disease. Fortunately, Corydoras seem practically immune from white spot, very probably because their bony plates protect them from the burrowing parasites.

Most of the genus are not difficult to breed provided they are large enough, in good condition, and given the correct requirements. In the past a mistaken idea has been circulated, and as a result it is now believed that to spawn these fishes the bottom of their tank should contain a good layer of mulm. This is quite wrong. Mulm with minute particles of food in it contains bacteria, and since the eggs take five or six days to hatch they are open to attack during the whole of this time. Should bacteria or infusoria puncture the shell of the egg, water will enter and it will fungus. When this fact was pointed out the adherents of the mulm theory then maintained that the mulm hid the youngsters and saved them from being devoured. But since the parents do not eat, fan, or look after their eggs, there is no point in leaving them in the tank after spawning.

Many aquarists are unable to distinguish sex differences in these fishes. Generally speaking, females are slightly larger than males, and their bellies are rounder below. In some cases the dorsal fin of the male is considerably more pointed than the female's. The best check, however, is to put the fish into a glass jar and look down on them from above. Males will be found to be torpedo-shaped; that is to say, from behind the gills they taper evenly to the tail. A female, however, is more diamond-shaped; in other words, she widens behind the gill-plates, and only tapers off again about half-way along her length (see

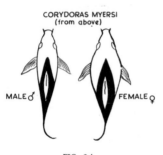

CORYDORAS MYERSI
(from above)

MALE ♂

FEMALE ♀

FIG. 24

Fig. 24). Once sexed breeding fish should be kept apart, males in one tank, females in another. They should be well fed on chopped earthworm. As the mating urge approaches many species begin to take on a slightly rosy hue from the belly to the anal fin.

For breeding a tank 24″ × 12″ × 12″ should be set up. It should have a 1″ layer of well-washed sand, and be filled with fresh tap-water, pH 7·2–7·4, hardness 150–180 p.p.m., temperature 70–72° F. In the tank should be planted a few Cryptocorynes and one or two broad-leafed Sagittarias. When all is ready a pair of fish may be introduced just before dusk. A good couple will start spawning next morning, and may continue to do so for several hours. Should they not mate after two or three days, another pair should be tried.

When spawning the male swims over the female's back and head, and the pair continue to keep in close proximity. After a while the male swims in front of the female, hovering just above her face. She rises slightly, puts her mouth to his vent, and receives some sperms. She then swims away, examining plant leaves or the walls of the aquarium to find a suitable spot to place her eggs. During this time she clasps her ventral fins together and expels four or five eggs into the pocket formed by her fins. Once satisfied with a depositing place, she spits out the sperms and, opening her ventral fins, sticks the adhesive eggs on to the plants among the sperms. She may even do this on the under sides of thin leaves. While performing this act her swim-bladder keeps her poised upside down in the water, so the leaf does not have to bend with her weight as might be expected. She then returns to the sand, and the male immediately starts to court her again. More sperm is taken in her mouth, more eggs are deposited, until some 300–400 are literally plastered on most of the leaves and in patches on the glass sides of the tank.

Once the pair separate and move about the aquarium singly spawning is over, and the couple should be removed. Even though the aquarist has taken pains to provide complete cleanliness, a few bacteria and infusoria infect the tank over the ensuing days. It is advisable, therefore, to eliminate the unwanted organisms by adding about five drops of 5 per cent. aqueous solution of methylene blue.

In two or three days numerous eggs will have turned white, but the aquarist should not despair, for in another 50–70 hours many of the eggs, difficult to see because they have not turned white, will hatch. Very probably 100 or more fry will develop, though possibly only one-tenth of these are initially visible. Newly hatched brine shrimp and micro-worms should now be fed to the babies, sparingly at first, and more generously when additional fry are seen. The young fish grow rapidly, and should reach $\frac{1}{2}''$ in length in six weeks.

CORYDORAS AENEUS

Bronze Catfish

TRINIDAD, VENEZUELA		♂ $2\frac{1}{2}''$ ♀ $2\frac{1}{2}''$
COMMUNITY	DIET: ALL FOODS	SWIMS: LOWER HALF OF TANK

Perhaps this is the commonest of all the Corydoras, and one of the hardiest. It is an excellent scavenger, and keeps the surface of the sand loose. Unfortunately, it is somewhat shy, and tends to hide beneath the background foliage.

It has a greeny-golden-coloured body. The curved edges of the bony plates divided by the lateral line give a faint herring-bone pattern on the sides.

Females are deeper and wider-bodied than males.

BREEDING. *Tank: 24″×12″×12″. pH: 7·2–7·4. Hardness: 150–180 p.p.m. Temperature: 76° F. Spawns: on plant leaves. Method: standard for Corydoras. Eggs: 200–350. Hatch: in 6 days. Fry hang on: 1 day. Free-swimming: 8th day. Food 1st week: brine shrimp, microworms. 2nd week: Grindal worms, fine dried food.*

This is one of the easiest Corydoras to breed.

CORYDORAS ARCUATUS

♂

Arched Catfish

GUIANA, AMAZON		♂ 2½″ ♀ 2½″
COMMUNITY	DIET: ALL FOODS	SWIMS: LOWER HALF OF TANK

A most attractive catfish, having a pearly-white body adorned by an arching black line which passes through the eye. This marking follows the curve of the back, passes under the dorsal and adipose fins, and ends in the caudal peduncle.

Sexing is obvious when viewed from above (p. 328).

BREEDING. The species has not been bred by the authors, but in all probability sexing and breeding follows that described on p. 328.

CORYDORAS AURATUS

Gold-line Catfish

GUIANA ♂ 2½″ ♀ 2½″

COMMUNITY DIET: ALL FOODS SWIMS: LOWER HALF OF TANK

Not so commonly seen, this catfish is rather like *C. aeneus*, but the body is darker in colour, and there is an arching gold line. This starts behind the upper portion of the gill-plate, passes under the dorsal and adipose fins, and ends in the caudal peduncle.

From a top view females are more diamond-shaped than males.

BREEDING. Tank: 24″×12″×12″. pH: 7·2–7·4. Hardness: 150–180 p.p.m. Temperature: 76° F. Spawns: on plant leaves. Method: standard for Corydoras. Eggs: 200–350. Hatch: in 6 days. Fry hang on: 1 day. Free-swimming: 8th day. Food 1st week: brine shrimp, microworms. 2nd week: Grindal worms, fine dried food.

CORYDORAS BREVIROSTRIS

GUIANA, VENEZUELA   ♂ 2¾″   ♀ 2¾″

COMMUNITY   DIET: ALL FOODS   SWIMS: LOWER HALF OF TANK

One of the most strikingly marked catfishes, this species has large black spots on a greyish body. A thick black line runs over the forehead and crosses the eye. A black bar adorns the upper portion of the back and continues into the lower front rays of the dorsal. The adipose fin is tipped with black. A few spots appear on the anal, but the tail is heavily covered with large black spots which form themselves into vertical bars.

Females are deeper and wider-bodied than males.

BREEDING. Tank: 24″ × 12″ × 12″. pH: 7·2–7·4. Hardness: 150–180 p.p.m. Temperature: 76° F. Spawns: on plant leaves. Method: standard for Corydoras. Eggs: 200–350. Hatch: in 6 days. Fry hang on: 1 day. Free-swimming: 8th day. Food 1st week: brine shrimp, microworms. 2nd week: Grindal worms, fine dried food.

CORYDORAS ELEGANS

Elegant Catfish

UPPER AMAZON, PERU, ECUADOR   ♂ 2¼″   ♀ 2¼″

COMMUNITY   DIET: ALL FOODS   SWIMS: LOWER HALF OF TANK

The name is misleading, as this 'cat' is not particularly elegant. It is a typical Corydoras shape, but of rather dull colouring.

The lower sides are silver-grey. A darker grey band tapers from front to rear. It starts immediately above the gill-plates, and runs just below the line of the back to the upper portion of the caudal peduncle. Green highlights appear on the gill-plates. The dorsal fin has an oblique black bar running across its centre, the upper portion being speckled. In males the top of the adipose fin is black.

Females are deeper-bodied than males, and appear wider when seen from above. With the exception of the dorsal, their other fins are clear.

BREEDING. *Tank: 24″ × 12″ × 12″. pH: 7·2–7·4. Hardness: 150–180 p.p.m. Temperature: 76° F. Spawns: on plant leaves. Method: standard for Corydoras. Eggs: 200–350. Hatch: in 6 days. Fry hang on: 1 day. Free-swimming: 8th day. Food 1st week: brine shrimp, microworms. 2nd week: Grindal worms, fine dried food.*

CORYDORAS HASTATUS

♀

Dwarf Catfish

AMAZON		♂ 1½″ ♀ 1½″
COMMUNITY	DIET: ALL FOODS	SWIMS: MID-WATER

We now come to one of the smallest catfishes, with an entirely different mode of living from the other species. It does not grub about continually on the sand, but often hovers in mid-water, fins quivering rapidly. Periodically it makes short darts to a new position, where it resumes its hovering action.

The body is olive-grey with a thin dark stripe along the sides. This ends in a large spot at the base of the tail, made even more conspicuous by being bordered on the outer edge by a crescent of white. The other fins are clear.

Adult females are considerably plumper than males.

BREEDING. Breeding has not yet been achieved by the authors, but in all probability it follows the standard pattern.

CORYDORAS JULII

Leopard Catfish

N.E. BRAZIL   ♂ $2\frac{1}{2}''$ ♀ $2\frac{3}{4}''$

COMMUNITY   DIET: ALL FOODS   SWIMS: LOWER HALF OF TANK

Of all the Corydoras this is probably the most attractively marked. Though not brightly coloured, its distinctive pattern makes it conspicuous. The overall body colour is a light creamy-grey. The head and forward portion of the body is spotted; some of the spots form irregular lines. The upper portion of the hindquarters is also spotted, but here these markings often form themselves into vertical stripes. Along the centre of the sides, starting in a line below the dorsal fin and ending at the base of the tail, is a horizontal black stripe. Above and below this stripe are two thinner lines formed by rows of black dots. These three lines are made more prominent as the space between them is devoid of dots. The caudal, ventral, and dorsal fins are spotted. In addition, a large black blotch appears in the upper part of the dorsal fin.

Sexing is best done from above, females being broader than males.

BREEDING. *Tank: 24″×12″×12″. pH: 7·2–7·4. Hardness: 150–180 p.p.m. Temperature: 76° F. Spawns: on plant leaves. Method: standard for Corydoras. Eggs: 200–350. Hatch: in 6 days. Fry hang on: 1 day. Free-swimming: 8th day. Food 1st week: brine shrimp, microworms. 2nd week: Grindal worms, fine dried food.*

CORYDORAS MELANISTIUS

GUIANA, VENEZUELA $\male\ 2\frac{1}{2}''$ $\female\ 2\frac{1}{2}''$

COMMUNITY   DIET: ALL FOODS   SWIMS: LOWER HALF OF TANK

This species closely resembles *C. brevirostris*, except that the spots on the body are smaller, and the tail fin is quite clear. It has all the attributes of the family, being peaceful, a good scavenger, and long-lived.

The body is silver-grey. From behind the gill-plates to the base of the tail small black dots are evenly sprinkled. An oblique black bar runs over the forehead. It passes through the eye and crosses the forward part of the gill-plate. Another large black blotch is splashed across the highest portion of the back and spreads into the front lower part of the dorsal. The rest of this fin and the adipose are lightly speckled.

Females are rounder under the belly than males, and appear more diamond-shaped from a top view.

BREEDING. *Tank: 24″ × 12″ × 12″. pH: 7·2–7·4. Hardness: 150–180 p.p.m. Temperature: 76° F. Spawns: on plant leaves. Method: standard for Corydoras. Eggs: 200–350. Hatch: in 6 days. Fry hang on: 1 day. Free-swimming: 8th day. Food 1st week: brine shrimp, microworms. 2nd week: Grindal worms, fine dried food.*

CORYDORAS MULTIPUNCTATUS

Spotted Catfish

N.E. BRAZIL   ♂ 2½″   ♀ 2¾″

COMMUNITY   DIET: ALL FOODS   SWIMS: LOWER HALF OF TANK

This is a pretty catfish, though rarely seen. It is somewhat like *C. julii*, the main differences being that the spots on the body are more clearly defined and spaced farther apart; also the large black blotch in the dorsal fin appears in the centre and not at the upper tip, as in *C. julii*. A study of our two plates will show the differences.

Sexing is not easy until the fish are adult. Then the females are deeper and wider in the body.

BREEDING. Tank: 24″×12″×12″. pH: 7·2–7·4. Hardness: 150–180 p.p.m. Temperature: 76° F. Spawns: on plant leaves. Method: standard for Corydoras. Eggs: 200–350. Hatch: in 6 days. Fry hang on: 1 day. Free-swimming: 8th day. Food 1st week: brine shrimp, microworms. 2nd week: Grindal worms, fine dried food.

The species has not been bred by the authors, but we understand from Continental breeders that the procedure follows the normal pattern given on p. 328.

CORYDORAS MYERSI

♂

♀

ECUADOR, PERU   ♂ 2½″   ♀ 2½″

COMMUNITY   DIET: ALL FOODS   SWIMS: LOWER HALF OF TANK

Though not very often seen, this is another pleasant little catfish.

The body colour is brownish to dull gold. A rather broad brownish-grey band starts at the back of the head, runs under the dorsal and adipose fins, and ends in the upper portion of the caudal peduncle. Just below this band is another one which is less clearly defined; it is narrower, and displays a golden sheen. The tip of the dorsal fin is more rounded than it is in other Corydoras.

Viewed from above, adult females are more diamond-shaped than males.

BREEDING. *Tank:* 24″× 12″× 12″. *pH:* 7·2–7·4. *Hardness:* 150–180 *p.p.m. Temperature:* 76° F. *Spawns: on plant leaves. Method: standard for Corydoras. Eggs: 200–350. Hatch: in 6 days. Fry hang on: 1 day. Free-swimming: 8th day. Food 1st week: brine shrimp, microworms. 2nd week: Grindal worms, fine dried food.*

The authors have made several attempts, following the usual procedure, to breed this fish, but it shows no desire to mate. Possibly the specimens used were too old or somewhat under-sexed. But there seems to be no reason why other healthy young specimens should not respond to the normal procedure.

CORYDORAS PALEATUS

♂

♀

Mottled Catfish

S. BRAZIL   ♂ $2\frac{1}{2}''$ ♀ $2\frac{3}{4}''$

COMMUNITY   DIET: ALL FOODS   SWIMS: LOWER HALF OF TANK

This catfish vies with *C. aeneus* for the distinction of being the commonest species of the genus. Not that this in any way detracts from its
usefulness. It is peaceful, a wonderful scavenger, not so shy as some others,
is long-lived, easy to breed, and often becomes a firm favourite with its
owner. It enjoys sitting in the front of the aquarium, where it amuses
onlookers with frequent winks of the eyes.

The body colour is olive green. Patches of blackish-green mottle the
flanks. The gill-plates shine with a metallic green in certain lights. The
front rays of the dorsal are olive; the tail fin is peppered with faint spots.
Otherwise the fins are clear.

Females are rounder below than males, and viewed from above are
more diamond-shaped. The males have a very sharp-pointed dorsal fin.

BREEDING. *Tank: 24″ × 12″ × 12″. pH: 7·2–7·4. Hardness: 150–180 p.p.m. Temperature: 76° F. Spawns: on plant leaves. Method: standard for Corydoras. Eggs: 200–350.
Hatch: in 6 days. Fry hang on: 1 day. Free-swimming: 8th day. Food 1st week: brine
shrimp, microworms. 2nd week: Grindal worms, fine dried food.*

The species breeds easily, often developing a reddish hue from under the belly to the anal fin as the spawning urge approaches. The procedure follows that described on p. 328, but the authors have noticed that males with well-developed sharp-pointed dorsal fins are the best drivers. Those lacking this feature often prove to be difficult to breed. The cause may be a deficit of hormones, since there seems to be some connexion between fin-development and virility.

CORYDORAS RETICULATUS

Mosaic Catfish

LOWER AMAZON		♂ 3″ ♀ 3″
COMMUNITY	DIET: ALL FOODS	SWIMS: LOWER HALF OF TANK

This is an attractively marked catfish. It grows slightly larger than most others.

The head and upper flanks are laced with irregular lines giving a mosaic appearance. A black zig-zagging line runs from the centre of the flanks to the base of the tail. The lower sides are covered with thin vertical stripes. There is a golden-green sheen over most of the body. The dorsal and tail fins are sprinkled with lines and spots.

Sexing is difficult until the fish are mature; then the female is deeper-bodied and broader from a top view.

BREEDING. *Tank: 24″ × 12″ × 12″. pH: 7·2–7·4. Hardness: 150–180 p.p.m. Temperature: 76° F. Spawns: on plant leaves. Method: standard for Corydoras. Eggs: 200–350. Hatch: in 6 days. Fry hang on: 1 day. Free-swimming: 8th day. Food 1st week: brine shrimp, microworms. 2nd week: Grindal worms, fine dried food.*

BAGRIDÆ

This family comprises several species found in the Far East. They are longer and slimmer than the Corydoras, and also have larger fins and longer barbels. They lack the armoured 'scales' common to the Corydoras.

LEIOCASSIS SIAMENSIS

THAILAND   ♂ 6″   ♀ 6″

COMMUNITY, WITH LARGER FISHES   DIET: ALL FOODS

SWIMS: LOWER HALF OF TANK

This very striking catfish from Siam is rarely found in aquaria, but it may become popular with the owners of large tanks. It is not aggressive, though it will on occasions chase for a short distance any fishes which annoy it. This action is sometimes accompanied with one or two short grunts which seem to warn off the intruder, who is never viciously attacked or harmed. *L. siamensis* enjoys chopped shrimp, small lumps of boiled cod-roe, small worms, and even dried food. It is continually scavenging the bottom for any particles of food left by other fishes. Unfortunately, it is rather inclined to excavate a pit in the sand where it likes to take a quiet rest. Around the nose and mouth it is equipped with eight barbels which give the face a rat-like appearance. In the first rays of the dorsal and pectoral fins there are hard, sharp spines. The adipose fin is extremely long.

The body is a light creamy colour, sometimes diffused with pale pink. It is crossed by several bands of dark grey to black, making a conspicuous contrast. These black bands enter most of the fins.

The female is much deeper and broader than the male, and her tail fin has a reddish hue.

Both sexes have an extraordinary fleshy appendage between the ventral and anal fins. It is about $\frac{1}{2}''$ long, and is soft and pointed. The purpose of this strange organ is unknown to the authors. Possibly it is used for depositing eggs and sperms in mud or between stones when spawning takes place.

BREEDING. On a few occasions a pair have been placed in a tank 30"×15"×15" containing a variety of plants. The male immediately started to drive the female. At times both fish have been seen side by side, heads together and fins curved towards each other. They have pressed their bodies against each other with a waggling motion, but no eggs have been observed. A few hours later the very fat female has been quite slim, so, unless she has spawned, her decrease in size is mystifying. So far no young have appeared. On the last occasion these fish were put out to spawn excited chasing began, but next morning both fish were found on the floor, having leapt from the breeding tank. They had jumped through a small opening in the cover glass, so warning must be given that these fish do jump when excited.

MYSTUS VITTATUS

N. INDIA, BURMA, CEYLON, AND THAILAND   ♂ 5"   ♀ 5"

COMMUNITY, WITH LARGER FISHES   DIET: ALL FOODS

SWIMS: LOWER HALF OF TANK

Though large, this is an interesting catfish. As it is quite a fast swimmer, it should not be kept with very small fishes. Although it will not eat them, it scares them by its bulk, particularly when moving at speed. It has a habit of sitting under low-leafed plants, and, by vigorously waving its body and fins, shifts the sand until it has formed a depression large enough in which to lie. This disturbance in a well-laid-out tank can be annoying. Nevertheless, the fish is a useful scavenger.

The sides are fawny-brown. Two lightish gold lines pass along the body. These run from behind the gill-plate, one above and the other under the lateral line, to the base of the tail. The fins are brownish.

The female is much deeper-bellied and broader than the male.

BREEDING. So far all attempts at breeding this fish have proved fruitless.

PIMELODIDÆ

This family is very similar to the Bagridæ, but inhabits South America.

MICROGLANIS PARAHYBŒ

♀

♂

Bumble-bee Catfish

GUIANA, AMAZON   ♂ 3″   ♀ 3″

COMMUNITY, WITH LARGER FISHES   SWIMS: LOWER HALF OF TANK

This catfish is rare, particularly in Europe. It has a large mouth, and will swallow small fishes so quickly that only a bulging stomach shows evidence of what has happened. The first ray of the dorsal and the pectoral fins are hard, sharp spines. All are erected stiffly when the fish is caught in a net or attacked by larger species. The trailing edge of the pectorals is serrated. Small hooks at the tips of these fins often catch so firmly in fine mesh nets that the material may have to be cut before the fish can be released. When lifted from the water the species sometimes makes a buzzing sound similar to that of a bee smothered with a cloth. Viewed from above, the head is round and large, the body tapering from the pectoral fins to a point at the tail.

The colouring is striking. The body is nearly jet-black, but in places there are one or two patches of pinkish grey. The first of these forms a band over the back of the head and runs down behind each gill-plate. Another appears on the flanks below the outer edge of the dorsal. One is to be seen on the forward portion of the adipose fin. There is yet another on the caudal peduncle; behind this two more show on the upper and lower edges of the base of the tail. The dorsal is black, but the outer edge is clear, and a colourless semicircle appears through the centre of this fin. The ventrals and pectorals are black; the tips of the latter are colourless. The anal fin is black, but has a clear patch in its centre. The tail has a black border near its outer edge, though the tips of the rays are clear. There are three pairs of barbels. One pair protrudes from the upper lip; these are longish, and are marked with alternate patches of black and white. A similar pair projects from the lower lip. The third pair also appears below the mouth, but these are shorter and colourless.

Sexing is difficult as both fish are similarly marked. At maturity females are deeper and rounder-bellied than males.

BREEDING. The fish is easy to keep, but the authors have not bred it.

PIMELODELLA GRACILIS

AMAZON, BRAZIL   ♂ 5″ ♀ 5″

COMMUNITY, WITH LARGER FISHES   DIET: ALL FOODS

SWIMS: LOWER HALF OF TANK

Another long-whiskered catfish, which grows large, so should not be kept with small fishes.

The body is pale blue-grey, and a blue-black line runs from behind the gill-plate to the base of the tail. The fins are grey.

The female is much deeper-bodied than the male.

BREEDING. All attempts at breeding have so far failed. A male and a plump female have often been given a 30″ × 15″ × 15″ tank well filled with mixed plants. Although next morning she is very much slimmer, no eggs have been observed. Possibly these have been eaten during and after the spawn.

CALLICHTHYIDÆ

A family of South American catfishes which have large heads, tapering bodies, and are covered with smooth, overlapping armour plates. The first ray of the dorsal, adipose, and pectoral fins is hard. They have four longish barbels.

CALLICHTHYS CALLICHTHYS

♂

♀

Bubble-nest-building Catfish

N.E. SOUTH AMERICA   ♂ $4\frac{1}{2}''$ ♀ $5''$

COMMUNITY, WITH MEDIUM-SIZED FISHES   DIET: ALL FOODS

SWIMS: LOWER HALF OF TANK

Though it grows rather large, this is an interesting and unusual catfish. It is peaceful, and a good scavenger, but rather shy.

The overall colour is a blackish grey-brown. The overlapping scales tend to give a herring-bone pattern along the sides.

The female is generally larger than the male, deeper under the belly, and much more diamond-shaped when viewed from above. The male is widest by the gill-plates, and then tapers towards the tail.

BREEDING. Tank: 24″×12″×12″. pH: 7·2–7·4. Hardness: 150–180 p.p.m. Temperature: 76°F. Spawns: under floating leaf. Method: builds bubble-nest. Eggs: 100–150. Hatch: in 4 days. Fry hang on: 1 day. Free-swimming: 6th day. Food 1st week: brine shrimp, microworms. 2nd week: Grindal worms, fine dried food.

The tank was planted merely to make the fish feel at home, and to keep the water cleaner. A large leaf was cut off from a pond lily and allowed to float in the breeding tank. A few hours later the male was noticed to be upside down under the leaf, placing bubbles beneath it with his mouth. The female took no interest whatsoever. So vigorously did the male busy himself in trying to build a nest that he pushed the lily leaf from one end of the tank to the other. This action caused most of the bubbles to slip out and escape.

The authors then made (and thoroughly recommend) a more stable but artificial spawning platter. A 4″ square was cut from a piece of slate $\frac{1}{8}$″ thick. At opposite sides two tiny holes were bored. Through each of these a piece of catgut or nylon was threaded and tied to form a loop. A $\frac{1}{2}$″ wooden slat was pushed through the loops so that the slate platform hung from it. The piece of wood was placed across the top of the tank and the square of slate slipped along so that it was wedged tightly in one of the front corners of the aquarium. The tank was then topped up so that the under side of the slate platform hung just below the surface of the water. The lily-pad was removed, and the male fish immediately turned his attention to the artificial slate platform. In spite of his vigorous actions the slate remained firm, and soon a large nest of bubbles was built beneath it. Every now and then the male would cease his building activities to pay attention to the female. During his courtship he serenaded her with audible grunts. At length both fish swam up and under the slate. Here, circling round each other, they laid and fertilized eggs while in an upside-down position. Spawning continued for two hours, after which the female was removed, as she was now being driven away by her mate. The large eggs were clearly visible among the bubbles in the nest. The male then spent all his time replenishing the bubbles and guarding the eggs. If a finger was dipped into the tank this normally timid fish immediately made an attack.

The eggs hatched in four days, the young falling to the bottom and becoming difficult to see among the grains of sand. The male did not attempt to eat the fry. On the contrary, he attacked any object which entered the tank. The babies were fed copiously with brine shrimp and microworms. A few days later, when the fry had reached $\frac{1}{4}$″ in length, the male was removed. Nearly 200 young were raised to maturity.

CALLICHTHYS SPECIES

N.E. SOUTH AMERICA   ♂ $3\frac{1}{2}''$ ♀ $3\frac{1}{2}''$

COMMUNITY, WITH MEDIUM-SIZED FISHES   DIET: ALL FOODS

SWIMS: LOWER HALF OF TANK

The specimens illustrated are a recent introduction. As yet we are uncertain that they are even Callichthys, but they arrived with a consignment of these fish, and until more is known about them we include them in this section. The head is large, round, and slightly flattened; the mouth is wide. Two barbels project from the upper lip, and four more from the lower. The body is slim and tapering. The dorsal fin is sharply pointed and higher than it is long. A fatty adipose fin appears at the end of the caudal peduncle. The outer fringe of the tail is serrated.

The back is brown, the flanks are purplish-mauve, and the belly is creamy but speckled. A mauvish line decorates the ridge of the back from just behind the dorsal to the tail. Chocolate markings on the sides form themselves into intermittent stripes. The head is marbled with brown and pale mauve markings.

Females appear plumper, especially when viewed from above.

BREEDING. No attempts have yet been made to breed this fish. Assuming it to be a Callichthys, the normal procedure would be tried first.

HAPLOSTERNUM LITTORALE

N. SOUTH AMERICA   ♂ 3¾″   ♀ 4″

COMMUNITY, WITH MEDIUM-SIZED FISHES   DIET: ALL FOODS

SWIMS: LOWER HALF OF TANK

This genus has a higher, more arching back than the Callichthys.

The body is a dull brown, and the sides are speckled with small dark brown spots.

Sexing adult fish is easy, as the female is much wider when viewed from above, whereas the male is more torpedo-shaped; also the front rays of his pectoral fins are tinged with yellowish-brown.

BREEDING. *Tank: 24″×12″×12″. pH: 7·2–7·4. Hardness: 150–180 p.p.m. Temperature: 76° F. Spawns: under floating leaf. Method: builds bubble-nest. Eggs: 100–150. Hatch: in 3 days. Fry hang on: 1 day. Free-swimming: 5th day. Food 1st week: brine shrimp, microworms. 2nd week: Grindal worms, fine dried food.*

The breeding procedure is exactly the same as for *C. callichthys*. At this time the normally peaceful and rather shy male becomes aggressive. Once possessing eggs or young, he has no hesitation in attacking any threatening object in the vicinity.

HAPLOSTERNUM MACULATUM

N.E. SOUTH AMERICA   ♂ 4½″   ♀ 5″

COMMUNITY, WITH MEDIUM–SIZED FISHES   DIET: ALL FOODS

SWIMS: LOWER HALF OF TANK

In comparison with the previous species, this fish has a larger, flatter head. The back is not so arched, and the dorsal fin appears longer and shallower.

The body is a dull grey-brown, and is sprinkled lightly with small dark dots. The eyes are much smaller, and, due to the flatness of the head, appear to be rather upwardly inclined. A close examination of our plates will show the main differences.

When viewed from the top females are much wider-bodied than males.

BREEDING. Although we have not bred this species, in all probability it follows the pattern described under *C. callichthys*.

HAPLOSTERNUM SPECIES

N.E. SOUTH AMERICA   ♂ 4½″   ♀ 5″

COMMUNITY, WITH MEDIUM-SIZED FISHES   DIET: ALL FOODS

SWIMS: LOWER HALF OF TANK

    This species is very similar to the foregoing in most respects; the body, however, is liberally covered with large brown to black spots.

    The males appear slimmer than females, and the front rays of his pectoral fins are tinted brown.

BREEDING. Though not achieved by the authors yet, is very likely to follow that of *H. littorale.*

DORADIDÆ

    These are spiny catfishes from South America. They are equipped with bony plates, each bearing its own spine. The front ray of the dorsal is hard and sharp. The pectoral fins are large, and the front rays are also hard. Just above these is a row of razor-like spines on the sides of the fish. The adipose fin, however, is soft-rayed. The mouth is equipped with long barbels.

ACANTHODORAS SPINOSISSIMUS

♀

♂

Talking Catfish

AMAZON ♂ 4″ ♀ 4″

COMMUNITY, WITH MEDIUM-SIZED FISHES DIET: ALL FOODS

SWIMS: LOWER HALF OF TANK

This is rather an ugly-looking fish, but popular because of its habit of emitting grunting sounds when irritated by a stick or when lifted out of the water in a net. Even so, the popular name has made it more famous than many other fishes which make louder and more frequent noises. It is rather lethargic, and is inclined to hide away under the sand. Worse still, it is shy, and rarely occupies the front of the tank. It is covered with hard plates, each equipped with vicious spines. The inner edges of the pectoral fins are serrated. When caught in a net the spines are erected, and become so entangled in the mesh that the net may have to be cut before the fish can be released. It is therefore advisable to use a plain material rather than a mesh net for this species.

The body is a very dark brown to chocolate; the fins are mottled in the same colour. It is quite a good scavenger, and will take any food. It seems to live for years.

BREEDING. As far as is known, the species has not been bred in captivity.

LORICARIIDÆ

This family consists of the sucking catfishes, their mouths being placed on the under side of the head. The lips form a sucking disc by which the fishes attach themselves firmly to the glass sides of the aquarium, plant leaves, or rocks. When they are determined to hang on quite an effort is required to remove them. The back is covered with bony plates, but the belly is soft and vulnerable. They inhabit most of north-eastern South America.

LORICARIA PARVA

♂

Whip-tail Loricaria

PARAGUAY   ♂ 4″   ♀ 4″

COMMUNITY   DIET: ALGÆ AND OTHER SMALL FOODS

SWIMS: LOWER HALF OF TANK

Not a common fish, but it deserves greater popularity than it receives. The body is long and tapering, being widest at the pectoral fins. The species is a good algæ-eater, cleaning the glass and plant leaves of this unsightly vegetable matter; also it will eat cod-roe, bits of shrimp, and even dried food.

The back and the fins are brown with mottled dark markings. The tail has an elongated ray on the top half only.

Mature females are thicker than males.

BREEDING. Although the authors have not bred this fish, it was achieved by a friend who found that a pair spawned in a community tank. The mating was not observed, but a patch of large adhesive eggs were seen on a flat rock. Over these the male kept guard, seeming to spend much time cleaning them with his sucker mouth, and fanning them with his ventral and pectoral fins. They hatched in just over a week. The fry were ⅜″ long; they were netted and placed in a separate tank. Growth was rapid, and they were fed on a paste made of mashed worms and fine dried food. The temperature was roughly 78°F. and the pH of the water 7·2.

OTOCINCLUS AFFINIS

♀

Mottled Sucking Catfish

S.E. BRAZIL   ♂ 1¾″ ♀ 1¾″

COMMUNITY   DIET: ALGÆ AND OTHER FOODS   SWIMS: MID-WATER

To the aquarist who is troubled with an unsightly overgrowth of algæ any of the Otocinclus will prove to be a boon, since they feed almost entirely on this growth. Like all vegetable-eaters, they are continuous feeders. When imported the containers in which they travel are dark, so no algæ develop. For this reason the fishes usually arrive in poor condition due to under-nourishment. Moreover, they are very prone to Ichthyoph-thirius (white spot disease), and in their weak condition very few arrivals escape infection. All newly purchased Otocinclus, therefore, should be rigidly quarantined for at least ten days. During this time they should be kept at 82° F. and treated with a pale solution of methylene blue. Due to their smallness, they should only be kept with species of comparable size.

So efficient are these fishes at clearing algæ that they will clean plants, rocks, the sides of the aquarium, and even turn upside down to eat any spores growing on the surface of the water. If algæ are not present in the tank they should be scraped from other aquaria and fed to the fish. Failing this, they require a substitute of boiled lettuce or spinach. There are several species of Otocinclus, all rather similar. But perhaps the commonest is O. *affinis*, which is fawn, sprinkled with brown spots.

Ripe females are considerably fatter than males.

BREEDING. The authors have not bred this fish, but have received reports that pairs have occasionally spawned, the female laying single eggs on rocks and the glass walls of the tank. These hatch in 48 hours, and the fry cling on for a further 2 days before dropping to the bottom in search of nourishment. This should consist of fine soaked dried food, mashed microworms, and scraped algæ.

OTOCINCLUS VITTATUS

Striped Sucking Catfish

S.E. BRAZIL   ♂ 1½″   ♀ 1½″

COMMUNITY   DIET: ALGÆ AND OTHER FOODS   SWIMS: MID-WATER

The species resembles *O. affinis*, but a dark black line starts on the lips, runs through the eye, passes along the sides, and ends in a large dark blotch at the base of the tail. All other details regarding *O. affinis* apply here.

PLECOSTOMUS PLECOSTOMUS

VENEZUELA, GUIANA   ♂ 10″   ♀ 10″

COMMUNITY   DIET: ALGÆ AND OTHER FOODS   SWIMS: LOWER HALF OF TANK

Aquarium specimens rarely exceed 10″ in length, but it is reported that they grow twice this size in their natural state. So great has been the demand for this fish that quite recently exports have been limited to preserve the species.

The fins are huge. From a side view the dorsal and tail appear like sails; so do the pectorals and ventrals when seen from above. All the fins have hard front rays. These are erected when the fish is caught or handled, and sometimes get wedged in a mesh net. The mouth is immediately beneath the tip of the snout, the large lips forming a most efficient sucker. There are two barbels. The back is armour-plated for protection. A row of fine spines runs from behind the eye to the adipose fin. *P. plecostomus* may therefore be kept with larger fishes.

The colour is a sandy grey, closely speckled with darker spots. Four faint bars cross the body obliquely, two fairly close together under the dorsal, one under the adipose fin, and one in the caudal peduncle.

BREEDING. The species has not been bred in captivity.

MALAPTERURIDÆ

The one species in this family is described below.

MALAPTERURUS ELECTRICUS

Electric Catfish

W. AFRICA   ♂ 10″   ♀ 10″

NON-COMMUNITY   DIET: PROTEIN   SWIMS: ALL DEPTHS

This is not a species for the ordinary aquarist, but it always receives attention when in a tank on its own in a public exhibition, for it is capable of giving quite severe electric shocks when disturbed and touched. Like the electric eel, the discharges tend to run out if too frequently set off, but after a period of rest the body becomes recharged. *M. electricus* is somewhat sluggish, often resting on the sand at the bottom of the tank, but it gets more lively at dusk or when fed. It lives mainly on smaller fishes, which it stuns with an electric shock and swallows. Some victims, if not eaten, may recover.

The body is suede-grey and, like this material, has a matt surface. As the fish swims and turns the inner flank becomes wrinkled and folded. A few dots appear on the sides. There is a whitish area in the caudal peduncle, and a black bar runs across the base of the tail. Another forms a crescent in the centre of this fin. The dorsal has a darker area at its base. The mouth is equipped with several pairs of barbels.

So far as we know breeding has not been achieved.

SILURIDÆ

This family comprises the glass catfishes, featured by their long, transparent bodies, antennæ-like barbels, minute dorsal and long anal fins. They come from Java, Sumatra, Thailand, and West Africa.

ETROPIELLA DEBAUWI

♀

♂

Congo Glass Catfish

BELGIAN CONGO   ♂ 1¾″   ♀ 1¾″

COMMUNITY   DIET: ALL FOODS   SWIMS: MID–WATER

This fish was first imported about five years ago; it has proved to be extremely hardy, and appears to be quite long-lived. The original specimens still thrive happily in our tanks without showing any signs of ageing. The species is extremely active, constantly swimming in mid-water from one end of the tank to the other, and never seems to rest. They are absolutely peaceful, and will take any food.

The body is remarkably transparent. A broad black stripe runs from behind the gill-plate to the fork of the tail. Above this a thinner one follows the line of the back, and ends on the outer edge of the upper lobe of the tail. A third travels from the pectoral fins along the lower portion of the body, and terminates above the last rays of the long anal fin. The intestines are enclosed in a silvery sac, the swim-bladder being clearly visible. The eyes are large. The dorsal fin, which consists of only two or three rays, sticks up like a spike just behind the head. Two short, stubby barbels protrude from the tip of the snout. Some fish appear deeper just below the pectoral fins. These may be females.

BREEDING. All attempts at breeding have proved unsuccessful.

KRYPTOPTERUS BICIRRHIS

♀

♂

Ghost Fish

SUMATRA, JAVA, THAILAND   ♂ 3½″   ♀ 3½″

COMMUNITY   DIET: ALL FOODS   SWIMS: MID-WATER

For many years this species was the only glass catfish kept by aquarists. It is hardy, very transparent, and once settled down will take any foods. Unfortunately, it is shy, seeking out a favourite shady spot beneath a large leaf at the back of the tank. Here it hovers, tail tilted downward and fins quivering, to keep afloat in mid-water. At feeding time it darts out, snatches a mouthful, and returns at once to its favourite haunt. It rarely swims actively about the aquarium, but when disturbed will dash to some other place of cover. The mouth is large; small fry up to ½″ in length will be devoured. Two long, hair-like barbels, resembling antennæ, project from the tip of the snout. The dorsal fin consists of a single short spine. This appears just behind the head, and looks like a hair. The anal fin runs practically the whole length of the under side of the body.

In some lights the fish appears silvery; in others it is colourless. At times light striking through the transparent body is split up into the colours of the spectrum, as if the rays had passed through a prism. When kept in darkish tanks the species develop brown stripes, which run lengthwise along the body. At these times the fish is not nearly so transparent.

BREEDING. We have heard of no instance where *K. bicirrhis* has been successfully bred in captivity.

SYNODONTIDÆ

Through the advent of air travel the amazing family of upside-down catfishes has been introduced, and is now providing us with several species of amusing and interesting scavengers. Nearly all come from tropical West Africa. They have armour-plated backs and hard spiny rays to their fins. The eyes are set higher up and closer together than in most other fishes. When grubbing about on the bottom they turn the normal way up. A number of sensitive barbels assist them in their search for food.

While swimming from one spot to another they roll over, and proceed belly upward. Frequently they rest in this position under large plant leaves.

SYNODONTIS NIGRIVENTRIS

Upside-down Catfish

BELGIAN CONGO   ♂ 2″   ♀ 2″

COMMUNITY   DIET: ALL FOODS   SWIMS: LOWER HALF OF TANK

First imported about five years ago, this fish caused quite a stir because of its habit of swimming upside down. In shape it closely resembles the Corydoras, but is considerably more spiny. The front rays of the dorsal and pectorals are hard and sharp. When the fish is caught in a net these spines are stiffly erected and become firmly hooked into the mesh, which may need cutting before release is possible. It is therefore better to use a net of plain material than one of fine mesh. The head and forward portion of the back are covered by a bony armour. Just above the pectoral fins this bony plate forms a long, sharp spine which lies against the fish's sides. From the lips protrude several pairs of barbels, the upper ones being quite long. When lifted from the water the fish makes croaking grunts.

The general colour is greyish, but the body, fins, and barbels are mottled with dark mauve blotches. The caudal peduncle bears broad mauve bars. The belly is mauvish black. The back is lighter than any other part. This feature is unusual, as normal swimming fishes are dark on the back and lighter in the belly.

A fish looking up from below sees the light-coloured belly of another fish above it against a background of light entering the surface of the water. The same fish looking down on one below sees the dark back against the bottom. Because *S. nigriventris* swims upside down its colour pattern has to be reversed to bring about the usual camouflage.

Females are rounder and deeper-bellied than males.

BREEDING. So far the species has not been bred. But when they were provided with a slate pad (see *C. callichthys*, p. 345), considerable interest was taken in it; some bubbles were occasionally seen underneath the pad.

SYNODONTIS SHOUTEDENI

Large Upside-down Catfish

EQUATORIAL W. AFRICA   ♂ 6″   ♀ 6″

COMMUNITY, WITH LARGER FISHES   DIET: ALL FOODS

SWIMS: LOWER HALF OF TANK

This upside-down catfish is greyish, mottled with dark mauve patches. The fins are longer and more pointed. The bony plating which covers the head and fore-part of the back carries a similar spine just above the pectoral fins. The shield of armour is clearly seen on the bottom fish in our plate. The species is not aggressive, but, knowing it is well protected, it will not hesitate to chase away other large fishes which annoy it. Such attacks do not mean harm, but serve merely to drive off the offender. There are two antennæ-like barbels on the upper lip; four smaller ones, each provided with side branches, project from the bottom lip. The adipose fin is very long at its base, but the rays are short. The points of the tail tend to curve inward.

This fish does not swim upside down nearly as much as *S. nigriventris*, and consequently its belly is not so dark. Never bred.

CHAPTER XXII

ANABANTIDÆ

THIS FAMILY, POPULARLY KNOWN AS THE LABYRINTH FISHES, IS EQUIPPED
with an auxiliary breathing apparatus which enables its members to gulp
a mouthful of air from above the surface of the water. On descending they
force this air into a special compartment known as the labyrinth, which is
situated in the head. From this store of air, oxygen is extracted and passed
to the blood-stream. The imprisoned air lasts for a considerable time
when the fish is inactive, but if it is excited or nervous, or should the
metabolism be speeded up by additional heat, the store of air in the labyrinth is used at a faster rate. When this occurs the fish frequently returns
to the surface for fresh supplies. On gulping more air through the mouth
and forcing it into the labyrinth the used store, now depleted of oxygen,
is forced out through the edge of the gill-covers. This family is therefore
able to live in dirtier, fouler, and warmer water than can most others.
Nevertheless, it is a mistake to think that they do not extract dissolved
oxygen from the water in which they live. On the contrary, they use up
nearly as much of this gas as do other fishes.

If several labyrinths are added to an aquarium already stocked to
capacity their presence will cause a shortage of oxygen. But it will be the
species not equipped with an auxiliary breathing apparatus that will die
first.

Most of the family are beautiful. The larger species are rather aggressive,
but their colours and the interesting method of reproduction have made
them firm favourites among aquarists.

Sexing is not difficult, as males are usually much more colourful, and
have longer points on the dorsal and anal fins. Furthermore, females
bulge just behind the pectoral and ventral fins.

Breeding the Bubble-nest-builders

The majority of the species in this family are bubble-nest-builders. The
male goes to the surface of the water and takes in a mouthful of air.
Breaking this into tiny bubbles, he coats each with saliva, and spits them
out. They float to the surface, but, due to their filmy covering, do not
burst immediately. The process is repeated continually, until in a few
hours the nest may measure several inches in diameter, and be mounded
up in the centre to a height of $\frac{1}{2}''$ or more. Some species construct the nest
solely of bubbles; others reinforce the structure with bits of plant. A
forceful male may even build such a nest in a community tank. He will
monopolize one top corner, and all other fishes will be driven away from
this area. Once he starts to build he will only break off to visit his mate for
further excitement and encouragement.

Eventually, when the nest is complete, the male entices his mate underneath the canopy of bubbles. Here, after some show and courtship, she will prod him in the flanks with her nose. The male then curves his body towards her and envelops her from slightly below. This is called the nuptial embrace. His curved position causes him to roll over on his side, while the female, gripped in his embrace, is tilted upside down. His grip tightens, and with quivering fins he squeezes her until she releases several eggs. At the same time he exudes his sperms so that the spawn is fertilized. In a few seconds the male relaxes his grip, and slowly the female drops away from his embrace. As she does so she rights herself from her upside-down position, and the eggs lodged between her fins start to sink slowly. Either the males alone, or more often both fish together, swim down and gather every falling egg in their mouths. These are surrounded with bubbles of air coated with saliva, and spat out beneath the nest, where they float. After a little more display the male and female re-embrace and spawning continues. Usually some 250–300 eggs are finally placed in the nursery; the male then takes charge. His first act is to drive away any fish he thinks may eat the spawn. More often than not his mate is the first to be attacked. Having cleared his domain, he continues to keep his nest in repair; as fast as any dilapidation takes place he makes good the damage with fresh bubbles.

In 24–30 hours the young hatch. Bursting their way out of the imprisoning bubbles, they tend to sink; but the ever-attentive male picks them up in his mouth and blows them back beneath the nest, where they hang in masses tail downward. If, as is presumed, all this has taken place in a community tank it is now time for the aquarist to intervene. For once these tiny fry are free-swimming they will spread all over the tank. It is quite impossible for the male to guard all the hatch at once. This means that they will be eaten by the other inhabitants of the aquarium. Taking a wide-mouthed jar, the aquarist should press the base below the surface of the water. Tilting the mouth towards the nest, the jar should be pressed slowly down until the nest and all the hanging bunches of young are drawn into the jar. Very few fry will be lost at this stage. The contents are then emptied into a breeding tank containing water which is chemically similar and of the same temperature as that in the aquarium.

In a further 48 hours the fry will be free-swimming, and must be fed copiously with fine infusoria. An occasional feed of hard-boiled yolk of egg squeezed through a piece of fine muslin is advisable. In yet another 10 days brine shrimp may be added to the diet. Later on, when the fry are $\frac{1}{2}''$ long, Cyclops and sifted Daphnia may be given. The babies of anabantids feed in mid-water, and food like microworms will be snapped up as they sink; but once the worms reach the bottom of the tank they are mostly ignored. Such foods are not strongly recommended.

The above procedure applies when a pair of bubble-nest-builders spawns unexpectedly in a community tank. The method is not the best under ordinary circumstances. It is preferable to select pairs and put them into a breeding tank. This should be about 24″ × 12″ × 10″. An inch of fine sand is placed on the bottom before filling with water, which should have a pH of 6·8–7·2, and a hardness of 100–150 p.p.m. Clumps of foliage are planted here and there so that the female may take refuge.

Where the male is aggressive it is a wise plan to place a female bulging with roe in a large glass jar and float this in one corner of the breeding tank, the male being allowed the freedom of the aquarium. A few floating plants may be needed in the construction of his nest, so these should be supplied. He is able to see his mate, and the sight of her excites him and prompts him to build a nest, but during this time he is unable to damage his partner. Only when the nest is complete should she be lifted with a net out of her jar and placed in the tank. In all probability the ardent male may be too impetuous, and unless the female responds immediately he is apt to feel frustrated and bad-tempered. If this occurs he will attack her and tear her fins. The pair should be given time to adjust themselves, when all may be well. But should the female be insufficiently worked up she is likely to be damaged. In such a case after an hour or two her fins will be torn, and she will be too scared to spawn. She should therefore be caught and returned to the safety of her jar. A further attempt may be made the next day, or the one after.

Once spawning has taken place the white eggs may be seen among the silvery bubbles, and the female will have been driven well away from the nest. She should now be placed in the jar and returned to her usual tank. Some males will raise and protect their fry until they are beyond the need of parental care; but it is often safer to remove the male when the babies have just become free-swimming. Feeding should be carried out as detailed above.

ANABAS TESTUDINEUS

Climbing Perch

INDIA, CEYLON, INDONESIA, PHILIPPINES   ♂ 5½″   ♀ 6″

COMMUNITY, WITH LARGER FISHES   DIET : ALL FOODS

SWIMS : LOWER HALF OF TANK

In its natural habitat this fish grows to between 12″ and 15″ in length, and is used for food. Aquarium specimens, however, rarely exceed half this size. The species has received a fair amount of publicity on account of its ability to come out of water and travel overland to other ponds. It has been nicknamed the "Climbing Perch," since it will ascend banks and even the lower branches of trees. On each gill-plate there is a spine. When these are extended the fish, by waggling its head, is able to hook first one and then the other spine on to some plant or object, thereby making a forward progression. When on land the pectoral fins are held rigid and used as front legs. These, as will be seen in our plate, keep the belly off the ground, and enable clumsy steps to be made. The picture was taken as the specimen was walking along a branch of a tree. Such rambles are not a necessity; the fish is more at home in the water. *A. testudineus* is not vicious or aggressive with fishes of its own size. On the contrary, it is inclined to hide behind tall plants at the back of the aquarium, Indian ferns being particularly favoured.

The back is a pale mauvish-blue. The sides and belly are silvery-yellow. There are two black spots; one appears immediately above the pectoral fins, the others shows up in the base of the tail. All the fins are a rich golden yellow.

The female is larger than the male. She is considerably deeper-bodied, and thicker just behind the pectoral and ventral fins.

BREEDING. Tank: 24″×12″×12″. pH: 6·8–7·2. Hardness: 120–150 p.p.m. Temperature: 80° F. Spawns: in floating plants. Method: eggs float at surface. Eggs: 100–150. Hatch: in 24 hours. Fry hang on: 2 days. Free-swimming: 4th day. Food 1st week: infusoria, brine shrimp. 2nd week: fine dried food, microworms.

The tank should contain some sand; plants should be provided in case one of the fish becomes too aggressive. The other can then avoid head-on attacks by dodging round the clumps of foliage. *A. testudineus* does not build a bubble-nest. The parents go into the usual embrace, and the small eggs rise to the surface of the water. Since the pair do not look after their eggs they may as well be removed.

BELONTIA SIGNATA

Comb-tail

CEYLON   ♂ 5″   ♀ 5″

COMMUNITY, WITH LARGER FISHES   DIET: ALL FOODS   SWIMS: ALL DEPTHS

This is not a colourful species, and it grows too large for the average aquarist. Kept with other fishes of its own size, it behaves moderately well. The popular name is derived from the extending rays of the tail fin, which give the appearance of a toothed comb.

The groundwork of the body is grey. Each scale, however, is edged with dull red, and this gives a network formation. Irregular wavy bands of dull red cross the sides from top to bottom. All the fins are a rusty hue, the edges being clear.

The male is usually larger than the female, and not so thick in the region behind the ventrals and pectorals. His dorsal and ventral fins are longer and more pointed than those of the female, and the extending rays of his tail are also slightly longer.

BREEDING. *Tank: 30″×15″×15″. pH: 6·8. Hardness: 100–150 p.p.m. Temperature: 80° F. Spawns: in typical embrace. Method: eggs float among bubbles in poor nest. Eggs: 300–400. Hatch: in 48 hours. Fry hang on: 2 days. Free-swimming: 5th day. Food 1st week: infusoria. 2nd week: brine shrimp, microworms.*

The tank should be filled with water to a depth of 8–10″. Clumps of plants should be set here and there to protect the female in case the male becomes too aggressive. He will blow a few bubbles, but they do not form into a mounded nest. After the usual embrace the floating eggs are massed together among the bubbles. Parents tend their young, but once the fry are free-swimming the adults should be removed.

BETTA PICTA

Mouth-breeding Betta

THAILAND, MALAYA, INDONESIA   ♂ 2″   ♀ 1¾″

COMMUNITY   DIET: ALL FOODS   SWIMS: MID-WATER

Though not over-colourful, this is an attractive fish. Its outstanding feature is that it is a mouth-breeder, the hatching being done in the mouth of the male. *B. picta* is not aggressive, but when kept in numbers males occasionally chase females.

The colouring is not brilliant, and, as in most Bettas, the intensity varies considerably. When content the fish is a mauvish-brown all over. A dark line runs from the lips through the eye and across the gill-plate. Should the fish be disturbed, caught, and put into a jar, it turns a more greyish colour, and faint bars appear vertically on the sides.

Sexing is easy, since the male has a dark maroon lower edge running the entire length of his anal fin. Females show no sign of this coloured border. This masculine feature remains when the fish is in full colour, or when it is put in a jar and lacks its normal hues.

BREEDING. *Tank: 24" × 8" × 8". pH: 6·8–7·0. Hardness: 120–150 p.p.m. Temperature: 80° F. Spawns: in typical embrace. Method: male incubates eggs in his mouth. Eggs: 80–100. Hatch: in 15–18 days. Food 1st week: brine shrimp. 2nd week: sifted Cyclops, fine dried food.*

The tank need be only lightly planted to make the fish feel at home. Sometimes they will start to lay their eggs in a few hours. But if the female is not ripe spawning will not take place for several days; even so, the male will not harm her. When spawning occurs the fish embrace in the usual Betta fashion. Immediately afterwards, as the pair separate, the male picks up the dropping eggs; but instead of blowing them out into a nest he retains them in his mouth. The pair embrace repeatedly, and each time the male collects and stores the eggs. After spawning the female may as well be removed, as she takes no further part in the rearing of the young. During the next 10–12 days the male's jaw and gill-plates are somewhat extended, and it is obvious that he is carrying the eggs. Although he rarely eats the fry once they are free-swimming, the risk can be entirely eliminated if he is removed: the babies in the breeding tank are safe without his protection.

BETTA SPLENDENS

♂

Red Betta   *Blue Betta*

♂

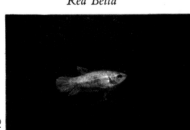

♀

♂

Red Female Betta   *Black Betta*

Siamese Fighting Fish

THAILAND, CAMBODIA, INDONESIA   ♂ $2\frac{3}{4}''$ ♀ $2\frac{1}{2}''$

COMMUNITY   DIET: ALL FOODS   SWIMS: ALL DEPTHS

The original wild specimens of these fish, although colourful, were generally darkish. Here and there the iridescent scales shone with jewel-like spots, and their fins were much shorter.

The modern aquarium-developed *B. splendens* is so different that it is hardly recognizable as being the same fish. It may be a brilliant corn-flower blue, a vivid red, a bright green, a black, or a cream with red fins. These self-coloured fish are the most prized in shows and exhibitions, but there are numerous beautiful individuals which blend two or more hues in one. Generally speaking, such specimens are more common and cheaper. When not in perfect colour Bettas are a dull, indistinct hue, but have a dark line running from the lips through the eye to the base of the tail. Females in particular often appear thus, but once excited the overall colour spreads and the line fades. It is unfair to assume that any Betta showing the lateral bar will always remain so; the slightest excitement will bring out the true colour, and he may well be a superb specimen.

In Siam these fish provided sport, much the same as cock-fighting did in England before becoming illegal. Large sums of money were waged by owners and onlookers as two male fish of different hues were placed in a bowl or tank of water to fight. This continued either to the death, or until one of the owners would admit defeat in order to save his fish from the *coup de grâce*, and so be able to stage a return match at a later date. Some fish after many bouts acquired a reputation comparable to professional boxers of to-day.

On facing each other unacquainted males will spread their gorgeous fins and waggle their bodies in aggressive threats. As the pair approach the gill-plates are extended and the gill membranes protrude fanwise round the throat, much like the feathers of a fighting-cock. With a lunge a combatant will bite and rip off a strip of one of the opponent's fins. In like manner the attacked fish will retaliate, and in a short while the gorgeous fins of both will be hanging in frayed rags and tatters. Eventually one becomes so damaged that he is unable to manoeuvre quickly. When this happens his opponent, being at an advantage, is able to twist and turn, and thereby inflict damage more easily. Occasionally in nature a badly beaten fish will retire before he is killed, but in a confined space he is unable to get away, and will have to fight to the death. The victor will recuperate surprisingly well. Most of his fins which are torn will knit together again; but the rays will thicken where they rejoin, and scars will show; he will never again be a perfect exhibition specimen. Fins which are torn too short may not reattain full length.

In spite of the fighting prowess of these fish the beginner need not be deterred from having one in his tank, for it will not battle with other fishes. It is true that *B. splendens* is not partial to other anabantids, and will occasionally chase them, but since most labyrinths prefer to swim away and avoid a fight, no damage is done. A male Betta may safely be kept with several females. They will not attack him, or fight to the death among themselves, though they will often squabble and tear one another's fins. Two males reared together from birth may also live fairly peacefully, but this depends mainly on their individual temperaments.

Sexing is easy, as the females have much shorter fins, and are considerably thicker in the region behind the pectorals and ventrals.

BREEDING. *Tank: 24″ × 8″ × 8″. pH: 6·8–7·0. Hardness: 150–180 p.p.m. Temperature: 80° F. Spawns: in typical embrace. Method: standard for bubble-nest-builders. Eggs: 150–250. Hatch: in 3 days. Fry hang on: 2 days. Free-swimming: 6th day. Food 1st week: infusoria. 2nd week: infusoria, brine shrimp.*

Only females well filled with roe should be tried for breeding. If unready to spawn they may be killed by the male.

The method of reproduction is fully described under the heading Breeding the Bubble-nest-builders, p. 362. After spawning the female should be removed immediately. Once the fry are free-swimming the male may be taken out.

CQLISA FASCIATA

Striped Gourami

INDIA ♂ 4¾″ ♀ 4½″

COMMUNITY DIET: ALL FOODS SWIMS: ALL DEPTHS

Although this is an attractive and extremely colourful fish, it has had to yield its place in the aquarium to its smaller cousins. It is hardy, peaceful, and easy to feed.

Male and female are very different in colour, she being as drab as he is gorgeous. She is a dull reddish-brown with a dark line running from the gill-plate to the base of the tail. Her fins are brown with a rusty-coloured edge. The back of the male is brown. The sides are more of an orange tinge, and are crossed by several thin, slightly oblique blue bars. The lower portions of the gill-plates are a bright blue. His dorsal is tipped with orange-red, the centre portion being more bluey-green. The anal fin is blue, the outer tips of the rays being bright red; the trailing point of this fin is edged with red. The tail is orange with red dots. His ventrals take the form of long, thin filaments (commonly known as feelers); they are bright orange-red.

BREEDING. Tank: 24″ × 12″ × 12″. pH: 6·8–7·0. Hardness: 150–180 p.p.m. Temperature: 78° F. Spawns: in typical embrace. Method: standard for bubble-nest-builders. Eggs: 150–250. Hatch: in 3 days. Fry hang on: 2 days. Free-swimming: 6th day. Food 1st week: infusoria. 2nd week: infusoria, brine shrimp.

The tank should be planted merely to make the fish feel at home.

All About Tropical Fish

COLISA LABIOSA

Thick-lipped Gourami

BURMA

COMMUNITY   DIET: ALL FOODS   SWIMS: ALL DEPTHS

♂ 2¾″   ♀ 2½″

Here we have another pleasing gourami, not too large for the average aquarium, yet big enough to be able to occupy a tank with other medium-sized fishes. The lips are not particularly thick, but are bordered by dark markings above and below which make them appear wider than they actually are.

The male is normally a chocolate-brown, but has blue vertical stripes on his sides. Blue appears in his dorsal, ventral, and caudal fins; the two former are edged with red, and are longer and more pointed than those of the female. Red streaks appear in his tail. His ventrals are bright red. At breeding time, however, the male turns much darker, sometimes nearly black. The edges of the dorsal and anal fins are then bordered by a golden-orange which stands out conspicuously and makes him appear a real beauty.

Colour and length of fins is a sure indication of sex. But with all fishes equipped with feeler-like ventrals the females are always thicker and more rounded in the area above these fins, and behind the pectorals, than are the males.

BREEDING. *Tank: 24″ × 12″ × 12″. pH: 6·8–7·2. Hardness: 150–180 p.p.m. Temperature: 80° F. Spawns: in typical embrace. Method: standard for bubble-nest-builders. Eggs: 150–550. Hatch: in 48 hours. Fry hang on: 1 day. Free-swimming: 4th day. Food 1st week: infusoria. 2nd week: infusoria.*

The species produces a bubble-nest, but sometimes incorporates into the structure a few bits of plant or duckweed, Riccia being preferred. The male takes mouthfuls of air from the surface, and instead of spitting out bubbles forces the air through his gills, exuding a mass of very fine bubbles which float to the surface. At other times he will build underneath the leaves of floating ferns. Nests are frequently constructed in a corner of a community tank, where spawning takes place. The young have little chance of survival in such a spot, so the nest and spawn should be drawn into a large jar and removed, as described on p. 363. When these fish are deliberately spawned in a breeding tank the procedure prescribed on p. 362 should be followed.

COLISA LALIA

♀

♂

Dwarf Gourami

INDIA		♂ 2″ ♀ 2″
COMMUNITY	DIET: ALL FOODS	SWIMS: ALL DEPTHS

Of the three Colisa mentioned in this book, this is undoubtedly the most beautiful; it is also the smallest, and is very peaceful. Its brilliance is best revealed when the fish is in the front of the tank and illuminated by light coming from over the viewer's shoulder. Unfortunately, it is shy, and is inclined to lurk round the darker parts of the aquarium.

The female cannot compare with her mate in appearance. She is a silvery colour, and faint bluish stripes occasionally glisten on her flanks. All her fins are clear. The male is superb, and this is not only at breeding-time.

Sex is easy to determine because of the colour differences. Furthermore, males have longer and more pointed tips to the dorsal and ventral fins. Females are thicker in the belly above the ventrals and behind the pectorals.

BREEDING. *Tank: 18″ × 10″ × 10″. pH: 6·8–7·2. Hardness: 150–180 p.p.m. Temperature: 80° F. Spawns: in typical embrace. Method: standard for bubble-nest-builders. Eggs: 100–150. Hatch: in 48 hours. Fry hang on: 2 days. Free-swimming: 5th day. Food 1st week: infusoria, yolk of egg. 2nd week: infusoria.*

The tank should be planted to make the fish feel at home, as they are inclined to be scarey. Some Riccia or other small floating plants should be included, as these are used to reinforce the bubble-nest blown by the male.

After laying her eggs the female should be removed. Once the fry are free-swimming the male may be taken out, as the young will not require his protection. The babies are minute, and need extremely fine food. Unless the tummies of the fry are kept well filled they die in great numbers during the first week or two. When $\frac{1}{8}''$ long they can be fed brine shrimp; later sifted Daphnia may be given.

HELASTOMA RUDOLPHI

Kissing Gourami

MALAYA, INDONESIA, THAILAND ♂ 6″ ♀ 6″

COMMUNITY, WITH LARGER FISHES   DIET: ALL FOODS   SWIMS: ALL DEPTHS

In nature these fish grow to 12″ or more in length, and are used for food. Those in aquaria rarely exceed 6″. The deep body is a golden cream, but laterally compressed, so that seen from a side view they look more bulky than when seen head on. They have gained wide publicity from their 'kissing' habit. The fish approach each other with their rather protruding thick lips turned back, so that they look somewhat like tiny rubber rings. The two place their lips together, and stay in that position for several seconds. Occasionally the authors have tried with a thin stick to part a pair which have just locked themselves together, but the fish could not be separated until they themselves decided to break apart. Why they unite their lips is a mystery. On occasions they will attempt to suck on to the sides of other fishes; frequently they will adhere to the glass walls of the aquarium, where they eat some algæ. Only when large do they tend to become a little aggressive, and should then be kept with bigger species.

These fish have tremendous appetites, and are often unknowingly starved by their owners. They adore dried food that floats, and will take 7 or 8 feeds of this daily. Constant meals prevent a hollow boniness which is frequently noticeable over their foreheads.

Since male and female are alike, sexing can only be told by the thickness of the female's body in the area above the ventrals and behind the pectorals.

BREEDING. *Tank: 30″ × 15″ × 15″. pH: 6·8–7·2. Hardness: 150–180 p.p.m. Temperature: 80° F. Spawns: in typical embrace. Method: eggs float at surface. Eggs: 300–350. Hatch: in 24 hours. Fry hang on: 2 days. Free-swimming: 4th day. Food 1st week: infusoria. 2nd week: infusoria, fine dried food.*

The species is often considered difficult to spawn, but this is because breeding is usually attempted long before the fish are mature. From 5″ in length upward they breed readily. They go into the usual embrace, and eggs are exuded and fertilized. These float to the surface, but are not housed in a nest, as the parents do not construct one. Some bits of floating plant help to hide the spawn, but if the adults are well fed they are not inclined to eat their eggs. As soon as the female is slim both parents may be removed. The large number of fry require an abundant supply of infusoria over the next few days. Some feeds of fine yolk of hard-boiled egg should also be given.

HELASTOMA TEMMINCKI

♀

♂

Green Kissing Gourami

MALAYA, INDONESIA, THAILAND   ♂ 6″   ♀ 6″

COMMUNITY, WITH LARGER FISHES   DIET: ALL FOODS   SWIMS: ALL DEPTHS

Somewhat similar to the foregoing, this species is slightly longer-bodied, and the forehead less dish-shaped. The body colour is a pale silvery-green which glistens in strong light. The tips of the rays of the dorsal and anal fins are black, and a dark bar appears across the caudal peduncle.

H. temmincki is peaceful and safe in a community tank until large; then it becomes a little aggressive. Sexing is only possible in mature specimens, when the female is notably thicker in the abdominal region.

BREEDING. As for *H. rudolphi.*

MACROPODUS CUPANUS DAYI

Spear-tailed Paradise Fish

SUMATRA, MALAYA   ♂ 2¾″   ♀ 2¾″

COMMUNITY   DIET: ALL FOODS   SWIMS: ALL DEPTHS

Though inclined to be a little shy, this is a pleasant, easy to breed, peaceful fish.

The colouring is dull reddish-brown, though at times it has a purplish hue. Two dark bands traverse the body from the head to the base of the tail. The dorsal and anal are reddish-brown, the outer portions being more red. The trailing points of these fins are edged with electric blue. The tail is spear-shaped, with its centre rays protruding some distance beyond the others. This fin also is edged in electric blue.

The female has shorter fins than the male; her belly is deeper and wider, particularly in the area behind and below the pectorals. Sexing is not easy until the fish have attained maturity.

BREEDING. *Tank: 24″ × 8″ × 8″. pH: 6·8–7·2. Hardness: 150–180 p.p.m. Temperature: 80° F. Spawns: in typical embrace. Method: standard for bubble-nest-builders. Eggs: 100–150. Hatch: in 48 hours. Fry hang on: 2 days. Free-swimming: 5th day. Food 1st week: infusoria, yolk of egg. 2nd week: infusoria, brine shrimp.*

Provided the female is full of roe, *M. cupanus dayi* is one of the easiest of the labyrinths to breed. The male builds a nest. He is not too aggressive, and rarely harms the female. They embrace in the usual fashion described on p. 362. Eggs are blown into the nest, after which the female may as well be taken out. The male tends the eggs. Once these have hatched he may be removed. The fry grow rapidly, and are breedable in 5–6 months.

MACROPODUS OPERCULARIS

Paradise Fish

S.E. CHINA, KOREA ♂ 5″ ♀ 4½″

COMMUNITY, WITH LARGER FISHES   DIET: ALL FOODS   SWIMS: ALL DEPTHS

Once king of the aquarium, this fish has recently lost favour owing to its size and somewhat aggressive nature, but kept in a large tank with medium-sized fishes it is still a popular beauty. It is extremely hardy, and will stand low temperatures.

Male and female are normally similar in colour, but the male has longer fin-tips than his mate. The female is considerably deeper and thicker in the body behind and rather below the pectorals. When breeding the male's colour is greatly intensified, while the female is inclined to become more drab.

There is an albino variety of this fish.

BREEDING. *Tank: 24″×12″×12″. pH: 6·8–7·2. Hardness: 150–180 p.p.m. Temperature: 78° F. Spawns: in typical embrace. Method: standard for bubble-nest-builders. Eggs: 250–350. Hatch: in 48 hours. Fry hang on: 2 days. Free-swimming: 5th day. Food 1st week: infusoria, yolk of egg. 2nd week: brine shrimp, microworms.*

The fish conform to the standard pattern of bubble-nest-builders (p. 362). The female should be given some protection while the male is building his nest. This may be accomplished either by plant thickets round which she can dodge, or she may be placed inside a large jar floating in the tank. The pair embrace, and eggs are blown into the nest. After spawning the female should be removed. The male tends the eggs. When the fry are free-swimming he also should be transferred to another tank.

SPHÆRICHTHYS OSPHROMENOIDES

Chocolate Gourami

MALAYA, SUMATRA		♂ 2¼″ ♀ 2¼″
COMMUNITY	DIET: ALL FOODS	SWIMS: ALL DEPTHS

To date this is rather a mystery fish. It is uncertain as to whether it is a bubble-nest-builder or a mouth-breeder. Claims have been made for both methods; possibly there are two species. Moreover, it is shy, and rather touchy as to water conditions. It is imported in large numbers from the Far East, but even with modern air travel losses are frequently very high. Those which arrive alive are somewhat weakened, and are very prone to Ichthyophthirius and gill infections. Quite a number refuse to eat, and die. The price is therefore never cheap. None the less, once acclimatized it lives well in the aquarium, proving to be a quiet, very peaceful, attractive fish. It seems to prefer soft peaty water with a pH of 5·0 and a hardness of under 5 p.p.m. It should only be kept with smaller, non-aggressive species. The fish swims most sedately, and thus is sometimes called the 'Malayan airship.'

In keeping with its retiring nature, the colouring of *S. osphromenoides* is subdued. The body is a brownish-grey. Crossing the flanks are creamy-grey stripes. One of these, just behind the head, is vertical. At the back of this lies a horizontal one, but two more vertical ones cross the hinder-quarters. In front of the dorsal there are two very tiny bars, only $\frac{1}{8}''$ long, and another in the upper part of the caudal peduncle. The dorsal is brownish-grey. The anal fin has a dark edge, and in the male the banded pattern across the hind-quarters extends into this fin. Nevertheless, sexing is difficult unless the fish are in full colour.

The species is extremely fond of gnat larvæ and blood worms. It will take Daphnia, Cyclops, and white worms. When trained even good dried food is consumed; but its mouth is small, and food should be graded accordingly.

BREEDING. Some people state that the species is a mouth-breeder; others maintain that it is a bubble-nest-builder. So far the authors' attempts at breeding have produced no result to establish which theory is correct.

TRICHOGASTER LEERI

♂   ♀

Lace Gourami

MALAYA, SUMATRA, THAILAND   ♂ 5″   ♀ 4½″

COMMUNITY   DIET: ALL FOODS   SWIMS: UPPER HALF OF TANK

Sometimes known as the Pearl, or Mosaic, Gourami, this attractive fish grows to a good size, and is usually extremely peaceful. On occasions, however, a frustrated male may make aggressive darts at other fishes, and may chase them for a few seconds. It is fairly hardy, but occasionally suffers from gill infections. These cause it to gyrate erratically before sinking to the bottom to die. All newly acquired specimens should be quarantined and treated with "Euflavin" in the proportion of a 1-gram tablet dissolved in 20 gallons of water.

In colour and finnage male and female are similar until they reach maturity, then the rays in the male's dorsal begin to lengthen until it extends well over the centre of the tail. The hind portion of his anal fin also grows; frequently on the trailing edge the rays protrude as short filaments. Now he starts to develop an orange-red throat and chest, this being particularly brilliant during courtship. His feeler-like ventrals are bright red; the female's are only a yellowish-orange.

BREEDING. *Tank: 24″×12″×12″. pH: 6·8–7·2. Hardness: 120–150 p.p.m. Temperature: 80°F. Spawns: in typical embrace. Method: standard for bubble-nest-builders. Eggs: 150–200. Hatch: in 48 hours. Fry hang on: 2 days. Free-swimming: 5th day. Food 1st week: infusoria, yolk of egg. 2nd week: brine shrimp, fine dried food.*

The fish are easy to spawn, and the male rarely, if ever, harms the female. He builds a large bubble-nest, frequently under the leaves of floating ferns; this he reinforces with bits of plant. Sometimes he even tears leaves from stalks of Myriophyllum, biting and tugging quite hard to break them off. Eventually the female is coaxed or driven under the nest, where the usual embrace takes place. The floating eggs are carefully stowed in the centre of the nest. After spawning the female may as well be removed. The male tends the eggs, continually blowing more bubbles to maintain the home. Although he looks after his young, it is as well to remove him once they are free-swimming. Then, siphoning through a fine nylon material, the water should be lowered to a depth of 6″. This reduces pressure, and prevents the fry from sinking into the depths. The babies are very small, and are usually produced in great numbers. Food must be abundant, and later, when they are 1″ long, they will enjoy numerous meals of floating dried food, white worms, mosquito larvæ, etc.

TRICHOGASTER MICROLEPIS

♂

♀

Moonlight Gourami

THAILAND   ♂ 5″ ♀ 4½″

COMMUNITY   DIET: ALL FOODS   SWIMS: UPPER HALF OF TANK

The species was first introduced into Britain by the authors in 1953, and is fast becoming one of the most popular gouramis of to-day. In shape and temperament it strongly resembles the lace gourami, but has a more turned-up snout, and the rear portion of the body from dorsal to tail is longer. It is extremely peaceful and hardy, beautiful and breedable, yet on account of its being difficult to raise it is prevented from becoming commonplace. Dried food is much enjoyed.

The first impression is that of a pearly fish. But, this popular name having already been appropriated by *T. leeri*, the wife of one of the authors suggested as an alternative 'moonlight gourami.' This has proved to be entirely suitable, since in some lights the fish is a cold steel-blue, while in others it takes on a pale, elusive gold. The eye is black, surrounded by gold. If kept in a dark tank a black line appears on the sides from nose to tail, but this marking disappears entirely in well-lighted aquaria.

Sexing is possible only in adult fish. The ventral feelers of the male and the forward edge of his anal fin become bright orange. The rays of his dorsal also grow, to make this fin longer and more pointed than that of the female. Her ventrals are colourless, and the body just above these is thicker and deeper than in the male. Frequently her snout is not so upturned as that of her mate.

BREEDING. Tank: 30"×15"×15". pH: 6·8–7·0. Hardness: 120–150 p.p.m. Temperature: 80°F. Spawns: in typical embrace. Method: standard for bubble-nest-builders. Eggs: 300–350. Hatch: in 48 hours. Fry hang on: 2 days. Free-swimming: 5th day. Food 1st week: infusoria, yolk of egg. 2nd week: infusoria, brine shrimp.

The tank should be provided with bunches of plants, round which the female may take refuge while the male builds his nest; not that he is vicious, but he seems to prefer to keep her at a distance during the construction period. The surface of the water should be covered with young floating ferns. These the male utilizes when blowing his bubble-nest. So vigorous is he in this work that he will even tear up stalks of Myriophyllum and Hygrophila and push them into the nest to reinforce it. Eventually, when all is ready, he allows the female to swim under the nest. Then, embracing her in the usual labyrinth manner, eggs are laid and fertilized. Coating each with a bubble, he blows them into the nest. When spawning is finished the female should be removed. The male continues to tend the eggs. Once the fry are free-swimming he should be removed from the breeding tank, and then the water be lowered to a depth of 6". The minute babies must be fed copiously. Even so, many die off, and a spawn of 350 may easily be reduced in a month to a mere dozen or so. The exact cause of this mortality is not clear, but the authors are still investigating and trying out different ways to counteract this trouble.

TRICHOGASTER PECTORALIS

♀

Snakeskin Gourami

THAILAND, CAMBODIA, INDONESIA

COMMUNITY   DIET: ALL FOODS

♂ $4\frac{1}{2}''$ ♀ $4\frac{1}{2}''$

SWIMS: ALL DEPTHS

Though this fish grows to a foot or more in length in its native haunts, when confined to the average big aquarium it rarely exceeds 5". Even so, its large size prevents it from becoming more popular. It is extremely peaceful, somewhat shy, and not particularly colourful.

The body is an olive grey-brown with a broken black line running from gill-plate to caudal peduncle. Somewhat faint fawn-coloured bars cross the flanks obliquely. The fins are clear, but tend to become yellowish on the outer edges.

The male is usually slightly larger than the female. His dorsal and anal fins are longer and more pointed. Both sexes have somewhat blunter-shaped heads than most gouramis.

BREEDING. Tank: 30"×15"×15". pH: 6·8–7·0. Hardness: 100–150 p.p.m. Temperature: 80°F. Spawns: in typical embrace. Method: standard for bubble-nest-builders. Eggs: 300–500. Hatch: in 48 hours. Fry hang on: 2 days. Free-swimming: 5th day. Food 1st week: infusoria. 2nd week: brine shrimp, fine dried food.

The species is easy to breed and very prolific. Parents do not harm their young.

TRICHOGASTER TRICHOPTERUS

Blue Gourami

INDIA, MALAYA, SUMATRA, THAILAND ♂ 5½″ ♀ 6½″

COMMUNITY, WITH LARGER FISHES   DIET: ALL FOODS   SWIMS: ALL DEPTHS

Being extremely hardy, attractively coloured, and obtainable very cheaply, this fish is often sold to beginners. This is all very well when it is young and small, but it grows quickly, and becomes far too large for the average aquarist. Furthermore, it often turns spiteful with smaller fishes, and sometimes becomes a bully and a nuisance. Kept with medium-sized species it generally behaves itself, and is then quite a favourite. Like all gouramis, it enjoys floating dried food.

The body is a pale silvery blue, and is crossed vertically by numerous wavy bands of a darker hue. These bands usually slant forward at the base. There is a large dark blue spot in the centre of the body, and another at the base of the tail. The belly has a yellowish-green tinge, and the dorsal, anal, and caudal fins are spotted in the same colour.

On reaching maturity the female becomes deeper and much thicker than the male, particularly in the area behind the pectorals and ventrals. Her dorsal fin is not so long and pointed as that of her mate.

There is a brown variety of this fish which when large is even more aggressive than the blue.

BREEDING. Tank: 24″ × 12″ × 12″. pH: 6·8–7·2. Hardness: 120–150 p.p.m. Temperature: 80° F. Spawns: in typical embrace. Method: standard for bubble-nest-builders. Eggs: 250–950. Hatch: in 48 hours. Fry hang on: 2 days. Free-swimming: 5th day. Food 1st week: infusoria, yolk of egg. 2nd week: infusoria, brine shrimp.

These are the easiest labyrinths to breed, and are so prolific that they are always obtainable cheaply. The tank should be well stocked with clumps of plants, as the male while building his nest is inclined to bully the female. Eventually the pair embrace beneath the bubbles, and the lighter-than-water eggs float. Some spread over the surface, but this does not seem to matter, as they nearly always hatch out. After spawning the female should be removed, or she may be damaged by her mate. The male keeps guard. After hatching he also should be taken out of the tank. The free-swimming fry appear in great numbers just below the surface of the water. Unlike most gouramis, the babies are so hardy that few die; they grow quickly, and are over 1″ in length in six weeks.

TRICHOPSIS PUMILUS

♂

♀

Sparkling Gourami

JAVA, BORNEO   ♂ 1″ ♀ 1¼″

COMMUNITY   DIET: ALL FOODS   SWIMS: ALL DEPTHS

A fairly recent introduction, this beautiful little fish vies with the dwarf gourami in colour. Unfortunately, it is so small that much of its beauty is overlooked. It undoubtedly has a future, for besides being colourful it frequently makes a grating noise, especially when courting. Surprisingly, this sound, coming from such a small fish, is clearly audible at a distance of 20 feet.

Male and female are similarly coloured, and sexing is therefore difficult. As the fish are small it is not easy to notice her fuller, deeper belly. A curious thing is that one day a male is so brilliant that any novice could pick him out, but the next day even an expert might fail to see any difference between a pair.

BREEDING. Tank: 24″ × 8″ × 8″. pH: 6·8–7·0. Hardness: 120–150 p.p.m. Temperature: 80° F. Spawns: in typical embrace. Method: bubble-nest under leaf. Eggs: 50–100. Hatch: in 72 hours. Fry hang on: 2 days. Free-swimming: 6th day. Food 1st week: infusoria. 2nd week: infusoria, brine shrimp.

This little fish has another claim to fame. It is a bubble-nest-builder with a difference: building its nest under a small leaf, growing horizontally a few inches above the sand.

As sexing is so difficult, five or six fish should be placed in a breeding tank. This should be planted with a few *Cryptocoryne beckettii* and one or two stalks of *Hygrophila polysperma*. In a short time a male will select a female and pay court to her. Quivering his fins in front of her, he will display himself, and make the grating noise previously referred to. The other fish in the tank will be constantly driven away from the selected spawning-site. Once it has become obvious which is the true pair the remainder should be removed. The couple now left alone play up to each other. The grunting becomes more frequent as they search for and decide upon a certain leaf under which the male builds his bubble-nest. This·is so small that it is often difficult to detect; but a few tiny bubbles at the surface of the water gives the astute aquarist a clue, for these have slipped from under the leaf and risen to the surface.

Therefore look for the nest below a leaf which is situated directly under the tell-tale surface bubbles. Now the nest may be seen densely packed beneath a leaf measuring only $1''$ long by $\frac{1}{4}''$ wide. If spawning is witnessed the aquarist will see the fish locked in the typical anabantid embrace. On breaking apart the male picks up the falling eggs, and any which have reached the sand. These he coats with a bubble, and blows them into the nest. When spawning is over it is as well to remove the female, but she should be placed apart from others, so that when next required for spawning the aquarist knows full well where he has a guaranteed female.

The eggs are rarely noticeable, but in two days the tails of the fry may be observed hanging downward from under this same leaf.

The male often transfers the fry to the under side of another leaf until they become free-swimming. At this stage it is best to remove him, once again taking care to place him in a tank where he may be identified immediately when required for a further spawning.

TRICHOPSIS VITTATUS

♂

♀

Croaking Gourami

THAILAND, MALAYA, INDONESIA   ♂ 2″   ♀ 1¾″

COMMUNITY   DIET: ALL FOODS   SWIMS: ALL DEPTHS

Though famed as the croaking gourami, this fish usually makes less noise, and not so often, as the previous species. It has been known in the past as *Ctenops vittatus*.

The body is a rusty red. A dark line passes from the lower lip through the eye across the gill-plate. The fins are long, the pectorals of the male having particularly long, feeler-like filaments. His dorsal, anal, and tail are also longer and more pointed than those of his mate. All the fins are rusty brown.

The female is thicker and deeper-bellied.

BREEDING. Tank: 24″ × 8″ × 8″. pH: 6·8–7·0. Hardness: 120–150 p.p.m. Temperature: 80° F. Spawns: in typical embrace. Method: standard for bubble-nest-builders. Eggs: 100–150. Hatch: in 48 hours. Fry hang on: 2 days. Free-swimming: 5th day. Food 1st week: infusoria. 2nd week: infusoria, brine shrimp.

The male builds a bubble-nest at the water surface. After spawning female should be removed. The male guards the eggs, but once the fry are free-swimming he may be taken out.

CHAPTER XXIII

CHANNIDÆ

THIS FAMILY, WHICH INCLUDES THE OPHIOCEPHALIDS, IS COMMONLY KNOWN as the snake heads, and is closely related to the anabantids. Compared with these, Channidæ possess a simpler form of suprabranchial cavity which permits them to breathe air from above the surface of the water. They come from Africa, India, Burma, Indonesia, Thailand, and Southern China. In shape their bodies are long, cylindrical, and snake-like, with biggish heads and extremely large mouths well-equipped with sharp conical teeth. They grow to a large size, and are commonly used for food in their native lands. None of the snake heads is safe in a community tank; they even fight among themselves, and often the victors devour the vanquished.

All the Channas are too dangerous, and grow too large, for the average aquarist, so we do not consider it worth while to illustrate and describe the numerous species. Though they differ in colour and markings, all are similar in habit. For this reason we are taking a typical example, if only to warn the aquarist of what to expect.

CHANNA ORIENTALIS

♀

♂

Snake Head

S.E. ASIA   ♂ 12″   ♀ 12″

NON–COMMUNITY   DIET: MEAT, FISH, AND OTHER PROTEIN

SWIMS: LOWER HALF OF TANK

The pair illustrated above were only 3″ long when photographed. They were then being fed on medium-sized earthworms and full-grown female guppies. At the time of writing, six weeks later, they are 8″ in length, and are feeding on chunks of horsemeat the size of grapes, as well as disposing of any unwanted fish up to 3″ in length. Given a large tank, they may be expected to grow to 18″ or more.

They are most attractively coloured, and get more beautiful as they increase in size. The general body hue is brown to chocolate, the back and sides being crossed by short bars. The dorsal and anal fins are bluish with a white edge surrounding both. The tail is brownish; it is peppered with red dots, and has a red border. As the fish grows patches of blue appear round the jaws. Flecks of the same colour adorn the body, and the blue in the fins is intensified.

BREEDING. *Tank: 30″×15″×15″. pH: 6·8–7·0. Hardness: 100–150 p.p.m. Temperature: 80° F. Spawns: above plants. Method: eggs float. Eggs: 100–150. Hatch: in 3 days. Fry float: 7–10 days. Food 1st week: Daphnia, white worms. 2nd week: fine minced meat, chopped earthworms.*

The tank should be well-planted to afford hiding-places until the pair are acquainted with each other. They come side by side in plant thickets just below the surface of the water. Waggling their bodies close together, large amber eggs are laid and fertilized. These float to the surface, and the male guards them zealously. Now the female should be removed. Once the fry are swimming about the male should be taken out. During the first few days the young fish float near the surface, and have difficulty in swimming at lower depths. But after a week or ten days they lose this buoyancy and stay near the bottom of the tank, frequently rising to gulp air at the surface of the water. In nature during droughts the fish bury themselves in mud and worm their way deeper as their surroundings tend to dry up. So long as they can keep damp they are able to breathe in little or no water by means of their suprabranchial cavity.

CHAPTER XXIV

NANDIDÆ

THE FAMILY IS COMPRISED OF SEVERAL GENERA WHICH COME FROM THREE different parts of the world. One group hails from the Far East, another from central West Africa, and the third is found in Guiana and the Amazon.

Most of the family have large mouths, and are not safe if kept with small fishes. The dorsal and anal fins usually consist of two portions, the fore-part being spined with hard rays, the hind portion bearing soft rays. The dorsal also extends to a great length along the back. The soft-rayed part of both the dorsal and anal projects beyond the normal outline of these fins, and is often transparent. At first glance these fishes look as though they have lost their tails.

BADIS BADIS

INDIA   ♂ 2¾″   ♀ 2½″

COMMUNITY, WITH MEDIUM-SIZED FISHES   DIET: LIVE FOOD

SWIMS: LOWER HALF OF TANK

These are the smallest of the family, but even so they are not safe in the same tank with small fishes. When several are kept together they are liable to squabble, and not infrequently one is killed. They are hardy, but not active, and have a habit of remaining for a time stationary in mid-water, then suddenly they will make a short dart to another position. Occasionally they will take a good dried food.

Mostly these fish are a chocolate-brown colour with darker bars. Like chameleons, they can vary their colours rapidly to suit their surroundings; occasionally they show off in most distinguished colours and patterns. The bars on the body form themselves into chains of red with red and brown links. The fins may take on a pinky-blue or brown hue. Unfortunately, these fish rarely stay in superb colour for long.

Males often look hollow-bellied, but ripe females are thick and deep just above the ventral fins.

BREEDING. *Tank: 24″ × 8″ × 8″. pH: 7·0–7·2. Hardness: 120–150 p.p.m. Temperature: 80° F. Spawns: in or under flower-pot. Method: male fans eggs. Eggs: 80–100. Hatch: in 48 hours. Fry wriggling: 2 days. Free-swimming: 5th day. Food 1st week: infusoria, brine shrimp. 2nd week: brine shrimp, microworms.*

The species is very easy to breed. Spawning takes place in a flower-pot which has had its base knocked out. The pot is placed on its side on the sand, with the larger end facing the front of the aquarium. Bunches of plants should be placed in the tank to afford protection to the female. Eventually the male coaxes her inside the pot, where she lays her eggs. Usually they are deposited high up, so that when spawning she turns on her side, or even upside down. After laying a few eggs she moves away, and the male comes in and fertilizes them. The process continues until about 100 eggs are laid, when the female should be removed. The male fans and guards the spawn. Once the babies are free-swimming the male may be taken out. Growth is slow. When the youngsters reach about 1″ in length squabbles break out, and the smaller and weaker ones are often killed.

The species will spawn in a community tank if given a flower-pot, and it is surprising how many young can be raised—mostly due to the care of the male, who drives off any fishes which would otherwise eat the fry.

POLYCENTROPSIS ABBREVIATA

♂

NIGERIA   ♂ 3″   ♀ 3″

NON–COMMUNITY   DIET : LIVE FOODS   SWIMS : MID–WATER

Those aquarists who specialize may like this rather rare fish. It is not safe in a community tank, as it has a very large mouth capable of swallowing fishes half its own size. It hangs about inactively in the water. The soft-rayed portions of the dorsal and anal fins, also the tail, are so transparent that *P. abbreviata* at first glance seems to have lost the rear portion of its anatomy : hence the name, implying abbreviation. It will eat worms, bluebottles, and water insects if these are large enough to be worth while swallowing.

The colour varies from yellowish-brown to dark brown, and is mottled with darker blotches.

BREEDING. The fish is occasionally bred, though this has not been achieved by the authors. The male is said to blow a nest of bubbles under floating plants such as Indian ferns. Among the bubbles the female deposits single eggs which are fertilized by the male. Spawning continues until 80–100 eggs are laid, after which the female should be removed. Hatching occurs in 3–4 days, and the fry will take brine shrimp, sifted Daphnia, and small white worms. The male should be taken out once the fry are able to look after themselves.

POLYCENTRUS SCHOMBURGKI

TRINIDAD, GUIANA   ♂ 3″   ♀ 3″

COMMUNITY, WITH LARGER FISHES   DIET : LIVE FOOD

SWIMS : LOWER HALF OF TANK

Although kept by some aquarists with large fishes, *P. schomburgki* is not to be recommended to the average amateur, as it is unsafe with the usual species kept. It requires live food, and, although it will eat worms and water insects, small fishes are much preferred.

The body is oval in shape, and is a brownish-grey in colour, though this can change to a near-black. The sides are irregularly spotted, and at times dark vertical bars appear. A black line in the form of an arrowhead, with its point as the pupil of the eye, shows up on the side of the head. The fins are brownish, but are edged with white. The soft-rayed parts of the dorsal, anal, and tail fins are transparent.

Females are deeper and thicker than males, and usually they are paler in colour.

BREEDING. Tank: 24″ × 12″ × 12″. pH: 7·0–7·2. Hardness: 120–150 p.p.m. Temperature: 78° F. Spawns: in flower-pot. Method: male fans eggs. Eggs: 80–100. Hatch: in 4 days. Fry wriggling: 3 days. Free-swimming: 8th day. Food 1st week: brine shrimp, microworms. 2nd week: microworms, sifted Daphnia.

Spawning takes place in a flower-pot laid on its side among plant thickets. The procedure follows that described under *Badis badis* (p. 394).

CHAPTER XXV

CICHLIDÆ

THIS IS A LARGE FAMILY OF SPINY-RAYED FISHES, MOST OF WHICH COME from Central and South America. Some hail from Africa, and at least two species are found in India and Ceylon. The family is intelligent, mating, breeding, and caring for their young in a more advanced manner than do other fishes which are lower down the evolutionary scale. Most cichlids are highly coloured and have gorgeous finnage. Contrary to general belief, the authors have found that nearly all of them prefer slightly alkaline water.

Breeding

Cichlids are not difficult to breed, but the procedure differs slightly where large, medium, and small species are concerned. Below is given a general description covering these groups. Where individual species differ from the general, details will be found under the fishes concerned. For the aquarist's convenience we will divide the family into three groups. These are:

(i) Large cichlids.
(ii) Medium cichlids.
(iii) Dwarf cichlids.

(i) LARGE CICHLIDS

The above-mentioned grow much too big for the average aquarist, and only specialists with enormous tanks can house them satisfactorily to maturity. These giants live 5–8 years or more; they will not usually tolerate plants, tearing them out by the roots. This means that their tank is unlikely to remain clear unless filters are kept in constant operation. In place of plants they should be given large rocks, round which they may dodge when attacked. Alternatively, beneath the ends of the rocks they like to dig depressions in the sand, where they lie when resting. Finally, it is usually on some flat surface of these boulders that they place their spawn when breeding.

Even a large tank 6 ft. × 2 ft. × 2 ft. will hold only six or seven of the biggest cichlids. Should a pair decide to spawn they may insist on having the aquarium entirely to themselves, inflicting such damage on the other occupants that the aquarist is forced to find an alternative home for these.

Mating

Quite a number of cichlids refuse to accept a mate chosen for them by their owner. If not allowed to pair naturally they may kill the partner offered. Natural selection usually means keeping 4 or 5 of the same species, so that choice is available. This is not only initially costly, but all the fish have to be kept to maturity, and then the unwanted ones discarded. Mating can sometimes be arranged by placing a pair of fish in a tank divided by a sheet of glass, allowing them to see each other, and yet do no harm. In a few days, when the pair have become familiar, the glass partition is removed, but the aquarist must watch and intervene should they prove incompatible. In this case the male will chase the female, biting her sides and ripping her fins till she cowers in some corner. If the pair are not separated she is likely to be killed. On the other hand, the couple may show off to each other, and then, gripping lips, tug and wrestle together. Providing the female does not flee, all may be well.

Spawning

Now the pair select a spawning-site, usually on some flat rock. This they clean with their mouths, and both male and female show protruding tubes just in front of the anal fin. In females this tube, called the ovipositor, is thicker and blunter-ended than is the male's counterpart. Having cleaned the rock thoroughly, spawning takes place. The female deposits eggs one after another in rows. On completing a line she moves away, and her mate comes in and fertilizes them. The process continues until some 300–1500 or more eggs are laid. Both parents now take turns to fan the spawn, which hatches some days later. Once the fry are wriggling a depression is dug in the sand, and the babies are transferred one by one to the new site, having been thoroughly washed in the parent's mouth while in transit. When the fry are free-swimming it is a wonderful sight to see how the parents guard them. As dusk approaches the cloud of youngsters is gathered in a tight cluster for greater protection. When these are $\frac{1}{2}''$ long the parents may be removed and the fry reared on their own.

(ii) MEDIUM CICHLIDS

With regard to the medium-sized cichlids, most of these will live in a large community tank with other big species. They will usually not tear out plants until urged to spawn. But as this occurs quite frequently, uprooting vegetation and digging pits in the sand becomes a nuisance.

Mating and Breeding

Mating is similar to the large cichlids just described, though spawning often occurs in flower-pots, or in a few cases on "Vitrolite" bars. Generally it is advisable to remove the males after spawning, as occasionally they become aggressive, and may kill their mates. Alternatively, the bar or flower-pot on which the eggs are deposited may be removed to a bare tank and the eggs hatched separately. Aeration must be provided, and a few drops of 5 per cent. methylene blue added to the water to prevent fungus.

(iii) DWARF CICHLIDS

Lastly we come to the dwarf cichlids. These are the most colourful, will live happily with other small to medium-sized fishes, will enjoy any food, and breed easily. Unfortunately, they rarely live longer than 2 years. Mating is not so difficult, most males accepting any female offered, providing she is full of roe. Spawning nearly always occurs in flower-pots. Having laid their eggs, both parents may be removed, but aeration must be employed to circulate the water normally provided by the fanning action of the adults. Five to seven drops of 5 per cent. aqueous solution of methylene blue should be added to every two gallons of water to kill bacteria. This method not only permits the eggs to hatch, but means that the pair can be spawned again in a short period. In our experience we find quite a number of species which, instead of spawning conveniently inside the pot, tunnel away the sand beneath and spawn on its under side. Here the eggs are out of sight unless the pot is lifted and examined daily; but such a disturbance is likely to deter the pair from breeding.

In order to surmount this difficulty the authors use a simple slate structure. This consists of two walls, roughly 3″ square, cut from $\frac{1}{2}$″ slate. A roof about 6″ long by 3″ wide is made from a piece of $\frac{1}{4}$″ slate. The two end walls are placed on edge near the centre of the planted breeding tank about 5″ apart. These must be bedded down through the sand until they stand firmly in an upright position on the bottom of the tank. The roof is then laid on top of the two walls (Fig. 25). The breeders are unable to dig underneath any part of this structure, and wherever their eggs are deposited the spawn is visible.

Spawning usually occurs on the inside face of one of the walls. Now the parents are removed, also the roof and blank wall. The wall coated with eggs is next turned to face the viewer, and an aerator tube placed under it so that the bubbles rise $\frac{1}{2}$″ in front of the eggs. Five to seven drops

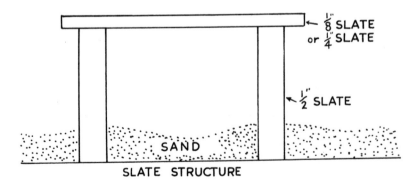

SLATE STRUCTURE

NOTE: UPRIGHT WALLS BEDDED THROUGH SAND
AND STANDING ON BOTTOM OF TANK

FIG. 25

of methylene blue are now added to the water. In a few days the eggs hatch and the young may be seen wriggling. Two or three days later the fry drop to the sand, and in a further 48 hours some begin to hop about. Do not feed until the whole batch leaves the sand and swims like a cloud of midges through the water. At this stage the fry are large enough to take brine shrimp and microworms. The methylene blue in the water will by now have faded, and the babies should be fed twice daily.

(i) and (ii) LARGE AND MEDIUM CICHLIDS
ÆQUIDENS CURVICEPS

♂

♀

Sheepshead Acara

AMAZON ♂ 3½″ ♀ 3½″

COMMUNITY, WITH MEDIUM–SIZED FISHES DIET: ALL FOODS

SWIMS: LOWER HALF OF TANK

This fish is just too large to be classified as a dwarf cichlid, but it is a border-line case. It is not harmful with medium-sized species, is only aggressive at spawning-time, and, like the dwarfs, does not tear out plants.

Æ. curviceps is attractively coloured, with a bluish tinge. A few short, dark bars come and go over the forward part of the back. The dorsal fin is blue; it has a yellow tip, and is edged with red. The anal is yellowish, and the tail has an orange border.

Males have longer points to the ends of the dorsal and anal fins. Females are thicker through the body just above the ventral fins.

BREEDING. *Tank: 24″×8″×8″. pH: 7·0–7·2. Hardness: 150–180 p.p.m. Temperature: 80°F. Spawns: in flower-pot. Method: standard for dwarf cichlids. Eggs: 150–250. Hatch: in 3 days. Fry wriggling: 3 days. Free-swimming: 7th day. Food 1st week: brine shrimp. 2nd week: microworms, fine dried food.*

Breeding follows the procedure given on p. 399.

ÆQUIDENS LATIFRONS

♀

♂

Blue Acara

CENTRAL AMERICA   ♂ 6″ ♀ 6″

COMMUNITY   DIET : ALL FOODS   SWIMS : LOWER HALF OF TANK

This fish is not suitable for the aquarist with small tanks, but may be kept with other large cichlids.

The colour is a greeny-blue. In the upper portion of the flanks it is liberally spangled with shining scales of light blue; these markings turn browner towards the belly. As with many cichlids, vertical bars running across the body come and go according to the fish's mood. A large dark spot appears in the upper portion of the body about half-way between the eyes and tail. The fins are orange with blue spangles.

Males have longer points to the dorsal and anal fins. Just behind and below the pectorals they are not so thick or deep-bodied as females.

BREEDING. Tank: 30″ × 15″ × 15″. pH: 7·0–7·2. Hardness: 150–180 p.p.m. Temperature: 80° F. Spawns: on rock. Method: standard for large cichlids. Eggs: 300–500. Hatch: in 3 days. Fry wriggling: 3 days. Free-swimming: 7th day. Food 1st week: brine shrimp. 2nd week: microworms, fine dried food.

The species is a prolific breeder, caring tenderly for its young. *Æ. latifrons* will often spawn again when the first brood has reached ¾″ in length and is still in the tank. The breeding procedure follows that described on p. 399.

ÆQUIDENS MARONII

Keyhole Cichlid

GUIANA, VENEZUELA   ♂ 4″ ♀ 4″

COMMUNITY, WITH LARGER FISHES   DIET: ALL FOODS

SWIMS: LOWER HALF OF TANK

Though the species has no bright colours, it is one of the pleasantest cichlids. It is quiet and peaceful, does not tear out plants, but is rather shy.

The overall tone is deep brown with darker patches coming and going according to the fish's moods. A bar of deeper hue runs across the face. A nearly black spot appears high on the flanks about two-thirds of the distance between head and tail. Occasionally a vertical bar, widening towards its base, emerges below the spot, and looks like the keyhole of a mortice lock—hence the name. Sometimes this feature is adorned by a golden outline. The fins are pale brown.

Sexing is difficult, except when the female is full of roe. At this time she is obviously thicker than the male behind and below the pectoral fins. In both sexes the trailing points of the dorsal and anal are long. These extremities in aged specimens sometimes curl inward, nearly wrapping the tail.

BREEDING. *Tank: 24″ × 12″ × 12″. pH: 7·0–7·2. Hardness: 150–180 p.p.m. Temperature: 80° F. Spawns: in flower-pot. Method: standard for medium cichlids. Eggs: 200–300. Hatch: in 4 days. Fry wriggling: 3 days. Free-swimming: 8th day. Food 1st week: brine shrimp. 2nd week: microworms, Cyclops.*

The fish do not breed regularly. They may spawn two or three times in quick succession, and then desist for several months. In order to obtain another spawn quickly it is best to remove the flower-pot in which the eggs are laid to a bare tank. Apply aeration close to the eggs, and add methylene blue to the water (see p. 400). Once the fry are hatched the flower-pot should be returned to the parents in the hope that they may spawn again within 10 days. Do not feed the babies until they are free-swimming.

ÆQUIDENS PORTALEGRENSIS

Green Acara

S.E. BRAZIL ·   ♂ 5½″   ♀ 5½″

COMMUNITY, WITH LARGER FISHES   DIET: ALL FOODS

SWIMS: LOWER HALF OF TANK

This is perhaps the commonest of the genus, mainly because it is a prolific breeder, and aquarists who spawn it have plenty of young fish to give away. Although the species is fairly peaceful, it is not safe with small fishes, and requires a good deal of room.

The general body colour is greenish, but the scales sparkle here and there with a bluish tinge. A dark spot appears in the centre of the flanks and at the base of the tail. Sometimes a horizontal stripe runs from the eyes to the caudal peduncle. Frequently numerous vertical bars cross the body, but these can disappear at will. The fins are greenish-yellow, the lower half of the tail being liberally spotted with bluish-green.

Male and female are very similar, but he is brighter, and has more spots in the tail. The female is wider behind and below the pectoral fins.

BREEDING. *Tank: 36″×15″×15″. pH: 7·0–7·2. Hardness: 150–180 p.p.m. Temperature: 78° F. Spawns: on flat rock. Method: standard for large cichlids. Eggs: 250–450. Hatch: in 3 days. Fry wriggling: 3 days. Free-swimming: 7th day. Food 1st week: brine shrimp. 2nd week: microworms, fine dried food.*

Probably the easiest and most prolific of all cichlids to breed. So attentive are the parents, and so great is the number of fry produced, that it is unnecessary to remove the eggs for safety or to obtain more frequent spawnings. Thus a large tank is recommended, so that the babies may attain $\frac{1}{2}''$ in length before it becomes necessary to transfer them to a larger home. The parents would spawn in an aquarium only 24" × 12" × 12", but the family would soon require larger quarters. In a big aquarium the adults may spawn again even though the first batch, now $\frac{3}{4}''$ long, are still in the tank. The procedure follows that described on p. 399.

ASTRONOTUS OCELLATUS

Marbled Cichlid

GUIANA, AMAZON   ♂ 12"   ♀ 12"

NON-COMMUNITY   DIET: MOSTLY PROTEIN   SWIMS: LOWER HALF OF TANK

This is the giant of aquarium cichlids. It requires a very large tank, particularly since it is difficult to sex until nearly full grown. This means that several may have to be reared in order to obtain a pair. It is not generally aggressive, but needs space.

Unlike most cichlids, the scales do not shine. The texture more resembles brown suede mottled with greyish markings and splashed here and there with vivid reddish-orange patches. A ring of this colour adorns the base of the tail. The fins are dusty brown, but at any time the fish may take on a much darker hue.

Sexing is possible only with large fish, and when the female becomes thick with roe. Sometimes the behaviour of a pair gives a clue to their sex.

BREEDING. Tank: 48"×15"×15", or larger. pH: 7·0–7·2. Hardness: 150–180 p.p.m. Temperature: 80° F. Spawns: on flat rock. Method: standard for large cichlids.

Eggs: 500–600. Hatch: in 3 days. Fry wriggling: 2 days. Free-swimming: 6th day. Food 1st week: brine shrimp, microworms. 2nd week: Cyclops, sifted Daphnia.

The authors could not afford the space to breed this species, but supplied large fish to Mr Stoker, of Sutton, who succeeded in spawning them many times. Below we give an abridged account based on his experiences.

The tank contained sand and large rocks, but no plants. A pair of fish 8″ long were conditioned on chunks of meat, liver, and large earthworms. A big, flat rock was selected and cleaned. Following the normal cichlid procedure, strings of small, pale eggs were deposited and fertilized on the rock. These were guarded, fanned, and hatched in the normal way.

CICHLASOMA BIOCELLATUM

Jack Dempsey

BRAZIL   ♂ 7″   ♀ 6″

NON-COMMUNITY   ·DIET: MAINLY PROTEIN   SWIMS: LOWER HALF OF TANK

A gorgeous fish, but much too large and aggressive to be kept in community tanks. It tears out plants.

Colour varies considerably when young, but as the fish ages it becomes a blue-black with shining scales of bottle-green. A black spot appears in the centre of the flanks, and another at the base of the tail. The fins are the same colour as the body, but the dorsal is edged with red.

The male is more brightly spangled, and the trailing point of the dorsal fin is longer than that of his mate.

BREEDING. Tank: 36″ × 15″ × 15″. pH: 7·0–7·2. Hardness: 150–180 p.p.m. Temperature: 80° F. Spawns: on flat rock. Method: standard for large cichlids. Eggs:

300–500. Hatch: in 3 days. Fry wriggling: 3 days. Free-swimming: 7th day. Food 1st week: brine shrimp, microworms. 2nd week: sifted Daphnia, Cyclops.

This is one of the species where males may kill females before mating, so care must be taken to prevent fatalities. Once in agreement they spawn readily, and make devoted parents, following precisely the procedure outlined on p. 399.

CICHLASOMA FESTIVUM

Festive Cichlid

AMAZON   ♂ 6″   ♀ 5″

COMMUNITY, WITH LARGE FISHES   DIET: ALL FOODS   SWIMS: MID-WATER

One of the quietest and most peaceful cichlids. It does not tear out plants. The name is misleading, for the colouring is not gay or festive. Nevertheless, the fish is smart because of its oblique dark line. This runs dead straight from the lips diagonally upward through the eye, crosses the upper flanks, enters the dorsal fin, and ends in the pointed tip.

The general body colour is greenish-grey, with a yellowish tinge. Faint vertical bars of grey appear on the sides. There is a dark spot on the upper portion of the caudal peduncle. The fins are yellowish-green speckled with brown dots. The lower half of the gill-plate in both sexes is pale blue.

Sexing is difficult, as both fish are similarly marked. On reaching maturity the male develops slightly longer points on the dorsal and anal fins. These, however, are not exaggerated. The female when full of roe is thicker behind and below the pectoral fins than her mate.

BREEDING. *Tank: 24"× 12"× 20" high. pH: 7·2–7·4. Hardness: 150–180 p.p.m. Temperature: 80° F. Spawns: on "Vitrolite" bar or leaf. Method: remove eggs, and hatch in separate tank. Eggs: 250–350. Hatch: in 4 days. Fry wriggling: 4 days. Free-swimming: 9th day. Food 1st week: infusoria, brine shrimp. 2nd week: brine shrimp, sifted Cyclops.*

These fish may spawn in a community tank providing they are not disturbed by other big, aggressive species. Even so, it is better to give them quarters of their own, for when the eggs are removed and hatched separately a good pair will spawn every ten days for months on end. The breeding tank should be nearly as high as it is long, but need not be particularly wide from front to back. It should have a 2" layer of sand on the bottom, and be planted to make a permanent home. The fish will spawn on a long, wide leaf like that of *Echinodorus intermedius*, but this is difficult to set correctly after transfer. The authors prefer to use a long bar of pale green "Vitrolite" (a glass-like substance generally used for panelling in bathrooms). This should be 18" long by 3" wide by $\frac{1}{4}$" thick. It is pushed 1" into the sand, and leant against the side of the tank nearly reaching the surface of the water. Here it stands, 10 degrees off perpendicular, has a natural plant colour, and is opaque enough to appear solid and strong to the spawners, who prefer it to transparent glass. In a few days the pair make half-hearted attempts to clean this bar with their mouths. Shortly afterwards the female presses her protruding ovipositor against the bar and, moving slowly upward, deposits a row of eggs upon it. The male moves in and fertilizes these. Spawning continues until a patch 3" long by $\frac{3}{4}$" wide, containing about 350 eggs, is laid.

During the spawning period, which lasts about $1\frac{1}{2}$ hours, the aquarist should prepare a small hatching tank 24" × 8" × 8". It should be quite bare, and filled to a depth of 4" with alkaline water of the same pH, hardness, and temperature as that in the tank where spawning is taking place. Five drops of 5 per cent. methylene blue and an aerator stone attached to an air-line are placed in the water in the hatching tank. When spawning is completed the "Vitrolite" bar is transferred and placed on its side lengthwise in the little aquarium, so that the eggs face the viewer. The aerator is pushed under the bar in order to allow the bubbles to rise about $\frac{3}{4}$" in front of the patch of eggs, thus creating water circulation. In 48 hours eyes appear in the eggs. Hatching occurs two days later, and the wriggling fry hang from the bar by a sticky thread attached to their heads. They remain in this state, absorbing the yolk-sac for food, until strong enough to break the thread. This occurs 3 days later, when they fall to the bottom. In a further 72 hours they rise in a cloud and become free-swimming. Now the strength of the methylene blue is reduced by changing three-quarters of the water in the tank. It will then be too weak to kill the infusoria and brine shrimp with which the fry should now be fed. After 10 days sifted Daphnia and Cyclops will be taken.

Fishes that spawn on bars and leaves usually take their food in mid-water, and do not readily grub about at the bottom of the tank. For this reason microworms are not a good food to feed the fry. They will seize the slowly sinking worms, but once these reach the bottom of the aquarium they are mostly ignored. Here the worms will die and cause pollution. As stated before, this type of cichlid should be given food that hops about in mid-water, and also some of the dried product that floats.

CICHLASOMA MEEKI

Fire-mouth Cichlid

YUCATAN   ♂ 4½″ ♀ 4″

COMMUNITY, WITH LARGER FISHES   DIET: ALL FOODS

SWIMS: LOWER HALF OF TANK

Looks belie this gaudy cichlid. It gives the impression of being very savage, but actually it is fairly mild-mannered when kept with large fishes. Nevertheless, two males may have occasional squabbles, and when the breeding urge approaches the protective instinct gives *C. meeki* a natural aggressiveness. At these times it will dig pits in the sand, tear out plants which may obstruct its view, and make determined charges at any fishes which approach its selected territory.

The general body colour is olive, but the scales shine in rows of blue dots. The outstanding feature is the vivid scarlet throat and belly. A black line runs from the eyes to a large spot on the flanks. Faint vertical bars appear at times on the sides. On the lower edge of the gill-plate is a prominent diamond-shaped black spot which is edged with silver-blue. The fins are reddish, but adorned with flecks and stripes of blue. The upper edge of the dorsal is scarlet. The lower edge of the ventrals and anal is bluish-black. The female is similarly coloured; but her dorsal and anal fins are not so long or pointed. She is usually smaller.

BREEDING. *Tank: 24″ × 12″ × 12″. pH: 7·0–7·2. Hardness: 120–150 p.p.m. Temperature: 80° F. Spawns: in flower-pot. Method: standard for medium cichlids. Eggs: 200–250. Hatch: in 4 days. Fry wriggling: 3 days. Free-swimming: 8th day. Food 1st week: brine shrimp. 2nd week: microworms, fine dried food.*

The species is easy to breed. It deposits eggs inside a flower-pot. Male and female should now be returned to their normal tanks. An aerator is placed near the eggs in the flower-pot and 5–7 drops of methylene blue added to the water. Do not feed until the fry are free-swimming.

CICHLASOMA NIGROFASCIATUS

Black-banded Cichlid

HONDURAS, NICARAGUA   ♂ 4″ ♀ 3½″

NON-COMMUNITY   DIET: ALL FOODS   SWIMS: LOWER HALF OF TANK

This is not a large cichlid, but aggressive enough to be unsafe with any small or medium-sized fishes. It is a frequent spawner, and if kept in a community tank causes havoc by tearing out plants and incessantly digging pits in the sand.

Long before maturity the fish can be easily sexed, as it is one of the species in which the female is more colourful than the male. He is a dark mauvish-black, the body being crossed by vertical bars. The foremost of these is inclined towards the head at an angle of 45 degrees. A dark blotch appears at the base of his tail. His dorsal bears shades of green, and when mature this fin and the anal grow longer points than those of the female. She is usually smaller, and flecks of gold adorn her lower sides and belly. Her dorsal and anal fins are bluish-green, and at mating-time she is round underneath and thicker than her mate.

BREEDING. *Tank: 24″×12″×12″. pH: 7·0–7·2. Hardness: 150–180 p.p.m. Temperature: 80° F. Spawns: in flower-pot. Method: standard for medium cichlids.*

Eggs: 250–350. Hatch: in 3 days. Fry wriggling: 3 days. Free-swimming: 7th day. Food 1st week: brine shrimp. 2nd week: microworms, fine dried food.

An easy and prolific breeder. Spawning follows the pattern described on p. 399. It is best to remove the male and allow the female to tend the eggs.

CICHLASOMA SEVERUM

♂

AMAZON   ♂ 6″   ♀ 5½″

COMMUNITY, WITH LARGER FISHES   DIET: ALL FOODS

SWIMS: LOWER HALF OF TANK

In spite of the name (meaning 'severe'), this is not a very aggressive cichlid if kept with fishes of its own size. Like any member of its family, it may become quarrelsome at breeding-time. It also pulls out plants.

When young the fish is a pale brown with a few vertical bars. But on reaching maturity the male has a greenish tinge, and along his flanks reddish-brown spots form themselves into horizontal but slightly arched stripes. The most outstanding feature is a slightly curved upright bar a little in front of the caudal peduncle. This bar links together a large spot in the rear portion of the anal fin with a similar one in the dorsal fin. When fully grown the fins of the male become brownish, and are sprinkled with spots of red and blue. His dorsal and anal fins grow long points; these extend back far enough to reach the outer edge of the tail.

The female is duller, and her fins are shorter.

BREEDING. Tank: 30"×15"×15". pH: 7·0–7·2. Hardness: 150–180 p.p.m. Temperature: 80° F. Spawns: on flat rock. Method: standard for large cichlids. Eggs: 300–350. Hatch: in 3 days. Fry wriggling: 3 days. Free-swimming: 7th day. Food 1st week: brine shrimp. 2nd week: microworms, fine dried food.

The species is not such a ready breeder, but when spawning occurs it follows the procedure described on p. 399.

ETROPLUS MACULATUS

Orange Chromide

INDIA, CEYLON   ♂ 3" ♀ 3"

COMMUNITY, WITH MEDIUM-SIZED FISHES   DIET: ALL FOODS

SWIMS: LOWER HALF OF TANK

A very striking fish, different in colour from most cichlids. Except at breeding-time, it is not aggressive with medium-sized fishes. Usually it does not pull out plants.

When young, or in an unfavourable situation, the fish is a dull buff with a black spot in the centre of the sides. But when happy, or in courting dress, the species is very beautiful. The whole body turns a brilliant golden-yellow, the sides being sprinkled with rows of carmine dots. These are more abundant in the male. The fins are gold to orange, the dorsal bearing numerous red dots, but the ventrals and lower edge of the anal turn jet-black. The spot on the side of the body fades to pale blue.

Sexing, according to most books, is extremely difficult, but the authors do not agree with this. An obvious and infallible colour mark seems to have escaped notice in the past. In the tail fin of the female there are two white bands, one running parallel to the upper edge, the other parallel to the lower. These white markings are always plainly visible whether she is in full colour or not. They are completely absent in the male. (See colour plate opposite.)

BREEDING. Tank: 24″ × 8″ × 8″. pH: 6·8–7·2. Hardness: 120–150 p.p.m. Temperature: 80° F. Spawns: in flower-pot. Method: standard for medium cichlids. Eggs: 200–250. Hatch: in 3 days. Fry wriggling: 3 days. Free-swimming: 7th day. Food 1st week: infusoria, brine shrimp. 2nd week: microworms, fine dried food.

Once a male has mated the pair should be kept apart from other 'orange chromides so that they may be easily identified again. This is because the species is very likely to mate for life and spawn frequently. Should a strange female be offered to the original male he may kill her in a few minutes.

If possible several fish should be placed together in a large tank, when one pair will soon mate up and keep all the rest away from their selected spawning-site. Once this occurs the pair should be removed to a breeding tank. They spawn in a flower-pot, following the procedure described on p. 399. After the parents have been removed they should not be placed with other chromides, or fighting may result. When the female is ready to breed again she will start digging pits in the sand. The pair should then be reunited in a breeding tank once more.

The young grow rapidly to ¾″ in length. At this stage the weaker ones may be killed off by their stronger brethren, so the aquarist is advised to keep a close watch and remove any which are being attacked. Even so, the young are more difficult to rear than most cichlids.

ETROPLUS SURATENSIS

Silver Chromide

CEYLON ♂ 3″ ♀ 2¾″

COMMUNITY, WITH MEDIUM-SIZED FISHES   DIET: ALL FOODS

SWIMS: LOWER HALF OF TANK

A more recent introduction, this fish resembles the foregoing in shape, but is of a quite different colour.

The body is greyish-black covered with rows of tiny silver dots, giving the first impression that the fish is in an advanced stage of Ichthyophthirius. About three-quarters of the way along the flanks in the upper half is a striking spot which is oval in shape and encircled by gold. The dorsal fin is dull gold edged with black. The ventrals are long and prominent; the forward rays are light yellow. The anal fin has a greenish tint.

BREEDING. The authors' specimens are still young, and so far it has not been possible to distinguish the sex or breed with these. It is very likely that the procedure follows that of E. maculatus.

GEOPHAGUS CUPIDO

Cupid Cichlid

N.E. SOUTH AMERICA		♂ 3½″ ♀ 3½″
COMMUNITY	DIET : ALL FOODS	SWIMS : LOWER HALF OF TANK

A rather rare and attractive little cichlid which, generally speaking, is not aggressive.

The upper half of the body is a pale mauvish-olive, the lower portion being a greenish-gold. The most striking markings are a short, thin line from the top of the head to the hind portion of the eye and a broader, more intense, line which runs from the top of the eye down to the lower jaw.

BREEDING. The authors have not yet bred this species.

GEOPHAGUS JURUPARI

♀

♂

AMAZON   ♂ 4½″   ♀ 4½″

COMMUNITY, WITH MEDIUM-SIZED FISHES   DIET: ALL FOODS

SWIMS: LOWER HALF OF TANK

An uncommon but very likeable cichlid. The head is long and pointed; the lips are prominent. The eye is large, and situated well up on the head. The dorsal is high and long; the body narrow and elongated. The species seems to be peaceful. It is not shy, and is amusing to watch. Using its pointed snout as a shovel, it scoops up mouthfuls of sand, sifting particles of food, and shooting out the refuse in showers from the gill-plates, making it a good scavenger.

The overall colour is greyish-olive; faint bars cross the flanks vertically. A black spot appears in the upper portion of the base of the tail. The flanks are adorned with numerous horizontal rows of tiny greenish-gold dots. On the face the rows of dots form gold stripes, which run downward at an angle of 45 degrees. Dots of similar colour appear in the rear portion of the dorsal, ventral, and tail fins. The first rays of the anal are pale yellow.

Males develop longer points on the dorsal and anal fins.

BREEDING. Spawning may occur in a community tank, for the species is a mouth-breeder. The pair circle round each other just above the sand, the female depositing eggs which are immediately fertilized by the male. She now picks up the eggs and incubates them in her mouth, occasionally spitting out a few and grabbing them again instantly. After spawning it is best to remove the female to a separate breeding tank. Incubation takes about 10 days, during which time the mother refuses all food. Once the young are free-swimming they will take brine shrimp. For further details see *Haplochromis multicolor*, p. 429.

HEMICHROMIS BIMACULATUS

♂

Jewel Cichlid

CENTRAL AFRICA ♂ 4″ ♀ 3¾″

NON–COMMUNITY   DIET: ALL FOODS   SWIMS: LOWER HALF OF TANK

A very beautiful but vicious cichlid. It will attack its own species as well as other fishes larger or smaller than itself.

When young or not excited it is a dull olive, with three black dots showing up on the sides. However, when it wears courting colours it is beautiful. Now the head and belly turn a fiery red; the scales on the flanks and gill-plates sparkle like blue-green jewels—hence the popular name. All the fins are edged with brilliant red, and shine profusely with blue-green spots. The black dot in the centre of the body disappears entirely.

The male is even more jewelled than the female, particularly in the regions of the gill-plates, the flanks, and the tail fin. His is not necessarily the brightest red; indeed, at times the female is so brilliant that the un-initiated might consider her to be the male.

BREEDING. *Tank:* 30″×15″×15″. *pH:* 7·0–7·2. *Hardness:* 120–150 *p.p.m. Temperature:* 80–82°F. *Spawns: in flower-pot. Method: standard for medium cichlids. Eggs:* 250–300. *Hatch: in 3 days. Fry wriggling: 3 days. Free-swimming: 7th day. Food 1st week: brine shrimp, microworms. 2nd week: microworms, fine dried food.*

The species is not difficult to breed, providing that a pair get on well together. But the aquarist is advised to watch for some little time, and to intervene if one fish is being bullied too fiercely. After spawning the male should be removed. Once the fry are free-swimming the female may also be taken away. The young grow rapidly, and soon develop aggressive tendencies. They will kill each other unless given plenty of plants and rocks round which they may dodge and take refuge. Spawns may be large, but it is not every aquarist or pet shop that will buy the surplus of such vicious fish.

HERICHTHYS CYANOGUTTATUS

Texas Cichlid

TEXAS, MEXICO ♂ 9″ ♀ 9″

COMMUNITY, WITH LARGE FISHES   DIET: ALL FOODS   SWIMS: MID-WATER

A mild-mannered cichlid, but one which grows far too large for the average aquarist.

The body is a pearly grey crossed by several vertical bars of a darker hue. A black, triangular spot appears at the base of the tail. The head, body, and part of the fins are liberally speckled with pale blue dots.

Longer points to the dorsal and anal fin of the male determine sex.

BREEDING. Tank: 36″×15″×15″. pH: 7·0–7·2. Hardness: 150–180 p.p.m. Temperature: 78° F. Spawns: on flat rocks. Method: standard for large cichlids. Eggs: 350–500. Hatch: in 3 days. Fry wriggling: 3 days. Free-swimming: 7th day. Food 1st week: brine shrimp, microworms. 2nd week: sifted Daphnia, Cyclops.

PTEROPHYLLUM EIMEKEI

<table>
<tr><td>*Angel Fish*</td><td></td><td>*Black Lace Angel*</td></tr>
</table>

AMAZON   ♂ 5″   ♀ 5″

COMMUNITY   DIET: ALL FOODS   SWIMS: MID–WATER

The elongated dorsal and anal fins of this graceful fish have earned it the popular name 'angel fish.' Because of its exotic appearance, nearly every aquarist likes to have at least one in his collection. This is one of the cichlids which does not tear out plants or dig pits in the sand. Angels are generally peaceful, but grow rapidly, and soon become out of proportion to other small species. However, if their owner has a larger tank they may be transferred, and will easily grow to maturity. They will eat all types of food, including the dried product.

Angels are sometimes temperamental, and get scared after being moved, and then refuse to eat. But they must not be coddled or kept in a quiet place, as this merely increases their nervousness when they have to be approached. It is far better to place them in a community tank with other less excitable fishes, preferably where people are continually passing. Here they soon settle down, behave normally, and feed well. Once this happens they become very tame, and will eat out of their owner's fingers. Some even allow him to pick them out of the water and replace them without fright. Such specimens will breed readily. The nervous ones are often too scared to mate.

The normal angel is so well-known that a full colour description is unnecessary. It suffices to say that the body is silvery with vertical black bars which adorn the fins and flanks. There is a glowing red in the upper half of the eye. The ventrals are pale blue; they are very long, and curve

Black Angel

back in graceful, unbroken points. On good specimens the upper and lower rays of the tail extend in filaments three times the length of this fin.

Just after the Second World War M. Carels, the renowned fish-breeder of Ghent, Belgium, produced a strain of *P. eimekei* which were normal-coloured in the front part of the body, but jet-black from the third bar to the tip of the tail. Some of these fish were exported to America, and very probably from this stock was developed the Black Lace Angel. In this the body and markings are darker, making the lighter parts appear like network seen through black lace. Further line breeding produced the pure Black Angel, in which the whole body and fins are jet-black. In the meantime in Germany a beautiful blue strain has been developed. Here, with the exception of the pale gold ventrals, body and fins are a lovely pale blue. The latest development is the Veil-tailed Angel produced by Herr Karl Buschendorf, of Germany.

Veil-tailed Angel

Sexing has always been considered difficult. Various writers have drawn attention to minute differences in the first short rays of the dorsal fin. Others have stated that the distance between ventral and anal fins indicates sex. Still others refer to the angle of this portion of the body. But the authors, after scrutinizing thousands of angels, failed to detect the vague difference referred to; yet a pronounced feature which we have found true has always been overlooked, or never mentioned. This is a characteristic which is clearly visible on all fishes bearing long, feeler-like ventral fins. The body of the female bulges noticeably behind and below the pectorals, or—what amounts to the same thing—above and behind the ventrals, as shown in Fig. 26. In this region the females are convex, while males are concave.

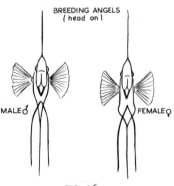

BREEDING ANGELS
(head on)

MALE ♂   FEMALE ♀

FIG. 26

To those following this system for the first time the angel should be viewed from head on, preferably while it is feeding at the water surface, as then it has its head inclined upward. Now the bulge shown in Fig. 26 should be clearly visible on a female. In this area a male appears as though he had been pinched between thumb and forefinger.

Once having observed the difference it is no longer necessary to see the fish head on. A side view is quite satisfactory, since the bulge on a female catches the light and shines slightly. On the other hand, the dent in the male casts a weak shadow. True, after a large feed both sexes are thicker, but the method still applies, as at all times females will bulge considerably more than males. By this system the authors are able to sex angels when the overall length from tip of nose to end of tail is only 2″. So far the method has proved to be infallible. Time and again a couple of youngsters of $1\frac{1}{2}$″ body diameter have been placed in a breeding tank, and when 8 months old have spawned, proving them to be a true pair.

Just prior to breeding the bulge on the female is very pronounced. The two fish face each other, jerk their fins, and kiss. At this time her ovipositor protrudes about $\frac{1}{8}$″; it is nearly as wide as it is long, and almost square at the extremity. The corresponding organ of the male is shorter, thinner, and much more pointed.

Two other species of angel fish exist, though they are rarely seen in aquaria. These are *P. scalare* and *P. altum*.

P. scalare grows larger than *P. eimekei*. The body is rounder and more disc-like, while the snout is more upturned. *P. altum*, similar in shape to *P. scalare*, has more soft rays in the hind-portion of the dorsal fin.

BREEDING. *Tank: 24″ × 12″ × 24″ high. pH: 7·0–7·4. Hardness: 150–180 p.p.m. Temperature: 78° F. Spawns: on tall leaf or "Vitrolite" bar. Method: remove eggs and hatch in separate tank. Eggs: 300–400. Hatch: in 3 days. Fry wriggling: 4 days. Free-swimming: 8th day. Food 1st week: infusoria, brine shrimp. 2nd week: brine shrimp.*

A proved pair should be housed in a tank of the dimensions given above. This is well-planted, and becomes their permanent home. They should be given a long "Vitrolite" bar on which to spawn. The procedure follows exactly that described under *Cichlasoma festivum*, except that angels cleanse the bar thoroughly with their mouths until every speck of sediment and algæ has been removed. If the bar is taken out, and the eggs hatched in a separate tank with methylene blue, a good pair of angels will spawn every 8 days for 18 months or more without a break. Should the bar be left where it is the parents take turns in fanning the eggs. Provided the eggs do not fungus, and that the parents do not tire of their duties and eat the spawn, it is a wonderful sight to see the adults with their fry, and to watch how they look after them and gather them into a tight ball as dusk approaches. When they raise their young the parents are unlikely to spawn again until the babies are 8–10 weeks old.

SYMPHYSODON DISCUS

♂

♀

Pompadour

AMAZON ♂ 7″ ♀ 7″

COMMUNITY, WITH MEDIUM-SIZED FISHES DIET: MAINLY PROTEIN

SWIMS: MID-WATER

Most superb of all fresh-water tropicals is an adult pair of *S. discus*. They are worthy of a large tank, and special care and attention. Though not aggressive, they should not be kept with small fishes, neither should they be placed among large, savage species which may damage them. Recently there have been more importations of young pompadours, but even so the price is high. The majority of these youngsters caught in the wild are infected with minute organisms. These multiply, especially where chills and frequent changes of water occur, and bring about the death of the fish.

When small *S. discus* is quite drab, having brownish flanks crossed vertically by several dark bars. Up to 2″ in length, the body is slightly elongated. After this stage it becomes deeper, the fish being greater in measurement from top to bottom than from nose to tail. On reaching 6–7 months old flecks of blue appear about the head and gill-plates. These markings extend with age until they spread over most of the back, as well as in the region of the anal fin. The fins become darkish blue on the inside, splashed with streaks of pale blue and orange. The outer portions turn pale blue and orange. The borders are bright red, though the first short rays of the dorsal and anal are tipped with white. The ventral fins are long; they are red with orange tips. The body turns mahogany colour.

Sometimes there is a golden hue; at other times a reddish one is noticeable.

In the past sexing has been regarded as extremely difficult. But Mr R. Skipper, of Hendon, finds that the shape of the ventral fins gives clear indication as to how to determine sex. According to him, these fins on a male hang down and curve backward in a crescent, whereas in the female the tips take a further downward sweep, forming a kind of letter S.

BREEDING. *Tank: 36″ × 15″ × 15″. pH: 6·4–7·0. Hardness: 50–80 p.p.m. Temperature: 80° F. Spawns: on long leaf or "Vitrolite" bar. Method: parents fan eggs. Eggs: 150–250. Hatch: in 3 days. Fry wriggling: 4 days. Free-swimming: 7th day. Food 1st and 2nd weeks: mucus secretion exuded by parents.*

Though this fish has not been bred by the authors, below is given an authentic account by Mr R. Skipper, who has successfully raised several spawnings.

The tank is filled with slightly acid water, and planted as a permanent home for the parents. The vegetation includes *Sagittaria sinensis*. After some love play the adults select and clean a tall, broad leaf. On this the female deposits her eggs in rows, and as they are laid the male fertilizes them. The spawn is fanned by the parents. The young, stuck by a thread to the leaf, wriggle violently. The parents now move the babies to a new site, washing them in their mouths during the transfer.

During this period the adults secrete a whitish mucus over their bodies, which provides the fry with their first food. Indeed, they will take nothing else, and may be seen pecking furiously from the sides and upper portion of the backs of their parents. Although other minute foods have been tried, Mr Skipper finds that the babies will not thrive on any alternative diet. Thus the only hope of raising the fry is to leave them with their parents. Occasionally the spawn is eaten, but this risk is inevitable. Once the youngsters are 3–4 weeks old they may be removed and fed on brine shrimp, sifted Daphnia, and finely scraped raw heart. They grow rapidly, and, unlike the imported specimens, all appear healthy and hardy.

TILAPIA MOSSAMBICA

E. AFRICA

COMMUNITY, WITH LARGE FISHES

SWIMS: UPPER HALF OF TANK

♂ 7″ ♀ 7″

DIET: ALL FOODS

Most Tilapia are mouth-breeders, but grow too large for the average aquarist. We show one species, which is perhaps the smallest. For a large fish, it is surprisingly fond of dried food. With mouth open and head tilted upward, it ploughs through the floating particles and gathers in mouthfuls.

The fish is greenish-grey, with a dull gold edge to the outer border of the tail fin. At times this edge has a reddish tint, and a thin red margin appears on the dorsal fin. Three faint vertical bars cross the rear portion of the flanks. Occasionally, when stimulated, a few white patches occur in the forward upper portions of the body, and the lower part of the male's gill-plate.

The dorsal and anal fins of the male are slightly longer and more pointed than those of the female, and the dull gold in his tail is a little more pronounced.

BREEDING. *Tank: 30″×15″×15″. pH: 7·0–7·2. Hardness: 150–180 p.p.m. Temperature: 78° F. Spawns: in depression in sand. Method: mouth-breeder. Eggs: 100–150. Hatch: in 14 days. Food 1st week: brine shrimp, microworms. 2nd week: sifted Daphnia, fine dried food.*

The tank should be planted to make the fish feel at home. The pair fan a depression in the sand and then, head to tail, circle just above it. Eggs are laid and fertilized, then after spawning the female should be removed. The male picks up the eggs and incubates them in his mouth for about 14 days before the young appear.

(iii) DWARF CICHLIDS

APISTOGRAMMA AGASSIZI

GUIANA   ♂ 3″   ♀ 2¾″

COMMUNITY   DIET: ALL FOODS   SWIMS: LOWER HALF OF TANK

A very beautiful, peaceful little fish, with an outstandingly long dorsal fin and an elongated tail.

The overall body colour is a pale olive-gold with scales of sparkling blue. The dorsal fin is golden with an edge of deep red. The oval tail is pale yellow with a bright yellow streak near the outer edge of the upper half. The lower portion is decorated with a purplish-blue streak, beneath which is a golden area.

The male is much more colourful than the female, and his fins are larger and longer.

BREEDING. *Tank: 24″ × 8″ × 8″. pH: 7·0–7·2. Hardness: 120–150 p.p.m. Temperature: 80° F. Spawns: in flower-pot. Method: standard for dwarf cichlids. Eggs: 80–150. Hatch: in 3 days. Fry wriggling: 3 days. Free-swimming: 7th day. Food 1st week: brine shrimp, microworms. 2nd week: microworms, fine dried food.*

The tank should be well planted, and provided with a flower-pot or slate structure, as described on p. 400.

APISTOGRAMMA ORNATIPINNIS

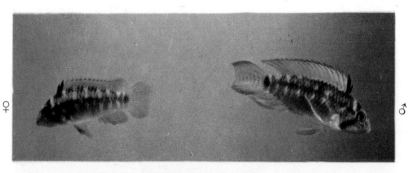

♀   ♂

Ornate Dwarf Cichlid

GUIANA   ♂ 3″   ♀ 2¾″

COMMUNITY   DIET: ALL FOODS   SWIMS: LOWER HALF OF TANK

A recent introduction, this is one of the prettiest dwarf cichlids, and is very peaceful.

The general body colour is reddish-brown, but large patches of blue adorn the sides. A black line starting above the head curves downward through the eye to the lower edge of the gill-plate. Behind this the throat is a vivid blue. The dorsal fin is blue, the first rays being black. The outer edge is bright red. The ventral fins are brilliant orange; the anal is bluish, with streaks of red and blue. The tail is spotted in its centre, the upper and lower edges being bright orange-red. The outer edge of the male's tail is concave, giving him the appearance of having two short points in the upper and lower lobes.

The female is less gaudy. Her body bears several broad, vertical bars of blue-black. A black line runs from the eye to a spot in the caudal peduncle. The colouring of her fins is similar to the male's, but more subdued.

BREEDING. *Tank: 24″ × 8″ × 8″. pH: 7·0–7·2. Hardness: 120–150 p.p.m. Temperature: 78° F. Spawns: in flower-pot or slate structure. Method: standard for dwarf cichlids. Eggs: 250–300. Hatch: in 3 days. Fry wriggling: 3 days. Free-swimming: 7th day. Food 1st week: infusoria, brine shrimp. 2nd week: brine shrimp, microworms.*

Like most dwarf cichlids, the species is short-lived, and spawning should be attempted before the parents get too old.

APISTOGRAMMA PERTENSE

♀ ♂

GUIANA ♂ 2″ ♀ 1¾″

COMMUNITY   DIET: ALL FOODS   SWIMS: LOWER HALF OF TANK

A quiet, inoffensive little fish which may be kept in community tanks with other small species.

The general body colour is greenish-grey, developing a yellowish tinge in maturity. A black line runs from the eye to the base of the tail and ends in a spot of the same colour. Faint vertical bars cross the flanks. The head and gill-plates are flecked with scales of shining blue. The fins are yellowish, but the first rays of the dorsal are black.

The dorsal and anal fins of the male are longer and more pointed than those of the female.

BREEDING. Tank: 24″ × 8″ × 8″. pH: 7·0–7·2. Hardness: 100–120 p.p.m. Temperature: 78° F. Spawns: in flower-pot. Method: standard for dwarf cichlids. Eggs: 100–120. Hatch: in 3 days. Fry wriggling: 3 days. Free-swimming: 7th day. Food 1st week: infusoria. 2nd week: brine shrimp, microworms.

The species is not quite so prolific as most.

APISTOGRAMMA RAMIREZI

♀

♂

VENEZUELA   ♂ $2\frac{1}{2}''$ ♀ $2\frac{1}{2}''$

COMMUNITY   DIET: ALL FOODS   SWIMS: LOWER HALF OF TANK

This truly gorgeous little fish is peaceful, and does not tear out plants. The species seems to do better in slightly acid soft water. It may be easily identified, as the top edge of the dorsal fin is concave.

The colour is not easy to describe, since it varies from blue to mauve; at times the belly is purplish-pink. The eye is red. A black stripe runs from the nape of the neck through the eye down to the lower edge of the gill-plate. The sides bear dark vertical bands which are most pronounced towards the head, and become fainter near the tail. The flanks are adorned with scales of shining blue. The dorsal, anal, and caudal fins are orange with blue dots. The first rays of the dorsal are jet-black, the tips being separated like the teeth of a comb. The second ray is elongated. The first rays of the ventrals are black, the third and fourth rays being bright blue.

Sexing is difficult until the fish are fully mature. Only then will it be noticed that the male is the more brightly coloured; the black spike in his dorsal is longer, and his anal is more pointed. The female becomes rounder and deeper when full of roe.

BREEDING. *Tank: 24″ × 8″ × 8″. pH: 6·5–6·8. Hardness: 80–100 p.p.m. Temperature: 80° F. Spawns: in flower-pot. Method: standard for dwarf cichlids. Eggs: 80–100. Hatch: in 3 days. Fry wriggling: 3 days. Free-swimming: 7th day. Food 1st week: infusoria. 2nd week: brine shrimp, microworms.*

Sometimes the species hollows out a depression in the sand where it spawns. Should this occur, remove the female. The male fans and guards the eggs; he should be transferred once the young are free-swimming.

HAPLOCHROMIS MULTICOLOR

♂

♀

Egyptian Mouth-breeder

EGYPT ♂ 3″ ♀ 3″

COMMUNITY   DIET: ALL FOODS   SWIMS: LOWER HALF OF TANK

For those aquarists with small tanks who wish to witness the incubation of eggs in a fish's mouth, and to watch how the babies seek refuge in their mother's jaws, this is the fish to keep. In its larger sizes the species occasionally becomes aggressive, but it will breed when only 1½″ long. At this size it is normally safe with other small fishes.

The males are considerably the more colourful. Their scales shine with bluish-green, body and fins being covered with red dots. A bright orange-red patch adorns the tip of the anal fin. Females are less colourful; they have a yellowish tinge, and lack the red patch in the anal.

BREEDING. Tank: 24″ × 8″ × 8″. pH: 7·0–7·4. Hardness: 150–180 p.p.m. Temperature: 78° F. Spawns: in depression fanned in sand. Method: female incubates eggs in mouth. Eggs: 25–75. Hatch: in 14–16 days. Free-swimming: immediately on leaving the mother's mouth. Food 1st week: brine shrimp and microworms. 2nd week: sifted Daphnia and dried food.

A pair will often spawn in a community tank. After fanning a slight depression in the sand, they circle each other head to tail. Eggs are laid and fertilized. The female then picks up the spawn in her mouth. She now refuses all food, and her lower jaw begins to get deeper. After a week her appearance is noticeable. Her jaw protrudes, and her normal rounded chin becomes angular and square; her belly through lack of food shrinks, and she looks all head. Her jaw also expands sideways, and viewed from the front the eggs may be seen in the cleft of her jaw plates. It is now best to remove her in a jar to a small breeding tank. Catching and transferring her, if done calmly, rarely upsets her. She should be watched daily from now on, and soon tiny eyes will be seen in the eggs in her jaws. About a week later she may be noticed swimming with 20 or 30 babies near her. If disturbed the young will jostle each other in their frantic attempts to reach the safety of the interior of her mouth.

Commercial breeders keep several females in one tank with a few males. When the females are seen to be carrying eggs each is caught and placed in a jam-jar, several of which are floated in a bare aquarium. As each produces her babies the mother is caught in a small net and the fry tipped into the tank. To ensure that the mother has not got a few babies still in her mouth she is returned to the jar, which should be floated in the original tank for an hour. If no more fry appear she may then be tipped out.

NANNACARA ANOMALA

GUIANA   ♂ 2¼″   ♀ 2″

COMMUNITY   DIET: ALL FOODS   SWIMS: LOWER HALF OF TANK

Though not one of the most colourful dwarf cichlids, the species is very prolific, and therefore one of the commonest.

The body is an olive green splashed with blue highlights here and there among the scales. The dorsal fin is edged with red.

The female is less colourful; her dorsal, anal, and ventral fins are not so long and pointed as those of the male.

BREEDING. *Tank: 24″ × 8″ × 8″. pH: 7·0–7·2. Hardness: 150–180 p.p.m. Temperature: 76° F. Spawns: in flower-pot. Method: standard for dwarf cichlids. Eggs: 75–120. Hatch: in 3 days. Fry wriggling: 3 days. Free-swimming: 7th day. Food 1st week: brine shrimp, microworms. 2nd week: microworms, fine dried food.*

The species often breeds in a community tank of medium-sized fishes. If no flower-pot is present the pair will spawn in a depression in the sand, and guard their eggs. The authors have frequently raised families in this manner. Even so, it remains remarkable that the parents are able to guard both the eggs and hatched fry throughout the hours of darkness as well as during the day. Perhaps the most surprising thing of all was that in a large community tank, measuring 36″ × 15″ × 15″, well stocked with fishes, no special food could be given solely to the babies, since all the other fishes present would have intercepted it. Nevertheless, the ever-attentive parents must have ensured that their offspring were nourished for the fry grew to maturity in this community tank.

NANNACHROMIS NUDICEPS

♂

♀

BELGIAN CONGO   ♂ 3¼″ ♀ 3″

COMMUNITY   DIET: ALL FOODS   SWIMS: LOWER HALF OF TANK

Introduced into Britain by the authors in 1952, this rather long-bodied dwarf cichlid caused quite a sensation. The somewhat protruding jaw gives it an aggressive appearance, but it is quite peaceful, though occasionally a male will ill-treat a female if she does not respond to his advances.

The long, slender body is bluish, but in certain lights it shows duck-egg green, while at other times it takes on a purplish hue. The lengthy dorsal fin is bluish and edged with red. The anal is mauve. In males the tail is adorned in the upper half with purplish-brown streaks. The absence of colour in this fin of the female is the first identification of sex in young fish.

BREEDING. *Tank: 24″ × 8″ × 8″. pH: 7·0–7·2. Hardness: 100–120 p.p.m. Temperature: 80° F. Spawns: in flower-pot or slate structure. Method: standard for dwarf cichlids. Eggs: 80–120. Hatch: in 3 days. Fry wriggling: 3 days. Free-swimming: 7th day. Food 1st week: brine shrimp. 2nd week: brine shrimp, microworms.*

The species breeds readily, and the young are not difficult to raise.

PELMATOCHROMIS GUNTHERI

GOLD COAST   ♂ 6″ ♀ 6″
COMMUNITY, WITH LARGER FISHES   DIET : ALL FOODS
SWIMS : LOWER HALF OF TANK

Some of the genus are mouth-breeders, and this species is one of them. In its smaller sizes it is moderately peaceful, but becomes aggressive with age.

At breeding-time the male is beautiful. The upper flanks are golden-olive, barred vertically and horizontally by bright bands of olive-green. The lower flanks and belly are suffused pink. The male's dorsal is edged with burnished gold, and black blocks adorn the lower areas of this fin for three-quarters of its length; in between, the fin is green-gold at first, turning to silver-pink in the centre, shading off to blue, and finally green-gold again at its tip. The ventrals and anal are silver-blue, and a blue-green stripe appears along the upper lip. The female is similarly coloured, but less brightly, and she lacks the colour and black markings in the dorsal fin. It is the male who incubates the eggs in his mouth, the babies being nearly $\frac{1}{4}$″ long when they first appear. At the first sign of danger they scramble hurriedly into the mouth of either parent for protection.

BREEDING. *Tank: 24″ × 12″ × 12″. pH: 7·0–7·2. Hardness: 120–150 p.p.m. Temperature: 78° F. Spawns: in depression in sand. Method: male incubates eggs. Eggs: 30–50. Hatch: in 2 to 3 weeks. Free-swimming immediately on leaving the male's mouth. Food 1st week: microworms, Grindal worms. 2nd week: Grindal worms, dried food.*

PELMATOCHROMIS KRIBENSIS

♀   ♂

Dwarf Rainbow Cichlid

BELGIAN CONGO   ♂ 3¾″   ♀ 3″

COMMUNITY   DIET: ALL FOODS   SWIMS: LOWER HALF OF TANK

The authors received the first specimens of this beautiful fish in 1953 from M. Van de Weyer, the well-known Belgian importer. Nearly every aquarist who saw them gave advance bookings for young when bred. The species has proved to be one of the most popular dwarf cichlids to date, and it can safely be predicted that it will always remain in favour. It is peaceful, does not tear out plants, eats any food, and breeds easily. So gorgeous is the colouring that it has been chosen to illustrate the jacket of this book. Moreover, it is one of those species in which both sexes are equally brilliant; if anything, the female at spawning-time is the prettier.

The general body colour is a golden-green, though the back is an olive-brown. The lower portion of the gill-plates and throat is a brilliant blue. A red patch appears in the belly of the male. His ventrals and anal fins are edged with peacock blue; the dorsal has a blue-green border. In adult males the top half of the tail is tinted with orange, and clear black spots numbering from one to seven appear in this region. The female is similarly coloured, but the reddish area in the abdomen spreads nearly to her back. Her dorsal has a golden edge, and 1, 2, or 3 black spots appear in the rear portion of this fin. The ventrals are bluish-red, but her tail remains almost clear.

Sexing adults is obvious. However, in young fish 1″ long, male and female can be distinguished. This is because the females show the black spot in the rear part of the dorsal. At this stage the corresponding fin of males is clear. In a few weeks he will develop these dorsal markings, but, as if to avoid confusion, he simultaneously shows the arcing orange area in the upper half of the tail. Though at first this is faint, it is un-mistakably there. Females never bear this orange arc in their tails.

BREEDING. *Tank: 24″ × 8″ × 8″. pH: 7·0–7·2. Hardness: 120–150 p.p.m. Temperature: 80° F. Spawns: in flower-pot or slate structure. Method: standard for dwarf cichlids. Eggs: 50–250. Hatch: in 3 days. Fry wriggling: 3 days. Free-swimming: 7th day. Food 1st week: brine shrimp. 2nd week: microworms, sifted Cyclops, a little fine dried food.*

This is a species where our slate structure is better than a flower-pot. Young fish will spawn every month and produce about 50–75 eggs. Older specimens breed less frequently, but families may be larger. The authors' best single spawn was 224 raised to maturity.

CHAPTER XXVI

KNIFE FISHES

THESE QUEER FISHES, THE GYMNOTIDÆ, WHICH HAIL FROM THE NORTH OF South America, are distantly related to the characins. Their long, compressed, tapering bodies resemble a thin blade or stiletto, so they have been nicknamed the knife fishes. Somewhat similar in shape, but distinct from the South American species, are those belonging to the family Notopteridæ, which comes from Indonesia, Burma, and Africa. The knife fishes have been erroneously called eels, but they are not even related to eels.

GYMNOTIDÆ

GYMNOTUS CARAPO

Striped Knife Fish

N. SOUTH AMERICA   ♂ 12″   ♀ 12″

NON–COMMUNITY   DIET : PROTEIN   SWIMS : LOWER HALF OF TANK

Occasionally imported, these unusual fishes are hardy and interesting, but they grow too large for all except those who specialize in keeping oddities. They are unsafe in community tanks, the mouth being large enough to swallow smaller fishes. When kept on their own they will eat pieces of meat, shrimp, aged guppies, etc. G. *carapo* is nocturnal in habits, and generally lethargic during daylight. The long, flat, tapering body hangs motionless in the water, the head slanting upward at an angle of 25 degrees, the long ventral fin beneath the body rippling to ensure stability. The fish occasionally moves forward or backward with equal ease.

The colour is a brownish-grey. Numerous wavy pale grey stripes cross the body slantwise. These stripes are wider and farther apart towards the tail. As far as is known, the species has not been bred in captivity.

HYPOPOMUS ARTEDI

Knife Fish

GUIANA ♂ 12″ ♀ 12″

NON–COMMUNITY DIET: PROTEIN SWIMS: LOWER HALF OF TANK

Very similar to the foregoing, but the body is a brownish olive-green. The sides are speckled with irregular dark spots and bear a faint horizontal line in the centre.

We have no record of the fish having ever been bred in captivity.

NOTOPTERIDÆ

XENOMYSTUS NIGRI

African Knife Fish

WEST AFRICA ♂ 6″ ♀ 6″

COMMUNITY, WITH MEDIUM–SIZED FISHES DIET: ALL FOODS

SWIMS: LOWER HALF OF TANK

As will be seen from the photograph, the African knife fish is not so long and narrow in outline as the typical South American knife fish. The colour is a uniform dark grey.

Our specimens are only 4″ long, but they do not as yet appear aggressive in a community tank of medium-sized blind cave tetras, black mollies, etc.; and they have soon learned to come forward and eat dried food, though they also like chopped shrimp and cod-roe. They are rather shy, and prefer to swim in the background. Unlike the South American knife fishes, *X. nigri* swims about continually, often with the head tilted downward.

BREEDING. The species have not been bred in captivity.

CHAPTER XXVII

GOBIOIDEA

UNDER THE ORDER GOBIOIDEA COME NUMEROUS FAMILIES WHICH ARE SPLIT into many genera and hundreds of species. These range over most of the world, particularly in the temperate and tropical regions. Some are purely marine, the majority inhabit brackish waters, but there are numbers which frequent fresh water. Quite a few species live in swamps, and often spend considerable time on land, where they hunt insects. Gobies differ from most fishes in having no lateral line, and their ventral fins are either under or in front of the pectoràls.

ELEOTRIDÆ

This family, often called 'sleepers,' may be distinguished from others in that the two ventral fins are separate and distinct; they never form a disc-like sucker. These fishes are found in most coastal areas of the tropics. They generally inhabit brackish water, but some ascend the rivers till they reach fresh water, though they frequently return to tidal areas for spawning.

DORMITATOR MACULATUS

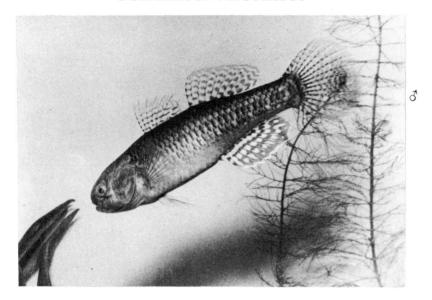

Spotted Sleeper

COASTAL AREAS ROUND GULF OF MEXICO
AND NORTHERN S. AMERICA   ♂ 5″   ♀ 5″

COMMUNITY, WITH MEDIUM-SIZED FISHES   DIET: ALL FOODS

SWIMS: LOWER HALF OF TANK

This is a quiet though somewhat sluggish fish.

The body is brownish-grey, rather heavily spotted. Faint bars appear horizontally on the gill-plates and vertically on the rear of the flanks. A shiny blue spot is to be seen just behind the upper edge of the gill-plate. The double dorsal fin is a brownish-grey, flecked with two rows of spots. The large, round anal fin bears shiny blue spots, and has an edging of the same colour. As in many other Gobioidea, the eyes look opaque. In this case they appear mauvish-blue in certain lights.

The female is less colourful, and deeper in the belly than her mate.

BREEDING. Tank: 24″×8″×8″. pH: 7·2–7·4. Hardness: 160–200 p.p.m. Temperature: 80°F. Spawns: in flower-pots or slate structure. Method: lays tiny adhesive eggs. Eggs: 100–150. Hatch: in 4 days. Fry hang on: 3 days. Free-swimming: 8th day. Food 1st week: infusoria. 2nd week: brine shrimp.

Very small adhesive eggs are attached to the inside of a flower-pot or the perpendicular walls of the slate structure (p. 400). On completion of spawning the female should be removed. The male guards and fans the eggs, but it is best to take him away when the fry are free-swimming. The tiny babies require large quantities of small infusoria.

MOGURNDA MOGURNDA

Persian Carpet

N. AUSTRALIA ♂ 4″ ♀ 4¼″

COMMUNITY, WITH LARGER FISHES DIET: ALL FOODS

SWIMS: LOWER HALF OF TANK

A rather sluggish species which is unsafe with smaller fishes.

The body is brownish, but flecked with spots of red, yellow, blue, orange, and purple. The mosaic pattern resembles a gaudy Persian carpet. The fins are brownish, sprinkled with maroon dots.

The male's fins are larger, and he has more coloured dots on his flanks. The female is considerably thicker and more swollen at breeding-time.

BREEDING. *Tank: 24″×8″×8″. pH: 7·2–7·4. Hardness: 160–180 p.p.m. Temperature: 78°F. Spawns: in flower-pot or slate structure. Method: adhesive eggs stuck to perpendicular surface. Eggs: 100–150. Hatch: in 5 days. Fry hang on: 3 days. Free-swimming: 9th day. Food 1st week: infusoria and brine shrimp. 2nd week: microworms and sifted Daphnia.*

Large brown, oval-shaped eggs are deposited and fertilized a few at a time until a patch about 1¼″ diameter appears. They are thick-shelled and opaque. At one end sticky fibres attach them to a vertical surface, where they hang overlapping one another. Once spawning is completed the female should be removed. The male guards and fans the eggs. As he does so the current he creates in the water wafts the spawn up and down like waving fronds of seaweed. As soon as the young are free-swimming the male also should be removed.

GOBIIDÆ

This is the largest family of gobioid fishes, and may be distinguished by the ventral fins, which are joined and form a sucking disc. With this the fishes are able to adhere to plants, rocks, and other flat surfaces. Many species are found in fresh water far inland; others inhabit brackish water in coastal areas. The majority are smallish and colourful.

BRACHYGOBIUS DORICE

Wasp Goby

MALAYA, JAVA, BORNEO, THAILAND		♂ 1¼″ ♀ 1¼″
COMMUNITY	DIET: LIVE FOOD	SWIMS: LOWER HALF OF TANK

An attractive little goby which is quite safe in a community tank of small fishes. It seems hardy, but is not very lively, and spends much of its time resting or making little hops on the sand. Small live food is preferred, but some dried will be taken. At feeding-time it will swim up regardless of bigger fishes and make sure that it receives its share.

The body is a creamy-yellow crossed with black bands. These are alternately broad and narrow, the latter crossing only the upper half of the body.

Males are slightly brighter-coloured; females have deeper, rounder bellies.

BREEDING. It is doubtful if these fish have been bred in captivity. The procedure is likely to follow that of the bumble bee goby.

BRACHYGOBIUS SUA

Miniature Goby

THAILAND   ♂ ¾″   ♀ ¾″

COMMUNITY   DIET: SMALL LIVE FOOD   SWIMS: LOWER HALF OF TANK

A recently imported goby which is the smallest species to date. In shape and colour it resembles *B. xanthozonus*, but grows to half the size. It is so small that, although it is a community fish in the sense that it will not hurt others, there is a danger that it may be molested itself. Not bred.

BRACHYGOBIUS XANTHOZONUS

Bumble Bee

MALAYA, THAILAND   ♂ 1¾   ♀ 1¾″

COMMUNITY   DIET: LIVE FOOD   SWIMS: LOWER HALF OF TANK

The commonest of the black-and-yellow-banded gobies, which has been imported for years in large numbers. It may be recognized by the very broad black bands that cross the body, the interspaces being bright gold. Though labelled 'community,' it occasionally nips the fins of smaller fishes. Furthermore, when housed with other species it is difficult to feed. It rarely eats anything but live food. As it is slow in movement, it seldom gets a good share of white worms or Daphnia, as these are gobbled up by the other inhabitants while this goby is making up its mind to seize a particular tit-bit.

At times the yellow areas on the flanks turn an orange-red; these are probably males in courting dress. But the authors have never succeeded in breeding the species, though it is said to spawn inside a flower-pot and take 5 or 6 days to hatch.

GOBIUS VAIMOSA BALTEATI

Rhino-horn Goby

CEYLON   ♂ 1½″   ♀ 1¼″

COMMUNITY   DIET: ALL FOODS   SWIMS: ALL DEPTHS

A new and pleasing little goby with a distinctively shaped dorsal fin, which resembles the horn of a rhinocerus, and led us to give it the popular name above.

The fish is peaceful, and quite lively for a goby; it swims about sedately, and never seems in any hurry. The body is pale yellow, somewhat faintly mottled in the hind-quarters. A striking black bar crosses the body and continues upward into the dorsal fin; another crosses the forehead, and after passing through the eye slants to the lower edge of the gill-plate. The front rays of the dorsal are vivid yellow.

The male is slightly brighter than the female, and his fins are longer and more pointed.

BREEDING. So far all attempts at breeding have failed—the fish just do not appear interested; maybe they are still too young.

STIGMATAGOBIUS SADANUNDIO

♀   ♂

THAILAND, JAVA   ♂ $3\frac{1}{2}''$ ♀ $3''$

COMMUNITY   DIET: ALL FOODS   SWIMS: ALL DEPTHS

A new, prettily marked, active goby, first imported into Britain by the authors in 1955. Although it grows to 4″, it is quite peaceful with smaller fishes, being more inclined to dart at its own kind than at strangers. *S. sadanundio* does not stay at the bottom of the aquarium like most gobies, but swims about at all depths, frequently taking short spells of rest. Its sucker-disc ventrals enable it to cling with ease to plants, rocks, or the glass sides of the aquarium.

The general colour is grey, with a few dark spots sprinkled over the body and on the fins. Shining pearly spots light up the fins so that at times they gleam like jewels.

The male is easily distinguishable by his more colourful markings, and by the much larger, longer, and more pointed fins. The trailing edge of his dorsal is split into pointed filaments. At breeding-time the female is thick, deep, and round; she literally bulges with eggs.

BREEDING. Reproduction has so far not been achieved either by the authors or by friends. The fish spawn readily, and lay a great number of minute white eggs. Strangely enough, these are sometimes stuck to the interior of a flower-pot laid on its side, and they completely encircle the internal circumference. On other occasions the male has dug a pit in the sand, though no eggs were seen in it. Yet again, eggs have been scattered over all the plants in the breeding tank, but have fungused within two days. On subsequent spawns salt was added to the water with no better results. Further attempts were made with the addition of methylene blue, yet once again all the eggs fungused. Similar results have been experienced by friends, who also have had numerous spawns but not a single hatching.

STIGMATAGOBIUS SPECIES

CEYLON   ♂ 4″   ♀ 4″

COMMUNITY, WITH MEDIUM-SIZED FISHES   DIET : ALL FOODS

SWIMS : LOWER HALF OF TANK

A recent introduction from Ceylon, though not yet positively identified. The fish seems peaceful, even though it has a large mouth. It spends
most of its time on the sand, but periodically does swim quite a distance
before taking a short rest. It appears to enjoy any food, and is an excellent
scavenger. When seen head on its drooping mouth gives it a lugubrious
expression. Suddenly the lower lip is dropped, and a mouthful of sand is
scooped up, exactly like the grab of an excavator. The rather transparent
mouth makes visible the sand which is being sifted; this is spat out when
the particles of food have been extracted. The ventral fins form a perfect
sucking disc for anchoring the fish to objects; this is clearly depicted in
our illustration. The eyes are high up on the head, as though supported
on minute stalks. This suggests that the species may at times leave the
water, climb on to a rock, and peer round, but so far this action has not
been observed in our specimens.

The colour is a sandy grey. A prominent black line runs through the
eye to the lower jaw. Brownish-grey spots appear in a broken line along
the sides. The fins are large and clear, the caudal being longish and oval in
outline.

Females appear to be thicker than males.

BREEDING. So far the authors' specimens have shown no sign of breeding.

PERIOPHTHALMIDÆ

The mud skippers, as this family of gobioid fishes is called, form one of the most remarkable groups. The eyes are large, and are supported on short stalks at the top of the head. They can be projected, so that while the body remains submerged the eyes break the surface to view the landscape, or they may be withdrawn beneath the surface of the water. Thus, Periophthalmidæ are able to spy out mosquitoes and other insects. Then, leaping along the surface of the water, they capture their prey. Furthermore, they are able to breathe atmospheric air. The powerful muscles of the pectoral fins allow them to raise themselves as though on short legs, crawl out of the water, and travel quite a distance over land. On these escapades small snails and insects are searched for and devoured. When alarmed in their native pools or streams the fishes often evade danger by leaping on to land. Alternatively, when on shore they may jump back into the water. These fishes are able to walk on land much more efficiently than the famous climbing perch (p. 365), which has only a clumsy waddling movement. Periophthalmidæ illustrate the stage in prehistoric times when some creatures left the water to take up a terrestrial abode.

PERIOPHTHALMUS KOELREUTERI

♂

♀

Mud Skipper

TROPICAL FAR EAST, W. AFRICA　　　　　　　　　♂ 5″　♀ 5″

NON-COMMUNITY　　　　　　　　　　　　DIET: ALL FOODS

SWIMS: IN SHALLOW WATER, AND CRAWLS ON LAND

This most interesting and amusing oddity requires special housing. It needs plenty of room, shallow water, and sloping sandy banks or rocks so that it may climb out of the water. The atmosphere must be warm and damp. Without warmth and moisture the fish will get too dry.

The general colour is a brownish-grey speckled with darker spots about the face and neck. The edge of the anterior dorsal fin is black. Beneath this is a white band, the rest of the fin being a mauvish-blue. The anterior dorsal is traversed by a blue line edged above and below with white.

BREEDING. The mud skippers have not been bred in captivity.

CHAPTER XXVIII

AMBASSIDÆ

THERE IS SOME CONFUSION AS TO WHETHER THE NAME OF THIS FAMILY should be Ambassidæ or Chandidæ. It comprises species of very transparent little fishes which inhabit salt, brackish, and fresh water. The majority are found in Malaya, Borneo, and Thailand, though some species come from India and Burma. Quite a few have been imported, and do well in the home aquarium. All have double dorsals.

AMBASSIS BUROENSIS

♀

♂

TROPICAL FAR EAST   ♂ 2″   ♀ 2″

COMMUNITY   DIET: ALL FOODS   SWIMS: UPPER HALF OF TANK

A hardy, transparent fish which is attractive and peaceful. The body is more elongated than in the better-known *Ambassis lala*. It does well in pure fresh water, but has no objection to small additions of salt. It feeds near the surface, and enjoys live food like Daphnia and Cyclops or floating fruit-flies. Nevertheless, it learns to accept a dried product which does not sink too rapidly. The species is nearly colourless, but the translucent scales produce reflected highlights in all the colours of the spectrum. The body is most transparent.

When full of roe females are considerably thicker than males.

BREEDING. The authors have not bred this species, but it is likely to follow the method described under *A. lala.*

AMBASSIS LALA

Glass Fish

INDIA, BURMA, THAILAND   ♂ 1½″   ♀ 1½″

COMMUNITY   DIET: SMALL LIVE FOOD   SWIMS: UPPER HALF OF TANK

The most popular of the glass fishes is this somewhat chunky little beauty. Compared with *A. buroensis*, it is shorter, deeper-bodied, and has a wider expanse of finnage. The eyes are large. Although the fish looks delicate, it is in fact quite hardy. It prefers alkaline water to which has been added one teaspoonful of salt per gallon.

The body is more or less colourless, but has a faint tinge of gold. Adult males have a slightly orange tint, and the trailing edges of their dorsal and anal fins are bordered with a thin line of electric blue. Both sexes show thin vertical bars across the body. At times the glassy flanks reflect the light in prismatic colours, pale blue being predominant.

BREEDING. *Tank: 24″ × 8″ × 8″. pH: 8·0–8·6. Hardness: 280–300 p.p.m. Temperature: 80° F. Spawns: in floating plants. Method: scatters tiny eggs at surface of water. Eggs: 100–150. Hatch: in 12 hours. Fry hang on: 1 day. Free-swimming: 2nd–3rd day. Food 1st week: infusoria. 2nd week: brine shrimp.*

The breeding tank should contain plants of feathery foliage like Myriophyllum, and have a 1″ layer of Riccia floating at the surface. After much driving male and female tremble side by side. Then he presses her to a horizontal position beneath the Riccia, where the minute eggs are deposited. After spawning the parents may be removed, and the tiny fry fed with very small infusoria. In some cases the parents will continue to spawn over a period, and if well fed do not molest eggs or fry. Youngsters may be trained to take fine dried food.

CHANDA WOLFFII

THAILAND   ♂ 2″   ♀ 2″

COMMUNITY   DIET: ALL FOODS   SWIMS: UPPER HALF OF TANK

First imported by the authors from Thailand in 1955, this fish took very happily to aquarium life. Much the same shape as *A. lala*, it lacks colour, but has a good spread of finnage which it keeps erect at all times. The species enjoys dried food, so is not difficult to keep. Our specimens are absolutely peaceful. It is said that *C. wolffii* grows to 8″ in its native rivers, but aquarium specimens are unlikely to exceed 3″.

Occasionally an individual fish will show a white spot on the body or fins. This, however, is not Ichthyophthirius or any infectious disease. On closer examination these rather large, somewhat creamy spots look more like air bubbles beneath the skin.

So far sex is not apparent.

BREEDING. Breeding has not been achieved by the authors, but it would seem that the procedure would follow closely that of *A. lala*.

CHAPTER XXIX

ATHERINIDÆ

To date very few species of this family are common to aquarists, as most are true salt-water fishes. A few, however, do come from fresh water, and three of these are described in this chapter. The silversides, as they are called, are attractive, peaceful, and swift swimmers, having the ability to leap from the water when frightened. They have two dorsal fins and long, narrow, laterally compressed bodies. The eyes are large; the mouth is small. All prefer the addition of some salt to the water.

MELANOTÆNIA MCCULLOCHI

Australian Rainbow

AUSTRALIA		♂ 3″ ♀ 3″
COMMUNITY	DIET: ALL FOODS	SWIMS: UPPER HALF OF TANK

Very active, peaceful fish which, when in suitable surroundings, show considerable colour. They will take any food, and are easy to breed. Slightly alkaline water with a pH of 7·0–7·4 and of medium hardness is preferred. When unduly scared these fish are inclined to jump, so their tank should be kept tightly covered.

The body has a greenish-golden sheen, and is crossed horizontally by numerous thin brown stripes. The fins are reddish—more so on the outer edges—and are sprinkled with fine dots. There is a bright red spot on the gill-plates.

The male is a little more colourful than his mate; his fins are of a more pronounced orange-red. The female is deeper-bodied at spawning-time, and the light catching her abdomen makes her look more silvery in this region.

BREEDING. *Tank: 24″ × 8″ × 8″. pH: 7·0–7·2. Hardness: 180 p.p.m. Temperature: 78° F. Spawns: over a period. Method: scatters semi-adhesive eggs. Eggs: 100–150. Hatch: 6–7 days. Fry hang on: 2 days. Free-swimming: 9th day. Food 1st week: infusoria, brine shrimp. 2nd week: microworms, sifted Daphnia.*

The breeding tank should be thickly planted, particularly with fine-leaved foliage. An addition of one teaspoonful of salt to each gallon of water seems to induce spawning. The male chases the female, and the pair, trembling side by side, scatter rather large, pale yellow eggs among the plant fronds. In their excited dashes some of the spawn gets disturbed and falls to the bottom. Provided the parents are well fed, they ignore the eggs, so the pair may be left together for 2 or 3 days. Over this period spawning often continues. They should be removed before the eggs hatch, as they will eat the young fry.

MELANOTÆNIA NIGRANS

Dark-striped Australian Rainbow

AUSTRALIA ♂ 3½″ ♀ 3¾″

COMMUNITY   DIET : ALL FOODS   SWIMS : UPPER HALF OF TANK

This fish is more colourful than the foregoing, but until recently was less frequently seen in Britain. In outline it is longer and slimmer. The stripes running horizontally along the sides are blacker, and the edges of the dorsal and anal fins are darker. Sexing is not difficult, as the male has longer fins, is brighter-coloured—with beautiful sheens of blue, yellow, and green—and considerably slimmer than his mate.

BREEDING. *Tank: 24″ × 8″ × 8″. pH: 7·0–7·2. Hardness: 180 p.p.m. Temperature: 78° F. Spawns: over a period. Method: scatters semi-adhesive eggs. Eggs: 100–150. Hatch: 6–7 days. Fry hang on: 2 days. Free-swimming: 9th day. Food 1st week: infusoria, brine shrimp. 2nd week: microworms, sifted Daphnia.*

For breeding the procedure is the same as that described under *M. mccullochi.*

TELMATHERINA LADIGESI

CELEBES   ♂ 2¼"   ♀ 2"

COMMUNITY   DIET: ALL FOODS   SWIMS: MID-WATER

A beautiful fish, but very susceptible to changes of water. This should be alkaline, with a pH of 7·2–7·4, to which has been added one teaspoonful of salt to every gallon. When the fish are purchased the buyer is strongly advised to take enough water with the specimens to house them comfortably for several days. Should this be very different in pH and hardness from that on the aquarist's premises the fish must on no account be transferred, or death is liable to occur. Before they are removed to another tank the water must be altered gradually; this is best done by changing a small cupful daily. Even so, they will not thrive under very acid conditions. Once in a situation to their liking they are not difficult to keep.

The body is a lovely translucent gold. The pectoral fins are set rather high up on the body, and from behind these to the base of the tail is a brilliant pale blue stripe. The posterior dorsal and anal fins have separate split rays, the foremost being black. The rest of these fins, pectorals, and tail are tinged with gold, though in the tail the colour is strongest on the outer edges of the upper and lower lobes.

Sexing presents no problem, as the dorsal and anal fins of the male grow extensions, the front rays forming separate filaments. The female's fins are quite normal.

BREEDING. *Tank: 24" × 8" × 8". pH: 7·2–7·4. Hardness: 180–200 p.p.m. Temperature: 78–80° F. Spawns: over a period. Method: eggs with sticky threads catch in plant fronds. Eggs: 80–100. Hatch: in 5 days. Fry hang on: 2 days. Free-swimming: 8th day. Food 1st week: infusoria. 2nd week: brine shrimp.*

A pair should be placed in a breeding tank in which numerous separate stalks of Myriophyllum are planted close together, or left floating. Male and female tremble side by side among the feathery foliage, and large, clear eggs may be seen hanging on threads in the fronds. These plant stems with the eggs attached should be gently removed and floated in a bare breeding tank containing water of the same composition and slightly tinted with methylene blue. Spawning continues over several days, and each morning the new eggs should be transferred. When the stalks are separate there is no difficulty in lifting out each one. But when they are planted in bunches to extract a single stem is difficult. It usually results in uprooting the whole clump, and at the same time losing sight of the precious eggs.

CHAPTER XXX

CENTRARCHIDÆ

THOUGH NOT REALLY TROPICALS, A FEW SPECIES OF SUNFISHES ARE KEPT BY some aquarists. Generally speaking, they prefer slightly lower temperatures and a good deal of light. They come from the south-eastern states of the U.S.A., and have two nostrils on each side of the snout.

MESOGONISTIUS CHÆTODON

Poor Man's Angel

EASTERN U.S.A.   ♂ 2½″   ♀ 2½″

COMMUNITY   DIET: LIVE FOODS   SWIMS: MID-WATER

Rather a quiet fish, which swims with an independent, stately air. The fins are kept well-spread in alkaline water to which has been added a teaspoonful of salt per gallon. It prefers live food, and is not easy to feed

454

in a community tank, being beaten to the post by quicker-moving fishes. It is not aggressive, and is inclined to be thrust aside and made unhappy by other species. Furthermore, it prefers a lower temperature than most inhabitants of a community tank. The popular name is no longer true. Since angels are now so easily bred and plentiful, their price has dropped considerably, leaving *M. chætodon* more expensive, at least in Britain.

The body is a creamy buff with thin black stripes crossing the flanks vertically.

Sexing is difficult, as male and female look alike.

BREEDING. The authors have not heard of any aquarist who has succeeded in breeding these fish.

ELASSOMA EVERGLADEI

Pygmy Sunfish

SOUTH-EASTERN U.S.A.   ♂ 1″   ♀ 1″

COMMUNITY   DIET: LIVE FOODS   SWIMS: LOWER HALF OF TANK

This sunfish generally fares rather better than *Mesogonistius chætodon* in a community tank. It does not mind an average temperature of 76°–78° F. and, being a little more agile, is better able to get its share of live food.

The normal colour is a dull grey. The male has larger and darker fins than his mate. In breeding garb he turns black, and his sides sparkle with greenish-gold dots.

BREEDING. Tank: 24″ × 8″ × 8″. pH: 7·2. Hardness: 150–180 p.p.m. Temperature: 78° F. Spawns: in nest. Method: lays adhesive eggs. Eggs: 50–70. Hatch: in 48 hours. Fry hang on: 1 day. Free-swimming: 4th day. Food 1st week: infusoria. 2nd week: brine shrimp, microworms.

The breeding tank should be planted normally, but contain some floating pieces of Myriophyllum and Riccia. These are gathered by the male and used to build a rough nest at the bottom of the aquarium. The pair enter their home and, quivering side by side, deposit and fertilize small, clear eggs. After this the female should be removed. The male then guards and fans the spawn. Once the young are free-swimming the male should be taken away, as he is liable to eat the fry.

OTHER BRACKISH-WATER FISHES

There are several fishes which will live in aquaria that contain sea-water, or half sea and half fresh water, or which can be slowly acclimatized until they will live in fresh water. Even so, most prefer the addition of salt, and alkaline conditions. They come from several families. None have been bred in captivity.

MONODACTYLIDÆ

MONODACTYLUS ARGENTEUS

Malayan Angel

INDIAN OCEAN   ♂ 5″   ♀ 5″

COMMUNITY, WITH LARGER FISHES   DIET: ALL FOODS   SWIMS: MID-WATER

Sometimes called *Psettus argenteus*, this moderately peaceful fish is a swift swimmer. As it flashes round the aquarium the compressed sides, covered with minute scales of gleaming silver, shine brightly.

A black line from above the head runs downward through the eye. Another curves at a slightly different angle behind the gill-plate into the thorax. The dorsal and ventral fins are a brilliant gold.

Females appear to be thicker in the region below the ventral fins. The species may be acclimatized to fresh, brackish, or sea-water, and does well in all.

MONODACTYLUS SEBÆ

♀

♂

WEST AFRICAN COASTAL AREAS   ♂ 5″   ♀ 5″

COMMUNITY, WITH LARGER FISHES   DIET: ALL FOODS   SWIMS: ALL DEPTHS

An attractive fish, though a little aggressive once settled in. It inhabits fresh, brackish, or pure salt water.

In comparison to *M. argenteus*, the fins are longer and the body shorter. There are no bright colours, but the contrasting black bars on a pure silver ground are sufficient to arrest the eye.

The species will eat any fresh food, and is soon trained to accept a good dried product.

Sexing is not obvious.

BREEDING. So far the fish has not been bred in captivity.

SCATOPHAGIDÆ
SCATOPHAGUS ARGUS

Scats

INDONESIA   ♂ 7″ ♀ 7″

COMMUNITY, WITH LARGER FISHES   DIET: ALL FOODS   SWIMS: MID-WATER

Usually imported in small sizes, few of these attractive fish grow to maturity. The body is round and laterally compressed. The fins when well-spread stand up smartly.

The majority of 'scats' are an olive green, but are coloured with darker olive spots. A perpendicular line always runs through the eye. There is a prettier variety popularly called the tiger scat in which the spots form themselves in vertical broken bars. The upper portion of the head and back glows with red which sometimes intermingles with the bars and appears again in the forward rays of the ventral and anal fins. The hind portions of the dorsal, anal, and tail are a chrome yellow.

Females are thicker in the belly region, and usually slightly less colourful than males.

SYNGNATHIDÆ

The pipe-fishes are found in most tropical waters in the Far East, some living in fresh water, others in brackish. The long, thin body is covered with bony plates, the skeleton being external. Most resemble the well-known sea horses, having a snouted head and long tail. Moreover, like sea horses, the male carries the eggs in a pouch situated in the abdominal region.

SYNGNATHUS SPECIES

♂

♀

♀

Pipe-fish

INDONESIA, THAILAND   ♂ 6"   ♀ 6"

COMMUNITY   DIET: SMALL LIVE FOOD   SWIMS: ALL DEPTHS

Our plate shows a trio of pipe-fishes imported from Singapore, but others almost identical have been received from Thailand. The species will live in fresh, brackish, or salt water, though brackish seems preferred. They are peaceful, but rather difficult to feed.

BREEDING. We have not witnessed mating or birth.

THERAPONIDÆ
THERAPON JARBUA

SHORES OF INDIAN OCEAN   ♂ 4″   ♀ 4″

COMMUNITY, WITH LARGE FISHES   DIET : ALL FOODS

SWIMS : LOWER HALF OF TANK

Though somewhat quarrelsome, this fish is common enough to be seen in many salt- and brackish-water aquaria. It can grow very large, but in normal tanks rarely exceeds the above dimensions.

The body is silver. Black rings encircle the fish horizontally like contour lines. In the front rays of the dorsal there is an intense black patch. Three stripes cross the tail from front to back.

Females are thicker and deeper than males.

TETRAODONTIDÆ

There are numerous puffers: a few inhabit fresh water, but many live in brackish or salt water. They are able to inflate themselves with air until they look like miniature balloons. At the same time small spines are erected over most of the body. Inflation is done for protection. In the first place, it scares an aggressor: the puffer becomes too large a mouthful for some jaws, and the spines turn its normally soft, flabby exterior into a prickly, less edible meal. When lifted from the water a puffer usually performs this act, and makes a croaking sound as the air is sucked in. If returned to the tank the fish is so buoyant that it floats upside down momentarily, then, deflating itself quickly, it dives for safety. The genus Tetraodon have strong, parrot-like beaks of bone just beneath the lips, and the powerful mandibles enable the fish to break off pieces of coral, crush up snails, and sometimes slice through the shells of medium-sized crabs. Nevertheless most puffers are not really aggressive.

TETRAODON FLUVIATILIS

Puffer Fish

SHORES OF INDIAN OCEAN, PHILIPPINES ♂ 3″ ♀ 3″

COMMUNITY, WITH LARGER FISHES DIET: MAINLY PROTEIN

SWIMS: MID-WATER

This species is the commonest seen in home aquaria. It is hardy, attractive, and not too aggressive, and does well in fresh or brackish water or in pure sea-water.

The back and upper sides are a beautiful golden-green, but well covered with sizeable brown spots which occasionally form themselves into rings. The belly is silver-white.

Sexing is difficult. It is shown in sea-water in our illustration of *Dascyllus carneus*, and in the composite plate of Marines, p. 476.

TETRAODON SPECIES

♂

Freshwater Puffer

THAILAND ♂ 3″ ♀ 3″

NON-COMMUNITY   DIET: MAINLY PROTEIN   SWIMS: LOWER HALF OF TANK

We show here one of the fresh-water puffers, coming from a pond in Thailand, miles from the sea.

It will only eat fish, meat, prawn, earthworm, etc., ignoring dried food and small white worms.

Though slow in movement, when tried in a community tank of medium-sized fast-swimming fishes it was able to make a stealthy approach and a final dart, usually upward, at a fish, its beak taking a clear semicircle out of the unfortunate target.

The body is green with mottled brown markings, but set off with a bright red eye, and a similar bright red spot towards the tail.

BREEDING. The species has not been bred in captivity.

TOXOTIDÆ

The archer fishes, as they are commonly called, have received great publicity. This is because they have specially shaped jaws, a groove inside the mouth, and a long tongue, enabling them to squirt drops of water at flies and other insects well above the surface. The accuracy of their aim is phenomenal. They can hit a fly $3\frac{1}{2}$–$4\frac{1}{2}$ feet away, nearly always scoring a bull. Occasionally they fire at insects on the wing, and, though marksmanship is not a hundred per cent. efficient, should they miss, repeated shots follow in such quick succession that the target is usually hit. The impact occurs with such force that the insect may be lifted a foot or more into the air.

TOXOTES JACULATOR

♀

♂

Archer Fish

SHORES OF INDIAN OCEAN TO PHILIPPINES   ♂ 4½″ ♀ 4½″

COMMUNITY   DIET: MOST FOODS   SWIMS: UPPER HALF OF TANK

This species seems to be the commonest, and most exported. It thrives well in an aquarium, and is hardy and peaceful. Despite shooting down insects, it will readily take pieces of meat, fish, shrimp, crab, etc.

The body is a silver-grey crossed vertically by five short black bars. The dorsal, anal, and ventrals are black, the pectorals white, and the tail dark grey.

Females appear to be deeper and rounder in the belly.

BREEDING. There is no record of the fish having been bred in captivity.

CHAPTER XXXI

TROPICAL MARINES

THOUGH FRESH-WATER FISHES HAVE BEEN KEPT IN AQUARIA FOR MANY years, comparatively few aquarists have ventured into the marine side of the hobby. In the past this has been understandable, as little was known about sea-water or the beautiful coral fishes. The majority of aquarists do not live near the coast, and acquiring sea-water was difficult and expensive. Although certain marine biological stations were prepared to sell and send sea-water great distances, the weight made costs high, and to ensure arrival in a pure condition special containers were necessary. Furthermore, if the water became quickly fouled replacements were not immediately at hand, and expenses were reincurred.

To-day it is possible to buy salts which when mixed with fresh water produce artificial sea-water in which most of the well-known coral fishes will survive. Formerly, marine fishes were extremely difficult to catch and transport. But, with the advent of the aqua-lung and the expansion of air services, they are becoming increasingly plentiful, and many now cost no more than their rarer fresh-water cousins.

The sight of a well-set-up marine tank, sparkling with crystal-clear water, enhanced by a background of various shapes of coloured coral, and containing half a dozen or more of the most striking coral fishes, is literally breath-taking. Even the most colourful fresh-water fishes rarely compare with the gaudy brilliance so artistically blended in the little marine beauties.

Contrary to the general belief, a marine tank is not difficult to maintain, though the inexperienced are advised to start modestly. To gain a little knowledge an all-glass tank or large battery jar will do for a start. This should contain pure sea sand, clean, unheated sea-water, a few small, well-cleansed rocks from the shore, and one or two common anemones. In addition, there may be a few tiny crabs and some shrimps or baby fishes that can be found in rock pools on most beaches—all are to be had for nothing. Having gained experience, the aquarist may then like to go a step further, and try a couple of the cheaper coral fishes. For this he will require a glass-cased heater and thermostat. If the tank is very slowly warmed up the majority of the shore creatures will continue to live quite happily at 76°F. This is because in the summer rock pools in temperate regions rise to over 80°F.—a temperature which is normal to the inhabitants.

FUNDAMENTALS

As in a fresh-water aquarium, there are a few basic rules to be observed with a marine tank. These are:

(i) Many metals are dissolved by sea-water, forming poisonous salts which quickly prove fatal to most forms of marine life. An all-glass tank has the usual disadvantages of distorted vision, and a crack is liable to spread and give way suddenly. A framed tank is therefore preferable. This can be made of plain angle iron, which may rust unless frequently painted. Even so, it is non-poisonous. If funds are available polished stainless steel is ideal, but should not be confused with chromium plate. The walls of the tank should be so tight-fitting that no putty-filled gap is visible. A pleasing effect can be created by making the back and two ends of coloured "Vitrolite" instead of glass. A pale shade of sea blue adds depth. If the aquarium is already made of glass the three walls may be painted on the outside. This also has the advantage of keeping out excess light, which encourages algæ.

(ii) The tank is filled with pure sea-water, or made up artificially with fresh water and purchased salts, as directed on the packet. In the past it has been stated that sea-water must be collected from at least three miles off shore. This is not essential, providing it is obtained from a clean, wind-swept beach facing the open sea, and not from a harbour, where con-tamination is likely to be considerable. When personally collecting sea-water the aquarist should take with him numerous polythene bags or large glass bottles, so that he may have enough water to fill his tank, and provide a similar amount in reserve. This may be needed either for a complete change should disaster occur, or for essential toppings-up and occasional changes which are beneficial. If possible the water collected should be left to stand in the jars for a fortnight in a dark, cool place before use. It will then be found to be crystal-clear; all the sand, sediment, and dead plankton will have settled at the bottom, and when the water is poured gently off into a clean enamel bucket it will be as clear as though filtered.

(iii) Sand should be very fine, so that it is not fouled by particles of uneaten food sinking between the grains. It must be thoroughly cleansed before use. Rocks must be of the non-disintegrating type; they require to be scrubbed and well rinsed.

(iv) Coral forms a natural background of beauty, but also serves as a refuge for little fishes. It is sharp, hard, and rather brittle, and should not be used in fresh-water aquaria, as the inhabitants are liable to damage themselves against it. This does not apply to coral fishes. They are used to it, diving in and out of the branches with impunity. Many corals con-tain dead organisms, and unless thoroughly bleached and cleansed may cause trouble and disease. Care should therefore be taken to ensure that the material is clean; in any case, a boiling in fresh water can do no harm. Corals in the sea are formed by minute polyps. Their secretions, mainly of lime, build up the actual hard deposit which is continually increasing through the ages. Slow as this process is, in time even larger waterways like the Gulf of Aden tend to become blocked, and have to be periodically cleared to maintain a passage for shipping. Pieces of coral suitable in size for the aquarium are chipped from these growths by divers.

But once broken off the polyps die, and the lime deposit turns back to a creamy white. Only a very few corals retain their coloration once removed from the sea. One of them is the beautiful red organ-pipe variety. Most others are dyed, and this dye in time comes off in the water. The aquarist should beware of tinted pieces, as they may cause serious trouble in the aquarium.

(v) In nature sea-water is never still. To imitate the constant movement to which the inhabitants are accustomed it is necessary to have either an aerator or a running filter to keep the water in the aquarium in constant agitation. Of the two means filtration is the better, particularly if a pump is used to force the water from the filter back into the tank, bringing about a rapid circulation, while the jet stream re-entering the tank carries with it bubbles which provide aeration. This automatically keeps the water fully charged with oxygen, and permits the constant escape of carbon dioxide. The normal air lift process is too feeble to do more than create a gentle trickle. The filter need only be charged with silver sand or spun glass which should be frequently cleaned, or replaced.

(vi) Sea-water varies in density according to its salt content, so a small but essential piece of equipment is a hydrometer. This floats, and the graduated neck gives a reading of the specific gravity, or weight of salt water, relative to an equal volume of fresh water. The hydrometer sinks deeper in fresh water than in sea-water. The majority of coral fishes thrive happily between 1·025 and 1·030 density. Therefore, a reading between the two—say 1·027—should be aimed at. If the hydrometer floats outside these limits the density should be corrected. The addition of more fresh water will make the hydrometer float deeper; conversely, it will rise if sea-water is added.

As in any aquarium, the water evaporates and the surface-level drops in time, but the salt remains. To top up continually with more sea-water gradually increases the salinity. Therefore, before making an addition, the hydrometer should be read to discover whether fresh or salt water is required. In theory, since salt does not evaporate much, all topping up should be done with fresh water. But in practice, every time a net, the hand, or a pair of tongs is submerged, when it is withdrawn both salt and water are removed. The authors find that once every seven times their tanks need replenishing with sea-water; on the other occasions fresh is used. It would seem, therefore, that only a few spare pints of salt water are needed annually. But it has been noticed that the inhabitants are stimulated by occasionally changing half the old water in the aquarium for new.

(vii) Temperatures should be a little lower than in the tropical fresh-water aquarium. Most marines are content between 72° and 76° F.

(viii) Left-over particles of food decompose quicker in salt water, and it is rather more easily fouled, so any dried food must be used sparingly. Small lumps of shrimp, prawn, fish, or meat if uneaten may easily be seen on the fine sand, and can be quickly removed with a dip tube or wooden forceps.

Some marine fishes will eat Daphnia. But the aquarist must be careful not to over-feed, as this crustacean soon dies in sea-water, and is not easily removed. All the same, if a few tiny crabs or live shrimps are kept as scavengers some food must be allowed to reach the bottom so that these creatures do not starve. Any anemones stuck on the rocks will require individual feeding. This is done by giving them particles of shrimp or meat, delivered into their tentacles by wooden forceps. It is surprising the number of individuals who think of sea-anemones as flowers. They are, of course, animal, and must be fed. Any corpse of fish, crab, or anemone must be removed at once. The astute marine aquarist will note daily that all his creatures are present. If one is absent he will search behind rock or coral to make certain that it is not lying there dead.

(ix) Since it is not possible to grow ordinary aquatic plants in the marine aquarium, the light which they would have absorbed for growth is available to form algæ. Therefore, marine tanks do not require an excess of illumination. Usually that available in the ordinary living-room is adequate, providing the fishes can be seen comfortably. The tank is better not situated in a window where it receives a good deal of direct sunlight.

If too much light enters a marine aquarium the coral will gradually become brown and lose its striking whiteness. However, it can easily be restored to its pristine beauty. Remove the discoloured coral from the tank, and place in an enamel bucket full of tap-water. Now pour into this one pint of ordinary household chlorine bleach (this is usually kept for cleaning sinks, etc.). In 24 hours all discoloration will have disappeared. The coral must now be soaked for a further 24 hours in clean tap-water to remove the chlorine. The next day rinse under a running tap before returning it to the marine tank. Discoloured sand can be siphoned off and washed under a tap in the ordinary way.

The one factor which saves money for the marine aquarist is that artificial light is generally unnecessary. Experiments are in hand with various seaweeds. Possibly it may shortly be practicable to decorate the aquarium with certain types. But, unless the owner is assured that this form of life is not going to die and foul the tank, he is wiser to do without it. Generally speaking, coral and rocks form adequate decoration.

(x) The fishes themselves should be purchased from a reputable dealer, and should have been kept long enough by him to be reasonably certain that they do not carry infection. One fish with a contagious disease will contaminate everything in the tank and soon cause disaster.

It is practically impossible for the average aquarist to breed egg-laying marines at present. Therefore we will not deal fully with every species, as has been done with fresh-water tropicals. A brief description will, however, be given of some of the more obtainable coral fishes that take to aquarium life and associate moderately well together. In this respect it must be borne in mind that quite a few are a little aggressive. Often this is more noticeable with their own kind than with other species. A beautiful and interesting community tank can be maintained with 5 or 6 single specimens chosen from those described in this chapter.

Diseases

The authors have had little experience of tropical marine diseases in their tanks; perhaps we have been lucky, or maybe the usual fish infections found inland do not thrive in sea-water.

However, one scourge is Oodinium, which is caused by a minute parasite, and is very similar to the fresh-water Ichthyophthirius, though the white spots are very much smaller and more numerous. The disease is usually introduced on new fishes, so all new purchases should be quarantined for ten days at least before they are placed in the established marine tanks.

Sometimes if caught early enough a cure can be effected by adding methylene blue to the water in the tank, until this is an inky blue-black.

The metal copper is very lethal to most marine life, so a very weak solution of copper sulphate—say 1 in 10,000—may be tried in the hope that the tiny parasites will succumb before the larger, stronger fishes. However, care must be used, and should the fishes show signs of distress they must be transferred immediately to clean new sea-water of the same temperature.

Butterfly-fish (p. 472)   *Blue Sergeant-major*

ABUDEFDUF UNIOCELLATUS

Blue Sergeant-major

CEYLON, INDONESIA, POLYNESIA   ♂ $2\frac{1}{2}''$ ♀ $2\frac{1}{2}''$

COMMUNITY   DIET: MOST FOODS   SWIMS: MID–WATER

The genus Abudefduf is widespread, and there are many species, quite a few of which have been nicknamed 'sergeant-majors.'

They are hardy, will eat most foods, but are a little aggressive, though unlikely to do much damage to other fishes of similar size. They are full of life, and nearly always on the move. The blue sergeant-major pictured right above is at first inclined to hide behind clumps of coral, but it soon settles down and becomes bolder, even to the extent of occasionally monopolizing the most prominent portion of the tank, thus taking the eye off other more colourful species.

BREEDING. The authors have not bred this fish.

AMPHIPRION BICINCTUS

♀  ♂

Dark Clown Fish

INDIAN OCEAN, RED SEA		♂ 3″ ♀ 3″
COMMUNITY	DIET: ALL FOODS	SWIMS: ALL DEPTHS

The Amphiprions—generally known as clown fishes—make some of the best inhabitants of the marine aquarium. They are most attractive in colour and behaviour, hardy, reasonably cheap, friendly, and easy to feed.

A. bicinctus has a black back, but shades to yellow on the face and belly. Two silver blue bands slash the body, and these are so clear and clean that they seem to be painted on. All the fins are yellow.

Clowns enjoy chopped shrimp, enchytræ, and most good dried foods; they soon become tame, and will eat from their owner's fingers.

BREEDING. We have not heard of *A. bicinctus* being bred in captivity.

AMPHIPRION EPHIPREUS

INDIAN OCEAN, RED SEA		♂ 1¾″ ♀ 1¾″
COMMUNITY	DIET: ALL FOODS	SWIMS: ALL DEPTHS

A pleasing little clown fish with a deep, stumpy body that is somewhat laterally compressed. Except for the one white band over the head, the fish is red all over.

It is friendly, attractive, easy to keep, and will take all the usual foods, including the dried product. We show one specimen in our composite plate, p. 476, *A. ephipreus* being the fish on the extreme left.

BREEDING. As far as is known, the species has never been bred in captivity.

AMPHIPRION PERCULA

Clown Fish

INDIAN OCEAN, POLYNESIA, RED SEA $\male\ 2\frac{3}{4}''\quad \female\ 2\frac{3}{4}''$

COMMUNITY DIET: SHRIMP, FISH, MEAT, SOME DRIED FOOD

SWIMS: ALL DEPTHS

One of the commonest of the clowns, and probably the most popular coral fish kept to-day. It is hardy and cheap. Having a happy disposition, it is not aggressive, and several will live happily together. The fish swims with an exaggerated waggle. It has an inquiring nature, and will investigate objects. When a little scared it will face the danger and, waggling its body more intensely, swim up and down like a professional boxer ducking and rising to prevent being a stationary target. Clowns soon become tame, and rush to greet their owner in the hope that they will receive a tit-bit.

A. percula is shown in our composite plate, p. 476, its orange and white banded pattern making it most conspicuous.

BREEDING. The fish lay their eggs in the mouth of a poisonous anemone and swim in and out of the stinging tentacles with impunity. They have come to an agreement whereby the anemone gives them and their young protection in return for scraps of food which they spit out for their host. When chased they flee into the dangerous tentacles. These, disregarding the clown, sieze the pursuer before it can stop or change direction. Occasionally *A. percula* has spawned on rocks in large public aquaria.

ANGELICHTHYS CILIARIS

Queen Angel Fish

WEST INDIES, FLORIDA   ♂ 8″   ♀ 8″

COMMUNITY   DIET: MAINLY PROTEIN   SWIMS: ALL DEPTHS

This beautiful fish grows to 20″ or more in the ocean, but smaller specimens are better for the marine aquarist. The species is somewhat quarrelsome, and, being equipped with a savage spine on the lower edge of the gill-plate, can inflict mortal wounds on other fishes.

Coloration is truly regal, blue and gold, and the head is crowned with a dark blue coronet, while the dorsal and anal fins bear flowing trains.

BREEDING. The marine angels have not been bred in captivity.

CHÆTODON VAGABUNDUS

Butterfly Fish

INDONESIA, POLYNESIA   ♂ 5″   ♀ 5″

COMMUNITY   DIET: MAINLY PROTEIN   SWIMS: ALL DEPTHS

The Chætodons comprise a genus with species spread throughout most tropical seas. Most have disc-shaped, compressed bodies and a pointed snout. *C. vagabundus* does well in the aquarium, and is not aggressive, but is somewhat choosey about food. It likes white worms and small pieces of chopped prawn. Since it is a slow mover, it often loses the tit-bit, which is grabbed by faster-moving fishes.

The fish is shown on our colour plate with *Abudefduf uniocellatus*.

BREEDING. The species has not been bred in captivity.

DASCYLLUS ARUANUS

♀

Striped Damsel

INDONESIA	♂ 2″ ♀ 2″
COMMUNITY	DIET: MOST FOODS, LIKES SOME SEAWEED OR ALGÆ
	SWIMS: ALL DEPTHS

Though not brilliantly coloured, no fish could be more striking.

D. aruanus is a little aggressive—more so with its own kind than with others. However, it settles down quickly, and claims its own special place. At feeding-time it dashes out, and soon becomes tame. The species is amusing to watch as it swims forward or backward with equal ease through the jagged branches of coral without touching the fronds. It is hardy and easy to keep.

The body is silver, slashed with three broad black bands. A white patch appears on the forehead. The tail is nearly colourless, and often almost invisible. The remaining fins are jet-black. The ventrals have a silver front edge.

BREEDING. The fish has not been bred in captivity.

DASCYLLUS CARNEUS

♂

♀

Cloudy Damsel

INDIAN OCEAN   ♂ 2″   ♀ 2″

COMMUNITY   DIET: ALL FOODS   SWIMS: ALL DEPTHS

This little damsel is smaller and stubbier than most, and is less aggressive. It is hardy, and easy to feed, soon learning to take even dried food.

The forepart of the body is dark grey, which shades into a black band, the hind-quarters are grey, but a patch of creamy white appears on the back just below the dorsal fin, and again on the caudal peduncle. The last rays of the dorsal and the tail fin develop a beautiful blue when the fish is in tip-top condition.

Also shown in our plate is a single specimen of *Tetraodon fluviatilis*, the spotted puffer fish.

BREEDING. The fish has not been bred in captivity.

DASCYLLUS TRIMACULATUS

♂

Three-spot Damsel

INDIAN OCEAN, INDONESIA   ♂ 2″   ♀ 2″

COMMUNITY   DIET: MOST FOODS, LIKES SOME SEAWEED OR ALGÆ

SWIMS: ALL DEPTHS

In characteristics and habits this fish is similar to *D. aruanus*. The head is more rounded, and the snout blunter.

The body and fins are jet-black all over, but three large silver-white spots appear, one on each upper flank and one on the front of the head. When this fish is not entirely happy the intense black fades to a dark grey.

BREEDING. Not bred in captivity.

COMPOSITE PLATE, MARINE FISHES

| *Amphiprion* | *A. percula* | *Pomacentrus* | *H. acuminatus* | *Tetraodon* |
| *ephipreus* | | *cæruleus* | | *fluviatilis* |

HENIOCHUS ACUMINATUS
Wimple Fish

INDIAN OCEAN   ♂ 4″ ♀ 4″

COMMUNITY   DIET: ALL FOODS   SWIMS: LOWER HALF OF TANK

This attractive fish is related to the fabulous Moorish Idol.

The long, pointed dorsal fin is kept mostly upright and contrasts magnificently with the shorter, rounded anal fin. The species is extremely docile; it does not attack other fishes, but swims around minding its own business, which seems to be a constant search for food. However, should any fish take a sly nip at it, it quickly retaliates, as if to stand for no nonsense, then immediately resumes its former occupation.

The clear-cut black-and-white body is enhanced by bright yellow in the rear portion of the lower rays of the dorsal fin and tail. The pectorals are pale yellow, but the ventral fins are solid jet-black. The fish is pictured above.

BREEDING. We have not heard of this fish being bred in captivity.

HIPPOCAMPUS BREVIROSTRIS

♀

Sea Horse

MADEIRA ♂ 6″ ♀ 6″

COMMUNITY, WITH SMALL FISHES   DIET : PROTEIN   SWIMS : ALL DEPTHS

The sea horses, of which there are many species, come from most warm seas where branching coral abounds. Like the pipe-fishes to which they are related, they have a bony skeleton on the outside of the body.

They swim in an upright position, and resemble prancing horses. Locomotion is by means of the dorsal fin, which vibrates very rapidly, and reminds one of a small boat being driven along by an outboard motor.

All have long, prehensile tails, with which they anchor themselves to branches of coral, and very often to each other.

Unfortunately, sea horses are slow and somewhat difficult to feed, requiring small food. The faster fishes get there first, and usually snatch their food from under their snouts; moreover, the authors have found that they usually get bullied. Sea horses have little or no defence, and other fishes bite the dorsal fin away, sometimes right down to the flesh; this prevents them from swimming, and the wounds eventually cause death. In our opinion they should be housed on their own, and not kept with coral fishes.

BREEDING. Mating is unusual: the pair come together face to face, the female then inserts her ovipositor in the male's abdominal pouch and places her eggs therein.

These the male fertilizes and hatches, his abdomen expanding as growth increases. Eventually he gives birth to fully formed young sea horses, about $\frac{1}{2}''$ in length.

Several males have delivered young in the London Zoo Aquarium, but the babies have never been grown to maturity.

HOLACANTHUS ANNULARIS

♂

Blue Angel

INDIAN OCEAN, POLYNESIA   ♂ 6″ ♀ 6″

COMMUNITY   DIET: SHRIMP, WHITE WORMS, ETC., AND SOME ALGÆ
                                OR VEGETABLE FOOD

                      SWIMS: MID-WATER

This is a very beautiful fish of disc-like shape, with compressed sides. Unfortunately, it grows rather large, and may become quarrelsome. It likes some vegetable food. If the thin, crinkly seaweed often found growing on breakwaters is not available blue angels will enjoy picking at lettuce leaves. These can be anchored with a piece of string to a stone or a bit of slate so placed that the leaf appears to be growing upward in the water.

The fish grows to a great size in nature, but small specimens are best in a marine community tank. The body, as will be seen from our colour plate, is vividly striped with brilliant blue lines.

BREEDING. Never bred in captivity.

POMACENTRUS CÆRULEUS

Blue Damsel

INDIAN OCEAN ♂ 2½″ ♀ 2½″

COMMUNITY DIET: SHRIMP, FISH, MEAT, ETC., AND SOME DRIED FOOD

SWIMS: LOWER HALF OF TANK

A brilliant, beautiful damsel. It is hardy and lively, but a little snappy with its own kind.

The whole body is a brilliant royal blue. The fins and tail are a rich yellow. When unhappy the blue turns darker, and may even become black, *P. cæruleus* is the centre fish in our composite plate, p. 476. This picture shows the corner of one of the author's tanks, and portrays the vivid beauty typical of marine aquaria.

PTEROIS VOLITANS

Dragon Fish

RED SEA, INDIAN OCEAN, POLYNESIA   ♂ and ♀ 8–10″

NON–COMMUNITY   DIET: SMALL FISHES, SHRIMPS, WORMS, ETC.

SWIMS: ALL DEPTHS

Weird and wonderful, this fish always creates a stir, and receives great publicity whenever exhibited. The head is large, and the body tapers towards the tail. But the outstanding features are the long, spiny-rayed dorsal and pectoral fins, which bear poisonous spikes. These can cause the death of other fishes, and the aquarist who has inadvertently run one of the spines into his flesh will experience a badly swollen, aching arm. However, it is not only the poison of *P. volitans* which makes it dangerous; it will pursue and swallow any fish which is capable of passing through the large mouth.

The colour is as dangerous-looking as the thorny appearance. The body and each spine is coloured with alternate bands of pale and darker brownish pink.

BREEDING. The species has not been bred in captivity.